한 권으로 끝내는

잉글리쉬앤 토익 실전 1000제

잉글리쉬앤 어학연구소 지음

LC+RC

English&북스

JN430399

한 권으로 끝내는
잉글리쉬앤
토익 실전
1000제 LC+RC

초판 1쇄 발행 2024년 12월 6일
초판 2쇄 발행 2025년 7월 17일

지은이 잉글리쉬앤 어학연구소
펴낸이 박성호
펴낸곳 잉글리쉬앤(주)

편   집 박고우니, 장서원
영업마케팅 여주형, 김성윤, 방성출, 박훈효, 조민형, 이달님, 강정구, 이진희, 조병운
조예선, 이현정, 조광민, 노회동, 김정민, 최희성, 윤종철, 엄주아, 오지현
최유미, 최가연, 안혜연, 조승채, 김희진, 남지현, 강예빈

주   소 서울 특별시 관악구 쑥고개로 67-1
대표전화 (02) 878-1945
출판등록 2002년 3월 3일 제 320-2002-00045호

ISBN 978-89-6715-223-9 13740

목차

온라인 모의고사 이용 방법

books.english.co.kr 접속 > 상단 메뉴 '도서인증받기' 클릭 > '잉글리쉬앤 토익 실전 1000제 LC+RC' 선택 >
인증 내용 입력 > 인증 완료 > 테스트 응시

● 북스 홈페이지(books.english.co.kr)에서 빈출 어휘 PDF 및 MP3 무료 다운로드가 가능합니다.

● 해설 강의는 cookie.english.co.kr에서 별도 구매 후 이용 가능합니다.

○ 토익 소개

토익이란?

Test Of English for International Communication의 약자로, 영어가 모국어가 아닌 사람들의 일상생활이나 국제업무 등에 필요한 실용 영어 능력을 평가하는 국제 평가 시험

▶ 시험 구성

구성	Part	유형		문항 수	시간	배점
듣기(LC)	1	사진 묘사		6	45분	495점
	2	질의 응답		25		
	3	대화문		39		
	4	담화문		30		
읽기(RC)	5	단문 공란 채우기		30	75분	495점
	6	장문 공란 채우기		16		
	7	지문 독해	단일 지문	29		
			복수 지문	25		
TOTAL		7 Parts		200문항	120분	990점

※ 문항 수 100, 시간 100은 듣기(LC)·읽기(RC) 각각 해당

▶ 시험 내용

Part	유형	내용
1	사진 묘사	제시된 사진을 알맞게 설명하는 보기 고르기
2	질의 응답	질문을 듣고 알맞은 대답 고르기
3	대화문	대화를 듣고 질문에 알맞은 내용 고르기
4	담화문	담화를 듣고 질문에 알맞은 내용 고르기
5	단문 공란 채우기	빈칸에 맞는 내용을 골라 문장 완성하기
6	장문 공란 채우기	빈칸에 맞는 내용을 골라 장문 완성하기
7	지문 독해	단일 지문 또는 이중·삼중 지문을 읽고 문제에 맞는 내용 고르기

접수 방법은?

▶ 한국 토익 위원회 사이트 혹은 앱으로 접수 ➜ www.toeic.co.kr
▶ 인터넷 접수할 때 시험일, 고사장, 개인 정보 등을 입력 (증명사진 필요)
　※ 접수 마감일 이후 추가 접수일에 접수 시 추가 비용 발생

응시 준비물은?

▶ 규정 신분증 (주민등록증, 운전면허증, 기간 만료 전의 여권, 중고등학생만 학생증 인정)
▶ 연필, 지우개 (볼펜이나 사인펜은 사용 금지)
▶ 아날로그 시계 (전자 시계 불가)

시험 진행은?

▶ 오전 9:20까지 입실 (오전 9:50 이후 입실 불가)

시간	내용
오전 9:30 ~ 9:45 (15분)	답안지 작성에 관한 오리엔테이션
오전 9:45 ~ 9:50 (5분)	수험자 휴식 시간
오전 9:50 ~ 10:05 (15분)	신분 확인 및 휴대폰 제출
오전 10:05 ~ 10:10 (5분)	문제지 배부 및 파본 확인
오전 10:10 ~ 10:55 (45분)	듣기 평가(LC)
오전 10:55 ~ 12:10 (75분)	읽기 평가(RC)

※ 읽기 평가(RC) 시간에 2차 신분 확인 실시

성적 확인은?

▶ 시험일로부터 약 10일 후에 토익 위원회 사이트(www.toeic.co.kr)에서 확인 가능
▶ 최초 성적표 발급은 우편 또는 온라인 통해 수령 가능

파트별 유형 및 전략

PART 1

사진 묘사 `6문제`

파트 1은 4개의 보기 중에서 사진을 가장 잘 묘사하는 보기를 고르는 문제이다. 총 6문제가 출제되며, 인물 및 사물/풍경 사진 등 다양한 유형들이 등장한다.

| 핵심 전략 |

+ 사진 유형별로 자주 출제되는 어휘와 표현들을 익힌다.

+ 난이도가 높은 경우 주어가 사물인 보기가 자주 등장하므로 수동태, 현재완료 수동태, 수동태 진행형과 같은 문법을 완벽하게 숙지한다.

+ 오답 소거법을 통해 사진을 완벽하게 묘사한 보기가 아닌, 그 중 정답에 가장 가까운 Best Answer를 고르도록 훈련한다.

+ 유사 발음, 연상 어휘 등을 이용한 오답이나, 사람과 사물의 상태 및 동작을 잘못 묘사하는 오답들이 자주 등장한다.

| 문제 형태 |

1

Look at the picture marked number one in your test book.

(A) She is cleaning her desk.
(B) She is sharpening a pencil.
(C) She is filing some papers.
(D) She is holding a phone.

PART 2

질의 응답 **25문제**

파트 2는 3개의 보기 중에서 질문에 적절한 응답을 고르는 파트이다. 문항 수는 총 25개로, 의문사 의문문, Yes/No 의문문이 출제된다.

│ 핵심 전략 │

+ 질문의 앞부분을 집중해서 듣고 질문 유형을 파악하는 연습을 한다.
+ 의문사 의문문은 가장 자주 출제되는 유형으로, 답변 패턴이 정해져 있다. 의문사별로 정답 유형을 숙지해 두자.
+ 평서문은 답변 패턴이 정해져 있지 않아서 어렵게 느껴질 수 있다. 오답 소거법을 이용하여 보기 중 가장 적절한 응답을 고르면 정답을 쉽게 찾을 수 있다.
+ 유사 발음 어휘, 질문의 단어 반복 등을 이용한 보기가 오답으로 자주 등장하므로 이를 주의하여 정답을 골라야 한다.

│ 문제 형태 │

7 Mark your answer on your answer sheet.

How much longer do you need on this project?

(A) About ten pages long.
(B) Roughly half an hour.
(C) The project was successful.

PART 3

대화문 **39문제**

파트 3는 2~3명이 나누는 대화를 듣고 이와 관련된 3개의 문제를 푸는 파트이다. 총 39문제가 출제되며, 3인 대화가 1~2세트 출제된다. 화자 의도 파악 문제와 시각 자료 연계 문제가 각각 2~3세트 출제된다.

| 핵심 전략 |

+ 대화를 듣기 전에 문제를 먼저 읽고, 키워드를 파악한 후 그 부분을 집중적으로 듣는 훈련을 하자.

+ 첫 번째 문제는 주로 주제나 장소, 신분에 관한 문제로, 정답의 단서가 대화 초반에 나오므로 처음 부분을 놓치지 않고 들어야 한다.

+ 의도 파악 문제는 먼저 제시된 표현을 확인하고, 음성을 들으면서 해당 표현이 나올 때까지 문맥을 정확히 파악해야 한다.

+ 표나 송장, 지도 등의 다양한 시각 자료가 출제되며, 미리 시각 자료를 읽고 지문의 내용을 예측해 본다. 또한, 시각 자료와 음성을 연계하여 정보를 파악하는 능력을 길러야 한다.

+ 3인 대화에서 화자는 국적에 따라 발음이 구분되므로, 미국, 영국, 호주 등의 다양한 발음에 익숙해지도록 연습한다.

| 문제 형태 |

32 What does the woman imply when she says, "I got one for my friend"?

(A) She is inviting the man to meet her friend.
(B) Her friend is the same size with his wife.
(C) She is willing to pay for the product.
(D) She is emphasizing it's a good product.

Questions 32 through 34 refer to the following conversation.

M: Hi, I'm looking for a birthday present for my wife. I think she'd like one of these sweaters, but do you have any in a smaller size?

W: I'm pretty sure everything we have is out here on the display table. But I can check the stockroom in the back if you'd like.

M: Thanks, that'll be great. You know they look perfect for early spring. Light, but warm. You can wear them indoors or outdoors.

W: That's right. I got one for my friend who wears it a lot, so I'm sure your wife would love one. And we're selling them for 30% off this week.

M: That's good to know. I hope you have one in my wife's size.

PART 4

담화문 30문제

파트 4는 담화를 듣고 이와 관련된 3개의 문제를 푸는 파트이다. 총 30문항이 출제되며, 녹음 메시지나 공지, 뉴스 등이 주로 출제된다. 파트 3와 마찬가지로, 화자 의도 파악 문제와 시각 자료 연계 문제가 등장한다.

핵심 전략

- 담화를 듣기 전에 문제를 먼저 읽고, 키워드를 파악한 후 그 부분을 집중적으로 듣는 훈련을 하자.
- 첫 번째 문제는 주로 주제나 장소, 신분에 관한 문제로, 정답의 단서가 담화 초반에 나오므로 처음 부분을 놓치지 않고 들어야 한다.
- 의도 파악 문제는 파트 3와 달리 한 사람의 담화이므로 문맥의 흐름을 더 쉽게 파악할 수 있다. 따라서 담화의 전반적인 문맥 흐름을 이해하고, 해당 문장의 앞뒤 상황을 정확히 파악하도록 하자.
- 표나 송장, 지도 등의 다양한 시각 자료가 출제되며, 미리 시각 자료를 읽고 지문의 내용을 예측해 본다. 또한, 시각 자료와 음성을 연계하여 정보를 파악하는 능력을 길러야 한다.

문제 형태

Tour Schedule	
Garden Tour	10:00 A.M.
Lunch	Noon
Museum Visit	1:30 P.M.
Theater Performance	4:00 P.M.

98 Look at the graphic. What time is this talk most likely being given?

(A) At 10:00 A.M.
(B) At noon
(C) At 1:30 P.M.
(D) At 4:00 P.M.

Questions 98 through 100 refer to the following talk and list.

Can I have everyone's attention at the front of the bus? I hope you enjoyed your lunch at Restaurant Baron. As I mentioned earlier, it first opened in 1880 and has been operating longer than any other restaurants in Charlestown. Now, if you look out the window on your right, you'll see the National Museum of History and according to our schedule, we're right on time. We'll be spending about 2 hours here. I'll pass out the brochures with the information about the permanent and temporary exhibits you'll be seeing today. We'll meet again at the main entrance at 3:30 for our next schedule. Enjoy yourselves.

PART 5

단문 공란 채우기 [30문제]

파트 5는 문장 안에 있는 빈칸에 적절한 단어나 어구를 채워 넣는 파트이다. 총 30문항이 출제되며, 문법 문제와 어휘 문제가 등장한다. 문제 유형에 따라 풀이 방식이 다르므로 이를 가장 먼저 파악하는 것이 중요하다.

| 핵심 전략 |

+ 문제를 풀기 전, 보기를 통해 문제 유형을 파악하는 연습을 한다.

+ 문법 문제는 문장 구조나 빈칸 주변의 문법을 통해 문제를 풀어야 한다. 문법 문제를 단 시간에 풀기 위해서 명사, 동사, 형용사 등의 기본적인 문법을 확실히 익혀 두도록 하자.

+ 어휘 문제는 해석을 통해 문맥에 가장 적절한 단어를 선택해야 한다. 가능한 한 많은 어휘를 암기하고, 예문을 통해 어휘가 어떻게 사용되는지를 이해하자.

+ 자주 함께 쓰이는 단어 및 표현들을 숙지하여 빠른 시간 내에 문제를 풀어야 한다.

| 문제 형태 |

101 Sky Motors offers a variety of training programs to help enhance ------- in the workplace.

(A) productivity
(B) produce
(C) productive
(D) productively

102 The fundraising event recorded such high ------- that the proceeds will be higher than expected.

(A) representative
(B) consultation
(C) safety
(D) attendance

PART 6

장문 공란 채우기 `16문제`

파트 6는 지문 안에 있는 4개의 빈칸에 알맞은 보기를 선택하는 파트이다. 문법, 어휘, 문장을 넣는 문제가 등장하며, 총 16문항이 출제된다. 문맥에 맞는 문장을 고르는 문제는 각 지문마다 1개씩 출제된다.

| 핵심 전략 |

+ 전체 문맥을 이해해야 풀 수 있는 문법 및 어휘 문제가 나오므로 지문의 흐름을 놓치지 않는 것이 중요하다.

+ 빈칸에 알맞은 문장을 넣는 문제는 빈칸 앞뒤와 전체 맥락을 파악하여 정답을 골라야 하므로 전반적인 독해력을 늘려야 한다.

+ 지문을 읽으면서 흐름상 다음에 나와야 할 내용을 예측하면 정답을 쉽게 찾을 수 있다.

| 문제 형태 |

Questions 135-138 refer to the following notice.

Important Notice about Hatter Industries

Please note that the contact information for Hatter Industries changed on March 21.

Due to the closure of our Dabbley office and the ------- of our operations in Buena,
135
all correspondence concerning our products and services should now be sent to the

following address: Hatter Industries, 642 Mandela Lane, Buena, CA.

Our employees' e-mail addresses, as well as our Web site's address,

www.hatterindustries.com, remain -------.
136

However, we are still waiting for our new telephone and fax numbers. ------- will be
137
updated on our Web site as soon as the new numbers are assigned as of March 25.

-------.
138

---

135 (A) decision
(B) relocation
(C) suspension
(D) result

136 (A) assigned
(B) even
(C) formal
(D) unchanged

137 (A) Yours
(B) Another
(C) These
(D) Theirs

138 (A) We apologize for any
inconvenience and thank you
for your understanding.
(B) Refer to the side of the packet
for full details of instructions
before applying.
(C) Her office location will also
remain the same.
(D) For more information about the
forthcoming event, visit www.
lizard.org.br/events.

PART 7

지문 독해 `54문제`

파트 7은 지문을 읽고 지문과 관련된 문제 2~5개를 푸는 파트이다. 총 54문항이 출제되며, 지문은 편지, 문자 메시지, 광고, 공지문 등 다양한 유형으로 나온다. 단일 지문 10개, 이중 지문 2개, 삼중 지문 3개의 세트가 등장한다.

| 핵심 전략 |

> ✚ 지문의 종류와 제목, 키워드를 파악하여 내용을 미리 예측하고 정답 단서를 찾는다.
>
> ✚ 지문의 단서가 보기에는 다르게 패러프레이징될 수 있으므로, 단어를 암기할 때 동의표현을 함께 익힌다.
>
> ✚ 복수 지문에서는 2개 이상의 지문을 연계하여 풀어야 하는 문제들이 출제되므로, 지문간의 관계를 파악하는 연습을 해야 한다.

| 문제 형태 |

Questions 176-180 refer to the following Web page and e-mail.

---

http://www.highlightcar.ca

| Home | About Us | Reviews | Contact Us |

Highlight Car Service: Taking You Where You Want to Go

Based in Toronto, Highlight Car Service provides a wide range of transportation solutions for business travelers and individuals attending special occasions such as weddings. Our drivers are expertly trained professionals who ensure a seamless journey to your desired destination, whether it's the airport or a hotel. We also offer guided sightseeing tours and will make your travel experience enjoyable and comfortable.

Highlight Car Service operates in numerous cities worldwide from New York to Tokyo, and we are continuously expanding our presence. We are excited to announce the upcoming opening of our newest branch in Nairobi later this year.

Founded three decades ago by former taxi driver Logan Haynes, Highlight Car Service is committed to meeting the demand for top-tier transportation services. To mark our 30th anniversary this April, all new customers who make reservations during that month will enjoy a 20% discount off their total bill. Simply use the code LUX300.

| From: Highlight Car Service <info@highlightcarservice.com> |
| To: Namiko Hideyoshi <Namiko_h@uchemical.jp> |
| Subject: Information |
| Date: April 20 |

Dear Ms. Hideyoshi,

We appreciate your trust in Highlight Car Service! This e-mail serves as confirmation of the reservation you made on April 18.

    Customer Number: 7416
    Pickup Location: Fiumicino Int'l Airport, Terminal C
    Pickup Date: May 3
    Pickup Time: 9:45 A.M.
    Number of Passengers: 5
    Destination/Route: Hilltop Hotel, Viale Europa / Piazza Benito Juarez Park
    Deposit Card: *** **** 8303
    Discount Code: LUX300

Should you have any inquiries or concerns or need a scheduling adjustment, please feel free to reach out to us at 1-800-904-0300 (U.S. and Canada) or internationally at (+1) 721-985-7413.

Stay connected with your driver by downloading our mobile app.

Thank you for choosing Highlight Car Service. We look forward to serving you.

Sincerely,

Highlight Car Service

176 According to the Web page, where will Highlight Car Service soon be available?

(A) In Toronto
(B) In Seoul
(C) In Tokyo
(D) In Nairobi

177 Who is Mr. Haynes?

(A) A car salesman
(B) An event planner
(C) A reservation staff
(D) A company founder

178 What does the Web page indicate about the company?

(A) It is three decades old.
(B) It has relocated its corporate offices.
(C) It focuses on budget-friendly travel.
(D) It has revised its driver training program.

179 What is the purpose of the e-mail?

(A) To book a hotel room
(D) To confirm a reservation
(C) To provide a flight itinerary
(D) To change an arrangement

180 What is suggested about Ms. Hideyoshi?

(A) She will be journeying by herself.
(B) She is employed at Fiumicino Airport.
(C) She is a first-time user of the service.
(D) She encountered an issue with the mobile app.

○ 학습 플랜

2주 완성

DAY 1	DAY 2	DAY 3	DAY 4	DAY 5
TEST 1 LC	TEST 1 RC	TEST 2 LC	TEST 2 RC	TEST 3 LC
DAY 6	**DAY 7**	**DAY 8**	**DAY 9**	**DAY 10**
TEST 3 RC	TEST 4 LC	TEST 4 RC	TEST 5 LC	TEST 5 RC

4주 완성

DAY 1	DAY 2	DAY 3	DAY 4	DAY 5
TEST 1 PART 1-2	TEST 1 PART 3-4	TEST 1 PART 5-6	TEST 1 PART 7	TEST 2 PART 1-2
DAY 6	**DAY 7**	**DAY 8**	**DAY 9**	**DAY 10**
TEST 2 PART 3-4	TEST 2 PART 5-6	TEST 2 PART 7	TEST 3 PART 1-2	TEST 3 PART 3-4
DAY 11	**DAY 12**	**DAY 13**	**DAY 14**	**DAY 15**
TEST 3 PART 5-6	TEST 3 PART 7	TEST 4 PART 1-2	TEST 4 PART 3-4	TEST 4 PART 5-6
DAY 16	**DAY 17**	**DAY 18**	**DAY 19**	**DAY 20**
TEST 4 PART 7	TEST 5 PART 1-2	TEST 5 PART 3-4	TEST 5 PART 5-6	TEST 5 PART 7

* 학습 플랜대로 학습하신 후 도서 인증을 통해 온라인 모의고사를 풀어 보세요. (p.3 하단의 이용 방법 참조)

books. english. co. kr

어휘리뷰와 듣기

실전 1000제

LC+RC

TEST

1

정답 및 해설 p.248

TEST1.mp3

MP3 바로 듣기

LISTENING TEST

In the Listening test, you will be asked to demonstrate how well you understand spoken English. The entire Listening test will last approximately 45 minutes. There are four parts, and directions are given for each part. You must mark your answers on the separate answer sheet.
Do not write your answers in your test book.

PART 1

Directions: For each question in this part, you will hear four statements about a picture in your test book. When you hear the statements, you must select the one statement that best describes what you see in the picture. Then find the number of the question on your answer sheet and mark your answer. The statements will not be printed in your test book and will be spoken only one time.

Statement (B), "They're shaking hands," is the best description of the picture, so you should select answer (B) and mark it on your answer sheet.

1.

2.

GO ON TO THE NEXT PAGE

3.

4.

5.

6.

GO ON TO THE NEXT PAGE

PART 2

Directions: You will hear a question or statement and three responses spoken in English. They will not be printed in your test book and will be spoken only one time. Select the best response to the question or statement and mark the letter (A), (B), or (C) on your answer sheet.

7. Mark your answer on your answer sheet.

8. Mark your answer on your answer sheet.

9. Mark your answer on your answer sheet.

10. Mark your answer on your answer sheet.

11. Mark your answer on your answer sheet.

12. Mark your answer on your answer sheet.

13. Mark your answer on your answer sheet.

14. Mark your answer on your answer sheet.

15. Mark your answer on your answer sheet.

16. Mark your answer on your answer sheet.

17. Mark your answer on your answer sheet.

18. Mark your answer on your answer sheet.

19. Mark your answer on your answer sheet.

20. Mark your answer on your answer sheet.

21. Mark your answer on your answer sheet.

22. Mark your answer on your answer sheet.

23. Mark your answer on your answer sheet.

24. Mark your answer on your answer sheet.

25. Mark your answer on your answer sheet.

26. Mark your answer on your answer sheet.

27. Mark your answer on your answer sheet.

28. Mark your answer on your answer sheet.

29. Mark your answer on your answer sheet.

30. Mark your answer on your answer sheet.

31. Mark your answer on your answer sheet.

PART 3

Directions: You will hear some conversations between two or more people. You will be asked to answer three questions about what the speakers say in each conversation. Select the best response to each question and mark the letter (A), (B), (C), or (D) on your answer sheet. The conversations will not be printed in your test book and will be spoken only one time.

32. Where does the conversation take place?

    (A) In a hotel
    (B) In an office building
    (C) In a bus depot
    (D) In a restaurant

33. What has arrived?

    (A) A computer
    (B) A flyer
    (C) A package
    (D) A fax

34. What will the man probably do next?

    (A) Check out
    (B) Get a receipt
    (C) Go downstairs
    (D) Send a fax

35. What does the woman want to buy?

    (A) Baked goods
    (B) Clothing
    (C) Office supplies
    (D) Auto parts

36. Why does the man advise the woman to hurry?

    (A) The train leaves in fifteen minutes.
    (B) She has a meeting.
    (C) The business will close soon.
    (D) The weather is bad.

37. According to the man, how will the woman most likely travel?

    (A) By taxi
    (B) By streetcar
    (C) By subway
    (D) On foot

38. What is the man's occupation?

    (A) Auto mechanic
    (B) Customer service representative
    (C) Architect
    (D) Taxi driver

39. Why is the woman calling?

    (A) Her phone bill is wrong.
    (B) Her order has not been delivered.
    (C) Her furnace is not working.
    (D) She needs an accountant.

40. What information does the man request?

    (A) The woman's account number
    (B) The woman's address
    (C) The product number
    (D) The amount that the woman paid

41. Where does this conversation most likely take place?

    (A) At a university
    (B) At a hotel
    (C) At a train station
    (D) At a concert hall

42. Why is the woman surprised?

    (A) There are no tickets available.
    (B) The price has been raised.
    (C) The man was rude.
    (D) There is no direct service.

43. Why does the woman say, "What do you mean"?

    (A) To encourage him to repeat the explanation
    (B) To complain about a service
    (C) To express her surprise
    (D) To ask for some help

GO ON TO THE NEXT PAGE

44. What is the main topic of the conversation?

(A) A complaint about a poor service
(B) The revision of a user manual
(C) Some travel plans
(D) Reimbursement for travel expenses

45. According to the woman, why is she happy to take the train?

(A) Because the price is reasonable
(B) Because it will not take a long time
(C) Because the weather will be perfect as anticipated
(D) Because she will get a complimentary beverage

46. What does the man offer to do for the woman?

(A) Book a ticket
(B) Record the agenda from a meeting
(C) Buy lunch
(D) Talk to her supervisor

47. Why does Mr. Shilton want to meet with Mr. Walton?

(A) To introduce a friend
(B) To collect some money
(C) To discuss a proposal
(D) To apply for a job

48. When can the man meet with Mr. Shilton?

(A) On Monday
(B) On Tuesday
(C) On Thursday
(D) On the weekend

49. What will the woman probably do next?

(A) Take a memo
(B) Meet Mr. Shilton
(C) Get in touch with Mr. Shilton
(D) Take a lunch break

50. What are the speakers mainly discussing?

(A) A trip to an art fair
(B) A journey to a foreign country
(C) A daily routine
(D) A café reservation

51. What does the woman say she will do?

(A) Change the reservation
(B) Buy discount tickets
(C) Copy an itinerary
(D) Call her friends

52. Why does Jeff say, "That sounds awesome"?

(A) Because he got a free coupon for dining
(B) Because he finally got a promotion
(C) Because he can have dinner together
(D) Because he will attend the seminar soon

53. Where does the woman work?

(A) At a tour company
(B) At a library
(C) At a bookshop
(D) At an English school

54. What task does the woman mention?

(A) Locating books for customers
(B) Giving a speech to the new hires
(C) Planning a training session
(D) Placing an order

55. When will the training session be held?

(A) On March 8
(B) On March 28
(C) On May 8
(D) On May 28

56. What is the main topic of the conversation?

(A) A business trip
(B) A promotion
(C) A delayed flight
(D) A present for a coworker

57. Why did the woman change her plan?

(A) Amelia Larkin was more qualified.
(B) She was reprimanded by her supervisor.
(C) The money was not available.
(D) She ran out of time.

58. What is Ms. Larkin going to do?

(A) Make a budget
(B) Increase sales
(C) Travel to Seattle
(D) Deliver a presentation

---

59. What is the woman doing?

(A) Interviewing a potential mentor
(B) Hiring a marketing company
(C) Applying for a job
(D) Receiving some training

60. What is the man's current title?

(A) Intern in Accounting
(B) Marketing manager
(C) Mail clerk
(D) President

61. What does the man want to do?

(A) Get a promotion
(B) Become a volunteer
(C) Sell his company
(D) Increase efficiency in the mailroom

	Title	Director
1	About the Future	Jason Lee
2	The Ocean Fellas	Joan Takamoto
3	Time Travel	Daniel Kang
4	Who Moved My Cup?	Yoshimoto

62. What industry do the speakers work in?

(A) Film marketing
(B) Book publishing
(C) Foreign investment
(D) Medical tourism

63. Look at the graphic. Who are the speakers most likely going to invite to the event?

(A) Jason Lee
(B) Joan Takamoto
(C) Daniel Kang
(D) Yoshimoto

64. What will the man probably do after the conversation?

(A) Consult with the manager
(B) Update a daily schedule
(C) Contact the director
(D) Arrange some books

GO ON TO THE NEXT PAGE

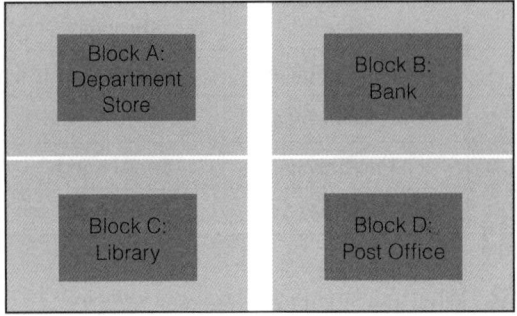

Quantity	Cost
10	$15
30	$40
50	$70
100	$150 $110 (Sale!)

65. What are the speakers concerned about?

(A) The expense of renting
(B) Limited parking space
(C) Strict laws against renting
(D) Few pedestrians

66. Look at the graphic. Which location do the speakers choose for their store?

(A) Block A
(B) Block B
(C) Block C
(D) Block D

67. What does the woman say she will do next?

(A) Contact a real estate agent
(B) Visit a building site
(C) Ask for a price
(D) Go back to her office

68. What does the man want to order?

(A) School uniforms
(B) Glasses
(C) Stamp cards
(D) Promotional pamphlets

69. Look at the graphic. How much will the man's order cost?

(A) $15
(B) $40
(C) $70
(D) $110

70. What is true about the man?

(A) He is the first customer of this store.
(B) He is worried about the location.
(C) He has placed an order from this store before.
(D) He prefers off-line shopping.

PART 4

Directions: You will hear some talks given by a single speaker. You will be asked to answer three questions about what the speaker says in each talk. Select the best response to each question and mark the letter (A), (B), (C), or (D) on your answer sheet. The talks will not be printed in your test book and will be spoken only one time.

71. Why is the woman calling?

(A) To place an order
(B) To book facilities
(C) To cancel an appointment
(D) To book a ticket

72. Who most likely is Ms. Grendel?

(A) A hotel employee
(B) A newspaper reporter
(C) A real estate agent
(D) A lawyer

73. When is Ms. Snell making plans for?

(A) Mid-August
(B) Late August
(C) Early September
(D) Mid-September

74. When is the flight scheduled to depart?

(A) In 15 minutes
(B) In half an hour
(C) In one hour
(D) In one and a half hours

75. What does the speaker say about carry-on luggage?

(A) It is completely full.
(B) It will be inspected.
(C) It is not allowed.
(D) It will be limited.

76. Which of the following items would not be allowed in carry-on luggage?

(A) A camera
(B) A box cutter
(C) A watch
(D) A tablet PC

77. Who is the announcement for?

(A) Shareholders
(B) Delivery personnel
(C) Moving company workers
(D) Office employees

78. According to the announcement, what will the company do over the weekend?

(A) Have a company picnic
(B) Train staff members
(C) Have employee evaluations
(D) Change locations

79. What does the speaker ask the listeners to do?

(A) Go home early
(B) Maintain equipment
(C) Pack items for moving
(D) Fill out some forms

80. How often is the meeting held?

(A) Once a week
(B) Twice a week
(C) Once a month
(D) Twice a month

81. Why does the speaker apologize to the listeners?

(A) She made a sudden change.
(B) She made her workers work late.
(C) She chose an inconvenient time.
(D) She forgot to post a notice.

82. What does the speaker mention in this talk?

(A) The time of the meeting is set for 5 P.M.
(B) The place for the meeting has changed.
(C) Employees have to fill out a form.
(D) Employees should work overtime.

GO ON TO THE NEXT PAGE

83. Where most likely is the speaker?

(A) At a police station
(B) At a radio station
(C) At an award ceremony
(D) At an airport

84. How long has this event been happening?

(A) For 10 years
(B) For 15 years
(C) For 20 years
(D) For 50 years

85. What will most likely happen next?

(A) There will be a demonstration.
(B) A plane will land.
(C) Dinner will be served.
(D) Someone will be given an award.

---

86. In which field does the speaker work?

(A) Manufacturing software
(B) Supplying software to buyers
(C) Selling software
(D) Testing the efficiency of software

87. What were the listeners required to do?

(A) Use antivirus software
(B) Test out some computer programs
(C) Discuss a better way of selling software
(D) Conduct a survey

88. What does the speaker mean when he says, "You cannot make any mistakes"?

(A) The listeners should think it is not a big deal.
(B) The listeners can get some help from the speaker.
(C) The listeners should comply with the instructions.
(D) The listeners will be able to finish the task quickly.

---

89. What is the caller promoting?

(A) A special sale
(B) A new line of clothing
(C) Free delivery
(D) A preferred customer membership

90. What will Ms. Nixon receive if she makes a purchase?

(A) An extended warranty
(B) A gift certificate
(C) A reduced price
(D) A free promotional flyer

91. How can Ms. Nixon take advantage of the offer?

(A) By coming to the store on Saturday
(B) By mailing in a special coupon
(C) By applying for membership through the company's Web site
(D) By showing a special identification to the delivery person

---

92. Who most likely is the speaker?

(A) A banker
(B) An advertising executive
(C) A university professor
(D) A property investor

93. What is the speaker mainly talking about?

(A) Time management skills
(B) Money-making techniques
(C) Maintaining good health
(D) The best travel destinations

94. What will the listeners do next?

(A) Visit some properties
(B) Look at some case studies
(C) Do a role play
(D) Do research on the Internet

```
+------------------------------------------+
|                                          |
|        Winter Music Festival             |
|                                          |
|        Featured Performers               |
|                                          |
|      Dec 20th – Joe Mraz                 |
|      Dec 21st – Jennifer Lauren          |
|      Dec 22nd – Linda                    |
|      Dec 23rd – Mathew Lee               |
|                                          |
+------------------------------------------+
```

Bin 1	Glass
Bin 2	Plastic
Bin 3	Paper
Bin 4	Can

95. What was the cause of the delay of the festival?

(A) Malfunction of instruments
(B) Unfavorable weather
(C) Complaints from residents
(D) Road repairs

96. Look at the graphic. According to the speaker, whose performance will be pushed back?

(A) Joe Mraz's
(B) Jennifer Lauren's
(C) Linda's
(D) Mathew Lee's

97. What does the speaker recommend the listeners do?

(A) Refer to a Web site
(B) Watch a TV show
(C) Copy the receipts
(D) Bring a friend

98. Where does the speaker work?

(A) In the Maintenance Division
(B) In the Human Resources Department
(C) In the cafeteria
(D) In the clinic

99. For whom is the talk intended?

(A) New hires
(B) Café owners
(C) Retired employees
(D) Environmentalists

100. Look at the graphic. Which bin does the speaker ask the listeners to be careful with?

(A) Bin 1
(B) Bin 2
(C) Bin 3
(D) Bin 4

This is the end of the Listening test. Turn to Part 5 in your test book.

GO ON TO THE NEXT PAGE

READING TEST

In the Reading test, you will read a variety of texts and answer several different types of reading comprehension questions. The entire Reading test will last 75 minutes. There are three parts, and directions are given for each part. You are encouraged to answer as many questions as possible within the time allowed.

You must mark your answers on the separate answer sheet. Do not write your answers in the test book.

PART 5

Directions: A word or phrase is missing in each of the sentences below. Four answer choices are given below each sentence. Select the best answer to complete the sentence. Then mark the letter (A), (B), (C), or (D) on your answer sheet.

101. Please send Mr. Dean ------- job application form within five business days.

    (A) you
    (B) yours
    (C) yourself
    (D) your

102. Most customers that we surveyed last month were ------- with the service of Gallerion Department Store.

    (A) satisfy
    (B) satisfied
    (C) satisfying
    (D) satisfaction

103. The new Z9 sedan that ------- last week has received many positive reviews.

    (A) released
    (B) were released
    (C) was released
    (D) releases

104. Staff members are encouraged to change their passwords every 90 days to ensure that company data is kept -------.

    (A) secure
    (B) useful
    (C) valid
    (D) available

105. James Hendel has shown much greater administrative ability than many of ------- with extensive management experience in leading companies.

    (A) they
    (B) that
    (C) this
    (D) those

106. Mr. Trump ------- an impressive lecture on how to effectively run a business at the Washington Memorial Hall.

    (A) mentioned
    (B) responded
    (C) delivered
    (D) considered

107. Now that the convention center has -------, it can seat up to 500 people.

    (A) is enlarged
    (B) enlarged
    (C) been enlarged
    (D) enlarging

108. Specific information about the charges is indicated ------- your invoice.

    (A) on
    (B) in
    (C) to
    (D) by

109. Prime Tech's new eco-friendly heaters consume much ------- energy than those produced by other manufacturers.

(A) strong
(B) higher
(C) lower
(D) less

110. ------- security, the company distributed security passes to all employees.

(A) To enhance
(B) Enhancing
(C) To enhancing
(D) Enhanced

111. Mr. Johnson ------- cannot participate in the awards ceremony because he is scheduled to go on a business trip to Seoul.

(A) regretfully
(B) significantly
(C) considerately
(D) purposely

112. When ------- a new employee, it is desirable to place emphasis on experience rather than academic background.

(A) hiring
(B) talking
(C) notifying
(D) training

113. Prestige Planning is an established company ------- in corporate advertising.

(A) specializes
(B) specializing
(C) specialized
(D) specialize

114. Since Max Construction frequently has leftover materials from its projects, it donates them ------- charity in need of support.

(A) to
(B) from
(C) as
(D) in

115. ------- the popularity of its latest laptop, Koreana Electronics Co. has decided to increase the production.

(A) Considering that
(B) Concerning
(C) In that
(D) Given

116. Wellbeing Food Management apologizes for any ------- which the current renovation work may cause to our customers.

(A) environment
(B) dedication
(C) distribution
(D) inconvenience

117. ------- attempts to contact the customer service representative have been unsuccessful.

(A) Repeated
(B) Repeating
(C) Repetition
(D) Having repeated

118. Pro Engineering is well qualified for operating the new management system, ------- will be introduced later this year.

(A) who
(B) that
(C) which
(D) where

119. The department manager and his team managed to have the project ------- on schedule.

(A) complete
(B) completing
(C) completed
(D) completes

120. TH Soft's ------- online game, "The Revolution," offers a variety of game experiences designed for people who want to pursue something different.

(A) sensitive
(B) upcoming
(C) stringent
(D) impartial

GO ON TO THE NEXT PAGE

121. North America's mobile phone market has grown more ------- over the last two years.

(A) compete
(B) competed
(C) competition
(D) competitive

122. Our weekly newsletters have ------- to be sent, so please be patient and wait a few more days.

(A) yet
(B) too
(C) still
(D) then

123. Because of the ongoing construction on Parker Street, motorists ------- to take Burrard Avenue to go downtown.

(A) direction
(B) directs
(C) directed
(D) are directed

124. At Future Telecom, customer satisfaction is something ------- is the most important.

(A) who
(B) when
(C) that
(D) this

125. The president of Lux Publishing was ------- that its sales have been at its highest for twelve consecutive weeks.

(A) welcomed
(B) flattered
(C) sophisticated
(D) operated

126. Of the two machine operators, the ------- qualified will be the one to run the new equipment in the factory.

(A) well
(B) better
(C) best
(D) even

127. Had I not met with the representative at the last minute, I ------- into a sales contract.

(A) entered
(B) will not enter
(C) could not have entered
(D) had not entered

128. ------- next Wednesday, a new dress code for employees will go into effect.

(A) Beginning
(B) Having
(C) Considering
(D) Regarding

129. The plans for the new building have to ------- with the current government regulations.

(A) belong
(B) apply
(C) consult
(D) comply

130. ------- sufficient information, it is difficult to find a good location and rent a nice apartment.

(A) Without
(B) On
(C) By
(D) During

PART 6

Directions: Read the texts that follow. A word, phrase, or sentence is missing in parts of each text. Four answer choices for each question are given below the text. Select the best answer to complete the text. Then mark the letter (A), (B), (C), or (D) on your answer sheet.

Questions 131-134 refer to the following e-mail.

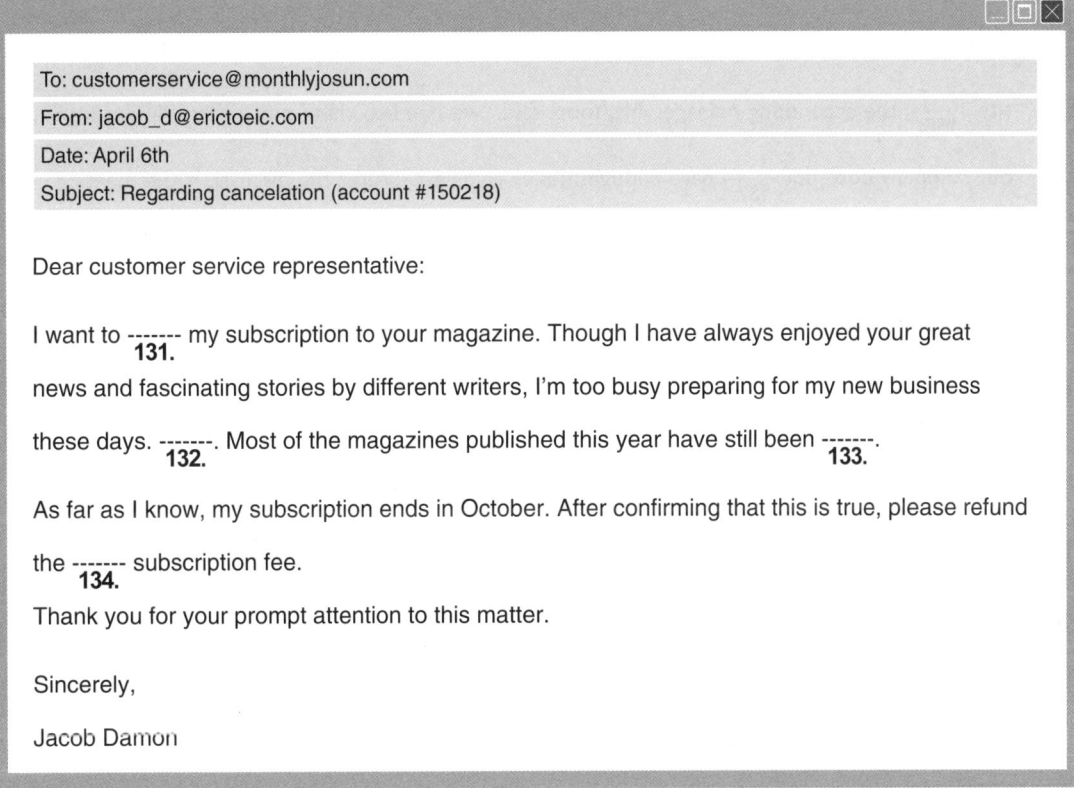

To: customerservice@monthlyjosun.com

From: jacob_d@erictoeic.com

Date: April 6th

Subject: Regarding cancelation (account #150218)

Dear customer service representative:

I want to ------- my subscription to your magazine. Though I have always enjoyed your great
     131.

news and fascinating stories by different writers, I'm too busy preparing for my new business

these days. -------. Most of the magazines published this year have still been -------.
     132.   **133.**

As far as I know, my subscription ends in October. After confirming that this is true, please refund

the ------- subscription fee.
     134.

Thank you for your prompt attention to this matter.

Sincerely,

Jacob Damon

131. (A) apply
    (B) renew
    (C) cancel
    (D) join

132. (A) I'm interested in business magazines.
    (B) However, I always try to read many
        books.
    (C) I want to write a story about my
        company.
    (D) Therefore, there is not enough free time
        to read them.

133. (A) valid
    (B) neglected
    (C) used
    (D) reading

134. (A) remain
    (B) remained
    (C) remaining
    (D) remains

GO ON TO THE NEXT PAGE

Questions 135-138 refer to the following meeting minutes.

The Meeting Minutes

Star Motor's management meeting was held at its headquarters on June 1. The purpose of the meeting was to decide ------- to relocate the second plant. Mr. Jung, the production manager,
135.

argued that the company had grown so much that it had to relocate the factory to a larger site. -------, the accounting manager, Ms. Yoon, said, "we need to think more carefully because
136.

our company does not ------- have enough money to invest." After the discussion, the meeting
137.

ended without a conclusion on moving the factory. -------.
138.

135. (A) that
(B) whether
(C) what
(D) this

136. (A) Therefore
(B) In addition to
(C) In that
(D) However

137. (A) currently
(B) previously
(C) shortly
(D) lately

138. (A) We should inform the staff that the headquarters will not be moved.
(B) We had a good opportunity to manage it.
(C) The factory needs more workers.
(D) The matter is to be dealt with again at the next meeting.

Questions 139-142 refer to the following information.

At Haro Books Online, we always do our best to ship orders as quickly as possible. ------- your
139.
order has already arrived, please refer to the following information. Delivery times range from

three to five days, depending on the ------- shipping method. -------. We try to make sure
140.   141.

that it is delivered on time, but sometimes it takes longer to arrive. If your order arrives more

than three days later than the scheduled delivery date, you will receive a refund of double

the shipping charge. If you want to track your shipment, please contact us with your invoice

number. We'll investigate and ------- you of your shipment status.
142.

139. (A) When
(B) Since
(C) Considering
(D) Unless

140. (A) selecting
(B) to select
(C) selected
(D) selection

141. (A) The expected delivery date is always
provided to you.
(B) You can return the damaged items at no
cost.
(C) The new books are introduced on the
Web site.
(D) Our delivery people are trained to drive
safely.

142. (A) announce
(B) speak
(C) notify
(D) explain

GO ON TO THE NEXT PAGE

Questions 143-146 refer to the following information.

Toronto Development Service Department
Building Construction Guidelines

Residents who want to change the structure of a building need to get approval to remodel it.

In general, minor modifications do not require -------. However, for any major alterations, things are
143.

different. The approval must be requested ------- by the building owner. -------.
144. **145.**

If you are caught doing construction work without consent, you may be fined more than $3,000.

These rules are for you and your neighbors' safety, so be sure to ------- them.
146.

Please check the City Hall Web site at www.torontocity.gov for examples of cases.

---

143. (A) plans
(B) funds
(C) permission
(D) materials

144. (A) shortly
(B) consistently
(C) directly
(D) separately

145. (A) After the application, it takes about five days to be determined.
(B) The process cannot be changed later.
(C) Some builders are not responsible for the permit.
(D) It is too costly to renovate buildings.

146. (A) see
(B) observe
(C) pay
(D) ignore

PART 7

Directions: In this part you will read a selection of texts, such as magazine and newspaper articles, e-mails, and instant messages. Each text or set of texts is followed by several questions. Select the best answer for each question and mark the letter (A), (B), (C), or (D) on your answer sheet.

Questions 147-148 refer to the following text message.

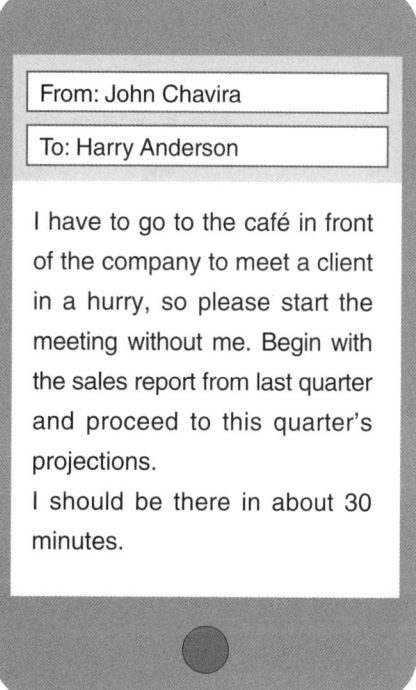

From: John Chavira

To: Harry Anderson

I have to go to the café in front of the company to meet a client in a hurry, so please start the meeting without me. Begin with the sales report from last quarter and proceed to this quarter's projections.
I should be there in about 30 minutes.

147. Why was the message sent?

(A) To give instructions
(B) To review a report
(C) To delay the meeting
(D) To ask for some advice

148. What is true about Mr. Chavira?

(A) He's never met his client before.
(B) He will revise the sales report.
(C) He can't attend the meeting on time.
(D) He already finished his project.

GO ON TO THE NEXT PAGE

MEMO

To: All staff
From: Pablo Recardo
Date: February 18
Subject: Overtime work

Good morning, April and May are usually the busiest months for the interior design service. Therefore, I think we'll have to work an extra three hours a day. Before we inform our customers about it, we need to look for employees who can work overtime. Employees working late will be given overtime pay for each hour as well as their normal hourly pay. If you are interested, please let me know before you leave on February 28. To hire as many new part-time workers as we need, we will post a job opening the next day on our Web site. Also, for those planning to go on vacation in May, it is recommended that it be postponed until the middle of June.

Sincerely,

Pablo Recardo

149. What is the purpose of the memo?
(A) To promote the new products
(B) To lay off some employees
(C) To suggest that employees make creative designs
(D) To encourage employees to do extra work

150. According to the memo, what will Mr. Recardo do after February 28?
(A) Announce the new service to customers
(B) Look for new employees
(C) Work overtime every day
(D) Increase the number of full-time employees

Questions 151-152 refer to the following text-message chain.

Stephen Kim [9:05 A.M.]

Can we get together to discuss the house at 186 Hamilton Street? The owners would like to put it on the market before the end of September.

Cindy Adams [9:14 A.M.]

I have a meeting from 10:00 A.M. to 11:50 A.M., but I'm free at lunchtime. How about meeting at Waining Café?

Stephen Kim [9:15 A.M.]

Good. I'll bring detailed information about the property, so please help me analyze it carefully.

Cindy Adams [9:15 A.M.]

No problem. I'll help you assess the value based on your property information.

Stephen Kim [9:16 A.M.]

Thanks. I really appreciate that you always give me so much useful advice.

Cindy Adams [9:17 A.M.]

Don't mention it. I'm off now. See you soon.

151. What is most likely true about Mr. Kim?

(A) He is looking for a new house.
(B) He wants to take a tour of a property.
(C) He has a house to move into.
(D) He has received help from Ms. Adams before.

152. At 9:17 A.M., what does Ms. Adams mean when she writes, "I'm off now"?

(A) She is leaving the office.
(B) She is going to the meeting.
(C) She is resting at home.
(D) She is going out to see a house.

GO ON TO THE NEXT PAGE

Questions 153-155 refer to the following e-mail.

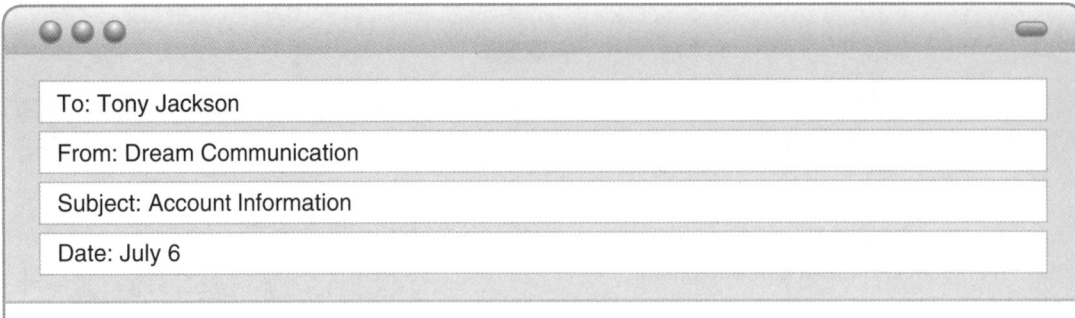

To: Tony Jackson

From: Dream Communication

Subject: Account Information

Date: July 6

Dear Mr. Jackson,

This e-mail is to inform you that your account's password has been changed. If you have not changed your password yourself, please contact our Customer Service Department, 051-1117-0406, as soon as possible. That way, we will be able to identify the cause and solve the problem quickly. This e-mail address is for outgoing use only, so please make sure to call us back because we cannot receive a reply.

If you have changed the information yourself, you do not need to contact us.

We always do our best to protect your personal information.

Sincerely,

Dream Communication Customer Service

153. Why was the e-mail sent to Mr. Jackson?

(A) To notify him of the new service
(B) To provide him with some benefits
(C) To inform him of changes in his account details
(D) To ask him about contact information

154. What is Mr. Jackson asked to do?

(A) Change the password regularly
(B) Visit the office within a short time
(C) Call if he didn't change the information
(D) Solve the problem quickly

155. What is NOT stated in the e-mail?

(A) Mr. Jackson forgot his password.
(B) The customer center can be contacted by phone.
(C) Mr. Jackson's personal information has been changed.
(D) This e-mail address can be used only for sending.

Questions 156-157 refer to the following text-message chain.

New Chat ⊖⊡⊗

Judy Clinton [2:28 P.M.]
I'm going to the silk trade fair in Winnipeg on February 18. Would you like to go with me?

Brad Rogers [2:33 P.M.]
I really want to go, but my design project for the new summer collection is due on February 25.
I should hope for another chance.

Judy Clinton [2:34 P.M.]
Then, you have no choice but to do so. I'll let you know if I get any information to refer to.

Brad Rogers [2:41 P.M.]
Good, and I'll send you a list of materials I can use for the new products this summer, so can you get them for me? Since the products from all over the world are displayed at the fair, I think there will be many things we can't usually get.

Judy Clinton [2:43 P.M.]
Of course. I'd be glad to. Send me the list by e-mail.

Send

156. Who most likely is Mr. Rogers?

(A) An organizer for a trade fair
(B) A clothing designer
(C) A cloth importer
(D) A CEO of a clothing company

157. At 2:34 P.M., what does Ms. Clinton mean when she writes, "Then, you have no choice but to do so"?

(A) She can't go to the fair with Mr. Rogers.
(B) She can help Mr. Rogers finish the task.
(C) She wants Mr. Rogers to put off some work.
(D) She'll get some materials for Mr. Rogers.

GO ON TO THE NEXT PAGE

Questions 158-160 refer to the following e-mail.

To: millers@mate.un
From: services1@oasissupply.km
Subject: Your order no.7163
Date: June 1

Dear Mr. Miller,

The following items from your order (#7163) have been shipped by Oasis Supply.

ITEM	QUANTITY
Yundai fax machine	1
SG LCD monitor (24 inches)	3
Soris Speaker	3

These items are currently on back order.

ITEM	QUANTITY
Jenix copier ink cartridge	5
ASUX computer keyboard	2

We apologize for the inconvenience. Please let us know if you would like to wait for these items or have them replaced with similar items currently in stock. We have copier ink cartridges manufactured by Kensis. There are also many different kinds of ink cartridges from other manufacturers on our Web site at www.oasissupply.km. You can choose the option just by logging on to our Web site. If you don't make any changes, the rest of your original order will be delivered to you two weeks late.

Your credit card has been charged only for the items that have already been shipped to you. The remainder of your items will not be charged until they get back in stock. So, please tell us whether you want to proceed with your original purchase as soon as possible.

Thank you for your constant patronage.

Oasis Supply Customer Service

158. What is the purpose of the e-mail?

(A) To give information about the status of an order
(B) To recall products from a retailer
(C) To request payment for goods
(D) To provide details of the product's price

159. What is indicated about a copier ink cartridge?

(A) It was discontinued last year.
(B) It comes in multiple colors.
(C) The wrong product was shipped.
(D) Other brands are in stock.

160. What is Mr. Miller asked to do?

(A) Select a credit card to be charged
(B) Pay the unpaid balance
(C) Consider ordering alternative products
(D) Return the items for a refund

Questions 161-163 refer to the following e-mail.

To	Juliana Roberts <j_roberts@goodmail.us>
From	John Breedlove <johns84@parker.ne.co>
Subject	Order #KS3609
Date	Novemver 17

Dear Ms. Roberts,

Thank you for sending me the e-mail yesterday regarding your recent purchase. — [1] —. I have reviewed the order you placed on Novemver 8, and it shows that you ordered ten marker pens, three staplers, and a box of copier paper. And we realized that a box of paper clips was sent instead of the copier paper. — [2] —. We sincerely apologize for the mistake. We have recently taken lots of orders, and mistakes sometimes happen. — [3] —. We will send you the copy paper immediately by overnight delivery, and you can also return the wrong order through the courier. Of course, you don't have to pay any extra fees. — [4] —. You can use it anytime in the future. Thank you for your patience.

Sincerely,

John Breedlove
Customer Service Representative
Parker Good Supplies

161. What does Mr. Breedlove most likely work for?

(A) An art supplies manufacturer
(B) A delivery service provider
(C) An office supplies vendor
(D) A publishing house

162. When did Ms. Roberts report a problem with her order?

(A) November 8
(B) November 16
(C) November 17
(D) November 18

163. In which of the positions marked [1], [2], [3], and [4] does the following sentence best belong?

"As an apology for our mistake, we will enclose a 30% discount coupon with the product."

(A) [1]
(B) [2]
(C) [3]
(D) [4]

GO ON TO THE NEXT PAGE

Questions 164-167 refer to the following article.

WASHINGTON (June 1) — Pendon Airlines CEO Gary Wilson announced on Thursday that his company has purchased Space Airlines. Pendon is headquartered in Toronto, Canada, and this acquisition will double the size of the airline. The airline will also expand its business into new markets. Most of Pendon's routes are to cities in North and South America such as New York, Mexico City, and Buenos Aires. Meanwhile, Space Airlines' head office is in Beijing, China, and the airline flies to countries throughout Asia.

"There will be no significant change in service, and the employment of current employees will be guaranteed," said the representative of the two airlines. The employees, including pilots and flight attendants, were very pleased about the purchase. Ava Martin, a flight attendant who has worked for Space for more than four years, said, "I think this acquisition is really good for us. We have always been anxious about restructuring because our company has been in financial trouble for about two years."

164. What is the purpose of the article?

(A) To announce staff reductions
(B) To compare the two companies
(C) To announce the expansion of the aircraft fleet
(D) To publicize the merger of two companies

165. What is indicated about Space Airlines?

(A) Its business was not doing very well.
(B) It may increase its ticket prices.
(C) It laid off some employees.
(D) It expanded its business to North America.

166. The word "purchased" in paragraph 1, line 4, is closest in meaning to

(A) stolen
(B) presented
(C) figured
(D) acquired

167. What is suggested about Ms. Martin?

(A) She is looking for another job.
(B) She wants to keep serving as a flight attendant.
(C) She should be transferred to New York.
(D) She wanted her company to expand the business.

GO ON TO THE NEXT PAGE

October 7

Sam Weinberg
245 Rockwell Avenue
Vancouver in BC, Canada

Dear Mr. Weinberg,

Thank you for visiting my office in Victoria last month. I really enjoyed talking with you about your career in publishing at Toronto Standard Publishing Co.

As I already mentioned then, our company is planning to open a new branch in Paris, France, so we are seeking new employees with French-language skills like you. Therefore, we would like to invite you to apply for a job. If you are selected for the position, you will undergo the training course for two weeks to familiarize yourself with our business.

Please send me your résumé at your earliest convenience if you want to take this opportunity. I will then send it to the personnel manager to arrange an interview. The interview will probably be held at our head office in Vancouver, so it will be convenient for you to come. I believe that the employment will be a great opportunity for your professional development. If you have any questions, please do not hesitate to contact me.

Regards,

Marisa Truman
Marisa Truman
Sales Department
Horizon Education & Publication

168. What is the purpose of the letter?

(A) To recruit a new employee
(B) To announce the schedule of an event
(C) To explain a new policy
(D) To request some information about a new market

169. According to the letter, what did Mr. Weinberg do in September?

(A) Send a résumé
(B) Register for a training course
(C) Visit the personnel office
(D) Meet with Ms. Truman

170. What is Ms. Truman's company planning to do?

(A) Hold an orientation for new employees
(B) Change its business strategy
(C) Open a new office
(D) Reduce its workforce

171. Where is Horizon Education & Publication based?

(A) In Victoria
(B) In Toronto
(C) In Paris
(D) In Vancouver

GO ON TO THE NEXT PAGE

Many large companies find it difficult to build a brand. For small business owners, the brand building may feel much harder. When Charles Clinton established his company, The Great People in Special Times, he tried to make the brand name distinctive. Now, Mr. Clinton considers the name a little too unique. "People seemed unable to adapt well to the name," says Mr. Clinton. — [1] —. "It was simply too long, so I shortened it to just 'Times.'"

According to market analyst Jimmy Handricks, changing a brand name is really difficult and risky for a company. — [2] —. "If consumers do not notice that the brand name has changed, they may turn to other brands," says Mr. Handricks. "Changes in packaging can be a dangerous challenge as well."

Despite the risks, the marketing department decided to drastically change the packaging designs and went ahead with the plan. They hired Cindy Garcia, the country's top designer, to create new packaging for the company's line of watches. — [3] —. Moreover, she always makes bold and funky designs. The company believed that her designs could attract more young consumers.

The company is trying to come up with an effective way to get as many customers as possible to recognize the new packaging design in a short time. In addition, Mr. Clinton is making a lot of effort to publicize that the appearance of the products has changed, but the performance has not changed. — [4] —. "We need to let our customers know that we are still making reliable, high-performance products, and at the same time, we need to make innovative changes to capture the attention of potential customers," he says.

172. What is the purpose of this article?

(A) To promote a new company
(B) To advertise policy changes
(C) To gather ideas for making brand names
(D) To inform the public of the change in a brand name

173. What is indicated about Ms. Garcia?

(A) She emphasizes design over product quality.
(B) She specializes in packaging design.
(C) She wants to increase her company's market share.
(D) She analyzes the market well.

174. Why does Mr. Clinton want to make changes?

(A) To attract more consumers
(B) To produce quality products
(C) To improve product quality
(D) To develop new equipment

175. In which of the positions marked [1], [2], [3], and [4] does the following sentence best belong?

"Ms. Garcia is famous for her use of abstract and brilliant patterns."

(A) [1]
(B) [2]
(C) [3]
(D) [4]

GO ON TO THE NEXT PAGE

Questions 176-180 refer to the following e-mail and flyer.

To: roses_1@dandyfurniture.net

From: jack_l@dandyfurniture.net

Date: July 6

Subject: Workshop

Attachment: the_flyer.jpg

Dear Ms. Wright,

I have attached a flyer that contains information about a workshop in which I am interested. I believe I can learn useful skills that will allow me to address an important concern.

Although the furniture we produce is very easy to assemble, the manual makes it seem very difficult to put it together. As you know, the most common complaints we receive from our customers are that the contents of the manual are too technical. By attending the workshop, I will be able to learn how to easily describe the assembly process to the majority of our customers so that they can complete the assembly quickly.

The total cost for my participation would be $380. This includes everything such as meals, transportation, and accommodation. I hope you will agree that my participation in this event would be valuable to our company.

Thank you for considering this request.

Best regards,

Jack Lewis

A workshop on improving working skills:
The easiest professional writing in the world

WR Conference Hall / 219-32 Haro Street, Seattle / July 24 – 26 / 10 A.M. – 4 P.M.

In this workshop, you will learn how to explain difficult information in a very easy way. No matter how complex the machines or equipment you describe is, you can make it easy for most users to understand and follow.

Sejun Lee, the instructor you will see in this course, has had a professional career over the last 12 years, providing explanations for various products from small computers to automobiles.

All participants in this course will have the opportunity to ask questions directly to their instructor and get answers from him. In addition, at the end of the workshop, you will receive a handbook that summarizes the key points of the training.

The workshop fee is $380 including meals and accommodations. It doesn't cover the transportation cost.

To register, visit our Web site, www.pro-trainings.or.kr.

176. What is the purpose of the e-mail?

(A) To request funds
(B) To reserve a room
(C) To report some problems
(D) To give information about products

177. In the e-mail, the word "majority" in paragraph 2, line 4, is closest in meaning to

(A) specialty
(B) distinction
(C) most
(D) chief

178. What is indicated about Mr. Lewis?

(A) He is not good at assembling furniture.
(B) He is a professional instructor.
(C) He created customer manuals.
(D) He wants to go to Seattle.

179. What information does Mr. Lewis misunderstand?

(A) The workshop location
(B) The purpose of the manual
(C) The necessary expenses
(D) The registration method

180. What is suggested about Mr. Lee?

(A) He organizes the workshop every year.
(B) He majored in technology education.
(C) He will be answering some questions by phone.
(D) He has a lot of experience in his field.

GO ON TO THE NEXT PAGE

Questions 181-185 refer to the following article and letter.

Local News

By John Wilson

JERSEY CITY (August 14) — After nearly eight months of renovation work, business has resumed in Jersey City Hall. On Friday, city officials and visitors were permitted to enter the prominent landmark to see the final result. Brendan Baker, the manager of the construction, is pleased about the move back to City Hall from the temporary facilities in the nearby Centum Plaza. "The majority of the transition was completed in two weeks," he said. "Compared with the series of delays we experienced during renovations, the move seemed relatively smooth, and the building now looks noble and elegant."

Visitors seemed equally pleased. Upon entering the lobby of the first floor, visitors were amazed to see the more brilliant marble floor with fantastic lighting. Simon Little, an architect, said, "I came to see the renovations, as I heard great things from my colleagues, and I've never seen such a nice building. There's no building that's been innovatively remodeled like this anywhere across the country today."

The most impressive feature was an addition that houses a museum honoring the special contributions of several figures. Colin Murray, President of Grand Nature Construction, said, "We did our best to build this building, not only to symbolize our city of Jersey, but also to be a tourist attraction."

Dear Editor,

I read your article recently, but I'm afraid your news on the renovation of Jersey City Hall was missing some information.

I personally regret there aren't any stories about ordinary citizens who have contributed a lot by making donations to renovate City Hall. The other thing, I think, is that the parking space in the building is now too small after the remodeling. If it becomes a favorite place for tourists to visit, I think it is more urgent to expand the parking space. In fact, I'll be discussing this issue with the supervisor of the renovation on Thursday, August 23.

I'd like you to add my comments to your new article in the newspaper if you write a follow-up on this matter.

Sincerely,

Peter Jones
Peter Jones

---

181. What is the purpose of the article?

(A) To encourage officials to expand parking areas
(B) To announce a facility's reopening
(C) To inform residents of defects in a structure
(D) To commemorate the donors

182. What is mentioned about the City Hall project?

(A) It was completed on time.
(B) It included the construction of amenities.
(C) It was supported only by personal funds.
(D) It took place over about eight months.

183. What does Mr. Jones indicate was missing from the article?

(A) A reference to donors to the project
(D) Details of renovation work
(C) The location of a new parking area
(D) The date of an upcoming event

184. What opinion about the renovation project does Mr. Jones give?

(A) It cost a lot of money for the work.
(B) Whether it will be successful remains to be seen.
(C) The building is expected to attract much attention.
(D) Visitors will have trouble parking their cars.

185. Who will Mr. Jones meet on Thursday?

(A) John Wilson
(B) Brendan Baker
(C) Simon Little
(D) Colin Murray

GO ON TO THE NEXT PAGE

Questions 186-190 refer to the following Web pages and e-mail.

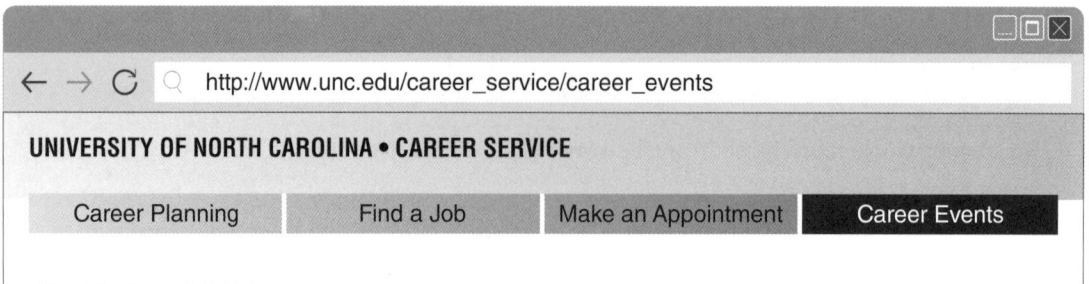

http://www.unc.edu/career_service/career_events

UNIVERSITY OF NORTH CAROLINA • CAREER SERVICE

| Career Planning | Find a Job | Make an Appointment | Career Events |

Health Care Job Fair

Here is your chance to find the job of a lifetime. Come to the Health Care Job Fair organized by the University of North Carolina. The event will take place on Friday, June 8, from 10:30 A.M. to 5:30 P.M. at the university's Charles Memorial Auditorium.

Learn how to finance your continuing studies, have your résumé and job application materials reviewed by recruiting experts, talk with many employers, and network with other job seekers.

A series of informative sessions will also be held, focusing on the following health care careers:

Topic	Time	Location
Dentistry	11:00 A.M. – 11:50 A.M.	Room 116
Nursing	1:00 P.M. – 1:50 P.M.	Room 114
Clinical pathology	2:30 P.M. – 3:20 P.M.	Room 108
Physical therapy	4:00 P.M. – 4:50 P.M.	Room 111

To: Dennis Wood

From: Harold White

Date: June 1

Subject: Requesting assistance

Dear Dennis,

Hi, I'm scheduled to give a presentation one week from today at the University of North Carolina about the work I do here at the Spring Medical Center. I'll be traveling with my secretary and will return to Atlantic City by car with her the following Tuesday, so please book me two one-way tickets for Friday, June 8. I would like to arrive in Charlotte between 2:00 and 2:30 P.M. and then I would have enough time to make a final check before my presentation at 4:00 P.M. I want to avoid journeys that have a train change in the middle. Also, given the budget constraints, the fare should not exceed $60 per person.

Thank you, and please feel free to contact me if you have any questions.

Harold White

← → C 🔍 https://www.united-rails.com/buytickets

Select Ticket	Seating Preferences	Delivery Options	Payment	Confirmation

Two passengers, from Atlantic City to Charlotte

Depart	Arrive	Connections	Ticket Fare Per Person	Rail Operator
10:30 A.M.	11:45 A.M.	0	$70.00	Speedy rails
11:00 A.M.	12:40 P.M.	0	$70.00	New trains
11:30 A.M.	2:10 P.M.	1	$50.00	Sky trains
12:00 P.M.	2:20 P.M.	0	$55.00	States connection

186. In the first Web page, the word "materials" in paragraph 2, line 1, is closest in meaning to

(A) fabrics
(B) substances
(C) documents
(D) methods

187. In the first Web page, what is NOT mentioned as a benefit of the Job Fair?

(A) Helpful advice for job hunting
(B) Opportunities to meet with employers
(C) Lectures on health care jobs
(D) Information about student loans

188. Who most likely is Mr. Wood?

(A) An event participant
(B) A speech expert
(C) An office assistant
(D) An entrepreneur

189. In what field does Mr. White work?

(A) Dentistry
(B) Nursing
(C) Clinical pathology
(D) Physical therapy

190. What railway company will Mr. White use to go to Charlotte?

(A) Speedy rails
(B) New trains
(C) Sky trains
(D) States connection

GO ON TO THE NEXT PAGE

Carol Harris
306 Kent Avenue
Los Angeles, CA 908688

January 28

Dear Ms. Harris,

I regret to inform you that the following item you ordered has been discontinued.
SN #0003609 (Sunpower) Digital Camera, $599.99

The manufacturer of the camera, Sunpower, stopped producing the product a month ago.
In the new year, they decided to make another product instead of that camera, but it has not yet been launched on the market.
Therefore, I encourage you to alternatively consider the following products that we have in stock.

• SN #0003689 (Sunpower) Digital Camera, $810.46
• SN #06081007 (Shotmaster) Digital Camera, $748.35
• SN #06081117 (Shotmaster) Digital Camera, $850.99

The products mentioned above have performance that is not significantly different from the one you originally wanted to order. The price is a little bit more expensive, but they allow for a picture with a slightly clearer quality.
If you'd like to compare them, please feel free to drop by our store any weekday.

Warmest regards,

Michelle Walker
Customer Service Representative
Prime Photos

To	: Michelle Walker <walker8000@primephotos.net>
From	: Carol Harris <happycarol@yahos.com>
Date	: January 30
Subject	: To select a camera

Thank you for sending me a letter explaining the recommended products. I'm very sorry that the product I wanted to buy is no longer being sold, but since I need a camera, I want to buy another one. Like everyone else, I prefer cameras that create photographs that are higher in resolution. However, the products you suggested are higher-priced than what I originally ordered. If I had to choose one, I'd like to get the second one, which is the most inexpensive of the three. And I want to get 5% off with the coupon I received last year, but I'm not sure if it is still valid. So, would you please check it for me? The coupon number is C137159. If possible, I'll visit your store and purchase it myself.

Sincerely,

Carol Harris

```
vvvvvvvvvvvvvvvvvvvvvvvvvvvvvvvvvvvvvvvvvvvvvvvvv
```

TRANSACTION RECEIPT

PRIME PHOTOS
550 Georgia Street
Los Angeles, CA 55027
[880] 5001-3609

01/31/2024 4:15 P.M.
Card No.: 1234 xxxx xxxx

Customer's Name: **Carol Harris**
Requested Product: **Digital Camera**
Discount: **$37.42**
Amount Paid: **$710.93**

We will exchange any unopened item with original receipt!
We do not offer refunds.

```
vvvvvvvvvvvvvvvvvvvvvvvvvvvvvvvvvvvvvvvvvvvvvvvvv
```

191. Why was the letter sent?

(A) To explain why a delivery was late
(B) To suggest more affordable options
(C) To report on the circumstance of a
    product
(D) To offer a special promotion

192. In the letter, the phrase "drop by" in paragraph 4, line 4, is closest in meaning to

(A) decline
(B) reserve
(C) visit
(D) restock

193. What is indicated about Ms. Harris in the e-mail?

(A) She will wait for a new product to be released.
(B) She wants to cancel the order due to the billing error.
(C) She is satisfied with the prices of recommended products.
(D) She prefers products with better performance.

194. Which camera is Ms. Harris most likely to buy?

(A) SN #0003609
(B) SN #0003689
(C) SN #06081007
(D) SN #06081117

195. What did NOT occur on January 31?

(A) A camera was purchased by credit card.
(B) A coupon was used for a purchase.
(C) Ms. Harris visited the store in person.
(D) Ms. Harris presented the receipt for an exchange.

GO ON TO THE NEXT PAGE

Humanity Appliances
245 Golden Street, Calgary
Phone: (921) 3666-4848
Business hours: Monday to Friday, 9 A.M. to 6 P.M.

DON'T MISS OUR ANNUAL INVENTORY CLEARANCE SALE!

Friday, April 6, to Sunday, April 8

- 48-inch LCD TV – 20% off
- KS Electric Rice Cooker – 25% off
- LGS Dishwasher – 30% off
- Stars Premium Refrigerator – 35% off
- SKY Laundry Dryer – 50% off

Please note that the store will close at 1 P.M. on Thursday, April 5, in order to prepare for the sale. Discounts apply equally to both online and offline purchases. You can buy items on a first-come first-served basis, and you cannot make reservations.

Sign up for Humanity Appliances' Gold Membership to become eligible for an additional 5% discount. If you have any questions, please contact our sales team. Our trained sales staff is available to answer any questions.

To: All employees
From: Mark Bolton
Date: March 30
Subject: Work Schedule

To all employees,

We are adding an overnight shift on April 5 and will need employees to record inventory, check prices, and set up product displays. I have arranged a special treat from Grand Foods so that all volunteers will have breakfast in addition to time-and-a-half pay during the shift. Please notify me by April 3 if you are available.

Sincerely,

Mark Bolton
General Manager

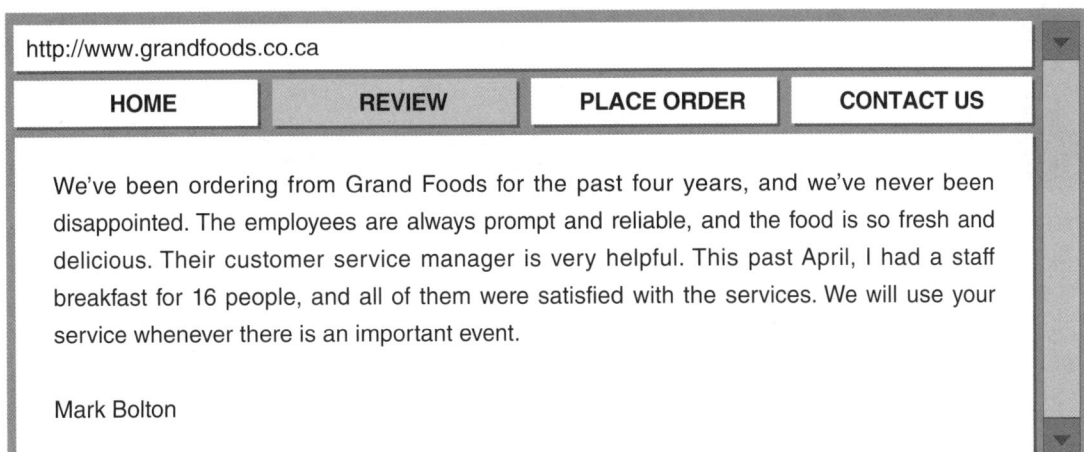

http://www.grandfoods.co.ca

| HOME | REVIEW | PLACE ORDER | CONTACT US |

We've been ordering from Grand Foods for the past four years, and we've never been disappointed. The employees are always prompt and reliable, and the food is so fresh and delicious. Their customer service manager is very helpful. This past April, I had a staff breakfast for 16 people, and all of them were satisfied with the services. We will use your service whenever there is an important event.

Mark Bolton

196. According to the advertisement, what will happen on April 5?

(A) A store will be moved to another location.
(B) There will be a sale on home appliances.
(C) Some new merchandise will be released.
(D) A store will close earlier than usual.

197. What is indicated about Gold Membership?

(A) It offers a 35% discount on dishwashers.
(B) People have to pay the membership fee to sign up.
(C) Free meals are included in the membership.
(D) Members can book products online in advance.

198. According to the e-mail, what does Mr. Bolton ask employees to do?

(A) Attend some training sessions
(B) Inform customers of an event
(C) Prepare for an annual event
(D) Recruit new volunteers

199. How many employees participated in the event preparation?

(A) 16
(B) 25
(C) 50
(D) 80

200. What is NOT mentioned in the online review?

(A) The level of customer service
(B) The competitiveness of the price
(C) The quality of the food
(D) The timeliness of the delivery

Stop! This is the end of the test. If you finish before time is called, you may go back to Parts 5, 6, and 7 and check your work.

이클리쉬의 토익

실전 1000제 LC+RC

TEST

2

정답 및 해설 p.288

TEST2.mp3

MP3 바로 듣기

books.english.co.kr에서 MP3 무료 다운로드가 가능합니다.

LISTENING TEST

In the Listening test, you will be asked to demonstrate how well you understand spoken English. The entire Listening test will last approximately 45 minutes. There are four parts, and directions are given for each part. You must mark your answers on the separate answer sheet.
Do not write your answers in your test book.

PART 1

Directions: For each question in this part, you will hear four statements about a picture in your test book. When you hear the statements, you must select the one statement that best describes what you see in the picture. Then find the number of the question on your answer sheet and mark your answer. The statements will not be printed in your test book and will be spoken only one time.

Statement (B), "They're shaking hands," is the best description of the picture, so you should select answer (B) and mark it on your answer sheet.

1.

2.

GO ON TO THE NEXT PAGE

3.

4.

5.

6.

GO ON TO THE NEXT PAGE

TEST 2

PART 2

Directions: You will hear a question or statement and three responses spoken in English. They will not be printed in your test book and will be spoken only one time. Select the best response to the question or statement and mark the letter (A), (B), or (C) on your answer sheet.

7. Mark your answer on your answer sheet.

8. Mark your answer on your answer sheet.

9. Mark your answer on your answer sheet.

10. Mark your answer on your answer sheet.

11. Mark your answer on your answer sheet.

12. Mark your answer on your answer sheet.

13. Mark your answer on your answer sheet.

14. Mark your answer on your answer sheet.

15. Mark your answer on your answer sheet.

16. Mark your answer on your answer sheet.

17. Mark your answer on your answer sheet.

18. Mark your answer on your answer sheet.

19. Mark your answer on your answer sheet.

20. Mark your answer on your answer sheet.

21. Mark your answer on your answer sheet.

22. Mark your answer on your answer sheet.

23. Mark your answer on your answer sheet.

24. Mark your answer on your answer sheet.

25. Mark your answer on your answer sheet.

26. Mark your answer on your answer sheet.

27. Mark your answer on your answer sheet.

28. Mark your answer on your answer sheet.

29. Mark your answer on your answer sheet.

30. Mark your answer on your answer sheet.

31. Mark your answer on your answer sheet.

PART 3

Directions: You will hear some conversations between two or more people. You will be asked to answer three questions about what the speakers say in each conversation. Select the best response to each question and mark the letter (A), (B), (C), or (D) on your answer sheet. The conversations will not be printed in your test book and will be spoken only one time.

32. What would the man like to do?

    (A) Rent some bicycles
    (B) Purchase some tickets
    (C) Get some discounts
    (D) Apply for a job

33. What does the woman say will happen if the man is late?

    (A) An appointment will be canceled.
    (B) An item will not be available.
    (C) A notice will be mailed.
    (D) An additional fee will be charged.

34. What does the woman offer the man?

    (A) Some beverages
    (B) Some maps
    (C) Free transportation
    (D) A coupon

35. What was the man having trouble with?

    (A) Finding a business center
    (B) Accessing the computer
    (C) Fixing audiovisual equipment
    (D) Purchasing supplies

36. What will the man do at ten o'clock?

    (A) Meet with some potential clients
    (B) Go to a nearby museum
    (C) Give a presentation
    (D) Participate in a group discussion

37. What does the woman say is available downstairs?

    (A) Some refreshments
    (B) A floor plan
    (C) A technical manual
    (D) A copy room

38. What product are the speakers discussing?

    (A) Electronics
    (B) Clothes
    (C) Fitness equipment
    (D) Packing materials

39. What does the man imply when he says, "There are only 12 boxes left"?

    (A) He is glad the sale is finally over.
    (B) He wants to hire more employees.
    (C) A product is selling very well.
    (D) Some inventory should be recounted.

40. What does the man say he will do?

    (A) Expand the storage area
    (B) Consult a lawyer
    (C) Launch a new advertising campaign
    (D) Talk to a sales representative

41. Which part of the company does the man most likely manage?

    (A) The cafeteria
    (B) The laboratory
    (C) The accounting office
    (D) The warehouse

42. What are the speakers discussing?

    (A) Increasing the current order
    (B) Hiring a new employee
    (C) Purchasing some machinery
    (D) Preparing for an inspection

43. What does the woman ask the man to do?

    (A) Update a document
    (B) Sign up for an event
    (C) Interview a candidate
    (D) Organize some files

GO ON TO THE NEXT PAGE

44. What are the speakers discussing?

(A) The renovation of the café
(B) A new location
(C) An order of supplies
(D) A price discrepancy

45. What problem does the woman mention?

(A) A delivery is incomplete.
(B) An Internet connection is not working.
(C) A bill has been misplaced.
(D) A container is damaged.

46. What does the man say he will give to the woman?

(A) A price discount
(B) Complimentary drinks
(C) A free trial period
(D) Extra products

---

47. Why is the woman meeting with the man?

(A) To request a job promotion
(B) To ask the man about his progress at work
(C) To follow up on a study they did together
(D) To congratulate the man on a nomination

48. What does the man say he had trouble with?

(A) Finding sources of information
(B) Utilizing an online software program
(C) Receiving funding for a project
(D) Making time for writing up a report

49. What does the woman suggest the man do?

(A) Talk to an expert
(B) Read an employee handbook
(C) Take some time off
(D) Access a database

---

50. Why is the woman calling?

(A) To reschedule an installation
(B) To offer a free service
(C) To request customer feedback
(D) To recommend extra work

51. What caused a delay?

(A) The weather was bad.
(B) Some equipment was defective.
(C) Some forms were filled out incorrectly.
(D) A product was temporarily unavailable.

52. What does the woman say she will do?

(A) Send some workers
(B) Issue a refund
(C) Demonstrate a new product
(D) Check with a sales representative

---

53. Where does the woman work?

(A) At a property management office
(B) At a shoe manufacturer
(C) At a government office
(D) At an interior design company

54. What is the man surprised about?

(A) A discounted price
(B) An essential inspection
(C) A rental price
(D) An updated contract

55. What does the man imply when he says, "We're opening in three days"?

(A) He needs more workers.
(B) He thinks the woman got the date wrong.
(C) He is worried about a deadline.
(D) He hopes to attract more customers.

---

56. Why is the woman meeting with Mr. Yamada?

(A) To conduct an interview
(B) To demonstrate a product
(C) To discuss a contract
(D) To view a rental property

57. What does the woman agree to do?

(A) Provide an address
(B) Sign in for a visit
(C) Revise the article
(D) Take a booklet

58. Why does Mr. Yamada apologize?

(A) He is unfamiliar with a publication.
(B) He forgot the woman's name.
(C) He needs to increase the price.
(D) He will be late for a meeting.

---

59. What will take place on the last weekend of May?

(A) A professional conference
(B) A holiday closure
(C) Computer maintenance
(D) Building construction

60. What do employees need to be reminded about?

(A) They will not be able to work on a weekend.
(B) They should turn off their computers.
(C) They have to report to the security office.
(D) They have to participate in a company reception.

61. What does the woman say she will do?

(A) Restart her computer
(B) Contact the technical support team
(C) Come back on Sunday afternoon
(D) Write an e-mail notification

Summerville City Library Events	
January 18	Book Discussion
February 15	Book Exchange
March 15	Children's Book Fair
April 19	Lecture Series — Local Writers

62. Look at the graphic. When is the conversation taking place?

(A) In January
(B) In February
(C) In March
(D) In April

63. Why is the man unable to attend the lecture series?

(A) He will be going on a vacation.
(B) He hasn't read the necessary books.
(C) He will be hosting some clients.
(D) He will be participating in a conference.

64. What does the woman say she will do?

(A) Recommend another class
(B) Revise a schedule
(C) Purchase some books
(D) Share some information

GO ON TO THE NEXT PAGE

PROMOTIONAL SPORT BOTTLES

Plastic	$3.30
Silicon	$4.00
Aluminum	$7.30
Stainless Steel	$9.00

http://Mtrain.com

Choose Your Train Car

Select	Car	Type	Full/Available
O	1	Quiet	Available
O	2	Quiet	Available
O	3	Quiet	Full
O	4	Regular	Available
O	5	Regular	Full

65. What does the woman plan to do with some water bottles?

(A) Sell them at her store
(B) Mail them to her customers
(C) Hand them out at an event
(D) Give them to her staff

66. Look at the graphic. Which material does the woman decide to use?

(A) Plastic
(B) Silicon
(C) Aluminum
(D) Stainless Steel

67. What does the man recommend?

(A) Choosing another material
(B) Increasing an order quantity
(C) Waiting for the next conference
(D) Getting additional price quotes

68. Why does the woman dislike Union Train Station?

(A) It is always understaffed.
(B) It has no Internet access.
(C) It is crowded with passengers.
(D) It needs to be renovated.

69. Look at the graphic. Which car will the speakers most likely choose?

(A) Car 2
(B) Car 3
(C) Car 4
(D) Car 5

70. What does the man ask the woman about?

(A) Where they should meet each other
(B) What time the train leaves
(C) How they would pay
(D) What client they should call first

PART 4

Directions: You will hear some talks given by a single speaker. You will be asked to answer three questions about what the speaker says in each talk. Select the best response to each question and mark the letter (A), (B), (C), or (D) on your answer sheet. The talks will not be printed in your test book and will be spoken only one time.

71. What kind of business is being advertised?

    (A) A cleaning service
    (B) A department store
    (C) A hair salon
    (D) A spa

72. When is the business closed?

    (A) On Monday
    (B) On Tuesday
    (C) On Friday
    (D) On Sunday

73. Why would listeners press 2?

    (A) To find out more about the business
    (B) To speak with a staff member
    (C) To schedule an appointment
    (D) To repeat the message

74. Who is Mr. Dorsett?

    (A) A former company president
    (B) A journalist
    (C) A former politician
    (D) A recruiter

75. What did Mr. Dorsett recently do?

    (A) Received an award
    (B) Won an election
    (C) Published a book
    (D) Applied for a job

76. What will happen next?

    (A) A speech will be given.
    (B) An interview will take place.
    (C) A ceremony will be held.
    (D) A meeting will end.

77. What kind of business does the speaker work for?

    (A) A truck rental company
    (B) A catering business
    (C) An automobile repair shop
    (D) A furniture store

78. What does the speaker mean when he says, "All of our trucks will be busy for the next few days"?

    (A) A rental vehicle is not available.
    (B) A business is doing well.
    (C) A delivery will be delayed.
    (D) Some employees will have to work overtime.

79. What does the speaker offer the listener?

    (A) A replacement product
    (B) A future discount
    (C) A design upgrade
    (D) A free installation

80. What is the talk mainly about?

    (A) Cost savings
    (B) A new product line
    (C) Price increases
    (D) Company sales

81. Where does the speaker say the company currently advertises?

    (A) On the Internet
    (B) On billboards
    (C) On the radio
    (D) On television

82. What will Victor do next?

    (A) Record a commercial
    (B) Present some data
    (C) Show the new products
    (D) Review some policies

GO ON TO THE NEXT PAGE

83. What is the speaker preparing to do?

(A) Organize a banquet
(B) Give a seminar
(C) Hire more staff
(D) Conduct a company tour

84. What does the speaker request?

(A) A plane ticket
(B) Visual equipment
(C) Copies of the materials
(D) A list of participants

85. Why does the speaker say, "I decided to reserve a car service"?

(A) To apologize for a delay
(B) To propose a schedule change
(C) To decline an offer
(D) To request the change of venue

---

86. Where most likely is the speaker?

(A) At a restaurant
(B) At a staffing firm
(C) At a convention center
(D) At a cooking competition

87. What is said about Infinity Staffing?

(A) They received an award for excellent service.
(B) They are hosting a special event.
(C) They will hire 100 people.
(D) Their office will close at 5 o'clock today.

88. What are the listeners asked to do next?

(A) Enjoy an excellent meal
(B) Open the business
(C) Check their assignments
(D) Serve lunch at the business office

---

89. What was recently approved?

(A) The expansion of an airport
(B) The renovation of a public park
(C) The construction of an office complex
(D) The improvement of a local highway

90. What advantage of the location does the speaker mention?

(A) Free parking is available.
(B) The rental fee is affordable.
(C) The landscape is attractive.
(D) Public transportation is close by.

91. Why will the listeners visit a Web site?

(A) To participate in an auction
(B) To see some floor plans
(C) To leave feedback
(D) To download some forms

---

92. Which field does the speaker most likely work in?

(A) Architecture
(B) Manufacturing
(C) Publishing
(D) Fashion

93. Why does the speaker say, "However, we've done this before"?

(A) To avoid repeating tasks
(B) To reject an idea
(C) To recommend a former vendor
(D) To reassure concerned employees

94. What should the listeners prepare by the end of the week?

(A) Some price lists
(B) Some draft designs
(C) An updated contract
(D) A budget proposal

BUS SCHEDULE	
Sherman St.	6:30 A.M.
Bridge St.	7:00 A.M.
Park Ave.	7:20 A.M.
Market Place	8:00 A.M.

95. Who most likely is the speaker?

(A) A job interviewer
(B) A property manager
(C) A travel agent
(D) A bus driver

96. What does the speaker ask the listener to do?

(A) Confirm a reservation
(B) Apply for a new job
(C) Sign the lease contract
(D) Pick up some items

97. Look at the graphic. When will the listener board the bus?

(A) At 6:30 A.M.
(B) At 7:00 A.M.
(C) At 7:20 A.M.
(D) At 8:00 A.M.

Checklist

☐ 1. Check the carton number.

☐ 2. Match contents with the packing list.

☐ 3. Inspect merchandise for damage.

☐ 4. Move items to the storeroom.

☐ 5. Update the list for any change.

98. What does the speaker say he is concerned about?

(A) Extra shipping costs
(B) Limited storage space
(C) Wasted time
(D) Customer complaints

99. Look at the graphic. Which step does the speaker say requires special attention?

(A) 1
(B) 2
(C) 3
(D) 4

100. What will happen next week?

(A) A sale event will begin.
(B) An inspection will be conducted.
(C) The store will be closed.
(D) The store will go through a renovation.

This is the end of the Listening test. Turn to Part 5 in your test book.

GO ON TO THE NEXT PAGE

READING TEST

In the Reading test, you will read a variety of texts and answer several different types of reading comprehension questions. The entire Reading test will last 75 minutes. There are three parts, and directions are given for each part. You are encouraged to answer as many questions as possible within the time allowed.

You must mark your answers on the separate answer sheet. Do not write your answers in the test book.

PART 5

Directions: A word or phrase is missing in each of the sentences below. Four answer choices are given below each sentence. Select the best answer to complete the sentence. Then mark the letter (A), (B), (C), or (D) on your answer sheet.

101. Ms. Gregory agreed to give ------- a phone call at 9 A.M. tomorrow.

(A) us
(B) we
(C) ourselves
(D) our

102. The customer canceled his last order ------- the office chair he wanted was no longer in stock.

(A) because
(B) therefore
(C) for instance
(D) in this case

103. Mr. Irving's ------- as a campaign manager makes him a perfect candidate for the marketing position.

(A) experiencing
(B) experienced
(C) experiment
(D) experience

104. Stardust Promotions began as a small, four-person office but ------- handles marketing campaigns for large corporations around the world.

(A) however
(B) large
(C) now
(D) since

105. Ms. Anthony should provide a ------- advantage for the company's sales revenues next year.

(A) distinct
(B) distinctively
(C) distinctly
(D) distinction

106. It is critical to voice ideas and suggestions ------- the planning portion of the structuring phase.

(A) afterwards
(B) during
(C) over
(D) inner

107. To attach the legs to the coffee table, ------- curved nails spaced at 2-inch intervals.

(A) used
(B) use
(C) using
(D) user

108. We are ------- to inform you that the latest issue of *Better Cooking Monthly* will be available for sale tomorrow.

(A) surprised
(B) pretended
(C) pleased
(D) built

109. The newly-designed Web site allows Online Bazaar customer representatives to respond to inquiries more -------.

(A) quickly
(B) quicker
(C) quicken
(D) quick

110. The annual company picnic is designed to allow employees to meet and socialize with ------- in other departments.

(A) generators
(B) professors
(C) secretaries
(D) colleagues

111. For gourmet delicacies at ------- prices, be sure to visit The Galloping Gourmet in Paradise City Mall.

(A) affordable
(B) afford
(C) afforded
(D) affording

112. All security personnel at Sentinel Labs ------- to wear uniforms and identification badges at all times on company property.

(A) expected
(B) expecting
(C) will expect
(D) are expected

113. Winter has only just begun, and the school ------- had to close twice due to poor weather.

(A) even
(B) at least
(C) already
(D) typically

114. Mendoza Construction was able to cut down on costs this year by pushing back the scheduled ------- of machinery.

(A) replaced
(B) replacement
(C) replaceable
(D) replace

115. The Granada Inn recommends booking guest rooms at least two weeks ------- in order to guarantee accommodation.

(A) afterwards
(B) already
(C) sooner
(D) in advance

116. Whenever the product assembly line breaks down, it is the line manager's ------- to quickly ascertain the cause of the problem.

(A) ability
(B) responsibility
(C) disappointment
(D) standard

117. While the information we collect today will help us to improve our product selection, your participation in the survey is completely -------.

(A) voluntary
(B) volunteering
(C) volunteered
(D) voluntarily

118. *Great Outdoors Magazine* offers advertising space only to companies that provide goods or services that ------- active lifestyles.

(A) belittle
(B) encourage
(C) appreciate
(D) reject

119. Due to sudden increased demand, ------- of our office supplies need to be replenished.

(A) some
(B) one
(C) another
(D) few

120. Most of the research materials will include summaries of ------- theories for those who are not familiar with the subject.

(A) boring
(B) repetitive
(C) relevant
(D) undetermined

GO ON TO THE NEXT PAGE

121. Ms. Park was ------- as the new head of the legal department after a series of interviews.

(A) implicated
(B) demanded
(C) appointed
(D) transferred

122. The town of Garden Grove continues to undergo a five percent annual population -------.

(A) rate
(B) increase
(C) experience
(D) revenue

123. Far Blue Fashions is ------- of the fastest growing apparel businesses in the industry.

(A) above
(B) new
(C) one
(D) some

124. Super Saver Supermarkets has enjoyed ------- increases in revenue since the fiscal year.

(A) steady
(B) accurate
(C) important
(D) frustrating

125. The new logo designed by Creative Solutions has been ------- to incorporate components of your company's core mission.

(A) customized
(B) customizing
(C) customizes
(D) customize

126. The goal of this meeting is to discuss ------- recent developments will require further budget cuts.

(A) instead
(B) however
(C) including
(D) whether

127. Since its merger with Leads Pharmaceuticals two years ago, ABC Medical Co. has experienced record-breaking -------.

(A) earners
(B) earned
(C) earning
(D) earnings

128. The new movie from director Mark Fernandez, *On the Shore*, ------- an award-winning cast.

(A) destroys
(B) expects
(C) excites
(D) features

129. Online sales will increase sharply during the holidays next week, so it is very important that our Web site be functioning -------.

(A) relied
(B) reliably
(C) rely
(D) reliable

130. Puma Automotive's attention to detail is consistent ------- its entire line of vehicles.

(A) among
(B) across
(C) under
(D) around

PART 6

Directions: Read the texts that follow. A word, phrase, or sentence is missing in parts of each text. Four answer choices for each question are given below the text. Select the best answer to complete the text. Then mark the letter (A), (B), (C), or (D) on your answer sheet.

Questions 131-134 refer to the following article.

Home Sales on the Rise

The National Real Estate Association expects nationwide sales of homes to reach 1,250,000 sold by

the end of the year. That would mean a 19 percent increase from the ------- year's figure and a new
                                                                    131.

all-time record, just exceeding the total from four years ago. The Association attributes the steady

rise in sales to a number of factors, ------- the continued decrease in interest rates on home loans.
                                       132.

Despite the increasing activity in the residential sector, the market for commercial real estate

properties has shown very little ------- over the past four years. -------.
                                 133.   **134.**

---

131. (A) next
    (B) first
    (C) previous
    (D) current

132. (A) included
    (B) include
    (C) includes
    (D) including

133. (A) growth
    (B) finance
    (C) interest
    (D) record

134. (A) Another home will be sold on the market
        tomorrow.
    (B) Industry experts are unsure as to the
        reason for this contrast.
    (C) There are many more residential
        properties on the market than
        commercial properties.
    (D) The Association expects interest rates
        on home loans to continue to decrease.

GO ON TO THE NEXT PAGE

Questions 135-138 refer to the following information.

The Zenith 2000 laptop computer will be the most important tool for you at your new job. --------, it
135.
is critical that you take good care of the computer so that it is always running smoothly. Here are a

few helpful tips from our team of product care team to keep your computer in great shape. First, be

sure to only use Zenith-approved --------, especially when cleaning the computer. Second, be careful
136.
when plugging in the charger. The manual contains instructions so that you do not accidentally shock

yourself or drain the battery. Third, make sure to install proper anti-virus software. --------. Finally, if
137.
you need your computer serviced, we recommend that you choose a ------- professional technician. If
138.
you just follow these easy steps, you can extend the life of your computer.

135. (A) On the other hand
(B) In summary
(C) Even so
(D) Therefore

136. (A) employees
(B) supplies
(C) access
(D) power

137. (A) Adequate protection is critical to safely
maintaining the information in your
computer.
(B) The computer comes with an extra
charger for you to use.
(C) If you are having problems, please
contact the number included in the
manual.
(D) Regular cleaning will prevent dust from
building up inside the computer.

138. (A) certify
(B) certifying
(C) certified
(D) certificate

Questions 139-142 refer to the following memo.

To: Theater Employees

From: M. Silver, Theater Director

Date: May 12

Subject: New Policy

I am writing to let you know that we will be making a change to our ------- policy for our summer
                                                                        139.
concert series, which is underway, effective immediately. As you know, many of our visitors

make seating requests on the day of the concert, particularly those who want the extra leg room

from aisle seats. From this moment, we will accept seating requests ------- at the time of ticket
                                                                     140.
purchase.

On the day of the concert, visitors ------- extra space can sit in the back row, on a first-come
                                     141.
first-served basis, since the back is usually empty. -------. This new policy should help us seat
                                                     142.
people more quickly before a concert and, hopefully, avoid complaints during the show.

139. (A) drinking
(B) appointment
(C) seating
(D) ticket price

140. (A) only
(B) maybe
(C) near
(D) today

141. (A) need
(B) who need
(C) when needed
(D) are needing

142. (A) Many of our visitors prefer to be closer to the stage.
(B) We are expecting more visitors this summer than last year.
(C) The new policy goes into effect next month.
(D) Although it is farther from the stage, there is extra leg room there.

GO ON TO THE NEXT PAGE

Questions 143-146 refer to the following press release.

Minton Laboratories, a private research laboratory based in Waltham, Massachusetts, has received a grant from the Food and Drug Administration(FDA). The grant was awarded in response to an application submitted to the FDA. The funds will be used to further research already being conducted at Minton on a new drug treatment for lung cancer. -------. The grant will
143.
therefore also be used to upgrade the laboratory's testing facilities ------- a new climate control
144.
system and new testing equipment. If any funds remain after these -------, they will be used to
145.
upgrade other portions of the laboratory. Dr. Janice Hartman, the Laboratory Director, ------- the
146.
work in consultation with Mark Hampton of the FDA.

143. (A) Minton Laboratories recently moved to Waltham from Boston.
(B) Minton has already produced the drug, which will soon be entering the testing phase.
(C) Mr. Hampton is experienced in developing conservation measures.
(D) Energy-saving construction to improve efficiency has increased in popularity.

144. (A) after
(B) following
(C) however
(D) such as

145. (A) suggestions
(B) innovations
(C) improvements
(D) applications

146. (A) will oversee
(B) has overseen
(C) oversee
(D) oversees

PART 7

Directions: In this part you will read a selection of texts, such as magazine and newspaper articles, e-mails, and instant messages. Each text or set of texts is followed by several questions. Select the best answer for each question and mark the letter (A), (B), (C), or (D) on your answer sheet.

Questions 147-148 refer to the following coupon.

Silver Diner
Special Anniversary Coupon

Present this coupon to your waiter or waitress during your next visit and receive a complimentary dessert with your order of any meal! This coupon can be used any time we are open, Monday through Friday(not valid on weekends).

Your opinion is important to us!

Visit www.silverdiner.com to view our menu and a listing of upcoming events. Complete and submit our customer survey to be entered into a drawing for a $50 gift certificate to the diner!

---

147. What free item can be obtained by using this coupon?

(A) A meal
(B) A sandwich
(C) A tableware
(D) A dessert

148. How can a customer get a chance to win a prize?

(A) By visiting the diner ten times
(B) By using the coupon this weekend
(C) By responding to a survey
(D) By spending $50 at the diner

GO ON TO THE NEXT PAGE

Questions 149-150 refer to the following e-mail.

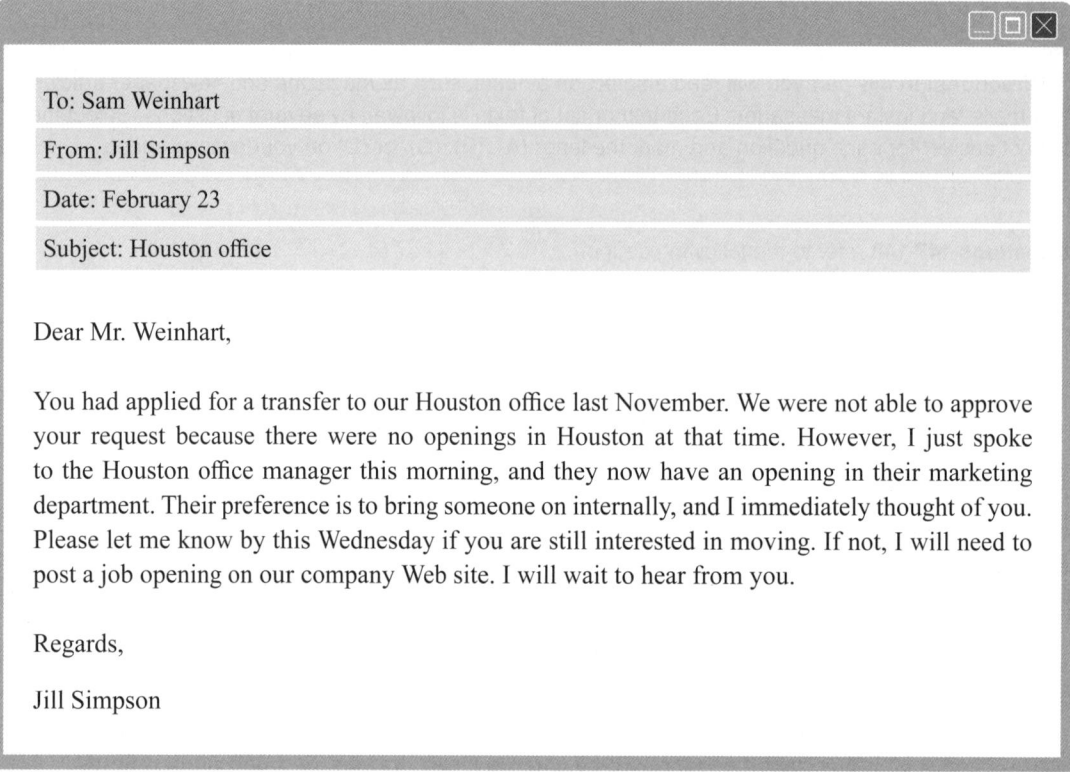

To: Sam Weinhart

From: Jill Simpson

Date: February 23

Subject: Houston office

Dear Mr. Weinhart,

You had applied for a transfer to our Houston office last November. We were not able to approve your request because there were no openings in Houston at that time. However, I just spoke to the Houston office manager this morning, and they now have an opening in their marketing department. Their preference is to bring someone on internally, and I immediately thought of you. Please let me know by this Wednesday if you are still interested in moving. If not, I will need to post a job opening on our company Web site. I will wait to hear from you.

Regards,

Jill Simpson

149. Why did Ms. Simpson send the e-mail to Mr. Weinhart?

(A) To ask him to perform a job
(B) To introduce a new employee
(C) To give notice of an available position
(D) To deny his request for transfer

150. What will Ms. Simpson wait to do?

(A) Post an advertisement
(B) Call Mr. Weinhart
(C) Hire Mr. Weinhart as the office manager
(D) Transfer to the Houston office

Questions 151-152 refer to the following text-message chain.

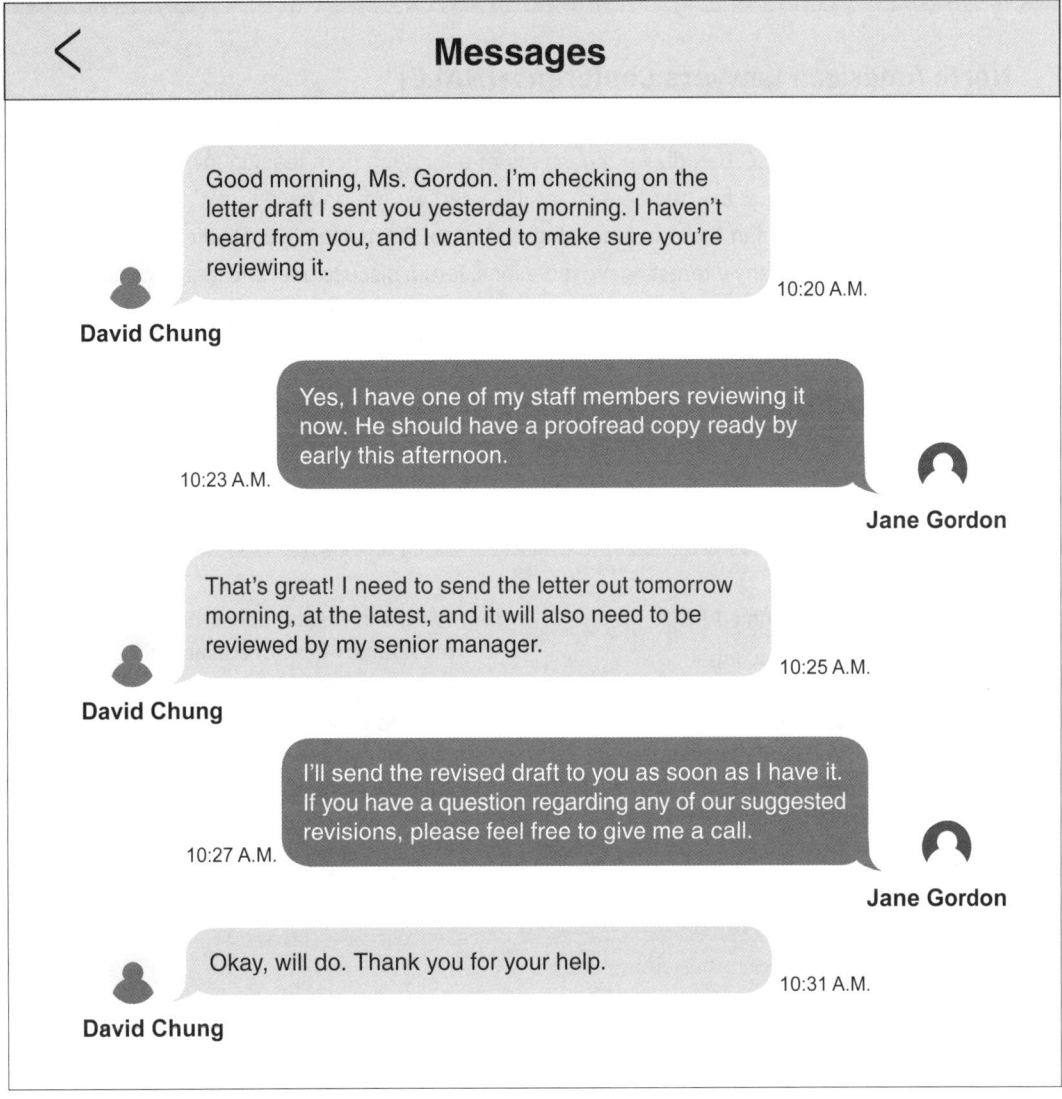

Messages

David Chung
Good morning, Ms. Gordon. I'm checking on the letter draft I sent you yesterday morning. I haven't heard from you, and I wanted to make sure you're reviewing it.
10:20 A.M.

Jane Gordon
Yes, I have one of my staff members reviewing it now. He should have a proofread copy ready by early this afternoon.
10:23 A.M.

David Chung
That's great! I need to send the letter out tomorrow morning, at the latest, and it will also need to be reviewed by my senior manager.
10:25 A.M.

Jane Gordon
I'll send the revised draft to you as soon as I have it. If you have a question regarding any of our suggested revisions, please feel free to give me a call.
10:27 A.M.

David Chung
Okay, will do. Thank you for your help.
10:31 A.M.

151. In which office does Ms. Gordon most likely work?

(A) Editorial services
(B) Sales
(C) Marketing
(D) Human Resources

152. At 10:31 A.M., what does Mr. Chung most likely mean when he writes, "will do"?

(A) He wants Ms. Gordon to review another letter.
(B) He will contact Ms. Gordon if he has any questions.
(C) He is grateful for Ms. Gordon's assistance.
(D) He will contact the staff member with questions about his rough draft.

GO ON TO THE NEXT PAGE

Questions 153-154 refer to the following advertisement.

North American Lawyers Conference(NALC)

In recent years, the NALC has drawn thousands of attendees from leading law firms across the country, and looking at the numbers so far this year, we are on pace to set a new record. Join keynote speaker Brian Ingram, managing partner of Davis Kronin & Seinfeld, and other prominent lawyers for many interesting presentations, forum discussions, and legal workshops. The theme of this year's conference is the evolving legal system and how to adapt to new client expectations.

When it comes to your peers in the legal industry, you will hold an advantage after attending the NALC. Don't miss out! Preregister by April 28 at www.nalc.com and save 15 percent off normal registration fees.

153. What is indicated about the NALC?

(A) It is the only nationwide legal conference.
(B) It will take place for one week.
(C) Participation has been dwindling in recent years.
(D) It is attended by only lawyers.

154. What information about the event is NOT provided by the advertisement?

(A) The name of the keynote speaker
(B) The date of the conference .
(C) The adress of the Web site
(D) The theme of the conference

Questions 155-157 refer to the following e-mail.

To: Samuel Preston <smpreston@covington.com>

From: Regina Kim <rekim@freemanlng.com>

Date: September 11

Subject: Welcome

Attachment: Helpful info for relocation

Dear Mr. Preston,

I would like to be the first to welcome you to the Austin office of Freeman LNG. Your new position will be project planner, and you will report directly to the project manager. As you know, we recently received government approval for the state's largest LNG project, and we are excited to get moving on laying the groundwork.

Your orientation session has been set for Monday, October 2 at 10 A.M. and will be led by John Green from Human Resources. At the session, you will receive information on the larger project group, as well as information on benefits and other details of your employment. Since you haven't yet been issued an identification badge, you will need to sign in at the security desk. Therefore, please plan to arrive by 9:30 A.M. so that you are on time for your orientation session.

Attached is a guide with some tips to help your move from our New York office. Included in the guide are some suggestions in case you haven't yet made housing arrangements. Please don't hesitate to reach out to me if you have any questions before you arrive.

Best regards,

Regina Kim
Director, Human Resources
Freeman LNG, Austin office

155. Why did Ms. Kim send the e-mail?

(A) To request government approval
(B) To apply for a new job
(C) To provide details about a new job
(D) To issue an identification badge

156. What is indicated about Freeman LNG?

(A) It has more than one location.
(B) It has an office in Boston.
(C) It will hire more employees.
(D) It is waiting for government approval.

157. What is Mr. Preston advised to do?

(A) Arrive early for orientation
(B) Speak with Mr. Green before the orientation
(C) Provide a list of references
(D) Read the orientation materials in advance

GO ON TO THE NEXT PAGE

Questions 158-160 refer to the following information.

National Dental Society
18th Annual Symposium, July 13–15
Jefferson Convention Center — Las Vegas, Nevada

Thank you for registering to attend the 18th Annual Symposium of the National Dental Society. For lunches during the symposium, you can purchase meal passes at the registration counter, located in the main lobby of the conference center. You have the option of purchasing a three-day meal pass for $18 or purchasing individual meal passes for $7. Make sure to provide your symposium registration number at the time of purchase. In the absence of a meal pass, you will be charged the standard price of $9. Please note that the meal passes are valid for use only at locations within the convention center.

The cafeteria is open for lunch from 11:30 A.M. to 2:30 P.M. during the symposium. For participants in need of a vegetarian dining option, the Natural Diner located on the second floor of the convention center provides healthy, vegetarian meal options. Refreshments can be purchased at Rainforest Café in the lobby, but the café does not serve lunch. A map of the convention center is included with your symposium materials so that you will not have any trouble finding your way around.

If you would prefer to have lunch away from the convention center, there are a number of restaurants located within a 15-minute drive.

Please ask at the registration counter for details.

158. What is indicated about the National Dental Society?

(A) It always hosts its symposium in Las Vegas.
(B) It held its first gathering eighteen years ago.
(C) It does not provide any meals at the symposium site.
(D) Its registration is open to participants from around the world.

159. Where can symposium participants NOT have lunch?

(A) At Rainforest Café
(B) At the cafeteria
(C) At the Natural Diner
(D) Outside the convention center

160. What is true about places to eat outside the symposium site?

(A) Lunch is served until 3:00 P.M.
(B) Lunch will cost more than $9.
(C) They do not accept symposium meal passes.
(D) They are within walking distance of the convention center.

Questions 161-163 refer to the following e-mail.

To: All Joy Toys employees

From: Lester Mann

Date: September 10

Subject: Security Access

To all employees:

We have installed a new security system for access to our building. Beginning next Monday, the new system will be in operation. The change will not affect regular employees. However, the process for checking in visitors to our building will be different.

As before, all visitors must register at the lobby security desk. The paper sign-in book that was previously used, though, will be replaced by a digitized system that will create a photograph of the visitor and issue a temporary pass card that must be visible at all times during the visitor's stay within our building.

The new system has been put in place for our corporate headquarters, as well as each of our manufacturing plants. Student groups that visit our factories on field trips will not be subject to the new digitized system. If you have any questions about the new system, you can find additional information in section 49.3b of the current security manual.

Regards,

Lester Mann
Head of Security, Joy Toys

---

161. What is the purpose of the e-mail?

(A) To respond to complaints about parking
(B) To explain a new procedure
(C) To address questions about a merger
(D) To discuss a new hiring policy

162. What is suggested about Joy Toys?

(A) It will now need to install a new security system.
(B) It is not open to visitors during weekends.
(C) It has only one manufacturing plant.
(D) It will no longer use a registration book.

163. Who must carry a temporary pass card while in the facilities?

(A) Student groups on a factory tour
(B) Security personnel
(C) Company visitors
(D) Regular employees

GO ON TO THE NEXT PAGE

Tastier Watermelons?

October 21—Consumer demand for watermelons continues to increase every year. —[1]—. Countries from very different parts of the world now export watermelons, including Finland, Brazil, Ghana, and Russia. Taking advantage of scientific advances in plant-breeding, watermelon farmers now enjoy a longer harvest season that lasts up to 11 months, with watermelons that are larger, stronger, and better capable of surviving the trip to your local supermarket.

—[2]—. However, one thing has been lost amidst the scramble to produce more watermelons. Nobody seems to have considered the taste. Russian scientist Alexis Porgov believes that the larger, prettier watermelons we see today fail to stack up against watermelons sold years ago. "The sweet juiciness of watermelons has largely been sacrificed in order to create a larger prettier shell," he says.

—[3]—. Dr. Porgov explains that each successive round of scientific advances slowly reduced the watermelon flavor. It may have been difficult for consumers to tell the difference because the reduction in taste took place over such a long period of time. Consumers may eventually have forgotten the sweetness that watermelons used to provide.

Dr. Porgov is currently working on a project to reinsert the flavor back into watermelons, while maintaining the advances in the size and outward appearance we have come to enjoy. —[4]—. "A few less watermelons per batch is a small price to pay for better flavor," he says. Dr. Porgov advocates the use of a natural breeding method, as opposed to the more scientific breeding methods that have become so popular. He reports that his initial efforts have shown great promise.

164. What characteristic of the watermelons is the focus of the article?

(A) Their size
(B) Their sturdiness
(C) Their appearance
(D) Their flavor

165. How has the farming of watermelons changed?

(A) Watermelons are harvested almost year round.
(B) Watermelons are grown only indoors.
(C) Watermelons are exported only from South America.
(D) Watermelons are harvested only by machines.

166. What is indicated about Dr. Porgov?

(A) He currently lives in Ghana.
(B) He has been experimenting with plant breeding.
(C) He was responsible for the scientific advances in watermelon farming.
(D) He is allergic to watermelons.

167. In which of the positions marked [1], [2], [3], and [4] does the following sentence best belong?

"The change in the way we harvest watermelons came about slowly and gradually."

(A) [1]
(B) [2]
(C) [3]
(D) [4]

GO ON TO THE NEXT PAGE

Questions 168-171 refer to the following online chat discussion.

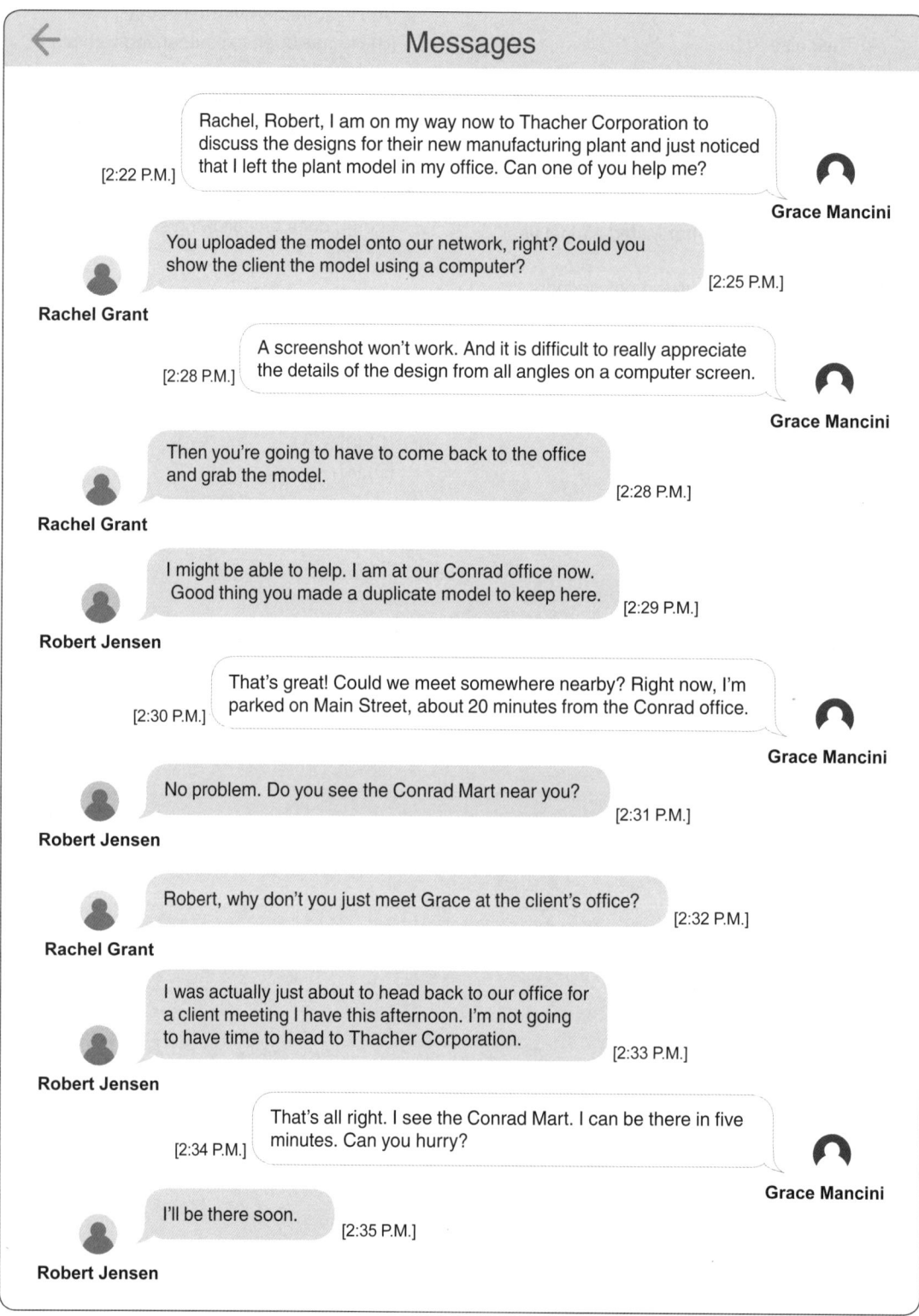

	Messages

Grace Mancini [2:22 P.M.]
Rachel, Robert, I am on my way now to Thacher Corporation to discuss the designs for their new manufacturing plant and just noticed that I left the plant model in my office. Can one of you help me?

Rachel Grant [2:25 P.M.]
You uploaded the model onto our network, right? Could you show the client the model using a computer?

Grace Mancini [2:28 P.M.]
A screenshot won't work. And it is difficult to really appreciate the details of the design from all angles on a computer screen.

Rachel Grant [2:28 P.M.]
Then you're going to have to come back to the office and grab the model.

Robert Jensen [2:29 P.M.]
I might be able to help. I am at our Conrad office now. Good thing you made a duplicate model to keep here.

Grace Mancini [2:30 P.M.]
That's great! Could we meet somewhere nearby? Right now, I'm parked on Main Street, about 20 minutes from the Conrad office.

Robert Jensen [2:31 P.M.]
No problem. Do you see the Conrad Mart near you?

Rachel Grant [2:32 P.M.]
Robert, why don't you just meet Grace at the client's office?

Robert Jensen [2:33 P.M.]
I was actually just about to head back to our office for a client meeting I have this afternoon. I'm not going to have time to head to Thacher Corporation.

Grace Mancini [2:34 P.M.]
That's all right. I see the Conrad Mart. I can be there in five minutes. Can you hurry?

Robert Jensen [2:35 P.M.]
I'll be there soon.

168. Who most likely is Ms. Mancini?

(A) A manager of Thacher Corporation
(B) A cashier of Conrad Mart
(C) A client of Mr. Jensen
(D) An employee of the design company

169. At 2:28 P.M., what does Ms. Mancini most likely mean when she writes, "A screenshot won't work"?

(A) She would prefer to show the client a physical model.
(B) She does not know how to access the office network.
(C) She will not come into work this afternoon.
(D) She did not upload the plant model to the office network.

170. Where is Ms. Mancini?

(A) At Thacher Corporation
(B) In her car
(C) At the Conrad office
(D) In front of a computer

171. What does Mr. Jensen offer to do?

(A) Go to Thacher Corporation
(B) Build a new model for Ms. Mancini
(C) Take an item to Ms. Mancini
(D) Reschedule a meeting

GO ON TO THE NEXT PAGE

Dragon Textiles Opens New Plant

BEIJING (March 17) — Dragon Textiles, one of the world's largest garment manufacturers headquartered in Beijing, has just announced the opening of its newest manufacturing facility in Danang, Vietnam on June 8. The new facility will operate under the name Phoenix and will be managed entirely by a local management team.

The new plant symbolizes the rapid growth of Dragon Textiles, as it continues to spread its wings throughout Asia. Simon Wong, the CEO of Dragon Textiles stated, "Manufacturing in Vietnam will allow for easier access to markets that we are targeting." —[1]—. Mr. Wong will attend the inauguration ceremony of the Danang plant, along with key company executives.

Dragon Textiles began in Beijing almost ten years ago. —[2]—. As Dragon rapidly expanded, it joined forces with many of the most famous clothing brands in China. —[3]—. However, overall sales in China have plateaued, reaching its peak last year. The company is betting that local garment production will save costs and boost its bottom line.

Dragon Textiles has two other manufacturing plants in Cheng Du, China. —[4]—. Mr. Wong noted his company is in the process of negotiating the construction of another plant with the Indonesian government. He expressed confidence that the new plant will be up and running by the end of next year.

172. What is stated about Dragon Textiles?

(A) It is headquartered in Europe.
(B) It already has another plant in Vietnam.
(C) It wants to expand into Southeast Asia.
(D) It has been in business for only three years.

173. What is indicated about Mr. Wong?

(A) He will directly manage the Danang plant.
(B) He plans on expanding his company into Europe.
(C) He spends most of his time in Vietnam.
(D) He will travel to Danang in June.

174. Where will Dragon Textiles most likely build its next production facility?

(A) In Vietnam
(B) In Indonesia
(C) In China
(D) In Thailand

175. In which of the positions marked [1], [2], [3], and [4] does the following sentence best belong?

"With this new location, we will further strengthen our position compared to our competitors in the region."

(A) [1]
(B) [2]
(C) [3]
(D) [4]

GO ON TO THE NEXT PAGE

To: Mark Vrabel <mvrabel@konoco.com>

From: Jordan Page <jpage@zoomrailways.com>

Date: November 12

Title: Your train ticket reservation

Dear Mr. Vrabel,

Due to the holidays, November is one of our busiest months. We expect a record number of travelers on our ZR 32 train tomorrow from Boston to Miami, and we are seeking volunteers among our ticketed passengers who might be willing to switch to a train departing at a different time in exchange for a special travel voucher. The voucher will be valid for six months and may be redeemed for any train ticket with Zoom Railways valued up to $500.

I have taken the liberty of searching for potential alternative dates and times you may be able to travel to Miami. The first option noted below leaves on the same day as your original departure date but includes a slight layover in Washington, D.C.

| ZR 22 | Boston | Nov. 21, 3:40 P.M. | Washington, D.C. | Nov. 21, 6:55 P.M. |
| ZR 23 | Washington, D.C. | Nov. 21, 7:45 P.M. | Miami | Nov. 21, 11:00 P.M. |

Another option would bring you directly into Miami, but you would need to leave one day later.

| ZR 33 | Boston | Nov. 22, 2:05 P.M. | Miami | Nov. 22, 8:15 P.M. |

If you are willing to switch trains, please call our reservation hotline at 1-855-338-4891. If you would like to keep your original reservation, we suggest you log onto our Web site(www.zoomrailways.com/reservations) prior to your departure to register your travel information.

As always, thank you very much for traveling with Zoom Railways.

With regards,

Jordan Page
Customer Service
Zoom Railways

Boarding Pass

TRAIN	DATE	BOARDING TIME	DEPARTS
ZR 33	NOV. 22	1:45 P.M.	2:05 P.M.

FROM	TO	PLATFORM	CAR/SEAT
BOSTON	MIAMI	3B	CAR 7/SEAT 16A

Board in order of cars with other Car 7 passengers.

Space is limited for carry-on baggage. Passengers may bring one carry-on bag with them into the train car. All other bags must be checked.

176. What is the purpose of the e-mail?

(A) To encourage a passenger to change trains
(B) To confirm reservation information
(C) To request payment for a reserved ticket
(D) To inform a passenger of new security policies

177. What is indicated about the voucher?

(A) It can be used for any train ticket.
(B) It has an expiration date.
(C) It can be used by anyone who presents the voucher.
(D) Its value is the same as the ticket purchased by Mr. Vrabel.

178. What did Mr. Vrabel most likely do after receiving the e-mail?

(A) Board a train immediately
(B) Log onto a Web site
(C) Reply to the e-mail
(D) Call the reservation hotline

179. What does the boarding pass indicate about Mr. Vrabel's train?

(A) It will leave from Washington, D.C.
(B) It will depart in the morning.
(C) Passengers will board in a predetermined order.
(D) Passengers cannot bring baggage aboard the train.

180. What time is Mr. Vrabel scheduled to arrive at his final destination?

(A) 6:55 P.M.
(B) 8:15 P.M.
(C) 11:00 P.M.
(D) 2:05 P.M.

GO ON TO THE NEXT PAGE

Questions 181-185 refer to the following advertisement and form.

Business Seminar on Marketing in a Digital Age

Are you seeking ways to reach new customers across a broader spectrum? Do you want to become familiar with all the new online social networking sites? If so, visit us at www. empoweredbusiness.edu and you can sign up for an online seminar discussing how to market to customers using all manner of digital media. You will have online access to our panel of experts, each of whom runs his or her own business, who will talk about the latest trends and how to go about building your online profile. The live seminar will take place on Monday, March 14 from 1:30 to 3:30 P.M. (Eastern Standard Time)

The seminar will consist of three presentations:

- "A First Step in Building Your Online Profile" by Mark Jacobs
- "The Most Popular Online Tools to Reach the New Generation" by Sanjay Gupta
- "Marketing to the New Generation: The Latest Trends" by Jennifer Rodriguez

If you are unable to register online, please e-mail Roger Cassidy at rcassidy@ empoweredbusiness.edu by Friday, March 11.

If you are not able to attend the live seminar but are still interested, you can visit our online seminar library. All seminars are available for viewing within 48 hours of broadcast.

---

www.empoweredbusiness.edu/seminar3912/evaluation-form

Ren Nakayama, thank you for attending our Business Seminar on Marketing in a Digital Age. We would greatly appreciate it if you would take a few minutes to complete the following survey. This information will help us continue to improve our services.

On a scale from 1(very dissatisfied) to 5(very satisfied), please rate the following.

The overall seminar topic	5
Quality of each presentation	4
The amount of useful information	4

What did you enjoy most about the seminar?

Mr. Gupta's presentation was particularly useful for my line of work. I had resisted getting caught up in the latest social networking sites, but Mr. Gupta was able to succinctly summarize the most relevant ones and how best to use them.

Is there anything you would like to see improved in future events?

I would really like it if there were alternate times available for participating in the seminar. The time given was actually quite inconvenient for me, as I logged on at 2:30 A.M. from Tokyo, where my business is located.

181. What is indicated about the seminar?

(A) It will be broadcast live over two days.
(B) It will be broadcast online.
(C) It will focus only on managing techniques.
(D) It is available only to residents of North America.

182. According to the advertisement, why should readers contact Mr. Cassidy?

(A) To cancel a registration
(B) To gain access to the seminar
(C) To take part in a survey
(D) To receive information on the speakers

183. What is true about the speakers?

(A) They have experience running their own businesses.
(B) They all work in the same company.
(C) They have presented numerous seminars on various topics before.
(D) They all live in the United States.

184. What is suggested about Mr. Nakayama?

(A) He was unable to attend the seminar.
(B) He would like to present at a future event.
(C) He has worked with Mr. Gupta before.
(D) He enjoyed hearing about online tools.

185. What aspect of the seminar does Mr. Nakayama suggest changing?

(A) The number of presentations
(B) The seminar topic
(C) The schedule
(D) The location

GO ON TO THE NEXT PAGE

SEVEN LOCKS MANAGEMENT OFFICE RENTAL AGREEMENT

37 Seven Locks Road, Unit 12
Bethesda, Maryland 20810

RENTAL TERMS

You agree to rent the office for twelve months, from March 1 to February 28, for a monthly rent of $14,000 due by the first of each month. Late payments are subject to a penalty of $1,000, which may be deducted from your security deposit. If you cancel the lease before the end of the term, you will be subject to a penalty of $1,000, also to be deducted from your security deposit. Your rent includes all utilities, including electricity, water, and heat. You are responsible for setting up any Internet connections and associated fees. Also included in your rent are the five parking spaces directly in front of your unit. If you need additional parking spaces, you can rent them at $200 a month each. Another option is to park in the parking garage adjacent to our building.

SECURITY DEPOSIT

You paid a security deposit equal to one months' rent on February 14. The deposit will be returned to you within 15 days of the end of the agreement term. Our management team will inspect the office space both before and after the rental period. Any cleaning or maintenance issues that we spot before the rental period begins will be documented and a copy will be provided to you. Issues other than these that are spotted after the rental period will be deducted from your security deposit.

SEVEN LOCKS MANAGEMENT INSPECTION FORM

Date: February 19
Property: 37 Seven Locks Road, Unit 12

Comments upon Inspection:
All facilities and equipment are in good working order. There is some discoloration in the carpet near the entrance and by the pantry. Also, some of the paint on the wall in the pantry has chipped off. Seven Locks Management will arrange to have these issues fixed by February 28.

Michael Mendez	John Kim
Manager	Office Tenant

To: mmendez@sevenlocks.com

From: jkim32@kmail.net

Date: January 21

Subject: My security deposit

Attachment: sevenlocks/inspection.form.pdf

Dear Mr. Mendez,

I terminated my rental agreement for Unit 12 a couple of weeks ago, and I just received a portion of my security deposit from Seven Locks Management. I had expected the $1,000 deduction, but I was surprised to see that an additional $2,000 was deducted. The accompanying letter notes that the $2,000 deduction was for paint work, but you agreed prior to my rental period that you would have the carpet cleaned but would not have the pantry repainted. No paint work was ever done, so I hope you will refund me my $2,000.

Sincerely,

John Kim

186. What is indicated in the rental agreement?

(A) The office is fully furnished.
(B) The agreement does not include parking spaces.
(C) The agreement is for a period of ten months.
(D) The renter must pay for Internet service separately.

187. What is true about the Seven Locks Office Building?

(A) It is next to a parking garage.
(B) It has exactly twelve office units.
(C) It just finished renovations last month.
(D) It will be moving to a new location next year.

188. In the rental agreement, the phrase "subject to" in paragraph 1, line 2, is closest in meaning to

(A) taught by
(B) responsible for
(C) Inspected by
(D) informed about

189. Why did Mr. Kim expect to receive a $1,000 penalty?

(A) He rented additional parking spaces.
(B) He was late in making a rent payment.
(C) He damaged the office during the rental period.
(D) He moved before his lease term expired.

190. What statement in the inspection form was not carried out by Seven Locks Management?

(A) The carpet was not properly cleaned.
(B) The pantry was not repainted.
(C) The manager dld not inspect the property.
(D) The pantry was repainted a different color.

GO ON TO THE NEXT PAGE

World Bird Watchers Forum Rules

1. Our forum does not limit the length of postings, but we do ask that discussions be focused on birds and bird habitats only. We will aggressively seek out and delete any postings discussing birds and bird-related equipment for sale.

2. All postings should be paired with a subject line that follows the format "bird type (or short description) – location". Our members post from all over the world, so please remember to be specific and brief.

   Good subject line example: "Red-tailed Robin – Helsinki, Finland"

   Bad subject line example: "Wow! – Look at this bird!"

3. As written descriptions can sometimes be insufficient to accurately identify a particular bird, we encourage all postings to include at least one photograph.

4. We have had a recent increase in active forum members. Please limit your postings to no more than two within any 24-hour period, so that we can continue to operate the Web site at maximum efficiency. Our bird experts are hard at work responding to all of your inquiries, usually within a few days.

World Bird Watchers Forum
Member Registration Form

Name: *Gavin Jennings*   E-mail: *gjennings@sandmail.com*

Have you had formal training in any bird-related fields? *Ph.D. in ornithology*

Where did you most recently work? *State University of New York*

Formal training or current employment is not required to register as a member. We use this information to distinguish members who may be considered experts when posting replies to posts.

I would like to receive regular e-mails from World Bird Watchers Forum. YES (✓) NO ( )

Privacy Policy: World Bird Watchers Forum is a secure Web site; member information will not be shared with or sold to third parties.

NEW FORUM POST MEMBER: Gavin Jennings

Subject line: Please someone help me name this bird   Date: June 7

I am an avid bird watcher. After retiring earlier this year, I went on a trip to Brazil. While there, I saw the most beautiful spotted bird. It was dark red with black spots and a white chest. I thought it might be a spatuletail, but one of my former students pointed out that spatuletails have red tails, while the bird I saw had a distinct black tail. Can anyone help me name this bird?

Please take a look at the attached photo.

 Spotted_Bird_05.30

191. What does the Web page indicate about the forum?

(A) It accepts international submissions.
(B) It features discussions related to birdhouses.
(C) Members must pay a registration fee.
(D) Postings cannot be longer than one paragraph.

192. What does the World Bird Watchers Forum promise to its members?

(A) It replies to inquiries within the same day.
(B) It provides a listing of bird-related jobs.
(C) It will never raise its registration fee.
(D) It protects private information.

193. Why did Mr. Jennings post on the forum?

(A) To offer another member expert advice
(B) To respond to another member's post
(C) To seek confirmation of an assumption
(D) To request bird feeding instructions

194. How did Mr. Jennings fail to follow the forum rules?

(A) He posted about a bird for sale.
(B) He attached a picture to his post.
(C) His post did not meet the length requirements.
(D) His subject line is too general.

195. What is probably true about Mr. Jennings?

(A) He used to teach at a university.
(B) He is planning on moving to Brazil.
(C) He currently works as a teacher.
(D) He has been a member of the forum for a long time.

GO ON TO THE NEXT PAGE

Questions 196-200 refer to the following job advertisement, information, and e-mail.

| Job title | *Part-time language instructor* | | Area | *Northern Virginia* |

Morton Industries, located about 25 minutes southwest of Washington, D.C., is seeking qualified language instructors to teach a class for our employees.

Languages we are interested in are Chinese(mandarin), Japanese, and Korean. Interested instructors must be available to teach the class every weekday before 9:30 A.M.

The format and structure of the class is completely up to the instructor. We will pay hourly rates commensurate with experience.

If you would like to apply, e-mail humanresources@mortonind.com with the subject line, "language instructor."

Your e-mail should include a résumé and at least two references.

Morton Industries
Falls Church Headquarters

September Language Class Schedule

Our language center is open from 7:00 A.M. to 9:00 P.M., Monday through Friday. You can sign up to join any of the following classes, which we are currently offering. If there is space, you may also drop in and attend without registering in advance. All classes are offered daily unless indicated otherwise. Class names will be posted outside the classrooms.

Time	Class	Instructor
7:00 A.M. – 8:00 A.M.	Beginning Japanese	Atsuki Mako
8:00 A.M. – 9:00 A.M. (Wednesdays and Fridays only)	Intermediate French	Margot Herbst
11:30 A.M. – 12:30 P.M.	Intermediate Spanish	Juan Dominguez
6:30 P.M. – 7:30 P.M. (Mondays and Thursdays only)	Beginning Russian	Vladimir Drago

All employees can use their Morton Industries ID cards to access the language center. Employees visiting from other Morton locations may also access the center, but they will need to first sign in at reception.

To: Jane Smith, Language Center Manager
From: Raul Sanchez, Managing Director
Date: Thursday, September 27
Re: New language classes

I received your report on the new schedule for language classes beginning this month. I am very pleased to hear that so many of our employees are making good use of the center. I have received a lot of positive feedback from employees, who have greatly enjoyed the experience. However, I've also heard from a few of our managers — in fact, I just got off the phone with one now — who have raised one common issue. As you know, our lunch breaks last one hour, but the class you have scheduled for lunchtime runs one full hour. Employees attending this class must then take extra time going to and coming from the language center, and they are eating their lunch at their desks. There have also been some complaints about difficulty in scheduling meeting times. The simplest solution may be to just shorten the lunchtime class to 40 minutes. Would that be possible?

Again, I appreciate all you're doing in keeping the language programs going.

Raul Sanchez

Managing Director
Morton Industries, Falls Church Headquarters

196. According to the job advertisement, what will the instructor decide?

(A) What the class format will be
(B) What the hourly rate will be
(C) How many students can register for the class
(D) How often the class meets

197. Who most likely is the newest language instructor?

(A) Mako
(B) Herbst
(C) Dominguez
(D) Drago

198. What is indicated on the schedule?

(A) Employees may take more than one class.
(B) There is only one classroom in the language center.
(C) Employees from other company locations may use the language center.
(D) Employees must register in advance for all classes.

199. According to the e-mail, with whom did Mr. Sanchez speak on the telephone?

(A) A language instructor
(B) A personnel director
(C) A new applicant
(D) A company manager

200. What class will most likely be shortened?

(A) Beginning Japanese
(B) Intermediate French
(C) Intermediate Spanish
(D) Beginning Russian

Stop! This is the end of the test. If you finish before time is called, you may go back to Parts 5, 6, and 7 and check your work.

TEST

3

정답 및 해설 p.330

TEST3.mp3

MP3 바로 듣기

books.english.co.kr에서 MP3 무료 다운로드가 가능합니다.

LISTENING TEST

In the Listening test, you will be asked to demonstrate how well you understand spoken English. The entire Listening test will last approximately 45 minutes. There are four parts, and directions are given for each part. You must mark your answers on the separate answer sheet.
Do not write your answers in your test book.

PART 1

Directions: For each question in this part, you will hear four statements about a picture in your test book. When you hear the statements, you must select the one statement that best describes what you see in the picture. Then find the number of the question on your answer sheet and mark your answer. The statements will not be printed in your test book and will be spoken only one time.

Statement (B), "They're shaking hands," is the best description of the picture, so you should select answer (B) and mark it on your answer sheet.

1.

2.

GO ON TO THE NEXT PAGE

3.

4.

5.

6.

GO ON TO THE NEXT PAGE

PART 2

Directions: You will hear a question or statement and three responses spoken in English. They will not be printed in your test book and will be spoken only one time. Select the best response to the question or statement and mark the letter (A), (B), or (C) on your answer sheet.

7. Mark your answer on your answer sheet.

8. Mark your answer on your answer sheet.

9. Mark your answer on your answer sheet.

10. Mark your answer on your answer sheet.

11. Mark your answer on your answer sheet.

12. Mark your answer on your answer sheet.

13. Mark your answer on your answer sheet.

14. Mark your answer on your answer sheet.

15. Mark your answer on your answer sheet.

16. Mark your answer on your answer sheet.

17. Mark your answer on your answer sheet.

18. Mark your answer on your answer sheet.

19. Mark your answer on your answer sheet.

20. Mark your answer on your answer sheet.

21. Mark your answer on your answer sheet.

22. Mark your answer on your answer sheet.

23. Mark your answer on your answer sheet.

24. Mark your answer on your answer sheet.

25. Mark your answer on your answer sheet.

26. Mark your answer on your answer sheet.

27. Mark your answer on your answer sheet.

28. Mark your answer on your answer sheet.

29. Mark your answer on your answer sheet.

30. Mark your answer on your answer sheet.

31. Mark your answer on your answer sheet.

PART 3

Directions: You will hear some conversations between two or more people. You will be asked to answer three questions about what the speakers say in each conversation. Select the best response to each question and mark the letter (A), (B), (C), or (D) on your answer sheet. The conversations will not be printed in your test book and will be spoken only one time.

32. Where are the speakers?

(A) At a hotel
(B) At a grocery store
(C) At a cafeteria
(D) At a restaurant

33. Why does the woman recommend the pasta?

(A) It is inexpensive.
(B) It doesn't take long to make.
(C) It is a newly added dish.
(D) It is very healthy.

34. What will the man get free of charge?

(A) More vegetables
(B) Bread
(C) Drinks
(D) A coupon

35. Why is the woman calling?

(A) To order equipment
(B) To check on an order
(C) To send a product
(D) To report a problem

36. What does the woman say she will do?

(A) Call the store again
(B) Contact the manufacturer
(C) Go to a shop
(D) Bring a coupon

37. What does the man offer to do?

(A) Call the woman later
(B) Ship a product
(C) Provide a voucher
(D) Give a discount

38. Why is the man in Toronto?

(A) To attend a seminar
(B) To visit a museum
(C) To reserve a hotel
(D) To inspect a system

39. According to the woman, what has caused a problem?

(A) The accommodation fee was not deposited.
(B) A duplicate reservation was made.
(C) The room number was wrong.
(D) The computer system did not operate properly.

40. What does the woman offer to do?

(A) Provide a coupon
(B) Upgrade his room
(C) Put his name on the waiting list
(D) Find lodging information

41. Where most likely are the speakers?

(A) At a conference hall
(B) At a library
(C) At a store
(D) At a construction site

42. What does the man say he has done?

(A) Closed all the doors
(B) Contacted some workers
(C) Informed customers of a special offer
(D) Posted some signs

43. What will the woman do next?

(A) Replace some products
(B) Send detailed information
(C) Give her e-mail address
(D) Arrange some files

GO ON TO THE NEXT PAGE

44. What are the speakers planning?

(A) An awards ceremony
(B) An annual banquet
(C) An orientation
(D) A workshop

45. What does the man say about the Japanese restaurant?

(A) It serves delicious food.
(B) It is a little far from the company.
(C) It provides food at reasonable prices.
(D) It has recently opened.

46. What is the problem with the Japanese restaurant?

(A) The quality of the food
(B) The distance from the company
(C) The size of space
(D) The variety of dishes

---

47. Where most likely are the speakers?

(A) At a subway station
(B) At a taxi stand
(C) At a restaurant
(D) At a bus stop

48. According to the woman, what has caused a delay?

(A) A traffic accident
(B) An ongoing strike
(C) A local event
(D) Some road construction

49. What does the woman suggest to the man?

(A) Waiting more
(B) Taking a taxi
(C) Walking to the destination
(D) Contacting the bus company

---

50. Where does the woman most likely work?

(A) At a travel agency
(B) At a catering company
(C) At an advertising agency
(D) At an insurance company

51. Why is the woman visiting the company?

(A) To make a complaint
(B) To meet with a sales representative
(C) To finalize the details of an event
(D) To pick up some products

52. According to the man, when is the woman supposed to meet with the manager?

(A) 9:50 A.M.
(B) 10:00 A.M.
(C) 10:30 A.M.
(D) 11:00 A.M.

---

53. Where does the conversation take place?

(A) At a stationery store
(B) At a mobile phone shop
(C) At an appliance repair shop
(D) At a supply warehouse

54. Why does the woman say, "Well, we cleaned and checked the store this morning"?

(A) She found a damaged product.
(B) She tried to find the pens that the man wants to buy.
(C) She put all the goods in place.
(D) She didn't see any missing items in the store.

55. What does the woman offer to do?

(A) Call the man later today
(B) Inform employees of a lost item
(C) Exchange the product for a new one
(D) Check the inventory

---

56. What problem does the woman mention?

    (A) The parking fee is too expensive.
    (B) It is difficult to park a car.
    (C) Many employees need company cars.
    (D) Construction is being delayed.

57. Why does the man say, "By sharing rides, the parking situation has become completely different"?

    (A) It became easier to find a parking space.
    (B) The lack of cars makes him uncomfortable.
    (C) The cost of transportation has decreased.
    (D) A large number of vehicles are needed.

58. What is true about Thomas?

    (A) He has a large car.
    (B) He is a good driver.
    (C) He knows the construction schedule.
    (D) He doesn't live near the woman.

59. Where do the speakers most likely work?

    (A) At a golf club
    (B) At a hospital
    (C) At a computer shop
    (D) At a software company

60. What have the men been doing?

    (A) Making an appointment
    (B) Filing some papers
    (C) Entering information into a database
    (D) Inspecting a computer system

61. What will the woman do next?

    (A) Hire more workers
    (B) Repair the computer
    (C) Contact another department
    (D) Convene a meeting

62. What industry do the speakers work in?

    (A) Financial services
    (B) Marketing
    (C) Clothing
    (D) Real estate

63. What are the speakers planning to do?

    (A) Expand their business
    (B) Release a new product
    (C) Advertise their goods
    (D) Recruit new members

64. What will the man do next?

    (A) Arrange a meeting
    (B) Meet with a customer
    (C) Figure out the expenses
    (D) Recommend a location

GO ON TO THE NEXT PAGE

Office	Location
Star Beauty Parlor	1105
Dr. Yoon's Clinic	1125
Royal Bank	1205
Blue Law Firm	1512

65. What is the purpose of the woman's visit?

(A) To see a lawyer
(B) To open a bank account
(C) To deliver an item
(D) To consult her doctor

66. What does the man say about parking?

(A) The parking duration is limited.
(B) Customers pay discounted rates.
(C) Visitors can park for free.
(D) Parking is not available on weekends.

67. Look at the graphic. Where will the woman most likely go at the building?

(A) 1105
(B) 1125
(C) 1205
(D) 1512

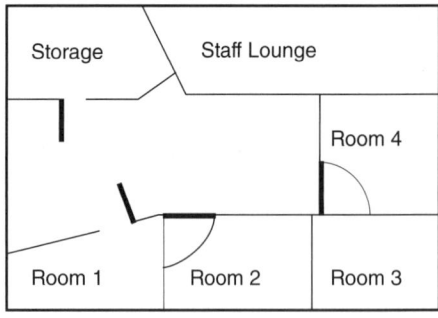

68. Why is the woman busy?

(A) She is preparing for an event.
(B) She is planning the renovation.
(C) She is organizing the marketing meeting.
(D) She is cleaning her office.

69. Look at the graphic. Which room has been assigned to the woman?

(A) Room 1
(B) Room 2
(C) Room 3
(D) Room 4

70. According to the woman, why will the staff like the plan?

(A) The lounge is larger than before.
(B) They will have big space to work.
(C) Their office is close to the woman.
(D) They can hold a meeting in their own office.

PART 4

Directions: You will hear some talks given by a single speaker. You will be asked to answer three questions about what the speaker says in each talk. Select the best response to each question and mark the letter (A), (B), (C), or (D) on your answer sheet. The talks will not be printed in your test book and will be spoken only one time.

71. Who most likely are the listeners?

(A) Club members
(B) Hotel patrons
(C) Store clerks
(D) Dress designers

72. What does the speaker ask the listeners to submit?

(A) A payment
(B) An account number
(C) Updated information
(D) A membership card

73. When will the next meeting be held?

(A) May 5
(B) May 10
(C) June 1
(D) June 10

74. Where does the speaker work?

(A) At a department store
(B) At a shipping company
(C) At an electronics factory
(D) At a power plant

75. What is the problem?

(A) The production facility does not work.
(B) The orders are missing.
(C) The wrong products were shipped.
(D) A delivery will be delayed.

76. What does the speaker ask the listener to do?

(A) Deliver the products earlier than usual
(B) Wait for the products to be delivered
(C) Find staff to work on the weekend
(D) Work the night shift during this week

77. Who is Grace Wilson?

(A) A radio announcer
(B) A reporter
(C) A businesswoman
(D) A professor

78. According to Ms. Wilson, what is the best way to help employees use their creativity?

(A) Holding workshops often
(B) Offering enough free time
(C) Rewarding good performance
(D) Making them work online

79. What should the listeners do if they have questions for Ms. Wilson?

(A) Ask her online
(B) Send a letter
(C) Visit her office
(D) Contact her after the show

80. Who is the speaker?

(A) A tour guide
(B) A critic
(C) A receptionist
(D) An artist

81. What does the speaker say about Mr. Watson's sculptures?

(A) They are simple.
(B) They have detailed designs.
(C) They are very famous.
(D) They are made of special materials.

82. What does the speaker suggest the listeners do?

(A) Present their identification card
(B) Take pictures at the front desk
(C) Keep their personal items in storage
(D) Pick up the brochure at the entrance

GO ON TO THE NEXT PAGE

83. What is the speaker mainly talking about?

(A) Reducing electricity use
(B) Shortening working hours
(C) Making new energy resources
(D) Sharing office equipment

84. What is true about the employees?

(A) They don't care about the expenses.
(B) They try to recycle the equipment.
(C) They make efforts to save electricity.
(D) They used to waste a lot of energy.

85. What is the company going to do this month?

(A) Prepare an opening ceremony
(B) Create an advertising campaign
(C) Hold an awards banquet
(D) Introduce a compensation plan

---

86. What order did the speaker take?

(A) Monitors
(B) Photocopiers
(C) Computers
(D) Printers

87. What does the speaker imply when he says, "I would like to check on something with you"?

(A) The products are sold out.
(B) He sent the wrong items.
(C) The listener didn't submit an order.
(D) There's something wrong with the payment.

88. What does the speaker ask the listener to do?

(A) Send the order form again
(B) Contact him to discuss the matter
(C) Pay for the items immediately
(D) Call the factory for repair

---

89. Where does the speaker work?

(A) At a medical device company
(B) At a doctor's office
(C) At a pharmacy
(D) At a community center

90. Why does the speaker ask the listener to visit a Web site?

(A) To look over the pictures
(B) To get information
(C) To make an appointment
(D) To place an order

91. What does the speaker imply when she says, "Maybe one minute is enough"?

(A) The treatment does not take long.
(B) The listener doesn't have enough time.
(C) The online system is easy to use.
(D) The office is very close to the listener.

Departures	Arrivals
10:00	14:20
12:00	16:20
13:30	17:50
16:00	20:20
18:50	23:10
22:00	02:20

92. What has caused a cancelation?

(A) Bad weather
(B) A shortage of fuel
(C) Equipment failure
(D) Communication interruption

93. Look at the graphic. What time can the listeners leave at the earliest?

(A) 10:00
(B) 16:00
(C) 18:50
(D) 22:00

94. What is offered to passengers who leave the next day?

(A) A special coupon
(B) Lodging facilities
(C) A free shuttle bus service
(D) Seat upgrades

Item	Quantity	Cost
Desk Lamp		
Paper		
Toner	2	$40
Monitor		

95. Look at the graphic. Which department filled out the order form?

(A) Public relations
(B) Quality control
(C) Personnel
(D) Management

96. What is the listener asked to do before ordering?

(A) Attend a meeting
(B) Check the price
(C) Fax an order form
(D) Get confirmation

97. What does the speaker think is likely to happen?

(A) There may be a lack of budget.
(B) Approval may be refused.
(C) An order form may be lost.
(D) An order list may be incomplete.

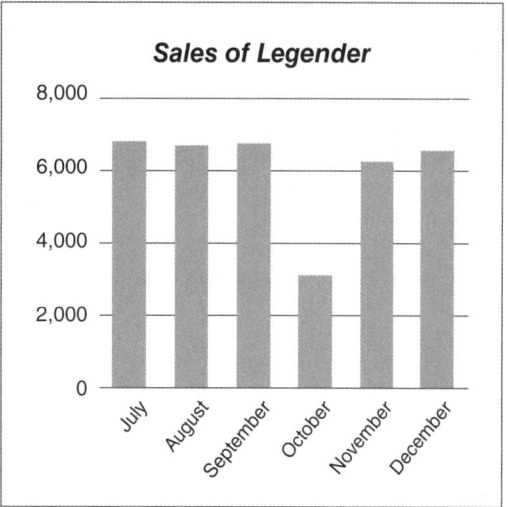

98. Where most likely is the talk taking place?

(A) At a computer manufacturer
(B) At a science museum
(C) At an advertising agency
(D) At an automobile company

99. According to the speaker, why did the sales drop?

(A) The warranty period was not long enough.
(B) Another company launched a new product.
(C) The price of the product was raised.
(D) Many defects were found by customers.

100. Look at the graphic. When did the company introduce the new policy?

(A) In July
(B) In October
(C) In November
(D) In December

This is the end of the Listening test. Turn to Part 5 in your test book.

GO ON TO THE NEXT PAGE

TEST 3

READING TEST

In the Reading test, you will read a variety of texts and answer several different types of reading comprehension questions. The entire Reading test will last 75 minutes. There are three parts, and directions are given for each part. You are encouraged to answer as many questions as possible within the time allowed.

You must mark your answers on the separate answer sheet. Do not write your answers in the test book.

PART 5

Directions: A word or phrase is missing in each of the sentences below. Four answer choices are given below each sentence. Select the best answer to complete the sentence. Then mark the letter (A), (B), (C), or (D) on your answer sheet.

101. Unfortunately, we have no choice but to ------- our annual subscription because of rising delivery fees.

(A) increase
(B) increases
(C) increased
(D) increasing

102. Mr. Smith is confident that he is really lucky to work in such a ------- environment.

(A) vulnerable
(B) decisive
(C) substantial
(D) friendly

103. The research ------- has reminded the management that the product needs to be comprehensively inspected.

(A) divided
(B) division
(C) divisive
(D) dividing

104. Due to its limited capacity, we cannot accept any additional registrations ------- further notice.

(A) despite
(B) through
(C) until
(D) around

105. As a strategy to respond to the fluctuating market, most of the companies are currently restructuring -------.

(A) their
(B) them
(C) theirs
(D) themselves

106. Ms. Jamie was honored for her twenty-five years of contributions to the company ------- after announcing her retirement.

(A) rather
(B) enough
(C) soon
(D) too

107. Bradley Woods Co. ------- shares the up-to-date information with other reputable companies.

(A) occasion
(B) occasions
(C) occasional
(D) occasionally

108. After receiving the results of his test, Mr. Edwards found Beth's advice very ------- in preparing his overseas employment.

(A) helpful
(B) lengthy
(C) immediate
(D) promotional

109. The survey released last week verified that Huxley Co. still ------- its high brand awareness in East Asia.

(A) maintains
(B) maintaining
(C) is maintained
(D) maintenance

110. ------- having small gatherings several times, Clarion Trading Co. decided to hold an annual event each December for all employees.

(A) Whether
(B) Just as
(C) Rather than
(D) Because

111. Ms. Catherine, who dresses ------- and is sitting in the front row, will receive the award named Journalist of the Year.

(A) grace
(B) graces
(C) graceful
(D) gracefully

112. Residents ------- would like to get a parking permit should contact the building administration office.

(A) who
(B) whose
(C) whom
(D) what

113. Our chief ------- is which place is the best and how large a budget we have for this annual conference.

(A) source
(B) concern
(C) partnership
(D) executive

114. Jean Russo's newly released movie was more fantastic and ------- than his previous ones, but actually cost less.

(A) impress
(B) impressed
(C) impressive
(D) impressively

115. The job opening ------- applicants to have at least two years of work experience in the relevant field.

(A) requires
(B) monitors
(C) startles
(D) evaluates

116. According to the news, ------- Biz Con Ltd. nor Max Stock Co. accepted the agreement for their mergers and acquisitions.

(A) both
(B) none
(C) neither
(D) whatever

117. Without additional devices, the XC-200 Laptop enables users to connect ------- to their televisions.

(A) closely
(B) eventually
(C) carefully
(D) remotely

118. While all computer accessories are 20% off, the discount rates on computers -------, depending on the model type.

(A) repair
(B) vary
(C) perform
(D) comply

119. It is not yet ------- how reliable Dr. Medina's presentation was, considering a lot of economic variables in the current market.

(A) clear
(B) clearly
(C) clearing
(D) cleared

120. Gloria Heather's latest book is well organized and ------- with interesting cases that we can easily face on a daily basis.

(A) illustrates
(B) illustrating
(C) illustrated
(D) illustration

GO ON TO THE NEXT PAGE

121. All graduate students are invited to attend a special seminar, forum, and ------- at the Department of Education.

(A) formality
(B) exposure
(C) reception
(D) assistance

122. The best way to reduce the social problems is to ------- the public to comply with the current laws and rules.

(A) interpret
(B) train
(C) care
(D) attend

123. ------- the data, the manager should explain how to responsibly share information among departments within the company.

(A) Protective
(B) Protected
(C) Protecting
(D) To protect

124. ------- the terms and conditions of the contract will be changed, all of our customers should sign the agreement electronically.

(A) Because
(B) When
(C) Therefore
(D) Despite

125. Overseas -------, nationals of countries outside of the U.S., should have a valid visa in order to work here.

(A) applies
(B) applicants
(C) applications
(D) applied

126. ------- deciding to make a purchase, you need to compare prices through a variety of Web sites.

(A) About
(B) Of
(C) Before
(D) Into

127. According to the federal law, all items sold in the U.S. must be labeled with their production date and the place of ------- of the contents.

(A) origin
(B) duplicate
(C) property
(D) religion

128. Ms. Heather ------- at the Fairfax branch for ten years by the time she transfers to our headquarters this March.

(A) will have worked
(B) had worked
(C) works
(D) have worked

129. Please call the personnel division at 710-1920 and let them know if the meeting schedule is ------- to you.

(A) agree
(B) agreed
(C) agreeable
(D) agreement

130. The World Football Championship final will be broadcast ------- all the states through Channel JCB this Saturday night.

(A) between
(B) with
(C) into
(D) across

PART 6

Directions: Read the texts that follow. A word, phrase, or sentence is missing in parts of each text. Four answer choices for each question are given below the text. Select the best answer to complete the text. Then mark the letter (A), (B), (C), or (D) on your answer sheet.

Questions 131-134 refer to the following advertisement.

Florida is now offering a variety of attractions to you — aquariums, amusement parks, and good restaurants. With the Special Florida Pass, you can enjoy all kinds of popular spots across the state at a reasonable price. If you ------- more attractions, you can get
131.
more discounts. -------. You can purchase the passes only through our Web site at www.
132.
specialflorida.com before leaving your home country. When you visit your first attraction, the passes you bought are going to be activated automatically. They will remain ------- at any
133.
place within the state of Florida for 30 days. When purchasing them, you can ------- get our
134.
premium coupon book, which can be used at in-state outlet stores.

131. (A) use
   (B) used
   (C) using
   (D) user

132. (A) A lot of travel agencies offer guided tours
      to you.
   (B) This offer is only available to overseas
      tourists.
   (C) In particular, Sea World is best known to
      foreign visitors.
   (D) In addition, you should submit it to our
      office in person.

133. (A) brilliant
   (B) decisive
   (C) valid
   (D) open

134. (A) very
   (B) as well
   (C) yet
   (D) also

GO ON TO THE NEXT PAGE

Questions 135-138 refer to the following e-mail.

To: Ulla Connor <u.connor@uccommunication.org>

From: Jane Lee <j.lee@innobizproduction.net>

Date: October 8

Subject: Workshop on September 30

Dear Ms. Connor,

I am writing to extend our ------- for the workshop John Swale conducted at our headquarters
135.
in Nashville on September 30. Some employees ------- concern about the effectiveness of the
136.
workshop before his lecture. These employees participated in the workshop throughout the
entire day and even asked whether another session would be held or not. So, we required
attendees to fill out our own evaluation form ------- to check the need for future workshops. Most
137.
of the participants positively responded to the issue while stating that they had a good chance
to improve their communication skills. -------. Please contact us in order to discuss the follow-up
138.
workshops in detail.

Best wishes,

Jane Lee

Innobiz Production

---

135. (A) appreciate
(B) appreciated
(C) appreciative
(D) appreciation

136. (A) express
(B) is expressing
(C) were expressed
(D) had expressed

137. (A) significantly
(B) usually
(C) afterwards
(D) frequently

138. (A) The workshop was scheduled to be organized next month.
(B) We will offer you a bonus of $400 by check.
(C) Other attendees said that they needed more actual practice.
(D) The president would like to take your lectures soon.

Questions 139-142 refer to the following e-mail.

To : Danny Rivera <d.rivera@boardworld.com>

From : Brad Triana <b.triana@uptondesign.com>

Date : March 20

Subject : Regular order

We'd like to make some changes to Upton Design's ------- order. Only some employees are using
139.
matte-black chalkboards in their presentations, and as a result, the use of CH-200 chalk on the

boards is lessening. -------, we want to ask you to reduce the number of this item in our order to
140.
only ten as of next month. Instead, please add 20 JX-120 multipurpose markers.

We will gradually decrease the use of CH-200 chalk until the end of this year. However, we -------
141.
your company continuous notices before that date. Could you send me a revised billing statement

for our monthly order? -------.
142.

Regards,

Brad Triana
Upton Design

---

139. (A) overdue
(B) standing
(C) excessive
(D) redundant

140. (A) For instance
(B) Therefore
(C) Nonetheless
(D) Likewise

141. (A) gives
(B) are given
(C) gave
(D) will give

142. (A) Our accounting department will require it.
(B) We will launch a new business for the board.
(C) Employees are satisfied with your products.
(D) You can ask us to submit the invoice.

GO ON TO THE NEXT PAGE

April 20

Chuck Conrad
Haman Utility Co.
Albany, New York

Dear Mr. Conrad,

We are pleased to announce that Willy Development ------- the proposal of Haman Utility for the
143.
bid for improvements to the Civic Center. Your workers for the construction will have access to
the ------- beginning on June 10. According to the policies regarding the building construction,
144.
Haman Utility Co. will take responsibility for obtaining the required permits. You can find
the layout of the project in the enclosed documents with this letter. -------, there are the lists
145.
of other companies associated with us, and your company can check their suitability for the
overall construction project. Please feel free to contact us if you have any questions or need more
information. -------.
146.

Sincerely,

John Svenson, Director
Willy Development

Enclosure

---

143. (A) would accept
(B) was accepting
(C) has accepted
(D) was accepted

144. (A) item
(B) site
(C) date
(D) person

145. (A) However
(B) Instead
(C) As a result
(D) In addition

146. (A) We will provide you with it as soon as
possible.
(B) You can connect to our Web site with
the address below.
(C) We ask you to visit our main office in
person.
(D) You should let us know about your
company's decision.

PART 7

Directions: In this part you will read a selection of texts, such as magazine and newspaper articles, e-mails, and instant messages. Each text or set of texts is followed by several questions. Select the best answer for each question and mark the letter (A), (B), (C), or (D) on your answer sheet.

Questions 147-148 refer to the following e-mail.

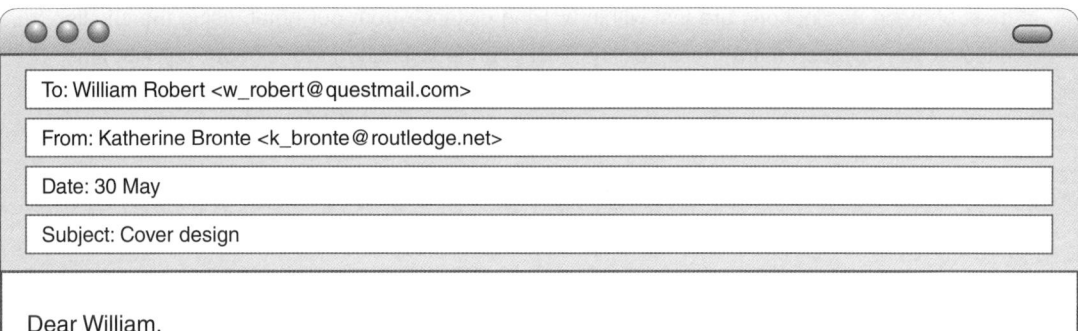

To: William Robert <w_robert@questmail.com>

From: Katherine Bronte <k_bronte@routledge.net>

Date: 30 May

Subject: Cover design

Dear William,

I would like to notify you that you will receive an e-mail from the Routledge marketing division in the near future. You can find the details about the marketing process and one Web address, which is linked to an online survey for authors. Although a marketing director and a designer will discuss your book cover, you need to have your own opinion about that. Do you have any suggestions that will make the cover design more striking and distinctive? Please let me know if you have any good ideas.

Sincerely,

Katherine Bronte
Chief Editor
Routledge Publishing

147. Who most likely is Mr. Robert?

(A) A designer
(B) An analyst
(C) An author
(D) A marketing manager

148. According to the e-mail, what should soon arrive?

(A) Sample pages of the book
(B) Marketing information
(C) The results of a survey
(D) A list of bookstores

GO ON TO THE NEXT PAGE

Thank you for choosing the Bayview Hotel!

In return for our guests' constant support, we have decided to extend our complimentary shuttle service to the downtown district. The shuttle makes stops at a variety of the city's excellent attractions such as museums, shopping centers, and sandy beaches. Although most of these destinations are just within walking distance from our hotel, using the shuttle enables you to reach them more quickly. This change is really good for both our first-time and regular guests. The shuttle will also stop at additional spots for seasonal events and festivals.

The schedules for the shuttle service are posted in our hotel lobby and on our Web site. As with our airport service, our Gold members can book a shuttle in advance.

Bayview Hotel

149. What is being offered?

(A) Discounted rates for the accommodation
(B) A free transportation service
(C) A guided tour of the attractions
(D) A membership upgrade program

150. What is suggested about the Bayview Hotel?

(A) It is near the center of the city.
(B) It is popular with guests for business travel.
(C) It is very valuable from a historical perspective.
(D) Its room rates are the most expensive in the area.

Questions 151-152 refer to the following text-message chain.

Messages

Julie May [11:30 A.M.]

> Glen, my train is delayed about one hour, and I might be late for the meeting. Could you prepare for it and start instead of me if I don't arrive there by 2 P.M.?

Glen Choi [11:32 A.M.]

> Of course. When will you arrive at the station?

Julie May [11:33 A.M.]

> I think I cannot get to Penn Station until 1:30. Then I need to ride the Red-Line bus to the office.

Glen Choi [11:35 A.M.]

> No need. I'll pick you up at the station. I'm sure we can get to the office before 2 P.M.

Julie May [11:37 A.M.]

> That sounds great! But I should set up the computer equipment for the meeting.

---

151. What is Ms. May concerned about?

(A) Updating the computer software
(B) Avoiding traffic congestion
(C) Preparing handouts for the meeting
(D) Making it to the office on time

152. At 11:35 A.M., what does Mr. Choi most likely mean when he writes, "No need"?

(A) They do not need to meet at Penn Station.
(B) They do not need to set up the computer.
(C) Ms. May does not need to take a bus.
(D) Ms. May does not need to join the meeting.

GO ON TO THE NEXT PAGE

Questions 153-155 refer to the following article.

Business Week of Baltimore

BALTIMORE (July 10) — Tahoma Max announced on Monday that it will have many job openings in the city of Baltimore. The company's spokesman, Simon Fraser, said a new restaurant is scheduled to open on August 20 at 301 Fleming Avenue. The branch manager of the Baltimore City location is currently looking for about 40 employees before it opens. There is a range of positions from servers and cooks to managers and chefs. In order to fill these positions, Tahoma Max is organizing a one-day job fair on July 20. After checking participants' applications, they will interview ideal candidates on the spot.

The new branch of Tahoma Max will be the only restaurant in Baltimore that grows its own farm products and uses them for its dishes. It stands behind its regional menu by using local produce. "We are really pleased to be devoted ourselves to developing the region-based job environment," said Gian Pagnucci, cofounder and CEO of Tahoma Max. "We hope that a lot of passionate and professional candidates apply for the positions. When fulfilling our requirements, we offer prospective employees a competitive salary and benefits package." Candidates who are interested but cannot attend the fair can instead apply online at www.tahomamax.com/Baltimore.

153. What is the article mainly about?

(A) Advertising of localized products
(B) Social contributions of the company
(C) The growth of the city's economy
(D) Job opportunities at a new restaurant

154. What is implied about the event on July 20?

(A) All the applicants must join the interview section.
(B) It is only intended for the city's grocery store owners.
(C) Participants can try a variety of dishes the company will serve.
(D) There will be many positions available to be filled.

155. Why is Tahoma Max special?

(A) It has donated to local charities.
(B) It has expanded its business abroad.
(C) It offers the best price for its dishes.
(D) It will grow its own vegetables and crops.

To: douglaird@findsplash.com

From: customerservice@rossapparel.com

Date: March 12

Subject: Order confirmation (No.10984821)

Dear Mr. Laird,

Thank you for purchasing our clothes! We are writing this e-mail regarding the confirmation of your order from www.rossapparel.com. Among apparel companies, we have been well recognized nationally, and we particularly specialized in the attire for cooking that you ordered.

We are now processing your order. Generally, orders are processed and sent out to our shipping department within three business days. After that, our staff will be ready to ship your goods. Once your product is shipped from our warehouse, you will receive another e-mail, which will include updated information about your tracking number.

Thank you for your business.

Regards,

Order&Shipping
Ross Apparel

156. What type of business does Mr. Laird most likely work for?

(A) A clothing company
(B) A restaurant
(C) A local farm
(D) A shipping company

157. According to the e-mail, when will Mr. Laird receive another e-mail from Ross Apparel?

(A) When he pays for the items
(B) When he confirms the order
(C) When his order leaves the warehouse
(D) When new merchandise is stocked

GO ON TO THE NEXT PAGE

Questions 158-160 refer to the following letter.

Bonnie Alyssa
2491 Courtland Boulevard
Daytona, FL 32118

September 20

Dear Ms. Alyssa,

Thank you for renewing your service contract with Allo Broadband Net. We have enclosed your quarterly invoice about our Web hosting services. — [1] —. You will find the additional cost of $15 on your billing statement for our regular maintenance service. — [2] —. As a reminder, Allo Broadband Net upgraded your Web site in August in order to be compatible with all kinds of the latest devices and software. And now there is nothing wrong with using the Web site and seeing the same contents. — [3] —.

We'd like to know your opinion regarding how effective these improvements have been to your Web site and business. — [4] —. Please fill out our online questionnaire by logging into your ABN account and clicking the red banner at the bottom of the page. As an expression of our gratitude for this, you can get 15 percent off of a future bill.

Thanks for your support!

Clark Davidson
Clark Davidson

Allo Broadband Net
Enclosure

---

158. Why was the additional fee charged?

(A) Ms. Alyssa added an extra Web site to her current account.
(B) Ms. Alyssa asked the company to upgrade her service plan.
(C) Allo Broadband Net improved its Web services.
(D) Allo Broadband Net employed new technical experts.

159. What does Mr. Davidson ask Ms. Alyssa to do?

(A) Complete an online survey form
(B) Send a notice to her clients
(C) Renew her monthly contract
(D) Update her personal information

160. In which of the positions marked [1], [2], [3], and [4] does the following sentence best belong?

"We already notified you of this increase in June by e-mail."

(A) [1]
(B) [2]
(C) [3]
(D) [4]

Questions 161-163 refer to the following e-mail.

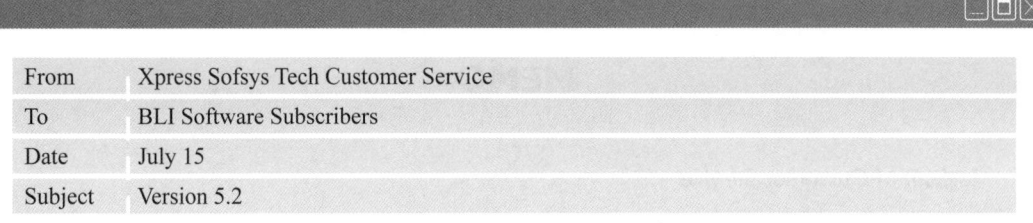

From	Xpress Sofsys Tech Customer Service
To	BLI Software Subscribers
Date	July 15
Subject	Version 5.2

At the end of this month, Xpress Sofsys Tech will release version 5.2 of BLI, our online software for managing inventories. Starting at midnight on July 31, BLI will be out of service temporarily while our IT team rolls out the new version. You don't need to do anything — just wait for its completion. During this period, our cloud server will automatically save your current data, and all users will be notified of this update at 7 A.M. on August 1 after the work is finished. Subsequent to this notification, all users can use our BLI software as usual without any action.

There are new innovative features which include an intuitive user interface allowing users to easily find functions and a fast data-processing engine enabling them to reduce their working time. Moreover, existing users can be given an additional 100 GB of Web cloud data storage as our promotional event for celebrating the release of the new version. We're sure that you will fully enjoy these new features without any difficulty.

Sincerely,

Customer Service
Xpress Sofsys Tech

161. What is the purpose of the e-mail?

(A) To promote national events
(B) To update a company's policies
(C) To inform customers of changes
(D) To remind subscribers about payment

162. The phrase "rolls out" in paragraph 1, line 3, is closest in meaning to

(A) circulates
(B) removes
(C) introduces
(D) expands

163. What will happen on August 1?

(A) An employee will demonstrate the new version.
(B) Users will be able to use the software as before.
(C) Xpress Sofsys Tech will employ extra staff.
(D) An update for a computer program will start.

GO ON TO THE NEXT PAGE

MEMO

To: Staff of Customer Service
Date: October 20
Subject: Meeting next Monday

Last week, we gathered and discussed our quality of customer service (CS). According to the data we secured, most customers positively responded to the communication with our CS staff. Our staff was really professional and prompt in answering various questions regarding the packaging service, shipping fees, and parcel status tracking.

One thing that we need to settle is the low level of recommendation to their acquaintances. Based on our survey, just a few customers told the advantages of our service to others. Most people are our regular customers using our shipping services only, or they recognize us through our media-based advertising. It is obvious that we have failed to attract new customers through referrals.

Therefore, our next Monday meeting will focus on this issue. I will devise some methods to improve the situation. I would also appreciate it if you would come up with creative and innovative approaches to increase the level of recommendation. Please submit your suggestions to my e-mail, and I will include them in our presentation slides for discussion. I look forward to hearing from you all.

Ronald Jackson
Director of Customer Service

164. Where does Mr. Jackson probably work?

    (A) At a telecommunication company
    (B) At an insurance company
    (C) At a logistics company
    (D) At an advertising company

165. What problem was mentioned?

    (A) There is a lack of employees in the CS department.
    (B) The expenses for advertising have gradually increased.
    (C) Few customers recommend the company to others.
    (D) Some orders tend to be frequently delayed.

166. What information did Mr. Jackson review?

    (A) Financing balance sheets
    (B) Survey results
    (C) Online advertisements
    (D) Competitor analysis

167. What are staff members asked to do?

    (A) Fill out the attached form
    (B) Send Mr. Jackson some ideas related to the issue
    (C) Hire more members for the customer service department
    (D) Confirm the date of their meeting

TEST 3

GO ON TO THE NEXT PAGE

Questions 168-171 refer to the following online chat discussion.

Hannah Park [11:20 A.M.]

You may be aware that the air conditioning is not working in some parts of our building.

Bob Taylor [11:21 A.M.]

I heard. For some time, it has become increasingly hot and humid.

Hannah Park [11:22 A.M.]

There is something wrong with the gas piping, and the repair has been delayed due to the difficulty of supplying parts. The last time one broke, it took about four days to be fixed. Probably, a technician will arrive in the late afternoon tomorrow. Until then, please use an existing fan.

Bob Taylor [11:25 A.M.]

I'm concerned that our computer equipment may overheat. Do we have any equipment for temporarily saving our work? I'm really afraid of losing our data.

Hannah Park [11:28 A.M.]

Not in this building. With Ms. Watson's approval, we could obtain extra storage equipment from the warehouse in Fleming. I think we have four or five devices there. I can pick them up tomorrow afternoon at the earliest.

Amy Watson [11:30 A.M.]

Hannah, I allow you to urgently purchase temporary storage server units for protecting our data right away. Please let me know the number of needed units and estimated costs as soon as you're ready for the purchase.

Hannah Park [11:31 A.M.]

I'll get started right now.

Amy Watson [11:32 A.M.]

If you cannot find any local appliance store to deliver them by 3 P.M., send someone directly to a store to pick them up.

Send

168. What is the problem?

(A) The warehouse is too far from the office.
(B) The purchase permit has been rejected.
(C) The delivery fee is more expensive than expected.
(D) The cooling system is not functioning.

169. At 11:28 A.M., what does Ms. Park mean when she writes, "Not in this building"?

(A) There are no extra storage devices nearby.
(B) Improvements will make the data safer.
(C) The company servers are stable anywhere.
(D) A pick-up truck is needed for moving the office supplies.

170. What is suggested about the equipment in Fleming?

(A) It will take too long to arrive at the office.
(B) It needs some additional parts from another store.
(C) Its storage is located near the office building.
(D) An expert should be used for its installment.

171. What will most likely happen next?

(A) The fans will be placed in each office.
(B) Ms. Park will be ready to place an order.
(C) The technician will set up new servers.
(D) Mr. Taylor will delete redundant data.

GO ON TO THE NEXT PAGE

Into the Virtual Reality: the Key to Success

COLUMBUS (2 May)—Jane Melissa had been a student who had majored in fashion design when she entered a university in New York City 25 years ago. However, she wanted to get down to business, at the time working at a small clothing store during her summer vacation. — [1] —. To achieve her new goal, she changed her major to business, and after getting the degree, she started her own small store in her hometown of Columbus under the name "Melissa's Open Arms".

Twenty years later, Ms. Melissa's store has steadily expanded into the fastest-growing company in the eastern part of the U.S. while earning millions of dollars every year. — [2] —. According to an interview with her, this success is partly thanks to suggestions about a virtual online store from Jessica Doris, who was hired seven years ago. By accepting her ideas, Ms. Melissa renamed her flagship store "V-Melissa" to match its digital identity.

Ms. Melissa has strong communication skills and the ability to interact with customers in person, and even loves having them share their feelings. — [3] —. However, she is aware that online shopping is important in these days of advanced telecommunications. V-Melissa expects that the annual sales on the Web alone will rise to $200 million. About one-third of these sales will be from outside the U.S., in places such as England, France, Japan, and South Korea.

In accordance with its expansion, V-Melissa has continuously employed a lot of new and experienced staff in order to update and manage the virtual online store and prepare for expanding to new branches inside and outside of the States.

"We need to consider the validity and profitability of opening our new branches in a timely fashion," said Ms. Melissa. "It is essential for us to promote our quality items and services all over the world." — [4] —.

Lastly, Ms. Melissa told us that, although she cannot predict the future accurately, she just keeps taking a step forward with her reliable team members.

172. What is the purpose of the article?

(A) To emphasize the importance of online sales
(B) To advertise new lines of clothes
(C) To describe how a company has grown
(D) To discuss up-to-date fashion trends

173. What is indicated about V-Melissa?

(A) It operated under another name.
(B) It opened its first store in New York City.
(C) It has hired only Web designers.
(D) It recently appointed Ms. Doris the vice president.

174. The word "fashion" in paragraph 5, line 2, is closest in meaning to

(A) manner
(B) kind
(C) function
(D) appearance

175. In which of the positions marked [1], [2], [3], and [4] does the following sentence best belong?

"She still believes that the best thing she can do is to meet their actual needs when they shop at her offline store."

(A) [1]
(B) [2]
(C) [3]
(D) [4]

GO ON TO THE NEXT PAGE

Questions 176-180 refer to the following online form and e-mail.

 http://www.miraclesoftware.com/support_request

Miracle Software Support Request Form

Name : Katie Yoon
Company : Wiki Corporation
E-mail : k.yoon@wikicorp.com
Subject : Issues with the video conference

Please describe the problem you are experiencing.

Since last March, we have used your Web-based video conference software and have been satisfied with it overall. However, we have intermittently gotten disconnected and had trouble in matching the screen with the voice. During a recent conference, the screen suddenly flickered with some noise. After being restarted, the message "Call the Service Center" was on the screen. Several of our clients from all over the world complained about this inconvenience in the last weekly conference, so we had no choice but to reschedule it. Don't you have any immediate action for improving these issues? If not, we would like to terminate our service contract soon. We want to get a guarantee that it would never happen again so that we can proceed with our projects smoothly. Please let us know about the solution as soon as possible.

To: Katie Yoon <k.yoon@wikicorp.com>

From: Miracle Software Support <support@miraclesoftware.com>

Date: May 2

Subject: Service Support 201904128 – Issues with the video conference

Dear Ms. Yoon,

Thank you for providing us with information about your difficulties. The problem you experienced at that time was caused by some conflicts among database servers. This problem could not be expected or discovered by our IT support team, so we had no way to warn our customers in advance. I am confident that this issue is very rare on our Web servers.

Considering your feedback, we have decided to change our on-screen alert messages from "Call the Service Center" to "Service Code No.100." This new message allows our clients to know the problem exactly and find the solution from our maintenance manual on the Web. By doing so, our customers could solve this kind of trouble easily. Actually, our Web-conferencing software is almost perfect in every aspect. In light of this sudden variable, we will update our software as soon as possible through the Internet. While being upgraded, the software will be temporarily inaccessible for just a few minutes. We sincerely apologize for the inconvenience caused and truly thank you for your comments. As a token of our appreciation, we will deduct $100 from this month's bill.

Best Wishes,

Steven Nash
Software Support
Miracle Software

176. What does Ms. Yoon request on the online form?

(A) A new conference device
(B) A customer service call
(C) A quick solution
(D) A membership upgrade

177. What is indicated about Wiki Corporation?

(A) They had cooperated with Miracle Software.
(B) They owned a copyright of the software.
(C) They have been in operation since mid-March.
(D) They use a video conference program regularly.

178. What problem did Ms. Yoon have with Miracle Software's program?

(A) It is incompatible with her computer.
(B) It is not suitable for her specific needs.
(C) It is more expensive than other competitors.
(D) It is unreliable and unstable on its server.

179. What does Mr. Nash say Miracle Software will change?

(A) Its terms and conditions
(B) Its confusing message
(C) Its maintenance schedule
(D) Its Webcam and speakerphone

180. What is suggested about Miracle Software?

(A) It will continue to do business with Wiki Corporation.
(B) It recently hired a new technical expert.
(C) It manages clients' financial plans.
(D) It upgraded its servers last month.

GO ON TO THE NEXT PAGE

Questions 181-185 refer to the following e-mail and instructions.

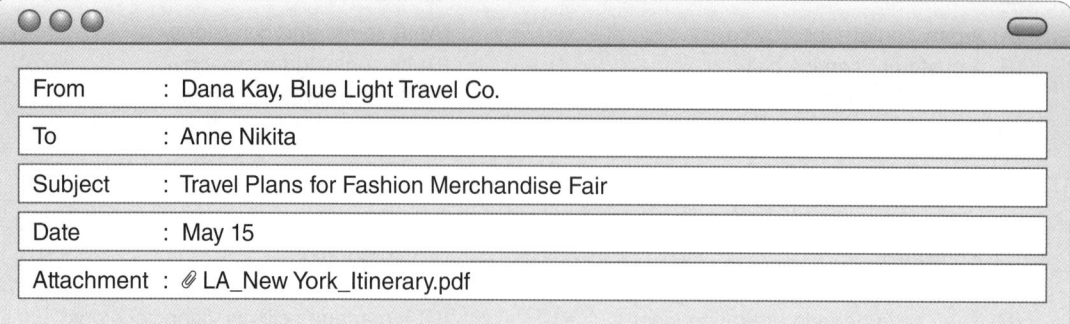

From	: Dana Kay, Blue Light Travel Co.
To	: Anne Nikita
Subject	: Travel Plans for Fashion Merchandise Fair
Date	: May 15
Attachment	: 📎 LA_New York_Itinerary.pdf

Dear Ms. Nikita,

As requested, I have made a reservation for your round-trip ticket to New York City. Your reservation number is LM3870401SW. You will depart from the L.A. domestic airport on June 2, and return from the New York airport on June 5. This schedule does not conflict with your tasks for the June Fashion Merchandise Fair. You can find the itinerary in the attached file of this e-mail.

In response to your inquiry about whether your small furniture can be sent together, clothes racks can be checked as luggage. The person in charge at South-West Airlines notified me that there is an additional fee of $100 for each piece of oversized luggage. On the condition that you pay for the fee beforehand, you can drop off these oversized items quickly at the express kiosk when checking in. Your items mentioned above do not exceed the airline's baggage policy limit in weight and size. If you have more items you want to check, please e-mail me about their weight and size. If so, I can make the payment for you in advance.

Regards,

Dana Kay
Blue Light Travel Co.

South-West Airlines
Instructions for Express Luggage Check-In Service

Upon arrival at the airport, please follow these simple procedures.

1. Print out your boarding pass at any check-in kiosk in the airport.

2. At the express drop-off kiosk, place your items on the scale. Show your valid photo ID (passport or driver's license) and boarding pass to one of our staff. He or she will ask you the number of bags or other items you want to check.

3. Our staff will put a tag on your baggage and give you the relevant document. And then, you can go to the airport security checkpoints.

NOTE: The express drop-off service is currently available only in Chicago, Atlanta, and L.A.

181. According to the e-mail, why is Ms. Nikita probably going to New York City?
    (A) To participate in the fashion show
    (B) To negotiate imported fabric prices
    (C) To promote her company's products
    (D) To hold a meeting with clients

182. What is true about Ms. Nikita's oversized luggage?
    (A) It consists of furniture for the fair.
    (B) It exceeds the weight limit.
    (C) It was bought by her clients.
    (D) It will be shipped by train.

183. What does Ms. Kay offer to do for Ms. Nikita?
    (A) Organize a trip budget
    (B) Make hotel reservations
    (C) Change a schedule
    (D) Deal with a fee

184. What is indicated about a boarding pass?
    (A) It is attached to Ms. Kay's e-mail.
    (B) It must be presented at the check-in area.
    (C) It must be printed out at home.
    (D) It is not required at the security point.

185. What is implied about Ms. Nikita's return flight?
    (A) Ms. Nikita will not use the express drop-off service.
    (B) Ms. Nikita will return back to L.A. overnight.
    (C) Ms. Nikita will change her itinerary.
    (D) Ms. Nikita will have additional luggage.

GO ON TO THE NEXT PAGE

Questions 186-190 refer to the following Web page, e-mail, and article.

http://pennylife.org/donations

Penny Life stores ask the public to donate new or pre-owned items such as furniture, appliances, supplies and so on. These should be clean for others to use them. Please note that damaged or stained items cannot be accepted. Profits from the sales of these goods are used to fund local community development projects, which include the renovation of houses, the creation of educational programs, and the improvement to the surrounding environments.

Step to donate:

1. Find the nearest Penny Life store by entering your address into the search box on the main page of our Web site.

2. Please check the operation hours of each store and its location on the Web site.

3. Bring your redundant or unneeded items yourself or call one of our managers at the number on the Web in order to schedule a pickup time for large items from your home or company.

From	: d.ditzel@ditzellodge.com
To	: k.tyler@pennylife.org
Date	: April 20
Subject	: Donation

Dear Mr. Tyler,

I am the owner of the Ditzel Suite Lodge in Morgantown. I am planning to close my accommodation business next month.

I would like to donate a great amount of good furniture in my building — beds, desks, chairs, tables, and more. A friend of mine advised me to donate these inventories to your organization. I figured out that the nearest branch of Penny Life is the Pittsburgh office when I used the location search system, and I now know the branch manager's contact information there. My place is located about 25 miles away from the office. I hope you will contact me regarding this issue as soon as possible.

Regards,

David Ditzel
Ditzel Suite Lodge

Ditzel Suite Lodge Closure

MORGANTOWN (May 2)—David Ditzel recently saw a lot of accommodation furniture moved from his Ditzel Suite Lodge by Penny Life's trucks. He has operated the hotel, a local landmark, for 50 years as its owner. "I am really happy to move into Erie County, which borders Lake Erie, one of the Great Lakes," said Mr. Ditzel. "And I have plans to spend the rest of my time volunteering and relaxing. But, it is hard for me to leave Morgantown because the hotel has been a big part of my life."

The property of Ditzel Suite Lodge has already been purchased by Max Virginia Development Co. The company is expected to entirely rebuild the building and construct a new shopping complex over the next few years.

186. According to the Web page, what does Penny Life do with items received?

(A) Donate them to local charities
(B) Clean them for recycling
(C) Sell them to the public
(D) Repair them for a display

187. How did Mr. Ditzel find the contact information of Penny Life?

(A) By visiting its Web site
(B) By hearing it from his acquaintance
(C) By downloading operating system updates
(D) By contacting its head office

188. What is indicated about Mr. Ditzel in the e-mail?

(A) He wants to sell his new furniture.
(B) He is going to transfer to another branch.
(C) He is seeking another job opportunity.
(D) He had decided to shut down a business.

189. What is suggested about the Penny Life branch in Pittsburgh?

(A) It provides customers with an excellent moving service.
(B) It is the largest branch in the United States.
(C) It will visit Mr. Ditzel's business for a pickup service.
(D) It will be temporarily closed for its renovation.

190. According to the article, where is Mr. Ditzel planning to live next?

(A) In Pittsburgh
(B) In Erie
(C) In Morgantown
(D) In Virginia

GO ON TO THE NEXT PAGE

Questions 191-195 refer to the following e-mails and order form.

To	: Tommy Lancer <t.lancer@blackdots.com>
From	: Grace Kim <g_kim@proassetfinanacial.net>
Date	: June 15
Subject	: Office supplies order
Attachment	: 📎 Orderform.doc

Dear Mr. Lancer,

I am writing about some changes of items we want to use for the next month on the attached form. We have placed orders with your Black Dots Supplies on a regular basis, and automatically received the items on the first day of each month. But this time, please be aware that we would like to replace the ink toner we have received with a different brand, as indicated on the form. In addition, we want to add more of item LP 350 than usual only for this time because new additional accountants have been recently employed. So, we need to prepare some office spaces for them. You can find our company credit card information in your records and use it for the payment.

We have been always satisfied with the quality of your items, especially the recycled paper-based stationery with our company's logo.

Best wishes,

Grace Kim
Manager of General Affairs
Proasset Financial Firm

Order for: Proasset Financial Firm   **Order Date:** June 15
Contact: Grace Kim

Item Description	Item Number	Quantity	Price Per Unit	Itemized Total
Letterhead paper	LP 350	10 Reams	$40.00	$400.00
Whiteboard markers	WM 500	8 Packages of 5	$5.99	$47.92
Maxdova ink toner cartridge	MI 750	10	$50.00	$500.00
Dusittani magnetic whiteboard	DM 900	5	$89.99	$449.95
Black Dots Supplies			TAX:	$60.13
			TOTAL:	$1,458.00

To	Grace Kim <g_kim@proassetfinanacial.net>
From	Tommy Lancer <t.lancer@blackdots.com>
Date	June 16
Subject	Re: Office supplies order

Dear Ms. Kim,

We would be pleased to process your orders including some changes as requested on your order form. However, it is regretful that the Dusittani's whiteboards you ordered are now out of stock. Instead of them, I would like to recommend using Gannon's whiteboards, which have had the highest level of preference from other clients. It is the top-ranked product in the office supplies market. The original price is $95.99 each, but I am willing to supply you with five at the same price as the Dusittani magnetic whiteboard. If you want to go along with this recommendation, just let me know through this e-mail.

Sincerely yours,

Tommy Lancer
Black Dots Supplies

191. What is the purpose of the first e-mail?

(A) To modify a regular order
(B) To complain about a product
(C) To contact a manufacturer
(D) To check an estimated delivery date

192. In the first e-mail, what is indicated about Proasset Financial Firm?

(A) It is currently expanding.
(B) It is preparing for its office relocation.
(C) It has recently hired a new salesperson.
(D) It upgraded some office appliances.

193. What product is Ms. Kim particularly satisfied with?

(A) Letterhead paper
(B) Whiteboard markers
(C) Maxdova ink toner cartridge
(D) Dusittani magnetic whiteboard

194. What item number is a replacement among regularly ordered products?

(A) LP 350
(B) WM 500
(C) MI 750
(D) DM 900

195. How much will the company pay for each Gannon brand whiteboard?

(A) $47.92
(B) $60.13
(C) $89.99
(D) $95.99

GO ON TO THE NEXT PAGE

Questions 196-200 refer to the following schedule and e-mails.

Benjamin Corporation

Timetable for Conference Room
Fridays in July

Below is the schedule chart for the meetings reserved and the available times for new ones in our conference rooms. The rooms can be used only for the scheduled meetings and conferences on Fridays in July. We ask for your understanding about the case that the management may request a room urgently. If this happens, please contact Kenny Rodgers at k_rodgers@benjaminco.com to inquire about the availability of rooms in other buildings on our premises.

Time Slot	Room 201 (Capacity: 30)	Room 202 (Capacity: 60)
Morning 1 9:30–10:30 A.M.	Available	Sales Team
Morning 2 10:50–11:50 A.M.	Human Resources	Public Relations
Afternoon 1 2:20–3:20 P.M.	Customer Service	IT Support Center
Afternoon 2 3:40–4:40 P.M.	Available	Marketing Group

To	: Department Managers
From	: Kenny Rodgers
Date	: June 29
Subject	: Conference Room Schedules

You should be aware that you cannot use both conference rooms in the Franklin Building the entire day on Friday, July 10, because there will be preliminary management seminars for the corporation's upcoming general meeting. These are scheduled to begin at ten o'clock and are expected to exceed the time appointed on the timetable. Anyone who wants to use a room on this date should notify me of your request by this Friday through this e-mail. A room will be reserved on a first-come, first-served basis.

Thanks,

Kenny Rodgers
Chief of Secretary's Office

To	: All Employees
From	: Kenny Rodgers
Date	: July 3
Subject	: Schedule Changes for Friday

Please be sure that there are following changes on our schedule chart because of the important management meetings on July 10.

Listed below are rooms reserved on that date.
- In Room 701 and 702, there will be Morning 1 meetings.
- In the Afternoon 1 slot, the marketing group will be gathered in Room 502.

You should check its limited capacity and conference equipment again, and send me an e-mail if you need a change or equipment.
Meetings not indicated above are all canceled under our policy and notice. All questions about this issue should be reported directly to your immediate managers. Meeting or conference contents will be posted on our intranet bulletin board for those who miss a meeting.

Kenny Rodgers
Chief of Secretary's Office

196. According to the schedule, what is true about Benjamin Corporation?

(A) Its employees meet once a month.
(B) It has a plan to expand.
(C) It has multiple buildings.
(D) It posts a yearly room schedule.

197. Why should department managers reply to the first e-mail?

(A) To meet with the management
(B) To inquire about job openings
(C) To ask about hiring additional staff
(D) To secure a meeting room

198. When will the management seminar most likely end?

(A) At 11:50 A.M.
(B) At 3:20 P.M.
(C) At 4:40 P.M.
(D) At 5:40 P.M.

199. Which group will NOT have a meeting on July 10?

(A) The sales team
(B) The marketing group
(C) Management
(D) Human resources

200. What is indicated about employees who do not attend a meeting?

(A) They should submit their absent statement to a manager.
(B) They can find meeting information on the Web site.
(C) They can attend the next session of the meeting.
(D) They should request Mr. Rodgers' meeting minutes.

Stop! This is the end of the test. If you finish before time is called, you may go back to Parts 5, 6, and 7 and check your work.

TEST

4

정답 및 해설 p.371

TEST4.mp3

MP3 바로 듣기

books.english.co.kr에서 MP3 무료 다운로드가 가능합니다.

LISTENING TEST

In the Listening test, you will be asked to demonstrate how well you understand spoken English. The entire Listening test will last approximately 45 minutes. There are four parts, and directions are given for each part. You must mark your answers on the separate answer sheet.
Do not write your answers in your test book.

PART 1

Directions: For each question in this part, you will hear four statements about a picture in your test book. When you hear the statements, you must select the one statement that best describes what you see in the picture. Then find the number of the question on your answer sheet and mark your answer. The statements will not be printed in your test book and will be spoken only one time.

Statement (B), "They're shaking hands," is the best description of the picture, so you should select answer (B) and mark it on your answer sheet.

1.

2.

GO ON TO THE NEXT PAGE

TEST 4

3.

4.

5.

6.

GO ON TO THE NEXT PAGE

PART 2

Directions: You will hear a question or statement and three responses spoken in English. They will not be printed in your test book and will be spoken only one time. Select the best response to the question or statement and mark the letter (A), (B), or (C) on your answer sheet.

7. Mark your answer on your answer sheet.

8. Mark your answer on your answer sheet.

9. Mark your answer on your answer sheet.

10. Mark your answer on your answer sheet.

11. Mark your answer on your answer sheet.

12. Mark your answer on your answer sheet.

13. Mark your answer on your answer sheet.

14. Mark your answer on your answer sheet.

15. Mark your answer on your answer sheet.

16. Mark your answer on your answer sheet.

17. Mark your answer on your answer sheet.

18. Mark your answer on your answer sheet.

19. Mark your answer on your answer sheet.

20. Mark your answer on your answer sheet.

21. Mark your answer on your answer sheet.

22. Mark your answer on your answer sheet.

23. Mark your answer on your answer sheet.

24. Mark your answer on your answer sheet.

25. Mark your answer on your answer sheet.

26. Mark your answer on your answer sheet.

27. Mark your answer on your answer sheet.

28. Mark your answer on your answer sheet.

29. Mark your answer on your answer sheet.

30. Mark your answer on your answer sheet.

31. Mark your answer on your answer sheet.

PART 3

Directions: You will hear some conversations between two or more people. You will be asked to answer three questions about what the speakers say in each conversation. Select the best response to each question and mark the letter (A), (B), (C), or (D) on your answer sheet. The conversations will not be printed in your test book and will be spoken only one time.

32. Where most likely are the speakers?

    (A) At a convention center
    (B) At a doctor's office
    (C) At a restaurant
    (D) At a movie theater

33. What did the man bring with him?

    (A) An appointment slip
    (B) A work order
    (C) A receipt
    (D) A form

34. What does the woman ask the man about?

    (A) How he heard about a business
    (B) What his appointment is for
    (C) When he first heard about Dr. Kim
    (D) What time his appointment is

35. Why is the man calling?

    (A) To reserve a flight
    (B) To express interest in a seminar
    (C) To ask about local activities
    (D) To complain about an error

36. What does the woman say will be distributed?

    (A) Brochures
    (B) Admission passes
    (C) Free meals
    (D) Prizes

37. Why does the woman apologize?

    (A) A seminar has been canceled.
    (B) Registration is now closed.
    (C) A flight has been delayed.
    (D) Some dates are not flexible.

38. Where do the speakers work?

    (A) At a zoo
    (B) At a television station
    (C) At a national park
    (D) At a book publisher

39. What does the woman hope Gordon Rabinsky will do?

    (A) Extend his show
    (B) Send staff to build the set
    (C) Take her with him on his next trip
    (D) Introduce interesting animals

40. What does the woman say she will do next week?

    (A) Read a book
    (B) Visit Mr. Rabinsky's office
    (C) Wait for an e-mail
    (D) Have lunch with Mr. Rabinsky

41. What problem are the speakers discussing?

    (A) Key employees have quit their jobs.
    (B) There was an accident at a factory.
    (C) Children no longer enjoy eating their cereal.
    (D) Product sales have decreased.

42. What does the woman suggest?

    (A) Expanding marketing efforts
    (B) Creating a new toy product
    (C) Hiring new employees
    (D) Launching a new line of cereals

43. What will take place next Wednesday?

    (A) A meeting with a cereal company
    (B) A factory safety inspection
    (C) A product demonstration
    (D) A management meeting

GO ON TO THE NEXT PAGE

44. What industry do the speakers work in?

   (A) Plumbing
   (B) Real estate
   (C) Education
   (D) Food service

45. What does the man mean when he says, "I have been having problems with my pipes for weeks"?

   (A) He does not want to work on Friday.
   (B) He is unhappy with his job.
   (C) His home is in need of repair.
   (D) He is getting engaged.

46. What does the man say about Santif?

   (A) He just recently started work.
   (B) He would like to work more hours.
   (C) He is good at his job.
   (D) He has been transferred to another department.

47. Who most likely is the man addressing?

   (A) Tour guides
   (B) Security guards
   (C) Athletic trainers
   (D) New employees

48. What does the man say about the exercise facilities?

   (A) They are only open on weekdays.
   (B) They can be used with employee identification.
   (C) They are undergoing renovations.
   (D) They are only accessible to executives.

49. What will the women probably do next?

   (A) Complete some paperwork
   (B) Guide their team members
   (C) Visit the gym
   (D) Leave the office for home

50. What are the speakers discussing?

   (A) Building a new house
   (B) Holding a retirement party
   (C) Remodeling a kitchen
   (D) Relocating new furniture

51. What will happen in about two weeks?

   (A) A home will be up for sale.
   (B) The man will receive an estimate.
   (C) There will be a party.
   (D) The man will be going on vacation.

52. What does the woman say she will send this afternoon?

   (A) A design contract
   (B) An estimate
   (C) Photos of cabinets
   (D) An interior designer

53. What is the man working on?

   (A) A budget report
   (B) New training software
   (C) Hiring guidelines
   (D) A mobile application

54. What does the man mean when he says, "I would suggest you check with someone in the technology department"?

   (A) He is on his way to the technology department now.
   (B) He does not know the answer.
   (C) He is on the phone with a customer.
   (D) He wants to transfer to another team.

55. What is the woman concerned about?

   (A) The tight deadline
   (B) Budget overruns
   (C) Customer complaints
   (D) Insufficient resources

56. What event did the man recently attend?

(A) A family wedding
(B) A restaurant opening
(C) A graduation
(D) An exhibition

57. According to the woman, what have customers been asking for?

(A) More diverse flavors
(B) More organic ingredients
(C) More wine choices
(D) Better service

58. What does the man say he will do after lunch?

(A) Make a reservation
(B) Clean out the kitchen
(C) Make some sauces
(D) Contact the customers

59. Who is the man?

(A) A gardener
(B) A customer service representative
(C) A financial consultant
(D) A technician

60. What does the man say about the Morton 2300?

(A) It measures moisture levels.
(B) It catches harmful insects.
(C) It works automatically during the night.
(D) It triggers an alarm when someone steps on the lawn.

61. Why does the woman say she will call back later?

(A) She is on her way out.
(B) She needs to discuss with her family.
(C) She doesn't think the Morton 2300 is what she is looking for.
(D) She needs to check with her bank.

Factory maintenance	$15,000
Office Rent	$9,000
Packaging	$20,000
Materials	$35,000

62. What product does the company make?

(A) Shoes
(B) Toys
(C) Cosmetics
(D) Clothes

63. What does the woman point out about the report?

(A) Expenses have increased.
(B) The report is incomplete.
(C) Some expenses are missing.
(D) Material costs decreased.

64. Look at the graphic. Which amount does the man say may change?

(A) $15,000
(B) $9,000
(C) $20,000
(D) $35,000

GO ON TO THE NEXT PAGE

Main Street	Closed from 6 A.M. to 3 P.M.
Gordon Boulevard	Closed from 7 A.M. to 1 P.M.
Seven Locks Road	Closed from 7:30 A.M. to 5 P.M.
Bethany Street	Closed from 9:30 A.M. to 3 P.M.

65. Why is the man giving the woman a ride?

(A) She does not know how to get to the office.
(B) She is having her car repaired.
(C) She has a lot of luggage.
(D) She is late for a meeting.

66. According to the man, what event is taking place today?

(A) A spring carnival
(B) A company picnic
(C) A music festival
(D) A running competition

67. Look at the graphic. Which road will the speakers take?

(A) Main Street
(B) Gordon Boulevard
(C) Seven Locks Road
(D) Bethany Street

Location	Opening Date
Cranston	January 28
Somersville	February 18
Silver City	April 4
Maytown	May 22

68. What are the speakers doing?

(A) Rescheduling a meeting
(B) Attending a staff meeting
(C) Taking a guided tour
(D) Making an appointment

69. Look at the graphic. Which date must be revised?

(A) January 28
(B) February 18
(C) April 4
(D) May 22

70. What has caused a delay in construction?

(A) The weather has been bad.
(B) City approval was not obtained.
(C) The construction workers have been sick.
(D) A budget overrun.

PART 4

Directions: You will hear some talks given by a single speaker. You will be asked to answer three questions about what the speaker says in each talk. Select the best response to each question and mark the letter (A), (B), (C), or (D) on your answer sheet. The talks will not be printed in your test book and will be spoken only one time.

71. Why is the speaker calling?
(A) To request a meeting
(B) To interview for a position
(C) To discuss the technical details of a program
(D) To reject a meeting

72. What is the speaker doing this afternoon?
(A) Going to the hospital
(B) Working on an online catalog
(C) Meeting with new employees
(D) Leaving the country on business

73. What does the speaker suggest that the listener do?
(A) Contact another colleague
(B) Attend a presentation
(C) Join him for lunch tomorrow
(D) Wait for a phone call

74. What type of business does the speaker work for?
(A) A supermarket chain
(B) A marketing agency
(C) A culinary academy
(D) A restaurant chain

75. What business plan is the speaker discussing?
(A) Beginning a delivery service
(B) Merging with a competitor
(C) Expanding distribution
(D) Hiring a new marketing manager

76. What will the listeners do on Monday?
(A) Change its business plan
(B) Conduct customer surveys
(C) Open a new store
(D) Revise a budget proposal

77. What is the workshop mainly about?
(A) Creating a software program
(B) Enhancing job interview skills
(C) Learning to speak in public
(D) Improving writing skills

78. What will the speaker give the listeners?
(A) An autograph
(B) A book
(C) A brochure
(D) A job

79. What will the listeners do next?
(A) Answer some questions
(B) Gather into groups
(C) Read a book
(D) Introduce themselves

80. Where do the listeners work?
(A) In a school
(B) In an office building
(C) In a restaurant
(D) In a real estate agency

81. According to the speaker, what is being changed?
(A) The procedure for reporting an accident
(B) The number of security guards
(C) The schedule for the renovation of lobby
(D) The limitation of access to the building

82. What will the listeners do next?
(A) Watch a demonstration
(B) Register at the reception desk
(C) Go back to work
(D) Head to lunch

GO ON TO THE NEXT PAGE

83. What does the speaker imply when he says, "Traffic is really backed up"?

(A) He is driving in reverse.
(B) He will be late to the office.
(C) He is on a train now.
(D) He will not be going to the office today.

84. What will the speaker e-mail to the listener?

(A) An agenda
(B) Meeting minutes
(C) A contract
(D) A receipt

85. What will the speaker ask Nancy to do?

(A) Order lunch
(B) Prepare a meeting agenda
(C) Take some notes
(D) Call a customer

---

86. Who most likely are the listeners?

(A) City officials
(B) Bank loan officers
(C) Newspaper journalists
(D) Conference organizers

87. What does the speaker imply when he says, "we landed Horizon Tech as a sponsor this year, which is a huge win"?

(A) They have won a competition.
(B) The listeners should be proud of themselves.
(C) The listeners do not need to be concerned.
(D) The listeners should call Horizon Tech.

88. Why should the listeners talk to the speaker after the meeting?

(A) To agree to sponsor the expo
(B) To hear the date of the next meeting
(C) To enter a competition
(D) To join a work team

---

89. What is being advertised?

(A) A dishwasher
(B) A mobile phone
(C) An automobile
(D) A computer

90. What does the speaker emphasize about the product?

(A) Cost efficiency
(B) Price
(C) Convenience
(D) Color scheme

91. Why should the listeners visit a Web site?

(A) To speak with a customer service representative
(B) To find a nearby store
(C) To get a free coupon
(D) To sign up for a test drive

---

92. What institution is the speaker reporting on?

(A) City hall
(B) University
(C) Museum
(D) Baseball stadium

93. According to the speaker, what benefit will the project provide to the public?

(A) Chances to meet the artists in person
(B) More job opportunities
(C) Discounts on admission
(D) Easier access to art

94. What does the speaker imply when she says, "considering the sheer number of art pieces at the museum"?

(A) A lot of time may be required.
(B) The project has not yet begun.
(C) Online access will cost money.
(D) More space will be needed.

Customized Mobile Phones	
Size	3 options – small, medium, large
Color	6 options – white, black, silver, gold, pink, green
Amount of memory	4 options – 64GB, 128GB, 256GB, 512GB
Shape	2 options – rectangular, circular

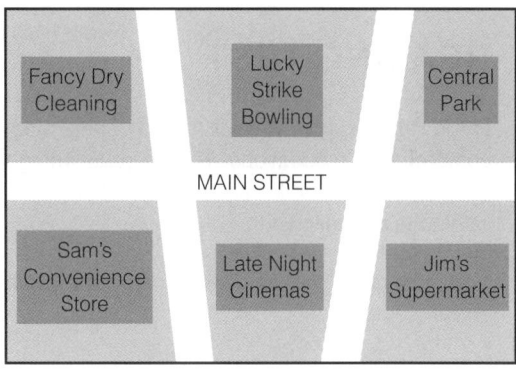

95. What is the speaker mainly discussing?

(A) A construction project
(B) An upcoming seminar
(C) Annual sales
(D) Customer feedback

96. Look at the graphic. Which option quantity will increase in August?

(A) 3 options
(B) 6 options
(C) 4 options
(D) 2 options

97. What is the speaker concerned about?

(A) The products are not selling well.
(B) There is an issue with the battery.
(C) Customers do not like the color options.
(D) Delivery of the products takes too long.

98. Who most likely is the speaker?

(A) A professor
(B) A real estate agent
(C) A store owner
(D) A food critic

99. Look at the graphic. Which location is the speaker talking about?

(A) Fancy Dry Cleaning
(B) Jim's Supermarket
(C) Lucky Strike Bowling
(D) Sam's Convenience Store

100. What plan does the speaker suggest changing?

(A) A budget
(B) A location
(C) A property size
(D) A construction schedule

This is the end of the Listening test. Turn to Part 5 in your test book.

GO ON TO THE NEXT PAGE

READING TEST

In the Reading test, you will read a variety of texts and answer several different types of reading comprehension questions. The entire Reading test will last 75 minutes. There are three parts, and directions are given for each part. You are encouraged to answer as many questions as possible within the time allowed.

You must mark your answers on the separate answer sheet. Do not write your answers in the test book.

PART 5

Directions: A word or phrase is missing in each of the sentences below. Four answer choices are given below each sentence. Select the best answer to complete the sentence. Then mark the letter (A), (B), (C), or (D) on your answer sheet.

101. It is true that two companies in New York City do not have any ------- of merging with each other.

(A) intend
(B) intention
(C) intending
(D) intended

102. ------- the contents for the next issue, Mr. Edmonds found a lot of errors in its illustrations.

(A) Editing
(B) Edited
(C) Edition
(D) Editor

103. At this meeting, his opinion on the upcoming promotional event is not so different from -------.

(A) I
(B) my
(C) me
(D) mine

104. The building is scheduled to be temporarily closed ------- six months due to its renovation.

(A) last
(B) since
(C) for
(D) during

105. Our Web site shows a wide ------- of new and used books for all age groups to provide our members with good information.

(A) selection
(B) deal
(C) conclusion
(D) enforcement

106. Mark's article about the 4th-generation trend has been ------- reviewed by most of the analysts.

(A) positive
(B) positively
(C) positiveness
(D) positivity

107. ------- a year, Tahoma Co. holds its general meeting in its headquarters for the next season.

(A) Every
(B) Yet
(C) Once
(D) Ago

108. Max Resolution Inc. ------- that it will recall the faulty items customers purchased as soon as possible.

(A) announce
(B) announced
(C) to announce
(D) announcing

109. Their new items released in May are much more ------- than the previous ones they have sold.

(A) expensive
(B) expensively
(C) expensiveness
(D) to expend

110. ------- of the workers are notified of newly revised regulations from the Department of Human Resources.

(A) Most
(B) Each
(C) Little
(D) Almost

111. Mr. Conor has been widely known ------- a creative writer in the field of science fiction.

(A) as
(B) of
(C) on
(D) like

112. The local government finally reached a ------- that new roads should be built up to cope with the heavy traffic.

(A) clue
(B) compensation
(C) consensus
(D) contradiction

113. It is reasonable that the Patent Office gives inventors ------- rights to their inventions for a fixed period of time.

(A) inclusive
(B) exclusive
(C) obvious
(D) dependent

114. We missed the opportunity to develop the property ------- we were eager to build a new center.

(A) as if
(B) even though
(C) only if
(D) even as

115. When you get a mailbox at the UPS Store, someone receives your mail, helps keep it -------, and signs for packages instead of you.

(A) careful
(B) vulnerable
(C) demanding
(D) secure

116. During the week of Black Friday, most of the outlet stores will offer customers products at a price of ------- 80% off.

(A) still
(B) even
(C) much
(D) up to

117. Their new customer service regulations ------- staff to respond to customers' needs effectively by improving the current services.

(A) encounter
(B) enable
(C) evoke
(D) explain

118. So far, Holly Motors is the only manufacturer that has announced plant ------- in the U.S. due to a sales shortage.

(A) breakdowns
(B) prohibition
(C) shutdowns
(D) construction

119. ------- the success of the marketing, our sales figures have not increased remarkably.

(A) Despite
(B) Although
(C) Nevertheless
(D) Otherwise

120. The research firm predicts the gap between Internet and newspaper advertising revenue will increase ------- next year.

(A) enthusiastically
(B) delicately
(C) drastically
(D) generously

GO ON TO THE NEXT PAGE

TEST 4

121. All students taking graduate courses are ------- to attend this upcoming scholar forum without any exception.

(A) requiring
(B) required
(C) to require
(D) require

122. If you ------- a meeting with one of our staff, you will contact our customer service center first.

(A) will schedule
(B) schedule
(C) scheduled
(D) are scheduled

123. The managers asked for ------- on how to increase the production capacity of the cell phone plant.

(A) interest
(B) suggestion
(C) importance
(D) advice

124. ------- carefully reviewing the article, Mr. John found some severe errors in its contents.

(A) When
(B) Because
(C) So that
(D) Whereas

125. We should have a plan ------- more customers such as holding various promotional events, including discounts.

(A) to attract
(B) attracting
(C) attractive
(D) attracted

126. Best Neighbors, which was founded in 1990, is an organization ------- mission is to help poor people in Africa.

(A) which
(B) whose
(C) who
(D) that

127. Kevin's article about the global warming issue ------- to as the standard format to publish articles in our journal.

(A) refers
(B) is referred
(C) has referred
(D) referring

128. Without wasting much of the resources, the ------- constructed buildings have eco-friendly offices reducing the amount of raw materials and energy.

(A) smoothly
(B) conveniently
(C) remotely
(D) efficiently

129. We should do our best to ------- all of our customers satisfied with our newly introduced services.

(A) keep
(B) demand
(C) notify
(D) hinder

130. We have a concrete business network to buy raw materials in ------- at lower prices, so we can provide good-quality but cheaper products for customers.

(A) bulk
(B) amount
(C) toll
(D) fee

PART 6

Directions: Read the texts that follow. A word, phrase, or sentence is missing in parts of each text. Four answer choices for each question are given below the text. Select the best answer to complete the text. Then mark the letter (A), (B), (C), or (D) on your answer sheet.

Questions 131-134 refer to the following notice.

Choosing Sides over Net Neutrality

The U.S. Federal Communications Commission, or FCC, approved controversial new rules for the Internet on Tuesday that supporters say will protect the interests of consumers, service providers, and investors.

Members of the FCC finally voted to approve a package of rules that would ------- bar Internet
131.
Service Providers(ISP) from selectively restricting bandwidth or consumer access to the Web.

Commission Chairman James Cooper proposed the guidelines — sometimes referred to as "net

neutrality" — to, in his words, create a strong but ------- future framework for the Internet.
132.

Under the provisions, networks such as Veracast or AC&T would not be allowed to slow or block Internet traffic from high-bandwidth or competitors' sites. The rules would allow ISPs to provide a

range of tiered services, offering ------- greater speeds and capacities at higher prices, although
133.

some members of the commission opposed the move, questioning the legal authority of the action

and the regulatory need. -------.
134.

131. (A) rarely
(B) largely
(C) nearly
(D) specially

132. (A) flexible
(B) competent
(C) individual
(D) costly

133. (A) very
(B) far
(C) too
(D) so

134. (A) In addition, their Internet service is very outstanding compared to other competitors in quality and price.
(B) For example, intranet services in many companies will be updated with their newest security software.
(C) However, the *Common Times Journal* reported that the rules would seem to discourage some services such as "high speed toll lanes".
(D) Moreover, the web-based protection system is also given to all of their prospective clients.

GO ON TO THE NEXT PAGE

Questions 135-138 refer to the following e-mail.

To: Jessica Garrison

From: John Pangunicci

Date: May 18

Subject: Please note

Dear Jessica,

-------. In an effort to keep the apartment in good condition, it is strongly advised that each apartment
135.
tenant shampoo their carpets periodically to avoid ------- damage caused by stains and dirt in
136.
ground. If excessive stains are on the carpet and no attempt is made to remove these stains within

a reasonable amount of time, it will shorten the life of the carpet and downgrade the condition of

the apartments. If ------- measures are taken throughout the lease term, serious damage and/or
137.
carpet replacement can be avoided. If you wish to have the Copper Beach Apartment set up an

appointment to have your carpets ------- and make payments on the cost, please feel free to
138.
contact our office.

Sincerely,

John Pangunicci
The Copper Beach Apartment

---

135. (A) We would like to welcome everyone who
has started living in the Copper Beach
Apartment.
   (B) Our cleaning service is widely known in
the state of Pennsylvania because of its
degree of completion.
   (C) Next month, we will hold a seminar on
how to maintain our residential areas
effectively.
   (D) During the recent home inspection, it
was noted that there are several stains
on your carpets.

136. (A) lengthy
   (B) permanent
   (C) absent
   (D) seasonal

137. (A) preventive
   (B) prevention
   (C) prevent
   (D) preventing

138. (A) shampoo
   (B) to shampoo
   (C) shampooing
   (D) shampooed

Is Ameriprise Financial right for you?

People seek financial planning and advice for many different reasons. Some are looking for help with retirement planning or specific future financial goals; ------- experience life changes or
139.
market changes that they're not sure how to plan for or adapt to. Everyone wants to make sure they make informative financial decisions throughout their lives.

You value financial advice and long-term planning!

If you're committed to ------- toward your long-term financial goals, and if you could use some
140.
guidance, we can help. -------. Can you handle your finances yourself while using a second
141.
opinion or more information? Would you rather turn over most financial matters to an advisor?

No matter what your personal financial style is, we can help you make ------- financial decisions
142.
throughout your lifetime.

139. (A) other
(B) others
(C) another
(D) the other

140. (A) work
(B) worked
(C) working
(D) works

141. (A) Through our Web site, you can download a great deal of stock information.
(B) The level of financial advice you receive depends on your needs and preferences.
(C) The recent financial crisis has been caused by its excessive investment.
(D) With our professionals, you can invest in a highly profitable business.

142. (A) sound
(B) lively
(C) trivial
(D) wealthy

GO ON TO THE NEXT PAGE

February 20

Dear Parents, Guardians, and Students

The Indiana Area School District uses an Integrated Pest Management(IPM) approach for managing insects, rodents, and weeds. Our goal is to protect every student from pesticide exposure by using an IPM approach to pest management. Our IPM approach focuses on making the school buildings and grounds an unfavorable habitat for these pests by removing food and water sources and ------- their hiding and breeding places.
143.

We accomplish this through cleaning and maintenance. We routinely ------- the school buildings
144.
and grounds to detect any pests that are present. Pest sightings are reported to our IPM coordinator, who evaluates the "pest problem" and determines the appropriate pest management techniques to ------- the problem.
145.

The techniques can include increased sanitation, modifying storage practices, sealing entry points, physically removing the pest, etc.

-------. If you have any questions, please contact John Pappal, IPM Coordinator at (724) 463-7591.
146.

Sincerely,

Kathleen R. Kelly

Superintendent of School

---

143. (A) eliminating
(B) including
(C) evaluating
(D) adding

144. (A) control
(B) monitor
(C) pursue
(D) register

145. (A) address
(B) tell
(C) speak
(D) say

146. (A) Next week, we will post the job advertisement for a sanitary inspector.
(B) The government funded the enlargement of playgrounds at state schools.
(C) Each year, the district will prepare a new notification registry.
(D) We asked you to fill out the survey form about sanitation satisfaction.

PART 7

Directions: In this part you will read a selection of texts, such as magazine and newspaper articles, e-mails, and instant messages. Each text or set of texts is followed by several questions. Select the best answer for each question and mark the letter (A), (B), (C), or (D) on your answer sheet.

Questions 147-148 refer to the following coupon.

Doria's Café

Thanks for Your Support

Show this coupon at the counter when visiting here next time. If you do so, you can get a free beverage with your other orders such as a burger, salad, or cake. Use your coupon anytime during the weekdays, Monday through Friday.

(* not valid on weekends)

We are waiting for your feedback!

If you want to know about more promotional events, you can see them on our Web site, www.doriascafe.net. Please fill out the online survey form, and you will be automatically entered for our drawing for a $50 Doria's Café Card. We would like your participation.

---

147. What kind of free item can be given to a coupon holder?

(A) Drink
(B) Burger
(C) Salad
(D) Cake

148. How can customers get a gift card?

(A) By completing a survey
(B) By presenting this coupon
(C) By attending an event
(D) By introducing other customers

GO ON TO THE NEXT PAGE

Questions 149-150 refer to the following text-message chain.

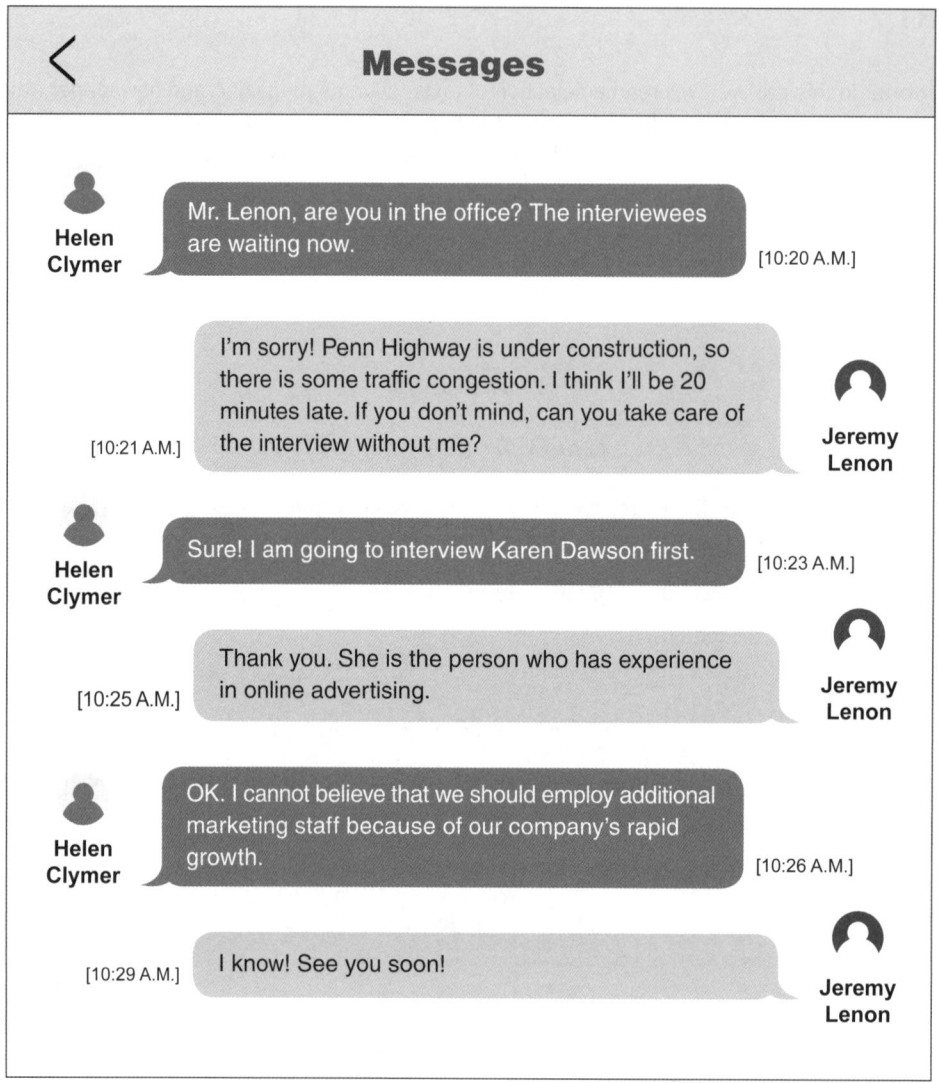

Messages

Helen Clymer: Mr. Lenon, are you in the office? The interviewees are waiting now. [10:20 A.M.]

Jeremy Lenon: [10:21 A.M.] I'm sorry! Penn Highway is under construction, so there is some traffic congestion. I think I'll be 20 minutes late. If you don't mind, can you take care of the interview without me?

Helen Clymer: Sure! I am going to interview Karen Dawson first. [10:23 A.M.]

Jeremy Lenon: [10:25 A.M.] Thank you. She is the person who has experience in online advertising.

Helen Clymer: OK. I cannot believe that we should employ additional marketing staff because of our company's rapid growth. [10:26 A.M.]

Jeremy Lenon: [10:29 A.M.] I know! See you soon!

---

149. What does Mr. Lenon want Ms. Clymer to do?

(A) Place some orders
(B) Talk with a job candidate
(C) Post job openings on the Web
(D) Ask another employee to participate

150. At 10:29 A.M., what does Mr. Lenon mean when he writes, "I know"?

(A) He is confident of his arrival in 10 minutes.
(B) He thought the company needs aggressive marketing.
(C) He has met Ms. Dawson before.
(D) He is also surprised at the company's growth.

Instructions of Pacific Union Research Lab
For a purchase request form

• Describe the items you need to purchase, including product code numbers, if available.

• If a certain brand is required, check "Designated Goods" on the form and write its reason in the box below.

• Give us the name of the vendor and contact information such as the Web site address or phone number.

• Sign the form at the bottom and submit it to the general affairs office. Without a signature, the order cannot be processed.

• Review your team's budget report for each quarter carefully.

* The expense of the purchase will be subtracted from your team budget as soon as the order has been placed.

TEST 4

151. According to the instructions, what information must be shown on all purchase request forms?

(A) A seller's contact number
(B) The signature of the purchaser
(C) The reason for the purchase
(D) A product serial number

152. What is suggested about the Department of General Affairs?

(A) They think that they need some price negotiations.
(B) They suggest the list of reliable vendors.
(C) They can deduct costs from each team's budget.
(D) They issue a security pass to employees.

GO ON TO THE NEXT PAGE

Questions 153-155 refer to the following notice.

NOTICE

Attention Visitors of Tucson Historical Museum in Arizona.

The Heritage Room is temporarily closed because we are organizing a special exhibit called "Arizona Aviation History" there from June 1 to August 20. We would like you to experience this innovative and brilliant exhibit, which will feature Air Force equipment, pictures, airplanes, and its technological sources sponsored by the U.S. Department of Defense. Especially, you can see a variety of military hardware used during World War II, including some lectures about the historical value of national defense systems, by Mr. McCluster, a former Air Force General, with his fellow soldiers, Mr. Dane and Mr. Condor, at that time. In addition, new technologies will be introduced by Ms. Rice, who is responsible for supervising the state's missile defense system and is widely regarded due to her authority in this field. If you need more detailed information about the event, please access our Web site at www.tucsonmuseum.org or pick up a special brochure at the entrance of our museum.

---

153. What is implied about the museum?

(A) It is recognized for its security system.
(B) It is promoting its upcoming exhibit.
(C) It will be closed for a renovation project.
(D) It always shows the army's historical features.

154. Who is Mr. McCluster?

(A) A veteran
(B) A journalist
(C) An art critic
(D) A museum director

155. According to the notice, who is respected by the public?

(A) Mr. Condor
(B) Mr. McCluster
(C) Ms. Rice
(D) Mr. Dane

Questions 156-157 refer to the following form.

Pennsylvania Appalachian Research Lab

Security Pass Request Form

1. Reason for Request

[ ] Issue New Pass   [✓] Lost Pass   [ ] Change Pass

2. Staff Information

Name: Arnold Linderman
Department: Geology
Position: Chief Researcher
Location: Stapleton Hall
Types of employment: [✓] Full-time   [ ] Part-time

3. If you lost your security pass, please explain how that occurred. (Date and time needed)

I lost my security pass when I participated in our general conference at the Acher Auditorium on Friday, May 10, around 4 P.M. When I left my office and arrived at the parking lot around 7 P.M., I realized my pass was missing. I returned to the auditorium, but it was locked. Although I went to work this morning and stopped by the auditorium again and searched for my pass thoroughly, I cannot find it. So, I assume that I lost it on the way to the parking lot or near the auditorium.

4. Security pass holder verification

I acknowledge that the provided information is entirely true and correct. I understand that I must pay a penalty of $100 for reissuing the replacement pass in case of it being my fault.

* The fees will be refunded in the event that the lost pass is found within a week.

Pass holder signature: *Arnold Linderman*   Date: May 11

5. For official use only

Approved by: Catherine Jones
New pass issued on: May 11

---

156. What is suggested about Mr. Linderman?

(A) He met with a colleague after work.
(B) He asked someone to open the auditorium.
(C) He left Stapleton Hall in the evening.
(D) He started his work in the lab recently.

157. What did NOT occur on May 11?

(A) Money was paid for a pass.
(B) A lost pass was found.
(C) A document was submitted.
(D) A new pass went into effect.

GO ON TO THE NEXT PAGE

Questions 158-160 refer to the following e-mail.

To: j_foster@zmobile.co.uk

From: t_svenson@wef.org.uk

Subject: Registration and Reception

Date: 20 August

Dear Ms. Foster,

This e-mail is to confirm that we have checked your registration status, including your payment and form for this year's World Economic Forum(WEF) in England. — [1] —. We sincerely welcome your regular attendance.

— [2] —. As we checked your form, we noticed that you did not include specifications about your dietary choice for the forum dinner. I should provide that information to the restaurant chief manager. By doing so, the cooking team can start preparing for the meal of our event participants. — [3] —. In addition to the meat or fish choices, the hotel restaurant is also offering an option for vegetarians. Additional information about these options is posted on our Web site at www.wef.org/uk2018. Could you reply to this e-mail as soon as possible and let me know about your meal choice?

Please be aware that this dinner fee is included in your registration payment. — [4] —. No extra fees will be charged.

Best wishes,

Tom Svenson
WEF-UK

158. Who most likely is Mr. Svenson?

(A) A restaurant director
(B) A conference official
(C) A hotel cook
(D) A Web master

159. What is Ms. Foster asked to do?

(A) Fill out a form
(B) Confirm her reservation
(C) Choose her seat
(D) Indicate her food choice

160. In which of the positions marked [1], [2], [3], and [4] does the following sentence best belong?

"I have one more detail to find out from you."

(A) [1]
(B) [2]
(C) [3]
(D) [4]

Strousberg (April 5) — Master Electronics Co. announced that it successfully purchased Superb Technology last week. That Master Electronics will start renovation of the Superb plant in Strousberg soon is very important for its local residents.

The local Superb factory was operated in order to process its massive production while giving a lot of job opportunities to local communities. However, some problems regarding their budget were caused a year ago, and the local plant started to reduce its work. Master's Deputy Kim Isabel said yesterday that the renovation project of the facility will be completed within a few months and the new hiring process will begin at that time.

"Our mission is to normalize the facility's operation and staffing completely by October," said Isabel. "The facility will possibly be operational at full capacity until December," she added.

In addition, it will manufacture Superb's most popular items under its original brand and produce Master's newly developed Solid State Drive(SSD) for personal computers there.

Master Electronics became a leading company in the U.S. electronics industry three years ago after its preceding years of effort. Its headquarters is currently situated in the city of Pittsburgh.

161. What is the purpose of the article?

(A) To announce the opening of a new business
(B) To describe a market trend in the electronics industry
(C) To explain the reason why the factory was closed
(D) To provide information about the merger and acquisition

162. According to Ms. Isabel, what will happen in October?

(A) A factory will be entirely deconstructed.
(B) A company will employ more staff.
(C) A new item will be released.
(D) A negotiation will be completed.

163. What is indicated about Master Electronics Co.?

(A) It will produce computer-related storage device.
(B) It will move into Pittsburgh.
(C) It has more branches in Strousberg.
(D) It was acquired by a larger corporation.

GO ON TO THE NEXT PAGE

Questions 164-167 refer to the following Web page.

 https://www.appletonartcenter.net

Appleton Art Center

Spring at the Appleton Art Center in Florida

Welcome to everyone visiting the Appleton Art Center. Check our extended spring operation hours and experience a variety of talks and learn special things you have never heard anywhere before.

Art Center Hours

Tuesday through Saturday, 9:00 A.M. – 6:00 P.M.

Sunday, 12:00 P.M. – 7:30 P.M.

Closed on Monday

Spring Exhibitions

• Bruno James: 19th Century – American Landscapes

• Louis Tiffany: Impressions on Film, Canvas, and Paper

• Hugh McKean: The Art Machine

Center Talks

March 28 at 7:00 P.M.

Beth Hansen, curator at the Slippery Rock Museum in North Carolina, will visit us to discuss the biography and career of renowned photographer Bruno James, whose pictures are on display here throughout this spring.

April 10 at 3:00 P.M.

Appleton's curator, Lily Savova, will join Louis Tiffany, a famous artist in our state, through a casual discussion of her experiences and techniques. Ms. Savova will then introduce our center by giving a tour of our center rooms.

May 17 at 3:00 P.M.

Ken Hyland, associate professor of Northern Florida College, will talk about additional information regarding the Appleton Art Center's variety of art machines, which can show history of art technique development in our main gallery.

164. What is indicated about the Appleton Art Center?

(A) It is operated by the state government.
(B) It exhibits local artists' works only.
(C) It has a lot of renowned painters.
(D) It is open later on Sundays.

165. What is NOT mentioned as a theme of the Appleton Center's exhibits?

(A) Stage designs for a play
(B) American paintings in the 19th century
(C) Feelings about movie and picture
(D) Equipment and skills for art

166. Who is Ms. Tiffany?

(A) A tour guide
(B) A center curator
(C) A college instructor
(D) A local artist

167. What will the discussion in May mainly be about?

(A) History of art skills
(B) Artists' creativeness
(C) Life of local artists
(D) Changes in American views

GO ON TO THE NEXT PAGE

Questions 168-171 refer to the following e-mail.

To	: Bandar Saleh; Massiata Bamba; Qiaqui Chen; Sandra Baaziz
From	: Indah Carrera
Date	: March 20
Subject	: Assigned tasks
Attachments	: position_list.doc; compensation_benefits_info.doc; contact_info.doc

Dear all,

I sincerely appreciate your support by volunteering for this project related to Giant Logistics, our subsidiary, which will open its branch in New Delhi on Thursday, June 10. —[1]—.
As I explained at the last meeting, 50 new positions will have to be filled at the new branch. —[2]—. You are in charge of the following tasks, which must be finished by the announced deadlines. —[3]—.

Bandar Saleh: Make out a final draft about the list of qualifications and responsibilities for each position by April 20. (See attached the list of positions)

Massiata Bamba: Create a spreadsheet of the wages and benefits package to be provided. (Using attached file)

Qiaqui Chen: Notify all in-state recruitment agencies about job positions available. (Using attached contact information)

Bandar Saleh: Post some notices and announcements on our company Web site. (E-mail a manuscript to Mr. Haziz in the Information Division)

Sandra Baaziz: Come up with an advertisement and its media for announcing the office opening and job vacancies. (Submit your proposals to Samuel Jones by April 15)

— [4] —. We will meet together to review and discuss your own progress on these assignments on April 10. If you have any questions, or whenever you face some problems, do not hesitate to contact me.

Indah Carrera
Human Resources Manager

168. When are the position descriptions due?

(A) April 10
(B) April 15
(C) April 20
(D) June 10

169. Who does NOT need to use one of the attached files?

(A) Bandar Saleh
(B) Massiata Bamba
(C) Qiaqui Chen
(D) Sandra Baaziz

170. What does Ms. Carrera ask the recipients to do before the next meeting?

(A) Ask her about issues at any times
(B) Visit the headquarters in person
(C) Work closely with one another
(D) Register for the voluntary work

171. In which of the positions marked [1], [2], [3], and [4] does the following sentence best belong?

"From now on, we have a lot of things to do before that date."

(A) [1]
(B) [2]
(C) [3]
(D) [4]

GO ON TO THE NEXT PAGE

Questions 172-175 refer to the following online chat discussion.

New Chat

Alan Schnitzer [11:15 A.M.]

Good morning, everyone. I'd like us to think about our next team meeting on Friday. Sales figures are not good for now. We should consider moving in a new direction.

Lloyd Alyssa [11:16 A.M.]

What should we prepare for that?

Alan Schnitzer [11:17 A.M.]

Because the demand for functional cosmetics is sharply decreasing, we need to research the current market trend, I think.

Nick Denton [11:18 A.M.]

If so, we should first divide customers into some categories such as age, gender, work environment, etc.

Dalton Rebecca [11:20 A.M.]

I think this is very important for us to develop and release new products. By the way, we should know the reason why customers turned their backs on the current items first.

Lloyd Alyssa [11:21 A.M.]

I totally agree. The cause analysis has to be completed before market research for new product development.

Alan Schnitzer [11:22 A.M.]

Good ideas, all. At the meeting, I'd like to listen to your own ideas. Each person should start preparing a presentation by taking advantage of the current data and potential information I sent to your e-mail addresses. In addition, I will need the information about the analysis data for the reduced demand.

Dalton Rebecca [11:23 A.M.]

OK. I will handle that.

Alan Schnitzer [11:24 A.M.]

Let me know if you have any questions. I'll send another attached file for our meeting guidelines by e-mail.

Send

172. At 11:15 A.M., what does Mr. Schnitzer mean when he writes, "We should consider moving in a new direction"?

(A) The company needs to move their office into another place.
(B) The company is scheduled to hold the general meeting in the headquarters.
(C) The company has to focus on changing its current business into other fields.
(D) The company should establish a strategy to increase its sales.

173. What type of business do they work for?

(A) A data analysis agency
(B) A cosmetics company
(C) A research laboratory
(D) A moving company

174. What will Ms. Rebecca most likely do next?

(A) She will distribute printouts.
(B) She will do data analysis.
(C) She will send an e-mail to the CEO.
(D) She will prepare for a proposal.

175. What will Mr. Schnitzer give to the team members?

(A) Instructions for the upcoming meeting
(B) A list of recent purchases and orders
(C) A detailed plan for improving products
(D) Suggestions for employing new staff

GO ON TO THE NEXT PAGE

To: David Robinson <d.robinson@zetamail.com>

From: AUTOINSU <autoservice@autoinsu.com>

Date: April 26, 2024

Subject: Confirmation

This e-mail refers to the following confirmation number(s): 1GHAK-3QPZ-3K4LC

AUTOINSU Casualty Insurance Company

Dear Mr. Robinson,

Thank you for using AUTOINSU's online services.

We processed the policy changes you requested. There will be no change in your premium. Your updated policy information will be available online within 24 hours. You can view changes by logging into the AUTOINSU Policyholder Service Center at www.autoinsu.com/mypolicy.

If you enroll in our Paperless Policy service, you will receive an e-mail when your updated policy documents are available online.

If you need assistance, please reply to this e-mail. We are available 24 hours a day, 7 days a week. To ensure a proper response, please do not change the confirmation number from the subject field or the reply-to address when replying to this e-mail.

It is our goal to provide you with an excellent service. We appreciate your business and loyalty, and look forward to offering our services that meet your needs for many years to come.

Sincerely,

Jon Wallers

_____

AUTOINSU Customer Service

1-800-813-3340

_____

[NOTE]

In order to protect your privacy, please do not include personal information such as your driver's license number, social security number, date of birth, or address details in your e-mail. If you need to provide us with this information, please log into our Web site, and click on Contact Us under My Resource Center tab. If you want, you can also phone us at 1-800-861-8380 for auto policies or 1-800-442-9253 for motorcycle ones.

To: AUTOINSU <autoservice@autoinsu.com>

From: David Robinson <d.robinson@zetamail.com>

Date: April 26, 2024

Subject: RE: Confirmation

To whom it may concern,

I am writing to request something on my online information you sent me. Most of the policies and contents have been correctly updated, but the address information is wrong. As I requested before through the live-chat service with your staff, I have recently moved into another place near the previous one. I would like you to change to my new address, 1038 Courtland Road, Indiana, PA. Please notify me about its change as soon as possible because I should submit the confirmation letter as a certificate of residence for being reissued my identification.

Regards,

David Robinson

176. What is the purpose of the first e-mail?

(A) To provide service promotion codes
(B) To advertise company's new services
(C) To confirm customer policy updates
(D) To explain how to access online service

177. What is NOT mentioned about AUTOINSU's online service?

(A) Clients can get support from the staff.
(B) Clients' status can be checked online.
(C) Clients can change their information.
(D) Clients can get a discount.

178. Why did Mr. Robinson send the second e-mail?

(A) To require change of his address
(B) To get a promotional code
(C) To apply for his new identification
(D) To set up an online chat program

179. What is indicated about Mr. Robinson?

(A) He wants to upgrade his service.
(B) He has transferred to another office.
(C) He has talked with the staff before online.
(D) He forgot his confirmation number.

180. In the second e-mail, which information can be problematic?

(A) Residential address
(B) Confirmation number
(C) E-mail address
(D) Policy information

GO ON TO THE NEXT PAGE

The Grand Cascade Hotel & Conference Center

Make a reservation!

Spacious and various meeting rooms at the Grand Cascade Hotel & Conference Center are available.

Choose from our four types of special rooms.

Room	Seating	Feature & Equipment	Cost
Tahoma Room	20 rolling chairs for executives	large conference table	£200
Edu Room	15 computer workstations	free Internet access and common software set up for demonstration	£230
Tech Room	30 computer workstations	black board, projector, free Internet access and common software set up for demonstration	£250
Innobiz Room	auditorium seating for 100-150	podium, microphone, projector, screen, computer	£300

Each room at the Grand Cascade Hotel & Conference Center is equipped with whiteboards, marker pens, paper and pens.

** Prices are for up to 5 hours of use (morning / afternoon) and rooms must be booked and paid for at least a week before.

** For £50 per session, our IT support staff will be in one of our three computer-equipped rooms. A representative for a meeting can receive detailed instructions about the use of software and equipment in advance. If you want to have technical help from one of our experts, he or she may stay during your session. The experts have more than 10 years of experience in the computer-related industry.

Please call 871-222-0047 to make a reservation for this service.

To: maxdavis@manchesteruniv.co.uk

From: lindawood@grandcascade.co.uk

Date: 10 September

Subject: Meeting Room

Dear Mr. Davis,

I am writing this e-mail to confirm your reservation number 1284 for £230. When you booked this reservation, I was not aware that a carpet cleaning service was scheduled for 18 September in the Edu Room. From what I remember, you can only hold your meeting on this date. So, I would like to offer you the Tech Room instead without any change in fee. In addition, if you need assistance from our experts, we can provide one person for £25, half of the original price. Our expert, Mr. Costa, would be pleased to help your group.

Please feel free to contact me at 871-222-1017 to discuss the procedures further.

Sincerely,

Linda Wood
Hotel Manager

181. In the advertisement, what is indicated about the meeting rooms?

(A) They should be inspected a week ahead of time.
(B) They will be furnished with writing stationery.
(C) They will all be closed for renovation.
(D) They can be reserved through the Web site.

182. What room would be most appropriate for a lecture with 80 people?

(A) Tahoma Room
(B) Edu Room
(C) Tech Room
(D) Innobiz Room

183. What is the purpose of the e-mail?

(A) To suggest an alternative for a reservation
(B) To remind a recipient of payment in full
(C) To inquire about whether an expert is needed
(D) To ask the number of attendants

184. According to the e-mail, how much will Mr. Davis be charged for using the Tech Room?

(A) £200
(B) £230
(C) £250
(D) £300

185. What is implied about Mr. Costa?

(A) He has helped with all kinds of tasks for an event.
(B) He is very experienced in dealing with computers.
(C) He wants to contact Mr. Davis to discuss a topic.
(D) He cannot be available during the session.

GO ON TO THE NEXT PAGE

Questions 186-190 refer to the following e-mail, flyer, and text message.

From: Robin Miller

To: Prospective Graduates

Date: May 25

Subject: Speeches

Dear Students,

I am really pleased to announce that Mr. Atsushi has decided to participate in our Speech Series this summer. As part of your internship program, you need to check his speech schedules on campus for June 10—30, and have all required paperwork completed and approved in order to receive your program certificate. You will also need to reserve a room for your final presentation. I advise you to book Leonard Hall because it can accommodate the most people and is well equipped with audio-visual tools, but any other rooms would be fine in that building as well.

Moreover, as soon as Mr. Atsushi provides his tentative speech schedule, you will take part in activities which include creating a flyer and posting it in all the buildings throughout the campus. I believe that you will be able to finish the tasks among the five of you without any issues.

Thanks,

Dr. Miller
Dean of College of Human Science

College of Human Science

Speech Series Announcement

Mr. Ilda Atsushi
Vice President, Osaka Progressive Asset, Japan

Developing M&A Techniques and Tips
June 15, 3:00 P.M.
Charlton Room

The term "M&A" is the abbreviation of mergers and acquisitions. A merger is the combining of two businesses, while an acquisition is the purchase of the ownership of one business by another. With the advent of new informational technology, workforce-based industries have become less competitive, so the small- and mid-sized companies have had difficulty operating their companies. One of the possible solutions to this matter is the M&A strategy. However, it may also have a side effect if processed without well-organized agreement. So, Mr. Atsushi will pass on his own know-how in this field and time-tested winning strategies with his real cases in Japan, and then discuss how we can apply these skills to our economic situation.

To: Isyah Colen

From: Donald Humphrey

Received: June 2, 5:00 P.M.

Ms. Colen, I'm in the computer lab, printing the flyer you sent to me, and I've noticed an error. Mr. Atsushi's profile information was deleted from the flyer! Can you correct this and resend it to me promptly? This lab is closing in 20 minutes, and we couldn't post the flyer this evening, which Dr. Miller emphasized.

186. What is suggested about the Charlton Room?

(A) It is located outside the Human Science building.
(B) It is smaller than Leonard Hall.
(C) It is the only room for this speech series.
(D) It will be renovated during the summer.

187. In the e-mail, the word "Issues" in paragraph 2, line 3, is closest in meaning to

(A) topics
(B) volumes
(C) conflicts
(D) publications

188. What is Mr. Atsushi's presentation about?

(A) The importance of internship programs
(B) Tips for recommendation letters
(C) Company takeover tips
(D) An MBA course description

189. What problem does Mr. Humphrey mention?

(A) Missing information in the flyer
(B) A misspelled name and its location
(C) Failure to meet the deadline
(D) Room reservation errors

190. Who most likely is Ms. Colen?

(A) A presenter for the Speech Series
(B) An assistant teacher to Mr. Atsushi
(C) A student at the College of Human Science
(D) An employee of the on-campus computer lab

GO ON TO THE NEXT PAGE

To	: r.steve@tubecare.net
From	: j.mckenzie@styleathome.com
Date	: April 10
Subject	: Re: Advertising in Style at Home
Attachments	: PRICELIST_styleathome.doc

Dear Mr. Steve,

Thank you for your interest in *Style at Home*. I strongly believe that proceeding with the advertisement into our magazine is the best way to promote your products and services because our magazines are delivered to a lot of households in Sydney twice a month. Referring to the attached price list file in this e-mail, you can find our reasonable and standard advertising fees. Additionally, we notify all advertisers of the following:

• *Style at Home* is published in greyscale. In order to ensure readability, pictures and illustrations should be kept simple.

• We will not change any images you send. Hence, you should send the correct images to us before the deadline.

• You should pay for the fees in full before an advertisement is published.

If you have any questions, please do not hesitate to contact me. We really look forward to featuring your quality products and services in our magazine.

Sincerely,

John McKenzie
Advertising Director

Style at Home
Advertising Price List

SIZE	ONE ISSUE	SIX ISSUES (three months)	TWELVE ISSUES (six months)
Quarter page	$500	$2,600	$5,400
Half page	$1,000	$5,500	$10,500
Full page	$2,000	$11,000	$21,000

** Note: These prices include taxes (if changed, we notify you in advance).
Depending on your additional requests, extra fees may be charged.

To : j.mckenzie@styleathome.com

From : r.steve@tubecare.net

Date : April 15

Subject : Re: Re: Advertising in Style at Home

Attachments : tubecare_image.png

Dear Mr. McKenzie,

Thank you for your detailed explanation. I would like to go forward with the advertisement with your company for the next six issues. Initially, I want to post our advertisement with a half page size, and then we will consider whether to enlarge the size or extend the term of this advertising in the future. And please let me know how to make the payment.

Best wishes,

Randall Steve
Public Relation Department, Tubecare Co.

191. What is the purpose of the first e-mail?

(A) To provide details to a prospective client
(B) To advertise their magazine to citizens
(C) To explain the cost of decoration sets
(D) To attract more subscribers to its publication

192. What does Mr. Mckenzie ask the client to do?

(A) Send a lot of information to the team
(B) Adjust the picture size and text length
(C) Review images before submitting an advertisement
(D) Correct errors on the advertisement

193. In the second e-mail, what is suggested about Mr. Steve?

(A) He is expected to open a new business.
(B) He has recently moved into the Sydney area.
(C) He may change the size and period of advertising later.
(D) He will join the magazine's regular membership.

194. How much will Mr. Steve likely be charged?

(A) $1,000
(B) $2,600
(C) $5,500
(D) $10,500

195. In the second e-mail, the word "term" in paragraph 1, line 3, is closest in meaning to

(A) agreement
(B) expression
(C) condition
(D) duration

GO ON TO THE NEXT PAGE

Gourmet Catering

3317 Hamilton Boulevard, Allentown
PA 18104
610-770-8888

Dear Ms. Monica,

Thank you for your order for our catering service. We make every effort to satisfy all our customers with our food and beverages. To provide healthy and organic dishes for you, we always bring all of the ingredients for the service from the original places of production. Please review the invoice enclosed with this letter carefully and contact us at 610-770-8888 or send an e-mail to cs3317@gourmetcatering.com if you have any problems with the order. Please be aware that you should include your order number for reference.

* Plates, cups, napkins, and utensils are included with every order.

John Milton
Reservation Department

Invoice

Customer Name: Anne Monica at Lehigh Valley Realty
Address: 1146 S Cedar Crest Drive 302, Allentown, PA
Delivery on: November 10 at 1:30 P.M.
Order Number: NOV391501

Item	Size	Quantity	Price	Total
Grilled Beef with Greek Salad	large	1	$50.00	$50.00
Freshly Made Lettuce Wraps with Chili Sauce	dozen	4	$15.00	$60.00
Coffee and Tea	per person	20	$3.00	$60.00

Delivery and Setup : $12.00
Total Price : $182.00
Paid : -$182.00
Balance : $0

Please note that if you want to change your order after November 6,
you should pay $30 for the late change under our order policy.

To	: cs3317@gourmetcatering.com
From	: a_monica@lehighvalleyrt.net
Date	: November 7
Subject	: Order #NOV391501

I'm writing about my order #NOV391501 for delivery to Cedar Crest Drive 302 on November 10. I have shown the menu to our staff, and unfortunately I just found out that one employee is a vegetarian. Would it be possible to have the Vegetable Stir-Fry as a replacement? I saw the dish listed for the same price and want to substitute the current one with the other. I'd appreciate it if you sent me an updated invoice.

Sincerely,

Anne Monica

196. Why was the letter sent?

(A) To announce a policy revision
(B) To request late-change fees
(C) To update a current receipt
(D) To confirm a recent order

197. What does Gourmet Catering ask the client to do when having questions?

(A) Contact the business only during operation hours
(B) Include a copy of her receipt
(C) Visit their store in person
(D) Mention her order number

198. What is suggested about Ms. Monica?

(A) She is arranging lunch for her employees.
(B) She is trying to reduce redundant costs.
(C) She frequently uses Gourmet Catering's services.
(D) She is planning to open a new branch.

199. What does Ms. Monica likely need to send to Gourmet Catering?

(A) An extra payment
(B) A signed order form
(C) An updated menu
(D) A list of her staff

200. What dish does Ms. Monica no longer want?

(A) Grilled Beef
(B) Fresh Wraps
(C) Coffee
(D) Vegetable Stir-Fry

Stop! This is the end of the test. If you finish before time is called, you may go back to Parts 5, 6, and 7 and check your work.

영국의 통의 실전 1000제 LC+RC

TEST

5

정답 및 해설 p.411

TEST5.mp3

MP3 바로 듣기

books.english.co.kr에서 MP3 무료 다운로드가 가능합니다.

LISTENING TEST

In the Listening test, you will be asked to demonstrate how well you understand spoken English. The entire Listening test will last approximately 45 minutes. There are four parts, and directions are given for each part. You must mark your answers on the separate answer sheet.
Do not write your answers in your test book.

PART 1

Directions: For each question in this part, you will hear four statements about a picture in your test book. When you hear the statements, you must select the one statement that best describes what you see in the picture. Then find the number of the question on your answer sheet and mark your answer. The statements will not be printed in your test book and will be spoken only one time.

Statement (B), "They're shaking hands," is the best description of the picture, so you should select answer (B) and mark it on your answer sheet.

1.

2.

GO ON TO THE NEXT PAGE

TEST 5

3.

4.

5.

6.

GO ON TO THE NEXT PAGE

PART 2

Directions: You will hear a question or statement and three responses spoken in English. They will not be printed in your test book and will be spoken only one time. Select the best response to the question or statement and mark the letter (A), (B), or (C) on your answer sheet.

7. Mark your answer on your answer sheet.

8. Mark your answer on your answer sheet.

9. Mark your answer on your answer sheet.

10. Mark your answer on your answer sheet.

11. Mark your answer on your answer sheet.

12. Mark your answer on your answer sheet.

13. Mark your answer on your answer sheet.

14. Mark your answer on your answer sheet.

15. Mark your answer on your answer sheet.

16. Mark your answer on your answer sheet.

17. Mark your answer on your answer sheet.

18. Mark your answer on your answer sheet.

19. Mark your answer on your answer sheet.

20. Mark your answer on your answer sheet.

21. Mark your answer on your answer sheet.

22. Mark your answer on your answer sheet.

23. Mark your answer on your answer sheet.

24. Mark your answer on your answer sheet.

25. Mark your answer on your answer sheet.

26. Mark your answer on your answer sheet.

27. Mark your answer on your answer sheet.

28. Mark your answer on your answer sheet.

29. Mark your answer on your answer sheet.

30. Mark your answer on your answer sheet.

31. Mark your answer on your answer sheet.

PART 3

Directions: You will hear some conversations between two or more people. You will be asked to answer three questions about what the speakers say in each conversation. Select the best response to each question and mark the letter (A), (B), (C), or (D) on your answer sheet. The conversations will not be printed in your test book and will be spoken only one time.

32. Where most likely are the speakers?
    (A) In an office
    (B) In a library
    (C) In a store
    (D) In a concert hall

33. What is the woman looking for?
    (A) CDs
    (B) Books
    (C) Concert tickets
    (D) A computer

34. What does the man offer to do for the woman?
    (A) Ship some products to her home
    (B) Reserve an item at a different store
    (C) Call a manufacturer
    (D) Give her a discount

35. Why does the woman thank the man?
    (A) He agreed to work overtime.
    (B) He designed a Web site for her.
    (C) He organized a fundraiser.
    (D) He made a donation.

36. Why is the woman calling?
    (A) To discuss a topic
    (B) To arrange an interview
    (C) To offer a job
    (D) To finalize a budget

37. What does the woman ask the man to provide?
    (A) A photo
    (B) A contact number
    (C) A reference letter
    (D) A schedule of events

38. Why is the woman making a phone call?
    (A) To order some extra supplies
    (B) To inquire about an order
    (C) To find out a contact number
    (D) To get a refund on defective items

39. Whom does the woman want to speak to?
    (A) A client
    (B) A sales representative
    (C) A secretary
    (D) A personnel manager

40. What will the woman most likely do?
    (A) Leave a message
    (B) Visit the store
    (C) Call another number
    (D) Give the man a phone number

41. What is being discussed?
    (A) A piece of luggage
    (B) A travel itinerary
    (C) A dinner reservation
    (D) A laptop computer

42. Why does the woman like the product?
    (A) It is small.
    (B) It is lightweight.
    (C) It is imported from another country.
    (D) It comes in different colors.

43. What was Ben asked to do?
    (A) Make a purchase
    (B) Stop by the shop
    (C) Forward a message
    (D) Lend an item

GO ON TO THE NEXT PAGE

44. What does the man request?

(A) Extra copies of the report
(B) A ride to the office
(C) Revisions to an agenda
(D) A client's contact information

45. What does the woman imply when she says, "I'm already at the office"?

(A) She is worried about a car accident.
(B) She cannot help the man.
(C) She will call other clients for the man.
(D) She is confused about a meeting time.

46. What does the woman recommend the man do?

(A) Postpone a meeting
(B) Set up a conference call
(C) Contact another colleague
(D) Work from a different location

---

47. What does the woman say she has done?

(A) Restocked some supplies
(B) Mailed some invoices
(C) Changed an appointment
(D) Interviewed new doctors

48. What does the man want to do?

(A) Close an office early
(B) Attend a medical conference
(C) Offer additional services
(D) Clean the office himself

49. What does the woman suggest will happen tonight?

(A) New scheduling software will be installed.
(B) A facility will be cleaned.
(C) A contract will be signed.
(D) Building renovations will start.

---

50. What problem does the man mention?

(A) Some documents are not ready yet.
(B) A signature is missing on the form.
(C) Some areas cannot be accessed.
(D) Files cannot be saved properly.

51. What will the woman ask Mr. Garcia to do?

(A) Schedule a follow-up interview
(B) Install some software
(C) Arrange a company tour
(D) Contact a personnel manager

52. What does the woman suggest the man do?

(A) Submit a recent photograph
(B) Restart the computer
(C) Attend a special gathering
(D) Make a dinner reservation

---

53. Where does the woman work?

(A) At a pharmacy
(B) At a museum
(C) At a travel agency
(D) At a movie theater

54. What is the purpose of the program?

(A) To sell some artworks
(B) To teach entrepreneurship skills
(C) To solicit funds for local artists
(D) To promote networking

55. According to the woman, what should the man do?

(A) Sign up for an event
(B) Take the promotional materials
(C) Join an association
(D) Bring some business cards

---

56. What are the speakers discussing?

(A) An advertising campaign
(B) A construction vehicle
(C) A renovation job
(D) Moving expenses

57. What does the woman say about the carpet?

(A) It looks outdated.
(B) It is too expensive.
(C) It is stored in the basement.
(D) It will be delivered tomorrow.

58. What does the woman imply when she says, "This is a really big room"?

(A) Some furniture should be removed.
(B) More people should be invited.
(C) A presentation should be rescheduled.
(D) A task will take longer to complete.

---

59. Why is the man surprised?

(A) An office space is large.
(B) A service is expensive.
(C) A business has been relocated.
(D) There are many people in the room.

60. Why does the man meet with the woman?

(A) He is interested in selling his business.
(B) He wants to hire a financial advisor.
(C) He needs to find a new office space.
(D) He is applying for a position at the woman's company.

61. What does the woman say about her clients?

(A) She meets with them regularly.
(B) Many of them have small businesses.
(C) Many of them acquired regular customers.
(D) Some of them need to open up new locations.

Shipping Rates		
National Zone	United States	$3.00
European Zone	Europe	$5.00
International Zone 1	Africa	$7.00
International Zone 2	Asia	$10.00

62. Who most likely is the woman?

(A) A postal worker
(B) A clothing designer
(C) A customer service representative
(D) An international banker

63. Look at the graphic. What shipping rate will the man pay?

(A) $3.00
(B) $5.00
(C) $7.00
(D) $10.00

64. What will the man most likely do next?

(A) Choose a design
(B) Provide information
(C) Order a catalog
(D) Write a customer review

GO ON TO THE NEXT PAGE

Rose Paradise Hotel
Let's enjoy tea time!

Tea, Sandwiches — Daily Baked goods

Classic Tea	$18
Premium Tea	$25
Family Tea	$30
Royal Tea	$50

65. How did the woman learn about the tea-time package?

(A) From a newspaper
(B) From a colleague
(C) From a Web site
(D) From a travel agency

66. Look at the graphic. Which tea-time package is selected?

(A) Classic Tea
(B) Premium Tea
(C) Family Tea
(D) Royal Tea

67. Why does the woman reserve the tea package?

(A) To have a meeting with her colleagues
(B) To celebrate her mother's retirement
(C) To congratulate a coworker on his promotion
(D) To entertain some clients

Factory Floor Safety Rules

1. Wear hardhats
2. Wear safety gloves and footwear
3. No mobile phones
4. No eating

68. What does the man thank the woman for?

(A) Working overtime
(B) Ordering extra supplies
(C) Updating some paperwork
(D) Helping new employees

69. What happened to the woman this morning?

(A) She forgot to bring some papers.
(B) She woke up late.
(C) She met with a customer.
(D) She left her lunch at home.

70. Look at the graphic. Which safety rule are the speakers discussing?

(A) Rule 1
(B) Rule 2
(C) Rule 3
(D) Rule 4

PART 4

Directions: You will hear some talks given by a single speaker. You will be asked to answer three questions about what the speaker says in each talk. Select the best response to each question and mark the letter (A), (B), (C), or (D) on your answer sheet. The talks will not be printed in your test book and will be spoken only one time.

71. What is the purpose of the message?

(A) To promote a new business
(B) To sell some household items
(C) To confirm a work plan
(D) To cancel an appointment

72. What type of business does the speaker work for?

(A) A flooring supplier
(B) A cleaning company
(C) A delivery service
(D) A home repair company

73. What does the listener have to do to change the appointment?

(A) Visit the store
(B) Go to the Web site
(C) Call the president of the company
(D) Leave a telephone message

74. What is the broadcast mainly about?

(A) A local author
(B) Traffic conditions
(C) Upcoming events
(D) Job opportunities

75. What are the listeners asked to do by Wednesday afternoon?

(A) Participate in a race
(B) Complete an application
(C) Make a donation
(D) Join an organization

76. What will the listeners hear next?

(A) A traffic report
(B) An advertisement
(C) A weather forecast
(D) An interview

77. What is the speaker's team working on?

(A) An accounting budget
(B) A computer program
(C) A travel itinerary
(D) A management workshop

78. According to the speaker, why was the listener recommended?

(A) He can conduct training sessions.
(B) He can offer a discount for the new product.
(C) He has business connections in the industry.
(D) He has experience with similar problems.

79. Why does the speaker say, "a lot of people on my team are on vacation"?

(A) To propose a schedule change
(B) To decline an offer
(C) To accept the revision requested
(D) To explain why the help is needed

80. What is the purpose of the talk?

(A) To explain the new equipment
(B) To announce some maintenance work
(C) To raise funds for the renovation of cafeteria
(D) To encourage saving electricity

81. When will the work most likely be done?

(A) On Monday
(B) On Wednesday
(C) On Thursday
(D) On Friday

82. What are the listeners asked to do?

(A) Report to the security officer
(B) Take a day off on Friday
(C) Call the electrician if there is a problem
(D) Leave the cafeteria sooner than usual

GO ON TO THE NEXT PAGE

83. What is the announcement about?

(A) A location of a restaurant
(B) A conference schedule
(C) An updated building plan
(D) A new meeting place

84. What is postponed?

(A) A registration deadline
(B) A departure time
(C) A business lunch
(D) A motivational speech

85. What will the listeners do in the afternoon?

(A) Listen to the presentation
(B) Register for the program
(C) Go to the cafeteria
(D) Speak with the keynote speaker

---

86. Who most likely are the listeners?

(A) Software programmers
(B) Government workers
(C) Factory employees
(D) Business owners

87. What does the speaker imply when he says, "Did you know that this program received only five applications last year"?

(A) The program is very competitive.
(B) The program needs to be canceled.
(C) The program is not very well-known.
(D) The program does not have a large budget.

88. What will the listeners do next?

(A) Ask some questions
(B) Discuss business strategies
(C) Review additional materials
(D) Watch a film

---

89. What department does the speaker work in?

(A) Human resources
(B) International sales
(C) Public relations
(D) Shipping

90. Who is the speaker talking to?

(A) Investors
(B) Journalists
(C) New employees
(D) Magazine subscribers

91. Why are the listeners asked to visit the speaker's office?

(A) To apply for an open position
(B) To sign the employment contract
(C) To receive employee identification
(D) To meet with the staff from other divisions

---

92. What is being mainly discussed?

(A) Reducing shipping costs
(B) Expanding services
(C) Opening a new branch
(D) Hiring new staff

93. Why has the company made a change?

(A) Competition has grown.
(B) Customer complaints have increased.
(C) Its products have become popular.
(D) The gas price has soared.

94. What will happen next week?

(A) The company will cover more areas.
(B) The company will renovate the office.
(C) The company will convene a follow-up meeting.
(D) The company will launch a new product.

Safety Inspection	
Company Name : Red Monkey Company	**Comments :** Inspection failed - Machinery
Checklist : ☑ Equipment ☑ Floors ☑ Lights ☑ Emergency exits	**Inspector :** Adam Waltz

Section 1	Cakes
Section 2	Pies
Section 3	Cookies
Section 4	Muffins

95. Where does the speaker work?

(A) At a manufacturing company
(B) At a moving company
(C) At a design company
(D) At a shipping company

96. Look at the graphic. Which section of the report does the speaker ask about?

(A) Company name
(B) Checklist
(C) Comments
(D) Inspector

97. What is the speaker concerned about?

(A) Ordering new equipment
(B) Completing an order
(C) Keeping track of inventory
(D) Paying a penalty

98. What is the store celebrating?

(A) A national holiday
(B) A grand opening
(C) A newly released product
(D) An upcoming merger

99. When will the event end?

(A) Next month
(B) Next week
(C) In two days
(D) Tonight

100. Look at the graphic. Which section contains items with an additional discount?

(A) Section 1
(B) Section 2
(C) Section 3
(D) Section 4

This is the end of the Listening test. Turn to Part 5 in your test book.

TEST 5

GO ON TO THE NEXT PAGE

READING TEST

In the Reading test, you will read a variety of texts and answer several different types of reading comprehension questions. The entire Reading test will last 75 minutes. There are three parts, and directions are given for each part. You are encouraged to answer as many questions as possible within the time allowed.

You must mark your answers on the separate answer sheet. Do not write your answers in the test book.

PART 5

Directions: A word or phrase is missing in each of the sentences below. Four answer choices are given below each sentence. Select the best answer to complete the sentence. Then mark the letter (A), (B), (C), or (D) on your answer sheet.

101. ------- who wish to attend the annual scholar forum should bring their photo identification card to the conference hall.

    (A) That
    (B) Those
    (C) This
    (D) These

102. The Financial Services Authority should resolve the current market crisis in a ------- manner, cooperating with private enterprises.

    (A) time
    (B) timing
    (C) timely
    (D) timeless

103. Placing an order online is the ------- way to get your items among the methods of purchasing our products.

    (A) quick
    (B) quickly
    (C) quicker
    (D) quickest

104. If you find errors in the articles, please contact the chief editor to ------- with the problems.

    (A) handle
    (B) deal
    (C) correct
    (D) revise

105. The newly appointed supervisor of the Ebensburgh plant has contributed to ------- our work efficiency.

    (A) improve
    (B) improves
    (C) improving
    (D) improved

106. Interest rates on 30-year-fixed-rate loans will increase by about 5 percent, and that alone will add $120 per month to the ------- mortgage payment on a $400,000 house.

    (A) original
    (B) universal
    (C) internal
    (D) casual

107. The contract ------- that tenants must notify the landlord of either any minor damage or major structural changes if they wish to renew their apartment leases.

    (A) deteriorates
    (B) controls
    (C) stipulates
    (D) overlooks

108. Creating new methods to increase productivity ------- the most important stage for our company.

    (A) is
    (B) are
    (C) been
    (D) to be

109. Mr. Baker corrected the errors of all related papers ------- due to the absence of his colleagues attending the company's general conference.

(A) he
(B) his
(C) him
(D) himself

110. Skavolo Co.'s management has not ------- decided to organize supplementary funds due to its tight fiscal policy.

(A) still
(B) yet
(C) already
(D) finally

111. The graduate students ------- that they could publish their papers in the journal from their program coordinator.

(A) inform
(B) informed
(C) were informed
(D) have informed

112. Our managers would like to know ------- to plan to recruit more employees for the Busan branch.

(A) while
(B) whether
(C) whereas
(D) that

113. The Xenon 306 color laser printer provides compact, flexible, and professional color printing that will revolutionize your ------- with exceptional quality.

(A) produce
(B) output
(C) yield
(D) creation

114. Because the flight is overbooked, there is a possibility that a seat will not be available even for a person with a ------- reservation.

(A) developed
(B) notified
(C) canceled
(D) confirmed

115. By the time the technician of the IT support center repairs our servers, all employees ------- our Web sites again.

(A) connected
(B) have connected
(C) had connected
(D) will have connected

116. ------- employee should participate in the promotional campaign for the upcoming season without any exception.

(A) Every
(B) A few
(C) All
(D) Whole

117. Alpha Apparel's CEO ------- all the employees that the company will change the current dress code soon.

(A) notified
(B) announced
(C) explained
(D) accounted

118. ------- redundant supplies, all the staff of Tahoma Electronics should check the amounts in stock before placing an order.

(A) To reduce
(B) Reducing
(C) Having reduced
(D) Reduced

119. A number of major credit card issuers recently made ------- increases to the amount of the fees they charge for foreign transactions.

(A) considerate
(B) important
(C) agreeable
(D) substantial

120. HT Tech finally began selling its small and multi-functional tablet PC ------- March 10 after completing its demonstration stage.

(A) for
(B) in
(C) at
(D) on

GO ON TO THE NEXT PAGE

TEST 5

121. No one ------- professionals in that field can understand how to handle this camera without any help.

(A) because of
(B) except
(C) next to
(D) subsequent to

122. In order to increase our production efficiency, we have a plan to purchase new -------.

(A) machine
(B) machinery
(C) machinelike
(D) machined

123. The entire audience for *The Old Man and the Sea* should turn off their electronic devices ------- before the performance.

(A) right
(B) once
(C) also
(D) too

124. By making customers receive gift certificates and exchange them for merchandise, increased gift-card ------- could boost retailers' sales.

(A) redemptions
(B) warranties
(C) prices
(D) payments

125. ------- our innovative advertisements are well reviewed by other ad agencies, they also received a lot of positive feedback from the public.

(A) If
(B) While
(C) Because
(D) In order that

126. All the employees are eligible for getting additional vacation days, ------- a paid holiday.

(A) including
(B) starting
(C) following
(D) beginning

127. A municipal officer announced that the construction work has been ------- suspended due to the long holiday weekend.

(A) noticeably
(B) temporarily
(C) concurrently
(D) relatively

128. Please leave your valuables at our reception desk ------- entering the pool in order to prevent loss of the items.

(A) before
(B) after
(C) since
(D) over

129. The board members ------- agreed on the M&A last month, so we have to be prepared for a new situation.

(A) unanimously
(B) sharply
(C) consciously
(D) slowly

130. All employees have been instructed to gather in the auditorium ------- at 5:00 P.M. for the safety training.

(A) inwardly
(B) punctually
(C) highly
(D) extremely

PART 6

Directions: Read the texts that follow. A word, phrase, or sentence is missing in parts of each text. Four answer choices for each question are given below the text. Select the best answer to complete the text. Then mark the letter (A), (B), (C), or (D) on your answer sheet.

Questions 131-134 refer to the following e-mail.

To: t_hiddlestone@clemson.edu

From: g.mckane@generalbooks.com

Date: June 1

Subject: Possible visit

Dear Mr. Hiddlestone,

I felt very fortunate for having heard your speech at the college conference two weeks ago. My colleagues and I ------- your remarks inspiring as well as insightful. We thought it would be a wonderful
131.
plan for you to ------- a larger number of our staff. Would it be possible for you to visit our office and make
132.
a short speech at our monthly general assembly?

As the semester has just ended, I guess you should be busy completing students' grading. -------, it may
133.
be difficult to make time for a visit just now. How would you feel about scheduling your visit two or three

weeks after the summer break starts? -------. Please let me know if I can reach you by phone next week.
134.

Sincerely,

George McKane

CEO, General Books

131. (A) hindered
(B) acclaimed
(C) considered
(D) generated

132. (A) motivate
(B) motivating
(C) motivated
(D) motivation

133. (A) However
(B) For example
(C) Therefore
(D) On the contrary

134. (A) In order to make an appointment, you can contact us anytime.
(B) All the students on campus highly respect your personality.
(C) Dy listening to your speech, we were all encouraged to increase our sales.
(D) I'd be happy to call you for a brief talk to discuss possible dates.

GO ON TO THE NEXT PAGE

Questions 135-138 refer to the following letter.

Dear friends,

We are pleased to announce that the annual Pitt Three Rivers Cleanup program will start this year on April 5. Regular and new volunteers who would like to participate this year will be required to use ------- gear. To request the gear, please fill in the Volunteer Registration Form
      135.
below.

Two days of river cleanup activities are planned at Yellow Creek followed by two days at Three Rivers. -------, various teams will work with the environmental department to move
            136.
trash retrieved from the waterfront to the city landfill. -------. With your help, this year's
                                                        137.
cleanup ------- another major success. See you there!
         138.

Sincerely,

James Rivera, Manager
Pitt Recycling Program

135. (A) protect
(B) protective
(C) protecting
(D) protection

136. (A) In addition
(B) First of all
(C) Instead
(D) Nevertheless

137. (A) By getting rid of waste, you can get paid for the work.
(B) To get there, you need to take the 21 Oak Drive route.
(C) We hope you will participate in this important initiative.
(D) They have promoted this event for the last two months.

138. (A) are
(B) has been
(C) had been
(D) will be

Questions 139-142 refer to the following e-mail.

To: John Mayer <jmayer@eurocar.com>

From: Monica Beth <mbeth@eurocar.com>

Date: January 30

Subject: Re: Outstanding Customer Ratings

Dear Mr. Mayer,

The executive board members were ------- to read the positive results of our latest customer
139.
satisfaction survey. We recognize that this is ------- due to your management of Euro Car Rentals,
140.
which has been exceptional. In appreciation, we are pleased to offer you a permanent contract for the

position starting March 1. -------. ------- you began as chief operating officer six months ago, car rentals
141. 142.
have tripled, 40% of which are repeat clients. Our ratings from client surveys have also improved

significantly.

All these indicate that Euro is in very capable hands, and we'd like it to remain so. Congratulations!

Monica Beth
Human Resources Department

139. (A) satisfy
(B) satisfied
(C) satisfying
(D) satisfaction

140. (A) considerately
(B) promptly
(C) largely
(D) shortly

141. (A) However, we regret to inform you that
we have no space for the promotion at
this time.
(B) Moreover, we are offering a higher
compensation package, including
full-time insurance and travel expenses.
(C) Nothing is more valuable than the
feedback and support from our regular
customers.
(D) To illustrate it, the sales figures for the
second quarter are the best among the
industry-related competitors.

142. (A) Since
(B) Because
(C) Although
(D) When

GO ON TO THE NEXT PAGE

Questions 143-146 refer to the following Web page.

Golden Save Card

The Golden Save Card has the most ------- coverage of all supermarket loyalty cards. -------. On any
                                    143.   **144.**
day of the week, you can use the card and earn double or triple credit on specially selected items.

You can use your credit for shopping, buying gas, renting a car, or booking a hotel. In addition, we

check your shopping patterns to ------- you coupons which fit your shopping habits and preferences.
                                 145.
Like shopping for clothes and sports equipment? We'll customize your coupons and send you

------- every time these items go on sale! There is absolutely no extra charge for using all these
146.
services. No wonder our loyalty card is the most popular.

143. (A) comprehend
(B) comprehensible
(C) comprehensive
(D) comprehensively

144. (A) Cardholders get credit for everything
from groceries to vehicle maintenance.
(B) If you want to apply for them, please
contact our registration division.
(C) Thanks to its benefits, our card sales
have sharply increased for this quarter.
(D) To protect your credit information,
you should install the newest security
software.

145. (A) activate
(B) reimburse
(C) deduct
(D) offer

146. (A) alerts
(B) alertly
(C) alerting
(D) to alert

PART 7

Directions: In this part you will read a selection of texts, such as magazine and newspaper articles, e-mails, and instant messages. Each text or set of texts is followed by several questions. Select the best answer for each question and mark the letter (A), (B), (C), or (D) on your answer sheet.

Questions 147-148 refer to the following information.

D A A

The INNOCREATE Awards are given annually to acknowledge remarkable accomplishments in automobile design. The awards are sponsored by the Detroit Auto Association and awarded exclusively to local companies in the city of Detroit.

The awards are divided into four categories and presented in November at the Detroit Auto Fair. All graphic design companies are encouraged to submit their works for consideration. Visit the DAA Web site for more information about these categories and for details about the submission process.

147. What is mentioned about the INNOCREATE Awards?

(A) They include a great amount of prize money.

(B) They are granted once every two years.

(C) They are given to those related to the design field.

(D) They are supported by an international foundation.

148. What are the readers invited to do?

(A) Join a contest

(B) Give feedback

(C) Attend an awards ceremony

(D) Organize an event

GO ON TO THE NEXT PAGE

State University of South Dakota

Training Programs in Predictive Analytics

Certificate of Completion

awarded to:

Annie Evelyn

to certify the completion of Predictive Analytics

for Business, Marketing and Research

Her series of sessions was rated "excellent" by the course participants.

Granted: June 20, 2024

John Swale

John Swale, Ph.D. Professor

Program Coordinator of SUSD Research Lab

---

149. What did Ms. Evelyn do on June 20?

(A) She registered for a graduate program.
(B) She took a business trip to South Dakota.
(C) She received a diploma.
(D) She taught one of the classes.

150. Who most likely is Ms. Evelyn?

(A) A graduate assistant
(B) A market researcher
(C) A computer technician
(D) A program director

Dave Ditzel [3:20 P.M.]
Are you still in the Stapleton Room?

[3:23 P.M.] **Stella Lanni**
Yes. The speaker is just finishing up his speech.

Dave Ditzel [3:24 P.M.]
OK. I'm going to Haman's presentation about "Language and Culture". Do you want to come with me? It's in Sutton Hall on the 2nd floor.

[3:25 P.M.] **Stella Lanni**
I wouldn't miss it. It should be very interesting.

Dave Ditzel [3:27 P.M.]
Of course! It'll be very informative as well.

Dave Ditzel [3:28 P.M.]
Should I save you a seat near me in the front row?

[3:30 P.M.] **Stella Lanni**
That would be great! Thanks.

Send

TEST 5

151. At 3:27 P.M., what does Mr. Ditzel most likely mean when he writes, "Of course"?

(A) All the forum participants want to join the reception.
(B) The speech in the Stapleton Room is very exciting.
(C) He regrets that he could not participate in the presentation.
(D) He completely agrees with Ms. Lanni's opinion of Haman's presentation.

152. What is true about Mr. Ditzel?

(A) He has been hired as Haman's assistant.
(B) He has guided the presentation attendees.
(C) He expects to arrive at Sutton Hall before Ms. Lanni.
(D) He has prepared for his presentation at Sutton Hall.

GO ON TO THE NEXT PAGE

Questions 153-154 refer to the following advertisement.

36-Hour Phone Card Sale
5% off everything!

Summer is coming! Students are in their last weeks of classes, and people are making their summer international travel plans, so Speed Tel will continue to provide the best rates for all phone card users. Do a rate search today to see the latest rates for your calling destination.

And don't forget to "like us" on INSTABOOK (our Social Network Service) to get the most up-to-date news and card updates from Speed Tel.

• Save 5% instantly

The whole store is on sale right now. Everything is marked down 5%, including recharging. No coupon required.

• Speed Tel mobile – 4-touch recharge

Recharge your phone card from your smartphone in just 4 clicks with our mobile interface.

153. What is indicated about Speed Tel?

(A) Customers should log onto their Web site to get a discount.
(B) It provides customers with a discount without any qualification.
(C) Through the social network service, customers can recharge their cards.
(D) Only students can take advantage of these offers.

154. What information is NOT provided by the advertisement?

(A) The discount rate
(B) The recharging method
(C) The Social Network
(D) The company location

Questions 155-157 refer to the following e-mail.

To	: Hee-Sun Yoon <y_heesun@advancedone.ca>
From	: Reuben Anderson <a.reuben@kinneyunionco.com>
Subject	: Information
Date	: March 10
Attachment	: 📎 move_details.doc

Dear Ms. Yoon,

I would like to welcome you to your new position as a planning manager at Kinney Union Co. The branch building in Seattle has been renovated to improve its efficiency. It can make the branch one of the most advanced Kinney facilities in the U.S.

Sally Beth from the Department of Human Resources will lead you through an employee orientation on Monday, March 30, at 10 A.M. Ms. Beth will kindly explain our company's structures, wages, benefits, and other details. You have not yet received our company identification card, so you'll need to register for it at the Security Division. I ask you to arrive there by 9:30 A.M. on March 30.

I have attached the information that will help you to move to Seattle from Vancouver. There are some recommendations in the file in the event that you cannot find a suitable residential space. If you have any questions, please feel free to contact me anytime by phone or e-mail.

Sincerely,

Reuben Anderson
Director, Department of Human Resources
Kinney Union Corporation
San Francisco Headquarters

155. Why did Mr. Anderson send the e-mail?

(A) To describe procedures of an application
(B) To request some personal information
(C) To provide details about a new position
(D) To explain a company's new business

156. What is indicated about Kinney Union Co.?

(A) It will be soon relocated to Vancouver.
(B) It has more than one branch.
(C) It has a plan to employ more staff.
(D) It has expanded its business to other Industries.

157. What is Ms. Yoon required to do?

(A) Submit the form to the HR team
(B) Contact Ms. Beth as soon as possible
(C) Arrive at the orientation in advance
(D) Make a call to the Security Division

GO ON TO THE NEXT PAGE

TEST 5

Questions 158-160 refer to the following flyer.

We invite you to
the Reopening of
Valentino's Restaurant
on October 13th

To celebrate the reopening of our restaurant, Valentino's is offering every customer a free bottle of wine to accompany any dinner on the first day of reopening. Bring the family and try out our selection of wines. Choose from over 20 countries including:

- South Africa
- France
- Italy
- New Zealand
- England

Valentino's is situated in the Latin Quarter opposite the Hill Brasserie and Mason's Department Store. We are open six days a week from 11 A.M. to 2 A.M.

Valentino's owner, Sergio Messi, will be appearing on television to promote the grand reopening on September 30th.

Offer is limited to one free bottle per booking.

---

158. What is sold at Valentino's?

(A) Tableware
(B) Uniforms
(C) Meals
(D) Groceries

159. What can customers do on October 13th?

(A) Reserve a table online
(B) Receive a free alcoholic beverage
(C) Get a 10% discount coupon
(D) Buy one meal and get one free

160. What is mentioned about Valentino's?

(A) It has various wines from different countries.
(B) It is situated in the banking district.
(C) Its owner will be featured in a magazine.
(D) It will be open seven days a week.

AT Healthcare

Wong Chan Boulevard
Indonesia

July 2
Ms. Yin-Chow Sui
5454 Kwon Avenue, Indonesia IN 435

Dear Ms. Sui,

Many thanks for your application to AT Healthcare. You have been recommended by our senior registrar, Mr. Hanes, as a suitable candidate for the position of head nurse in our hospital. We would like to invite you for an interview on Monday, July 22nd at 1:30 P.M. Please contact my PA, Leone Tia to confirm this appointment. Her number is 195-3530234.

Can you also send copies of your references? Unfortunately, the original references you submitted have been misplaced in our recent relocation to the new facility.

Lastly, please see attached forms to be completed and brought along to the interview. We look forward to seeing you.

Sincerely,

Sun Lo-Chan
Director of Recruitment

Enclosures

---

161. Why does Mr. Lo-Chan write to Ms. Sui?

(A) To arrange an interview
(B) To inquire about a job position
(C) To ask for visa documents
(D) To suggest a change of location

162. Whom is Ms. Sui asked to contact?

(A) The senior registrar
(B) The healthcare director
(C) Mr. Hanes
(D) Ms. Tia

163. What problem does Mr. Lo-Chan mention?

(A) Some papers were missing in a recent move.
(B) The hospital's Web site is not working properly.
(C) The person interviewing Ms. Sui cannot be reached.
(D) The application was received after the deadline.

GO ON TO THE NEXT PAGE

Questions 164-167 refer to the following article.

Superfood!
Green Tea around the World

April 10 — As the effects of green tea have been widely covered in a variety of health-related books; its demand has been increasing for several years as well. — [1] —. Green tea is a type of tea made from Camellia Sinensis leaves, and it originated from East Asian countries such as China, Korea, and Japan. There is a wide range of green tea in its plant species, based on its growing conditions, cultivation methods, and production processing. — [2] —. With its development of various cultivation methods, it has recently spread to many other countries throughout the world.

According to some journals, drinking green tea daily has anti-cancer effects and cholesterol-lowering impacts on the body. In addition, it can enable the body to enhance metabolism activities. — [3] —. So, you should drink it moderately, no more than three times a day.

One of the drinking methods is steeping its tea bag in hot water. The other is brewing its leaves by using teapots with hot water. You should recognize that if the temperature of the water is too high, it can destroy original nutrients of leaves. So, maintain its proper temperature from 60°C to 90°C and dip the tea bag about three times in hot water for 30 seconds every five minutes.

— [4] —. Its taste entirely depends on its steeping and brewing techniques. Therefore, it is very important that proper information about green tea be given to the public because it can help maintain or damage our health. You can find its detailed information at our Web site, www.ourvoicemagazine.com/health.

164. What aspect of green tea did the writer explain?

(A) Its history of discovery
(B) Its process of production
(C) Its botanical importance
(D) Its drinking method

165. What is NOT mentioned about green tea's medical effects?

(A) Lowering cholesterol
(B) Reducing the risk of cancer
(C) Helping metabolism activities
(D) Controlling appetite

166. What is indicated about green tea?

(A) It can adversely affect our health.
(B) Its origin was found in many old books.
(C) Its color can be changed with modern technology.
(D) The general public is not agreeable to its taste.

167. In which of the positions marked [1], [2], [3], and [4] does the following sentence best belong?

"However, drinking it too much may cause other serious health problems."

(A) [1]
(B) [2]
(C) [3]
(D) [4]

GO ON TO THE NEXT PAGE

Questions 168-171 refer to the following online chat discussion.

New Chat ⊜⊡⊗

Emma Lynn [10:35 A.M.]
Good morning, everyone! Did anyone hear the news about Pitt Business Complex?

Joyce Roche [10:36 A.M.]
I talked to Mr. Smith last Tuesday. He said that he expects to make a decision by this Wednesday, but we haven't heard anything yet.

Emma Lynn [10:37 A.M.]
Well, if we don't order steel and cement, we'll fail to meet the deadline, although we've already made the blueprint.

Scott William [10:38 A.M.]
I've already placed the orders yesterday.

Emma Lynn [10:40 A.M.]
That could be a problem. If we don't get the contract, we'll have to pay for the construction materials, even though we won't be able to use them. By when do we have to cancel them to avoid being charged?

Scott William [10:41 A.M.]
I need to take more time to figure that out, considering that it varies. Let me check.

Emma Lynn [10:42 A.M.]
Ms. Roche, can you call Mr. Smith and ask what's going on now?

Scott William [10:43 A.M.]
We can cancel them without any penalty by the end of tomorrow.

Joyce Roche [10:46 A.M.]
Mr. William, could you do that for me? And Ms. Lynn, I just got a call from Ms. Jade, Mr. Smith's secretary. She said Mr. Smith decided to go with Cornwell Development Co. this time.

Emma Lynn [10:48 A.M.]
That's so disappointing, but don't be discouraged! We'll have a better result next time.

	Send

168. What kind of business do they most likely work for?

(A) Construction
(B) Landscaping
(C) Catering service
(D) Distribution

169. At 10:41 A.M., what does Mr. William most likely mean when he writes, "Let me check"?

(A) He will estimate the cost of materials.
(B) He will readjust a delivery schedule.
(C) He will calculate a return deadline.
(D) He will count the number of members.

170. What information did Ms. Jade provide?

(A) How to get a contract
(B) Who will develop Mr. Smith's property
(C) When the construction will begin
(D) Why a decision was delayed

171. What will Mr. William most likely do next?

(A) Contact Mr. Smith again
(B) Submit their proposal
(C) Cancel their orders
(D) Show their blueprints

GO ON TO THE NEXT PAGE

Coming to New Orleans

by Paul Kei

New Orleans (10 June) — From 20 to 24, a number of writers, teachers, and professors will join the upcoming 10th Contemporary Writing Conference. — [1] —. There will be a variety of participants in this conference, so it will be one of the biggest events in the writing field.

Andrea Carnale, a prominent linguist and writer, posted the complimentary column about the conference on the New York Tribune. Thanks to that writing, public's interest has considerably increased. "A lot of people e-mailed us every day in order to register for the conference," said John Swain, who is organizing and directing this event for the first time. — [2] —. Last year, around 100 writers and teachers participated in the conference, and the total number of registrants was over 350. — [3] —.

This year's conference will focus on various genres in the writing field. "We would like to show a wide range of literary works and their approaches to the second language writing education," said the program coordinator Jerry Tannacito. Prospective writers presenting their works are from twenty different countries throughout the world. — [4] —. It is strongly believed that the conference can be very informative and successful.

For more information about the event, please visit the Web site at www.CWC.org.

172. Who helped the conference become more popular?

    (A) Mr. Kei

    (B) Mr. Carnale

    (C) Mr. Swain

    (D) Mr. Tannacito

173. What is indicated about the conference?

    (A) A ticket should be purchased only online.

    (B) New Orleans hosts it for the first time.

    (C) It has a new director this year.

    (D) It lasts one week.

174. What is stated about the writers at the conference?

    (A) They have been already renowned.

    (B) They have been sponsored by certain company.

    (C) They have a certified license.

    (D) They come from various countries.

175. In which of the positions marked [1], [2], [3], and [4] does the following sentence best belong?

"This year, we expect that both of these figures have just about tripled."

    (A) [1]

    (B) [2]

    (C) [3]

    (D) [4]

GO ON TO THE NEXT PAGE

Employment Opportunity – INNOBIZ Services

	Date: October 5	**Reference Number:** 2922513
Job Title	Office Maintenance Technician	
Type of Employment	Full-Time (permanent)	
Qualifications	Applicants must have extensive knowledge of electronic devices and machines and at least two years of experience in photocopier repair, and be certified to operate a commercial truck.	
Job Description	We provide repairs of photocopiers and other office equipment for companies.	
Additional Information	Because the areas we cover are so large, it will be essential for applicants to live near the Slippery Rock, which is the most central of our service areas.	
Contact Information	Henry Kane INNOBIZ Services – Personnel Division 391 Washington Drive, Pittsburgh, PA 15712 h_kane@innobizservices.com	
Interview Schedule	Preliminary Interviews: October 15 – October 20	
Starting Date for Work	October 30	

To: Jane Foster <j_foster@innobizservices.com>

From: Henry Kane <h_kane@innobizservices.com>

Date: October 10

Subject: New Technician

Dear Ms. Foster,

Currently, a lot of applications for the technician position are being submitted. The first few applicants showing their interest have asked whether the company would provide accommodation or not.

Probably, the details about it in our job advertisement are unclear to the applicants. Please update this part of the advertisement before the preliminary interviews start.

In addition, I want to ask whether it would be possible to create an online application form that automatically sends all detailed information to a database on our network. Our current system requires receiving applicants' information in person and entering it into our hiring database, so it may result in a lot of errors.

Sincerely,

Henry Kane
Director, Personnel Division
INNOBIZ Services

176. According to the advertisement, what is NOT listed as a requirement for the position?

(A) A degree from a university
(B) A background in electronics
(C) Experience in equipment repair
(D) Authorization to drive a commercial car

177. What is one of the purposes of the e-mail?

(A) To approve a request
(B) To confirm an appointment
(C) To suggest a new system
(D) To offer a position

178. When will the accommodation information be updated by?

(A) October 5
(B) October 14
(C) October 16
(D) October 20

179. Who most likely is Mr. Kane?

(A) A college student
(B) A department head
(C) A computer expert
(D) A job applicant

180. What part of the advertisement does Mr. Kane refer to?

(A) Qualifications
(B) Type of Employment
(C) Additional Information
(D) Contact Information

GO ON TO THE NEXT PAGE

The Stony Grand Hotel
Membership Benefits

Monthly Payments: BLUE - $30 / RED - $50 / BLACK - $70

	BLUE	RED	BLACK
Complimentary Parking	Yes	Yes	Yes
Pool and Spa	Yes	Yes	Yes
Hotel Gym	Yes	Yes	Yes
Free Shuttle	Yes	Yes	Yes
Discounts on Special Events *	No	Yes	Yes
Guest Passes	No	No	Yes

Please note that the one-day registration payment is $80, and you can take advantage of our BLACK membership services. This payment is non-refundable when changing or canceling the registration. If you register for our regular membership, the fees can be refunded within two months of your enrollment.

* For more information and schedules of special events, visit our Web site at www.stonygrandhotel.com.

From: Melisa Milton <m.milton@stonygrandhotel.com>

To: Gary Jacob <g.jacob@gammanet.com>

Subject: Re: Guest Passes

Date: July 10

Attachment: 📎 Receipt

Dear Mr. Jacob,

I would like to thank you again for becoming a member of the Stony Grand Hotel. I have attached a receipt for your full payment of $360, which reflects 12 months' dues at $30 per month.

You asked us to issue guest passes for your friends who will take a vacation on July 30. Unfortunately, your BLUE membership does not cover the free guest passes you required. To apply for this and other benefits in your package, you need to upgrade your membership to our premium level. If you would like to change your service to the BLACK plan, you should pay for its difference of $480. However, if you do not want to upgrade to the BLACK one, your friends cannot be entitled to exactly the same membership status. In this case, your friends need to purchase the one-day passes at our reception desk on the first floor.

Melisa Milton
Chief Director of Service

181. What is true about the Stony Grand Hotel's service?

(A) It is more expensive than other hotels.
(B) It is only applicable on the Web.
(C) It is open to nonmembers.
(D) It is operated by local communities.

182. In the e-mail, the word "reflects" in paragraph 1, line 2, is closest in meaning to

(A) demonstrates
(B) illuminates
(C) represents
(D) considers

183. What can Mr. Jacob NOT do at the Stony Grand Hotel?

(A) Exercise at the hotel fitness club
(B) Take a free shuttle bus to downtown areas
(C) Park his car in the hotel parking lot
(D) Attend an event at a reduced price

184. Which plan should Mr. Jacob upgrade to in order to help his friends?

(A) BLUE
(B) RED
(C) BLACK
(D) One-day pass

185. What is indicated about the guests of premium-level members?

(A) They should be accompanied by a member.
(B) They can use every facility and service in the hotel.
(C) They can stay in the hotel on certain dates only.
(D) They need to present their passes at the front desk.

GO ON TO THE NEXT PAGE

Global Vision Foundation
Entrepreneurs Development Training

The Global Vision Foundation is organizing a variety of lectures and seminars for entrepreneurs who need to make their operation strategies more innovative and creative through the online marketing. This upcoming event is scheduled to be held at Kovalchick Convention Center from July 10 to 13.

Jansen Gauge, a marketing professional, will talk about the basic elements for company's item promotion. Catherine Upton, an online expert who is working at GVF, will instruct attendees to increase efficiency about Internet-based operation with a reasonable budget. On the last day of the event, a simulation practice to devise business plans for its degree of effectiveness and potential growth will analyze participants based on all the materials we have.

The program registration fees are all free except for the simulation practice which will be charged $15. Please register now by visiting www.gvf.org/EDTprograms.

GVF Program Schedule
Entrepreneurs Development Training

Topic	Time	Place
Monday, July 10		
Marketing Strategy for Beginner	4 P.M.	Sutton Hall
A Way of Online Promotion	5 P.M.	Sutton Hall
Coaching Program – 1 : 1	6 P.M.	IT Support Center
Tuesday, July 11		
Saving Online Marketing Budget	5 P.M.	Sutton Hall
Coaching Program – 1 : 1	6 P.M.	IT Support Center
Wednesday, July 12		
Improving Brand Awareness on the Web	5 P.M.	Sutton Hall
Coaching Program – 1 : 1	6 P.M.	IT Support Center
Thursday, July 13		
Simulation Practice	6 P.M.	Unity Grand Ballroom

GVF Hosts Prestigious Programs

Johnstown (July 14) – Promising entrepreneurs joined four-day events with a variety of lectures, seminars and activities to allow them to establish and improve their current online business methods thanks to the Global Vision Foundation (GVF).

Malcom Harrison, who recently started a space rental service, was very satisfied with the seminars. "These kinds of programs helped small business owners like me to understand the importance of online promotion strategies by reducing the risk of new business," he said.

Angela Beth, who is preparing for delivery network business, was especially impressed with the simulation practice, which utilized its SWOT Analysis(strengths, weaknesses, opportunities, threats). "The evaluation sheet from the experts will let me know how to approach my prospective customers," she said.

Lyman Faith, Director of GVF, was very surprised at its degree of participation and told that this kind of event is being considered again for December.

---

186. According to the brochure, what is the event mainly about?

(A) To announce the importance of online server maintenance

(B) To hire additional staff for organizing upcoming events

(C) To improve Global Vision Foundation's brand perception

(D) To teach entrepreneurs how to use web-based strategies

187. In the brochure, the word "devise" in paragraph 2, line 4, is closest in meaning to

(A) withdraw

(B) convene

(C) design

(D) manufacture

188. What can be inferred about the program schedule?

(A) Only one session is held each day.

(B) Attendees can have several chances for training.

(C) The simulation practice will begin before the other events.

(D) All the sessions will be held in the same hall.

189. What is suggested about Ms. Beth?

(A) She met a budget consultant.

(B) She has worked with the foundation.

(C) She submitted the evaluation sheet.

(D) She made a payment to GVF.

190. What is suggested about GVF?

(A) It will appoint Mr. Harrison new director.

(B) It offered financial support to all start-up businesses.

(C) It has made every effort to promote itself.

(D) It will probably host a similar event later this year.

GO ON TO THE NEXT PAGE

Questions 191-195 refer to the following ticket and e-mails.

From	: confirmation@ticketexpress.com
To	: c.hunter@betamail.com
Date	: May 18, 2024
Subject	: Your Order
Attachments : ∅ ticket_may_cleveland.pdf	

This message is an automatically generated e-mail receipt for your order at www.ticketexpress.com, which is currently being processed.

Thank you for ordering from Ticket Express.

PIN(Personal Identification Number) INFORMATION
You can track the status of your order at any time by using our tracking system at www.ticketexpress.com/myticket. To access your order, you will need to enter the e-mail address used to place this order as well as the PIN for this order. Your PIN for this order is 29981524.

ORDER INFORMATION
Order ID#: 7592591 - May 18 2024 3:07 P.M.

Tickets: 2 tickets at $35.00 each	$70.00
Will-Call:	$15.00
Total:	$85.00

Additional Purchase Information:
Your credit card will be charged in USD.
*Your total does not include any applicable state, local, or other sales taxes.

If you have any questions about the receipt, please feel free to contact us and state your PIN on the subject line.

Division of Order Confirmation

This is your ticket   Name: Colin Hunter & Sunny Bale

SECTION	ROW	SEAT	EVENT
183	V	10/11	Cleveland vs. Pittsburgh

Progressive Stadium   Sat. May 25, 2024 4:30 P.M.

Don't miss the Reds at Progressive Stadium this season!
For more information, visit www.TheReds.com.

* The barcode only allows one entry per scan.
* Unauthorized duplication or sale of this ticket may prohibit your admittance to the event.
* No outside food or drink allowed inside the stadium. (You can use the snack bars at the ballpark for food.)

** The holder takes all risk and danger incidental to the baseball game before, during, or after the game.

Thanks for your e-mail and baseball game ticket. I carefully read the details of my order. However, I cannot understand what "Will-Call" is. I definitely ordered only two tickets without any options and paid with my credit card at $70. However, $15 of "Will-Call" is on my receipt for this order. Can you explain what it is and why it was added?

Best Wishes,

Colin Hunter

191. What information is stated in the first e-mail?

(A) The personal identification of the customer is revealed.

(B) There is something wrong with the purchaser's contact information.

(C) The tickets have been delivered through e-mail.

(D) Only credit cards are accepted for purchases.

192. What is implied about the ticket?

(A) A promotional code is included.

(B) It can be used anytime during the season.

(C) It can be handed over to others.

(D) One ticket covers two seats.

193. What are people prevented from doing?

(A) Taking a photo in the game

(B) Leaving the stadium during the game

(C) Bringing some snacks to the ballpark

(D) Drinking beer at each seat

194. At the bottom of the ticket, the word "takes" in line 4, is closest in meaning to

(A) simulates

(B) maintains

(C) believes

(D) accepts

195. Which information is missing in the second e-mail?

(A) A seat number

(B) A credit card number

(C) A personal identification number

(D) A telephone number

TEST 5

GO ON TO THE NEXT PAGE

Questions 196-200 refer to the following advertisement, letter, and e-mail.

MARKETING DIRECTOR WANTED

Whitewall Publishing is looking for an additional experienced marketing director because it has recently been acquired by the Mastermind Group, widely recognized in the publishing world. As a director of marketing, this position will be in charge of a new team called Mastermind Whitewall Task Force. He or she will supervise these new members and publication promotion procedures by arranging and advertising our upcoming special event for the book lists of the humanities. The successful candidate will have at least two years of experience in the field of marketing and promotion. In addition, the person in this position is required to think creatively and analytically, and lead his/her members systematically. A high standard of knowledge about the humanities is also necessary for general management. Lastly, having expertise in social media tools is highly preferred in order to fit into the recent mobile-based era.

If you have any questions or want to know our benefits package, please feel free to contact us at mw_taskforce@mastermind.com.

To apply for the position, visit www.mastermind/application/mw_taskforce.

* An application must be submitted by March 10.

Whitewall Publishing
1038 Washington Boulevard
Newark, New Jersey

March 4

To Whom It May Concern:

Amanda Caroline has been a member of my team at Corner Media for four years. She is very dedicated, experienced, and professional in using a variety of social media for promotional events. Although she has not had a career as a director yet, she has worked closely with me and my members as a deputy of our department. She even completed a double major in the humanities and digital media at the University of East Virginia. With her educational background, she has generated a wide range of creative advertisements and promotions that led to sales increases. In particular, she directed and supervised Dr. Gloria's speech series at Washington College two months ago, which was favorably regarded in nationwide magazines. In addition, her communication skills with colleagues and clients are definitely notable among other staff members.

I hope that her efficiency will help to support your newly-organized department.

Sincerely,

James Blanchard
Chief Director
Corner Media

From	: Patrick Upton <p_upton@mastermind.com>
To	: Amanda Caroline <a.caroline@cornermedia.net>
Date	: March 15
Subject	: Marketing Director Position

Dear Ms. Caroline,

Thank you for your application for the position of marketing director in our new team at the Mastermind Group. Your qualifications are very interesting, and Mr. Blanchard's reference is highly impressive. I had actually attended Ms. Gloria's speech series on January 2. It was very exciting and informative for me.

We would like to interview you for the position. I have tentatively scheduled you to visit our Virginia office building at 2 P.M. on March 20. Please reply to this e-mail to let me know if that time is convenient for you.

Best wishes,

Patrick Upton
Director, Human Resources Department
Whitewall Publishing, Mastermind Group

196. What is indicated about Whitewall Publishing?

(A) It needs several job positions for its new team.
(B) It has promoted the importance of the humanities.
(C) Its business has expanded into the Asian areas.
(D) It was purchased by the Mastermind Group.

197. What requirement for the position did Ms. Caroline fulfill?

(A) Outstanding educational and academic achievements
(B) The ability to use social media tools for marketing
(C) The knowledge of mergers and acquisitions of businesses
(D) Good relationships with media-related departments

198. What is the purpose of the letter?

(A) To offer a position
(B) To meet an author
(C) To discuss an event
(D) To recommend a person

199. What event did Mr. Upton most likely attend on January 2?

(A) A trade fair in Virginia
(B) A lecture at Washington College
(C) A talk by the CEO of Mastermind
(D) A social media conference

200. What does Mr. Upton ask Ms. Caroline to do?

(A) Open a new account online
(B) Provide personal information
(C) Submit a proposal
(D) Confirm an appointment

Stop! This is the end of the test. If you finish before time is called, you may go back to Parts 5, 6, and 7 and check your work.

books. english. co. kr

ANSWER SHEET

No.

수험번호
성 명 | 한글
영자

TEST 1

LISTENING (PART I ~ IV)

NO.	ANSWER				NO.	ANSWER				NO.	ANSWER				NO.	ANSWER			
	A	B	C	D		A	B	C	D		A	B	C	D		A	B	C	D
1	Ⓐ	Ⓑ	Ⓒ	Ⓓ	21	Ⓐ	Ⓑ	Ⓒ	Ⓓ	41	Ⓐ	Ⓑ	Ⓒ		61	Ⓐ	Ⓑ	Ⓒ	Ⓓ
2	Ⓐ	Ⓑ	Ⓒ	Ⓓ	22	Ⓐ	Ⓑ	Ⓒ	Ⓓ	42	Ⓐ	Ⓑ	Ⓒ		62	Ⓐ	Ⓑ	Ⓒ	Ⓓ
3	Ⓐ	Ⓑ	Ⓒ	Ⓓ	23	Ⓐ	Ⓑ	Ⓒ	Ⓓ	43	Ⓐ	Ⓑ	Ⓒ		63	Ⓐ	Ⓑ	Ⓒ	Ⓓ
4	Ⓐ	Ⓑ	Ⓒ	Ⓓ	24	Ⓐ	Ⓑ	Ⓒ	Ⓓ	44	Ⓐ	Ⓑ	Ⓒ		64	Ⓐ	Ⓑ	Ⓒ	Ⓓ
5	Ⓐ	Ⓑ	Ⓒ	Ⓓ	25	Ⓐ	Ⓑ	Ⓒ	Ⓓ	45	Ⓐ	Ⓑ	Ⓒ		65	Ⓐ	Ⓑ	Ⓒ	Ⓓ
6	Ⓐ	Ⓑ	Ⓒ	Ⓓ	26	Ⓐ	Ⓑ	Ⓒ	Ⓓ	46	Ⓐ	Ⓑ	Ⓒ		66	Ⓐ	Ⓑ	Ⓒ	Ⓓ
7	Ⓐ	Ⓑ	Ⓒ		27	Ⓐ	Ⓑ	Ⓒ		47	Ⓐ	Ⓑ	Ⓒ		67	Ⓐ	Ⓑ	Ⓒ	Ⓓ
8	Ⓐ	Ⓑ	Ⓒ		28	Ⓐ	Ⓑ	Ⓒ		48	Ⓐ	Ⓑ	Ⓒ	Ⓓ	68	Ⓐ	Ⓑ	Ⓒ	Ⓓ
9	Ⓐ	Ⓑ	Ⓒ		29	Ⓐ	Ⓑ	Ⓒ		49	Ⓐ	Ⓑ	Ⓒ	Ⓓ	69	Ⓐ	Ⓑ	Ⓒ	Ⓓ
10	Ⓐ	Ⓑ	Ⓒ		30	Ⓐ	Ⓑ	Ⓒ		50	Ⓐ	Ⓑ	Ⓒ	Ⓓ	70	Ⓐ	Ⓑ	Ⓒ	Ⓓ
11	Ⓐ	Ⓑ	Ⓒ		31	Ⓐ	Ⓑ	Ⓒ		51	Ⓐ	Ⓑ	Ⓒ	Ⓓ	71	Ⓐ	Ⓑ	Ⓒ	Ⓓ
12	Ⓐ	Ⓑ	Ⓒ		32	Ⓐ	Ⓑ	Ⓒ		52	Ⓐ	Ⓑ	Ⓒ	Ⓓ	72	Ⓐ	Ⓑ	Ⓒ	Ⓓ
13	Ⓐ	Ⓑ	Ⓒ		33	Ⓐ	Ⓑ	Ⓒ		53	Ⓐ	Ⓑ	Ⓒ	Ⓓ	73	Ⓐ	Ⓑ	Ⓒ	Ⓓ
14	Ⓐ	Ⓑ	Ⓒ		34	Ⓐ	Ⓑ	Ⓒ		54	Ⓐ	Ⓑ	Ⓒ	Ⓓ	74	Ⓐ	Ⓑ	Ⓒ	Ⓓ
15	Ⓐ	Ⓑ	Ⓒ		35	Ⓐ	Ⓑ	Ⓒ		55	Ⓐ	Ⓑ	Ⓒ	Ⓓ	75	Ⓐ	Ⓑ	Ⓒ	Ⓓ
16	Ⓐ	Ⓑ	Ⓒ		36	Ⓐ	Ⓑ	Ⓒ		56	Ⓐ	Ⓑ	Ⓒ	Ⓓ	76	Ⓐ	Ⓑ	Ⓒ	Ⓓ
17	Ⓐ	Ⓑ	Ⓒ		37	Ⓐ	Ⓑ	Ⓒ		57	Ⓐ	Ⓑ	Ⓒ	Ⓓ	77	Ⓐ	Ⓑ	Ⓒ	Ⓓ
18	Ⓐ	Ⓑ	Ⓒ		38	Ⓐ	Ⓑ	Ⓒ		58	Ⓐ	Ⓑ	Ⓒ	Ⓓ	78	Ⓐ	Ⓑ	Ⓒ	Ⓓ
19	Ⓐ	Ⓑ	Ⓒ		39	Ⓐ	Ⓑ	Ⓒ		59	Ⓐ	Ⓑ	Ⓒ	Ⓓ	79	Ⓐ	Ⓑ	Ⓒ	Ⓓ
20	Ⓐ	Ⓑ	Ⓒ		40	Ⓐ	Ⓑ	Ⓒ		60	Ⓐ	Ⓑ	Ⓒ	Ⓓ	80	Ⓐ	Ⓑ	Ⓒ	Ⓓ

NO.	ANSWER			
	A	B	C	D
81	Ⓐ	Ⓑ	Ⓒ	Ⓓ
82	Ⓐ	Ⓑ	Ⓒ	Ⓓ
83	Ⓐ	Ⓑ	Ⓒ	Ⓓ
84	Ⓐ	Ⓑ	Ⓒ	Ⓓ
85	Ⓐ	Ⓑ	Ⓒ	Ⓓ
86	Ⓐ	Ⓑ	Ⓒ	Ⓓ
87	Ⓐ	Ⓑ	Ⓒ	Ⓓ
88	Ⓐ	Ⓑ	Ⓒ	Ⓓ
89	Ⓐ	Ⓑ	Ⓒ	Ⓓ
90	Ⓐ	Ⓑ	Ⓒ	Ⓓ
91	Ⓐ	Ⓑ	Ⓒ	Ⓓ
92	Ⓐ	Ⓑ	Ⓒ	Ⓓ
93	Ⓐ	Ⓑ	Ⓒ	Ⓓ
94	Ⓐ	Ⓑ	Ⓒ	Ⓓ
95	Ⓐ	Ⓑ	Ⓒ	Ⓓ
96	Ⓐ	Ⓑ	Ⓒ	Ⓓ
97	Ⓐ	Ⓑ	Ⓒ	Ⓓ
98	Ⓐ	Ⓑ	Ⓒ	Ⓓ
99	Ⓐ	Ⓑ	Ⓒ	Ⓓ
100	Ⓐ	Ⓑ	Ⓒ	Ⓓ

READING (PART V ~ VII)

NO.	ANSWER				NO.	ANSWER				NO.	ANSWER				NO.	ANSWER			
	A	B	C	D		A	B	C	D		A	B	C	D		A	B	C	D
101	Ⓐ	Ⓑ	Ⓒ	Ⓓ	121	Ⓐ	Ⓑ	Ⓒ	Ⓓ	141	Ⓐ	Ⓑ	Ⓒ	Ⓓ	161	Ⓐ	Ⓑ	Ⓒ	Ⓓ
102	Ⓐ	Ⓑ	Ⓒ	Ⓓ	122	Ⓐ	Ⓑ	Ⓒ	Ⓓ	142	Ⓐ	Ⓑ	Ⓒ	Ⓓ	162	Ⓐ	Ⓑ	Ⓒ	Ⓓ
103	Ⓐ	Ⓑ	Ⓒ	Ⓓ	123	Ⓐ	Ⓑ	Ⓒ	Ⓓ	143	Ⓐ	Ⓑ	Ⓒ	Ⓓ	163	Ⓐ	Ⓑ	Ⓒ	Ⓓ
104	Ⓐ	Ⓑ	Ⓒ	Ⓓ	124	Ⓐ	Ⓑ	Ⓒ	Ⓓ	144	Ⓐ	Ⓑ	Ⓒ	Ⓓ	164	Ⓐ	Ⓑ	Ⓒ	Ⓓ
105	Ⓐ	Ⓑ	Ⓒ	Ⓓ	125	Ⓐ	Ⓑ	Ⓒ	Ⓓ	145	Ⓐ	Ⓑ	Ⓒ	Ⓓ	165	Ⓐ	Ⓑ	Ⓒ	Ⓓ
106	Ⓐ	Ⓑ	Ⓒ	Ⓓ	126	Ⓐ	Ⓑ	Ⓒ	Ⓓ	146	Ⓐ	Ⓑ	Ⓒ	Ⓓ	166	Ⓐ	Ⓑ	Ⓒ	Ⓓ
107	Ⓐ	Ⓑ	Ⓒ	Ⓓ	127	Ⓐ	Ⓑ	Ⓒ	Ⓓ	147	Ⓐ	Ⓑ	Ⓒ	Ⓓ	167	Ⓐ	Ⓑ	Ⓒ	Ⓓ
108	Ⓐ	Ⓑ	Ⓒ	Ⓓ	128	Ⓐ	Ⓑ	Ⓒ	Ⓓ	148	Ⓐ	Ⓑ	Ⓒ	Ⓓ	168	Ⓐ	Ⓑ	Ⓒ	Ⓓ
109	Ⓐ	Ⓑ	Ⓒ	Ⓓ	129	Ⓐ	Ⓑ	Ⓒ	Ⓓ	149	Ⓐ	Ⓑ	Ⓒ	Ⓓ	169	Ⓐ	Ⓑ	Ⓒ	Ⓓ
110	Ⓐ	Ⓑ	Ⓒ	Ⓓ	130	Ⓐ	Ⓑ	Ⓒ	Ⓓ	150	Ⓐ	Ⓑ	Ⓒ	Ⓓ	170	Ⓐ	Ⓑ	Ⓒ	Ⓓ
111	Ⓐ	Ⓑ	Ⓒ	Ⓓ	131	Ⓐ	Ⓑ	Ⓒ	Ⓓ	151	Ⓐ	Ⓑ	Ⓒ	Ⓓ	171	Ⓐ	Ⓑ	Ⓒ	Ⓓ
112	Ⓐ	Ⓑ	Ⓒ	Ⓓ	132	Ⓐ	Ⓑ	Ⓒ	Ⓓ	152	Ⓐ	Ⓑ	Ⓒ	Ⓓ	172	Ⓐ	Ⓑ	Ⓒ	Ⓓ
113	Ⓐ	Ⓑ	Ⓒ	Ⓓ	133	Ⓐ	Ⓑ	Ⓒ	Ⓓ	153	Ⓐ	Ⓑ	Ⓒ	Ⓓ	173	Ⓐ	Ⓑ	Ⓒ	Ⓓ
114	Ⓐ	Ⓑ	Ⓒ	Ⓓ	134	Ⓐ	Ⓑ	Ⓒ	Ⓓ	154	Ⓐ	Ⓑ	Ⓒ	Ⓓ	174	Ⓐ	Ⓑ	Ⓒ	Ⓓ
115	Ⓐ	Ⓑ	Ⓒ	Ⓓ	135	Ⓐ	Ⓑ	Ⓒ	Ⓓ	155	Ⓐ	Ⓑ	Ⓒ	Ⓓ	175	Ⓐ	Ⓑ	Ⓒ	Ⓓ
116	Ⓐ	Ⓑ	Ⓒ	Ⓓ	136	Ⓐ	Ⓑ	Ⓒ	Ⓓ	156	Ⓐ	Ⓑ	Ⓒ	Ⓓ	176	Ⓐ	Ⓑ	Ⓒ	Ⓓ
117	Ⓐ	Ⓑ	Ⓒ	Ⓓ	137	Ⓐ	Ⓑ	Ⓒ	Ⓓ	157	Ⓐ	Ⓑ	Ⓒ	Ⓓ	177	Ⓐ	Ⓑ	Ⓒ	Ⓓ
118	Ⓐ	Ⓑ	Ⓒ	Ⓓ	138	Ⓐ	Ⓑ	Ⓒ	Ⓓ	158	Ⓐ	Ⓑ	Ⓒ	Ⓓ	178	Ⓐ	Ⓑ	Ⓒ	Ⓓ
119	Ⓐ	Ⓑ	Ⓒ	Ⓓ	139	Ⓐ	Ⓑ	Ⓒ	Ⓓ	159	Ⓐ	Ⓑ	Ⓒ	Ⓓ	179	Ⓐ	Ⓑ	Ⓒ	Ⓓ
120	Ⓐ	Ⓑ	Ⓒ	Ⓓ	140	Ⓐ	Ⓑ	Ⓒ	Ⓓ	160	Ⓐ	Ⓑ	Ⓒ	Ⓓ	180	Ⓐ	Ⓑ	Ⓒ	Ⓓ

NO.	ANSWER			
	A	B	C	D
181	Ⓐ	Ⓑ	Ⓒ	Ⓓ
182	Ⓐ	Ⓑ	Ⓒ	Ⓓ
183	Ⓐ	Ⓑ	Ⓒ	Ⓓ
184	Ⓐ	Ⓑ	Ⓒ	Ⓓ
185	Ⓐ	Ⓑ	Ⓒ	Ⓓ
186	Ⓐ	Ⓑ	Ⓒ	Ⓓ
187	Ⓐ	Ⓑ	Ⓒ	Ⓓ
188	Ⓐ	Ⓑ	Ⓒ	Ⓓ
189	Ⓐ	Ⓑ	Ⓒ	Ⓓ
190	Ⓐ	Ⓑ	Ⓒ	Ⓓ
191	Ⓐ	Ⓑ	Ⓒ	Ⓓ
192	Ⓐ	Ⓑ	Ⓒ	Ⓓ
193	Ⓐ	Ⓑ	Ⓒ	Ⓓ
194	Ⓐ	Ⓑ	Ⓒ	Ⓓ
195	Ⓐ	Ⓑ	Ⓒ	Ⓓ
196	Ⓐ	Ⓑ	Ⓒ	Ⓓ
197	Ⓐ	Ⓑ	Ⓒ	Ⓓ
198	Ⓐ	Ⓑ	Ⓒ	Ⓓ
199	Ⓐ	Ⓑ	Ⓒ	Ⓓ
200	Ⓐ	Ⓑ	Ⓒ	Ⓓ

ANSWER SHEET

No.

수험번호
성 명 한글
영자

TEST 2

LISTENING (PART I ~ IV)

NO.	ANSWER	NO.	ANSWER	NO.	ANSWER	NO.	ANSWER	NO.	ANSWER
	A B C D		A B C D		A B C D		A B C D		A B C D
1	Ⓐ Ⓑ Ⓒ Ⓓ	21	Ⓐ Ⓑ Ⓒ Ⓓ	41	Ⓐ Ⓑ Ⓒ Ⓓ	61	Ⓐ Ⓑ Ⓒ Ⓓ	81	Ⓐ Ⓑ Ⓒ Ⓓ
2	Ⓐ Ⓑ Ⓒ Ⓓ	22	Ⓐ Ⓑ Ⓒ Ⓓ	42	Ⓐ Ⓑ Ⓒ Ⓓ	62	Ⓐ Ⓑ Ⓒ Ⓓ	82	Ⓐ Ⓑ Ⓒ Ⓓ
3	Ⓐ Ⓑ Ⓒ Ⓓ	23	Ⓐ Ⓑ Ⓒ Ⓓ	43	Ⓐ Ⓑ Ⓒ Ⓓ	63	Ⓐ Ⓑ Ⓒ Ⓓ	83	Ⓐ Ⓑ Ⓒ Ⓓ
4	Ⓐ Ⓑ Ⓒ Ⓓ	24	Ⓐ Ⓑ Ⓒ Ⓓ	44	Ⓐ Ⓑ Ⓒ Ⓓ	64	Ⓐ Ⓑ Ⓒ Ⓓ	84	Ⓐ Ⓑ Ⓒ Ⓓ
5	Ⓐ Ⓑ Ⓒ Ⓓ	25	Ⓐ Ⓑ Ⓒ Ⓓ	45	Ⓐ Ⓑ Ⓒ Ⓓ	65	Ⓐ Ⓑ Ⓒ Ⓓ	85	Ⓐ Ⓑ Ⓒ Ⓓ
6	Ⓐ Ⓑ Ⓒ Ⓓ	26	Ⓐ Ⓑ Ⓒ Ⓓ	46	Ⓐ Ⓑ Ⓒ Ⓓ	66	Ⓐ Ⓑ Ⓒ Ⓓ	86	Ⓐ Ⓑ Ⓒ Ⓓ
7	Ⓐ Ⓑ Ⓒ Ⓓ	27	Ⓐ Ⓑ Ⓒ	47	Ⓐ Ⓑ Ⓒ Ⓓ	67	Ⓐ Ⓑ Ⓒ Ⓓ	87	Ⓐ Ⓑ Ⓒ Ⓓ
8	Ⓐ Ⓑ Ⓒ Ⓓ	28	Ⓐ Ⓑ Ⓒ	48	Ⓐ Ⓑ Ⓒ Ⓓ	68	Ⓐ Ⓑ Ⓒ Ⓓ	88	Ⓐ Ⓑ Ⓒ Ⓓ
9	Ⓐ Ⓑ Ⓒ Ⓓ	29	Ⓐ Ⓑ Ⓒ	49	Ⓐ Ⓑ Ⓒ Ⓓ	69	Ⓐ Ⓑ Ⓒ Ⓓ	89	Ⓐ Ⓑ Ⓒ Ⓓ
10	Ⓐ Ⓑ Ⓒ Ⓓ	30	Ⓐ Ⓑ Ⓒ	50	Ⓐ Ⓑ Ⓒ Ⓓ	70	Ⓐ Ⓑ Ⓒ Ⓓ	90	Ⓐ Ⓑ Ⓒ Ⓓ
11	Ⓐ Ⓑ Ⓒ Ⓓ	31	Ⓐ Ⓑ Ⓒ	51	Ⓐ Ⓑ Ⓒ Ⓓ	71	Ⓐ Ⓑ Ⓒ Ⓓ	91	Ⓐ Ⓑ Ⓒ Ⓓ
12	Ⓐ Ⓑ Ⓒ Ⓓ	32	Ⓐ Ⓑ Ⓒ	52	Ⓐ Ⓑ Ⓒ Ⓓ	72	Ⓐ Ⓑ Ⓒ Ⓓ	92	Ⓐ Ⓑ Ⓒ Ⓓ
13	Ⓐ Ⓑ Ⓒ Ⓓ	33	Ⓐ Ⓑ Ⓒ	53	Ⓐ Ⓑ Ⓒ Ⓓ	73	Ⓐ Ⓑ Ⓒ Ⓓ	93	Ⓐ Ⓑ Ⓒ Ⓓ
14	Ⓐ Ⓑ Ⓒ Ⓓ	34	Ⓐ Ⓑ Ⓒ	54	Ⓐ Ⓑ Ⓒ Ⓓ	74	Ⓐ Ⓑ Ⓒ Ⓓ	94	Ⓐ Ⓑ Ⓒ Ⓓ
15	Ⓐ Ⓑ Ⓒ Ⓓ	35	Ⓐ Ⓑ Ⓒ	55	Ⓐ Ⓑ Ⓒ Ⓓ	75	Ⓐ Ⓑ Ⓒ Ⓓ	95	Ⓐ Ⓑ Ⓒ Ⓓ
16	Ⓐ Ⓑ Ⓒ Ⓓ	36	Ⓐ Ⓑ Ⓒ	56	Ⓐ Ⓑ Ⓒ Ⓓ	76	Ⓐ Ⓑ Ⓒ Ⓓ	96	Ⓐ Ⓑ Ⓒ Ⓓ
17	Ⓐ Ⓑ Ⓒ Ⓓ	37	Ⓐ Ⓑ Ⓒ	57	Ⓐ Ⓑ Ⓒ Ⓓ	77	Ⓐ Ⓑ Ⓒ Ⓓ	97	Ⓐ Ⓑ Ⓒ Ⓓ
18	Ⓐ Ⓑ Ⓒ Ⓓ	38	Ⓐ Ⓑ Ⓒ	58	Ⓐ Ⓑ Ⓒ Ⓓ	78	Ⓐ Ⓑ Ⓒ Ⓓ	98	Ⓐ Ⓑ Ⓒ Ⓓ
19	Ⓐ Ⓑ Ⓒ Ⓓ	39	Ⓐ Ⓑ Ⓒ	59	Ⓐ Ⓑ Ⓒ Ⓓ	79	Ⓐ Ⓑ Ⓒ Ⓓ	99	Ⓐ Ⓑ Ⓒ Ⓓ
20	Ⓐ Ⓑ Ⓒ Ⓓ	40	Ⓐ Ⓑ Ⓒ	60	Ⓐ Ⓑ Ⓒ Ⓓ	80	Ⓐ Ⓑ Ⓒ Ⓓ	100	Ⓐ Ⓑ Ⓒ Ⓓ

READING (PART V ~ VII)

NO.	ANSWER	NO.	ANSWER	NO.	ANSWER	NO.	ANSWER	NO.	ANSWER
	A B C D		A B C D		A B C D		A B C D		A B C D
101	Ⓐ Ⓑ Ⓒ Ⓓ	121	Ⓐ Ⓑ Ⓒ Ⓓ	141	Ⓐ Ⓑ Ⓒ Ⓓ	161	Ⓐ Ⓑ Ⓒ Ⓓ	181	Ⓐ Ⓑ Ⓒ Ⓓ
102	Ⓐ Ⓑ Ⓒ Ⓓ	122	Ⓐ Ⓑ Ⓒ Ⓓ	142	Ⓐ Ⓑ Ⓒ Ⓓ	162	Ⓐ Ⓑ Ⓒ Ⓓ	182	Ⓐ Ⓑ Ⓒ Ⓓ
103	Ⓐ Ⓑ Ⓒ Ⓓ	123	Ⓐ Ⓑ Ⓒ Ⓓ	143	Ⓐ Ⓑ Ⓒ Ⓓ	163	Ⓐ Ⓑ Ⓒ Ⓓ	183	Ⓐ Ⓑ Ⓒ Ⓓ
104	Ⓐ Ⓑ Ⓒ Ⓓ	124	Ⓐ Ⓑ Ⓒ Ⓓ	144	Ⓐ Ⓑ Ⓒ Ⓓ	164	Ⓐ Ⓑ Ⓒ Ⓓ	184	Ⓐ Ⓑ Ⓒ Ⓓ
105	Ⓐ Ⓑ Ⓒ Ⓓ	125	Ⓐ Ⓑ Ⓒ Ⓓ	145	Ⓐ Ⓑ Ⓒ Ⓓ	165	Ⓐ Ⓑ Ⓒ Ⓓ	185	Ⓐ Ⓑ Ⓒ Ⓓ
106	Ⓐ Ⓑ Ⓒ Ⓓ	126	Ⓐ Ⓑ Ⓒ Ⓓ	146	Ⓐ Ⓑ Ⓒ Ⓓ	166	Ⓐ Ⓑ Ⓒ Ⓓ	186	Ⓐ Ⓑ Ⓒ Ⓓ
107	Ⓐ Ⓑ Ⓒ Ⓓ	127	Ⓐ Ⓑ Ⓒ Ⓓ	147	Ⓐ Ⓑ Ⓒ Ⓓ	167	Ⓐ Ⓑ Ⓒ Ⓓ	187	Ⓐ Ⓑ Ⓒ Ⓓ
108	Ⓐ Ⓑ Ⓒ Ⓓ	128	Ⓐ Ⓑ Ⓒ Ⓓ	148	Ⓐ Ⓑ Ⓒ Ⓓ	168	Ⓐ Ⓑ Ⓒ Ⓓ	188	Ⓐ Ⓑ Ⓒ Ⓓ
109	Ⓐ Ⓑ Ⓒ Ⓓ	129	Ⓐ Ⓑ Ⓒ Ⓓ	149	Ⓐ Ⓑ Ⓒ Ⓓ	169	Ⓐ Ⓑ Ⓒ Ⓓ	189	Ⓐ Ⓑ Ⓒ Ⓓ
110	Ⓐ Ⓑ Ⓒ Ⓓ	130	Ⓐ Ⓑ Ⓒ Ⓓ	150	Ⓐ Ⓑ Ⓒ Ⓓ	170	Ⓐ Ⓑ Ⓒ Ⓓ	190	Ⓐ Ⓑ Ⓒ Ⓓ
111	Ⓐ Ⓑ Ⓒ Ⓓ	131	Ⓐ Ⓑ Ⓒ Ⓓ	151	Ⓐ Ⓑ Ⓒ Ⓓ	171	Ⓐ Ⓑ Ⓒ Ⓓ	191	Ⓐ Ⓑ Ⓒ Ⓓ
112	Ⓐ Ⓑ Ⓒ Ⓓ	132	Ⓐ Ⓑ Ⓒ Ⓓ	152	Ⓐ Ⓑ Ⓒ Ⓓ	172	Ⓐ Ⓑ Ⓒ Ⓓ	192	Ⓐ Ⓑ Ⓒ Ⓓ
113	Ⓐ Ⓑ Ⓒ Ⓓ	133	Ⓐ Ⓑ Ⓒ Ⓓ	153	Ⓐ Ⓑ Ⓒ Ⓓ	173	Ⓐ Ⓑ Ⓒ Ⓓ	193	Ⓐ Ⓑ Ⓒ Ⓓ
114	Ⓐ Ⓑ Ⓒ Ⓓ	134	Ⓐ Ⓑ Ⓒ Ⓓ	154	Ⓐ Ⓑ Ⓒ Ⓓ	174	Ⓐ Ⓑ Ⓒ Ⓓ	194	Ⓐ Ⓑ Ⓒ Ⓓ
115	Ⓐ Ⓑ Ⓒ Ⓓ	135	Ⓐ Ⓑ Ⓒ Ⓓ	155	Ⓐ Ⓑ Ⓒ Ⓓ	175	Ⓐ Ⓑ Ⓒ Ⓓ	195	Ⓐ Ⓑ Ⓒ Ⓓ
116	Ⓐ Ⓑ Ⓒ Ⓓ	136	Ⓐ Ⓑ Ⓒ Ⓓ	156	Ⓐ Ⓑ Ⓒ Ⓓ	176	Ⓐ Ⓑ Ⓒ Ⓓ	196	Ⓐ Ⓑ Ⓒ Ⓓ
117	Ⓐ Ⓑ Ⓒ Ⓓ	137	Ⓐ Ⓑ Ⓒ Ⓓ	157	Ⓐ Ⓑ Ⓒ Ⓓ	177	Ⓐ Ⓑ Ⓒ Ⓓ	197	Ⓐ Ⓑ Ⓒ Ⓓ
118	Ⓐ Ⓑ Ⓒ Ⓓ	138	Ⓐ Ⓑ Ⓒ Ⓓ	158	Ⓐ Ⓑ Ⓒ Ⓓ	178	Ⓐ Ⓑ Ⓒ Ⓓ	198	Ⓐ Ⓑ Ⓒ Ⓓ
119	Ⓐ Ⓑ Ⓒ Ⓓ	139	Ⓐ Ⓑ Ⓒ Ⓓ	159	Ⓐ Ⓑ Ⓒ Ⓓ	179	Ⓐ Ⓑ Ⓒ Ⓓ	199	Ⓐ Ⓑ Ⓒ Ⓓ
120	Ⓐ Ⓑ Ⓒ Ⓓ	140	Ⓐ Ⓑ Ⓒ Ⓓ	160	Ⓐ Ⓑ Ⓒ Ⓓ	180	Ⓐ Ⓑ Ⓒ Ⓓ	200	Ⓐ Ⓑ Ⓒ Ⓓ

books. english. co. kr

ANSWER SHEET

No.

수험번호
성 명 | 한글
     | 영자

TEST 3

LISTENING (PART I ~ IV)

NO.	ANSWER	NO.	ANSWER	NO.	ANSWER	NO.	ANSWER	NO.	ANSWER
	A B C D		A B C D		A B C D		A B C D		A B C D
1	Ⓐ Ⓑ Ⓒ Ⓓ	21	Ⓐ Ⓑ Ⓒ	41	Ⓐ Ⓑ Ⓒ Ⓓ	61	Ⓐ Ⓑ Ⓒ Ⓓ	81	Ⓐ Ⓑ Ⓒ Ⓓ
2	Ⓐ Ⓑ Ⓒ Ⓓ	22	Ⓐ Ⓑ Ⓒ	42	Ⓐ Ⓑ Ⓒ Ⓓ	62	Ⓐ Ⓑ Ⓒ Ⓓ	82	Ⓐ Ⓑ Ⓒ Ⓓ
3	Ⓐ Ⓑ Ⓒ Ⓓ	23	Ⓐ Ⓑ Ⓒ	43	Ⓐ Ⓑ Ⓒ Ⓓ	63	Ⓐ Ⓑ Ⓒ Ⓓ	83	Ⓐ Ⓑ Ⓒ Ⓓ
4	Ⓐ Ⓑ Ⓒ Ⓓ	24	Ⓐ Ⓑ Ⓒ	44	Ⓐ Ⓑ Ⓒ Ⓓ	64	Ⓐ Ⓑ Ⓒ Ⓓ	84	Ⓐ Ⓑ Ⓒ Ⓓ
5	Ⓐ Ⓑ Ⓒ Ⓓ	25	Ⓐ Ⓑ Ⓒ	45	Ⓐ Ⓑ Ⓒ Ⓓ	65	Ⓐ Ⓑ Ⓒ Ⓓ	85	Ⓐ Ⓑ Ⓒ Ⓓ
6	Ⓐ Ⓑ Ⓒ Ⓓ	26	Ⓐ Ⓑ Ⓒ	46	Ⓐ Ⓑ Ⓒ Ⓓ	66	Ⓐ Ⓑ Ⓒ Ⓓ	86	Ⓐ Ⓑ Ⓒ Ⓓ
7	Ⓐ Ⓑ Ⓒ	27	Ⓐ Ⓑ Ⓒ	47	Ⓐ Ⓑ Ⓒ Ⓓ	67	Ⓐ Ⓑ Ⓒ Ⓓ	87	Ⓐ Ⓑ Ⓒ Ⓓ
8	Ⓐ Ⓑ Ⓒ	28	Ⓐ Ⓑ Ⓒ	48	Ⓐ Ⓑ Ⓒ Ⓓ	68	Ⓐ Ⓑ Ⓒ Ⓓ	88	Ⓐ Ⓑ Ⓒ Ⓓ
9	Ⓐ Ⓑ Ⓒ	29	Ⓐ Ⓑ Ⓒ	49	Ⓐ Ⓑ Ⓒ Ⓓ	69	Ⓐ Ⓑ Ⓒ Ⓓ	89	Ⓐ Ⓑ Ⓒ Ⓓ
10	Ⓐ Ⓑ Ⓒ	30	Ⓐ Ⓑ Ⓒ	50	Ⓐ Ⓑ Ⓒ Ⓓ	70	Ⓐ Ⓑ Ⓒ Ⓓ	90	Ⓐ Ⓑ Ⓒ Ⓓ
11	Ⓐ Ⓑ Ⓒ	31	Ⓐ Ⓑ Ⓒ	51	Ⓐ Ⓑ Ⓒ Ⓓ	71	Ⓐ Ⓑ Ⓒ Ⓓ	91	Ⓐ Ⓑ Ⓒ Ⓓ
12	Ⓐ Ⓑ Ⓒ	32	Ⓐ Ⓑ Ⓒ	52	Ⓐ Ⓑ Ⓒ Ⓓ	72	Ⓐ Ⓑ Ⓒ Ⓓ	92	Ⓐ Ⓑ Ⓒ Ⓓ
13	Ⓐ Ⓑ Ⓒ	33	Ⓐ Ⓑ Ⓒ	53	Ⓐ Ⓑ Ⓒ Ⓓ	73	Ⓐ Ⓑ Ⓒ Ⓓ	93	Ⓐ Ⓑ Ⓒ Ⓓ
14	Ⓐ Ⓑ Ⓒ	34	Ⓐ Ⓑ Ⓒ	54	Ⓐ Ⓑ Ⓒ Ⓓ	74	Ⓐ Ⓑ Ⓒ Ⓓ	94	Ⓐ Ⓑ Ⓒ Ⓓ
15	Ⓐ Ⓑ Ⓒ	35	Ⓐ Ⓑ Ⓒ	55	Ⓐ Ⓑ Ⓒ Ⓓ	75	Ⓐ Ⓑ Ⓒ Ⓓ	95	Ⓐ Ⓑ Ⓒ Ⓓ
16	Ⓐ Ⓑ Ⓒ	36	Ⓐ Ⓑ Ⓒ	56	Ⓐ Ⓑ Ⓒ Ⓓ	76	Ⓐ Ⓑ Ⓒ Ⓓ	96	Ⓐ Ⓑ Ⓒ Ⓓ
17	Ⓐ Ⓑ Ⓒ	37	Ⓐ Ⓑ Ⓒ	57	Ⓐ Ⓑ Ⓒ Ⓓ	77	Ⓐ Ⓑ Ⓒ Ⓓ	97	Ⓐ Ⓑ Ⓒ Ⓓ
18	Ⓐ Ⓑ Ⓒ	38	Ⓐ Ⓑ Ⓒ	58	Ⓐ Ⓑ Ⓒ Ⓓ	78	Ⓐ Ⓑ Ⓒ Ⓓ	98	Ⓐ Ⓑ Ⓒ Ⓓ
19	Ⓐ Ⓑ Ⓒ	39	Ⓐ Ⓑ Ⓒ	59	Ⓐ Ⓑ Ⓒ Ⓓ	79	Ⓐ Ⓑ Ⓒ Ⓓ	99	Ⓐ Ⓑ Ⓒ Ⓓ
20	Ⓐ Ⓑ Ⓒ	40	Ⓐ Ⓑ Ⓒ	60	Ⓐ Ⓑ Ⓒ Ⓓ	80	Ⓐ Ⓑ Ⓒ Ⓓ	100	Ⓐ Ⓑ Ⓒ Ⓓ

READING (PART V ~ VII)

NO.	ANSWER	NO.	ANSWER	NO.	ANSWER	NO.	ANSWER	NO.	ANSWER
	A B C D		A B C D		A B C D		A B C D		A B C D
101	Ⓐ Ⓑ Ⓒ Ⓓ	121	Ⓐ Ⓑ Ⓒ Ⓓ	141	Ⓐ Ⓑ Ⓒ Ⓓ	161	Ⓐ Ⓑ Ⓒ Ⓓ	181	Ⓐ Ⓑ Ⓒ Ⓓ
102	Ⓐ Ⓑ Ⓒ Ⓓ	122	Ⓐ Ⓑ Ⓒ Ⓓ	142	Ⓐ Ⓑ Ⓒ Ⓓ	162	Ⓐ Ⓑ Ⓒ Ⓓ	182	Ⓐ Ⓑ Ⓒ Ⓓ
103	Ⓐ Ⓑ Ⓒ Ⓓ	123	Ⓐ Ⓑ Ⓒ Ⓓ	143	Ⓐ Ⓑ Ⓒ Ⓓ	163	Ⓐ Ⓑ Ⓒ Ⓓ	183	Ⓐ Ⓑ Ⓒ Ⓓ
104	Ⓐ Ⓑ Ⓒ Ⓓ	124	Ⓐ Ⓑ Ⓒ Ⓓ	144	Ⓐ Ⓑ Ⓒ Ⓓ	164	Ⓐ Ⓑ Ⓒ Ⓓ	184	Ⓐ Ⓑ Ⓒ Ⓓ
105	Ⓐ Ⓑ Ⓒ Ⓓ	125	Ⓐ Ⓑ Ⓒ Ⓓ	145	Ⓐ Ⓑ Ⓒ Ⓓ	165	Ⓐ Ⓑ Ⓒ Ⓓ	185	Ⓐ Ⓑ Ⓒ Ⓓ
106	Ⓐ Ⓑ Ⓒ Ⓓ	126	Ⓐ Ⓑ Ⓒ Ⓓ	146	Ⓐ Ⓑ Ⓒ Ⓓ	166	Ⓐ Ⓑ Ⓒ Ⓓ	186	Ⓐ Ⓑ Ⓒ Ⓓ
107	Ⓐ Ⓑ Ⓒ Ⓓ	127	Ⓐ Ⓑ Ⓒ Ⓓ	147	Ⓐ Ⓑ Ⓒ Ⓓ	167	Ⓐ Ⓑ Ⓒ Ⓓ	187	Ⓐ Ⓑ Ⓒ Ⓓ
108	Ⓐ Ⓑ Ⓒ Ⓓ	128	Ⓐ Ⓑ Ⓒ Ⓓ	148	Ⓐ Ⓑ Ⓒ Ⓓ	168	Ⓐ Ⓑ Ⓒ Ⓓ	188	Ⓐ Ⓑ Ⓒ Ⓓ
109	Ⓐ Ⓑ Ⓒ Ⓓ	129	Ⓐ Ⓑ Ⓒ Ⓓ	149	Ⓐ Ⓑ Ⓒ Ⓓ	169	Ⓐ Ⓑ Ⓒ Ⓓ	189	Ⓐ Ⓑ Ⓒ Ⓓ
110	Ⓐ Ⓑ Ⓒ Ⓓ	130	Ⓐ Ⓑ Ⓒ Ⓓ	150	Ⓐ Ⓑ Ⓒ Ⓓ	170	Ⓐ Ⓑ Ⓒ Ⓓ	190	Ⓐ Ⓑ Ⓒ Ⓓ
111	Ⓐ Ⓑ Ⓒ Ⓓ	131	Ⓐ Ⓑ Ⓒ Ⓓ	151	Ⓐ Ⓑ Ⓒ Ⓓ	171	Ⓐ Ⓑ Ⓒ Ⓓ	191	Ⓐ Ⓑ Ⓒ Ⓓ
112	Ⓐ Ⓑ Ⓒ Ⓓ	132	Ⓐ Ⓑ Ⓒ Ⓓ	152	Ⓐ Ⓑ Ⓒ Ⓓ	172	Ⓐ Ⓑ Ⓒ Ⓓ	192	Ⓐ Ⓑ Ⓒ Ⓓ
113	Ⓐ Ⓑ Ⓒ Ⓓ	133	Ⓐ Ⓑ Ⓒ Ⓓ	153	Ⓐ Ⓑ Ⓒ Ⓓ	173	Ⓐ Ⓑ Ⓒ Ⓓ	193	Ⓐ Ⓑ Ⓒ Ⓓ
114	Ⓐ Ⓑ Ⓒ Ⓓ	134	Ⓐ Ⓑ Ⓒ Ⓓ	154	Ⓐ Ⓑ Ⓒ Ⓓ	174	Ⓐ Ⓑ Ⓒ Ⓓ	194	Ⓐ Ⓑ Ⓒ Ⓓ
115	Ⓐ Ⓑ Ⓒ Ⓓ	135	Ⓐ Ⓑ Ⓒ Ⓓ	155	Ⓐ Ⓑ Ⓒ Ⓓ	175	Ⓐ Ⓑ Ⓒ Ⓓ	195	Ⓐ Ⓑ Ⓒ Ⓓ
116	Ⓐ Ⓑ Ⓒ Ⓓ	136	Ⓐ Ⓑ Ⓒ Ⓓ	156	Ⓐ Ⓑ Ⓒ Ⓓ	176	Ⓐ Ⓑ Ⓒ Ⓓ	196	Ⓐ Ⓑ Ⓒ Ⓓ
117	Ⓐ Ⓑ Ⓒ Ⓓ	137	Ⓐ Ⓑ Ⓒ Ⓓ	157	Ⓐ Ⓑ Ⓒ Ⓓ	177	Ⓐ Ⓑ Ⓒ Ⓓ	197	Ⓐ Ⓑ Ⓒ Ⓓ
118	Ⓐ Ⓑ Ⓒ Ⓓ	138	Ⓐ Ⓑ Ⓒ Ⓓ	158	Ⓐ Ⓑ Ⓒ Ⓓ	178	Ⓐ Ⓑ Ⓒ Ⓓ	198	Ⓐ Ⓑ Ⓒ Ⓓ
119	Ⓐ Ⓑ Ⓒ Ⓓ	139	Ⓐ Ⓑ Ⓒ Ⓓ	159	Ⓐ Ⓑ Ⓒ Ⓓ	179	Ⓐ Ⓑ Ⓒ Ⓓ	199	Ⓐ Ⓑ Ⓒ Ⓓ
120	Ⓐ Ⓑ Ⓒ Ⓓ	140	Ⓐ Ⓑ Ⓒ Ⓓ	160	Ⓐ Ⓑ Ⓒ Ⓓ	180	Ⓐ Ⓑ Ⓒ Ⓓ	200	Ⓐ Ⓑ Ⓒ Ⓓ

books. english. co. kr

ANSWER SHEET

No.

수험번호							
성명	한글						
	영자						

TEST 4

LISTENING (PART I ~ IV)

NO.	ANSWER				NO.	ANSWER				NC.	ANSWER				NO.	ANSWER			
	A	B	C	D		A	B	C	D		A	B	C	D		A	B	C	D
1	Ⓐ	Ⓑ	Ⓒ		21	Ⓐ	Ⓑ	Ⓒ	Ⓓ	41	Ⓐ	Ⓑ	Ⓒ	Ⓓ	61	Ⓐ	Ⓑ	Ⓒ	Ⓓ
2	Ⓐ	Ⓑ	Ⓒ		22	Ⓐ	Ⓑ	Ⓒ	Ⓓ	42	Ⓐ	Ⓑ	Ⓒ	Ⓓ	62	Ⓐ	Ⓑ	Ⓒ	Ⓓ
3	Ⓐ	Ⓑ	Ⓒ		23	Ⓐ	Ⓑ	Ⓒ	Ⓓ	43	Ⓐ	Ⓑ	Ⓒ	Ⓓ	63	Ⓐ	Ⓑ	Ⓒ	Ⓓ
4	Ⓐ	Ⓑ	Ⓒ		24	Ⓐ	Ⓑ	Ⓒ	Ⓓ	44	Ⓐ	Ⓑ	Ⓒ	Ⓓ	64	Ⓐ	Ⓑ	Ⓒ	Ⓓ
5	Ⓐ	Ⓑ	Ⓒ		25	Ⓐ	Ⓑ	Ⓒ	Ⓓ	45	Ⓐ	Ⓑ	Ⓒ	Ⓓ	65	Ⓐ	Ⓑ	Ⓒ	Ⓓ
6	Ⓐ	Ⓑ	Ⓒ		26	Ⓐ	Ⓑ	Ⓒ	Ⓓ	46	Ⓐ	Ⓑ	Ⓒ	Ⓓ	66	Ⓐ	Ⓑ	Ⓒ	Ⓓ
7	Ⓐ	Ⓑ	Ⓒ		27	Ⓐ	Ⓑ	Ⓒ		47	Ⓐ	Ⓑ	Ⓒ	Ⓓ	67	Ⓐ	Ⓑ	Ⓒ	Ⓓ
8	Ⓐ	Ⓑ	Ⓒ		28	Ⓐ	Ⓑ	Ⓒ		48	Ⓐ	Ⓑ	Ⓒ	Ⓓ	68	Ⓐ	Ⓑ	Ⓒ	Ⓓ
9	Ⓐ	Ⓑ	Ⓒ		29	Ⓐ	Ⓑ	Ⓒ		49	Ⓐ	Ⓑ	Ⓒ	Ⓓ	69	Ⓐ	Ⓑ	Ⓒ	Ⓓ
10	Ⓐ	Ⓑ	Ⓒ		30	Ⓐ	Ⓑ	Ⓒ		50	Ⓐ	Ⓑ	Ⓒ	Ⓓ	70	Ⓐ	Ⓑ	Ⓒ	Ⓓ
11	Ⓐ	Ⓑ	Ⓒ		31	Ⓐ	Ⓑ	Ⓒ		51	Ⓐ	Ⓑ	Ⓒ	Ⓓ	71	Ⓐ	Ⓑ	Ⓒ	Ⓓ
12	Ⓐ	Ⓑ	Ⓒ		32	Ⓐ	Ⓑ	Ⓒ		52	Ⓐ	Ⓑ	Ⓒ	Ⓓ	72	Ⓐ	Ⓑ	Ⓒ	Ⓓ
13	Ⓐ	Ⓑ	Ⓒ		33	Ⓐ	Ⓑ	Ⓒ		53	Ⓐ	Ⓑ	Ⓒ	Ⓓ	73	Ⓐ	Ⓑ	Ⓒ	Ⓓ
14	Ⓐ	Ⓑ	Ⓒ		34	Ⓐ	Ⓑ	Ⓒ		54	Ⓐ	Ⓑ	Ⓒ	Ⓓ	74	Ⓐ	Ⓑ	Ⓒ	Ⓓ
15	Ⓐ	Ⓑ	Ⓒ		35	Ⓐ	Ⓑ	Ⓒ		55	Ⓐ	Ⓑ	Ⓒ	Ⓓ	75	Ⓐ	Ⓑ	Ⓒ	Ⓓ
16	Ⓐ	Ⓑ	Ⓒ		36	Ⓐ	Ⓑ	Ⓒ		56	Ⓐ	Ⓑ	Ⓒ	Ⓓ	76	Ⓐ	Ⓑ	Ⓒ	Ⓓ
17	Ⓐ	Ⓑ	Ⓒ		37	Ⓐ	Ⓑ	Ⓒ		57	Ⓐ	Ⓑ	Ⓒ	Ⓓ	77	Ⓐ	Ⓑ	Ⓒ	Ⓓ
18	Ⓐ	Ⓑ	Ⓒ		38	Ⓐ	Ⓑ	Ⓒ		58	Ⓐ	Ⓑ	Ⓒ	Ⓓ	78	Ⓐ	Ⓑ	Ⓒ	Ⓓ
19	Ⓐ	Ⓑ	Ⓒ		39	Ⓐ	Ⓑ	Ⓒ		59	Ⓐ	Ⓑ	Ⓒ	Ⓓ	79	Ⓐ	Ⓑ	Ⓒ	Ⓓ
20	Ⓐ	Ⓑ	Ⓒ		40	Ⓐ	Ⓑ	Ⓒ		60	Ⓐ	Ⓑ	Ⓒ	Ⓓ	80	Ⓐ	Ⓑ	Ⓒ	Ⓓ

NO.	ANSWER			
	A	B	C	D
81	Ⓐ	Ⓑ	Ⓒ	Ⓓ
82	Ⓐ	Ⓑ	Ⓒ	Ⓓ
83	Ⓐ	Ⓑ	Ⓒ	Ⓓ
84	Ⓐ	Ⓑ	Ⓒ	Ⓓ
85	Ⓐ	Ⓑ	Ⓒ	Ⓓ
86	Ⓐ	Ⓑ	Ⓒ	Ⓓ
87	Ⓐ	Ⓑ	Ⓒ	Ⓓ
88	Ⓐ	Ⓑ	Ⓒ	Ⓓ
89	Ⓐ	Ⓑ	Ⓒ	Ⓓ
90	Ⓐ	Ⓑ	Ⓒ	Ⓓ
91	Ⓐ	Ⓑ	Ⓒ	Ⓓ
92	Ⓐ	Ⓑ	Ⓒ	Ⓓ
93	Ⓐ	Ⓑ	Ⓒ	Ⓓ
94	Ⓐ	Ⓑ	Ⓒ	Ⓓ
95	Ⓐ	Ⓑ	Ⓒ	Ⓓ
96	Ⓐ	Ⓑ	Ⓒ	Ⓓ
97	Ⓐ	Ⓑ	Ⓒ	Ⓓ
98	Ⓐ	Ⓑ	Ⓒ	Ⓓ
99	Ⓐ	Ⓑ	Ⓒ	Ⓓ
100	Ⓐ	Ⓑ	Ⓒ	Ⓓ

READING (PART V ~ VII)

NO.	ANSWER				NO.	ANSWER				NO.	ANSWER				NO.	ANSWER			
	A	B	C	D		A	B	C	D		A	B	C	D		A	B	C	D
101	Ⓐ	Ⓑ	Ⓒ	Ⓓ	121	Ⓐ	Ⓑ	Ⓒ	Ⓓ	141	Ⓐ	Ⓑ	Ⓒ	Ⓓ	161	Ⓐ	Ⓑ	Ⓒ	Ⓓ
102	Ⓐ	Ⓑ	Ⓒ	Ⓓ	122	Ⓐ	Ⓑ	Ⓒ	Ⓓ	142	Ⓐ	Ⓑ	Ⓒ	Ⓓ	162	Ⓐ	Ⓑ	Ⓒ	Ⓓ
103	Ⓐ	Ⓑ	Ⓒ	Ⓓ	123	Ⓐ	Ⓑ	Ⓒ	Ⓓ	143	Ⓐ	Ⓑ	Ⓒ	Ⓓ	163	Ⓐ	Ⓑ	Ⓒ	Ⓓ
104	Ⓐ	Ⓑ	Ⓒ	Ⓓ	124	Ⓐ	Ⓑ	Ⓒ	Ⓓ	144	Ⓐ	Ⓑ	Ⓒ	Ⓓ	164	Ⓐ	Ⓑ	Ⓒ	Ⓓ
105	Ⓐ	Ⓑ	Ⓒ	Ⓓ	125	Ⓐ	Ⓑ	Ⓒ	Ⓓ	145	Ⓐ	Ⓑ	Ⓒ	Ⓓ	165	Ⓐ	Ⓑ	Ⓒ	Ⓓ
106	Ⓐ	Ⓑ	Ⓒ	Ⓓ	126	Ⓐ	Ⓑ	Ⓒ	Ⓓ	146	Ⓐ	Ⓑ	Ⓒ	Ⓓ	166	Ⓐ	Ⓑ	Ⓒ	Ⓓ
107	Ⓐ	Ⓑ	Ⓒ	Ⓓ	127	Ⓐ	Ⓑ	Ⓒ	Ⓓ	147	Ⓐ	Ⓑ	Ⓒ	Ⓓ	167	Ⓐ	Ⓑ	Ⓒ	Ⓓ
108	Ⓐ	Ⓑ	Ⓒ	Ⓓ	128	Ⓐ	Ⓑ	Ⓒ	Ⓓ	148	Ⓐ	Ⓑ	Ⓒ	Ⓓ	168	Ⓐ	Ⓑ	Ⓒ	Ⓓ
109	Ⓐ	Ⓑ	Ⓒ	Ⓓ	129	Ⓐ	Ⓑ	Ⓒ	Ⓓ	149	Ⓐ	Ⓑ	Ⓒ	Ⓓ	169	Ⓐ	Ⓑ	Ⓒ	Ⓓ
110	Ⓐ	Ⓑ	Ⓒ	Ⓓ	130	Ⓐ	Ⓑ	Ⓒ	Ⓓ	150	Ⓐ	Ⓑ	Ⓒ	Ⓓ	170	Ⓐ	Ⓑ	Ⓒ	Ⓓ
111	Ⓐ	Ⓑ	Ⓒ	Ⓓ	131	Ⓐ	Ⓑ	Ⓒ	Ⓓ	151	Ⓐ	Ⓑ	Ⓒ	Ⓓ	171	Ⓐ	Ⓑ	Ⓒ	Ⓓ
112	Ⓐ	Ⓑ	Ⓒ	Ⓓ	132	Ⓐ	Ⓑ	Ⓒ	Ⓓ	152	Ⓐ	Ⓑ	Ⓒ	Ⓓ	172	Ⓐ	Ⓑ	Ⓒ	Ⓓ
113	Ⓐ	Ⓑ	Ⓒ	Ⓓ	133	Ⓐ	Ⓑ	Ⓒ	Ⓓ	153	Ⓐ	Ⓑ	Ⓒ	Ⓓ	173	Ⓐ	Ⓑ	Ⓒ	Ⓓ
114	Ⓐ	Ⓑ	Ⓒ	Ⓓ	134	Ⓐ	Ⓑ	Ⓒ	Ⓓ	154	Ⓐ	Ⓑ	Ⓒ	Ⓓ	174	Ⓐ	Ⓑ	Ⓒ	Ⓓ
115	Ⓐ	Ⓑ	Ⓒ	Ⓓ	135	Ⓐ	Ⓑ	Ⓒ	Ⓓ	155	Ⓐ	Ⓑ	Ⓒ	Ⓓ	175	Ⓐ	Ⓑ	Ⓒ	Ⓓ
116	Ⓐ	Ⓑ	Ⓒ	Ⓓ	136	Ⓐ	Ⓑ	Ⓒ	Ⓓ	156	Ⓐ	Ⓑ	Ⓒ	Ⓓ	176	Ⓐ	Ⓑ	Ⓒ	Ⓓ
117	Ⓐ	Ⓑ	Ⓒ	Ⓓ	137	Ⓐ	Ⓑ	Ⓒ	Ⓓ	157	Ⓐ	Ⓑ	Ⓒ	Ⓓ	177	Ⓐ	Ⓑ	Ⓒ	Ⓓ
118	Ⓐ	Ⓑ	Ⓒ	Ⓓ	138	Ⓐ	Ⓑ	Ⓒ	Ⓓ	158	Ⓐ	Ⓑ	Ⓒ	Ⓓ	178	Ⓐ	Ⓑ	Ⓒ	Ⓓ
119	Ⓐ	Ⓑ	Ⓒ	Ⓓ	139	Ⓐ	Ⓑ	Ⓒ	Ⓓ	159	Ⓐ	Ⓑ	Ⓒ	Ⓓ	179	Ⓐ	Ⓑ	Ⓒ	Ⓓ
120	Ⓐ	Ⓑ	Ⓒ	Ⓓ	140	Ⓐ	Ⓑ	Ⓒ	Ⓓ	160	Ⓐ	Ⓑ	Ⓒ	Ⓓ	180	Ⓐ	Ⓑ	Ⓒ	Ⓓ

NO.	ANSWER			
	A	B	C	D
181	Ⓐ	Ⓑ	Ⓒ	Ⓓ
182	Ⓐ	Ⓑ	Ⓒ	Ⓓ
183	Ⓐ	Ⓑ	Ⓒ	Ⓓ
184	Ⓐ	Ⓑ	Ⓒ	Ⓓ
185	Ⓐ	Ⓑ	Ⓒ	Ⓓ
186	Ⓐ	Ⓑ	Ⓒ	Ⓓ
187	Ⓐ	Ⓑ	Ⓒ	Ⓓ
188	Ⓐ	Ⓑ	Ⓒ	Ⓓ
189	Ⓐ	Ⓑ	Ⓒ	Ⓓ
190	Ⓐ	Ⓑ	Ⓒ	Ⓓ
191	Ⓐ	Ⓑ	Ⓒ	Ⓓ
192	Ⓐ	Ⓑ	Ⓒ	Ⓓ
193	Ⓐ	Ⓑ	Ⓒ	Ⓓ
194	Ⓐ	Ⓑ	Ⓒ	Ⓓ
195	Ⓐ	Ⓑ	Ⓒ	Ⓓ
196	Ⓐ	Ⓑ	Ⓒ	Ⓓ
197	Ⓐ	Ⓑ	Ⓒ	Ⓓ
198	Ⓐ	Ⓑ	Ⓒ	Ⓓ
199	Ⓐ	Ⓑ	Ⓒ	Ⓓ
200	Ⓐ	Ⓑ	Ⓒ	Ⓓ

ANSWER SHEET

No.

수험번호
성 명 한글
       영자

TEST 5

LISTENING (PART I ~ IV)

NO.	ANSWER				NO.	ANSWER				NO.	ANSWER				NO.	ANSWER			
	A	B	C	D		A	B	C	D		A	B	C	D		A	B	C	D
1	A	B	C	D	21	A	B	C		41	A	B	C	D	61	A	B	C	D	81	A	B	C	D
2	A	B	C	D	22	A	B	C		42	A	B	C	D	62	A	B	C	D	82	A	B	C	D
3	A	B	C	D	23	A	B	C		43	A	B	C	D	63	A	B	C	D	83	A	B	C	D
4	A	B	C	D	24	A	B	C		44	A	B	C	D	64	A	B	C	D	84	A	B	C	D
5	A	B	C	D	25	A	B	C		45	A	B	C	D	65	A	B	C	D	85	A	B	C	D
6	A	B	C	D	26	A	B	C		46	A	B	C	D	66	A	B	C	D	86	A	B	C	D
7	A	B	C		27	A	B	C		47	A	B	C	D	67	A	B	C	D	87	A	B	C	D
8	A	B	C		28	A	B	C		48	A	B	C	D	68	A	B	C	D	88	A	B	C	D
9	A	B	C		29	A	B	C		49	A	B	C	D	69	A	B	C	D	89	A	B	C	D
10	A	B	C		30	A	B	C		50	A	B	C	D	70	A	B	C	D	90	A	B	C	D
11	A	B	C		31	A	B	C		51	A	B	C	D	71	A	B	C	D	91	A	B	C	D
12	A	B	C		32	A	B	C	D	52	A	B	C	D	72	A	B	C	D	92	A	B	C	D
13	A	B	C		33	A	B	C	D	53	A	B	C	D	73	A	B	C	D	93	A	B	C	D
14	A	B	C		34	A	B	C	D	54	A	B	C	D	74	A	B	C	D	94	A	B	C	D
15	A	B	C		35	A	B	C	D	55	A	B	C	D	75	A	B	C	D	95	A	B	C	D
16	A	B	C		36	A	B	C	D	56	A	B	C	D	76	A	B	C	D	96	A	B	C	D
17	A	B	C		37	A	B	C	D	57	A	B	C	D	77	A	B	C	D	97	A	B	C	D
18	A	B	C		38	A	B	C	D	58	A	B	C	D	78	A	B	C	D	98	A	B	C	D
19	A	B	C		39	A	B	C	D	59	A	B	C	D	79	A	B	C	D	99	A	B	C	D
20	A	B	C		40	A	B	C	D	60	A	B	C	D	80	A	B	C	D	100	A	B	C	D

READING (PART V ~ VII)

NO.	ANSWER				NO.	ANSWER				NO.	ANSWER				NO.	ANSWER			
	A	B	C	D		A	B	C	D		A	B	C	D		A	B	C	D
101	A	B	C	D	121	A	B	C	D	141	A	B	C	D	161	A	B	C	D	181	A	B	C	D
102	A	B	C	D	122	A	B	C	D	142	A	B	C	D	162	A	B	C	D	182	A	B	C	D
103	A	B	C	D	123	A	B	C	D	143	A	B	C	D	163	A	B	C	D	183	A	B	C	D
104	A	B	C	D	124	A	B	C	D	144	A	B	C	D	164	A	B	C	D	184	A	B	C	D
105	A	B	C	D	125	A	B	C	D	145	A	B	C	D	165	A	B	C	D	185	A	B	C	D
106	A	B	C	D	126	A	B	C	D	146	A	B	C	D	166	A	B	C	D	186	A	B	C	D
107	A	B	C	D	127	A	B	C	D	147	A	B	C	D	167	A	B	C	D	187	A	B	C	D
108	A	B	C	D	128	A	B	C	D	148	A	B	C	D	168	A	B	C	D	188	A	B	C	D
109	A	B	C	D	129	A	B	C	D	149	A	B	C	D	169	A	B	C	D	189	A	B	C	D
110	A	B	C	D	130	A	B	C	D	150	A	B	C	D	170	A	B	C	D	190	A	B	C	D
111	A	B	C	D	131	A	B	C	D	151	A	B	C	D	171	A	B	C	D	191	A	B	C	D
112	A	B	C	D	132	A	B	C	D	152	A	B	C	D	172	A	B	C	D	192	A	B	C	D
113	A	B	C	D	133	A	B	C	D	153	A	B	C	D	173	A	B	C	D	193	A	B	C	D
114	A	B	C	D	134	A	B	C	D	154	A	B	C	D	174	A	B	C	D	194	A	B	C	D
115	A	B	C	D	135	A	B	C	D	155	A	B	C	D	175	A	B	C	D	195	A	B	C	D
116	A	B	C	D	136	A	B	C	D	156	A	B	C	D	176	A	B	C	D	196	A	B	C	D
117	A	B	C	D	137	A	B	C	D	157	A	B	C	D	177	A	B	C	D	197	A	B	C	D
118	A	B	C	D	138	A	B	C	D	158	A	B	C	D	178	A	B	C	D	198	A	B	C	D
119	A	B	C	D	139	A	B	C	D	159	A	B	C	D	179	A	B	C	D	199	A	B	C	D
120	A	B	C	D	140	A	B	C	D	160	A	B	C	D	180	A	B	C	D	200	A	B	C	D

books.english.co.kr

잉글리쉬앤 토익

실전 1000제

LC+RC

정답 및
해설

TEST 1

p.16

LISTENING TEST

01 (D)	02 (C)	03 (A)	04 (A)	05 (D)
06 (B)	07 (C)	08 (B)	09 (C)	10 (C)
11 (A)	12 (B)	13 (A)	14 (A)	15 (B)
16 (C)	17 (C)	18 (A)	19 (B)	20 (B)
21 (B)	22 (B)	23 (A)	24 (B)	25 (A)
26 (C)	27 (C)	28 (C)	29 (C)	30 (B)
31 (C)	32 (B)	33 (D)	34 (C)	35 (A)
36 (C)	37 (D)	38 (B)	39 (C)	40 (A)
41 (C)	42 (D)	43 (C)	44 (C)	45 (B)
46 (A)	47 (C)	48 (C)	49 (C)	50 (A)
51 (A)	52 (C)	53 (C)	54 (A)	55 (B)
56 (A)	57 (C)	58 (C)	59 (A)	60 (D)
61 (B)	62 (A)	63 (C)	64 (C)	65 (A)
66 (D)	67 (A)	68 (C)	69 (B)	70 (C)
71 (B)	72 (A)	73 (D)	74 (B)	75 (D)
76 (B)	77 (D)	78 (A)	79 (C)	80 (A)
81 (A)	82 (A)	83 (C)	84 (D)	85 (D)
86 (D)	87 (B)	88 (C)	89 (A)	90 (C)
91 (A)	92 (D)	93 (C)	94 (B)	95 (B)
96 (A)	97 (A)	98 (C)	99 (A)	100 (B)

READING TEST

101 (D)	102 (B)	103 (C)	104 (A)	105 (D)
106 (C)	107 (C)	108 (A)	109 (D)	110 (A)
111 (A)	112 (A)	113 (B)	114 (A)	115 (D)
116 (D)	117 (A)	118 (C)	119 (C)	120 (B)
121 (D)	122 (A)	123 (D)	124 (C)	125 (B)
126 (B)	127 (C)	128 (A)	129 (D)	130 (A)
131 (C)	132 (D)	133 (B)	134 (C)	135 (B)
136 (D)	137 (A)	138 (D)	139 (D)	140 (C)
141 (A)	142 (C)	143 (C)	144 (C)	145 (A)
146 (B)	147 (A)	148 (C)	149 (D)	150 (B)
151 (D)	152 (B)	153 (C)	154 (A)	155 (B)
156 (B)	157 (A)	158 (C)	159 (D)	160 (C)
161 (C)	162 (B)	163 (D)	164 (D)	165 (A)
166 (D)	167 (B)	168 (A)	169 (D)	170 (C)
171 (D)	172 (D)	173 (B)	174 (D)	175 (D)
176 (A)	177 (C)	178 (D)	179 (C)	180 (D)
181 (B)	182 (D)	183 (A)	184 (D)	185 (B)
186 (C)	187 (D)	188 (C)	189 (D)	190 (D)
191 (C)	192 (C)	193 (C)	194 (C)	195 (D)
196 (D)	197 (A)	198 (C)	199 (A)	200 (B)

PART • 1

1 인물(1인) 사진

(A) A man is installing a computer program.
(B) A man is carrying a backpack.
(C) A man is turning on the monitor.
(D) A man is sitting in front of the monitors.

(A) 남자가 컴퓨터 프로그램을 설치하고 있다.
(B) 남자가 배낭을 메고 있다.
(C) 남자가 모니터를 켜고 있다.
(D) 남자가 모니터 앞에 앉아 있다.

해설 남자가 모니터 앞에 앉아 있는 사진으로 (D)가 정답이다. (A)는 컴퓨터 프로그램을 설치하고 있지 않으므로 오답, (B)는 사진에 배낭이 보이지 않으므로 오답, (C)는 모니터가 켜져 있지만 남자가 모니터를 켜는 동작을 하고 있지 않아서 오답이다.

어휘 install 설치하다 backpack 배낭 turn on 켜다

2 인물(2인 이상) 사진

(A) They're sitting on a couch.
(B) They're focusing on the computer screen.
(C) They're examining some pictures.
(D) They're moving a table.

(A) 그들은 소파 위에 앉아 있다.
(B) 그들은 컴퓨터 화면에 집중하고 있다.
(C) 그들은 사진을 보고 있다.
(D) 그들은 탁자를 옮기고 있다.

해설 남자와 여자가 사진을 보고 있는 사진이므로 (C)가 정답이다. examine은 '보다'라는 뜻으로 자주 사용된다. (A)는 사람들이 소파가 아닌 바닥에 앉아 있어서 오답, (B)는 노트북 화면을 보고 있지 않아서 오답, (D)는 테이블이 보이지만 사람들이 옮기고 있지 않아서 오답이다.

어휘 couch 소파 focus on ~에 집중하다 examine 검사하다, 보다 move 옮기다

3 사물/풍경 사진

(A) There are potted plants in front of the door.
(B) The rug is being cleaned.
(C) A door has been left open.
(D) There are lights hanging from the ceiling.

(A) 문 앞에 화분들이 있다.
(B) 깔개가 세탁되고 있다.
(C) 문이 열려 있다.
(D) 천장에 조명들이 걸려 있다.

해설 문 앞에 화분들이 놓여 있는 사진이므로 (A)가 정답이다. (B)는 사진에 깔개가 없으므로 오답이다. 보이는 단어가 들린다고 해서 꼭 답이 되는 것은 아니므로 door가 들어간 (C)는 주의해야 한다. 사진에 조명은 천장이 아니라 벽에 매달려 있으므로 (D)는 오답이다.

어휘 potted plant 화분 rug 깔개 leave open 열려 있다
ceiling 천장

4 인물(2인 이상) 사진

(A) People are viewing some artworks.
(B) People are drawing pictures.
(C) People are painting the wall.
(D) People are negotiating the prices of paintings.

(A) 사람들이 예술 작품을 보고 있다.
(B) 사람들이 그림을 그리고 있다.
(C) 사람들이 벽에 페인트칠하고 있다.
(D) 사람들이 그림의 가격을 흥정하고 있다.

해설 사람들이 그림을 보고 있는 사진이므로 (A)가 정답이다. (B)는 그림을 그리는 모습이 보이지 않으므로 오답, (C)는 벽에 페인트칠하고 있는 모습이 아니므로 오답, (D)는 이 사진만으로 가격을 협상 중인 것을 알 수 없으므로 오답이다.

어휘 view 보다 artwork 예술작품 negotiate 협상하다

5 혼합 사진

(A) The woman is making a hotel reservation.
(B) Some books have been piled up on the counter.
(C) The woman is wiping the window frame.
(D) Some documents have been posted on the
    bulletin board.

(A) 여자가 호텔 예약을 하고 있다.
(B) 몇 권의 책이 카운터 위에 쌓여 있다.
(C) 여자가 창틀을 닦고 있다.
(D) 서류들이 게시판에 붙어 있다.

해설 사무실의 모습을 보여주는 사진으로, 여자 뒤 게시판에 메모들이 붙어 있으므로 (D)가 정답이다. 사진에 사람이 나와 있지만 정답은 사물에 초점을 맞추고 있음에 주의한다. (A)는 이 사진만으로 여자가 호텔 예약을 한다고 판단할 수 없으므로 오답, (B)는 책이 쌓여 있지 않으므로 오답, (C)는 창틀이 보이기는 하지만 닦고 있지 않아서 오답이다.

어휘 make a reservation (= reserve, book) 예약하다
be piled up 쌓여 있다 wipe 닦다 post 붙이다, 게재하다
bulletin board 게시판

6 사물/풍경 사진

(A) The bridge is under construction.
(B) The bridge overlooks the river.
(C) Some boats are tied up to a dock.
(D) Some boats are being built.

(A) 다리가 공사 중이다.
(B) 다리가 강을 내려다보고 있다.
(C) 몇 척의 배가 부두에 묶여 있다.
(D) 몇 척의 배가 건조되고 있다.

해설 다리가 강을 내려다보고 있으므로 (B)가 정답이다. (A) 다리는 보이지만 공사 중이 아니므로 오답, (C)와 (D)는 사진에 배가 보이지 않으므로 오답이다.

어휘 under construction 공사 중인 overlook 내려다보다
be tied up 묶이다 dock 부두

PART • 2

7 일반 의문문

Is the meeting room big enough for the seminar?
(A) I'm in the meeting room.
(B) She's one of the presenters.
(C) Only fifty people have enrolled.

세미나를 하기에 회의실이 충분히 큰가요?
(A) 저는 회의실에 있습니다.
(B) 그녀는 발표자들 중 한 명입니다.
(C) 50명만 등록했는데요.

해설 세미나를 하기에 회의실이 충분히 큰지 묻는 질문에 50명만 등록했다고 대답하며 '공간이 충분하다'는 것을 우회적으로 말하고 있는 (C)가 정답이다. (A)는 질문에 나온 meeting room을 반복한 함정이며, (B)는 질문에 등장하지 않는 She에 대해 말하고 있으므로 오답이다.

어휘 big enough 충분히 큰   presenter 발표자   enroll 등록하다

8 **요청 의문문**

Can you pass the scissors?
(A) They're sizable.
(B) Sure, here they are.
(C) A pair of scissors.

가위 좀 건네 주실래요?
(A) 그것들은 꽤 크네요.
(B) 네, 여기 있어요.
(C) 가위 하나요.

해설 가위를 달라는 요청에, 여기 있다고 대답하는 (B)가 정답이다. (A)는 질문의 scissors와 발음이 유사한 sizable을 이용한 오답이며, (C)는 scissors를 반복한 함정이다.

어휘 pass 건네다   scissors 가위   sizable 꽤 큰   a pair of 한 쌍의, 한 벌의

9 **Who 의문문**

Who's organizing the annual company picnic?
(A) It is held annually.
(B) Jessica missed it.
(C) I heard it was Carter.

누가 연례 회사 야유회를 준비하고 있죠?
(A) 그것은 매년 열려요.
(B) 제시카는 그것을 놓쳤어요.
(C) 카터라고 들었어요.

해설 누가 회사의 연례 야유회를 준비하고 있는지 묻는 질문에 카터라고 들었다고 대답한 (C)가 정답이다. (A)는 질문의 annual과 발음이 유사한 annually를 이용한 오답이고, (B)는 사람 이름으로 오답을 유도하는 함정이다.

어휘 organize 준비하다   annual 연례의   miss 놓치다

10 **제안/권유 의문문**

What if we moved these tables to make more space?
(A) On the table.
(B) It's very spacious.
(C) That sounds great.

공간을 더 만들기 위해 이 테이블들을 옮기면 어떨까요?
(A) 테이블 위에요.
(B) 그것은 매우 넓어요.
(C) 그거 좋네요.

해설 공간 확보를 위해 테이블을 옮기면 어떨지 묻는 질문에, 좋은 생각이라고 답하는 (C)가 정답이다. (A)는 질문에서 들렸던 table을 반복하여 오답을 유도하고 있으며, (B)는 질문의 space와 발음이 유사한 spacious를 이용한 오답이다.

어휘 what if ~하면 어떨까요?   move 옮기다   make space 공간을 만들다   spacious 공간이 넓은

11 **When 의문문**

When did you return home?
(A) The day before yesterday.
(B) You can return it within a week.
(C) It took three days.

언제 집에 돌아왔어요?
(A) 그저께요.
(B) 당신은 그것을 일주일 안에 반품할 수 있습니다.
(C) 3일 걸렸습니다.

해설 언제 돌아왔는지 묻는 질문에, 그저께라고 돌아온 시점을 대답한 (A)가 정답이다. (B)는 질문의 return을 사용하여 오답을 유도하고 있으며, (C)는 How long ~?에 대한 대답이므로 오답이다.

어휘 the day before yesterday 그저께   return 돌아오다, 반품하다   within a week 일주일 안에

12 **Where 의문문**

Where did Jackson leave the revised budget report?
(A) It is out of my budget.
(B) Check the top drawer.
(C) He reported it a while ago.

잭슨이 수정된 예산 보고서를 어디에 두었죠?
(A) 그건 제 예산에 안 맞네요.
(B) 맨 위 서랍을 확인해 봐요.
(C) 그가 그것을 조금 전에 보고했어요.

해설 수정된 예산 보고서가 어디 있는지 묻는 질문에, 맨 위 서랍을 확인해 보라고 장소를 알려주는 (B)가 정답이다. (A)와 (C)는 질문의 budget과 report를 반복하여 혼동을 준 오답이다.

어휘 revised 수정된   budget 예산   be out of ~을 벗어난   drawer 서랍   a while ago 조금 전에

13 **How 의문문**

How do you like working at the headquarters?
(A) So far so good.
(B) I have to work alone.
(C) Let me check later.

본사에서 일하는 건 어때요?
(A) 지금까지는 좋아요.
(B) 저는 혼자 일해야 합니다.
(C) 제가 나중에 확인해 볼게요.

해설 본사에서 일하는 것이 어떤지 묻는 질문에, 지금까지는 좋다고 답하는 (A)가 정답이다. So far so good.(지금까지는 좋다.)이라는 표현이 답으로 자주 등장하므로 반드시 익혀 두자. (B)는 질문에서 들렸던 work를 반복하여 혼동을 주었고, (C)는 질문의 내용과 관련이 없으므로 오답이다.

어휘 headquarters 본사 alone 혼자 later 나중에

14 Why 의문문

Why did you bring an umbrella today?
(A) It is going to be cloudy with a chance of rain this afternoon.
(B) No, I didn't bring them.
(C) It was rainy yesterday.

오늘 우산을 왜 가지고 왔나요?
(A) 오늘 오후에 흐려지면서 비 올 가능성이 있대요.
(B) 아니요, 저는 그것들을 가져오지 않았어요.
(C) 어제는 비가 왔어요.

해설 우산을 가져온 이유를 묻자 비 올 가능성이 있어서라고 대답한 (A)가 정답이다. (B)는 질문에서 들렸던 bring을 반복하여 혼동을 준 오답이며, (C)는 질문에 나오는 우산과 관련된 단어 rainy로 오답을 유도하고 있다.

어휘 cloudy 흐린 with a chance of rain 비 올 가능성이 있는

15 Which 의문문

Which of the applicants was offered the job?
(A) You should fill out the application first.
(B) The first one we interviewed.
(C) Excellent job.

이떤 지원자가 취업 제안을 받았나요?
(A) 당신은 먼저 신청서를 작성해야 합니다.
(B) 우리가 면접 봤던 첫 번째 사람이요.
(C) 잘했어요

해설 어떤 지원자가 제안을 받았는지 묻는 질문에, 우리가 처음 면접을 보았던 사람이라고 대답하는 (B)가 정답이다. (A)는 질문에서 들렸던 applicants와 발음이 유사한 application을 이용한 오답이며, (C)는 질문의 job을 반복하여 혼동을 준 오답이다.

어휘 applicant 지원자 fill out 작성하다 application 신청서 excellent 뛰어난

16 평서문

I'd like to cancel my reservation.
(A) Yes, I like it.
(B) The cans were collected in the hotel lobby.
(C) What's your reservation number?

예약을 취소하고 싶습니다.
(A) 네, 저는 그것이 마음에 듭니다.
(B) 호텔 로비에서 캔을 수거했습니다.
(C) 예약 번호가 어떻게 되죠?

해설 예약을 취소하고 싶어 하는 사람에게 예약 번호를 묻는 (C)가 정답이다. 최근 토익에는 질문으로 답하는 경우가 많으므로 이러한 패턴을 잘 숙지해야 한다. 질문에서 들렸던 like를 반복한 (A), 질문의 cancel과 발음이 유사한 cans를 이용한 (B)는 오답이다.

어휘 cancel 취소하다 reservation 예약 collect 모으다, 수집하다

17 부가 의문문

It's supposed to be a good restaurant, isn't it?
(A) It might serve mainly European dishes.
(B) Only if you've made a reservation.
(C) Yes, but it's certainly not cheap.

그곳은 좋은 식당이겠죠, 그렇죠?
(A) 주로 유럽식 요리를 제공할 겁니다.
(B) 예약한 경우만요.
(C) 네, 그런데 가격이 확실히 싸지는 않네요.

해설 좋은 식당인지 묻는 질문에, 그렇다고 동의하지만 가격은 싸지 않다고 말하는 (C)가 정답이다. (A)와 (B)는 질문에 나온 restaurant과 관련된 dishes, make a reservation를 이용한 오답이다.

어휘 be supposed to ~하기로 되어 있다 mainly 주로 European 유럽의 dish 접시; 요리 make a reservation 예약하다 certainly 틀림없이 cheap 싼

18 일반 의문문

Do you have enough space on your hard drive for this program?
(A) Yes, it shouldn't be a problem.
(B) Yes, it is fast enough.
(C) Yes, but too much is never enough.

당신의 하드 드라이브에 이 프로그램을 위한 충분한 공간이 있나요?
(A) 네, 문제없을 거예요.
(B) 네, 그것은 충분히 빨라요.
(C) 네, 하지만 너무 과한 것은 결코 좋지 않아요.

해설 하드 드라이브에 프로그램을 위한 충분한 공간이 있는지 묻는 질문에, 문제가 되지 않는다, 즉 '공간이 충분하다'고 말하는 (A)가 정답이다. (B), (C)는 질문에서 들렸던 enough를 반복하여 오답을 유도하고 있다.

어휘 enough 충분한 space 공간 fast 빠른

19 How 의문문

How long will it take to rewrite the invoice?
(A) It will take off soon.
(B) No time at all.
(C) Right, she has a lovely voice.

송장을 다시 작성하는 데 얼마나 걸리나요?
(A) 곧 이륙할 거예요.
(B) 금방이요.
(C) 맞아요, 그녀는 사랑스러운 목소리를 가지고 있어요.

해설 송장을 새로 만드는 데 시간이 얼마나 걸리는지 묻는 질문에, 금방이라고 답한 (B)가 정답이다. (A)는 질문에서 들렸던 take를 반복하여 오답을 유도하고 있고, (C)는 질문의 invoice와 발음이 유사한 voice를 사용한 오답이다.

어휘 take (시간이) 걸리다 invoice 송장 take off 이륙하다 lovely 사랑스러운, 아름다운

20 Which 의문문

Which caterer is supplying food for the awards banquet?
(A) At the banquet.
(B) It hasn't been decided yet.
(C) We need some office supplies.

어떤 출장 뷔페 업체가 시상식 연회에서 음식을 제공하나요?
(A) 연회에서요.
(B) 아직 결정되지 않았어요.
(C) 우리는 몇 가지 사무용품이 필요해요.

해설 연회에서 음식을 제공할 출장 뷔페 업체가 어디인지 묻는 질문에, 업체가 아직 결정되지 않았다고 대답하는 (B)가 정답이다. (A)와 (C)는 질문에서 들렸던 banquet과 supply를 이용한 오답이다.

어휘 caterer 출장 뷔페 업체 supply 공급하다 award banquet 시상식 연회 office supplies 사무용품

21 일반 의문문

Is there a musical event at the auditorium this evening?
(A) No, I prefer art collections.
(B) Let me check the schedule first.
(C) I can't play any musical instrument.

오늘 저녁에 강당에서 음악 행사가 있나요?
(A) 아니요, 저는 예술품들을 선호해요.
(B) 먼저 일정을 확인해 볼게요.
(C) 저는 연주할 수 있는 악기가 없어요.

해설 오늘 저녁에 강당에서 음악 행사가 있는지 묻는 질문에, 먼저 일정을 확인해 보겠다고 대답한 (B)가 정답이다. (A)는 질문과 무관한 내용이며, (C)는 질문에서 들렸던 musical을 반복하여 혼동을 주는 오답이다.

어휘 auditorium 강당 prefer 선호하다 art collection(s) 예술품 musical instrument 악기

22 평서문

I think James hasn't fixed the photocopier yet.
(A) The manager will have James repair the fax machine.
(B) He's having a day off because of working last Saturday.
(C) You can see my photos online.

제임스가 아직 복사기를 고치지 않은 것 같네요.
(A) 부장님이 제임스에게 팩스기를 고치라고 시킬 거예요.
(B) 그는 지난 토요일에 근무해서 하루 쉬고 있어요.
(C) 제 사진들을 온라인으로 보실 수 있을 겁니다.

해설 제임스가 아직 복사기를 고치지 않은 것 같다는 말에, 그가 하루 쉬는 중이라서 고치지 못했다고 암시한 (B)가 정답이다. (A)는 질문의 fix와 발음이 유사한 fax를 이용하여 오답을 유도하고 있고, (C)는 질문과 전혀 상관없는 내용의 오답이다.

어휘 fix 고치다 photocopier 복사기 a day off 하루 휴가

23 평서문

I'm wondering if you could help me move the bed to the side.
(A) I'll be there in 10 minutes.
(B) I think I had a bad cold.
(C) Yes, you can help me.

이 침대를 옆으로 옮기는 걸 당신이 도와줄 수 있을지 모르겠네요.
(A) 제가 10분 후에 거기로 갈게요.
(B) 저는 독감에 걸렸던 것 같아요.
(C) 네, 당신은 저를 도와줄 수 있어요.

해설 자신을 도와줄 수 있는지 묻는 질문에, 10분 후에 가서 도와준다는 의미의 (A)가 정답이다. (B)는 질문의 bed와 발음이 유사한 bad를 이용한 오답이며, 질문의 help를 반복하여 혼동을 준 (C) 또한 오답이다.

어휘 wonder 궁금하다 move 옮기다 bad cold 심한 감기, 독감

24 부정 의문문

Doesn't Mr. Gonzalez work in advertising?
(A) The advertisements have been completed.
(B) No, he is a financial advisor.
(C) No, I think he works in New York.

곤잘레스 씨는 광고업에 종사하지 않나요?
(A) 그 광고들은 마무리되었어요.
(B) 아니요(광고업에 종사하지 않아요), 그는 재무 자문관이에요.
(C) 아니요, 그는 뉴욕에서 일하는 것 같아요.

해설 곤잘레스 씨가 광고업에 종사하는지 묻는 질문에, 그가 재무 자문관이라고 대답하는 (B)가 정답이다. 질문의 advertising 과 발음이 유사한 advertisement가 들어간 (A)는 오답이다. (C)는 No만 들으면 답이라고 생각할 수 있으나, 뒤의 내용이 질문과 관련 없기 때문에 오답이다.

어휘 advertising 광고업 advertisement 광고 complete 끝내다, 마무리하다 financial advisor 재무 자문관, 재정 고문

25 선택 의문문

Should I make a presentation to a new client today or tomorrow?
(A) I'll let you know later.
(B) It's a little present.
(C) I'm going to meet with a client today.

새로운 고객에게 프레젠테이션을 오늘 해야 하나요, 아니면 내일 해야 하나요?
(A) 제가 나중에 알려줄게요.
(B) 작은 선물이에요.
(C) 저는 오늘 고객을 만날 거예요.

해설 새 고객에게 프레젠테이션을 오늘 할지, 아니면 내일 할지 묻는 선택 의문문으로, 나중에 알려 주겠다고 말하는 (A)가 정답이다. 선택 의문문에서 바로 선택하지 않고 '나중에 알려 주겠다', '확인해 보겠다' 또는 '아직 결정되지 않았다' 등의 내용이 답으로 자주 출제되고 있으니 주의하자. 질문의 presentation과 발음이 유사한 present로 혼동을 준 (B)는 오답이다. (C)는 today가 들리긴 했지만 질문과 관련 없는 내용이므로 오답이다.

어휘 make a presentation 프레젠테이션을 하다 client 고객 present 선물 meet with ~와 만나다

26 Who 의문문

Who's picking up the package?
(A) It's a backpack.
(B) Thanks for the tip.
(C) I think it's my turn.

누가 소포를 가지러 가죠?
(A) 그것은 배낭입니다.
(B) 조언해 주셔서 감사합니다.
(C) 제 차례인 것 같습니다.

해설 누가 소포를 가지러 갈 건지 묻는 질문에, 자기 차례인 것 같다고 대답하는 (C)가 정답이다. (A)는 질문의 package와 발음이 유사한 backpack으로 오답을 유도했다. (B)는 질문과 관련 없는 보기이므로 오답이다.

어휘 pick up ~을 찾다, 찾아오다 package 소포 backpack 배낭 tip 조언 turn 차례

27 제안/권유 의문문

Would you like me to organize a farewell party for Mr. Adams?
(A) The report is well organized.
(B) No, it was a retirement party.
(C) Yes, if you have time.

제가 아담스 씨를 위한 송별회를 준비할까요?
(A) 그 보고서는 잘 정리되어 있어요.
(B) 아니요, 그것은 은퇴 기념 파티였어요.
(C) 네, 당신이 시간이 된다면요.

해설 자신이 파티를 준비할지 묻는 질문에, 시간이 된다면 그렇게 하라고 한 (C)가 정답이다. 'Would you like to(당신이 ~하기를 원하는지)'와 'Would you like me to(내가 ~하기를 원하는지)'를 정확하게 구분해서 들을 수 있도록 연습해야 한다. 질문에서 들렸던 organize, party를 이용하여 혼동을 준 (A)와 (B)는 오답이다.

어휘 organize a party 파티를 준비하다 farewell party 송별회 well organized 잘 구성된(정리된) retirement party 은퇴 기념 파티

28 When 의문문

When will the acquisition be final?
(A) We called some of our acquaintances.
(B) I won't be available then.
(C) Probably next Monday.

언제 인수가 마무리되죠?
(A) 우리가 지인 몇 명에게 전화했어요.
(B) 저는 그때 안될 거예요.
(C) 아마 다음 주 월요일일 겁니다.

해설 언제 인수가 마무리되는지 묻는 질문에, 다음 주 월요일이라고 정확한 시점을 언급한 (C)가 정답이다. (A)는 질문의 acquisition과 발음이 유사한 acquaintances를 이용하여 혼동을 주었고, (B)는 질문의 내용과 관련이 없는 오답이다.

어휘 acquisition 인수 final 최종의 acquaintance 아는 사람, 지인 available 이용 가능한

29 부가 의문문

We have met before, haven't we?
(A) Please meet the deadline this time.
(B) No, before the door.
(C) Yes, I think we went to the same university.

우리는 전에 만난 적이 있어요, 그렇죠?
(A) 이번에는 마감일을 지켜 주세요.
(B) 아니요, 문 앞에요.
(C) 네, 우리는 같은 대학교에 다녔던 것 같아요.

해설 전에 만난 적이 있는지 묻는 질문에 '같은 대학교에 다녔다' 즉, 서로 만난 적이 있다고 말한 (C)가 정답이다. 질문에서 들렸던 met(meet), before를 반복하여 혼동을 준 (A)와 (B)는 오답이다.

어휘 meet the deadline 마감일을 맞추다 before (시간상) ~전에, (위치상) ~앞에

30 Where 의문문

Where will the out-of-town participants be staying?
(A) It was well attended.
(B) We won't know until June.
(C) I believe it's on cutting-edge technology.

외부 참가자들은 어디서 머물게 되나요?
(A) 많은 사람들이 참석했어요.
(B) 6월이 되어야 알 겁니다.
(C) 최첨단 기술이라고 생각합니다.

해설 외부에서 오는 참가자들이 어디에 머무는지 묻는 질문에, 장소를 언급하지 않고 6월이 되어야 알 수 있다고 한 (B)가 정답이다. 의문사로 물어보는 질문에 모른다는 식의 답변이 정답으로 자주 출제되고 있으므로 유의한다. (A)는 질문의 participants에서 연상되는 attend로 오답을 유도하고 있다. (C)는 질문과 관련 없는 내용이므로 오답이다.

어휘 out-of-town 다른 곳에서 온 participant 참가자 well attended 많은 사람들이 참석한 cutting-edge 최첨단의

31 부정 의문문

Didn't Sophia order more business cards on Tuesday?
(A) Yes, the birthday cards were lovely.
(B) No, I ordered her to try.
(C) I'll check with her and get back to you.

소피아가 화요일에 명함을 더 주문하지 않았나요?
(A) 네, 그 생일 카드들은 멋졌어요.
(B) 아니요, 제가 그녀에게 시도해 보라고 했어요.
(C) 그녀에게 확인해 보고 다시 알려 드릴게요.

해설 소피아가 명함을 더 주문하지 않았는지 묻는 질문에, 그녀에게 확인해 보고 연락 주겠다고 대답한 (C)가 정답이다. 질문에서 들렸던 cards, order를 반복하여 혼동을 준 (A)와 (B)는 오답이다. PART 2에서는 질문에서 들리는 단어가 선택지에서 반복되거나 유사한 발음의 단어가 나오면 오답인 경우가 많으니 주의해야 한다.

어휘 business card 명함 lovely 사랑스러운, 멋진 order 주문하다, 명령하다 get back to ~에게 다시 연락하다

PART • 3

[32-34]

W Hello, this is Lorna down at reception. I received a fax here that looks like it probably has something to do with you guys up in accounting, but there's no recipient name on it.
M Does it say who it's from?
W Well, it's a copy of some sort of invoice, and it has the name Brenda Walker on it.
M Oh, yes. I was expecting something from Ms. Walker. I'm not sure why she sent it to the main fax number. Actually, I had given her my direct fax number.
W Okay, I will keep it here for you to pick up.

W 안녕하세요, 저는 아래층 프런트에 있는 로나입니다. 위층의 회계 부서 분들과 관련이 있어 보이는 팩스를 하나 받았는데, 수취인의 이름이 없어서요.
M 어디에서 온 건지 적혀 있나요?
W 일종의 송장 사본인데 거기에 브렌다 워커라고 이름이 쓰여 있네요.
M 아, 네. 워커 씨로부터 받을 게 있어요. 그녀가 왜 메인 팩스 번호로 보냈는지 모르겠네요. 실은, 그녀에게 저의 직통 팩스 번호를 알려 주었거든요.
W 알겠습니다. 당신이 가져갈 수 있게 여기에 보관할게요.

어휘 reception 프런트, 접수처 probably 아마 have something to do with ~와 관련이 있다 accounting 회계; 경리 recipient 수취인 invoice 송장

32 대화 장소

대화가 일어나는 장소는 어디인가?
(A) 호텔에서
(B) 사무실 건물에서
(C) 버스 터미널에서
(D) 식당에서

해설 장소를 묻는 문제는 보통 특정 장소와 관련된 단어/표현 등을 통해 유추할 수 있는데, 여자가 프런트라고 하면서(Hello, this is Lorna down at reception.) 회계 부서에 있는 사람과 관련 있는 팩스를 받았다(I received a fax here that looks like it probably has something to do with you guys up in accounting,)고 하는 것으로 보아 프런트와 회계 부서가 있는 사무실 건물임을 알 수 있다. 따라서 (B)가 정답이다.

33 세부 사항

무엇이 도착했는가?
(A) 컴퓨터
(B) 전단지
(C) 소포
(D) 팩스

해설 특정 물건을 묻는 문제는 단어가 직접적으로 언급되는 경우가 많은데, 팩스를 받았다(I received a fax here)는 여자의 말을 통해 (D)가 정답임을 알 수 있다.

34 다음에 할 일

남자가 다음에 할 일은 무엇인가?
(A) 체크아웃한다
(B) 영수증을 받는다
(C) 아래층으로 내려간다
(D) 팩스를 보낸다

해설 다음에 할 행동을 묻는 문제는 대화의 마지막에 단서가 나오는 경우가 많은데, 직접적으로 언급되지 않은 경우 내용을 통해 유추할 수도 있다. 지문에서 아래층에 있는 프런트에 팩스가 왔다고 했고 남자가 그것을 가져갈 수 있게 보관하겠다(I will keep it here for you to pick up.)는 여자의 말을 통해 남자가 팩스를 가지러 아래층으로 내려갈 것임을 유추할 수 있다. 따라서 (C)가 정답이다.

[35-37]

> W John, I have to rush straight over to a dinner party with some friends. Do you know if there's a place I could stop by and pick up some pies or pastries near here?
> M Um… Oh, yeah, there's a really good bakery, Home Fresh Bakery, just about a few blocks from here on Milton Avenue. You'd better hurry, though; it closes in about fifteen minutes.
> W I should probably take a taxi over there then.
> M Actually, in this traffic, you'd probably get there quicker if you walk. If you leave now, you'll be there in ten minutes.
> ---
> W 존, 저는 친구들과 저녁 파티에 곧장 가봐야 해요. 이 근처에 파이나 빵을 살 수 있는 곳이 있는지 알고 있나요?
> M 음… 아, 네, Home Fresh Bakery라고 정말 맛있는 제과점이 있는데, 여기서 몇 블록 정도 떨어진 Milton Avenue에 있어요. 하지만 서두르는 게 좋을 거예요, 약 15분 후에 문을 닫거든요.
> W 그럼 거기에 택시를 타고 가야겠군요.
> M 사실, 이런 교통 상태에서는 걸어가는 게 더 빨리 도착할 거예요. 지금 출발하면 그곳에 10분 후에 도착할 겁니다.

어휘 rush straight over ~로 곧장 가다   stop by 들르다
pick up ~을 사다   pastry 빵류   bakery 제과점
had better V ~하는 편이 낫다   traffic 교통

35 세부 사항

여자는 무엇을 사고 싶어 하는가?
(A) 제빵류
(B) 의류
(C) 사무용품
(D) 자동차 부품

해설 여자가 파이나 빵(some pies or pastries)을 사고 싶다고 했으므로 (A)가 정답이다. 정답에서는 Baked goods로 패러프레이징되었다.

36 세부 사항

남자는 여자에게 왜 서두르기를 권하는가?
(A) 기차가 15분 후에 떠난다.
(B) 그녀는 회의가 있다.
(C) 영업이 곧 끝날 것이다.
(D) 날씨가 나쁘다.

해설 남자가 제과점이 15분 후에 문을 닫으니 서두르라고 말하고 있으므로(You'd better hurry, though; it closes in about fifteen minutes.) (C)가 정답이다.

37 세부 사항

남자의 말에 따르면, 여자는 어떻게 이동할 것 같은가?
(A) 택시로
(B) 시내 전차로
(C) 지하철로
(D) 도보로

해설 남자가 걸어가면 더 빨리 도착할 수 있을 것(you'd probably get there quicker if you walk.)이라고 했으므로 (D)가 정답이다. 본문의 walk를 on foot으로 바꿔 표현했다.

[38-40]

> M Hello, Reliable Home Heating, Customer Service Department. This is Roger speaking. How can I help you?
> W Hello. Your servicemen installed a new natural gas furnace in my home yesterday. It was working when they left, but it stopped overnight. It's freezing in here right now.
> M Oh, that's not good at all. If you'd be so kind as to give me your account number, I'll call up your account details, and we'll see how quickly we can get someone out there to take care of that.
> W It's 555-4799. I would appreciate that. The weather is terribly cold.
> ---
> M 안녕하세요, Reliable Home Heating의 고객 서비스 부서입니다. 저는 로저입니다. 무엇을 도와드릴까요?
> W 안녕하세요. 수리 기사님들이 어제 저희 집에 새 천연가스 난로를 설치하셨어요. 가실 때는 잘 작동했는데 밤사이에 작동이 멈추어 버렸네요. 여기는 지금 너무 추워요.
> M 오, 정말 힘드시겠네요. 고객님의 계정 번호를 불러 주시면 계정 정보를 통해 그것을 처리할 사람을 그곳에 얼마나 빨리 보낼 수 있는지 알아보겠습니다.
> W 555-4799입니다. 감사합니다. 날씨가 상당히 춥네요.

어휘 serviceman 수리공 install 설치하다 furnace 난로 overnight 밤사이에 account number 계정 번호 detail 세부 사항 take care of ~을 처리하다 terribly 매우

38 화자의 직업

남자의 직업은 무엇인가?
(A) 자동차 정비사
(B) 고객 서비스 직원
(C) 건축가
(D) 택시 운전사

해설 직업을 묻는 문제는 직업과 관련된 특정 단어가 반드시 나오는데, 남자가 전화를 받으면서 고객 서비스 부서 (Hello, Reliable Home Heating, Customer Service Department.)라고 말하고 있으므로 (B)가 정답이다.

39 주제/목적

여자는 왜 전화하는가?
(A) 전화 요금 고지서가 잘못되었다.
(B) 주문품이 배송되지 않았다.
(C) 난로가 작동하지 않는다.
(D) 그녀는 회계사가 필요하다.

해설 전화를 건 이유를 묻는 문제의 단서는 대화의 초반에 나오는 경우가 많다. 여자가 어제 설치한 난로가 작동되지 않는다고(It was working when they left, but it stopped overnight.) 했으므로 (C)가 정답이다. 대화에서는 stopped 로 나오지만 보기에는 is not working으로 나온 것에 유의한다.

40 세부 사항

남자는 어떤 정보를 요구하고 있는가?
(A) 여자의 계정 번호
(B) 여자의 주소
(C) 제품 번호
(D) 여자가 지불한 금액

해설 남자가 계정 번호를 알려주면 해결하겠다고(If you'd be so kind as to give me your account number, I'll call up your account details, and we'll see how quickly we can get someone out there to take care of that.) 했으므로 (A)가 정답이다.

[41-43]

W Hello, sir. I'd like to buy a ticket for the next train to Smithville.
M I'm sorry, ma'am, but the train doesn't go directly to Smithville. To get there, you need to take a train to Jonestown and then catch a bus to Smithville.
W What do you mean? I've taken the train there many times. That can't be right.
M You're right, ma'am. The train used to go there, but unfortunately, due to budget constraints, the stations in some of the smaller towns have been closed.

W 안녕하세요, Smithville로 가는 다음 기차표를 사고 싶은데요.
M 죄송합니다만, 그 기차는 Smithville에 직행으로 가지 않습니다. 거기로 가시려면 Jonestown으로 가는 기차를 탄 다음 Smithville로 가는 버스로 갈아타야 합니다.
W 무슨 말씀이시죠? 거기에 기차를 타고 여러 번 갔는데요. 그럴 리가 없어요.
M 맞습니다. 예전에는 기차가 그곳에 갔지만, 안타깝게도 예산 제약으로 인해 몇몇 작은 마을의 역들이 폐쇄되었습니다.

어휘 directly 직접 take a train 기차를 타다 catch a bus 버스를 타다 used to V ~하곤 했다 budget constraint 예산 제약

41 대화 장소

대화가 일어나는 있는 장소는 어디인가?
(A) 대학교에서
(B) 호텔에서
(C) 기차역에서
(D) 콘서트장에서

해설 장소를 묻는 문제는 보통 특정 장소와 관련된 단어나 표현을 통해 유추할 수 있는데, 여자가 기차표를 사려고 하는 것을 보아(I'd like to buy a ticket for the next train to Smithville.) 기차역에서 일어나는 대화임을 알 수 있다. 따라서 (C)가 정답이다.

42 세부 사항

여자가 놀라는 이유는 무엇인가?
(A) 남은 기차표가 없다.
(B) 가격이 올랐다.
(C) 남자가 무례했다.
(D) 직행편이 없다.

해설 직행으로 가는 기차가 없다는 남자의 말에(but the train doesn't go directly to Smithville.) 여자가 놀라고 있으므로 (D)가 정답이다. go directly(직행으로 가다)라는 표현이 direct service로 바뀌어서 나왔다.

43 의도 파악

여자는 왜 '무슨 말씀이시죠?'라고 말하는가?
(A) 남자가 다시 설명하게 하기 위해
(B) 서비스에 대해 불평하기 위해
(C) 놀라움을 표현하기 위해
(D) 도움을 요청하기 위해

해설 여자는 자신이 몇 번 가본 적이 있는 곳에 더 이상 기차가 가지 않는다는 사실에 놀라 무슨 뜻이냐고 묻고 있으므로 (C)가 정답이다.

[44-46]

> W Hello, I was told that you're also going to the conference in Milan. I have no idea how I can get there. How are you planning to get there?
> M My coworker already arranged my train ticket to Milan, and he told me that it's only a two-hour train ride.
> W Oh, really? I'm pleased to hear that it only takes a short time. Actually, I've been so busy with all the work revising the user manual for our new machine. I have to finish it before the conference.
> M Then, since I have some time to spare now, shall I book the ticket for you?
> W I'd appreciate that. I will buy you lunch as a thank-you.
> ----
> W 안녕하세요, 당신도 밀라노 회담에 참석한다고 들었습니다. 저는 그곳에 어떻게 가야 할지 모르겠습니다. 거기에 어떻게 가실 계획인가요?
> M 제 직장동료가 이미 제 밀라노행 기차표를 예약했고 기차로 2시간 밖에 안 걸린다고 했어요.
> W 아, 정말요? 시간이 얼마 걸리지 않는다니 좋네요. 사실, 제가 새로운 기계에 관한 사용자 매뉴얼을 수정하는 일로 너무 바빴거든요. 저는 회담 전에 이것을 마무리해야 해요.
> M 그러면 제가 시간이 조금 있으니, 대신 표를 예약해 드릴까요?
> W 그래 주시면 고맙죠. 감사의 표시로 제가 점심을 사겠습니다.

어휘 be told that ~을 듣다 conference 회담 coworker (직장) 동료 arrange 준비하다 be pleased to ~해서 기쁘다 revise 수정하다 appreciate 감사하다, 평가하다

44 주제/목적

대화의 주제는 무엇인가?
(A) 형편없는 서비스에 대한 불평
(B) 사용자 매뉴얼 개정
(C) 이동 계획
(D) 출장 경비 상환

해설 대화의 전반적인 흐름이 밀라노 회담에 맞추어져 있으며, 여자가 그곳에 어떻게 갈지에 대해 물었고(How are you planning to get there?) 남자가 여자를 위해 티켓을 예약해 준다고(shall I book the ticket for you?) 하는 것을 보아 주제가 (C) 이동 계획임을 알 수 있다.

45 세부 사항

여자의 말에 따르면, 왜 그녀는 기차를 타는 것에 기뻐하는가?
(A) 가격이 합리적이기 때문에
(B) 시간이 오래 걸리지 않기 때문에
(C) 예상대로 날씨가 좋을 것이기 때문에
(D) 무료 음료를 받을 것이기 때문에

해설 여자가 시간이 얼마 걸리지 않는다니 기쁘다고 했으므로(I'm pleased to hear that it only takes a short time.) (B)가 정답이다.

46 제안

남자는 여자를 위해 무엇을 하겠다고 하는가?
(A) 티켓을 예약한다
(B) 회의 안건을 기록한다
(C) 점심을 산다
(D) 그녀의 상관에게 이야기한다

해설 지문의 후반부에 남자가 시간이 있어 티켓을 대신 예약해 주겠다고 했으므로(Then, since I have some time to spare now, shall I book the ticket for you?) (A)가 정답이다.

[47-49]

> W Hi, Mr. Walton. I had a call again from Jerry Shilton. He wants to know when he can meet with you to discuss his proposal.
> M Wow, he certainly is persistent. I guess he's not going to leave me alone until I listen to what he has to say. Do I have any windows in my schedule this week?
> W You're pretty booked up. You could see him over lunch on Thursday if you wanted.
> M Okay, I might as well get this over with. Please give him a call back and set that up.
> ----
> W 안녕하세요, 월튼 씨. 제리 실튼 씨로부터 또 전화를 받았습니다. 그는 제안을 의논하기 위해 언제 당신을 만날 수 있는지 알고 싶어 합니다.
> M 이런, 참 끈질긴 사람이군요. 그가 해야 할 말을 들어줄 때까지 나를 가만히 내버려 두지 않을 것 같아요. 이번 주에 제 일정 중에 비는 시간이 있나요?
> W 일정이 거의 꽉 찼는데요. 원하신다면 목요일에 점심 식사를 하면서 그를 보실 수 있습니다.
> M 그렇게 하죠. 이 상황을 끝내버리는 편이 낫겠어요. 그에게 전화해서 약속을 잡아주세요.

어휘 have a call 전화를 받다 proposal 제안 persistent 끈기 있는, 고집이 센 window 기회, 시간 over lunch 점심을 먹으면서 get ~ over with ~을 끝내다 set up 약속을 정하다

47 세부 사항

실튼 씨는 왜 월튼 씨를 만나고 싶어 하는가?
(A) 친구를 소개하기 위해서
(B) 돈을 모으기 위해서
(C) 제안에 대해 의논하기 위해서
(D) 일자리에 지원하기 위해서

해설 여자가 남자에게 실튼 씨가 제안에 관한 이야기를 나누기 위해 만나고 싶어 한다고(He wants to know when he can meet with you to discuss his proposal.) 했으므로 (C)가 정답이다.

48 세부 사항

남자는 언제 실튼 씨를 만날 수 있는가?
(A) 월요일에
(B) 화요일에
(C) 목요일에
(D) 주말에

해설 여자가 남자에게 원하면 목요일에 실튼 씨를 만날 수 있다고 했으므로(You could see him over lunch on Thursday if you wanted.) (C)가 정답이다.

49 다음에 할 일

여자가 다음에 할 일은 무엇인가?
(A) 메모한다
(B) 실튼 씨를 만난다
(C) 실튼 씨에게 연락한다
(D) 점심 시간을 가진다

해설 남자가 여자에게 전화해서 약속을 잡아달라고 부탁하는 것으로(Please give him a call back and set that up.) 보아, 여자가 실튼 씨에게 전화할 것이라는 사실을 유추할 수 있다. 그러므로 (C)가 정답이다. 본문에 나온 give ~ a call이라는 표현이 get in touch with으로 패러프레이징되었다.

[50-52] 3인 대화

M1 Hello, Stacey. Do you happen to know if there's any bus that goes to the art fair? We're dying to go there to see the Mexican art exhibit.
W Jeff, actually, some of my friends and I have plans to go there next weekend. And Lisa told me she's going to drive! You two should join us if you want!
M2 Oh, that's such a great idea! Then, should we have dinner before the exhibit, or are you planning to have it afterwards?
W We already made a reservation at Ox Hill, right next to the museum. If you guys want to go as well, I will call the restaurant and say two more people will be going.
M1 That sounds awesome. I can't wait!
M2 How kind of you! I would appreciate that.

M1 안녕하세요, 스테이시. 혹시 미술 박람회로 가는 버스가 있는지 아시나요? 저희는 멕시코 미술 전시회를 정말 보러 가고 싶어요.
W 제프, 사실 저와 제 친구 몇 명이 다음 주말에 그 곳에 가려고 해요. 그리고 리사가 운전할 거라고 말했어요! 괜찮으시면, 두 분도 합류하세요!
M2 오, 그거 좋은 생각이네요! 그러면, 저희가 전시회 전에 저녁을 먹어야 하나요? 아니면 그 후에 먹을 예정인가요?
W 저희는 미술관 바로 옆에 있는 옥스힐을 이미 예약했어요. 만약 두 분도 가고 싶으시면, 제가 레스토랑에 전화해서 두 명이 더 갈 거라고 말할게요.
M1 정말 좋네요. 기대됩니다!
M2 참 친절하시네요! 그렇게 해주시면 감사하죠.

어휘 Do you happen to know ~? 혹시 ~ 알아요? art fair 미술 박람회 be dying to ~를 정말 하고 싶다 exhibit 전시회 have plans to ~할 계획이다 afterwards 나중에, 그 후에 make a reservation 예약하다 awesome 좋은, 굉장한

50 주제/목적

화자들은 주로 무엇에 대해 이야기하고 있는가?
(A) 미술 박람회 방문
(B) 해외 여행
(C) 하루 일과
(D) 카페 예약

해설 대화의 주제를 묻는 문제는 주로 대화 초반에 답이 나오는 경우가 많은데, 대화의 초반에 전시회를 너무 가고 싶다(We're dying to go there to see the Mexican art exhibit.)고 하는 것을 보아 (A)가 정답임을 알 수 있다.

51 다음에 할 일

여자는 무엇을 할 것이라고 말하는가?
(A) 예약을 변경한다
(B) 할인 티켓을 구매한다
(C) 일정표를 복사한다
(D) 그녀의 친구들에게 전화한다

해설 여자가 레스토랑에 전화해 두 사람이 더 간다고 말하겠다고 (I will call the restaurant and say two more people will be going.) 했으므로 예약을 변경한다는 (A)가 정답이다.

52 의도 파악

왜 제프는 '정말 좋네요'라고 말하는가?
(A) 그가 무료 식사 쿠폰을 받았기 때문에
(B) 그가 마침내 승진했기 때문에
(C) 그가 저녁을 함께 먹을 수 있기 때문에
(D) 그가 곧 세미나에 참석할 예정이기 때문에

해설 인용 표현 앞뒤 문장에서 저녁 식사를 언급하며 여자가 We already made a reservation at Ox Hill, right next to the museum. If you guys want to go as well, I will call the restaurant and say two more people will be going.이라고 말한 것으로 보아, 저녁을 같이 먹을 수 있기 때문에 남자가 좋다고 말했음을 알 수 있다. 그러므로 (C)가 정답이다.

[53-55]

W Hi, Mark. It's Laura from Rexiton Book Store. I'm calling to let you know that I was hugely impressed with your interview last Friday, and I'd like to offer you the job. Are you still between jobs?

M Thanks for calling me about the job offer. Could you please tell me what my job would be at your shop in detail?

W Yes, there are not many things to do. All you need to do is to help customers find the books they are looking for, check the stocks, and clean the place.

M Okay, I'm sure I'm the best fit for it. Thank you again for the offer.

W That's good to hear. Can you please come a little early on the 28th of March since there is a training session for the new hires?

W 안녕하세요, 마크. Rexiton 서점의 로라입니다. 저는 지난주 금요일에 있었던 당신과의 면접에서 상당히 감명 받았고, 당신에게 일자리를 제공하고 싶다는 것을 알려 드리기 위해 전화 드립니다. 아직 구직 중이신가요?

M 취업 제안과 관련하여 전화 주셔서 감사합니다. 서점에서 제 업무가 어떤 것인지 말씀해 주시겠어요?

W 네, 할 일은 많지 않습니다. 당신이 해야 할 일은 고객들이 찾고 있는 책을 찾아 주고, 재고를 확인하고 서점을 청소하는 것입니다.

M 좋아요, 그 일에는 제가 딱 맞는 사람이라고 확신합니다. 제안해 주셔서 다시 한 번 감사드립니다.

W 좋습니다. 3월 28일에 조금 일찍 오실 수 있으신가요? 신입 사원들을 위한 교육이 마련되어 있거든요.

어휘 hugely 크게 be impressed with ~에 감명받다 offer 제공하다 between jobs 구직 중인 check the stocks 재고를 확인하다 be the best fit for ~ ~에 제격이다, 딱 맞다 training session 교육 new hire 신입 사원

53 화자의 근무지

여자가 일하는 곳은 어디인가?
(A) 여행사에서
(B) 도서관에서
(C) 서점에서
(D) 영어 학원에서

해설 첫 번째 문장(It's Laura from Rexiton Book Store.)에서 여자가 서점에 근무한다는 것을 알 수 있으므로 (C)가 정답이다.

54 세부 사항

여자는 어떤 업무를 언급하는가?
(A) 고객들을 위해 책 찾기
(B) 신입 사원들에게 연설하기
(C) 교육 계획하기
(D) 주문하기

해설 여자가 남자의 할 일은 고객들이 책을 찾는 것을 도와주는 것이라고(All you need to do is to help customers to find the books they are looking for) 언급했으므로 (A)가 정답이다. locate(~을 찾다)는 토익 빈출 어휘이기 때문에 꼭 알아 두어야 한다.

55 세부 사항

교육은 언제 열리는가?
(A) 3월 8일
(B) 3월 28일
(C) 5월 8일
(D) 5월 28일

해설 여자의 마지막 말(Can you please come a little early on the 28th of March since there is a training session for the new hires?)을 통해 (B)가 정답임을 알 수 있다.

[56-58]

M Hey, Mary. When do you head out to Seattle for your business trip?

W I'm afraid I won't be going. Sales are down, and management has drastically cut the company travel budget.

M However, I thought you were doing a presentation on behalf of the company there.

W I was, but we're having Amelia Larkin from the Seattle office take care of it. She can just go in for the presentation, so there won't be any travel expenses.

M 안녕, 메리. 출장으로 시애틀은 언제 가요?

W 유감이지만 갈 수 없을 것 같아요. 매출이 떨어져서 경영진이 출장 예산을 급격히 삭감했거든요.

M 하지만, 그곳에서 회사를 대표해 프레젠테이션을 하는 걸로 알고 있었는데요.

W 그러기로 했지만, 그건 시애틀 지사의 아멜리아 라킨이 담당하기로 했어요. 그녀가 프레젠테이션만 하면 되니까 출장비가 들지 않을 거예요.

어휘 head out ~로 가다, 향하다 management 경영진 drastically 극단적으로, 급격히 travel budget 출장 예산 on behalf of ~을 대표하여, 대신하여 take care of ~을 다루다, 처리하다 travel expense 출장 경비

56 주제/목적

대화의 중심 주제는 무엇인가?

(A) 출장
(B) 승진
(C) 연착된 비행기
(D) 동료를 위한 선물

> **해설** 대화의 주제에 관한 내용은 주로 지문의 초반에 등장한다. 남자는 여자에게 출장으로 시애틀에 언제 가는지(When do you head out to Seattle for your business trip?) 묻고 있고, 이후에도 출장 예산과 같은 내용을 언급하고 있으므로 정답은 (A)이다.

57 세부 사항

여자는 왜 계획을 바꾸었는가?
(A) 아멜리아 라킨이 더 적격이다.
(B) 그녀의 상관에게 질책을 받았다.
(C) 돈을 사용할 수 없다.
(D) 그녀가 시간이 부족하다.

> **해설** 여자가 출장 예산이 삭감되어서 갈 수 없을 것 같다(I'm afraid I won't be going. Sales are down, and management has drastically cut the company travel budget.)고 말했으므로 (C)가 정답임을 알 수 있다.

58 다음에 할 일

라킨 씨는 무엇을 할 것인가?
(A) 예산을 편성한다
(B) 매출을 늘린다
(C) 시애틀로 여행을 간다
(D) 프레젠테이션을 한다

> **해설** 여자의 마지막 대사에서 아멜리아 라킨이 프레젠테이션을 할 것(but we're having Amelia Larkin from the Seattle office take care of it. She can just go in for the presentation,)이라고 말했으므로 (D)가 정답이다. 대화 속의 go in for the presentation이 보기에서 deliver a presentation으로 바뀐 것에 주의하자.

[59-61]

W Hi, Mr. Phillips. Thank you so much for taking the time to talk about your interest in our mentoring program. First of all, could you tell me a little about your professional background?

M No problem at all. I've been with Stellar Marketing for fifteen years, and I've been the president of the company for eight of those years.

W Wow, it sounds like you would have a lot to offer young people.

M Well, when I started with Stellar in the mailroom, Martin Zegglar—who was the vice president of customer relations at that time—really took me under his wing. I want to take the opportunity to give something back.

W 안녕하세요, 필립 씨. 우리의 멘토십 프로그램에 대한 당신의 관심에 대해 이야기 나눌 시간을 내주셔서 감사합니다. 우선, 당신의 경력에 대해서 조금 말씀해 주실 수 있나요?

M 물론이죠. 저는 Stellar Marketing 사에 15년째 근무하고 있고, 그 중에 8년을 사장으로 일하고 있습니다.

W 와, 당신은 젊은 사람들에게 제안할 것이 많겠는데요.

M 글쎄요, 우편물실에서 Stellar와 함께 시작했을 때, 그 당시 고객 상담부 부사장이셨던 마틴 지글러 씨께서 저를 많이 이끌어 주셨죠. 저는 무언가를 보답할 기회를 갖고 싶습니다.

> **어휘** interest 관심   mentor 정신적 지주, 멘토   first of all 우선   professional background 경력   president 사장   sound like ~처럼 들리다   vice president 부사장   take ~ under one's wing ~을 잘 돌보다, 이끌어주다   opportunity 기회

59 세부 사항

여자는 무엇을 하고 있는가?
(A) 잠재적 멘토를 인터뷰하고 있다
(B) 마케팅 회사를 고용하고 있다
(C) 일자리에 지원하고 있다
(D) 교육을 받고 있다

> **해설** 여자가 멘토십 프로그램에 참여하고자 하는 사람을 인터뷰하고 있으므로(Thank you so much for taking the time to talk about your interest in our mentorship program.) (A)가 정답이다.

60 화자의 직업

남자의 현재 직함은 무엇인가?
(A) 회계부 인턴
(B) 마케팅 부장
(C) 우체국 직원
(D) 사장

> **해설** 남자가 15년 중 8년 동안 사장으로 일하고 있다고 했으므로(I've been with Stellar Marketing for fifteen years, and I've been the president of the company for eight of those years.) (D)가 정답이다.

61 세부 사항

남자는 무엇을 하고 싶어 하는가?
(A) 승진하기
(B) 자원자 되기
(C) 그의 회사를 매각하기
(D) 우편물실의 효율성 증대하기

> **해설** 여자가 남자에게 멘토십 프로그램에 대한 관심에 대해 얘기할 시간을 내 주셔서 감사하다(Thank you so much for taking the time to talk about your interest in our mentorship program.)고 하고 남자는 마지막에 받았던 것을 돌려주고 싶다(I want to take the opportunity to give something back.)고 말한다. 이를 통해 남자가 멘토십 프로그램에 지원하고 싶어 한다는 것을 알 수 있다. 따라서 (B)가 정답이다.

[62-64]

W Good morning, Mr. Tim. As we discussed during last week's meeting, we need to figure out a way to attract more customers who are interested in our best movies of the year.

M Well, I have thought about it and come up with a brilliant idea. As you know, *Time Travel*, which is number 3 on the list, really sparked customers' interest. So why don't we invite the director of the movie and give the fans some time to share some comments with him?

W I think that's such a wonderful idea. Why don't you get in touch with him right away and see if he is available in the near future?

W 좋은 아침입니다, 팀 씨. 지난주 회의에서 논의한 바와 같이, 우리는 올해 최고의 영화에 관심이 있는 고객들을 더 유치하기 위한 방법을 강구해야 합니다.

M 음, 제가 생각해 보았는데 좋은 아이디어가 하나 떠올랐습니다. 아시다시피, 목록의 3번째에 있는 <Time Travel>은 고객들의 흥미를 유발했습니다. 그래서 우리가 그 영화의 감독을 초대하여 팬들에게 그와 논평을 공유하는 시간을 제공하는 것은 어떨까요?

W 좋은 아이디어인 것 같아요. 지금 바로 그에게 연락해서 가까운 시일 내에 시간이 되는지 물어봐 주시겠어요?

	제목	감독
1	About the Future	제이슨 리
2	The Ocean Fellas	존 타카모토
3	Time Travel	다니엘 강
4	Who Moved My Cup?	요시모토

어휘 figure out 강구하다, 생각해 내다 attract 유치하다, 끌어모으다 be interested in ~에 흥미가 있다 come up with ~을 생각해내다 brilliant 멋진, 훌륭한 as you know 아시다시피 spark interest (in) (~에) 관심을 불러일으키다 share 공유하다 available 이용 가능한, 시간이 있는 in the near future 가까운 시일 내에

62 화자의 직업

화자들은 어떤 산업에 종사하는가?
(A) 영화 마케팅
(B) 도서 출판
(C) 해외 투자
(D) 의료 관광

해설 첫 번째 대사에서 올해 최고의 영화에 관심이 있는 고객들을 더 유치할 수 있는 방법을 찾자(we need to figure out a way to attract more customers who are interested in our best movies of the year.)고 했고, 감독을 초대해서 팬들과 이야기하게 하자(So why don't we invite the director of the movie and give the fans some time to share some comments with him?)고 말한 것을 보아 화자들이 영화 마케팅 산업에 종사하고 있음을 알 수 있다. 그러므로 (A)가 정답이다.

63 시각 자료 연계

시각 자료를 보시오. 화자들이 행사에 누구를 초대할 것 같은가?
(A) 제이슨 리
(B) 존 타카모토
(C) 다니엘 강
(D) 요시모토

해설 대화에서 남자가 목록의 3번째 영화가 고객들의 흥미를 유발했다고(As you know, *Time Travel*, which is number 3 on the list, really sparked customers' interest.) 했고, 그 영화의 감독을 초대하자고(why don't we invite the director of the movie) 제안했으므로 도표에서 3번째 영화의 감독인 (C) 다니엘 강이 정답이다.

64 다음에 할 일

남자는 대화 후에 무엇을 할 것 같은가?
(A) 매니저와 상담하기
(B) 하루 일과 업데이트하기
(C) 감독에게 연락하기
(D) 책 정리하기

해설 여자의 마지막 대사에서 가까운 시일 안에 시간이 되는지 알아보기 위해 감독에게 연락해 보라(Why don't you get in touch with him right away and see if he is available in the near future?)고 하고 있으므로 남자에게 연락한다는 (C)가 정답이다.

[65-67]

M Hello, Rynn. Do you remember when we talked about the relocation of our store? Here are the available spots for rent.

W Thank you for your work. I thought the department store would best fit our needs, but I was told that there will be other competitors as well. So I'm worried that the price will be much higher than expected.

M Yeah, you have a point since we have a limited budget for this year.

W Then, how about we move to the opposite side of the library? I heard there are many good spots.

M Yeah, great idea. I'm sure many workers will come as well during their lunchtime.

W Sure. I'll phone the real estate agent now to find out if that place is still available.

M 안녕하세요, 린. 우리가 상점 이전에 대해 이야기했던 때를 기억하나요? 여기 보시면 임대 가능한 장소들이 있습니다.

W 작업해 주셔서 감사합니다. 저는 백화점이 저희의 요구사항에 가장 적합할 것이라 생각했는데요, 다른 경쟁사들도 있을 거라고 들었어요. 그래서 예상보다 가격이 훨씬 높아질까 봐 걱정됩니다.
M 네, 당신 말도 일리가 있어요. 올해는 예산이 제한되어 있으니까요.
W 그러면 도서관 맞은편으로 이전하는 것은 어떠세요? 거기에 좋은 장소들이 많다고 들었어요.
M 네, 좋은 생각이네요. 점심 시간에 직장인들도 많이 올 거라고 확신해요.
W 맞습니다. 제가 지금 부동산 중개업자에게 전화해서 그 장소가 아직 임대 가능한지 물어 볼게요.

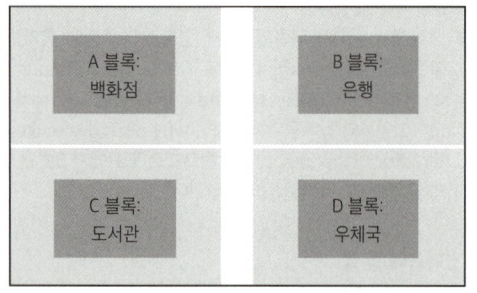

| A 블록:
백화점 | B 블록:
은행 |
| C 블록:
도서관 | D 블록:
우체국 |

어휘 relocation 이전 available 이용 가능한 spot 장소 rent 임대 fit 맞다 competitor 경쟁자 than expected 예상보다 limited budget 제한된 예산 real estate agent 부동산 중개업자

65 문제점
화자들이 걱정하는 것은 무엇인가?
(A) 임대료
(B) 제한된 주차 공간
(C) 엄격한 임대 관련 법
(D) 적은 보행자

해설 남자가 올해는 예산이 제한되어 있다고 했고(since we have a limited budget for this year.) 여자는 가격이 예상보다 더 높을까 봐 걱정하는(I'm worried that the price will be much higher than expected.) 것으로 보아, 화자들이 임대 비용에 대해 걱정하고 있음을 알 수 있다. 따라서 (A)가 정답이다.

66 시각 자료 연계
시각 자료를 보시오. 화자들은 그들의 상점을 위해 어느 장소를 선택하는가?
(A) A 블록
(B) B 블록
(C) C 블록
(D) D 블록

해설 여자가 도서관 맞은편으로 옮기는 것을 제안하자(Then, how about we move to the opposite side of the library?) 남자가 동의하고 있으므로 정답이 (D)임을 알 수 있다.

67 다음에 할 일
여자는 다음에 무엇을 할 거라고 말하는가?
(A) 부동산 중개업자에 연락하기
(B) 건축 부지 방문하기
(C) 가격 묻기
(D) 그녀의 사무실로 돌아가기

해설 여자의 마지막 대사에서 임대가 아직 가능한지 알아 보기 위해 부동산 중개업자에게 전화하겠다(I'll phone the real estate agent now to find out if that place is still available.)고 했으므로 (A)가 정답이다.

[68-70]

M Hello, this is Tom Carson in Vexcel Corporation. I'm calling to place an order for our new stamp cards. I'd like to order 30 as usual, please.
W Sure. By the way, have you checked out our Web site? There is currently a special offer going on. If you place an order for more than 100 cards at once, you will get them at a lower price.
M Thanks, but since we don't have many students now, I'll take advantage of that later.
W No problem. Would you like the design on the card as usual, or do you have another one this time?
M We've made a change to our logo. How can I send you the image?
W You can send it to our e-mail at info@alwaysdesign.com. Thank you.

M 안녕하세요, Vexcel 사의 톰 카슨입니다. 저희의 새로운 도장 카드를 주문하고 싶어서 전화 드렸습니다. 평소와 같이 30장 부탁드립니다.
W 네. 그런데, 저희 웹 사이트를 확인해 보셨나요? 지금 특별 판매가 진행되고 있습니다. 한 번에 100장 이상의 카드를 주문하시면, 더 낮은 가격에 구입하실 수 있습니다.
M 감사하지만 저희가 지금 학생들이 많지 않아서 나중에 이용하겠습니다.
W 알겠습니다. 평소와 같은 카드 디자인을 원하시나요? 아니면 이번엔 다른 디자인을 가지고 계신가요?
M 저희는 로고를 변경했습니다. 이미지를 어떻게 보내 드리면 되나요?
W 저희의 이메일인 info@alwaysdesign.com으로 보내 주시면 됩니다. 감사합니다.

수량	가격
10	15달러
30	40달러
50	70달러
100	~~150달러~~ 110달러 (할인!)

어휘 place an order 주문하다 as usual 평소처럼 currently 현재 a special offer 특가 판매 at once 한번에 take advantage of ~를 이용하다 make a change 변경하다

68 세부 사항

남자는 무엇을 주문하길 원하는가?
(A) 교복
(B) 안경
(C) 도장 카드
(D) 홍보용 팸플릿

해설 첫 번째 대사에서 남자가 도장 카드를 주문하려고 전화했다(I'm calling to place an order for our new stamp cards.)고 말하고 있으므로 (C)가 정답이다.

69 시각 자료 연계

시각 자료를 보시오. 남자의 주문 가격은 얼마인가?
(A) 15달러
(B) 40달러
(C) 70달러
(D) 110달러

해설 첫 번째 대사에서 남자가 30개를 주문했고(I'd like to order 30 as usual, please.) 여자가 특가에 대해 이야기했지만 나중에 이용하겠다며(I'll take advantage of that later.) 거절했다. 따라서 원래의 주문 수량인 30개에 해당하는 (B) 40달러가 정답이다.

70 세부 사항

남자에 대한 설명 중 옳은 것은?
(A) 이 상점의 첫 고객이다.
(B) 위치에 대해 걱정하고 있다.
(C) 이 상점에서 이전에 주문한 적이 있다.
(D) 오프라인 쇼핑을 선호한다.

해설 평소와 같이(as usual) 주문하겠다는 남자의 말과 평소와 같은 디자인을 사용할 건지(Would you like the design on the card as usual, or do you have another one this time?) 묻는 여자의 말을 미루어 볼 때, 남자가 이전에도 이 상점을 이용했다는 것을 알 수 있다. 따라서 정답은 (C)이다.

PART • 4

[71-73] 전화 메시지

Hi, Ms. Grendel. This is Geraldine Snell calling from Best View Realty. We're planning a training for our staff on the weekend of September 15th, and I'm wondering if you could accommodate us. There will be 32 people who will need rooms for two nights. We'll also need a conference room that can handle that many people from 9 A.M. to 6 P.M. on Saturday and Sunday. We'll be wanting breakfast and lunch catered as well. I realize it is short notice. Please give me a call at 555-4342 and let me know if your hotel will be able to handle this.

안녕하세요, 그렌델 씨. 저는 Best View Realty에서 전화 드리는 제랄딘 스넬입니다. 우리는 9월 15일 주말에 직원들을 위한 교육을 계획하고 있는데 저희가 그곳에 묵을 수 있는지 알고 싶습니다. 2박 3일 동안 방이 필요한 사람은 32명입니다. 토요일과 일요일 오전 9시부터 오후 6시까지 그 많은 사람들을 수용할 수 있는 회의실도 필요합니다. 아침 식사와 점심 식사도 제공되었으면 합니다. 갑작스럽게 통지한다는 걸 압니다. 555-4342로 전화 주셔서 당신의 호텔이 이것을 처리할 수 있는지 알려 주시기 바랍니다.

어휘 wonder 궁금하다 accommodate ~을 수용하다, 숙박시키다 handle 처리하다 cater 음식을 공급하다 realize 알다, 인식하다 short notice 급박한 공지 give ~ a call ~에게 전화하다

71 주제/목적

여자는 왜 전화했는가?
(A) 주문하기 위해서
(B) 시설을 예약하기 위해서
(C) 약속을 취소하기 위해서
(D) 티켓을 예약하기 위해서

해설 화자가 9월 15일에 있는 교육을 위해 호텔에 수용 가능한지 묻고 있으므로(We're planning a training for our staff on the weekend of September 15th, and I'm wondering if you could accommodate us.) 시설을 예약한다는 내용의 (B)가 정답이다.

72 청자의 직업

그렌델 씨는 누구인 것 같은가?
(A) 호텔 종업원
(B) 신문 기자
(C) 부동산 중개인
(D) 변호사

해설 화자가 청자에게 숙박 예약에 관해 말하는(There will be 32 people who will need rooms for two nights.) 것으로 보아 그렌델 씨는 (A) 호텔 종업원임을 알 수 있다.

73 세부 사항

스넬 씨가 계획하는 날은 언제인가?
(A) 8월 중순
(B) 8월 말
(C) 9월 초
(D) 9월 중순

해설 9월 15일에 교육이 예정되어 있다(We're planning a training for our staff on the weekend of September 15th)는 화자의 말을 통해 9월 중순에 계획했음을 알 수 있다. 따라서 (D)가 정답이다.

[74-76] 안내

Attention, passengers on Air Iberia Flight 593 to Madrid. The flight will be departing in 30 minutes. Please proceed immediately to the gate to board the plane. Please note that due to the fact that the plane is completely full, the amount of carry-on luggage will be restricted. Furthermore, please make sure that you are not carrying any prohibited items such as lighters or sharp objects in any of your baggage. Once again, passengers on Flight 593 to Madrid please proceed immediately to the gate, and thank you for flying Air Iberia. Thank you for your cooperation.

마드리드 행 Air Iberia 593편에 탑승하실 승객 여러분께서는 주목해 주시기 바랍니다. 비행기는 30분 후에 출발할 예정입니다. 비행기 탑승을 위해 즉시 게이트로 와 주시기 바랍니다. 비행기가 만원인 관계로 기내 휴대용 수하물의 양이 제한됨을 유의하십시오. 뿐만 아니라, 당신의 어느 짐에도 라이터나 날카로운 물체 같은 금지된 물품을 소지하시는 일이 없도록 해 주시기 바랍니다. 다시 한번, 마드리드 행 593편을 이용하실 승객 여러분께서는 즉시 게이트로 와 주시기 바랍니다. Air Iberia를 이용해 주셔서 감사합니다. 협조해 주셔서 감사합니다.

어휘 attention 주목, (안내 방송에서) 주목해 주세요 passenger 승객 depart 출발하다 proceed to ~로 향하다 board 탑승하다 amount 양 carry-on luggage 기내 휴대용 수하물 restrict 제한하다 furthermore 뿐만 아니라, 게다가 prohibited 금지된 sharp object 날카로운 물체 baggage 짐 immediately 즉시 cooperation 협조

74   세부 사항
비행기는 언제 출발할 예정인가?
(A) 15분 후에
(B) 30분 후에
(C) 1시간 후에
(D) 1시간 30분 후에

해설 지문의 초반에 비행기가 30분 후에 출발할 것(The flight will be departing in 30 minutes.)임을 알려 주고 있으므로 (B)가 정답이다. 지문의 30 minutes가 보기에서는 half an hour로 바뀐 것에 주의한다.

75   세부 사항
화자는 기내 휴대용 수하물에 대해 뭐라고 말하는가?
(A) 완전히 가득 차 있다.
(B) 검사될 것이다.
(C) 허용되지 않는다.
(D) 제한될 것이다.

해설 기내 휴대용 수하물의 양이 제한될 것(the amount of carry-on luggage will be restricted.)이라고 했으므로 (D)가 정답이다.

76   세부 사항
다음 물품 중 기내 휴대용 수하물로 허용되지 않는 것은?
(A) 카메라
(B) 커터칼
(C) 손목시계
(D) 태블릿 PC

해설 지문에서 날카로운 물체는 금지된다고 했으므로(please make sure that you are not carrying any prohibited items such as lighters or sharp objects in any of your baggage.) 칼을 휴대하는 것은 허용되지 않는다. 따라서 (B)가 정답이다. 지문에서는 sharp objects였지만 답에서는 a box cutter로 사용된 것에 주의한다.

[77-79] 공지

Attention, everyone. Please don't forget that this is the weekend that we will be moving locations. Please make sure to take all personal belongings from desks, workstations, and lockers. We will be letting everyone stop work two hours early so that you can get everything organized. For small work-related items, please pack them into the boxes that we have provided and write your name on the outside. The boxes will be dropped at your new work location. On Monday from 9 A.M. to 11 A.M., we will allow everyone to get settled back in. Have a great weekend.

주목해주세요, 여러분. 이번이 우리가 이사 가는 주말이라는 것을 잊지 마시기 바랍니다. 책상, 작업장, 사물함에서 모든 개인 소지품을 가져가시기 바랍니다. 여러분이 모든 것을 정리할 수 있도록 2시간 일찍 업무를 끝내 드릴 겁니다. 업무와 관련된 작은 물품들은 우리가 제공한 상자에 넣고 상자 바깥쪽에 여러분의 이름을 써 주시기 바랍니다. 상자들은 여러분의 새로운 작업장에 옮겨질 겁니다. 월요일 오전 9시부터 오전 11시까지 모든 사람들이 짐을 풀도록 할 것입니다. 좋은 주말 보내세요.

어휘 personal belongings 개인 소지품 workstation 작업장 organize 정리하다, 구성하다 related 관련된 pack 짐을 싸다 provide 제공하다 drop 두다 allow 허락하다 settle in 짐을 풀다

77   청자의 직업
누구를 위한 공지인가?
(A) 주주들
(B) 배달 직원들
(C) 이삿짐 센터 직원들
(D) 사무실 직원들

해설 지문에서 이번 주말에 사무실 이전이 있고(Please don't forget that this is the weekend that we will be moving locations.), 이와 관련하여 자신의 물건을 챙기라고(Please make sure to take all personal belongings) 했으므로 공지를 듣는 사람이 사무실 직원들임을 알 수 있다. 그러므로 (D)가 정답이다.

78 다음에 할 일

공지에 따르면, 회사는 주말 동안 무엇을 할 것인가?
(A) 회사 야유회를 간다
(B) 직원을 교육한다
(C) 직원을 평가한다
(D) 위치를 이전한다

해설 지문 초반에 이번 주말에 사무실 이전이 있다(this is the weekend that we will be moving locations.)고 알려 주고 있으므로 (D)가 정답이다.

79 요청 사항

화자는 청자들에게 무엇을 하라고 요청하는가?
(A) 집에 일찍 가기
(B) 장비 관리하기
(C) 이사를 위해 물건 챙기기
(D) 양식 작성하기

해설 지문에서 사무실 이전과 관련하여 자신의 물건을 챙기라고(please pack them into the boxes that we have provided and write your name on the outside.) 했으므로 이사를 위해 짐을 챙긴다는 내용의 (C)가 정답이다.

[80-82] 공지

Good morning, everyone. Before we get started with our weekly meeting, I want to deliver you a sincere apology for changing the time of the meeting all of a sudden. We found out that the meeting room had already been booked, so we had to change the time to 5 P.M. However, the place for the meeting is the same, so this won't cause any confusion. As you arrive, you will see the documents for the meeting all arranged on the table. We're terribly sorry again for any inconvenience this may have caused.

좋은 아침입니다, 여러분. 주간 회의에 앞서, 갑자기 회의 시간을 변경한 것에 대해 진심 어린 사과의 말씀을 드립니다. 회의실이 이미 예약되었다는 것을 알게 되어서 우리는 오후 5시로 시간을 변경해야 했습니다. 그러나 회의 장소는 변경되지 않았기 때문에 어떤 혼란도 일으키지 않을 것입니다. 도착하시면 테이블 위에 회의 자료가 모두 준비되어 있을 것입니다. 다시 한번 불편을 드려 죄송합니다.

어휘 weekly meeting 주간 회의 deliver an apology 사과하다 sincere 진실된 all of a sudden 갑자기 find out ~를 발견하다, 알아내다 book 예약하다 confusion 혼동, 혼란 terribly 대단히 inconvenience 불편

80 세부 사항

회의는 얼마나 자주 열리는가?
(A) 일주일에 한 번
(B) 일주일에 두 번
(C) 한 달에 한 번
(D) 한 달에 두 번

해설 지문 초반부(Before we get started with our weekly meeting,)에서 weekly라는 표현을 통해 일주일에 한 번 열리는 회의라는 것을 알 수 있다. 따라서 정답은 (A)이다.

81 세부 사항

화자는 왜 청자들에게 사과하는가?
(A) 그녀가 갑작스럽게 변경해서
(B) 그녀가 직원들을 야근 시켜서
(C) 그녀가 불편한 시간대를 골라서
(D) 그녀가 통지하는 것을 잊어서

해설 지문의 초반부에 화자가 갑자기 회의 시간을 바꾸게 되어 미안하다(I want to deliver you a sincere apology for changing the time of the meeting all of a sudden.)고 말하고 있으므로 (A)가 정답이다.

82 세부 사항

화자가 담화에서 언급하는 것은?
(A) 회의 시간은 오후 5시로 정해졌다.
(B) 회의 장소가 변경되었다.
(C) 직원들은 서류를 작성해야 한다.
(D) 직원들은 초과 근무를 해야 한다.

해설 화자가 오후 5시로 시간을 변경해야 했다고(so we had to change the time to 5 P.M.) 말했으므로 회의 시간이 5시로 정해졌다는 것을 알 수 있다. 그러므로 (A)가 정답이다.

[83-85] 소개

Good evening, everyone, and welcome to the Kansas State Private Pilots Awards Dinner. Every year we honor a pilot who has exhibited great skill, bravery or exceptional kindness by giving an award. This year is very special. This award was established 50 years ago by the first female pilot in the state of Kansas, Bertha Gable. Bertha is actually with us tonight and will be presenting this year's Pilot of the Year Award. She even doesn't know who will be receiving an award today. Then, Bertha, would you please come to the podium to announce the winner?

안녕하세요, 여러분. Kansas State Private Pilots Awards Dinner에 오신 것을 환영합니다. 매년 우리는 대단한 기술, 용기 또는 특별한 친절을 보여 준 조종사에게 상을 수여함으로써 명예를 드립니다. 올해는 매우 특별합니다. 이 상은 50년 전, 캔자스 주의 최초 여성 조종사인 베르타 게이블 씨에 의해 시작되었습니다. 사실 베르타 씨는 올해의 Pilot of the Year Award를 수여하기 위해 오늘밤 우리와 함께 있습니다. 그녀도 오늘 누가 상을 받을지 모릅니다. 그러면 베르타 씨, 수상자 발표를 위해 강단으로 나와 주시겠습니까?

어휘 award 상 honor 명예를 주다 exhibit 보여 주다 skill 기술 exceptional 예외의, 특별한 establish 설립하다 female pilot 여성 조종사 present 수여하다 podium 강단

83 담화 장소

화자는 어디에 있는가?
(A) 경찰서에
(B) 라디오 방송국에
(C) 시상식장에
(D) 공항에

> **해설** 시상식에 온 것을 환영한다(welcome to the Kansas State Private Pilots Awards Dinner.)고 하고 있으므로 (C)가 정답이다.

84 세부 사항

이 행사는 얼마나 오랫동안 진행되었는가?
(A) 10년 동안
(B) 15년 동안
(C) 20년 동안
(D) 50년 동안

> **해설** 지문의 중간 부분에 50년 전에 시작되었다(This award was established 50 years ago)고 하고 있으므로 (D)가 정답이다.

85 다음에 할 일

다음에 어떤 일이 일어날 것 같은가?
(A) 시연이 있을 것이다.
(B) 비행기가 착륙할 것이다.
(C) 저녁 식사가 제공될 것이다.
(D) 누군가가 상을 받을 것이다.

> **해설** 지문의 마지막에 수상자 발표를 위해 베르타 씨에게 강단으로 오라고(Bertha, would you please come to the podium to announce the winner?) 하고 있으므로 누군가가 상을 받게 될 것을 예상할 수 있다. 그러므로 (D)가 정답이다.

[86-88] 안내

Welcome, everyone. Thank you for volunteering for our software testing group. I'm Mark and during the test session, I'll be requiring you to perform various tasks using computers to ensure that the newly-downloaded software works properly. Don't worry, <u>you cannot make any mistakes</u> during the test since I will be right next to you the whole time. Our ultimate goal is to enhance our software, so all we want is to see how you handle the task. Now, let's get started!

여러분, 반갑습니다. 저희 소프트웨어 실험 그룹에 자원해 주셔서 감사합니다. 저는 마크이고, 테스트 기간 동안, 저는 새로 다운로드된 소프트웨어가 적절하게 작동되는지 확인하기 위해 여러분께 컴퓨터를 사용하여 다양한 업무들을 수행하도록 요구할 것입니다. 걱정하지 마세요, 제가 계속 옆에 있을 것이기 때문에 여러분은 테스트 동안에 실수하지 않을 것입니다. 저희의 궁극적인 목표는 소프트웨어 개선이며, 그렇기 때문에 저희는 여러분이 업무를 어떻게 다루는지 보려고 합니다. 이제, 시작합시다!

> **어휘** volunteer 자원하다; 자원 봉사자   require 요구하다   various 다양한   task 업무   ensure 확인하다   newly-downloaded 새로 다운로드된   software 소프트웨어   properly 적절히, 적당히   ultimate 궁극적인   enhance 향상시키다, 개선하다   handle 다루다, 처리하다

86 화자의 직업

화자는 어느 분야에서 일하는가?
(A) 소프트웨어 제조
(B) 구매자들에게 소프트웨어 공급
(C) 소프트웨어 판매
(D) 소프트웨어 효율성 실험

> **해설** 지문의 첫 번째 문장에서 화자가 소프트웨어 실험 그룹에 자원해 주셔서 고맙다고(Thank you for volunteering for our software testing group.) 하고 있으므로 화자가 일하는 분야는 소프트웨어를 실험하는 곳임을 알 수 있다. 그러므로 (D)가 정답이다.

87 요청 사항

청자들은 어떤 일을 하도록 요구 받았는가?
(A) 바이러스 백신 소프트웨어 사용하기
(B) 컴퓨터 프로그램 테스트하기
(C) 보다 나은 소프트웨어 판매 방안 논의하기
(D) 설문조사하기

> **해설** 지문의 중간 부분에 화자가 청자들에게 컴퓨터를 사용하여 새로 다운로드된 소프트웨어가 적절히 작동되고 있는지 확인하기 위해 다양한 업무들을 수행하도록 요구할 것(I'll be requiring you to perform various tasks using computers to ensure that the newly-downloaded software works properly.)이라고 하므로 청자들이 컴퓨터 프로그램을 테스트할 것을 알 수 있다. 따라서 (B)가 정답이다.

88 의도 파악

화자가 "여러분은 실수하지 않을 것입니다"라고 말하는 의미는 무엇인가?
(A) 청자들은 이 일이 큰 문제가 아니라고 생각해야 한다.
(B) 청자들은 화자로부터 도움을 받을 수 있다.
(C) 청자들은 지시 사항에 따라야 한다.
(D) 청자들은 업무를 빠르게 끝낼 수 있을 것이다.

> **해설** 해당 문장을 보면 테스트 동안에 계속 옆에 화자가 있으니 걱정하지 말라고(Don't worry, you cannot make any mistakes during the test since I will be right next to you the whole time.) 하므로 화자가 청자들을 도와줄 것임을 알 수 있다. 그러므로 (B)가 정답이다.

[89-91] 전화 메시지

Hi, this is a message for Colette Nixon. This is Donald Milton calling from Widget's Fine Fashion. Because you are a member of our preferred customer group, you are being invited to our Old Season/New Season sale. You will have the opportunity to buy clearance items at blowout prices and have the first chance to get the new season's offerings. Best of all, you will be eligible for a 15% discount on all items in the store. This includes already discounted clearance items. This exclusive event will take place from 10 A.M. to 6 P.M. this Saturday only at Widget's. Just show your preferred customer card to get in. We hope to see you there.

안녕하세요. 콜레트 닉슨 씨에게 메시지 남깁니다. 저는 Widget's Fine Fashion에서 전화 드리는 도날드 밀턴입니다. 당신이 특별 고객 그룹 회원이시기 때문에 저희의 Old Season/New Season 세일에 초대합니다. 당신은 파격적인 가격에 재고 정리 제품들을 구매할 기회와 새로운 시즌의 제품을 받으실 첫 기회를 가지게 됩니다. 무엇보다도 상점의 모든 품목에 15%의 할인을 받으실 수 있습니다. 이것은 이미 할인된 재고 정리 제품들에도 적용됩니다. 이 독점 행사는 이번 주 토요일 오전 10시부터 오후 6시까지 오직 Widget's에서만 진행됩니다. 입장을 위해 당신의 특별 고객 카드를 보여주시기만 하면 됩니다. 그곳에서 당신을 뵙기를 바랍니다.

어휘 preferred customer group 특별 고객 그룹 clearance 재고 정리 blowout price 파격가 be eligible for ~할 자격이 있다 include 포함하다 exclusive 독점적인 take place 일어나다

89 세부 사항

전화를 건 사람은 무엇을 홍보하고 있는가?
(A) 특별 세일
(B) 새 의류 라인
(C) 무료 배송
(D) 특별 고객 멤버십

해설 메시지의 초반부에 세일에 초대한다(you are being invited to our Old Season/New Season sale.)고 하므로 (A) 특별 세일이 정답이다.

90 세부 사항

닉슨 씨는 구매하면 무엇을 받을 수 있는가?
(A) 연장된 보증서
(B) 상품권
(C) 할인된 가격
(D) 무료 홍보 전단지

해설 메시지에서 가게의 모든 품목에 대해서 15% 할인을 받을 수 있다(you will be eligible for a 15% discount on all items in the store.)고 하고 있으므로 닉슨이 물건을 구매하면 할인된 가격으로 살 수 있음을 알 수 있다. 그러므로 (C)가 정답이다. 메시지에서는 a 15% discount로 나오지만 정답에서는 a reduced price로 바뀌는 것에 주의한다.

91 세부 사항

닉슨 씨는 이 제안을 어떻게 이용할 수 있는가?
(A) 토요일에 상점을 방문함으로써
(B) 특별 쿠폰을 우편으로 보냄으로써
(C) 회사 웹 사이트를 통해 회원권을 신청함으로써
(D) 배달원에게 특별 신분증을 보여 줌으로써

해설 메시지 마지막 부분에서 토요일에 이 행사에 입장할 때 특별 고객 카드를 보여 주면 된다(This exclusive event will take place from 10 A.M. to 6 P.M. this Saturday only at Widget's. Just show your preferred customer card to get in.)고 말하고 있다. 즉, 토요일에 가게를 방문하면 되므로 정답은 (A)이다.

[92-94] 설명/소개

Hello, everyone, and welcome. Today I'm going to teach you my secrets about how to make money in real estate. I've been in the real estate business for more than 25 years now. It took me quite a while to figure out what I'm going to teach you today, but for the last 15 years, I've made a lot of money in this business whether the market was up or down. I'm still making money with this system today, but after all these years, I've decided to share my system with other people. It's just too good not to. Now, I'm going to show you some example cases on the screen. I'll be showing you what types of property were involved, every step I took, and how much money I ended up with.

안녕하세요 여러분, 환영합니다. 오늘 저는 여러분에게 부동산으로 돈 버는 방법에 대한 비법을 알려드릴 것입니다. 제가 부동산 업계에 종사한 지도 이제 25년이 넘었습니다. 오늘 여러분에게 무엇을 가르쳐야 할지 생각해 내는 데 시간이 꽤 걸렸지만, 지난 15년 동안 시장 경기가 좋든 나쁘든 간에 저는 이 사업을 통해 많은 돈을 벌었습니다. 현재도 이 시스템으로 돈을 벌고 있지만, 결국 요즘에는 저의 시스템을 다른 사람들과 공유하기로 결심했습니다. 그러지 않기엔 그것이 너무 좋거든요. 이제, 스크린에 몇 가지 사례를 보여 드리겠습니다. 어떤 유형의 부동산들이 포함되었는지, 제가 착수했던 모든 단계, 그리고 결국에는 얼마나 많은 돈으로 귀결되었는지 여러분들께 보여드릴 겁니다.

어휘 real estate 부동산 quite a while 꽤 오랫동안 figure out 알아내다 whether ~인지 아닌지 share A with B A를 B와 공유하다 property 부동산 involve 포함하다 end up with 결국 ~하게 되다

92 화자의 직업

화자는 누구인 것 같은가?
(A) 은행가
(B) 광고 경영진
(C) 대학 교수
(D) 부동산 투자자

해설 초반부에 부동산을 통해 돈을 버는 비법을 가르쳐 주겠다고 (Today I'm going to teach you my secrets about how to make money in real estate.) 하는 것을 보아 화자가 (D) 부동산 투자자임을 알 수 있다. 지문에 나온 real estate가 답에서는 property로 바뀌는 것을 주의한다.

93　주제/목적
화자가 주로 무엇에 대해 이야기하는가?
(A) 시간 관리 기술
(B) 돈 버는 기술
(C) 건강 유지하기
(D) 최고의 여행지

해설 지문 상단에서 화자가 부동산 투자자임을 알 수 있고, 화자는 부동산을 통해 돈을 버는 방법(how to make money in real estate)에 대해서 이야기하고 있으므로 (B)가 정답이다.

94　다음에 할 일
청자들은 다음에 무엇을 할 것인가?
(A) 부동산을 방문한다
(B) 몇 가지 사례 연구를 본다
(C) 역할극을 한다
(D) 인터넷으로 조사한다

해설 화자가 마지막 부분에서 스크린에 몇 가지 사례를 보여 주겠다(Now, I'm going to show you some example cases on the screen.)고 하고 있으므로 청자들이 사례 연구를 볼 것이라는 내용의 (B)가 정답이다.

[95-97] 방송 & 시간표

You're currently listening to our music broadcasting on the All Music Channel. I have an announcement about the upcoming Winter Music Festival held in front of the City Hall. We have just found out that due to weather conditions, the first event will be postponed. The festival organizers are planning to hold that event on the same day as Jennifer Lauren's show. Please visit our Web site for the updated schedule and for further information about the musicians. Please stay tuned.

여러분은 현재 All Music 채널에서 저희 음악 방송을 듣고 계십니다. 시청 앞에서 열릴 이번 겨울 음악 축제에 관한 소식이 있습니다. 기상 조건으로 인해 첫 번째 행사가 연기될 것이라고 합니다. 축제 주최자들은 그 행사를 제니퍼 로렌의 쇼와 같은 날에 개최할 예정이라고 합니다. 업데이트된 스케줄과 뮤지션에 대한 더 많은 정보를 원하시면 저희 웹 사이트를 방문하시기 바랍니다. 채널 고정하세요.

겨울 음악 축제

출연자
12월 20일 - 조 므라즈
12월 21일 - 제니퍼 로렌
12월 22일 - 린다
12월 23일 - 매튜 리

어휘 currently 현재　broadcasting 방송　announcement 발표, 소식　upcoming 다가오는　postpone 연기하다　organizer 조직자, 주최자　further information 더 많은 정보　stay tuned 채널을 고정하다　details 세부사항

95　세부 사항
축제가 연기된 원인은 무엇인가?
(A) 악기의 고장
(B) 악천후
(C) 주민들의 불만
(D) 도로 보수 공사

해설 화자가 기상 조건으로 인해 첫 행사가 연기 될 것(We have just found out that due to weather conditions, the first event will be postponed.)이라고 말하므로 정답은 (B)이다.

96　시각 자료 연계
시각 자료를 보시오. 화자에 따르면 누구의 공연이 연기될 것인가?
(A) 조 므라즈의 공연
(B) 제니퍼 로렌의 공연
(C) 린다의 공연
(D) 매튜 리의 공연

해설 화자가 첫 번째 행사가 연기될 것(the first event will be postponed.)이라고 언급했고 도표에서 첫 번째 행사에 해당하는 것은 (A) 조 므라즈의 공연이다.

97　제안
화자는 청자들에게 무엇을 하라고 권하는가?
(A) 웹 사이트 참고하기
(B) TV 쇼 시청하기
(C) 영수증 복사하기
(D) 친구 데려오기

해설 지문의 후반에서 화자가 업데이트된 스케줄과 뮤지션에 대한 더 많은 정보를 원하면 웹 사이트를 방문하라(Please visit our Web site for the updated schedule and for further information about the musicians.)고 한다. 따라서 웹 사이트를 참고하라는 내용의 (A)가 정답이다. visit our Web site가 refer to a Web site로 바뀐 것에 주목하자.

[98-100] 안내 & 도표

Welcome, I'm the manager of this cafeteria here at ThankYou Enterprises. I know you've already seen a lot today on the new employee tour. Well, our cafeteria not only serves various types of coffee but also many kinds of delicious food for you. And as you are all aware, we always do our best to keep the environment clean. As you can see, all waste is sorted into these four labeled bins. Most importantly, please pay extra attention to plastic, since we aim to recycle it to prevent environmental pollution.

환영합니다. 저는 ThankYou 기업의 구내식당 매니저입니다. 오늘 신입 사원 투어에서 여러분들이 이미 많은 것을 보셨으리라 생각합니다. 음, 저희 구내식당은 여러분들을 위해 다양한 종류의 커피 뿐만 아니라 많은 종류의 맛있는 음식도 제공합니다. 그리고 모두가 아시다시피, 저희는 식당의 환경을 깨끗하게 유지하기 위해 항상 최선을 다하고 있습니다. 보시다시피, 모든 쓰레기는 4개의 라벨이 붙어 있는 쓰레기통에 분류됩니다. 가장 중요한 것은, 저희는 환경오염을 막기 위해 플라스틱 재활용을 목표로 하기 때문에, 플라스틱에 특별히 주의해주세요.

1번 통	유리
2번 통	플라스틱
3번 통	종이
4번 통	캔

어휘 cafeteria 구내식당　new employee tour 신입사원 견학　not only A but also B A뿐만 아니라 B도　various 다양한　kind 종류　delicious 맛있는　environment 환경　waste 쓰레기　sort 분류하다　labeled 라벨이 붙어 있는　bin 쓰레기통　aim to ~을 목표로 하다　recycle 재활용하다

98 화자의 근무지

화자는 어디에서 일하는가?
(A) 관리부에서
(B) 인사부에서
(C) 구내식당에서
(D) 진료소에서

해설 지문의 초반부에서 화자가 자신을 구내식당의 매니저(I'm the manager of this cafeteria here at ThankYou Enterprises.)라고 소개하고 있으므로 화자가 일하는 곳은 구내식당임을 알 수 있다. 그러므로 (C)가 정답이다.

99 청자의 신분

이 담화는 누구를 대상으로 하는가?
(A) 신입 사원
(B) 카페 주인
(C) 퇴직한 사원
(D) 환경 운동가

해설 화자가 오늘 신입 사원 투어에서 여러분들이 많은 것을 보셨으리라 생각한다(I know you've already seen a lot today on the new employee tour.)고 하는 것으로 보아 이 담화는 (A) 신입 사원들을 대상으로 한다는 것을 알 수 있다. 지문의 new employee가 보기에서는 new hires로 바뀐 것에 주의한다.

100 시각 자료 연계

시각 자료를 보시오. 화자는 청자에게 어떤 쓰레기통을 주의하라고 하는가?

(A) 1번 통
(B) 2번 통
(C) 3번 통
(D) 4번 통

해설 지문의 후반부에서 화자는 환경오염을 예방하기 위해 플라스틱을 재활용하니 주의를 기울여달라(please pay extra attention to plastic, since we aim to recycle it to prevent environmental pollution.)고 언급한다. 도표에서 플라스틱을 넣는 통은 2번이므로 정답은 (B)이다.

PART · 5

101 대명사

영업일 기준 5일 내로 딘 씨에게 당신의 지원서를 보내주세요.

해설 알맞은 대명사를 선택하는 문제이다. 명사 'job application' 앞에서 한정사 역할을 할 수 있는 소유격 대명사 (D)가 정답이다.

어휘 application 지원서, 신청서　form 양식　within ~이내에

102 분사

우리가 지난달에 조사했던 대부분의 고객들은 Gallerion 백화점의 서비스에 만족했습니다.

해설 알맞은 분사를 선택하는 문제이다. satisfy는 감정 동사로, 주체가 사물일 때는 감정을 유발하는 현재분사, 사람일 때는 감정을 느끼는 주체이므로 과거분사를 쓴다. 여기서는 주체가 사람인 'Most customers'이므로 과거분사 (B)가 정답이다.

어휘 survey 조사, 조사하다

103 동사의 형태, 시제, 수

지난주에 출시된 새로운 Z9 세단은 긍정적인 평가를 많이 받았습니다.

해설 관계절의 동사를 선택하는 문제이다. release는 타동사이기 때문에 목적어를 필요로 하지만, 빈칸 뒤에 목적어가 없으므로 수동태를 써야 한다. 또한, 관계대명사 that의 선행사 'The new Z9 sedan'이 단수이기 때문에 단수 동사인 (C)가 가장 적절하다.

어휘 release 출시하다, 공개하다　positive 긍정적인

104 형용사 어휘

직원들은 회사 데이터를 안전하게 유지하기 위해 비밀번호를 90일마다 변경하도록 권장 받습니다.

해설 보어 자리에 알맞은 형용사 어휘를 선택하는 문제이다. 데이터를 '안전하게' 유지하기 위해 비밀번호를 바꾸라는 것이 문맥상 자연스러우므로 (A)가 정답이다. (B)는 '유용한', (C)는 '유효한', (D)는 '이용 가능한'이라는 의미이다.

어휘 be encouraged to V ~하도록 권유 받다

105 대명사

제임스 헨델은 일류 회사에서의 방대한 관리 경력이 있는 많은 사람들보다 훨씬 더 훌륭한 관리 능력을 보여주었습니다.

해설 알맞은 대명사를 고르는 문제이다. 빈칸 뒤 전치사구의 수식을 받을 수 있는 대명사는 that과 those인데, 'many of' 뒤에는 복수형이 나와야 하므로 (D) those가 정답이다.

어휘 administrative 관리의 ability 능력 leading 일류의, 선두의

106 동사 어휘

트럼프 씨는 사업을 효율적으로 운영하는 방법에 대해 워싱턴 기념관에서 인상적인 강연을 했습니다.

해설 동사 어휘 문제로, 'deliver a lecture(강의를 하다)'라는 표현으로 연결되는 (C)가 정답이다. (A)는 '언급하다', (B)는 '반응하다, 응답하다', (D)는 '생각하다, 고려하다'라는 뜻으로, 문맥상 적절하지 않다.

어휘 impressive 인상적인 lecture 강의 run a business 사업을 운영하다

107 동사의 형태, 시제, 수

컨벤션 센터가 확장되었기 때문에, 사람들을 500명까지 수용할 수 있습니다.

해설 동사의 형태를 고르는 문제이다. 빈칸 앞에 has가 있는 것으로 보아 현재완료(have p.p) 시제임을 알 수 있고, 빈칸 뒤에 타동사 enlarge의 목적어가 없으므로 수동태로 쓰였음을 알 수 있다. 따라서 정답은 현재완료 수동태인 (C)이다.

어휘 now that ~이므로, ~이기 때문에 seat 앉히다 up to ~까지 enlarge 확대하다, 확장하다

108 전치사

요금에 관한 구체적인 정보는 당신의 청구서에 명시되어 있습니다.

해설 문맥상 알맞은 전치사를 선택하는 문제이다. 청구서 '위'에 명시되어 있다는 의미이므로 (A) on이 적합하다.

어휘 specific 구체적인 indicate 나타내다, 명시하다 invoice 송장, 청구서

109 형용사 어휘

Prime Tech 사의 새로운 친환경 난방기는 다른 제조업체에서 생산한 것들보다 훨씬 적은 에너지를 소비합니다.

해설 알맞은 형용사 어휘를 선택하는 문제이다. 빈칸 뒤에 than이 있고 앞에는 비교급 강조부사 much가 있으므로 비교급인 (B), (C), (D) 중 골라야 한다. '에너지 소비량'을 수식할 때 '많고 적음'으로 수식하는 것이 자연스러우므로 little의 비교급인 (D) less가 적합하다.

어휘 eco-friendly 친환경적인 consume 소비하다

110 to부정사 자리

보안을 강화하기 위해, 그 회사는 모든 직원들에게 보안 출입증을 나눠주었습니다.

해설 본동사 distributed가 있으므로 빈칸에는 security를 목적어로 취하는 준동사가 들어가야 한다. 의미상 '강화하기 위해'라는 목적을 나타내는 to부정사가 적합하므로 (A)가 정답이다.

어휘 security 보안, 경비, 안보 distribute 나누어 주다, 분배하다 enhance 강화하다, 보강하다

111 부사 어휘

존슨 씨는 서울로 출장을 갈 예정이기 때문에 유감스럽게도 시상식에 참석할 수 없습니다.

해설 문맥상 알맞은 부사를 선택하는 문제이다. 다른 일정으로 인해 '유감스럽게도' 시상식에 참석하지 못한다는 뜻이므로 (A) regretfully가 의미상 가장 자연스럽다.

어휘 participate in ~에 참석하다 be scheduled to V ~할 예정이다 significantly 상당히 considerately 사려 깊게 purposely 고의로

112 동사 어휘

신입 사원을 고용할 때, 학력보다 경력에 중점을 두는 것이 바람직합니다.

해설 분사구문에 어울리는 동사 어휘를 고르는 문제로, 의미상 신입사원을 '고용하다'가 적절하므로 정답은 (A)이다. (B) '말하다'는 자동사이므로 뒤에 목적어를 취할 수 없고, (C) '통보하다'와 (D) '훈련시키다'는 문맥상 적합하지 않다.

어휘 desirable 바람직한 place emphasis on ~을 강조하다 rather than ~보다는

113 현재분사

Prestige Planning 사는 기업 광고를 전문으로 하는 저명한 회사입니다.

해설 문장에 동사(is)가 있으므로 동사 (A)와 (D)는 답이 될 수 없고, specialize는 자동사이므로 과거분사(수동의 의미)로 쓰이지 않는다. 따라서 정답은 (B)이다.

어휘 established 인정받는, 저명한 specialize in ~을 전문으로 하다, 전공하다

114 전치사

Max 건설은 프로젝트에서 자재가 남는 경우가 빈번해서, 그것들을 후원이 필요한 자선단체에 기부합니다.

해설 동사 donate는 전치사 to와 함께 'donate A to B(A를 B에 기부하다)'의 형태로 쓰이므로 정답은 (A)이다.

어휘 frequently 빈번하게, 자주 leftover 나머지의, 남은 charity 자선단체

115 전치사

최신 노트북의 인기를 고려해서, Koreana Electronics 사는 생산량을 늘리기로 결정했습니다.

해설 콤마 앞에 동사가 없으므로 접속사는 들어갈 수 없고, 전치사인 (B) '~에 대한', (D) '~를 고려해 볼 때' 중 인기를 '고려해 볼 때'라는 뜻의 (D)가 의미상 적합하다. (A)와 (C)는 that 뒤에 완전한 문장이 나와야 하므로 답이 될 수 없다.

어휘 popularity 인기   decide 결정하다   increase 증가하다   production 생산(량)

116 명사 어휘

Wellbeing Food 경영진은 현재의 보수 작업이 고객 여러분에게 일으킬 수 있는 불편에 대해 사과드립니다.

해설 문맥상 적절한 명사 어휘를 선택하는 문제이다. 빈칸 앞의 'apologizes for(~에 대해 사과하다)' 뒤에 나올 어휘로는 (D) inconvenience(불편)가 가장 자연스럽다.

어휘 apologize for ~에 대해 사과하다   environment 환경   dedication 헌신, 전념   distribution 분배

117 분사

고객 서비스 직원에게 연락하려는 반복된 시도는 성공하지 못했습니다.

해설 attempts를 수식하는 적절한 분사를 선택하는 문제로, '반복된 시도'라는 뜻의 (A)가 가장 적합하다. 빈칸을 주어 자리라고 생각하면 (B)를 동명사로 보고 정답으로 선택할 수 있지만, 동사가 have이기 때문에 주어는 복수 명사가 와야 한다.

어휘 attempt 시도   repeat 반복하다, 되풀이하다   repetition 되풀이, 반복

118 관계대명사

Pro Engineering 사는 올해 말에 도입될 새로운 관리 시스템을 운영하기에 충분한 자격을 갖추고 있습니다.

해설 적절한 관계대명사를 선택하는 문제이다. 빈칸 뒤에 동사가 있고, 선행사가 사물(the new management system)이므로 (C) which가 적합하다. (B) that은 계속적 용법으로 콤마 뒤에 쓸 수 없다는 것에 주의한다.

어휘 be qualified for ~할 자격이 있다   operate 운영하다, 조작하다   introduce 도입하다, 소개하다

119 분사

부서장과 그의 팀은 프로젝트를 가까스로 예정대로 마무리 지었습니다.

해설 문장에 동사 managed가 있으므로 (A), (D)는 오답이다. 빈칸은 사역동사 have의 목적격 보어 자리로, 프로젝트가 '완성된다'는 수동의 의미이기 때문에 과거분사 (C)가 와야 한다.

어휘 manage to 간신히 ~하다   on schedule 예정대로

120 형용사 어휘

TH Soft에서 새로 출시되는 온라인 게임 'The Revolution'은 색다른 무언가를 추구하길 원하는 사람들을 위해 고안된 다양한 게임 경험을 제공합니다.

해설 문맥상 어울리는 형용사를 고르는 문제로, (A) '민감한, 예민한' (B) '다가오는, 곧 있을' (C) '엄격한' (D) '공정한' 중에서 '곧 있을', 즉 새로 출시된다는 의미의 (B)가 가장 적절하다.

어휘 revolution 혁명   designed for ~을 위해 만들어진   pursue 추구하다

121 형용사 자리

북미 지역의 휴대폰 시장은 지난 2년간 경쟁이 더 치열해졌습니다.

해설 <grow + 형용사>는 '~해지다'라는 의미로, 상태나 상황의 변화를 나타낸다. 따라서 정답은 형용사 (D) competitive이다.

어휘 compete 경쟁하다   competition 경쟁   competitive 경쟁이 치열한, 경쟁력 있는

122 부사 어휘

저희의 주간 소식지가 아직 발송되지 않았으니, 인내심을 갖고 며칠만 더 기다려 주세요.

해설 'have yet to do(아직 ~하지 않았다)'의 구조로, 빈칸은 (A)가 정답이다.

어휘 weekly 매주의, 주간의   newsletter 소식지   patient 참을성 있는

123 동사의 형태, 시제, 수

Parker 가에서 진행 중인 공사 때문에, 운전자들은 시내로 가기 위해 Burrard 가를 이용하도록 안내 받습니다.

해설 문장에 동사가 없으므로 빈칸은 동사 자리이다. direct는 3형식 동사로 목적어를 필요로 하지만, 빈칸 뒤에는 목적어가 없으므로 수동태인 (D)가 정답이다.

어휘 ongoing 진행 중인   construction 건설, 공사   motorist 운전자   direct 지시하다, 안내하다

124 관계대명사

Future Telecom에서는 고객 만족이 가장 중요합니다.

해설 문장에 동사가 두 개이므로 빈칸에는 접속사가 들어가야 하는데, 빈칸 뒤에 주어가 없으므로 주격 관계대명사 (A)와 (C) 중 골라야 한다. 선행사 something이 사람이 아니므로 (C) that이 정답이다. something, anything 등이 선행사인 경우 주로 관계대명사 that을 쓴다는 것을 알아두자.

어휘 customer satisfaction 고객 만족

125 동사 어휘

Lux Publishing 사의 사장은 12주 연속 최고 매출액을 이어가고 있음에 우쭐했습니다.

해설 '(A) 환영 받는 (B) ~에 우쭐해하는 (C) 세련된 (D) 운영된, 작동된'의 수동태 어휘들 중에서, 최고 판매 기록에 대해 "우쭐해한다"는 뜻이 가장 자연스러우므로 (B)가 정답이다.

어휘 president 사장   consecutive 연속의

126 비교급

두 명의 기계공 중에서, 더 좋은 자질을 가진 사람이 공장의 새 장비를 작동시킬 것입니다.

해설 비교 대상이 둘이므로(Of the two ~) 빈칸에는 비교급을 써야 한다. 따라서 정답은 (B) better이다. 전치사 of 뒤의 비교 대상이 둘이면 비교급 앞에는 반드시 정관사(the)를 쓴다는 것을 알아 두자.

어휘 operator 운영자, (기계를) 조작하는 사람   qualified 적격의, 자질이 있는   run 작동하다, 작동시키다   equipment 장비

127 가정법 도치

마지막 순간에 담당자를 만나지 않았다면, 저는 판매 계약을 체결할 수 없었을 것입니다.

해설 가정법 과거완료(If+S+had p.p.)에서 If가 생략되고 주어와 had가 도치된 구문이다. 가정법 과거완료의 주절은 'S+조동사 과거형+have p.p.' 형태가 되어야 하므로 정답은 (C)이다.

어휘 representative 대표자, 대리인   enter into 시작하다, 들어가다   contract 계약

128 전치사

다음 주 수요일부터 직원들의 새로운 복장 규정이 시행될 것입니다.

해설 시점 표현(next Wednesday) 앞에서 전치사 역할을 하는 (A) Beginning이 정답이다. 유사 표현으로는 starting, as of, effective, from 등이 있다.

어휘 dress code 복장 규정   go into effect 효력이 발생되다, 시행되다   considering ~을 고려할 때   regarding ~에 관하여

129 동사 어휘

새 건물에 대한 설계는 현재의 정부 규정을 준수해야 합니다.

해설 빈칸 뒤의 전치사 with와 함께 쓸 수 있는 자동사로는 (A), (C), (D)가 있는데, (A) belong with(~와 관계가 있다), (C) consult with(~와 상의하다)는 의미상 적합하지 않고, 정부 규정을 '준수한다'는 뜻의 (D)가 가장 적절하다.

어휘 plan 계획, 설계도   current 현재의, 지금의   regulation 규정

130 전치사

충분한 정보 없이, 좋은 장소를 찾고 멋진 아파트를 임대하는 것은 어렵습니다.

해설 문맥에 맞는 적절한 전치사를 고르는 문제이다. 충분한 정보가 '없으면' 좋은 장소와 아파트를 찾기 어렵다는 내용이므로 정

답은 (A)이다.

어휘 sufficient 충분한   location 장소, 위치   rent 임대하다, 빌리다

PART • 6

[131-134] 이메일

수신: customerservice@monthlyjosun.com
발신: jacob_d@erictoeic.com
날짜: 4월 6일
제목: 취소 관련 (계정 번호 150218)

고객 서비스 담당자에게:

저는 귀사의 잡지 구독을 취소하고 싶습니다. 저는 늘 다양한 작가들이 쓴 훌륭한 뉴스와 흥미로운 이야기들을 즐겨 읽었지만, 요즘 제가 새로운 사업을 준비하느라 너무 바쁩니다. 그러므로 그것들을 읽을 만한 충분한 여유 시간이 없습니다. 올해 발행된 잡지들의 대부분은 아직 방치되어 있습니다.
제가 알기로, 제 정기 구독은 10월에 끝납니다. 그게 맞는지 확인한 후, 남은 구독료를 환불해 주세요.

이 문제를 신속히 처리해 주시면 감사하겠습니다.

진심으로,

제이콥 데이먼

어휘 subscription 구독   fascinating 매력적인   be busy ~ing ~하느라 바쁘다   publish 발행하다, 출판하다   confirm 확인해 주다   prompt 즉각적인, 신속한

131 동사 어휘

해설 이메일 제목이 "Regarding cancelation"이고, 뒤에 나오는 문장의 "I'm too busy preparing for my new business these days."에서 새로운 사업 준비로 너무 바쁘다고 했고, 이는 곧 잡지를 읽을 시간이 부족하다는 뜻이다. 따라서 잡지 구독을 '취소하겠다'는 내용이 자연스러우므로 정답은 (C)이다.

132 문맥에 맞는 문장 고르기

(A) 저는 비즈니스 잡지에 관심이 있습니다.
(B) 하지만 저는 항상 많은 책을 읽으려고 노력합니다.
(C) 저는 제 회사에 대해 글을 쓰고 싶습니다.
(D) 그러므로 그것들을 읽을 만한 충분한 여유 시간이 없습니다.

해설 앞 문장에서 사업을 준비하느라 너무 바쁘다고 했으므로, 그로 인한 결과를 설명하는 내용이 적합하다. 따라서, 바빠서 잡지를 읽을 시간이 없다고 말하는 (D)가 정답이다.

133 형용사 어휘

해설 앞에서 너무 바빠서 잡지를 읽기 어렵다고 했으므로, 문맥 흐름상 책이 '방치되어' 있다는 의미의 (B) neglected가 가장 적합하다.

134 분사

해설 빈칸 뒤의 명사를 수식하는 자리로 형용사나 분사가 올 수 있는데, remain은 수동형으로 쓸 수 없는 자동사이므로 정답은 (C) remaining(남아 있는)이다.

[135-138] 회의록

회의록

Star Motor 사의 간부 회의가 6월 1일에 본사에서 열렸다. 회의의 목적은 제2공장을 이전시킬 결정하는 것이었다. 생산부장 정 씨는 회사가 많이 성장해서 더 큰 부지로 공장을 이전해야 한다고 주장했다. 하지만, 회계부장 윤 씨는 "우리는 현재 투자할 충분한 자금이 없기 때문에 더 신중하게 생각해야 합니다."라고 말했다. 논의 끝에, 공장 이전에 대한 결론을 내지 못한 채 회의가 끝났다. 그 안건은 다음 회의에서 다시 다뤄질 예정이다.

어휘 headquarters 본사, 본부 relocate 이전하다 argue 주장하다 site 장소, 부지 invest 투자하다 conclusion 결론

135 명사절 접속사

해설 빈칸 앞에 있는 동사(decide)의 목적어 역할을 하면서, 뒤에 있는 to부정사를 취할 수 있는 접속사 (B) whether이 적합하다. 나머지는 의미상, 문법상 적합하지 않다.

136 접속부사

해설 빈킨 앞에는 공장을 더 큰 지역으로 이진해야 한다고 헸고, 뒤에는 자금 문제로 인해 더 신중히 생각해야 한다며 상반된 내용이 나오고 있으므로 역접의 접속부사 (D) However가 적합하다.

137 부사 어휘

해설 현재시제의 의미와 어울리는 부사를 써야 하므로 정답은 (A) currently이다. (B)는 과거시제, (C)는 미래시제, (D)는 현재완료나 과거시제와 함께 자주 쓰인다.

138 문맥에 맞는 문장 고르기

(A) 우리는 직원들에게 본사는 이전하지 않을 것임을 알려야 힌다.
(B) 우리는 그것을 다룰 좋은 기회를 가졌다.
(C) 그 공장은 더 많은 인력이 필요하다.
(D) 그 안건은 다음 회의에서 다시 다뤄질 예정이다.

해설 공장 이전에 대해 회의를 했지만 결론이 나지 않은 채로 끝났기 때문에, 다음 회의에서 다시 논의될 것이라는 (D)가 적합하다.

[139-142] 정보

Haro Books 온라인 서점에서는, 주문품을 최대한 신속하게 배송하도록 항상 최선을 다하고 있습니다. 만약 여러분의 주문품이 도착하지 않았다면, 다음의 정보를 참조하세요.
배송 시간은 선택된 배송 방법에 따라 3일에서 5일 정도 소요됩니다. 배송 예정일은 여러분에게 항상 제공됩니다. 저희는 제시간에 배송될 수 있도록 노력하지만, 때로는 도착하는 데 더 오래 걸리기도 합니다. 만약 당신의 주문품이 배송 예정일보다 3일 이상 늦게 도착한다면 배송료를 두 배로 환불해 드립니다. 배송을 조회하시려면, 송장 번호를 가지고 저희에게 연락주세요. 저희가 확인해서 배송 상태를 알려드리겠습니다.

어휘 as quickly as possible 가능한 한 빨리 refer to ~을 참조하다 following 다음의 method 방법 track (~의 흔적을) 추적하다 investigate 조사하다

139 부사절 접속사

해설 빈칸 뒤 문장에서 주문품이 도착하지 않았을 때 참조할 수 있는 정보를 안내하고 있으므로 문맥상 (D) Unless(~하지 않는다면)가 가장 적합하다.

140 분사

해설 명사를 수식하는 분사를 선택하는 문제이다. '선택된 배송 방법'이라는 의미가 자연스러우므로, 과거분사인 (C) selected가 적합하다.

141 문맥에 맞는 문장 고르기

(A) 배송 예정일은 여러분에게 항상 제공됩니다.
(B) 손상된 제품온 무료로 반품히실 수 있습니다.
(C) 신간 도서들은 웹 사이트에 소개됩니다.
(D) 배송 기사들은 안전하게 운전하도록 교육 받습니다.

해설 빈칸 앞에는 일반적인 배송 기간에 대해 설명했고, 뒤에는 제시간에 배송되도록 노력한다고 했으므로, 빈칸에는 배송 예정일을 제공한다는 내용의 (A)가 문맥상 가장 적합하다.

142 동사 어휘

해설 (A)와 (D)는 사물을 목적어로 취하는 동사이고, (B)는 자동사이므로 오답이다. 따라서 정답은 (C)이다. 'notify A of B(A에게 B를 알려주다)'는 자주 등장하는 표현이므로 기억해 두자.

[143-146] 정보

토론토 개발부
건물 공사 안내 지침

건물의 구조를 변경하고자 하는 거주민들은 개조하기 위한 승인을 받아야 합니다. 일반적으로, 사소한 변경은 허가가 필요하지 않습니다. 하지만, 주요한 변경에 대해서는 상황이 다릅니다. 허가는 반드시 건물주가 직접 신청해야 합니다. 신청 후, 확정되기까지는 5일 정도 소요됩니다. 만약 동의 없이 건축 작업을 하는 것이 적발되면, 3천 달러 이상의 벌금이 부과될 수 있습니다. 이 규정들은 여러분과 이웃의 안전을 위한 것이므로, 반드시 준수하시기 바랍니다.
사례는 시청 홈페이지 www.torontocity.gov에서 확인하세요.

어휘 resident 거주자, 주민 structure 구조, 구조물 approval 승인 remodel 개조하다 modification 수정, 변경 alteration 변화, 개조 permit 허가증; 허가하다 permission 허가 consent 동의, 허락 example 사례, 예시

143 명사 어휘

해설 사소한 변경에는 '허가'가 필요 없다는 내용으로, 불가산 명사 (C) permission이 정답이다. (A) plans(계획), (B) funds(자금), (D) materials(재료)는 문맥상 적합하지 않다.

144 부사 어휘

해설 문맥상 알맞은 부사를 선택하는 문제이다. 건물주로부터 '직접' 신청되어야 한다는 의미가 적절하므로, 정답은 (C)이다. (A) shortly(곧), (B) consistently(변함없이), (D) separately(별도로)는 의미상 적합하지 않다.

145 문맥에 맞는 문장 고르기

(A) 신청 후, 확정되기까지는 5일 정도 소요됩니다.
(B) 절차는 나중에 변경할 수 없습니다.
(C) 일부 건축업자들은 그 허가증에 책임이 없습니다.
(D) 건물들을 보수하는 것은 너무 비쌉니다.

해설 빈칸 앞 문장은 '반드시 건물주가 허가를 직접 신청해야 한다'는 내용이므로, 신청에 대한 부연 설명이 이어지는 것이 자연스럽다. 따라서 신청이 승인되는 데 5일 정도 걸린다는 (A)가 정답이다.

146 동사 어휘

해설 문맥상 알맞은 동사를 찾는 문제이다. 빈칸 뒤의 목적어 them은 앞의 'These rules(이 규정들)'를 가리키므로 규정들을 '준수한다'는 의미를 만드는 (B) observe가 적합하다. (D) ignore는 '무시하다'의 의미로 rules를 목적어로 취할 수 있지만, 내용상 적절하지 않다.

PART • 7

[147-148] 문자 메시지

발신: 존 차비라
수신: 해리 앤더슨

저는 고객을 만나러 회사 앞 카페로 급히 가야 하니 저 없이 회의를 시작하세요. 지난 분기 매출 보고부터 시작해서 이번 분기 예상 수치까지 진행하세요. 저는 약 30분 후 그곳에 도착할 겁니다.

어휘 in front of ~앞에 client 고객 proceed 진행하다 instructions 지시사항, 설명서 delay 미루다, 연기하다 attend 참석하다 on time 정시에

147 주제/목적

메시지는 왜 보내졌는가?
(A) 지시사항을 전달하기 위해
(B) 보고서를 검토하기 위해
(C) 회의를 연기하기 위해
(D) 조언을 구하기 위해

해설 고객과 약속이 있어서 본인은 제시간에 회의에 참석하지 못하지만, 예정대로 회의를 진행하라는 지시사항을 전달하는 내용이므로 정답은 (A)이다.

148 Not/True 확인

차비라 씨에 대한 설명 중 옳은 것은?
(A) 그의 고객과 전에 만난 적이 없다.
(B) 매출 보고서를 수정할 것이다.
(C) 제시간에 회의에 참석할 수 없다.
(D) 프로젝트를 이미 마무리했다.

해설 지문 상단에서 존 차비라가 메시지의 발신자임을 알 수 있고, 메시지의 'please start the meeting without me(저 없이 회의를 시작하세요)' 부분을 통해 회의에 제시간에 참석할 수 없음을 알 수 있다. 따라서 정답은 (C)이다. 그가 전에 고객을 만났는지 여부는 지문에서 알 수 없으므로 (A)는 오답이다.

[149-150] 회람

수신: 전 직원
발신: 파블로 리카르도
날짜: 2월 18일
제목: 초과 근무

안녕하세요, 4월과 5월은 보통 실내 디자인 서비스에 있어서 가장 바쁜 달입니다. 그러므로, 우리는 하루에 3시간씩 초과 근무를 해야 할 것 같습니다. 고객들에게 이에 대해 알리기 전에, 우리는 초과 근무가 가능한 직원들을 찾아봐야 합니다. 야근을 하는 직원들은 기본 시급뿐만 아니라 매 시간 초과 근무 수당을 받을 겁니다. 관심 있으면 2월 28일 퇴근 전까지 저에게 알려주세요. 우리가 필요한 만큼 많은 새로운 시간제 근로자들을 채용하기 위해, 다음 날 우리 홈페이지에 채

용 공고를 올릴 겁니다. 또한, 5월에 휴가를 갈 계획인 분들은 6월 중순 이후로 연기할 것을 권장합니다.

진심으로,
파블로 리카르도

어휘 inform 알리다 work overtime 초과 근무하다 part-time worker 시간제 근로자 job opening 일자리, 채용 공고 promote 홍보하다 lay off 해고하다 announce 알리다 look for ~을 찾다

149 주제/목적
회람의 목적은 무엇인가?
(A) 신제품을 홍보하기 위해
(B) 일부 직원들을 해고하기 위해
(C) 직원들에게 창의적인 디자인을 하라고 제안하기 위해
(D) 직원들이 추가 업무하도록 독려하기 위해

해설 글의 목적은 주로 지문의 초반부에 나온다. 첫 문장에서 4월과 5월은 가장 바쁜 시기라고 한 후, 초과 근무가 필요하다고 언급하는 것으로 보아 정답이 (D)임을 알 수 있다.

150 세부 사항
회람에 따르면, 리카르도 씨는 2월 28일 이후에 무엇을 할 것인가?
(A) 고객들에게 새로운 서비스를 알린다
(B) 새로운 직원들을 찾는다
(C) 매일 초과 근무를 한다
(D) 정규 직원의 수를 늘린다

해설 지문 후반부에, 2월 28일 다음 날에 새로운 시간제 근로자를 채용하기 위해 홈페이지에 공지할 것이라는 내용이 있으므로 정답은 (B)이다. 정규 직원이 아닌 시간제 근로자를 채용하는 것이므로 (D)는 오답이다.

[151-152] 문자 메시지

스티븐 킴 (오전 9:05)
Hamilton 가 186번지 주택에 대해 논의하기 위해 만날 수 있을까요? 집주인들이 9월 말이 되기 전에 집을 매물로 내놓길 원합니다.

신디 아담스 (오전 9:14)
전 오전 10시부터 11시 50분까지 회의가 있지만, 점심시간에는 한가해요. Waining 카페에서 만나는 게 어때요?

스티븐 킴 (오전 9:15)
좋아요. 제가 그 집에 대한 상세 정보를 가져갈 테니, 신중히 분석할 수 있도록 도와주세요.

신디 아담스 (오전 9:15)
알겠습니다. 당신이 부동산 정보에 근거해서 가치를 평가할 수 있도록 도와드릴게요.

스티븐 킴 (오전 9:16)
고마워요. 항상 많은 유용한 조언을 해주셔서 정말 감사드립니다.

신디 아담스 (오전 9:17)
별말씀을요. 전 이제 갑니다. 이따 봐요.

어휘 bring 가져오다 detailed 구체적인, 상세한 property 부동산 analyze 분석하다 based on ~에 근거하여 appreciate 고마워하다

151 Not/True 확인
킴 씨에 대해 사실인 것은 무엇 같은가?
(A) 새 집을 알아보고 있다.
(B) 건물을 둘러보길 원한다.
(C) 입주할 집을 소유하고 있다.
(D) 이전에 아담스 씨의 도움을 받은 적이 있다.

해설 9시 16분의 메시지 'Thanks. I really appreciate that you always give me so much useful advice.'에서 항상 유용한 조언을 해줘서 고맙다는 것으로 보아 이전에도 아담스 씨의 도움을 받았다는 것을 알 수 있다. 따라서 정답은 (D)이다.

152 의도 파악
오전 9시 17분에, 아담스 씨가 "전 이제 갑니다"라고 쓴 의미는 무엇인가?
(A) 퇴근한다.
(B) 회의에 참석하러 간다.
(C) 집에서 휴식을 취한다.
(D) 집을 보기 위해 나간다.

해설 신디 아담스의 9시 14분 메시지를 보면 오전 10시부터 11시 50분까지 회의가 있다고 했으므로, 이제 간다는 것은 곧 있을 회의에 참석하러 간다는 의미이다. 따라서 정답은 (B)이다.

[153-155] 이메일

수신: 토니 잭슨
발신: Dream Communication
제목: 계정 정보
날짜: 7월 6일

잭슨 씨에게,

이 이메일은 당신의 계정 비밀번호가 변경되었음을 알려드리기 위한 것입니다. 만약 당신이 비밀번호를 직접 변경하지 않았다면, 저희 고객 서비스 부서 051-1117-0406으로 가능한 한 빨리 연락주세요. 그렇게 하면, 우리는 신속하게 원인을 파악하고 문제를 해결할 수 있을 것입니다. 이 이메일 주소는 발신 전용이어서 답신을 받을 수 없기 때문에 반드시 저희에게 전화로 연락주세요.
만약 당신이 정보를 직접 변경했다면, 저희에게 연락할 필요가 없습니다.
저희는 당신의 개인정보를 보호하기 위해 항상 최선을 다하고 있습니다.

진심으로,
Dream Communication 고객 서비스

153 주제/목적

이메일이 왜 잭슨 씨에게 보내졌는가?
(A) 그에게 새로운 서비스를 알려주기 위해
(B) 그에게 몇 가지 혜택을 제공하기 위해
(C) 그에게 계정 정보의 변경을 알려주기 위해
(D) 그에게 연락처를 묻기 위해

해설 지문 초반부의 "This e-mail is to inform you that your account's password has been changed."에서 계정 비밀번호 변경을 알리기 위한 이메일이라고 했기 때문에 정답은 (C)이다.

154 세부 사항

잭슨 씨는 무엇을 하라고 요구 받는가?
(A) 비밀번호를 정기적으로 변경하기
(B) 빠른 시일 내에 사무실 방문하기
(C) 정보를 변경하지 않은 경우 연락하기
(D) 문제를 신속히 해결하기

해설 명령문은 요구사항을 나타내는 기본적인 표현으로, 초반부의 'If you have not changed your password yourself, please contact our Customer Service Department(만약 당신이 비밀번호를 직접 변경하지 않았다면, 저희 고객 서비스 부서로 연락주세요)'를 통해 정답이 (C)임을 알 수 있다.

155 Not/True 확인

이메일에 언급되지 않은 내용은?
(A) 잭슨 씨는 비밀번호를 잊어버렸다.
(B) 고객센터에 전화로 연락할 수 있다.
(C) 잭슨 씨의 개인 정보가 변경되었다.
(D) 이 이메일 주소는 발신 전용이다.

해설 이메일에서 비밀번호가 변경되었다는 것을 알려주고 있고, 비밀번호를 직접 변경하지 않았다면 고객센터로 연락을 달라고 했다. 하지만 잭슨 씨가 비밀번호를 잊어버렸는지의 여부는 알 수 없으므로 (A)가 정답이다.

[156-157] 온라인 채팅

주디 클린턴 [오후 2:28]
저는 2월 18일에 Winnipeg에서 열리는 실크 무역 박람회에 가려고 합니다. 저와 함께 가실래요?

브래드 로저스 [오후 2:33]
저도 정말 가고 싶은데, 여름 신상품 컬렉션을 위한 디자인 프로젝트 마감일이 2월 25일이에요. 다음 기회를 기대해야겠어요.

주디 클린턴 [오후 2:34]
그렇다면 어쩔 수 없네요. 참조할 만한 정보를 얻으면 알려 드릴게요.

브래드 로저스 [오후 2:41]
좋아요, 그리고 제가 이번 여름 신상품에 사용할 수 있는 자재 목록을 보내 드릴 테니 좀 구해 주시겠어요? 전 세계 제품들이 그 박람회에 전시되기 때문에, 우리가 일반적으로 구할 수 없는 것들이 많을 거예요.

주디 클린턴 [오후 2:43]
물론이죠. 그럴게요. 목록을 이메일로 보내 주세요.

156 추론/암시

로저스 씨는 누구일 것 같은가?
(A) 무역 박람회 주최자
(B) 의류 디자이너
(C) 옷감 수입업자
(D) 의류회사 대표이사

해설 로저스 씨의 오후 2시 33분 메시지에서 'my design project for the new summer collection is due on February 25.' 부분을 보면 그가 의류 디자인 프로젝트에 작업 중임을 알 수 있다. 따라서 정답은 (B) 의류 디자이너이다.

157 의도 파악

오후 2시 34분에, 클린턴 씨가 "그렇다면 어쩔 수 없네요"라고 쓴 의미는 무엇인가?
(A) 그녀는 로저스 씨와 함께 박람회에 가지 못한다.
(B) 그녀는 로저스 씨가 업무를 끝내는 것을 도울 수 있다.
(C) 그녀는 로저스 씨가 업무를 미루길 원한다.
(D) 그녀는 로저스 씨를 위해 자재를 준비한다.

해설 해당 부분의 바로 앞 메시지를 보면, 로저스 씨가 '디자인 프로젝트 때문에 박람회에 갈 수 없어서 다음 기회를 기대해야겠다'고 했으므로 정답은 (A)이다.

[158-160] 이메일

수신: millers@mate.un
발신: services1@oasissupply.km
제목: 귀하의 주문 번호 7163
날짜: 6월 1일

밀러 씨에게,

당신이 주문한 아래의 물품들(주문번호 7163)이 Oasis Supply에 의해 배송되었습니다.

물품	수량
Yundai 팩스기	1
SG LCD 모니터 (24인치)	3
Soris 스피커	3

이 물품들은 현재 주문이 밀려 있습니다.

물품	수량
Jenix 복사용 잉크 카트리지	5
ASUX 컴퓨터 키보드	2

불편을 드려 죄송합니다. 이 물품들을 기다리길 원하는지, 혹은 현재 재고가 있는 비슷한 물품으로 대체하길 원하는지 알려 주세요. 우리는 Kensis 사에서 제조된 복사기 잉크 카트리지를 보유하고 있습니다. 또한 다른 제조업체에서 만든 많은 다양한 종류의 잉크 카트리지가 저희 웹 사이트 www.oasissupply.km에 있습니다. 웹 사이트에 접속하기만 하면 옵션을 선택할 수 있습니다. 만약 당신이 어떠한 것도 변경하지 않는다면, 기존 주문에서 남은 물품들이 당신에게 2주 늦게 배송될 겁니다.

이미 배송된 물품들에 한해 당신의 신용카드로 대금이 청구되었습니다. 남은 물품들은 재고가 들어올 때까지 청구되지 않을 것입니다. 그러니 기존 구매를 계속 진행할 것인지 저희에게 가능한 한 빨리 알려주세요.

귀하의 변함없는 애용에 감사드립니다.

Oasis Supply 고객 서비스

어휘 back order 이월 주문, 처리하지 못한 주문 apologize for ~에 대해 사과하다 inconvenience 불편 replace 교체하다 in stock 재고가 있는 charge 청구하다, 부과하다 constant 끊임없는, 변함없는 patronage 애용 recall 회수하다 retailer 소매업체 discontinue 중단하다 multiple 많은, 여러 개의 select 선택하다 balance 잔액, 균형 alternative 대안의, 대안

158 주제/목적
이메일의 목적은 무엇인가?
(A) 수분 상태에 대한 성보를 주기 위해
(B) 소매업체로부터 제품을 회수하기 위해
(C) 상품 결제를 요청하기 위해
(D) 제품 가격에 대한 정보를 제공하기 위해

해설 지문의 상단에 주문한 제품 중 배송된 것과 배송되지 않은 것의 목록이 있고, 그 뒤에 이에 대한 세부 내용이 나오고 있으므로 정답은 (A)이다.

159 Not/True 확인
복사용 잉크 카트리지에 대해 알 수 있는 것은?
(A) 작년에 단종되었다.
(B) 다양한 색상으로 나온다.
(C) 잘못된 제품이 배송되었다.
(D) 다른 브랜드 제품들은 재고가 있다.

해설 지문 중반에, 타사 제품도 있고(We have copier ink cartridges manufactured by Kensis.), 다른 제조업체 제품들도 많다(There are also many different kinds of ink cartridges from other manufacturers)고 했으므로 정답은 (D)이다.

160 세부 사항
밀러 씨는 무엇을 하도록 요청 받았는가?
(A) 청구될 신용카드 선택하기
(B) 미납금 지불하기
(C) 대체품 주문을 고려하기
(D) 환불을 위해 반품하기

해설 원래 주문했던 제품은 재고가 없기 때문에, 재고가 있는 유사 제품들을 고려해볼 것(have them replaced with similar items currently in stock)을 제안하고 있다. 또한 다른 제조업체의 다양한 제품들이 웹 사이트에 있다며 다른 제품을 확인해 볼 것을 제안하고 있으므로 정답은 (C)이다.

[161-163] 이메일

수신: 줄리아나 로버츠 <j_roberts@goodmail.us>
발신: 존 브리드러브 <johns84@parker.ne.co>
제목: 주문 번호 KS3609
날짜: 11월 17일

로버츠 씨에게,

어제 최근 구매에 관한 이메일을 보내주셔서 감사드립니다. 저는 11월 8일에 당신이 주문한 것을 확인했고, 마커 펜 열 개, 스테이플러 세 개 그리고 복사용지 한 상자를 주문했다고 나와 있었습니다. 그리고 우리는 복사용지 대신 종이 클립 한 상자가 배송되었다는 것을 깨달았습니다. 실수에 대해 진심으로 사과 드립니다. 우리는 최근에 너무 많은 주문을 받아서 가끔 실수가 일어나기도 합니다. 우리는 익일 배송으로 즉시 복사용지를 보내드릴 것이며, 잘못된 주문품은 그 택배업체를 통해 반품하시면 됩니다. 물론, 추가요금을 납부하실 필요는 없습니다. 실수에 대한 사과의 표시로 30% 할인 쿠폰을 제품과 함께 동봉할 것입니다. 그것은 향후 언제든지 사용 가능합니다.
양해해 주셔서 감사드립니다.

진심으로,

존 브리드러브
고객 서비스 담당자
Parker Good Supplies

어휘 regarding ~에 관하여 purchase 구매하다; 구매 review 검토하다, 확인하다 apologize 사과하다 immediately 즉시 overnight delivery 익일 배송 return 돌려주다, 반납하나 courier 택배 회사 extra 추가의 patience 참을성, 인내 office supplies 사무용품 vendor 판매자, 상인

161 추론/암시

브리드러브 씨는 어디에서 근무하고 있는 것 같은가?
(A) 미술용품 제조업체
(B) 배송업체
(C) 사무용품 판매업체
(D) 출판사

해설 지문 상단에서 브리드러브 씨가 이메일의 발신자임을 알 수 있고, 이메일 초반부에서 마커 펜, 스테이플러, 복사용지 주문을 받았다고 이야기하는 것으로 보아 사무용품 판매업체에서 일하고 있음을 알 수 있다. 따라서 정답은 (C)이다.

162 세부 사항

로버츠 씨는 주문품에 대한 문제를 언제 알렸는가?
(A) 11월 8일
(B) 11월 16일
(C) 11월 17일
(D) 11월 18일

해설 이메일의 발신일이 11월 17일이고, 'Thank you for sending me the e-mail yesterday regarding your recent purchase(어제 최근 구매에 관한 이메일을 보내주셔서 감사드립니다)'라고 했으므로, 로버츠 씨가 주문품에 대한 문제를 알린 날짜는 (B) 11월 16일이다.

163 문장 삽입

다음 표시된 [1], [2], [3], [4]의 위치들 중에서 다음의 문장이 들어갈 가장 알맞은 곳은?
"실수에 대한 사과의 표시로 30% 할인 쿠폰을 제품과 함께 동봉할 것입니다."
(A) [1]
(B) [2]
(C) [3]
(D) [4]

해설 주어진 문장은 할인 쿠폰을 제공한다는 내용이고, [4]의 뒤 문장 'You can use it anytime in the future(그것은 향후 언제든지 사용 가능합니다)'에서 '그것'이 '할인 쿠폰'임을 유추할 수 있다. 따라서 (D)가 가장 적합하다.

[164-167] 기사

WASHINGTON (6월 1일)—Pendon 항공사의 대표이사 개리 윌슨은 그의 회사가 Space 항공사를 인수했다고 목요일에 발표했다. Pendon 사는 캐나다 토론토에 본사가 있고, 이번 인수는 항공사의 규모를 두 배로 키울 것이다. 그 항공사는 또한 새로운 시장으로 사업을 확장할 것이다. Pendon 사의 항로 대부분은 뉴욕, 멕시코시티 그리고 부에노스아이레스와 같은 북남미 도시들로 향한다. 한편, Space 항공사의 본사는 중국 베이징에 있으며 아시아 전역의 나라들로 운항한다. "서비스에 큰 변화는 없을 것이며, 현 직원들의 고용은 보장될 것입니다."라고 두 항공사의 대표는 말했다. 파일럿과 승무원을 포함한 직원들은 인수에 매우 기뻐했다. Space 사에서 4년 이상 근무한 승무원 에바 마틴은 "이번 인수는 우리에게 정말 좋다고 생각합니다. 회사가 약 2년간 경영난을 겪어서, 우리는 항상 구조조정에 대해 불안해했습니다."라고 말했다.

어휘 announce 발표하다, 알리다 purchase 구입하다, 매입하다 be headquartered in ~에 본사를 두다 acquisition 인수 double ~을 두 배로 하다 expand 확장하다 route 경로 meanwhile 한편 throughout 도처에, ~동안 쭉, 내내 significant 상당한, 현저한 current 현재의, 지금의 guarantee 보장하다, 약속하다 representative 대표, 대리인 including ~을 포함하여 flight attendant 승무원 pleased 기쁜, 만족해하는 anxious 염려하는, 불안해 하는 restructure 구조조정하다 financial trouble 재정적인 문제 reduction 감소, 감축 lay off 해고하다 keep ~ing 계속 ~하다 transfer 옮기다, 이동하다

164 주제/목적

기사의 목적은 무엇인가?
(A) 직원 감축을 알리기 위해
(B) 두 회사를 비교하기 위해
(C) 항공기 수의 확대를 알리기 위해
(D) 두 회사의 합병을 발표하기 위해

해설 기사의 주제나 목적은 지문의 초반부에 단서가 나온다. 'Pendon Airlines CEO Gary Wilson announced on Thursday that his company has purchased Space Airlines.'에서 Pendon 사의 대표가 Space 항공사를 인수했다는 것을 발표했고, 이후에도 인수에 대해 이야기하고 있으므로 정답은 (D)이다.

165 Not/True 확인

Space 항공사에 대해 알 수 있는 것은?
(A) 사업이 잘되고 있지 않았다.
(B) 티켓 가격을 인상할 수도 있다.
(C) 일부 직원들을 해고했다.
(D) 북미 지역으로 사업을 확장했다.

해설 지문의 마지막 부분에, Space 항공사에서 근무하는 직원이 회사가 약 2년간 경영난을 겪어왔다(our company has been in financial trouble for about two years)고 말하는 부분에서 해당 항공사의 사업이 잘되고 있지 않았음을 알 수 있다. 따라서 정답은 (A)이다.

166 동의어 찾기

첫 번째 문단, 네 번째 줄의 "purchased"와 가장 가까운 의미를 가진 단어는?
(A) 훔치다
(B) 제시하다
(C) 계산하다
(D) 인수하다

해설 해당 부분은 기업을 구매했다는 의미이므로, (D) '인수하다'와 의미가 가깝다고 볼 수 있다.

167 추론/암시

마틴 씨에 대해 암시되는 것은?
(A) 다른 일자리를 찾고 있다.
(B) 승무원으로 계속 근무하기를 원한다.
(C) 뉴욕으로 전근가야 한다.
(D) 그녀의 회사가 사업을 확장하길 원했다.

해설 지문의 후반부에 마틴 씨는 Space 항공사의 승무원이라고 언급되었고, 합병이 직원들에게 좋은 소식(this acquisition is really good for us)이고, 직원들이 구조조정에 대해 불안해했다(We have always been anxious about restructuring)고 말한 것을 봤을 때, 그녀가 승무원으로 계속 근무하길 원했음을 유추할 수 있다. 따라서 정답은 (B)이다.

[168-171] 편지

10월 7일

샘 와인버그
Rockwell 가 245번지
캐나다 BC 밴쿠버

와인버그 씨에게,

지난달 빅토리아에 있는 제 사무실을 방문해 주셔서 감사드립니다. 저는 Toronto Standard 출판사에서의 당신의 출판 경력에 대해 얘기를 나누게 되어 정말 즐거웠습니다.

제가 그때 이미 언급했듯이, 우리 회사는 프랑스 파리에 새로운 지점을 오픈할 예정이기 때문에, 당신처럼 프랑스어 실력을 갖춘 새로운 직원들을 찾고 있습니다. 그러므로, 우리는 당신이 일자리에 지원하셨으면 합니다. 만약 당신이 그 직책에 뽑히면, 당신은 우리 회사에 익숙해지기 위해 2주 동안 교육을 받을 것입니다.

이 기회를 잡고 싶으시면, 저에게 가급적 빨리 당신의 이력서를 보내주세요. 그러면 제가 그것을 인사부장에게 전달해서 면접을 잡겠습니다. 면접은 아마 저희 밴쿠버 본사에서 열릴 예정이니, 오시기 편할 것입니다. 저는 그 일자리가 전문성을 기르는 데 좋은 기회가 될 것이라 믿습니다. 질문이 있으시면, 주저 마시고 저에게 연락주세요.

안부를 전하며,

마리사 트루먼
영업부
Horizon Education & Publication

어휘 mention 언급하다 seek 찾다, 구하다 undergo ~을 겪다 familiarize A with B A에게 B를 숙지시키다 résumé 이력서 opportunity 기회 arrange 마련하다, 준비하다 convenient 편리한, 간편한 employment 고용, 근무 hesitate 주저하다 recruit 채용하다 register for ~에 등록하다 strategy 전략 reduce 줄이다, 감소시키다

168 주제/목적

편지의 목적은 무엇인가?
(A) 신입 사원을 채용하기 위해
(B) 행사 일정을 알리기 위해
(C) 새로운 정책을 설명하기 위해
(D) 새로운 시장에 대한 정보를 요청하기 위해

해설 프랑스에 새로운 지점을 개설하기 때문에 프랑스어에 능숙한 사람을 구한다고 언급하면서 편지의 수신자에게 채용에 관해 이야기하고 있으므로 정답은 (A)이다.

169 세부 사항

편지에 따르면, 와인버그 씨는 9월에 무엇을 했는가?
(A) 이력서를 보냈다
(B) 교육 과정에 등록했다
(C) 인사부를 방문했다
(D) 트루먼 씨와 만났다

해설 편지의 초반에 'Thank you for visiting my office in Victoria last month.'에서 와인버그 씨가 지난달에 트루먼 씨와 만났다는 것을 알 수 있고, 편지를 작성한 날이 10월 7일이므로 그들이 9월에 만났음을 알 수 있다. 따라서 정답은 (D)이다.

170 세부 사항

트루먼 씨의 회사는 무엇을 계획하고 있는가?
(A) 신입 사원들을 위한 오리엔테이션을 개최한다
(B) 사업 전략을 변경한다
(C) 새 사무실을 연다
(D) 인력을 감축한다

해설 두 번째 문단에, '프랑스에 새로운 지점을 열 것이다(our company is planning to open a new branch in Paris, France)'라고 했으므로 (C)가 정답이다.

171 세부 사항

Horizon Education & Publication는 본사가 어디에 있는가?
(A) 빅토리아에
(B) 토론토에
(C) 파리에
(D) 밴쿠버에

해설 지문 후반부의 'The interview will probably be held at our head office in Vancouver(면접은 밴쿠버 본사에서 열릴 예정이다)'에서 본사가 밴쿠버에 있음을 알 수 있다. 따라서 정답은 (D)이다.

[172-175] 기사

많은 대기업들은 브랜드를 만들어 내는 것이 어렵다고 생각한다. 중소 기업 사장들은 브랜드 구축을 훨씬 더 어렵게 느낄지도 모른다. 찰스 클린턴이 그의 회사 The Great People in Special Times 사를 설립 했을 때, 그는 브랜드명을 독특하게 만들려고 했다. 이제 클린턴 씨는 그 이름이 너무 특이하다고 생각한다. "사람들이 그 이름에 잘 적응하지 못했던 것 같습니다."라고 클린턴 씨는 말한다. "그것은 단지 너무 길어서, 저는 그냥 'Times'로 줄였습니다."

시장 분석가 지미 핸드릭스에 따르면, 브랜드명을 변경하는 것은 기업에게 매우 어렵고 위험하다. "만일 소비자들이 브랜드명이 변경된 것을 알아채지 못한다면, 그들은 다른 브랜드로 발길을 돌릴지도 모릅니다."라고 핸드릭스 씨는 말한다. "포장의 변경 또한 위험한 도전이 될 수 있습니다."

그런 위험에도 불구하고, 마케팅 부서는 과감하게 포장 디자인을 변경하기로 결정했고, 계획을 진행했다. 그들은 회사의 시계 제품들에 사용할 새로운 포장을 만들기 위해 국내 최고의 디자이너 신디 가르시아를 고용했다. 가르시아 씨는 추상적이면서도 선명한 무늬를 사용하는 것으로 유명하다. 게다가, 그녀는 항상 대담하고 파격적인 디자인을 만든다. 회사는 그녀의 디자인이 더 많은 젊은 소비자들을 끌어들일 수 있다고 믿었다.

그 회사는 가능한 한 많은 고객들이 새로운 포장 디자인을 단기간에 인식할 수 있도록 하기 위한 효과적인 방법을 생각해내기 위해 노력하고 있다. 뿐만 아니라, 클린턴 씨는 제품의 외관은 바뀌었지만 성능은 변하지 않았다는 것을 홍보하기 위해 많은 노력을 하고 있다. "우리가 여전히 믿을 만한 고성능 제품을 만들고 있다는 점을 고객들에게 알려야 하고, 동시에 잠재 고객들의 관심을 사로잡기 위한 혁신적인 변화를 만들어야 합니다."라고 그는 말한다.

어휘 establish 설립하다 distinctive 독특한 consider 생각하다, 여기다 unique 유일무이한, 독특한 adapt 적응하다 shorten 짧게 하다, 단축하다 according to ~에 따르면 analyst 분석가 risky 위험한 despite ~에도 불구하고 drastically 과감하게 go ahead with ~을 추진하다 bold 대담한 funky 파격적인 attract 끌어들이다 come up with ~을 찾아내다, 생각해내다 effective 효과적인, 실질적인 recognize 인정하다 make an effort 노력하다 publicize 알리다, 광고[홍보]하다 appearance (겉)모습, 외모 reliable 믿을 수 있는 high-performance 고성능의 capture 사로잡다 potential 잠재적인 promote 홍보하다 advertise 광고하다 inform A of B A에게 B에 대해 알려주다 emphasize 강조하다 specialize in ~을 전문으로 하다, 전공하다 analyze 분석하다

172 주제/목적

기사의 목적은 무엇인가?
(A) 새로운 기업을 홍보하기 위해
(B) 규정 변화를 알리기 위해
(C) 브랜드명을 만들기 위한 아이디어를 모으기 위해
(D) 대중에게 브랜드명의 변화를 알리기 위해

해설 지문의 초반에 브랜드명이 너무 길고 특이해서 짧게 변경했다는 이야기가 나오고, 이후 브랜드명의 변경을 대중에게 알리지 못할 경우 생기는 위험에 대해 설명하고 있으므로 정답은 (D)이다.

173 Not/True 확인

가르시아 씨에 대해 알 수 있는 것은?
(A) 제품의 품질보다 디자인을 강조한다.
(B) 포장 디자인을 전문으로 한다.
(C) 그녀의 회사 시장 점유율을 높이길 원한다.
(D) 시장을 잘 분석한다.

해설 세 번째 문단에서 가르시아 씨는 새 포장 디자인을 위해 채용되었다는 내용을 통해 포장 디자인 전문가임을 알 수 있다. 따라서 정답은 (B)이다.

174 세부 사항

클린턴 씨는 왜 변화를 주고 싶어 하는가?
(A) 더 많은 소비자를 유치하기 위해
(B) 양질의 제품을 생산하기 위해
(C) 제품의 품질을 향상시키기 위해
(D) 새 장비를 개발하기 위해

해설 지문의 후반부에서 '잠재 고객들의 관심을 사로잡기 위한 혁신적인 변화를 만들어 내야 한다(we need to make innovative changes to capture the attention of potential customers)'고 하는 것을 보아 변화의 목적이 더 많은 고객들을 유치하는 것임을 알 수 있다. 따라서 정답은 (A)이다.

175 문장 삽입

다음 표시된 [1], [2], [3], [4]의 위치 중에서 다음 문장이 들어 갈 가장 알맞은 곳은?
"가르시아 씨는 추상적이면서도 선명한 무늬를 사용하는 것으로 유명하다."
(A) [1]
(B) [2]
(C) [3]
(D) [4]

해설 [3] 바로 뒤에, '뿐만 아니라, 그녀는 항상 대담하고 파격적인 디자인을 만든다(Moreover, she always makes bold and funky designs)'에서 가르시아 씨의 디자인 특징을 언급하는데, Moreover을 통해 앞서 유사한 내용이 나왔음을 알 수 있다. 따라서 주어진 문장은 (C) [3]에 오는 것이 자연스럽다.

[176-180] 이메일 & 전단

수신: roses_1@dandyfurniture.net
발신: jack_l@dandyfurniture.net
날짜: 7월 6일
제목: 워크숍
첨부: the_flyer.jpg

라이트 씨에게,

제가 관심있는 워크숍에 관한 정보가 담겨 있는 전단지를 첨부했습니다. 저는 중요한 걱정거리를 해결할 유용한 기술들을 배울 수 있을 것이라 믿습니다.

우리가 생산하는 가구는 조립하기 매우 쉽지만, 설명서는 매우 어려워 보입니다. 아시다시피, 우리가 고객들에게 받는 가장 많은 불평은 설명서 내용이 너무 전문적이라는 겁니다. 저는 그 워크숍에 참석함으로써, 대다수의 고객들이 조립을 빨리 끝낼 수 있도록 조립 과정을 쉽게 설명하는 방법을 배울 수 있을 것입니다.

참가비는 총 380달러일 겁니다. 이는 식비, 교통비, 숙박비와 같은 모든 것을 포함합니다. 제가 이 행사에 참여하는 것이 우리 회사에 가치있는 일이 될 것임을 당신도 동의해 주시길 바랍니다.

저의 요청을 고려해 주셔서 감사합니다.

안부를 전하며,

잭 루이스

**업무 기술 향상에 대한 워크숍:
세상에서 가장 쉬운 전문적 글쓰기**

WR 컨퍼런스 홀 / Seattle, Haro 가 219-32번지 /
7월 24일 ~ 26일 / 오전 10시 ~ 오후 4시

이번 워크숍에서, 여러분은 어려운 정보를 아주 쉬운 방식으로 설명하는 법을 배울 겁니다. 당신이 설명하는 기계나 장비가 아무리 복잡할지라도, 여러분은 대부분의 사용자들이 쉽게 이해하고 따라하도록 할 수 있습니다.

이번 교육 과정에서 여러분이 만날 이세준 강사는 소형 컴퓨터부터 자동차에 이르는 다양한 상품들에 대한 설명을 제공하면서 지난 12년간 전문 경력을 쌓았습니다.

이번 과정의 모든 참가자들은 강사에게 직접 질문하고 답변을 얻는 기회를 가질 겁니다. 뿐만 아니라, 워크숍이 끝날 때, 여러분은 교육의 핵심 내용을 요약한 책자를 받을 것입니다.

워크숍 비용은 식비 및 숙박비 포함 380달러입니다. 교통비는 포함되지 않습니다.

어휘 attach 첨부하다, 붙이다 contain 포함하다 allow 허용하다 assemble 조립하다, 모으다 manual 설명서 technical 기술적인 attend 참석하다 the majority of 대다수의 participation 참여 accommodation 숙소, 시설 transportation 교통 valuable 가치 있는 consider 고려하다, 생각하다 request 유처 요구 improve 개선되다, 향상시키다 no matter how 아무리 ~해도 instructor 강사 professional 전문적인 explanation 설명 participant 참가자 summarize 요약하다 including ~을 포함하여 fund 자금 reserve 예약하다 location 위치, 장소 expert 전문가 experience 경험, 경력

---

176 주제/목적

이메일의 목적은 무엇인가?
(A) 자금을 요청하기 위해
(B) 방을 예약하기 위해
(C) 문제점을 보고하기 위해
(D) 제품에 대한 정보를 주기 위해

해설 워크숍 참석에 관심이 있다는 내용으로 지문이 전개되고 있고, 후반부에 워크숍 참석에 필요한 비용을 요청하며 이를 고려해 달라고 하고 있으므로 정답은 (A)이다.

177 동의어 찾기

이메일의 두 번째 문단 네 번째 줄의 "majority"와 가장 가까운 의미를 가진 단어는?
(A) 특성
(B) 차이
(C) 대부분
(D) 최고위자

해설 해당 부분은 '대다수의' 고객들(the majority of our customers)을 의미하므로 정답은 (C)이다. chief는 형용사일 때 '주된'이라는 의미로 쓰이지만 명사일 때는 '최고위자'로 쓰인다는 점에 유의해야 한다.

178 Not/True 확인 (연계)

루이스 씨에 대해 알 수 있는 것은?
(A) 그는 가구 조립에 서투르다.
(B) 그는 전문 강사이다.
(C) 그는 고객 매뉴얼을 작성했다.
(D) 그는 Seattle에 가기를 원한다.

해설 첫 번째 지문에서 루이스 씨는 워크숍에 참석하기를 원한다고 했고, 두 번째 지문의 초반에 그 워크숍이 Seattle에서 열린다는 내용이 나오므로 정답은 (D)이다.

179 세부 사항 (연계)

루이스 씨가 잘못 알고 있는 정보는 무엇인가?
(A) 워크숍 장소
(B) 설명서의 목적
(C) 필요한 경비
(D) 등록 방법

해설 첫 번째 이메일에서 루이스 씨는 워크샵 참석에 드는 비용이 식비, 교통비, 숙박비를 모두 포함한다고 했지만, 두 번째 지문 후반부에서 교통비는 포함되지 않는다고 했다. 따라서 그는 경비에 대해 잘못 알고 있으므로 정답은 (C)이다.

180 추론/암시

리 씨에 대해 암시되는 것은?
(A) 그는 매년 워크숍을 개최한다.
(B) 그는 기술 교육을 전공했다.
(C) 그는 전화로 질문에 답해 줄 것이다.
(D) 그는 자신의 분야에 경력이 많다.

해설 리 씨가 언급되는 두 번째 지문에서 답을 찾아야 한다. 'Sejun Lee ~ has had a professional career over the last 12 years'에서 12년간 경력을 쌓았다고 했으므로 답은 (D)이다.

[181-185] 기사 & 편지

지역 뉴스
존 윌슨

JERSEY CITY (8월 14일) — 약 8개월간의 개조 작업 후, Jersey 시청의 업무가 재개되었다. 금요일에, 시청 공무원들과 방문객들은 최종 결과물을 보기 위해 그 유명 랜드마크에 입장을 허가 받았다. 공사 담당자인 브랜던 베이커는 Centum Plaza 인근의 임시 시설물에서 시청으로 복귀한 것을 기뻐했다. "대부분의 이전 작업이 2주 만에 완료되었습니다."라고 그는 말했다. "우리가 보수공사 동안 겪은 일련의 지연에 비해 작업은 비교적 원활한 것처럼 보였으며, 이제 그 건물은 웅장하고 품위 있어 보입니다."

방문객들도 마찬가지로 기뻐하는 것 같았다. 1층 로비에 들어서자마자, 방문객들은 멋진 조명이 비추는 더욱 화려한 대리석 바닥을 보고 놀라워했다. 건축가 사이먼 리틀은 "저는 동료들에게 엄청난 이야기를 듣고 개조 공사를 보러 왔는데, 저는 이런 멋진 건축물은 처음 봅니다. 오늘날, 전국 어느 곳에도 이처럼 혁신적으로 개조된 건물은 없습니다."라고 말했다.

가장 인상 깊은 특징은 몇몇 인사들의 특별 기부를 기념하는 박물관이 추가되었다는 것이다. Grand Nature 건설사의 회장 콜린 머레이는 "우리는 이 건물이 Jersey 시를 상징할 뿐 아니라 관광 명소가 될 수 있도록, 건물을 짓는 데 최선을 다했습니다."라고 말했다.

편집자 님께,

저는 최근에 당신의 기사를 읽었는데, Jersey 시청 공사에 대한 당신의 기사에 몇 가지 정보가 빠진 것 같습니다.
시청을 개조하기 위해 기부로 많은 공헌을 한 일반 시민들에 대한 이야기가 없다는 것이 개인적으로 유감스럽습니다. 또 다른 하나는, 재건축 후 현재 건물의 주차 공간이 너무 협소한 것 같습니다. 만약 관광객이 가장 선호하는 방문지가 된다면, 주차 공간의 확충은 더욱 시급할 것입니다. 사실 저는 이 안건을 8월 23일 목요일에 보수 담당자와 논의할 것입니다.
추후에 이 내용에 대해 글을 쓴다면 신문에 나올 당신의 새로운 기사에 제 의견을 추가해 주셨으면 합니다.

진심으로,

피터 존스

어휘 nearly 거의 renovation 개조, 수리 resume 재개하다 official 공무원 permit 허가되다, 허락하다 enter 들어가다 prominent 중요한, 유명한 landmark 주요 지형지물, 랜드마크 temporary 일시적인, 임시의 majority 다수 transition 이행, 과도 compared with ~과 비교하여 a series of 일련의 relatively 비교적 smooth 순조로운, 매끄러운 noble 고결한, 고귀한 elegant 우아한, 품격 있는 upon ~ing ~하자마자 곧 amazed 놀란 brilliant 훌륭한,

멋진 marble 대리석 lighting 조명 architect 건축가 honor 기념하다, 예우하다 contribution 공헌, 기여 figure 인물, 사람 symbolize 상징하다 tourist attraction 관광 명소 ordinary citizen 평범한 시민 donation 기부 expand 확장하다 encourage 권유하다 commemorate 기념하다 amenity 편의 시설 donor 기부자 have trouble ~ing ~하는 데 어려움이 있다

181 주제/목적

기사의 목적은 무엇인가?
(A) 공무원들에게 주차 공간을 확장할 것을 권하기 위해
(B) 시설물의 재개를 알리기 위해
(C) 주민들에게 건축물의 결함을 알리기 위해
(D) 기부자들을 기념하기 위해

해설 기사의 목적은 대부분 초반에 단서가 나온다. 'After nearly eight months of renovation work, business has resumed in Jersey City Hall(8개월간의 개조 작업 후, Jersey 시청 업무가 재개되었다)'는 내용에서 기사의 목적이 시청의 재개를 알리려는 것임을 알 수 있다. 따라서 정답은 (B)이다.

182 Not/True 확인

시청 공사 프로젝트에 대해 언급된 것은?
(A) 제시간에 완료되었다.
(B) 편의시설 건축을 포함했다.
(C) 개인 자금에 의해서만 지원받았다.
(D) 약 8개월간 이루어졌다.

해설 첫 번째 지문 초반에, '거의 8개월간의 개조 작업 후에(After nearly eight months of renovation work)'를 통해 정답이 (D)임을 알 수 있다.

183 세부 사항

존스 씨는 기사에서 무엇이 빠졌다고 말하는가?
(A) 프로젝트에 기부한 사람들에 대한 언급
(B) 보수 작업에 대한 세부 사항
(C) 새로운 주차 구역의 위치
(D) 곧 있을 행사의 날짜

해설 편지의 첫 부분에, '많은 공헌을 한 일반 시민들에 대한 이야기가 빠진 것이 유감스럽다(I personally regret there aren't any stories about ordinary citizens who have contributed a lot by making donations)'는 부분을 통해 (A)가 정답임을 알 수 있다.

184 세부 사항

존스 씨는 개조 프로젝트에 대해 어떤 의견을 말하는가?
(A) 작업에 돈이 많이 들었다.
(B) 성공 여부는 지켜볼 일이다.
(C) 그 건물이 많은 관심을 끌 것으로 예상된다.
(D) 방문자들이 주차하는 데 문제가 있을 것이다.

해설 존스 씨는 편지를 쓴 사람으로, 편지의 중반부에 '시청 건축 후, 주차 공간이 부족해졌다(the parking space in the building is now too small after the remodeling)'는 내용이 있으므로 답이 (D)임을 알 수 있다.

185 세부 사항 (연계)

존스 씨는 목요일에 누구를 만날 예정인가?
(A) 존 윌슨
(B) 브랜던 베이커
(C) 사이먼 리틀
(D) 콜린 머레이

해설 존스 씨가 쓴 편지의 마지막 부분에, '8월 23일 목요일에 보수 담당자와 이 건에 대해 논의할 것이다(I'll be discussing this issue with the supervisor of the renovation on Thursday, August 23.)'라고 했고, 기사를 보면 개조공사 담당자의 이름이 '브랜던 베이커'라고 나와 있으므로 정답은 (B)이다.

[186-190] 웹 페이지 & 이메일 & 웹 페이지

---

http://www.unc.edu/careers_service/career_events

NORTH CAROLINA 대학교 · 직업 서비스

진로 계획	구직	예약	직업 행사

의료 보건 취업 박람회

평생 직장을 찾을 수 있는 기회가 여기 있습니다. North Carolina 대학교가 주최하는 의료 보건 취업 박람회로 오세요. 행사는 6월 8일 금요일 오전 10시 30분부터 오후 5시 30분까지 대학교 Charles 메모리얼 강당에서 열립니다.

여러분의 지속적인 학업 비용을 어떻게 마련할지 배우고, 이력서와 입사 지원 자료를 채용 전문가에게 검토 받고, 많은 고용주들과 이야기 나누며, 다른 구직자들과의 인맥도 형성하세요.

아래의 의료 보건 직업에 중점을 둔 일련의 유익한 교육과정들도 열릴 것입니다.

주제	시간	장소
치의학	오전 11시 ~ 오전 11시 50분	116호
간호학	오후 1시 ~ 오후 1시 50분	114호
임상 병리학	오후 2시 30분 ~ 오후 3시 20분	108호
물리 요법	오후 4시 ~ 오후 4시 50분	111호

수신: 데니스 우드
발신: 해롤드 화이트
날짜: 6월 1일
제목: 지원 요청

데니스 씨에게,

안녕하세요, 저는 오늘부터 일주일 후 North Carolina 대학교에서 Spring 의료센터에서의 제 업무에 관해 발표할 예정입니다. 저는 제 비서와 함께 갈 것이며, 그 다음 주 화요일에 차편으로 그녀와 Atlantic City에 돌아올 예정이므로, 6월 8일 금요일에 편도 티켓 두 장을 예매해 주세요. 저는 Charlotte에 오후 2시에서 2시 30분 사이에 도착했으면 하는데, 그러면 제가 4시에 발표를 하기 전에 최종 점검을 할 시간이 충분할 겁니다. 중간에 환승하는 여정은 피하고 싶습니다. 또한, 한정된 예산을 고려해서, 요금은 한 사람당 60달러를 초과하지 않아야 합니다.

감사 드리며, 질문 있으시면 편히 연락 주세요.

해롤드 화이트

---

https://www.united-rails.com/buytickets

티켓 선택	선호 좌석	배송 옵션	결제	확인

2인 승객, Atlantic City 출발 Charlotte 도착

출발	도착	환승	1인당 요금	철도 회사
오전 10시 30분	오전 11시 45분	없음	70달러	Speedy rails
오전 11시	오후 12시 40분	없음	70달러	New trains
오전 11시 30분	오후 2시 10분	1회	50달러	Sky trains
오후 12시	오후 2시 20분	없음	55달러	States connection

어휘 fair 박람회 lifetime 일생, 평생 organize 조직하다, 준비하다 take place (사건이) 일어나다, 발생하다 finance 자금을 대다 résumé 이력서 application 지원서, 신청서 material 자료 review 검토하다 recruit 모집하다 expert 전문가 network 통신망을 연결하다, 인맥을 형성하다 job seeker 구직자 a series of 일련의 informative 유익한 be scheduled to ~하기로 예정되어 있다 secretary 비서 following 그 다음의 constraint 제약, 제한, 통제 exceed 넘다, 초과하다 preference 선호 benefit 혜택 helpful 도움이 되는 loan 대출

186 동의어 찾기

첫 번째 웹 페이지에서, 두 번째 문단 첫 번째 줄의 "materials"
와 가장 가까운 의미를 가진 단어는?
(A) 직물
(B) 물질
(C) 서류
(D) 방법

해설 해당 부분은 채용 전문가가 입사 지원 서류를 검토하게 될
것(job application materials reviewed by recruiting
experts)이라는 의미이므로, materials는 documents와
의미가 가깝다고 볼 수 있다. 따라서 정답은 (C)이다.

187 Not/True 확인

첫 번째 웹 페이지에서, 취업 박람회의 이점으로 언급되지 않
은 것은?
(A) 구직 활동에 도움이 되는 조언
(B) 고용주들과 만날 기회
(C) 의료 보건 직업들에 관한 강의
(D) 학자금 대출에 대한 정보

해설 학업 비용을 마련하는 법을 배울 수 있다고 했을 뿐, 학자금 대
출에 대한 정보는 언급되지 않았으므로 정답은 (D)이다.

188 추론/암시

우드 씨는 누구일 것 같은가?
(A) 행사 참가자
(B) 연설 전문가
(C) 사무 보조원
(D) 기업가

해설 두 번째 지문에서 이메일을 받는 사람이 우드 씨이고, 제목은
도움을 요청한다고 되어 있으며, 발신자인 화이트 씨는 행사
참석을 위해 교통편 티켓 예약을 부탁하고 있다. 이를 통해 우
드 씨는 그러한 업무를 수행하는 사무 보조 직원임을 짐작할
수 있다. 따라서 정답은 (C)이다.

189 세부 사항 (연계)

화이트 씨는 어떤 분야에 근무하는가?
(A) 치의학
(B) 간호학
(C) 임상 병리학
(D) 물리 요법

해설 이메일 후반부에 화이트 씨가 "오후 4시에 있을 자신의 발표
(my presentation at 4:00 P.M.)"에 대해 언급했고, 첫 번째
지문의 강의 일정표를 보면 4시에 해당하는 것은 Physical
therapy(물리 요법)이므로 정답은 (D)이다.

190 세부 사항 (연계)

화이트 씨는 Charlotte에 가기 위해 어떤 철도 회사를 이용
할 것인가?
(A) Speedy rails
(B) New trains
(C) Sky trains
(D) States connection

해설 이메일을 보면, '오후 2시에서 2시 30분 사이에 도착하고 싶
다(I would like to arrive in Charlotte between 2:00
and 2:30 P.M.)'고 했고, '중간에 환승하는 여정은 원하지 않
는다(I want to avoid journeys that have a train change
in the middle)'고 했으므로, 이 두 조건을 충족하는 (D)가 정
답이다. (C)는 도착 시간은 충족되지만, 환승이 필요하므로 오
답이다.

[191-195] 편지 & 이메일 & 영수증

캐롤 해리스
306 Kent 가
Los Angeles, 캘리포니아 주 908688

1월 28일

해리스 씨에게,

당신이 주문한 다음 물품이 단종되었다는 것을 알려드리게 되어 유
감입니다.
SN #0003609 (Sunpower) 디지털 카메라, 599달러 99센트

그 카메라의 제조업체인 Sunpower 사가 한 달 전에 그 제품의 생산
을 중단했습니다.
그들은 새해에 그 카메라 대신 다른 제품을 만들기로 결정했는데, 아
직 시장에 출시되지는 않았습니다.
그러므로 우리가 재고로 가지고 있는 아래의 제품들을 대신 고려해
볼 것을 권장합니다.

· SN #0003689 (Sunpower) 디지털 카메라, 810달러 46센트
· SN #06081007 (Shotmaster) 디지털 카메라, 748달러 35센트
· SN #06081117 (Shotmaster) 디지털 카메라, 850달러 99센트

위에 언급된 제품들은 당신이 기존에 주문하길 원했던 제품과 크게 다
르지 않은 성능을 가지고 있습니다. 가격은 약간 더 비싸지만, 조금 더
선명한 화질의 사진을 찍을 수 있습니다.
제품들을 비교하고 싶으시면, 주중에 저희 매장에 편하게 들러주세요.

안부를 전하며,

마이클 워커
고객 서비스 담당자
Prime Photos

수신: 마이클 워커 <walker8000@primephotos.net>
발신: 캐롤 해리스 <happycarol@yahos.com>
날짜: 1월 30일
제목: 카메라 선택

추천 제품을 설명하는 편지를 보내 주셔서 감사합니다. 제가 구입하고 싶었던 제품이 더 이상 판매되지 않아 매우 유감이지만, 저는 카메라가 필요하기 때문에, 다른 제품을 사려고 합니다. 다른 사람들처럼, 저도 해상도가 더 높은 사진을 찍는 카메라를 선호합니다. 하지만 당신이 제안하신 제품들은 제가 원래 주문했던 것보다 가격이 비싸군요. 만약 제가 하나를 선택해야 한다면, 셋 중에서 가장 저렴한 두 번째 제품을 선택하고 싶습니다. 그리고 작년에 받은 5퍼센트 할인 쿠폰을 사용하고 싶은데, 그것이 아직도 유효한지 잘 모르겠네요. 그래서, 이것을 확인해 주시겠어요? 쿠폰 번호는 C137159입니다. 만약 가능하다면, 제가 매장에 방문해서 그것을 직접 구매하겠습니다.

진심으로,

캐롤 해리스

거래 영수증

PRIME PHOTOS
550 Georgia 가
Los Angeles, 캘리포니아 주 55027
[880] 5001-3609

2024년 1월 31일   오후 4시 15분
신용카드 번호: 1234 XXXX XXXX

고객 이름: 캐롤 해리스
요청 상품: 디지털 카메라
할인: 37달러 42센트
지불 금액: 710달러 93센트

영수증과 함께 개봉되지 않은 물건을 가져오시면
기꺼이 교환해 드립니다! 환불은 해드리지 않습니다.

어휘 discontinue 중단하다, 단종하다 manufacturer 제조업체 instead of ~대신에 launch 출시하다 encourage 권장하다 alternatively 그 대신에 in stock 재고로 mention 언급하다 significantly 상당히 slightly 약간, 조금 clear 또렷한 compare 비교하다 recommend 추천하다 prefer 선호하다 resolution 해상도, 결의안 valid 유효한 request 요청하다, 신청하다 affordable (가격 등이) 적당한 circumstance 상황

191 주제/목적
편지는 왜 보내셨는가?
(A) 배송이 늦은 이유를 설명하기 위해
(B) 더 저렴한 선택권을 제안하기 위해
(C) 제품의 상황을 알리기 위해
(D) 특가 상품을 제안하기 위해

해설 지문 초반부에 'I regret to inform you that the following item you ordered has been discontinued(당신이 주문한 상품이 단종되었다는 것을 알려드리게 되어 유감입니다)'라는 부분을 보면, 제품의 상황을 알리기 위해 쓴 편지라는 것을 알 수 있다. 따라서 정답은 (C)이다.

192 동의어 찾기
편지에서, 네 번째 문단 네 번째 줄의 "drop by"와 의미가 가장 가까운 것은?
(A) 감소하다
(B) 예약하다
(C) 방문하다
(D) 다시 채우다

해설 해당 부분은 '저희 매장에 편하게 들러주세요(please feel free to drop by our store)'라는 의미이다. drop by는 '~에 들르다'라는 뜻이므로, (C) visit(방문하다)와 의미상 가깝다.

193 Not/True 확인
이메일에서 해리스 씨에 대해 명시된 것은?
(A) 그녀는 신제품이 출시되기를 기다릴 것이다.
(B) 그녀는 청구상 오류 때문에 주문을 취소하길 원한다.
(C) 그녀는 추천 받은 제품의 가격에 만족한다.
(D) 그녀는 더 좋은 성능의 제품을 선호한다.

해설 지문 초반부에 'Like everyone else, I prefer cameras that create photographs that are higher in resolution(다른 사람들처럼, 저도 해상도가 더 높은 사진을 찍는 카메라를 선호합니다)'이라고 되어 있으므로 정답은 (D)이다.

194 세부 사항 (연계)
해리스 씨는 어떤 카메라를 구입할 것 같은가?
(A) SN #0003609
(B) SN #0003689
(C) SN #06081007
(D) SN #06081117

해설 이메일 중반에 해리스 씨는 'I'd like to get the second one(두 번째 것을 선택하고 싶다)'이라고 했는데, 첫 번째 편지의 제품 목록 중 두 번째 제품은 SN #06081007이므로 정답은 (C)이다.

195 Not/True 확인 (연계)
1월 31일에 일어난 일이 아닌 것은?
(A) 카메라가 신용카드로 구매되었다.
(B) 구매에 쿠폰이 사용되었다.
(C) 해리스 씨가 매장에 직접 방문했다.
(D) 해리스 씨가 교환을 위해 영수증을 제시했다.

해설 세 번째 지문인 영수증을 보면, 1월 31일에 해리스 씨가 카메라를 구입한 것에 대한 정보가 나와 있다. (A) 영수증에 카드 번호(Card No.)가 나와 있는 것으로 보아 해리스 씨는 신용카드로 카메라를 구입했음을 알 수 있고, 두 번째 지문인 이메일에서 해리스 씨가 쿠폰 할인 가능 여부를 문의하며 가능할 시

매장에 직접 방문하겠다고 했고, 영수증에 할인 금액이 명시되어 있으므로 (B), (C)도 일치한다. 영수증 하단의 'We will exchange any unopened item with original receipt.' 부분만 통해 해리스 씨가 교환을 위해 영수증을 제시했다는 것은 알 수 없다.

[196-200] 광고 & 이메일 & 온라인 리뷰

Humanity Appliances
Calgary, Golden 가 245
전화번호: (921) 3666-4848
영업시간: 월요일 ~ 금요일, 오전 9시 ~ 오후 6시

저희 연례 창고 정리 세일을 놓치지 마세요!

4월 6일 금요일 ~ 4월 8일 일요일

- 48인치 LCD TV — 20% 할인
- KS 전기밥솥 — 25% 할인
- LGS 식기세척기 — 30% 할인
- Stars 프리미엄 냉장고 — 35% 할인
- SKY 세탁 건조기 — 50% 할인

4월 5일 목요일은 세일 행사를 준비하기 위해 매장이 오후 1시에 마감한다는 점을 알아두세요. 할인은 온라인과 오프라인 구매에 동일하게 적용됩니다. 제품은 선착순으로 구매할 수 있으며, 예약은 불가능합니다.

Humanity Appliances의 골드 회원에 가입하셔서 5% 추가 할인을 받으세요. 질문 있으시면, 저희 판매팀에 연락해주세요. 유능한 우리 판매 직원들은 어떤 질문이든 답변해 드릴 수 있습니다.

수신: 전 직원
발신: 마크 볼튼
날짜: 3월 30일
제목: 근무 일정

전 직원 여러분께,

우리는 4월 5일에 야간 근무를 할 것이며, 재고 기록, 가격 확인, 제품 진열을 할 직원들이 필요합니다. 저는 모든 지원자들이 야간 근무 동안 1.5배의 수당을 받는 것과 함께 아침식사를 할 수 있도록 Grand Foods에서의 특별 대접을 마련했습니다. 가능하신 분들은 저에게 4월 3일까지 알려주세요.

진심으로,

마크 볼튼
총 책임자

---

http://www.grandfoods.co.ca

홈	후기	주문하기	연락하기

우리는 지난 4년간 Grand Foods를 이용했고, 결코 실망한 적이 없습니다. 직원들은 항상 신속하고 믿을 만하며, 음식은 아주 신선하고 맛있습니다. 고객 서비스 담당 부장님도 많은 도움을 주셨습니다. 지난 4월, 저는 16명의 직원들을 위한 아침식사를 대접했고, 그들 모두가 서비스에 만족했습니다. 우리는 중요한 행사가 있을 때마다 귀사의 서비스를 이용할 겁니다.

마크 볼튼

어휘 annual 매년의, 연례의 inventory 재고(품) clearance sale 창고 정리 세일 in order to ~하기 위해서 prepare for ~을 준비하다 discount 할인 apply 적용하다 equally 똑같이, 동등하게 on a first-come first-served basis 선착순으로 sign up 참가하다, 가입하다 eligible for ~에 자격이 있는 additional 추가의 available 시간이 있는, 이용 가능한 overnight shift 철야 근무 arrange 정리하다, 마련하다 notify 알리다 prompt 지체 없는, 신속한 reliable 믿을 만한 be satisfied with ~에 만족하다 home appliance 가전 제품 merchandise 상품 competitiveness 경쟁력 quality 질

196 세부 사항
광고에 따르면, 4월 5일에 무슨 일이 일어날 것인가?
(A) 매장이 다른 장소로 이전할 것이다.
(B) 가전 제품 할인 행사가 있을 것이다.
(C) 일부 신상품이 출시될 것이다.
(D) 매장이 평소보다 일찍 마감할 것이다.

해설 질문의 키워드인 'April 5'를 지문에서 먼저 찾는다. 광고문 중간에 '4월 5일은 오후 1시에 문을 닫을 것(the store will close at 1 P.M. on Thursday, April 5)'이라는 언급이 있으므로 평소보다 일찍 마감한다는 (D)가 정답이다.

197 Not/True 확인
골드 멤버십에 대해 알 수 있는 것은?
(A) 식기세척기에 35% 할인을 제공한다.
(B) 가입하려면 회비를 지불해야 한다.
(C) 무료 식사가 회원권에 포함된다.
(D) 회원들은 온라인으로 제품을 사전 예약할 수 있다.

해설 광고 후반부에 '5% 추가 할인을 받기 위해(to become eligible for an additional 5% discount)' 회원 가입을 하라는 내용이 있고, 광고 중간의 제품 목록을 보면, '식기세척기의 할인율은 30%(LGS Dishwasher – 30% off)'이다. 골드 회원은 여기서 5% 추가된 총 35%의 할인을 받을 수 있으므로 정답은 (A)이다.

198 세부 사항 (연계)

이메일에 따르면, 볼튼 씨는 직원들에게 무엇을 하라고 요청하는가?

(A) 교육 과정에 참석하기
(B) 고객들에게 행사에 대해 알리기
(C) 연례 행사 준비하기
(D) 새로운 자원봉사자 모집하기

해설 볼튼 씨가 쓴 이메일을 보면, 'We are adding an overnight shift on April 5 and will need employees to record inventory, check prices, and set up product displays(4월 5일에 야간 근무를 할 것이다)'라고 되어 있다. 첫 번째 광고에서 4월 5일은 '연례 창고 정리 할인 행사(ANNUAL INVENTORY CLEARANCE SALE)'가 시작되기 바로 전 날이므로, 볼튼 씨가 직원들에게 행사 준비를 요청하고 있음을 알 수 있다. 따라서 정답은 (C)이다.

199 세부 사항 (연계)

몇 명의 직원들이 행사 준비에 참여했는가?

(A) 16명
(B) 25명
(C) 50명
(D) 80명

해설 두 번째 지문인 볼튼 씨의 이메일을 보면, 'I have arranged a special treat from Grand Foods so that all volunteers will have breakfast(참여하는 직원들이 아침식사를 할 수 있도록 Grand Foods에 특별 대접을 마련했다)'고 되어 있고, 세 번째 지문인 볼튼 씨가 작성한 온라인 후기를 보면, 'I had a staff breakfast for 16 people(16명의 직원들을 위한 아침식사를 대접했다)'는 내용이 있으므로, (A)가 정답이다.

200 Not/True 확인

온라인 후기에서 언급되지 않은 것은?

(A) 고객 서비스 수준
(B) 가격 경쟁력
(C) 음식의 품질
(D) 배달의 적시성

해설 (A) 온라인 후기에서 '고객 서비스 담당 부장이 도움이 되었고(Their customer service manager is very helpful)', (C) '음식은 신선하고 맛있으며(the food is so fresh and delicious)', (D) '직원들은 신속하다(The employees are always prompt)'고 언급되어 있으나, 가격에 대해 언급된 부분은 없으므로 (B)가 정답이다.

Memo

TEST 2

p.60

LISTENING TEST

01	(B)	02	(B)	03	(D)	04	(C)	05	(A)
06	(C)	07	(B)	08	(C)	09	(C)	10	(A)
11	(B)	12	(C)	13	(B)	14	(B)	15	(C)
16	(A)	17	(B)	18	(C)	19	(C)	20	(C)
21	(C)	22	(A)	23	(B)	24	(C)	25	(B)
26	(A)	27	(A)	28	(B)	29	(A)	30	(C)
31	(C)	32	(A)	33	(D)	34	(B)	35	(B)
36	(C)	37	(D)	38	(B)	39	(C)	40	(D)
41	(D)	42	(B)	43	(A)	44	(C)	45	(A)
46	(B)	47	(B)	48	(A)	49	(D)	50	(C)
51	(D)	52	(B)	53	(A)	54	(B)	55	(C)
56	(A)	57	(B)	58	(D)	59	(C)	60	(A)
61	(D)	62	(C)	63	(D)	64	(D)	65	(C)
66	(A)	67	(B)	68	(A)	69	(C)	70	(C)
71	(D)	72	(A)	73	(D)	74	(C)	75	(C)
76	(B)	77	(D)	78	(C)	79	(B)	80	(D)
81	(C)	82	(B)	83	(B)	84	(B)	85	(C)
86	(A)	87	(B)	88	(C)	89	(C)	90	(D)
91	(B)	92	(A)	93	(D)	94	(B)	95	(B)
96	(D)	97	(A)	98	(C)	99	(A)	100	(A)

READING TEST

101	(A)	102	(A)	103	(D)	104	(C)	105	(A)
106	(B)	107	(B)	108	(C)	109	(A)	110	(D)
111	(A)	112	(D)	113	(C)	114	(B)	115	(D)
116	(B)	117	(A)	118	(B)	119	(A)	120	(C)
121	(C)	122	(B)	123	(C)	124	(A)	125	(A)
126	(D)	127	(D)	128	(C)	129	(B)	130	(B)
131	(C)	132	(D)	133	(A)	134	(B)	135	(D)
136	(B)	137	(A)	138	(C)	139	(C)	140	(A)
141	(B)	142	(D)	143	(B)	144	(D)	145	(C)
146	(A)	147	(D)	148	(C)	149	(C)	150	(C)
151	(A)	152	(B)	153	(A)	154	(B)	155	(C)
156	(A)	157	(A)	158	(B)	159	(A)	160	(C)
161	(B)	162	(D)	163	(B)	164	(C)	165	(A)
166	(B)	167	(C)	168	(D)	169	(A)	170	(B)
171	(C)	172	(C)	173	(D)	174	(B)	175	(A)
176	(A)	177	(B)	178	(C)	179	(C)	180	(B)
181	(B)	182	(B)	183	(A)	184	(D)	185	(C)
186	(D)	187	(A)	188	(B)	189	(D)	190	(B)
191	(A)	192	(D)	193	(C)	194	(D)	195	(A)
196	(A)	197	(A)	198	(C)	199	(D)	200	(C)

PART • 1

1 인물(1인) 사진

(A) She's opening a window.
(B) She's cutting vegetables.
(C) She's stirring something in a pot.
(D) She's serving some food.

(A) 여자가 창문을 열고 있다.
(B) 여자가 채소를 썰고 있다.
(C) 여자가 냄비 속의 무언가를 젓고 있다.
(D) 여자가 음식을 제공하고 있다.

해설 여자가 부엌에서 야채를 썰고 있는 사진이다. "썰다"를 의미하는 cut, chop 등의 동사를 익혀두는 것이 중요하다. (A)는 창문을 여는 행동이 아니므로 오답, (C)는 냄비가 있지만 젓고 있지도 않으므로 오답, (D)는 음식을 제공하고 있지 않으므로 오답이다.

어휘 open 열다; 열린 stir 휘젓다, 섞다 serve 제공하다, 서빙하다

2 인물(2인 이상) 사진

(A) They are entering a house.
(B) They are cycling outdoors.
(C) They are resting against a railing.
(D) They are parking a vehicle on a street.

(A) 그들은 집에 들어가고 있다.
(B) 그들은 야외에서 자전거를 타고 있다.
(C) 그들은 난간에 기대어 있다.
(D) 그들은 길가에 차를 주차하고 있다.

해설 길에서 자전거를 타는 모습을 야외에서 자전거를 탄다고 묘사한 (B)가 정답이다. (A)는 집과 들어가는 사람이 없으므로 오답, (C)는 난간도 보이지 않고 기대어 있지도 않으므로 오답, (D)는 길거리가 배경이지만 자동차를 주차하고 있지 않으므로 오답이다.

어휘 enter 들어가다, 입장하다 cycle 자전거를 타다; 자전거 outdoors 야외에서 rest against ~에 기대다 railing 난간, 손잡이 vehicle 탈것, 자동차

3 사물/풍경 사진

(A) Some boats are sailing in the ocean.
(B) Some people are swimming in the water.
(C) Some pedestrians are crossing the bridge.
(D) Some buildings overlook the water.

(A) 배들이 바다에서 항해하고 있다.
(B) 사람들이 물에서 수영하고 있다.
(C) 보행자들이 다리를 건너고 있다.
(D) 건물들이 물을 내려다 보고 있다.

해설 물가에 건물이 있는 것을 "overlook(내려다 보다)"이라는 동사로 표현한 (D)가 정답이다. (A)는 배는 있지만 항해하고 있지 않아 오답이며, (B)와 (C)는 사람들이 보이지 않아 오답이다.

어휘 sail 항해하다 ocean 대양, 바다 pedestrian 보행자, 행인 cross 건너다 overlook 내려다보다

4 혼합 사진

(A) Some signs are being hung on the wall.
(B) Items are being placed into plastic bags.
(C) A cart is being pushed down an aisle by a shopper.
(D) A woman is next to a checkout counter.

(A) 몇 개의 간판들이 벽에 걸리고 있다.
(B) 식료품들이 비닐봉투 안에 넣어지고 있다.
(C) 카트가 쇼핑객에 의해 통로에서 밀어지고 있다.
(D) 여자가 계산대 옆에 있다.

해설 수동태 진행형(be being p.p.)을 사용하여 카트가 밀어지고 있는 모습, 즉 카트를 밀고 있는 인물의 행동을 묘사한 (C)가 정답이다. 수동태 진행형은 인물의 행동을 묘사하여 인물 사진 문제의 정답이 되는 경우가 많다. (A)는 광고판은 보이지 않아서 오답, (B)는 물건을 비닐봉투에 넣고 있는 사람이 없으므로 오답, (D)는 사진에 계산대가 보이지 않아서 오답이다.

어휘 sign 표지판, 간판 hang(hung) 걸다 plastic bag 비닐봉투 cart 카트 aisle 복도, 통로 checkout counter 계산대

5 사물/풍경 사진

(A) A seating area is surrounded by plants.
(B) Some rocks are being moved into a corner.
(C) Workers are repairing some walls.
(D) The park is crowded with people.

(A) 앉는 공간이 식물로 둘러싸여 있다.
(B) 바위들이 구석으로 옮겨지고 있다.
(C) 일꾼들이 벽을 수리하고 있다.
(D) 공원이 사람들로 붐비고 있다.

해설 앉는 공간이 식물들로 둘러싸여 있다고 묘사한 (A)가 정답이다. (B)는 돌을 구석으로 옮기는 사람이 없으므로 오답, (C)는 일꾼들도 보이지 않고 수리하는 행동도 없으므로 오답, (D)는 사진 속 장소에 사람이 등장하지 않으므로 오답이다.

어휘 area 지역, 공간 plant 화초, 식물 move 옮기다, 이동하다 corner 구석 repair 수리하다 crowded 붐비는

6 혼합 사진

(A) A woman is writing something on a board.
(B) A woman is sitting at the table.
(C) Some papers are spread out on the table.
(D) The floor is being cleaned.

(A) 여자가 칠판에 무언가를 쓰고 있다.
(B) 여자가 테이블에 앉아 있다.
(C) 종이들이 테이블 위에 펼쳐져 있다.
(D) 바닥이 정소되고 있나.

해설 인물이 등장하지만 정답은 테이블에 펼쳐진 종이들을 묘사한 (C)이다. (A)는 칠판도 없고 그 위에 쓰는 행동도 없으므로 오답, (B)는 여자가 서 있으므로 오답, (D)는 바닥을 청소하는 사람이 보이지 않아서 오답이다. 수동태 진행형 "be being p.p"는 인물의 행동을 묘사할 때 사용된다.

어휘 board 칠판, 판 spread 펼치다, 퍼지다 floor 바닥 clean 청소하다; 깨끗한

7 How 의문문

How long will it take to fix this elevator?
(A) Why don't you fax it?
(B) About 30 minutes.
(C) Just last week.

이 엘리베이터를 수리하는 데 시간이 얼마나 걸릴까요?
(A) 그것을 팩스로 보내는 게 어때요?
(B) 약 30분 정도요.
(C) 지난주예요.

해설 How long ~으로 시작하는 의문문으로, 시간이 얼마나 오래 걸리는지를 묻고 있다. 따라서 '약 30분 정도' 걸린다고 응답하는 (B)가 정답이다. (A)는 문제의 fix와 발음이 유사한 fax가 들어간 오답이며, (C)는 시점을 묻는 When 의문문의 대답으로 적합하다.

어휘 take (시간이) 걸리다   fix 고치다, 수리하다   just 바로, 방금

8 Where 의문문

Where can I buy an umbrella?
(A) It is going to rain.
(B) That's a brilliant idea.
(C) Try the shop next door.

어디에서 우산을 살 수 있나요?
(A) 비가 올 겁니다.
(B) 그것 참 좋은 아이디어군요.
(C) 옆 가게에 한번 가보세요.

해설 의문사 Where로 시작하는 의문문으로, 우산을 살 수 있는 장소를 묻고 있다. 따라서 옆 가게에 가보라고 응답하는 (C)가 정답이다. (A)는 질문에 등장한 우산(umbrella)에서 연상되는 어휘 rain을 활용한 오답이다. (B)는 권유문의 응답으로 적합하다.

어휘 umbrella 우산   rain 비가 오다; 비   brilliant 멋진, 명석한   try 시도해 보다   shop 가게   next door 옆집에

9 When 의문문

When did you sign up for the marathon?
(A) On the sign-up sheet.
(B) It's in August.
(C) Last month.

당신은 언제 마라톤을 신청했나요?
(A) 등록 신청서예요.
(B) 8월에 있어요.
(C) 지난달예요.

해설 시점을 묻는 When 의문문으로, 마라톤을 언제 신청했는지 묻고 있다. (A)는 Where 의문문에 대한 응답이므로 오답이다. When과 Where에 대한 대답을 혼동하지 않도록 주의하자. (B)와 (C)는 둘 다 시점을 나타내는 표현이지만, 질문에 과

거 시제가 사용되었으므로 과거 시점을 말하는 (C)가 정답이다. (B)는 행사가 열릴 시기를 묻는 질문에 적합하다.

어휘 sign up for ~에 신청하다   marathon 마라톤

10 부가 의문문

You've been here before, haven't you?
(A) Yes, a few years ago.
(B) Let's wait here.
(C) No, they don't have it.

당신은 전에 여기 와본 적이 있죠, 그렇죠?
(A) 네, 몇 년 전에요.
(B) 여기서 기다립시다.
(C) 아니요, 그들은 그것을 가지고 있지 않아요.

해설 "You have ~, haven't you?"의 구조로, 경험을 묻는 부가의문문이다. '전에 와본 적이 있지 않나요?'라는 질문에 대해 '몇 년 전에 와봤다'고 말하는 (A)가 의미상 가장 적합하다. (B)는 질문의 here를 반복한 오답이며, (C)는 질문에서 경험을 묻는 have가 '소유하다'의 의미로 사용된 오답이다.

어휘 a few 몇몇의, 약간의   ago 전에   wait 기다리다

11 일반 의문문

Is this the bus to Manchester?
(A) You can pay on the bus.
(B) That's what the driver told me.
(C) Only about once an hour.

맨체스터로 가는 버스인가요?
(A) 버스에서 계산하면 됩니다.
(B) 운전사가 그렇게 말했어요.
(C) 한 시간에 한 번 정도만요.

해설 버스가 맨체스터행인지 물어보는 질문에, 버스 운전기사가 그렇게 말했다고 하는 (B)가 정답이다. 이처럼 Yes/No 의미를 포함한 표현을 암기해 두면 쉽게 정답을 맞출 수 있다. 'That's what I heard(내가 들은 바로는 그래)', 'Not that I know of(내가 아는 바로는 아니야)'를 대표적으로 알아두자. (A)는 지불 방법을 물어보는 How 의문문의 대답으로 적합하며, (C)는 빈도를 묻는 How often ~? 의문문의 대답으로 적합하다.

어휘 pay 지불하다   once 한번, 한때

12 선택 의문문

Should I fax or mail the invitation?
(A) To the mayor's office.
(B) Yes, that's better.
(C) I'd deliver it by hand.

초대장을 팩스로 보내야 하나요, 아니면 우편으로 보내야 하나요?
(A) 시장의 사무실로요.
(B) 네, 그것이 더 좋습니다.
(C) 제가 직접 전달하겠습니다.

해설 'A or B' 구조의 선택 의문문으로, 초대장을 팩스로 보낼지 우편으로 보낼지 묻는 문제이다. 선택 의문문에서는 A도 B도 아닌 새로운 선택이 답이 될 수 있는데, 이 문제에서는 '직접 전달하겠다(deliver ~ by hand)'라며 새로운 선택을 한 (C)가 정답이다. (A)는 질문의 mail과 발음이 유사한 mayor를 활용하여 혼동을 주고 있고, 선택의문문에는 Yes/No로 대답할 수 없으므로 (B)는 오답이다.

어휘 mail 우편으로 보내다; 우편물 invitation 초대, 초대장 mayor 시장 deliver 전달하다 by hand 손으로, 직접

13 일반 의문문

Did Charles finish writing the report?
(A) I need to see the reporter.
(B) I don't think so.
(C) No, it is not.

찰스가 보고서 작성을 마쳤나요?
(A) 저는 그 기자를 봐야 합니다.
(B) 전 그렇게 생각하지 않아요.
(C) 아니요, 그렇지 않습니다.

해설 보고서 작성을 마쳤는지 묻는 질문에, 부정의 의미를 포함한 (B) '그렇게 생각하지 않는다'가 정답이다. (A)는 질문의 명사 report와 발음이 비슷한 reporter를 사용한 오답이고 (C)는 be동사가 나왔으므로 일반동사 의문문에 대한 답이 될 수 없다.

어휘 finish 끝내다, 마치다 report 보고서; 보고하다 reporter 기자

14 Who 의문문

Who has the key to the archives room?
(A) I am free tonight.
(B) I gave it back to Shannon.
(C) It's actually quite far.

문서 보관소 열쇠를 누가 가지고 있나요?
(A) 저는 오늘 밤에 시간이 있습니다.
(B) 제가 그것을 샤넌에게 돌려주었습니다.
(C) 그곳은 사실 꽤 멉니다.

해설 열쇠를 누가 가지고 있는지 묻는 Who 의문문에, '샤넌에게 열쇠를 다시 돌려주었다', 즉, 샤넌이 가지고 있다고 한 (B)가 정답이다. (A)는 문제와 관계 없는 내용이며, (C)는 거리를 묻는 의문문에 대한 대답으로 적합하다.

어휘 archives 기록 보관소 be free 시간이 있는, 한가한 actually 사실 quite 꽤

15 제안/권유 의문문

Would you like to join us for dinner on Friday?
(A) I'm already a member.
(B) No, I haven't seen her.
(C) Let me check my calendar.

금요일에 저희와 함께 저녁 식사를 하시겠어요?
(A) 저는 이미 회원입니다.
(B) 아니요, 저는 그녀를 본 적이 없습니다.
(C) 일정표 좀 확인해 보고요.

해설 'Would you like to ~' 형태의 권유/청유문으로, 함께 저녁 식사를 할 것을 권유하는 질문에 '일정을 확인해 보겠다'고 대답하는 (C)가 정답이다. 일반 의문문에는 긍정 또는 부정으로 답하는 경우가 일반적이지만, 이처럼 "몰라요"의 내용으로도 대답할 수 있다. (A)는 질문의 join(가입하다)의 관련 어휘인 member(회원)로 오답을 유도하고 있다. (B)는 No로 대답했지만, 뒤의 내용이 질문과 관계가 없으므로 오답이다.

어휘 join 함께하다, 가입하다 already 이미 check 확인하다 calendar 일정표, 달력

16 What 의문문

What's Mr. Chang's new position?
(A) I think he is an assistant manager.
(B) This is the latest edition.
(C) He's looking forward to it.

창 씨의 새 직책은 무엇인가요?
(A) 부매니저인 것 같습니다.
(B) 이것은 최신판입니다.
(C) 그는 그것을 고대하고 있습니다.

해설 특정 인물의 새로운 직책을 묻는 질문에, '부매니저인 것 같다'고 답하는 (A)가 정답이다. (B)는 질문의 position과 발음이 유사한 edition으로 오답을 유도하고 있다. (C)는 질문과 관계 없다.

어휘 position 지위, 직책 assistant 보조의 latest 최신의 edition 판 look forward to ~을 고대하다, 기대하다

17 부정 의문문

Wouldn't these flowers be good for the wedding?
(A) It was very useful.
(B) I think they're perfect.
(C) A table for five, please.

이 꽃들이 결혼식에 어울리지 않을까요?
(A) 그것은 매우 유용했습니다.
(B) 완벽하다고 생각합니다.
(C) 5인용 테이블로 부탁합니다.

해설 꽃들이 결혼식에 어울리지 않을지 묻는 부정의문문으로, 정답은 '완벽하다'며 긍정을 표현하는 (B)이다. (A)는 과거시제이므로 적합하지 않고, (C)는 식당에서 좌석을 요청할 때 쓰는 표현으로 질문과는 무관한 내용이다.

어휘 wedding 결혼(식) useful 유용한 perfect 완벽한

18 **Why 의문문**

Why are you taking an accounting class?
(A) I learned how to fix it.
(B) The classroom is on the fifth floor.
(C) It'll help me get a promotion.

당신은 왜 회계학 수업을 들어요?
(A) 저는 그것을 어떻게 고치는지 배웠어요.
(B) 교실은 5층에 있습니다.
(C) 제가 승진하는 데 도움이 될 거예요.

해설 회계학 수업을 듣는 이유는 묻는 Why 의문문으로, 승진에 도움이 될 거라고 이유를 말한 (C)가 정답이다. (A)는 질문의 class에서 연상되는 어휘 learned을 이용한 함정, (B)는 수업의 장소를 묻는 Where 의문문의 응답으로 적절하며, class와 classroom의 유사 발음을 이용한 함정이다.

어휘 accounting 회계   fix 고치다   classroom 교실   get a promotion 승진하다

19 **부정 의문문**

Don't you have more candidates to interview today?
(A) Yes, the view was fantastic from the top.
(B) That was a very interesting article.
(C) Yes, there are two more scheduled for this afternoon.

오늘 면접 볼 지원자들이 더 있지 않아요?
(A) 네, 꼭대기에서의 전망은 환상적이었어요.
(B) 정말 흥미로운 기사였어요.
(C) 네, 오늘 오후에 예정된 두 명이 더 있어요.

해설 오늘 면접 볼 지원자가 더 있지 않냐는 부정 의문문에 "Yes + 세부 내용"으로 긍정을 표현한 (C)가 정답이다. 부정 의문문의 경우, 부정으로 물어도 긍정을 뜻하는 질문이라는 것을 기억해 두자. (A)는 질문의 interview와 발음이 유사한 view를 이용한 오답이며, (B)는 interview와 유사 발음의 interesting을 이용한 오답이다.

어휘 candidate 후보자, 지원자   interview 면접보다, 취재하다   view 전망   top 정상, 꼭대기   article 기사   scheduled 예정된

20 **평서문**

I think we should get to the stadium early.
(A) I'm afraid she has an appointment.
(B) That's my favorite.
(C) Yes, if we want good seats.

우리는 경기장에 일찍 도착해야 할 것 같군요.
(A) 유감스럽게도 그녀는 약속이 있습니다.
(B) 그것은 제가 제일 좋아하는 겁니다.
(C) 네, 좋은 자리를 원하면요.

해설 'I think we should ~'의 평서문으로, '일찍 도착하는 게 좋겠다'고 제안하고 있다. 정답은 '좋은 자리를 원한다면 그렇게 하는 게 좋겠다'라는 의미의 (C)이다. (A)는 질문과 무관한 she가 등장한 오답이며, (B)는 질문과 관련 없는 내용의 응답이다.

어휘 get to ~에 도착하다   stadium 경기장   appointment 약속   favorite 가장 좋아하는 것   seat 좌석

21 **How 의문문**

How do I access my e-mail account on my laptop?
(A) The mail carrier hasn't come yet.
(B) On the top of the table, next to the front door.
(C) Download the e-mail program.

제 노트북 컴퓨터에서 이메일 계정을 어떻게 이용할 수 있나요?
(A) 우체부는 아직 오지 않았어요.
(B) 정문 옆에 있는 테이블 위에요.
(C) 이메일 프로그램을 다운로드 하세요.

해설 "How + 일반동사" 형태의 질문으로, 자신의 이메일 계정을 이용하는 방법을 묻고 있다. 이에 명령문으로 이메일 프로그램을 다운로드하라고 제안한 (C)가 정답이다. 최신 기출에서는 질문의 어휘를 반복한 보기도 정답으로 많이 등장한다. (A)의 mail은 질문의 e-mail과 유사한 발음을 이용한 오답이고, (B)는 위치를 묻는 Where 의문문의 대답으로 적합하다.

어휘 mail carrier 우체부   access 이용하다, 접근하다   account 계정, 계좌   mail carrier 우체부

22 **When 의문문**

When will the press conference take place?
(A) It's marked on your calendar.
(B) In at least two conference centers.
(C) The keynote speech was very impressive.

기자회견은 언제 열리나요?
(A) 당신의 달력에 표시되어 있어요.
(B) 적어도 2개의 회의장에서요.
(C) 기조연설은 굉장히 인상적이었어요.

해설 기자회견이 언제 열리는지 묻는 When 의문문이다. 정답은 "몰라요" 유형을 변형한 "달력에 써 있으니 확인해 보라"는 의미의 (A)이다. "몰라요" 유형은 매달 출제되는 정답 유형이므로 반드시 기억해 두자. (B)는 질문의 conference를 반복했으나 장소를 묻는 Where 의문문에 대한 대답이므로 오답이다. (C)는 conference에서 연상되는 어휘 keynote speech를 이용한 오답이다.

어휘 take place 일어나다   mark 표시하다   at least 적어도   keynote speech 기조연설   impressive 인상적인, 놀라운

23 평서문

I need to do some repairs on my garage.

(A) A two-story house.

(B) Is that going to be expensive?

(C) It was parked right in front of my house.

차고를 수리해야 해요.

(A) 이층집이요.

(B) 비쌀까요?

(C) 그것은 제 집 바로 앞에 주차되어 있어요.

해설 수리를 해야 한다는 평서문에, 가격이 비쌀지 묻는 (B)가 정답이다. 평서문에 대한 응답으로 질문이 자주 등장한다는 것을 알아 두자. (A)는 garage에서 연상되는 어휘 house를 사용한 오답이고 (C) 또한 garage에서 연상되는 park(주차하다)를 사용한 오답이며, Where 의문문에 대한 대답으로 적합하다.

어휘 repair 수리; 수리하다   garage 차고   story 층   park 주차하다

24 Where 의문문

Where can I buy a cell phone charger?

(A) She's making a phone call at the moment.

(B) They charge more at night.

(C) I have an extra one.

휴대폰 충전기를 어디에서 살 수 있을까요?

(A) 그녀는 지금 통화 중입니다.

(B) 그들은 야간에 요금을 더 부과해요.

(C) 저한테 여유분이 하나 있는데요.

해설 충전기를 살 수 있는 장소를 묻는 Where 의문문으로, 장소를 알려주는 대신 '여유분이 있다'고 말한 (C)가 정답이다. (A)는 질문과 관계없는 she가 나와 오답이며, (B)는 질문의 charger와 유사한 발음인 charge를 이용한 오답이다.

어휘 charger 충전기   make a phone call 전화를 걸다   at the moment 현재, 지금   charge 청구하나, 값을 매기다   extra 추가의, 여유의

25 부정 의문문

Didn't you order more printing papers?

(A) It should be printed on both sides.

(B) They haven't been delivered yet.

(C) In alphabetical order.

인쇄 용지를 더 주문하지 않았나요?

(A) 그것은 양면으로 인쇄되어야 합니다.

(B) 그것들은 아직 배달되지 않았어요.

(C) 알파벳 순서로요.

해설 주문을 하지 않았냐고 묻는 부정 의문문으로, Yes를 생략하고 '주문을 했으나 배달되지 않았다'고 대답한 (B)가 정답이다. (A)는 질문의 print를 반복한 오답이며, (C)는 질문의 order(주문하다)를 '순서'의 의미로 사용한 오답이다.

어휘 order 주문하다; 순서   print 인쇄하다   deliver 배달하다

26 What 의문문

What security software do you recommend for my company?

(A) I forgot what it's called.

(B) Somewhere between the first and second streets.

(C) One of my colleagues recommended your place.

저희 회사를 위해 어떤 보안 소프트웨어를 추천하나요?

(A) 이름을 잊어버렸어요.

(B) 1번가와 2번가 사이의 어딘가요.

(C) 제 동료 중 한 명이 당신의 업체를 추천했습니다.

해설 어떤 상품을 추천하는지 묻는 What 의문문으로, 제품을 구체적으로 말하는 것이 전형적이지만, "몰라요"의 유형으로 이름이 기억나지 않는다고 말한 (A)가 정답이다. (B)는 위치를 묻는 Where 의문문의 대답으로 적합하며, (C)는 질문의 recommend를 반복한 오답이다.

어휘 security 보안   recommend 추천하다   call ~라고 부르다   colleague 동료

27 선택 의문문

Do you want to take a fitness class or just use the pool?

(A) I don't like to swim.

(B) It fits very well.

(C) There is a gym down the street.

운동 수업을 듣길 원하나요, 아니면 수영장만 사용하길 원하나요?

(A) 저는 수영하는 것을 좋아하지 않아요.

(B) 그것은 굉장히 살 낮아요.

(C) 길 아래쪽에 체육관이 하나 있어요.

해설 운동 수업을 들을 것인지 수영장만 사용할 것인지 묻는 선택 의문문에, 수영하는 것을 좋아하지 않는다, 즉 수영장을 사용하지 않고 수업만 듣겠다고 한 (A)가 정답이다. (B)는 질문의 fitness와 발음이 유사한 fit을 이용한 오답이다. (C)는 질문과 연관된 어휘 gym이 나왔지만 장소를 묻는 Where 의문문에 대한 대답으로 적합하다.

어휘 fitness 운동, 건강   pool 수영장   swim 수영하다   fit 잘 맞다, 어울리다   gym 체육관

28 요청 의문문

Can you help me with this paperwork?

(A) The paper is in the bottom drawer.

(B) I'd be happy to help later today.

(C) Thanks, but I don't need any help.

제 서류 작업 좀 도와줄 수 있나요?
(A) 그 서류는 맨 아래 서랍에 있습니다.
(B) 이따가 오늘 중으로 기꺼이 도와드리겠습니다.
(C) 고맙지만, 저는 도움이 필요하지 않습니다.

해설 상대방에게 도움을 요청하는 권유/청유문으로, '나중에 기꺼이 도와주겠'다고 응답한 (B)가 정답이다. (A)와 (C)는 각각 질문의 paper과 help를 반복한 오답이며, 도움을 요청한 상대방에게, 본인이 도움이 필요하지 않다고 말하는 (C)는 응답으로 부적절하다.

어휘 paperwork 서류 작업 bottom 아래 drawer 서랍 later 나중에

29 **Who 의문문**

Who's planning the employee appreciation dinner?
(A) It was canceled.
(B) At an Italian restaurant near the office.
(C) A choice of appetizers.

누가 직원 감사 만찬을 계획하고 있나요?
(A) 그것은 취소됐어요.
(B) 사무실 근처의 이탈리아 식당에서요.
(C) 애피타이저 선택이요.

해설 누가 행사를 계획하고 있는지 묻는 질문이다. 사람 이름이나 조직명을 대는 것이 전형적이지만, 여기서는 '행사가 취소되었다'는 (A)가 정답이다. 이외에도 특정 행사가 언제(When), 어디에서(Where) 열리는지 묻는 질문에도 취소되었거나 이미 끝났다는 대답이 가능하다. (B)와 (C)는 각각 질문의 dinner에서 연상되는 restaurant과 appetizers를 이용한 오답이다.

어휘 plan 계획하다 appreciation 감사 cancel 취소하다 choice 선택, 선택권 appetizer 애피타이저, 전채

30 **부가 의문문**

The new soda commercial is almost finished, isn't it?
(A) The yearly inspection.
(B) Across from the restaurant.
(C) We had to start over.

새 청량음료 광고 작업은 거의 끝났어요, 그렇죠?
(A) 연례 검사요.
(B) 식당 맞은편이요.
(C) 우리는 다시 시작해야 했어요.

해설 광고 작업이 끝나가는지 묻는 부가 의문문이다. (C)의 '우리는 다시 시작해야 했다'는 내용은 결국 작업이 끝나려면 아직 멀었다는 의미로 정답이다. (A)는 질문과 무관한 내용이며, (B)는 질문의 soda에서 연상되는 restaurant를 이용했지만, 위치를 묻는 Where 의문문의 대답으로 적합하다.

어휘 commercial 광고 yearly 연례의, 연간의 inspection 검사 start over 다시 시작하다

31 **Why 의문문**

Why did you schedule tomorrow's meeting at noon?
(A) Thanks, I really appreciate it.
(B) Of course, they arrived on time.
(C) I can move it to one o'clock if you want.

내일 회의를 왜 정오로 잡았나요?
(A) 고마워요, 정말 감사합니다.
(B) 물론이죠, 그들은 정시에 도착했어요.
(C) 원하시면 1시로 옮길 수도 있어요.

해설 왜 회의를 정오에 잡았냐는 Why 의문문에 이유를 대답하는 대신, '원하면 1시로 옮길 수도 있다'고 제3안을 제안하는 (C)가 정답이다. (A)는 호의에 대한 반응이므로 오답이며, (B)의 Of course는 의문사 의문문의 응답으로 적절하지 않다.

어휘 schedule 일정을 잡다 at noon 정오에 appreciate 감사하다 on time 정시에, 제시간에 move 옮기다, 이동하다

PART • 3

[32-34]

M Hi, I'd like to rent some bicycles for me and my friend. How much would it be to rent two bicycles for two days, today and tomorrow?
W The total would be eighty dollars; that's forty dollars per person. Let me get the bikes and adjust them for you. Also, you'll need to bring them by five tomorrow afternoon. If you're late, you'll be charged an extra fee of six dollars per hour.
M We'll definitely try to be on time. Also, can you recommend any good bike paths nearby?
W Yes, we have several scenic bike paths nearby. There are maps for each one available over there on the counter. Please feel free to take some since they're free of charge.

M 안녕하세요, 저와 제 친구가 탈 자전거를 빌리고 싶습니다. 오늘과 내일 이틀 동안 자전거 두 대를 빌리는 데 얼마나 들까요?
W 1인당 40달러로, 총 80달러입니다. 제가 자전거를 가져와서 손님에게 맞게 조정해 드릴게요. 또한, 내일 오후 5시까지 자전거를 가지고 오셔야 합니다. 늦으면 시간당 6달러의 추가 비용이 부과될 거예요.
M 시간을 꼭 지키도록 할게요. 또한, 근처의 좋은 자전거 전용도로를 추천해 주실 수 있나요?
W 네, 근처에 경치가 좋은 자전거 전용도로가 몇 군데 있습니다. 각 도로의 지도가 저쪽 카운터에 있어요. 무료니까 얼마든지 가져가세요.

어휘 rent 임대하다, 빌리다   total 총액   adjust 조절하다, 조정하다
charge 부과하다; 비용, 요금   extra 추가의   fee 요금
per ~당   definitely 확실하게, 반드시   on time 정시에,
시간에 맞게   path 길, 경로   scenic 경치가 좋은   available
이용할 수 있는   take 가지고 가다   purchase 구매하다
apply for ~에 지원하다   item 물건, 상품   notice 공지

32   **세부 사항**

남자는 무엇을 하고 싶어하는가?
(A) 자전거 빌리기
(B) 티켓 구매하기
(C) 할인 받기
(D) 입사 지원하기

해설 남자의 첫 대사에서 친구와 본인이 탈 자전거를 빌리고 싶다
(I'd like to rent some bicycles for me and my friend)는
부분을 통해 정답이 (A)임을 알 수 있다.

33   **세부 사항**

여자는 남자가 늦으면 어떤 일이 생길 것이라고 말하는가?
(A) 약속이 취소될 것이다.
(B) 물건을 이용할 수 없을 것이다.
(C) 통지서가 우편으로 보내질 것이다.
(D) 추가 요금이 부과될 것이다.

해설 질문의 키워드인 'late'를 기억하고 본문을 듣자. 여자의 대사
에서 늦으면 추가 비용이 청구될 것(If you're late, you'll be
charged an extra fee of six dollars per hour)이라는 부
분을 통해 정답이 (D)임을 알 수 있다.

34   **세부 사항**

여자는 남자에게 무엇을 제공하는가?
(A) 음료수
(B) 지도
(C) 무료 교통편
(D) 쿠폰

해설 여자의 마지막 대사에서 지도가 준비되어 있으니 얼마든지
가져가라(There are maps for each one available ~.
Please feel free to take some ~)는 부분을 통해 정답이
(B)임을 알 수 있다.

[35-37]

W Hello, I am from the IT support team for the
conference. I'm going around the rooms to make
sure everything is working fine. Are you having any
problems using the equipment here?
M Hi, I'm so glad you're here. I was actually having
some trouble logging onto the computer.
W Oh, sorry. You need a password to do that. Here, let
me put that in for you.

M Thanks. I was getting worried because my accounting
presentation starts at ten o'clock. Oh, I also need to
make extra copies of my handouts. Where can I do
that?
W There's a copier in the business center downstairs.
It's right across from the elevator.

- -

W 안녕하세요, 저는 컨퍼런스를 위해 IT 지원팀에서 나왔습니다. 모
든 것이 제대로 작동되는지 확인하기 위해 회의실들을 돌고 있습니
다. 이곳의 장비를 사용하는 데 어떤 문제라도 있으십니까?
M 안녕하세요, 와 주셔서 정말 기뻐요. 사실은 제가 컴퓨터에 로그인
하는데 문제가 있어요.
W 아, 죄송해요. 그러기 위해서는 비밀번호가 필요해요. 이리 줘보세
요, 제가 입력해 드리죠.
M 고마워요. 제 회계 발표가 10시에 시작해서 걱정하고 있었어요.
아, 저는 제 인쇄물도 추가로 복사해야 하는데요. 어디에서 할 수
있을까요?
W 아래층 비즈니스 센터에 복사기가 있어요. 엘리베이터 바로 맞은
편에 있습니다

어휘 support team 지원팀   accounting 회계   make copies
복사하다   handout 유인물, 인쇄물   downstairs 아래층에서
fix 수리하다   audiovisual 시청각의   supplies 용품, 물품
potential 잠재적인   nearby 근처의   participate 참가하다
refreshments 다과, 스낵   manual 설명서

35   **문제점**

남자는 무엇에 문제를 겪고 있었는가?
(A) 비즈니스 센터 찾기
(B) 컴퓨터에 접속하기
(C) 시청각 장비 수리하기
(D) 물품 구매하기

해설 세부 내용을 묻는 문제는 지문에서 해당 내용을 정확하게 찾
아 파악하는 것이 중요하다. 남자의 첫 대사에서 컴퓨터에
로그인하는 데 문제가 있다(I was actually having some
trouble logging onto the computer)는 부분을 통해 정답
이 (B)임을 알 수 있다.

36   **다음에 할 일**

남자는 10시에 무엇을 할 것인가?
(A) 잠재 고객들과 만난다
(B) 근처의 박물관에 간다
(C) 발표한다
(D) 그룹 토론에 참여한다

해설 남자가 할 일은 남자의 대사에서 언급될 확률이 높다. 남자의
두 번째 대사 중 10시에 회계 발표가 있다(my accounting
presentation starts at ten o'clock)는 부분을 통해 정답이
(C)임을 알 수 있다.

37 세부 사항

여자는 아래층에서 무엇을 이용할 수 있다고 말하는가?
(A) 다과
(B) 평면도
(C) 기술 설명서
(D) 복사실

해설 '아래층(downstairs)'이라는 키워드를 지문에서 정확하게 듣도록 한다. 복사할 장소를 묻는 남자의 말(I also need to make extra copies of my handouts. Where can I do that?)에 여자가 아래층 비즈니스 센터에 복사기가 있다(There's a copier in the business center downstairs)고 말하는 것으로 보아 아래층에 복사할 장소가 있음을 알 수 있다. 따라서 정답은 (D)이다.

[38-40]

M Sandra, I am very much pleased with how well the annual clearance sale for our women's clothing line has been going. This is just the first day, and we've been busy all day.
W I've never seen anything like it either. You know, featuring the Pro-EX sportswear was a smart idea. Customers just love the concept of breathable materials for their exercise outfits. Just look in the storage room.
M You're right. <u>There are only 12 boxes left.</u>
W It's surprising since Pro-EX is a company that just started its business. We should order more from them.
M Good idea. I'll ask the sales representative to bring more samples of their other styles. Maybe we should discuss the idea of becoming their exclusive distributor in the area.

M 산드라, 우리 여성복 라인의 연례 재고 정리 세일이 잘 진행되어서 너무 기뻐요. 첫날일 뿐인데, 우리는 하루 종일 바빴네요.
W 저도 이런 상황은 본 적이 없어요. 아시다시피, Pro-EX 스포츠 의류를 판매한 것은 현명한 생각이었어요. 고객들은 그들의 운동복의 통기성 있는 재질 컨셉을 정말 좋아해요. 창고를 한번 보세요.
M 맞아요. 12박스 밖에 안 남았네요.
W Pro-EX는 이제 갓 사업을 시작한 회사인데 정말 놀라워요. 그 회사에서 더 주문해야겠어요.
M 좋은 생각이에요. 제가 영업사원에게 그들의 다른 스타일의 샘플을 더 가져오라고 요청할게요. 우리가 이 지역에서 그들의 독점 유통업체가 되는 방안도 논의해봐야 할 것 같아요.

어휘 annual 연례의 clearance sale 재고 정리 세일 feature 특징으로 하다 concept 개념, 컨셉 breathable 통기성이 있는 material 재료, 재질 outfit 의류 storage 저장, 보관 representative 직원 exclusive 독점의, 단독의 distributor 유통업체 electronics 전자제품 clothes 의류 pack 포장하다 imply 암시하다, 의미하다 finally 마침내 inventory 재고(품) expand 확장하다 consult 상담하다 launch 출시하다, 시작하다

38 주제/목적

화자들은 어떤 상품에 대해 이야기하고 있는가?
(A) 전자제품
(B) 의류
(C) 운동 기구
(D) 포장재

해설 주제를 묻는 질문은 주로 지문 초반에 힌트가 있다. 남자가 첫 대사에서 가게의 여성복의 재고 세일이 잘 진행되어 기쁘다(I am very much pleased with how well the annual clearance sale for our women's clothing line has been going)고 말하고, 의류 판매에 대한 이야기가 계속 나오는 것으로 보아 대화 주제가 (B)임을 알 수 있다.

39 의도 파악

남자가 "12박스 밖에 안 남았네요"라고 말하는 의미는 무엇인가?
(A) 그는 세일이 마침내 끝나서 기쁘다.
(B) 그는 더 많은 직원들을 고용하길 원한다.
(C) 제품이 매우 잘 팔리고 있다.
(D) 몇몇 재고품을 다시 세야 한다.

해설 화자의 의도를 묻는 문제는 해당 문장의 앞뒤 문맥을 정확히 파악해야 한다. 앞서 세일에 손님들이 많았다고 했고, 창고를 보니 "물건이 12박스 밖에 남지 않았다"고 하는 것은 물건이 잘 팔려서 재고가 얼마 남지 않았다는 의미이다. 따라서 정답은 (C)이다.

40 다음에 할 일

남자는 무엇을 할 것이라고 말하는가?
(A) 창고를 확장한다
(B) 변호사와 상담한다
(C) 새 광고 캠페인을 시작한다
(D) 영업 사원과 이야기한다

해설 상품의 매출이 좋아서 주문을 더 해야겠다는 여자의 말에 남자가 영업사원에게 샘플을 더 가져오라고 말하겠다(I'll ask the sales representative to bring more samples ~)고 했으므로 정답은 (D)이다.

[41-43]

W Greg, you mentioned in our managers' meeting that you need another person to help in the warehouse now that our business is growing fast.
M Yes, we could really use someone to load and unload trucks. That would make Sandy available to focus on processing orders and managing our inventory.
W Alright. I'll send you the job description I have on file. Could you update it with the current requirements? Then I can post it on our Web site.
M Sure. Thanks, Ms. Shin.

W 그렉, 당신은 관리자 회의에서 우리 사업이 빠르게 성장하고 있어서 창고에서 도와줄 다른 사람이 필요하다고 말했어요.

M 네, 트럭에 짐을 싣고 내리는 사람이 정말 필요해요. 그러면 샌디가 주문 처리와 재고 관리에 집중할 수 있을 거예요.

W 알았어요. 제가 파일에 가지고 있는 직무 설명서를 당신에게 보낼게요. 현재 자격 요건을 반영해서 업데이트해 주겠어요? 그러면 제가 그걸 웹 사이트에 올릴 수 있어요.

M 물론이죠. 감사합니다, 신 씨.

어휘 mention 언급하다, 말하다　manager 관리자　warehouse 창고　now that ~이므로　grow 성장하다, 자라다　load (짐을) 싣다　unload (짐을) 내리다　available 가능한　focus on ~에 집중하다　inventory 재고　job description 직무 설명서　update 갱신하다, 업데이트하다　current 현재의　requirement 자격 요건　post 올리다, 게시하다　cafeteria 구내식당　laboratory 실험실　accounting 회계　increase 증가시키다　hire 고용하다　purchase 구매하다　inspection 검사　sign up 등록하다　interview 면접 보다　candidate 후보자, 지원자　organize 정리하다

41 화자의 근무지

남자는 회사의 어떤 분야를 관리하는 것 같은가?

(A) 구내식당
(B) 실험실
(C) 회계 사무소
(D) 창고

해설 남자가 관리하는 분야는 지문 앞쪽에 힌트가 있다. 여자의 첫 대사에서 남자가 창고에 사람이 더 필요하다고 언급했다(you mentioned in our managers' meeting that you need another person to help in the warehouse ~)는 것을 통해 남자가 (D) 창고를 관리한다는 것을 알 수 있다.

42 주제/목적

화자들은 무엇에 대해 이야기하고 있는가?

(A) 현재의 주문량 늘리기
(B) 새 직원 고용하기
(C) 기계 구매하기
(D) 검사 준비하기

해설 대화의 주제는 주로 지문 초반에 힌트를 준다. 남자가 짐을 싣고 내리는 일을 할 직원이 필요하다(we could really use someone to load and unload the trucks)고 말하는 것을 통해 두 사람이 새 직원 고용에 관해 대화하고 있음을 알 수 있다. 따라서 정답은 (B)이다.

43 요청 사항

여자는 남자에게 무엇을 하라고 요청하는가?

(A) 서류 업데이트하기
(B) 행사에 등록하기
(C) 후보자 면접 보기
(D) 파일 정리하기

해설 여자가 남자에게 직무 설명서를 보낼 테니 현재의 자격 요건을 반영해서 업데이트 하라(I'll send you the job description I have on file. Could you update it with the current requirements?)는 것으로 보아 서류 업데이트를 요청하고 있음을 알 수 있다. 따라서 정답은 (A)이다.

[44-46]

W Hi, this is Gloria Lynn from Gloria's Café. I'm calling about my order for coffee filters.

M Sure, what can I do for you?

W I've just received the order, and you only sent 30 boxes of medium-sized filters, but I was also expecting 20 boxes of large-sized filters, too.

M Let me take a look at your invoice, Ms. Lynn. You're right. We have the order as 30 medium filters and 20 large filters. I'm terribly sorry about that.

W Well, I really need those large filters.

M I can send them by express shipping, and you should get them by 4 P.M. tomorrow.

W Thank you. That would be great.

M And because this was our mistake, I'll include 5 more boxes of large filters for you. Thank you for doing business with us.

W 안녕하세요, Gloria 카페의 글로리아 린입니다. 제 커피 필터 주문 때문에 전화 드립니다.

M 네, 무엇을 도와드릴까요?

W 제가 주문한 물건을 방금 받았는데, 중간 사이즈 필터 30박스만 보냈네요. 하지만 저는 라지 사이즈 필터 20박스도 받았어야 해요.

M 당신의 송장을 한번 볼게요, 린 씨. 당신 말이 맞네요. 저희는 중간 사이즈 필터 30개와 라지 사이즈 필터 20개의 주문을 받았어요. 정말 죄송합니다.

W 음, 저는 그 라지 사이즈 필터가 필요해요.

M 제가 속달 배송으로 보내드릴 수 있는데, 그러면 내일 오후 4시까지는 받을 수 있을 겁니다.

W 고마워요. 그래주시면 좋겠네요.

M 그리고 이선 서희 쪽의 실수이므로, 제가 라지 사이즈 필터 5박스를 더 넣어 드리겠습니다. 저희 회사를 이용해 주셔서 감사합니다.

어휘 expect 기다리다, 기대하다　take a look (한번) 보나　invoice 송장, 주문 내역서　express 속달의, 급행의　shipping 배송　renovation 개조, 개축　supplies 물품, 용품　discrepancy 차이, 불일치　incomplete 불완전한　connection 연결　bill 고지서　misplace 잃어버리다　container 용기, 그릇　damaged 손상된　complimentary 무료의　trial 시험　period 기간　extra 추가의, 여유분의

44 주제/목적

화자들은 무엇에 대해 이야기하고 있는가?

(A) 카페 개조
(B) 새로운 장소
(C) 물품 주문
(D) 가격 차이

해설 지문 첫 대사에서 여자가 커피 필터 주문에 대해서 전화했다 (I'm calling about my order for coffee filters)고 하는 것으로 보아 물품(supplies)의 주문에 대한 대화임을 알 수 있다. 따라서 정답은 (C)이다.

45 문제점

여자는 어떤 문제점을 언급하는가?
(A) 배달이 완전하지 않았다.
(B) 인터넷 연결이 되지 않는다.
(C) 고지서를 잃어버렸다.
(D) 용기가 손상되었다.

해설 주문한 중간 사이즈 필터는 도착했으나 라지 사이즈 필터도 왔어야 했다(I've just received the order, and you only sent 30 boxes of medium-sized filters, but I was also expecting 20 boxes of large-sized filters, too)는 여자의 말을 통해 주문한 물건의 배달이 완전하지 않았다(incomplete)는 것을 알 수 있으므로 정답은 (A)이다.

46 세부 사항

남자는 여자에게 무엇을 주겠다고 말하는가?
(A) 가격 할인
(B) 무료 음료
(C) 무료 체험 기간
(D) 추가 제품

해설 회사의 실수이니 라지 사이즈 필터를 5박스 더 보내겠다 (because this was our mistake, I'll include 5 more boxes of large filters for you)는 남자의 마지막 대사를 통해 남자가 여자에게 추가 제품을 제공할 것임을 알 수 있다. 따라서 정답은 (D)이다.

[47-49]

W Thanks for coming to my office today, David. I'd like to check in with all the stuff you are working on. So, how's everything going?
M Very well, Ms. Thomson. It took some time, but I just submitted my first article for publication. I had trouble finding people to interview to show our readers different viewpoints of the incident.
W Yes, locating good sources can be difficult. Did you use our company's database? It has a list of experts on various subjects we deal with. You can use that to find the right people to contact.

W 오늘 제 사무실을 방문해 줘서 고마워요, 데이비드. 당신이 작업하고 있는 일을 모두 확인하고 싶어서요. 그래서, 어떻게 되어가고 있나요?
M 아주 좋습니다, 톰슨 씨. 시간이 좀 걸리기는 했지만, 출간을 위한 제 첫 기사를 이제 막 제출했답니다. 저희 독자들에게 그 사건의 다양한 관점을 보여 주기 위해 취재할 사람들을 찾느라 애먹었어요.
W 맞아요, 좋은 정보원을 찾는 것은 어려울 수 있답니다. 우리 회사의

데이터베이스를 사용해 보았나요? 우리가 다루는 다양한 주제에 대한 전문가들의 목록을 보유하고 있답니다. 당신은 그것을 사용해서 연락을 취할 적당한 사람들을 찾을 수 있어요.

어휘 submit 제출하다 article 기사 publication 출판 viewpoint 관점, 견해 source 정보원, 소식통 expert 전문가 various 다양한 subject 주제 deal with ~을 다루다 contact 연락하다 request 요청하다 promotion 승진 progress 진행, 진전 follow up 더 알아보다, 후속 조치를 취하다; 후속, 추적 study 연구 congratulate 축하하다 nomination 지명, 추천 utilize 이용하다 funding 자금 employee handbook 직원 안내서 take some time off 쉬다, 휴식을 갖다 access 이용하다

47 세부 사항

여자는 왜 남자와 만나고 있는가?
(A) 승진을 요청하기 위해
(B) 남자의 업무 진행 상황을 묻기 위해
(C) 그들이 함께한 연구에 후속 조치를 취하기 위해
(D) 남자의 임명을 축하하기 위해

해설 지문의 첫 대사에서 여자가 일은 어떻게 되어가는지(I'd like to check in with all the stuff you are working on. So, how's everything going?) 묻는 것으로 보아 남자의 업무 진행 상황에 대해 묻기 위해 만났음을 알 수 있다. 따라서 정답은 (B)이다.

48 문제점

남자는 무엇에 어려움을 겪었다고 말하는가?
(A) 정보원 찾기
(B) 온라인 소프트웨어 프로그램 이용하기
(C) 프로젝트를 위한 자금 받기
(D) 보고서 작성할 시간 내기

해설 남자가 취재할 사람들을 찾는 데 어려움이 있었다(I had trouble finding people to interview ~)고 이야기하고, 이어 여자가 좋은 정보원을 찾는 것은 힘들 수 있다(locating good sources can be difficult)고 언급하는 것으로 보아 남자가 정보원을 찾는 데 어려움을 겪었음을 알 수 있다. 따라서 정답은 (A)이다.

49 제안

여자는 남자에게 무엇을 하라고 제안하는가?
(A) 전문가와 이야기하기
(B) 직원 안내서 읽기
(C) 휴식 시간 갖기
(D) 데이터베이스 사용하기

해설 정보원을 찾는 데 어려움을 겪었다는 남자에게 여자는 회사가 데이터베이스를 보유하고 있으니 이를 활용할 수 있다(Did you use our company's database? ~ You can use that to find the right people to contact)고 알려주고 있다. 즉, 데이터베이스 사용을 제안하고 있으므로 정답은 (D)이다.

[50-52]

W Hi, this is Andrea from Peral Construction. We installed new carpeting in your house last month. I'm calling to find out if you're satisfied with the service you received.

M On the whole, yes. But the carpeting I ordered was temporarily out of stock. That caused a delay, but when it was delivered, the carpet was installed quickly and neatly.

W I'm glad everything worked out well. And I see in our records that you bought the carpeting when it was on sale for 10 percent off, right?

M Really? That wasn't reflected in my bill. I remember paying the full amount.

W That shouldn't have happened. I'll make sure that you get a 10 percent refund.

W 안녕하세요, Peral 건축사의 안드레아입니다. 저희는 지난달에 당신의 집에 새 카펫을 설치했습니다. 당신이 받으신 서비스에 만족하는지 알아보기 위해 전화 드립니다.

M 전반적으로 만족해요. 하지만 제가 주문한 카펫이 일시적으로 품절되었어요. 그로 인해 지연되었지만, 카펫이 배달되자 빠르고 깔끔하게 설치되었어요.

W 모든 것이 잘 진행되었다니 기쁩니다. 그리고 저희 기록에는 당신이 카펫이 10퍼센트 할인 중일 때 구매했다고 나와 있어요, 맞나요?

M 그래요? 제 고지서에는 반영되어 있지 않던데요. 저는 전액을 지불한 것으로 기억해요.

W 있어서는 안 되는 일이네요. 당신이 10퍼센트를 환불 받을 수 있도록 하겠습니다.

어휘 install 설치하다 on the whole 대체로, 전반적으로 temporarily 일시적으로, 임시적으로 out of stock 재고가 없는, 품절된 reflect 반영하다, 보여주다 bill 고지서 amount 금액, 양 refund 환불; 환불하다 reschedule 일정을 변경하다 offer 제공하다, 제안하다 feedback 의견, 피드백 recommend 추천하다 extra 추가의 detective 결함 있는, 불량의 form 양식 fill out 작성하다 unavailable 이용할 수 없는 issue 지급하다, 발급하다 demonstrate 시연하다 representative 직원

50 주제/목적

여자는 왜 전화하는가?
(A) 설치 일정을 변경하기 위해
(B) 무료 서비스를 제공하기 위해
(C) 고객 의견을 요청하기 위해
(D) 추가 작업을 추천하기 위해

해설 여자의 첫 내사에서 카펫을 지난달에 설치했는데 서비스가 만족스러웠는지 물어보기 위해 전화했다(I'm calling to find out if you're satisfied with the service you received)는 부분을 통해 고객의 의견을 듣기 위해 전화했음을 알 수 있다. 따라서 정답은 (C)이다. 의견(opinion, feedback, idea,

suggestion, advice)은 다양한 동의어로 표현되니 반드시 익혀 두도록 하자.

51 세부 사항

무엇이 지연을 야기했는가?
(A) 날씨가 안 좋았다.
(B) 일부 장비에 결함이 있었다.
(C) 일부 양식이 잘못 작성되었다.
(D) 제품을 일시적으로 이용할 수 없었다.

해설 남자는 주문한 물건이 일시적으로 품절되어서 지연되었다(the carpeting I ordered was temporarily out of stock. That caused a delay)고 언급하고 있으므로 재고가 없다는 말을 unavailable(이용할 수 없는)로 바꾸어 표현한 (D)가 정답이다.

52 다음에 할 일

여자는 무엇을 할 것이라 말하는가?
(A) 직원들을 보낸다
(B) 환불해 준다
(C) 신제품을 시연한다
(D) 영업 사원과 확인한다

해설 여자가 다음에 할 일은 여자의 대사에서 힌트를 찾을 수 있는데, 남자가 할인을 받지 못했다고 말하자 여자가 10퍼센트를 환불해 주겠다(I'll make sure that you get a 10 percent refund)고 했으므로 정답은 (B)이다.

[53-55]

W Hello, this is Melanie from the shopping mall's management team. I know you're planning to open up your shoe store soon, so I'm calling to schedule a time when the mall management can inspect your premises.

M Oh, I didn't know that was necessary. All the plans were approved before we started renovations.

W Well, if you check your lease agreement, you'll see that an inspection is required to make sure the final construction and layout match the original plan.

M I hadn't realized that. We're opening in three days.

W I can send someone over later today, and the inspection shouldn't take long.

W 안녕하세요, 저는 쇼핑몰 관리팀의 멜라니입니다. 당신이 곧 신발 가게를 열 계획이라고 알고 있어서, 쇼핑몰 관리진이 당신의 건물을 검사할 수 있는 시간을 잡으려고 전화 드렸어요.

M 아, 그게 필수인지는 몰랐어요. 모든 계획은 저희가 개조를 시작하기 전에 허가를 받았는데요.

W 음, 임대 계약서를 확인해 보시면, 최종 건축물과 구조가 원래 계획에 맞는지 확인하기 위해 검사가 필요하다는 것이 보일 거예요.

M 그건 몰랐네요. 저희는 3일 후에 개점하는데요.

W 제가 이따가 오늘 중으로 직원을 보내드릴 수 있고, 검사는 오래 걸리지 않을 겁니다.

어휘 inspect 검사하다 premises 건물, 부지 approve 승인하다, 인가하다 renovation 개조, 개축 lease agreement 임대 계약서 required 필수의, 필요한 final 최종의 layout 배치, 설계 match 맞다 original 원래의, 처음의 realize 인식하다, 알다 take long (시간이) 오래 걸리다 property 부동산 manufacturer 제조업체 rental 임대 updated 최신의, 갱신된 contract 계약서 deadline 마감일 attract 끌어 모으다

53 화자의 근무지

여자는 어디에서 일하는가?
(A) 부동산 관리 사무소에서
(B) 신발 제조업체에서
(C) 관공서에서
(D) 인테리어 디자인 회사에서

해설 일하는 장소에 대한 힌트는 일반적으로 지문 초반에서 주어진다. 여자는 첫 대사에서 본인의 소속이 쇼핑몰의 관리팀(this is Melanie from the shopping mall's management team)이라고 언급한다. 이는 부동산 관리 사무소(a property management office)라는 동의 표현으로 바꿀 수 있으므로 정답은 (A)이다. 신발 가게는 남자가 일하는 장소이므로 (B)를 선택하지 않도록 주의한다.

54 세부 사항

남자는 무엇에 대해 놀라는가?
(A) 할인된 가격
(B) 필수 검사
(C) 임대 가격
(D) 갱신된 계약서

해설 건물의 검사 일정을 잡으려는 여자의 말에, 그게 필수인지 몰랐다(I didn't know that was necessary)는 남자의 반응을 통해 남자가 필수 검사에 대해 놀라고 있음을 알 수 있다. 따라서 정답은 (B)이다.

55 의도 파악

남자가 "저희는 3일 후에 개점하는데요"라고 말하는 의미는 무엇인가?
(A) 그는 더 많은 직원이 필요하다.
(B) 그는 여자가 날짜를 잘못 알았다고 생각한다.
(C) 그는 마감일에 대해 걱정한다.
(D) 그는 더 많은 고객들을 끌어 모으길 원한다.

해설 화자의 의도 문제는 주어진 문장의 앞뒤 문맥상 의미를 정확히 알아야 한다. 해당 문장은 필수로 검사를 받아야 한다는 말에 대한 반응이고, 그 다음에 여자가 검사가 오래 걸리지 않을 것이라고 안심시키는 것으로 보아, 남자가 검사가 3일 후에 개점할 가게에 부정적인 영향을 미칠까 걱정한다는 것을 알 수 있다. 따라서 (C)가 정답이다.

[56-58] 3인 대화

W Hello, my name is Charlotte Anderson, and I'm a reporter from *Current Architect* magazine. I'm here to see Mr. Yamada for an interview.
M1 Okay, I'll let him know you're here. In the meantime, can you sign the visitors' book? And I need to see your identification. We keep track of all visitors for security reasons.
W Sure, no problem.
M1 Mr. Yamada is on his way down to meet you. Oh, here he comes. Mr. Yamada, this is Charlotte Anderson, your eleven o'clock appointment.
M2 Hello, Ms. Anderson. Thanks for coming. I'm so sorry, but I need a few more minutes before we interview. I have to respond to an urgent phone call.
W Okay, take your time, Mr. Yamada.

W 안녕하세요, 제 이름은 샬롯 앤더슨이고, 저는 Current Architect 잡지사의 기자입니다. 야마다 씨를 취재하기 위해 왔습니다.
M1 네, 당신이 도착했다고 그에게 알려드릴게요. 그동안 방명록에 서명해 주시겠어요? 신분증도 보여주셔야 합니다. 저희는 보안상의 이유로 모든 방문객들을 기록합니다.
W 네, 문제 없습니다.
M1 야마다 씨가 당신을 만나기 위해 내려오는 중입니다. 아, 저기 오시네요. 야마다 씨, 이쪽은 당신과 11시 약속을 잡으신 샬롯 앤더슨 씨입니다.
M2 안녕하세요, 앤더슨 씨. 와 주셔서 감사합니다. 죄송하지만 우리가 인터뷰를 하기 전에 시간이 좀 더 필요해요. 급한 전화를 받아야 하거든요.
W 네, 천천히 하세요, 야마다 씨.

어휘 reporter 기자 interview 취재, 면접 in the meantime 그동안에 identification 신분증 keep track of ~을 기록하다 security 보안 respond to ~에 응답하다 urgent 긴급한 take time 천천히 하다, 시간이 걸리다 conduct (활동을) 하다, 시행하다 demonstrate 시연하다 contract 계약(서) rental 임대의 property 부동산 agree to ~에 동의하다 provide 제공하다 revise 개정하다, 바꾸다 booklet 소책자 publication 출판물

56 세부 사항

여자는 왜 야마다 씨와 만나는가?
(A) 취재를 하기 위해
(B) 제품을 시연하기 위해
(C) 계약에 관해 논의하기 위해
(D) 임대 건물을 보기 위해

해설 여자의 첫 대사에서 본인이 잡지사 소속임을 밝히며 야마다 씨를 취재하러 왔다(I'm here to see Mr. Yamada for an interview)고 언급하는 것으로 보아, 여자가 취재를 위해 야마다 씨를 만나려고 한다는 것을 알 수 있다. 따라서 정답은 (A)이다.

57 세부 사항

여자는 무엇을 하는 것에 동의하는가?
(A) 주소를 제공한다
(B) 방문을 위해 서명한다
(C) 기사를 수정한다
(D) 소책자를 가져간다

해설 첫 번째 남자가 서명을 요구하며 보안상의 이유로 방문객들을 기록하고 있다(In the meantime, can you sign the visitor's book? ~ We keep track of all visitors for security reasons)고 말하자 여자가 문제 없다(Sure, no problem)고 했으므로 정답이 (B)임을 알 수 있다.

58 세부 사항

야마다 씨는 왜 사과하는가?
(A) 그는 출판물에 대해 익숙하지 않다.
(B) 그는 여자의 이름을 잊어버렸다.
(C) 그는 가격을 올려야 한다.
(D) 그는 미팅에 늦을 것이다.

해설 야마다 씨가 급한 전화를 받아야 해서 인터뷰가 좀 늦어질 거라고(I'm so sorry, but I need a few more minutes before we interview. I have to respond to an urgent phone call) 말하며 사과하는 것으로 보아 정답이 (D)임을 알 수 있다.

[59-61]

M Hi, Sophia. Could you let all employees know that the technical support team is doing a maintenance check on our servers the last weekend of May?

W Sure, which computer applications will be affected this time?

M Actually, this time the whole system will be affected. It is really important to remind everyone that they won't be able to work from Friday night to Sunday morning on that weekend.

W Okay. I'll emphasize that point in an e-mail and send it out to all employees right away.

M Thanks, Sophia.

M 안녕하세요, 소피아. 직원 모두에게 5월 마지막 주말에 기술지원팀이 서버 점검 작업을 할 것이라고 알려 줄 수 있어요?

W 물론이죠, 이번에는 어떤 컴퓨터 응용 프로그램이 영향을 받을까요?

M 실은, 이번에는 전체 시스템이 영향을 받을 거예요. 모두에게 그 주말 금요일 밤부터 일요일 아침까지 일할 수 없다는 것을 상기시켜 주는 것이 정말 중요해요.

W 알겠어요. 제가 이메일에 그 점을 강조해서 모든 직원들에게 지금 당장 보내도록 하겠습니다.

M 고마워요, 소피아.

어휘 maintenance 시설 관리, 점검   check 확인; 확인하다
application 응용, 응용 프로그램   affect 영향을 미치다

---

remind 다시 알리다, 상기시키다   emphasize 강조하다
point 요점, 중점   take place 일어나다   professional 전문적인   closure 폐쇄, 휴업   turn off 끄다   report 보고하다   participate in ~에 참가하다   reception 연회, 파티   restart 다시 시작하다   contact 연락하다   notification 통보

59 세부 사항

5월 마지막 주말에 무슨 일이 일어나는가?
(A) 전문 컨퍼런스
(B) 휴일 휴업
(C) 컴퓨터 점검
(D) 건축 공사

해설 5월 마지막 주말이라는 키워드를 기억하고 본문을 듣도록 하자. 첫 대사에서 기술지원팀이 서버 점검을 한다(the technical support team is doing a maintenance check on our servers the last weekend of May)는 언급을 통해 정답이 (C)임을 알 수 있다.

60 세부 사항

직원들은 무엇에 대해 주의해야 하는가?
(A) 그들은 주말에 일할 수 없을 것이다.
(B) 그들은 컴퓨터를 꺼야 한다.
(C) 그들은 경비실에 보고해야 한다.
(D) 그들은 회사 연회에 참석해야 한다.

해설 남자의 두 번째 대사에서 주말에는 일할 수 없다는 것을 상기시키는 것이 중요하다(It is really important to remind everyone that they won't be able to work from Friday night to Sunday morning on that weekend)는 부분을 통해 정답이 (A)임을 알 수 있다.

61 다음에 할 일

여자는 무엇을 할 것이라고 말하는가?
(A) 그녀의 컴퓨터를 다시 시작한다
(B) 기술지원팀에 연락한다
(C) 일요일 오후에 돌아온다
(D) 이메일 통지를 작성한다

해설 남자가 직원들에게 알려야 하는 내용을 설명하자 여자가 해당 내용을 강조하여 이메일을 보내겠다(I'll emphasize that point in an e-mail and send it out to all employees right away)고 말하는 것을 보아 정답이 (D)임을 알 수 있다.

[62-64] 대화 & 포스터

M Heidi, I noticed the city library is hosting a book fair this month. I know you're a fan of reading, so would you like to go with me after we finish work on that day?

W Well, the fair is mostly for school-aged children. So, we won't have much to see. Next month, though, they will have a lecture series that I'm thinking of going to.

M Oh, I guess I will skip the book fair then. And I can't go to the lecture series because some of my clients will be visiting from out of town. I have to treat them to dinner.

W Well, don't worry. I'll be happy to let you know which authors and books will be in the lecture series. We can read those books together if you like.

M 하이디, 시립 도서관이 이번 달에 도서 박람회를 주최한다고 해요. 당신이 독서를 정말 좋아하는 걸로 아는데, 그날 일 끝나고 저랑 같이 가실래요?

W 글쎄요, 그 박람회는 대부분 취학 연령의 아이들을 대상으로 해요. 그래서 저희가 볼 건 별로 없을 거예요. 하지만 다음 달에는 제가 가려고 생각 중인 강연 시리즈가 있을 거예요.

M 아, 그러면 도서 박람회를 가지 말아야겠네요. 그리고 다른 도시에서 오는 고객들이 방문할 예정이라서 저는 강연 시리즈에 갈 수 없어요. 저는 그들에게 저녁식사를 대접해야 해요.

W 그래요, 걱정하지 말아요. 제가 어떤 작가와 도서가 강연 시리즈에 나오는지 당신에게 기꺼이 알려드릴게요. 원하시면 저희는 그 책들을 같이 읽어도 돼요.

Summerville 시립 도서관 행사	
1월 18일	독서 토론
2월 15일	도서 교환
3월 15일	어린이 도서 박람회
4월 19일	강연 시리즈 — 지역 작가

어휘 notice 알아채다 host 주최하다 fair 박람회 mostly 대부분, 주로 lecture 강연 skip 빠지다, 건너뛰다 exchange 교환; 교환하다 local 지역의 necessary 필요한 participate in ~에 참가하다 revise 개정하다, 바꾸다 share 공유하다

62 시각 자료 연계

시각 자료를 보시오. 이 대화는 언제 일어나고 있는가?
(A) 1월에
(B) 2월에
(C) 3월에
(D) 4월에

해설 남자의 첫 대화문에서 이번 달에 도서 박람회가 있다(I noticed the city library is hosting a book fair this month)는 부분을 통해 대화가 일어나는 시점이 도서 박람회가 있는 (C) 3월임을 알 수 있다.

63 세부 사항

남자는 왜 강연 시리즈에 참석할 수 없는가?
(A) 그는 휴가를 갈 것이다.
(B) 그는 필수 도서를 읽지 않았다.
(C) 그는 고객들을 접대할 것이다.
(D) 그는 컨퍼런스에 참석할 것이다.

해설 남자의 두 번째 대사에서 고객들에게 저녁 식사를 대접해야 한다며(I can't go to the lecture series because some of my clients will be visiting from out of town. I have to treat them to dinner) 강연 시리즈에 참석할 수 없는 이유를 밝히고 있다. 따라서 정답은 (C)이다.

64 다음에 할 일

여자는 무엇을 할 것이라 말하는가?
(A) 다른 수업을 추천한다
(B) 일정을 변경한다
(C) 책을 구매한다
(D) 정보를 공유한다

해설 강연에 참석할 수 없다는 남자의 말에 여자가 강연에 등장한 작가와 책을 알려주겠다(I'll be happy to let you know which authors and books will be in the lecture series)고 말하고 있다. 이는 정보를 공유할 것이라는(share some information) 뜻이므로 정답은 (D)이다.

[65-67] 대화 & 가격표

M Hi, Ms. Jones. You mentioned you'd like to order water bottles with your company's name and logo to give away at a conference. I brought a few samples to show you, and also a price list.

W Thank you, Mr. Park. As you know, I have a limited budget for promotional items for this conference, so I'll definitely have to go with the cheapest material.

M Sure, I understand.

W Even at this price, though, they seem a little expensive. Is there any way you could come down on the price?

M Well, the price I gave you here is for a retail price. If you order more than 200, I can lower the unit price quite a bit. You could use the extra bottles for another conference.

M 안녕하세요, 존스 씨. 컨퍼런스에서 증정하기 위해 당신의 회사 이름과 로고가 있는 물병을 주문하고 싶다고 하셨죠. 당신에게 보여 드리기 위해 샘플과 가격표를 가지고 왔습니다.

W 고마워요, 박 씨. 아시다시피, 저희는 이번 컨퍼런스를 위한 홍보 물품에 사용할 예산이 제한되어 있어서 반드시 가장 싼 재질로 주문해야 해요.

M 괜찮아요, 이해합니다.

W 하지만 이 가격에도 그것들은 약간 비싼 것 같아요. 당신이 가격을 낮추어 줄 수 있는 방법이 있을까요?

M 글쎄요, 제가 여기 드린 가격은 소매가입니다. 200개 이상을 주문하시면, 단가를 꽤 낮춰 드릴 수 있어요. 남은 물병은 다른 컨퍼런스에서 사용하실 수 있을 거예요.

홍보용 스포츠 보틀	
플라스틱	3달러 30센트
실리콘	4달러
알루미늄	7달러 30센트
스테인리스 스틸	9달러

어휘 mention 언급하다 bottle 병 give away 무료로 나누어 주다 a few 몇몇의 price list 가격표 limited 제한된, 한정된 budget 예산 promotional 홍보의 definitely 확실하게, 분명히 go with ~로 하다, 결정하다 material 재질, 재료 retail 소매의 lower 낮추다 quite a bit 꽤 extra 추가의, 여유분의 another 다른 mail 우편으로 보내다 hand out 나누어 주다, 배포하다 recommend 추천하다 increase 증가시키다 quantity 수량 additional 추가의 price quote 견적서

65 세부 사항

여자는 물병으로 무엇을 할 계획인가?
(A) 그녀의 가게에서 판매한다
(B) 고객들에게 우편으로 보낸다
(C) 행사에서 나누어 준다
(D) 그녀의 직원들에게 준다

해설 남자의 첫 번째 대사를 통해 여자가 컨퍼런스에서 증정하기 위해 물병을 주문하려고 한다는 것(You mentioned you'd like to order water bottles with your company's name and logo to give away at a conference)을 알 수 있다. 따라서 정답은 (C)이다.

66 시각 자료 연계

시각 자료를 보시오. 여자는 어떤 재질을 사용하기로 결정하는가?
(A) 플라스틱
(B) 실리콘
(C) 알루미늄
(D) 스테인리스 스틸

해설 여자가 한정된 예산으로 인해 가장 싼 재질로 주문해야 한다고(so I'll definitely have to go with the cheapest material) 했으므로, 도표에서 가장 저렴한 (A) 플라스틱이 정답이다.

67 제안

남자는 무엇을 추천하는가?
(A) 다른 재질 고르기
(B) 주문 수량 늘리기
(C) 다음 컨퍼런스 기다리기
(D) 추가 견적서 받기

해설 가격이 비싸서 고민하는 여자에게 남자가 주어진 가격표는 소매가로 200개 이상 주문하면 가격을 낮추어 줄 수 있다(If

you order more than 200, I can lower the unit price quite a bit)고 말하고 있다. 즉, 주문 수량(order quantity)을 늘리는 것을 추천하고 있으므로 정답은 (B)이다.

[68-70] 대화 & 차트

W I'm so excited about our business trip on Wednesday. But I hate Union Train Station. They never have enough people working there.
M Yes, we're so lucky that we can get our tickets online instead of visiting the station.
W It's easier and faster to get tickets on the Web site. Now, we need to choose a car. How about the first quiet car?
M Actually, I have to make some calls on the way, and I can't do that in a quiet car.
W Okay. Well, only one regular car has seats still available, so we should take that.
M Should I use the company credit card for this reservation?
W No, I'll use my own card and get reimbursed later. It's better for me that way.

- -

W 저는 수요일에 있을 저희 출장이 너무 기대돼요. 하지만 Union 기차역은 싫군요. 거기서 일하는 사람들은 항상 충분하지 않아요.
M 맞아요, 역을 방문하는 대신 온라인으로 티켓을 살 수 있어서 다행이에요.
W 웹 사이트에서 티켓을 사는 게 더 쉽고 빨라요. 이제 탑승 칸을 선택해야 해요. 조용한 첫 번째 칸은 어때요?
M 실은 제가 가는 길에 전화를 해야 하는데 조용한 칸에서는 그럴 수 없어요.
W 알겠어요. 그럼, 아직 좌석이 남은 일반 칸은 하나밖에 없으니 그 칸에 탑승해야 해요.
M 예약하는 데 법인카드를 사용해야 할까요?
W 아니요, 제 개인 카드를 사용하고 나중에 상환 받을 거예요. 그렇게 하는 게 더 나아요.

기차 칸을 선택하세요			
선택	칸	종류	만석/예약 가능
○	1	조용	예약 가능
○	2	조용	예약 가능
○	3	조용	만석
○	4	일반	예약 가능
○	5	일반	만석

어휘 enough 충분한 instead 내신에 car (기차의) 칸 quiet 조용한; 고요 regular 일반적인 available 이용할 수 있는 reservation 예약 reimburse 상환하다, 배상하다 way 방법 dislike 싫어하다 understaffed 인원이 부족한 access 이용, 접속 passenger 승객 renovate 개조하다

68 세부 사항

여자는 왜 Union 기차역을 싫어하는가?
(A) 직원이 항상 부족하다.
(B) 인터넷에 접속할 수 없다.
(C) 승객들로 붐빈다.
(D) 보수 공사가 필요하다.

해설 여자가 첫 번째 대사에서 Union 기차역이 싫다고 언급한 후 일하는 직원들이 충분하지 않다(They never have enough people working there)고 말하고 있다. 이는 인원이 부족하다(understaffed)는 동의 표현으로 바꾸어 쓸 수 있으므로 정답은 (A)이다.

69 시각 자료 연계

시각 자료를 보시오. 화자들은 어떤 칸을 선택할 것 같은가?
(A) 2번 칸
(B) 3번 칸
(C) 4번 칸
(D) 5번 칸

해설 여자가 조용한 칸을 제안했으나 남자는 전화를 해야 해서 안 된다고 했고, 일반 칸 중에는 좌석이 남은 칸이 하나밖에 없다(only one regular car has seats still available, so we should take that)고 했으므로 일반 칸 중 유일하게 좌석이 남은 (C) 4번 칸이 정답이다.

70 세부 사항

남자는 여자에게 무엇에 대해 묻는가?
(A) 어디에서 서로 만나야 하는지
(B) 몇 시에 기차가 출발하는지
(C) 어떻게 그들이 지불할지
(D) 어떤 고객에게 먼저 전화해야 하는지

해설 남자는 마지막 대사에서 기차표를 예약하는 데 법인카드를 사용할지(Should I use the company credit card for this reservation?)를 물어보았다. 이는 지불 방법에 대해 묻는 것이므로 정답은 (C)이다.

PART • 4

[71-73] 녹음 메시지

Hello, and thank you for calling the Main Street Spa & Wellness Center. We offer a full range of services including nail care, massages, and facials as well as spa packages. We are open Tuesday through Friday from 11 A.M. to 9 P.M. and on weekends from 12 P.M. to 6 P.M. We are closed on Mondays. We are located at 501 Main Street at the corner of Jefferson and Main. To schedule an appointment, please press 1. To hear this message again, please press 2.

안녕하세요, Main Street Spa & Wellness Center에 전화 주셔서 감사합니다. 저희는 스파 프로그램뿐만 아니라 손톱 관리, 마사지, 얼굴 마사지를 포함한 모든 종류의 서비스를 제공합니다. 저희는 화요일부터 금요일 오전 11시부터 오후 9시까지, 그리고 주말에는 오후 12시부터 오후 6시까지 영업합니다. 월요일은 휴무입니다. 저희는 Jefferson 가와 Main 가의 교차 지점인 Main 가 501번지에 위치해 있습니다. 예약 일정을 잡으시려면, 1번을 눌러 주세요. 메시지를 다시 들으시려면 2번을 눌러 주시기 바랍니다.

어휘 spa 온천 wellness 건강 offer 제공하다 range 범위 nail 손톱 care 관리 facial 얼굴 마사지 located 자리한, 위치한 schedule 일정을 잡다 appointment 약속 press 누르다 find out 알아내다 repeat 반복하다

71 주제/목적

어떤 종류의 사업이 광고되고 있는가?
(A) 청소 서비스
(B) 백화점
(C) 미용실
(D) 스파

해설 녹음 메시지의 초반 "Hello, and thank you for calling the Main Street Spa & Wellness Center. We offer a full range of services including nail care, massages, and facials as well as spa packages"에서 해당 업체가 스파 및 미용 관련 서비스를 제공하고 있음을 알 수 있으므로 정답은 (D)이다.

72 세부 사항

업체는 언제 문을 닫는가?
(A) 월요일에
(B) 화요일에
(C) 금요일에
(D) 일요일에

해설 녹음 메시지의 중반부 "We are closed on Mondays"에서 월요일에는 문을 닫는다고 했으므로 정답은 (A)이다. 문제의 키워드를 정확하게 기억하고 본문에서 정답을 찾도록 하자.

73 세부 사항

청자들은 왜 2번을 누르겠는가?
(A) 업체에 대해 더 알기 위해
(B) 직원과 말하기 위해
(C) 예약 일정을 잡기 위해
(D) 메시지를 다시 듣기 위해

해설 녹음 메시지의 마지막 부분 "To hear this message again, please press 2"를 통해 2번을 누르면 메시지를 다시 들을 수 있음을 알 수 있다. 따라서 정답은 (D)이다.

[74-76] 설명/소개

We're honored to have Mr. Brian Dorsett in our studio today. Many of you know Mr. Dorsett as a former congressman in our government. However, he can now add another career as an author to his impressive résumé. Mr. Dorsett is visiting BBT Radio today to promote his newly released autobiography, *Against the Odds*. In the book, he discusses his humble beginnings from a poor family and how he overcame tremendous adversity to become a successful politician. At the conclusion of the interview, Mr. Dorsett has agreed to take calls from our listening audience. If you'd like to speak to Mr. Dorsett, please call 555-2020.

오늘 저희 스튜디오에 브라이언 돌셋 씨를 모시게 되어 영광입니다. 여러분 중 많은 분들이 돌셋 씨를 우리 정부의 전직 국회의원으로 알고 있습니다. 그러나, 이제 그는 그의 인상적인 이력서에 저자로서 또 다른 경력을 추가할 수 있습니다. 돌셋 씨는 그의 신간 자서전인 '역경을 딛고'를 홍보하기 위해 오늘 BBT 라디오 방송국을 방문하셨습니다. 그 책에서, 그는 가난한 가정에서의 초라한 시작과 성공한 정치가가 되기 위해 엄청난 역경을 어떻게 극복했는지 이야기합니다. 인터뷰 마지막에, 돌셋 씨는 청취자분들의 전화를 받는 것에 동의하셨습니다. 만약 돌셋씨와 이야기를 나누고 싶으시면, 555-2020으로 전화 주시기 바랍니다.

어휘 honored 명예로운, 영광스러운 former 과거의 congressman 국회의원 government 정부 add 더하다, 추가하다 author 저자, 작가 impressive 인상적인 résumé 이력서 visit 방문하다 release 출시하다, 발간하다 autobiography 자서전 discuss 논의하다 humble 초라한 overcome 극복하다 tremendous 엄청난 adversity 역경 successful 성공한 conclusion 결말, 마무리 agree 찬성하다, 동의하다 president 사장 journalist 기자 politician 정치인 recruiter 스카우터, 모집자 recently 최근에 receive 받다 election 선거 publish 출판하다 apply for ~에 지원하다 speech 연설 ceremony 의식

74 특징 인물의 직업

돌셋 씨는 누구인가?
(A) 전 회사 사장
(B) 기자
(C) 전직 정치인
(D) 직원 모집자

해설 특징 인물이 누구인지 묻는 질문은 주로 지문 초반에 힌트가 있다. 두 번째 문장 "Many of you know Mr. Dorsett as a former congressman in our government"를 통해 돌셋 씨가 전직 국회의원임을 알 수 있다. 따라서 정답은 (C)이다.

75 세부 사항

돌셋 씨는 최근에 무엇을 했는가?
(A) 상을 받았다
(B) 선거에서 이겼다
(C) 책을 출판했다
(D) 일자리에 지원했다

해설 돌셋 씨가 최근에 어떤 일을 했는지 묻고 있다. 본문의 중반 부분 "Mr. Dorsett is visiting BBT Radio today to promote his newly released autobiography, ~"에서 돌셋 씨는 새로 출간된 자신의 자서전을 홍보하기 위해 라디오 방송국을 방문했다고 언급하고 있다. 이를 통해 그가 최근에 도서를 출판했음을 알 수 있으므로 정답은 (C)이다.

76 다음에 할 일

다음에 어떤 일이 일어날 것인가?
(A) 연설이 있을 것이다.
(B) 인터뷰가 있을 것이다.
(C) 의식이 열릴 것이다.
(D) 회의가 끝날 것이다.

해설 다음에 일어날 일을 묻는 질문은 주로 지문의 후반에 힌트가 있다. 마지막 부분 "At the conclusion of the interview, Mr. Dorsett has agreed to take calls from our listening audience"에서 인터뷰를 한 후 돌셋 씨가 청취자들의 전화를 받을 것이라고 언급되었다. 이를 통해 대화 후에는 인터뷰가 진행된다는 것을 알 수 있으므로 정답은 (B)이다.

[77-79] 전화 메시지

Hello, this is Jack Greco from Greco's Custom Furniture Store. I am calling to give you an update on your order. We've received the office desks and chairs you ordered. From what I see in the invoice notes, you wanted them to be delivered tomorrow, but all of our trucks will be busy for the next few days. In addition, the bookshelves you requested have not arrived yet. The factory has just finished producing them, and it will take a couple more days to get them ready. To apologize for these delays, we'll give you 15 percent off your next purchase with us.

안녕하세요, 저는 Greco 맞춤 가구점의 잭 그레코입니다. 당신의 주문에 대한 업데이트 사항을 알리기 위해 전화 드립니다. 저희는 당신이 주문하신 사무실 책상과 의자를 받았습니다. 송장의 메모에서 본 바로는, 당신은 그것들이 내일 배송 되기를 원했는데, 저희 모든 트럭은 앞으로 며칠 동안 바쁠 것입니다. 또한, 당신이 요청하신 책장은 아직 도착하지 않았습니다. 공장에서 이제 막 생산을 마쳐서 그것들이 준비되기까지는 며칠 더 걸릴 것입니다. 지연에 대한 사과로, 다음에 저희 매장에서 구매하실 때 15퍼센트를 할인해 드리겠습니다.

어휘 custom 맞춤의, 주문 제작의 update 업데이트 invoice 송장 in addition 추가로, 게다가 bookshelf 책장 request 요청하다 apologize 사과하다 delay 지연시키다, 지연 off 할인하여 purchase 구매; 구매하다 rental 임대 catering 출장 요리 vehicle 차량 available 이용할 수 있는 do well 잘하다 delayed 지연된, 늦은 work overtime 초과 근무를 하다 offer 제공하다 replacement 교체 upgrade 업그레이드, 개선 free 무료의 installation 설치

77 화자의 근무지

화자는 어떤 종류의 사업에서 일하는가?
(A) 트럭 대여 회사
(B) 출장 요리 업체
(C) 자동차 수리점
(D) 가구점

해설 화자가 어떤 분야에서 일하는지 묻는 질문은 주로 지문의 앞쪽에 힌트가 있다. 첫 문장에서 "Hello, this is Jack Greco from Greco's Custom Furniture Store"라고 말하는 부분에서 화자가 가구점에서 일한다는 것을 알 수 있다. 따라서 정답은 (D)이다.

78 의도 파악

화자가 "저희 모든 트럭은 앞으로 며칠 동안 바쁠 것입니다"라고 말한 의미는 무엇인가?
(A) 대여 차량을 이용할 수 없다.
(B) 사업이 잘 되고 있다.
(C) 배달이 지연될 것이다.
(D) 일부 직원들은 잔업을 해야 할 것이다.

해설 의도 파악 문제는 앞뒤 문장과의 문맥상 의미를 찾아야 한다. 고객은 주문품이 내일 배달되기를 원했지만, 모든 트럭이 며칠 동안 바쁠 예정이라고 말한 것은 결국 내일은 배달을 할 수 없다는 것을 의미하므로 정답은 배달이 지연될 것이라는 (C)이다.

79 세부 사항

화자는 청자에게 무엇을 제공하는가?
(A) 교체 상품
(B) 미래의 할인
(C) 디자인 개선
(D) 무료 설치

해설 지문의 마지막 "To apologize for these delays, we'll give you 15 percent off your next purchase with us"에서 배달 지연에 대한 사과로 15퍼센트를 할인해 준다고 언급하므로 정답은 off의 동의어 discount를 사용한 (B)이다.

[80-82] 설명/소개

The next item on our agenda is our jewelry sales. In a moment, I will turn the floor over to Victor, who is going to present the quarterly sales statistics. But before he does, I want to give you a brief overview. We have seen a 20% increase in our jewelry sales this quarter. The spike in sales correlates with our new venture in radio advertising. In fact, the radio ads have been so successful that we are now considering the possibility of extending the advertising contract. Victor will now share some specific sales figures so that we can better understand our status.

저희의 다음 안건은 보석 매출에 관한 것입니다. 잠시 후, 저는 분기별 매출 통계를 발표할 빅터에게 연단을 넘길 것입니다. 하지만 그가 발표하기 전에, 저는 여러분에게 간략한 내용을 알려 드리고자 합니다. 저희는 이번 분기에 보석 매출이 20%가 증가한 것을 보았습니다. 매출 급등은 우리가 라디오 광고를 새롭게 시도한 것과 관련이 있습니다. 실제로, 라디오 광고가 매우 성공적이어서 현재 저희는 광고 계약을 연장할 가능성을 고려하고 있습니다. 우리의 상황을 좀 더 잘 이해할 수 있도록 빅터가 이제 몇 가지 구체적인 매출 수치를 공유할 겁니다.

어휘 item 항목 agenda 의제, 안건 jewelry 보석 turn over 넘겨주다 floor 발언권 quarterly 분기별의 sales 매출 statistics 통계, 통계 자료 brief 간략한 overview 개관, 개요 increase 인상; 인상시키다 spike 급증, 급등 correlate with ~와 관련되다 venture 모험 advertising 광고 successful 성공적인 consider 고려하다 possibility 가능성 extend 연장하다 contract 계약 specific 구체적인 figures 수치 status 상태, 상황 savings 절감 product line 제품 라인 currently 현재 advertise 광고하다 billboard 광고판 record 녹음하다, 녹화하다 commercial 광고 present 발표하다 review 검토하다 policy 정책

80 주제/목적

발표는 주로 무엇에 대한 것인가?
(A) 비용 절감
(B) 신제품 라인
(C) 가격 인상
(D) 회사 매출

해설 지문을 보면 'our jewelry sales(보석 매출)', 'quarterly sales statistics(분기별 매출 통계 자료)', 'a 20% increase in our jewelry sales(보석 매출이 20%가 증가)' 등 매출과 관련된 표현이 많이 나오고 있다. 이를 통해 정답이 (D) 회사 매출임을 알 수 있다.

81 세부 사항

화자는 회사가 현재 어디에 광고하고 있다고 말하는가?
(A) 인터넷에
(B) 광고판에

(C) 라디오에
(D) 텔레비전에

해설 발표의 중반 "The spike in sales correlates with our new venture in radio advertising. In fact, the radio ads have been so successful that we are now considering the possibility of extending the advertising contract"에서 매출의 증가가 라디오 광고 시도와 관련이 있고, 실제로 라디오 광고가 매우 성공적이어서 광고 계약을 연장할 가능성에 대해서 고려하고 있다고 했으므로 정답은 (C)이다.

82 다음에 할 일
빅터는 다음에 무엇을 할 것인가?
(A) 광고를 녹화한다
(B) 자료를 발표한다
(C) 신제품을 보여준다
(D) 몇 가지 정책을 검토한다

해설 발표의 마지막 "Victor will now share some specific sales figures so that we can better understand our status"에서 빅터가 매출 수치를 공유할 것임을 알 수 있다. 따라서 figures를 동의 표현인 data로 바꾼 (B)가 정답이다.

[83-85] 전화 메시지

Good morning, Naomi. This is Pete, returning your call about the seminar I'm giving at your company. You asked if I need any special equipment or materials for this workshop. I'm actually bringing all the materials with me. So, the only thing I'll really need is a projector. And about your suggestion to pick me up from the airport, I decided to reserve a car service, so don't worry about that. I'll see you on Monday, then.

좋은 아침입니다, 나오미 씨. 저는 피트입니다. 저는 제가 당신의 회사에서 할 세미나에 대해 당신이 주신 전화에 회신 드립니다. 당신은 제가 이번 워크숍을 위해 특별 장비나 자료가 필요한지 물어보셨는데요. 사실 모든 자료는 제가 가지고 갈 겁니다. 그래서, 제가 정말 필요한 유일한 것은 프로젝터입니다. 그리고 공항으로 저를 태우러 오시겠다는 당신의 제안에 대해, 저는 차량 서비스를 예약하기로 결정했으니 그것에 대해서는 걱정하지 마십시오. 그럼 월요일에 뵙겠습니다.

어휘 return 돌려주다 special 특별한 material 자료, 재료 workshop 워크숍, 수업 bring 가지고 오다 working 작동하는, 효과가 있는 suggestion 제안 pick up 데리러 가다, (차에) 태우다 organize 조직하다, 준비하다 tour 견학 participant 참가자 apologize 사과하다 delay 지연; 시연시키나 propose 제안하다 decline 거절하다 offer 제공, 제안 request 요청하다

83 세부 사항
화자는 무엇을 하려고 준비하고 있는가?
(A) 연회를 준비한다
(B) 세미나를 한다
(C) 직원을 더 고용한다
(D) 회사 견학을 진행한다

해설 두 번째 문장 "This is Pete, returning your call about the seminar I'm giving at your company"에서 화자가 청자의 회사에서 세미나를 진행할 것이라 했으므로 그가 세미나를 준비한다는 것을 알 수 있다. 따라서 정답은 (B)이다.

84 요청 사항
화자는 무엇을 요청하는가?
(A) 비행기 티켓
(B) 영상 장비
(C) 자료 사본
(D) 참가자 목록

해설 메시지의 중반 "the only thing I'll really need is a projector"에서 화자는 프로젝터를 요청한다는 것을 알 수 있다. 따라서 정답은 projector를 패러프레이징한 (B)이다.

85 의도 파악
화자는 왜 "저는 차량서비스를 예약하기로 결정했어요"라고 말하는가?
(A) 지연에 대해 사과하기 위해
(B) 일정 변경을 제안하기 위해
(C) 제안을 거절하기 위해
(D) 장소 변경을 요청하기 위해

해설 화자의 의도 파악 문제는 한 문장이 아닌 앞뒤 맥락을 파악해야 한다. 해당 문장의 앞 부분 "And about your suggestion to pick me up from the airport"에서 청자가 화자를 데리러 오겠다고 제안했지만, 화자는 차량 서비스를 예약했다며 이를 거절함을 알 수 있다. 따라서 정답은 (C)이다.

[86-88] 공지

Good morning, everyone. In case you forgot, Infinity Staffing is hosting a private luncheon here today. To accommodate them, our restaurant will be closed to the public until five o'clock. As you may know, they often host events here because of the delicious food and superior service that we always deliver. Let's do our best to satisfy them today so they will continue to host events with us in the future. It's important that we all communicate and work together today because we are expecting about a hundred people. With that being said, we have a lot of preparation to do this morning, so please check your assignments and get started.

안녕하세요, 여러분. 여러분이 잊었을 경우에 대비하여 다시 말씀 드리면, Infinity Staffing 사가 오늘 이곳에서 비공개 오찬 행사를 주최합니다. 그들을 수용하기 위해서, 우리 레스토랑은 5시까지 일반 손님에게는 개방되지 않을 겁니다. 아시다시피, 우리가 늘 제공하는 맛있는 음식과 우수한 서비스 덕분에 그들은 이곳에서 행사를 자주 엽니다. 앞으로도 우리 레스토랑에서 계속 행사를 주최하도록 오늘도 그들을 만족시키는 데 최선을 다합시다. 우리는 약 백 명의 손님들을 예상하고 있기 때문에 오늘은 우리 모두가 소통하고 함께 일하는 것이 중요합니다. 앞서 말한 것처럼, 오늘 아침에는 준비해야 할 것이 많으므로 여러분의 업무를 확인하고 일을 시작합시다.

어휘 in case ~할 경우에 대비하여 host 주최하다 private 비공개의, 사적인 luncheon 오찬 accommodate 수용하다 delicious 맛있는 superior 우수한, 탁월한 deliver 제공하다 satisfy 만족시키다 in the future 미래에, 앞으로 communicate 의사소통하다 expect 기대하다 preparation 준비 check 확인하다 assignment 임무, 업무 staffing 직원 채용 excellent 훌륭한 hire 고용하다 meal 식사

86 장소

화자는 어디에 있는 것 같은가?
(A) 레스토랑에
(B) 인력 파견 회사에
(C) 컨벤션 센터에
(D) 요리 경연대회에

해설 지문의 초반 "our restaurant will be closed to the public until five o'clock"에서 자신들의 레스토랑이 5시까지는 일반 손님을 받지 않겠다는 것과 "As you may know, they often host events here because of the delicious food and superior service that we always deliver"에서 맛있는 식사와 우수한 서비스를 늘 제공하고 있다는 것으로 미루어 볼 때, 화자가 있는 장소는 레스토랑임을 알 수 있다. 따라서 정답은 (A)이다.

87 세부 사항

Infinity Staffing 사에 대해 무엇이 언급되는가?
(A) 그들은 훌륭한 서비스에 대해 상을 받았다.
(B) 그들은 특별 행사를 개최할 것이다.
(C) 그들은 백 명의 인력을 고용할 것이다.
(D) 그들의 사무실은 오늘 5시에 문을 닫는다.

해설 지문의 초반 "Infinity Staffing is hosting a private luncheon here today"에서 Infinity Staffing 사는 오늘 비공개 오찬 행사, 즉 특별 행사를 주최한다고 말하고 있으므로 정답은 (B)이다.

88 다음에 할 일

청자들은 다음에 무엇을 하도록 요청 받는가?
(A) 훌륭한 식사 즐기기
(B) 영업 개시하기
(C) 그들의 업무 확인하기
(D) 사무실에서 점심 제공하기

해설 청자들이 다음에 할 일을 묻는 문제는 부탁 혹은 명령조로 언급된다. 화자는 담화의 마지막 부분 "we have a lot of preparation to do this morning, so please check your assignments and get started"에서 오늘 아침에 준비해야 할 것이 많으므로 본인의 업무를 확인하고 일을 시작하라고 요청하고 있다. 따라서 (C)가 정답이다.

[89-91] 방송

And now for the local news, this morning, Bloomsbury City Council members approved plans for the construction of an entire complex of new office buildings on Ferris Street and Carter Avenue. Construction is scheduled to begin in March and is expected to be completed by the end of next year. The great advantage of this location is that it's directly adjacent to the Main Street train station. Commuters will have to walk only a few steps from the train station. Listeners can visit our radio station's Web site to see a floor plan of the new office.

이어서 지역 뉴스 시간입니다. 오늘 아침 Bloomsbury 시의원들은 Ferris 가와 Carter 가에 새로운 사무실 건물 단지 건설 계획을 승인했습니다. 공사는 3월에 시작될 예정이며 내년 말에 완공될 것으로 예상됩니다. 이 위치의 큰 이점은 Main 가 기차역에 바로 인접하다는 것입니다. 통근자들은 기차역에서 단 몇 걸음만 걸으면 될 것입니다. 청취자분들은 새 사무실의 평면도를 보려면 우리 라디오 방송국의 웹 사이트에 방문하시면 됩니다.

어휘 local 지역의 council 의회 approve 승인하다, 허가하다 entire 전체의 complex 단지 complete 완성하다; 완성된 advantage 장점 location 위치, 장소 directly 바로, 곧장 adjacent to ~에 인접한 commuter 통근자 a few 몇몇의 step 걸음, 계단 floor plan 평면도 expansion 확장 renovation 개조, 수리 improvement 향상, 개선 landscape 풍경 attractive 매력적인 transportation 교통 participate 참가하다 leave 남기다 feedback 의견, 피드백 form 양식

89 세부 사항

최근에 무엇이 승인되었는가?
(A) 공항 확장
(B) 공원 개조
(C) 사무 단지 건설
(D) 지역 고속도로 개선

해설 최근에 승인된(recently approved) 것을 묻고 있음을 기억하고 본문을 듣도록 하자. 첫 문장의 "this morning, Bloomsbury City Council members approved plans for the construction of an entire complex of new office buildings"에서 오늘 아침에 시의회에서 사무 단지 건설을 승인했다고 했으므로 정답은 (C)이다.

90 세부 사항

화자는 그 위치의 어떤 장점을 언급하는가?
(A) 무료 주차가 가능하다.
(B) 임대료가 저렴하다.
(C) 경치가 매력적이다.
(D) 대중교통이 가깝다.

해설 지문 중간의 "The great advantage of this location is that it's directly adjacent to the Main Street train station"에서 위치가 기차역 바로 근처라고 언급되었다. 이는 대중교통이 가깝다는 의미이므로 (D)가 정답이다.

91 세부 사항

청자들은 왜 웹 사이트를 방문할 것인가?
(A) 경매에 참가하기 위해
(B) 평면도를 보기 위해
(C) 의견을 남기기 위해
(D) 양식을 다운로드하기 위해

해설 문제의 키워드인 웹 사이트를 기억하고 본문을 듣도록 하자. 본문에서 웹 사이트가 언급되는 부분인 "Listeners can visit our radio station's Web site to see a floor plan of the new office"에서 청취자들이 평면도를 보기 위해 웹 사이트를 방문할 것임을 알 수 있다. 따라서 정답은 (B)이다.

[92-94] 회의 발췌

This morning, I want to discuss a potential new client, Jin Apparel. They're a small but rapidly growing company that's looking for architects to design their new office space. They've recently purchased an abandoned factory and want to convert it into their corporate headquarters. Yes, I know this could be a challenging project. <u>However, we've done this before.</u> We need to send Jin Apparel a design as soon as possible. So, by the end of the week, I'd like you to prepare some preliminary designs for us to consider at next week's meeting.

오늘 아침, 저는 새로운 잠재 고객인 Jin Apparel 사에 대해서 논의하고 싶습니다. 그들은 소규모이지만 빠르게 성장하고 있는 회사로, 그들의 새 사무실 공간을 디자인할 건축가들을 찾고 있습니다. 그들은 최근 버려진 공장을 매입했고 그것을 그들의 회사 본사로 개조하고 싶어 합니다. 네, 이것이 어려운 프로젝트가 될 수 있다는 걸 압니다. 하지만 우리는 전에 이것을 해낸 적이 있습니다. 우리는 가능한 한 빨리 Jin Apparel 사에 도안을 보내야 합니다. 그래서, 여러분이 이번 주말까지 우리가 다음 주 회의에서 고려할 디자인 초안을 준비해 주셨으면 합니다.

어휘 potential 잠재적인 client 고객 apparel 의류 rapidly 빠르게 architect 건축가 abandoned 버려진 convert 바꾸다, 개조하다 corporate 기업의 headquarters 본사 challenging 어려운, 도전적인 as soon as possible 가능한 한 빨리 preliminary 기초의, 예비의 field 분야

architecture 건축업 manufacturing 제조업 publishing 출판업 avoid 피하다 repeat 반복하다 task 일, 과제 reject 거절하다 recommend 추천하다 vendor 상인 assure 확신시키다 concerned 걱정하는 draft 초안 updated 최신의, 갱신된 budget 예산 proposal 제안, 제안서

92 화자의 직업

화자는 어떤 분야에서 일하는 것 같은가?
(A) 건축업
(B) 제조업
(C) 출판업
(D) 의류업

해설 화자가 일하는 분야를 묻는 질문은 주로 앞에서 힌트를 준다. 본문 앞부분의 "I want to discuss a potential new client, Jin Apparel. They're a small but rapidly growing company that's looking for architects to design their new office space"에서 화자의 고객은 의류업체이지만 화자의 회사는 그들의 사무실을 디자인하는 건축업체임을 알 수 있다. 따라서 정답은 (A)이다.

93 의도 파악

화자는 왜 "하지만, 우리는 전에 이것을 해낸 적이 있습니다"라고 말하는가?
(A) 반복되는 업무를 피하기 위해
(B) 아이디어를 거절하기 위해
(C) 이전 판매자를 추천하기 위해
(D) 걱정하는 직원들을 안심시키기 위해

해설 해당 문장의 바로 앞부분인 "Yes, I know this could be a challenging project"에서 그 일이 힘들 수 있다고 언급한 후, 그렇지만 이전에 해낸 적이 있는 일이라고 말하는 것으로 보아 결국은 이번에도 잘 할 수 있다며 걱정하는 청자들을 안심시키는 것으로 볼 수 있다. 따라서 정답은 (D)이다.

94 세부 사항

청자들은 이번 주말까지 무엇을 준비해야 하는가?
(A) 가격표
(B) 디자인 초안
(C) 최신 계약서
(D) 예산 제안서

해설 "by the end of the week"라는 키워드를 기억하고 본문을 듣도록 하자. 본문 후반의 "by the end of the week, I'd like you to prepare some preliminary designs for us to consider"에서 디자인 초안을 준비해 달라고 했으므로 정답은 이를 동의 표현으로 바꾼 (B)임을 알 수 있다.

[95-97] 전화 메시지 & 시간표

Hi, this is Douglas Johnson from the management office at Sherman Street Garden Apartments. Mr. Clark, I wanted to remind you that you still need to come by to pick up your key before you move in next week. Also, I remember you mentioned that you need to get to your new job on Park Avenue every morning. The good news is that the Sherman Street bus stop is right in front of our apartments. I printed out a copy of the morning schedule for you. You can pick that up too when you come by to get your key.

안녕하세요, 저는 Sherman 가 Garden 아파트 관리사무소에 있는 더글러스 존슨입니다. 클라크 씨, 다음 주에 입주하기 전에 당신의 열쇠를 가지러 오셔야 한다는 것을 다시 한번 알려드리고 싶었습니다. 또한, 당신이 매일 아침 Park 가에 있는 새 직장에 출근해야 한다고 말씀하신 걸 기억합니다. 좋은 소식은 Sherman 가 버스 정류장이 저희 아파트 바로 앞에 있다는 것입니다. 제가 당신을 위해 오전 시간표 사본을 한 장 출력했습니다. 열쇠를 찾으러 오실 때 그것도 가져가시면 됩니다.

버스 시간표	
Sherman 가	오전 6:30
Bridge 가	오전 7:00
Park 가	오전 7:20
시장	오전 8:00

어휘 remind 알려주다, 상기시키다 still 아직도 come by 잠깐 들르다 pick up 가지러 가다, 찾으러 가다 mention 언급하다 bus stop 버스 정류장 right 바로 print out 출력하다 interviewer 면접관 property 부동산, 건물 agent 직원, 대리인 confirm 확인하다 reservation 예약 apply for ~에 지원하다 lease contract 임대 계약서

95 화자의 직업

화자는 누구일 것 같은가?
(A) 채용 면접관
(B) 건물 관리자
(C) 여행사 직원
(D) 버스 운전사

해설 화자가 누구인지 묻는 질문은 앞에서 힌트를 주는 것이 일반적이다. 첫 문장의 "this is Douglas Johnson from the management office at Sherman Street Garden Apartments"에서 화자가 아파트 관리사무소에서 일하고 있음을 알 수 있다. 따라서 정답은 (B)이다.

96 요청 사항

화자는 청자에게 무엇을 하라고 요청하는가?
(A) 예약을 확인하라고

(B) 새 일자리에 지원하라고
(C) 임대 계약서에 서명하라고
(D) 물건을 가져가라고

해설 "I printed out a copy of the morning schedule for you. You can pick that up too when you come to get your key"에서 버스 시간표와 열쇠를 가져가라고 하는 것을 보아 정답이 (D)임을 알 수 있다.

97 시각 자료 연계

시각 자료를 보시오. 청자는 언제 버스를 탈 것인가?
(A) 오전 6시 30분에
(B) 오전 7시에
(C) 오전 7시 20분에
(D) 오전 8시에

해설 본문의 "The good news is that the Sherman Street bus stop is right in front of our apartments"에서 청자의 아파트 앞에 Sherman 가 버스 정류장이 있다고 언급하고 있으므로 청자는 Sherman 가에서 버스를 탈 것임을 알 수 있다. 시간표에서 Sherman 가 정류장의 버스 탑승 시간은 (A) 오전 6시 30분이다. Park 가는 직장이 위치한 곳이므로 혼동하지 않도록 주의해야 한다.

[98-100] 설명/소개 & 체크리스트

Before opening the store today, let's review our procedures for receiving clothing shipments. Following the proper procedures will save us a great deal of time and effort. For example, sometimes cartons of merchandise shipped from the company warehouse are delivered to the wrong branch store. We don't want our staff spending time inspecting merchandise that isn't meant for our store. So, please pay special attention to the number marked on each box. It must be the same as the number on the shipping report that's been e-mailed to us. If not, simply return the box unopened to the warehouse. It is important that you remember these rules since we are expecting a large amount of merchandise for the big sale next week.

오늘 가게 문을 열기 전에, 의류 배송을 받는 절차를 검토해 봅시다. 적절한 절차를 따르는 것은 우리가 많은 시간과 수고를 절약하게 해줄 것입니다. 예를 들어, 가끔 회사 창고에서 발송된 제품 박스들이 잘못된 지점으로 배송됩니다. 우리 가게의 것이 아닌 물건을 검수하는 데 직원들이 시간을 보내는 것을 우리는 원치 않습니다. 그러니, 각 박스에 표시된 숫자에 특별히 주의를 기울여 주세요. 그것은 우리가 이메일로 받은 배송 보고서의 번호와 일치해야 합니다. 그렇지 않다면, 박스를 개봉하지 않은 채로 창고에 반품해 주세요. 우리는 다음주에 대규모 세일로 인해 많은 상품들이 들어올 것으로 예상하고 있으니 이러한 규칙을 기억하는 것이 중요합니다.

```
                  체크 리스트

    ☐  1. 상자 번호를 확인한다.
    ☐  2. 내용물이 포장 목록과 맞는지 확인한다.
    ☐  3. 제품이 손상되었는지 검수한다.
    ☐  4. 물품들을 창고로 옮긴다.
    ☐  5. 변경사항 목록을 업데이트한다.
```

어휘 review 검토하다 procedure 절차 shipment 배송, 배송물 follow 따르다 proper 적절한 save 절약하다 carton 상자 merchandise 상품, 물건 warehouse 창고 branch 지점 staff 직원 inspect 검사하다 be meant for ~로 의도되다 attention 주의 mark 표시하다 shipping 배송 return 반품하다 expect 기대하다, 기다리다 check 확인하다 match 일치하다 packing 포장 damage 손상 storeroom 창고 update 업데이트하다, 갱신하다 concerned 걱정하는 extra 추가의 limited 한정된 storage 저장, 보관 wasted 낭비된 conduct 시행하다 go through ~을 겪다 renovation 개조, 수리

98 문제점

화자는 무엇이 걱정된다고 말하는가?
(A) 추가 배송비
(B) 한정된 저장 공간
(C) 낭비된 시간
(D) 고객 불만

해설 담화 초반에 "Following the proper procedures will save us a great deal of time and effort"에서 적절한 절차를 따르면 직원들의 시간과 노력을 아낄 수 있다고 했고, 중반부에 "We don't want our staff spending time inspecting merchandise ~"에서 직원들이 물건을 검수하는 데 시간을 낭비하는 것을 원치 않는다고 했으므로 화자는 직원들의 시간이 낭비되는 것에 대해 걱정하고 있음을 알 수 있다. 따라서 정답은 (C)이다.

99 시각 자료 연계

시각 자료를 보시오. 화자는 어떤 단계가 특별한 주의를 요한다고 말하는가?
(A) 1
(B) 2
(C) 3
(D) 4

해설 지문 중반에 키워드(special attention)가 나오는 문장 "please pay special attention to the number marked on each box"를 통해 박스에 표시된 번호를 확인하는 데 특별히 주의해야 한다는 것을 알 수 있다. 따라서 정답은 box의 동의 표현인 carton을 사용한 (A) 1이다.

100 다음에 할 일

다음 주에 무슨 일이 일어날 것인가?
(A) 할인 행사가 시작될 것이다.
(B) 검사가 시행될 것이다.
(C) 가게가 폐업할 것이다.
(D) 가게가 개조 작업을 할 것이다.

해설 '다음 주'라는 문제의 키워드를 기억하도록 하자. 본문의 후반 "It is important that you remember these rules since we are expecting a large amount of merchandise for the big sale next week"에서 다음 주에 대규모 세일이 있을 것임을 알 수 있다. 따라서 정답은 (A)이다.

PART • 5

101 대명사

그레고리 씨가 내일 오전 9시에 우리에게 전화하기로 했습니다.

해설 본동사(타동사) 또는 부정사와 같은 준동사(타동사) 뒤는 목적어 자리이므로 목적격 인칭대명사 (A)가 정답이다.

어휘 agree 동의하다 give a phone call 전화를 걸다

102 접속사

고객이 원했던 사무실 의자가 더 이상 재고가 없기 때문에 지난번 주문을 취소했습니다.

해설 본동사가 cancel(취소하다)과 was(be동사) 두 개이므로 접속사가 필요하다. 따라서 (A)가 정답이다. 나머지 선택지는 접속부사이기 때문에 오답.

어휘 customer 고객 order 주문 no longer 더 이상 ~하지 않는 in stock 재고가 있는 therefore 그러므로 for instance 예를 들어 in this case 이러한 경우에는

103 명사 자리

캠페인 관리자로서의 어빙 씨의 경험은 그를 마케팅 직책의 완벽한 후보자로 만듭니다.

해설 소유격 뒤는 명사 자리이므로 -ence로 끝나는 명사 (D)가 정답이다. (C)의 -ment 형태도 명사이지만 의미상 오답이다.

어휘 perfect 완벽한 candidate 후보자 marketing position 마케팅 직책

104 부사 어휘

Stardust Promotions는 소규모 4인 사무실에서 시작했지만 지금은 전세계에 대기업의 마케팅 캠페인을 다룹니다.

해설 부사 어휘 문제로, 의미상 과거와 다른 현재의 상황을 말해주는 (C)가 답이다.

office 사무실   handle 처리하다, 다루다, 해결하다
corporation 기업   however 하지만

105 형용사 자리
앤서니 씨는 내년에 회사 판매 수익에 뚜렷한 이점을 제공해야 합니다.

해설 관사와 명사 사이에서 명사를 수식하는 형용사 자리이다. (C)의 부사에서 -ly를 뺀 '뚜렷한'이라는 뜻의 (A)가 정답이다.

어휘 provide 제공하다   advantage 이점, 장점   sales 판매
revenue 수익

106 전치사 어휘
구조화 단계의 계획 부분에서 아이디어와 제안을 표명하는 것이 중요하다.

해설 빈칸 뒤에 나오는 명사구를 이끄는 전치사 어휘 문제이다. 의미상 "구조화 단계(structuring phase) 동안"을 나타내는 (B)가 정답이다. (C)의 over가 "~동안, ~에 걸쳐"로 사용되기 위해서는 뒤에 구체적인 숫자가 들어간 기간 표현이 와야 한다.

어휘 critical 중요한   voice 목소리를 내다   suggestion 제안
portion 부분   structuring 구조화   phase 단계
afterwards 나중에

107 동사의 형태, 시제, 수
커피 테이블에 다리를 부착하려면 2인치 간격으로 곡선의 못을 사용하십시오.

해설 빈칸에 본동사가 들어가야 하는 자리이므로 명령문의 동사원형인 (B)가 정답이다.

어휘 attach 부착시키다, 첨부하다   curved 구부러진, 곡선의
nail 손톱, 못   space 간격을 두다   interval 간격

108 동사 어휘
Better Cooking Monthly의 최신 호가 내일 판매될 예정임을 알려 드리게 되어 기쁩니다.

해설 동사 어휘 문제로, 의미상 "~하게 되어 기쁘다"라는 의미를 이루는 (C)가 정답이다. be pleased to 표현을 묶어서 알아두자.

어휘 inform 알리다   the latest 최근의   issue 발행물, 호
available 이용 가능한, 구매 가능한   surprise 놀라다
pretend ~인척 하다

109 부사 자리
새롭게 디자인된 웹 사이트를 통해 Online Bazaar 고객 담당자는 더 신속하게 질문에 응답할 수 있습니다.

해설 'respond to + 명사'로 문장 구조가 완전하기 때문에 다음에 올 수 있는 것은 부사밖에 없다. 따라서 정답은 -ly로 끝나는 부사 (A)이다. 그외에도 '동명사/부정사(타동사) + 목적어 + 부사'의 구조도 암기해 두자.

newly 새롭게   allow 허용하다   customer representative
고객 담당자   respond to ~에 응답하다   inquiry 질문

110 명사 어휘
연례 회사 야유회는 직원들이 다른 부서의 동료들과 만나고 사귈 수 있도록 마련되었다.

해설 socialize with 뒤에 오는 명사 어휘 문제이다. 의미상 in other departments(다른 부서에 있는)와 어울리는 (D)가 정답이다.

어휘 annual 연례의   employee 직원   socialize with ~와
사귀다   department 부서   generator 발전기
professor 교수   secretary 비서   colleague 동료

111 형용사 자리
합리적인 가격으로 고급 별미를 즐기기 위해 Paradise City Mall 안에 있는 The Galloping Gourmet을 꼭 방문해 주세요.

해설 명사 prices를 수식하는 형용사 자리로, '합리적인 가격'이라는 의미를 완성하는 (A)가 정답이다.

어휘 gourmet 미식가   delicacies 진미   visit 방문하다

112 동사의 형태
Sentinel Labs의 모든 보안 담당자들은 회사 건물에서 항상 유니폼과 신분증을 착용해야 합니다.

해설 빈칸은 본동사 자리이다. 의미상 수동태로 '~하도록 요구된다'는 의미를 이루는 (D)가 정답이다. be expected + to V의 형태는 자주 나오는 구조이므로 암기하자.

어휘 security 보안   personnel 직원들   wear 입다, 착용하다
identification 신분증   at all times 항상   property 부동산, 건물

113 부사 어휘
겨울이 이제 막 시작했을 뿐인데, 학교는 악천후로 인해 벌써 두 번이나 문을 닫아야 했습니다.

해설 부사 어휘 문제로, 앞부분의 just와 상응하여 겨울이 이제 막 시작했는데 벌써 두 번이나 문을 닫아야 했다는 문맥이 자연스럽다. 따라서 (C)가 정답이다.

어휘 just 지금 막   poor 부실한, 좋지 않은   even 심지어
at least 적어도   typically 일반적으로

114 명사 자리
Mendoza Construction은 기계의 예정된 교체를 미룸으로써 올해 비용을 절감할 수 있었습니다.

해설 <관사 + 형용사> 뒤에 오는 명사 자리로, 정답은 -ment 형태의 (B)이다.

어휘 be able to ~할 수 있다   cut down 절감하다   push back
미루다   scheduled 예정된   machinery 기계

115 부사 어휘

Granada Inn은 숙박을 보장하기 위해 최소 2주 전에 미리 객실을 예약할 것을 권장합니다.

(해설) 부사 어휘 문제로, '최소 2주 전에'라는 의미를 완성하는 (D)가 정답이다.

(어휘) recommend 권장하다, 추천하다 book 예약하다 at least 적어도 in advance 미리 in order to ~하기 위해 guarantee 보장하다

116 명사 어휘

제품 조립 라인이 고장 날 때마다 문제의 원인을 신속하게 확인하는 것이 작업 라인 관리자의 책임입니다.

(해설) 소유격 뒤에 오는 명사 어휘 문제로, 문제의 원인을 파악하는 것은 관리자의 '책임'이다라는 문맥이 자연스럽다. 따라서 (B)가 정답이다.

(어휘) whenever ~할 때마다 product 제품 assembly line 조립 라인 break down 고장 나다 ascertain 알아내다, 확인하다 cause 원인 disappointment 실망 standard 기준

117 형용사 자리

오늘 수집한 정보는 제품 선정을 개선하는 데 도움이 되지만 설문 참여는 완전히 자발적입니다.

(해설) <be동사 + 부사> 뒤는 형용사 자리이므로 형용사 (A)가 정답이다. <be + -ing> 구조는 능동 진행형이므로 뒤에 목적어가 와야 하기 때문에 (B)는 오답이고, (C)가 오면 수동태가 되기 때문에 의미상 어색하다.

(어휘) while ~하는 반면, ~동안 information 정보 collect 수집하다 improve 개선시키다 product selection 제품 선정 participation 참여, 참석 survey 설문 조사 completely 완전히 voluntary 자발적인

118 동사 어휘

Great Outdoors Magazine은 활동적인 라이프 스타일을 권장하는 제품이나 서비스를 제공하는 회사에만 광고 지면을 제공합니다.

(해설) 명사를 뒤에서 수식하는 that절(관계대명사절)의 본동사 어휘 문제로, 의미상 목적어 "active lifestyles"와 어울리는 동사 (B)가 정답이다.

(어휘) goods 물품 active 적극적인, 활발한 belittle 하찮게 만들다 encourage 격려하다, 고무하다 appreciate 고맙게 여기다 reject 거절하다

119 대명사

급격한 수요 증가로, 일부 사무용품을 보충해야 합니다.

(해설) 빈칸 뒤에 있는 <of + 복수명사>와 어울려, '사무용품 중 일부'라는 (A)가 정답이다. (B)는 <one of + 복수명사 + 단수동

사>의 구조가 와야 하므로 오답이고, (D)는 "거의 없는" 부정의 의미를 가지고 있기 때문에 오답이다.

(어휘) increased 증가된 demand 수요 office supplies 사무용품 replenish 보충하다

120 형용사 어휘

그 주제에 익숙하지 않은 사람들을 위한 관련 이론 요약이 대부분의 연구 자료에 포함될 것입니다.

(해설) 명사(theories) 앞에서 수식하는 형용사 어휘 문제이다. 의미상 '관련된 이론'이 어울리므로 정답은 (C)이다.

(어휘) research materials 연구 자료 include 포함시키다 summary 요약 theory 이론 be familiar with ~에 익숙하다 subject 주제 repetitive 반복적인 undetermined 미정의, 결정되지 않은

121 동사 어휘

박 씨는 일련의 면접을 거쳐 법무부의 새로운 부서장으로 임명되었습니다.

(해설) 동사 어휘 문제로, 빈칸 뒤에 as the new head ~로 보아, 의미상 주어가 "~로서 임명되다"가 적합하므로 정답은 (C)이다.

(어휘) appoint 임명하다 head 책임자 legal 법적의 a series of 일련의 implicate 시사하다 demand 요구하다 transfer 옮기다, 이동하다

122 명사 어휘

Garden Grove 마을은 매년 5%의 인구 증가가 계속되고 있습니다.

(해설) 복합명사 어휘 문제로, 바로 앞에 있는 명사(population)과 함께 '인구 증가'를 의미하는 (B)가 정답이다.

(어휘) continue 계속되다, 계속하다 undergo 겪다 annual 연간의 population 인구 rate 가격, 속도, 비율 revenue 이익

123 대명사

Far Blue Fashions는 업계에서 가장 빠르게 성장하는 의류 업체 중 하나입니다.

(해설) 주어가 단수로, 의미상 '~ 중 하나'라는 의미를 이루는 (C)가 정답이고, (D)는 복수를 의미하므로 오답이다.

(어휘) growing 성장하는 apparel 의류 industry 산업, 업계

124 형용사 어휘

Super Saver 슈퍼마켓은 회계 연도 이후 꾸준한 매출을 보였습니다.

(해설) 명사 increase(증가) 앞에서 수식하는 형용사 자리로, 의미상 '꾸준한 증가'를 뜻하는 (A)가 정답이다.

어휘 increase 증가 revenue 이익 fiscal year 회계 연도
steady 꾸준한 accurate 정확한 frustrating 불만스러운

125 동사의 형태

Creative Solutions가 디자인한 새로운 로고는 귀사의 핵심
임무에 맞는 구성 요소를 포함하도록 맞춤 제작되었습니다.

해설 has been 뒤의 p.p. 자리로, 정답은 과거분사 형태의 (A)이
다. <be + 과거분사> 구조가 수동태임을 숙지하자.

어휘 logo 로고 customize 맞춤 제작하다 incorporate 포함
하다 component 구성 요소 core 핵심 mission 임무

126 명사절 접속사

이 회의의 목표는 최근 개발이 추가로 예산 삭감을 필요로 하
는지 여부를 논의하는 것입니다.

해설 to discuss 뒤에서 목적어 기능을 하는 명사절 접속사 (D)가
정답이다.

어휘 goal 목표 discuss 논의하다 development 개발
require 요구하다 further 더 먼, 그 이상의 budget 예산
cut 삭감 instead 대신에 however 하지만

127 명사 자리

2년 전 Leads Pharmaceuticals와 합병한 이후, ABC Medical
기업은 기록적인 수익을 거두었습니다.

해설 빈칸 앞에 형용사가 있으므로 빈칸은 명사 자리이다. 관사가
없기 때문에 정답은 복수 형태의 (D)이다.

어휘 since ~이래로, 때문에 merge with ~와 합병하다
experience 경험하다 record-breaking 기록적인
earnings 소득, 수익, 이익

128 동사 어휘

마크 페르난데즈 감독의 새 영화인 "On the Shore"에는 수상
경력이 있는 출연자들이 나옵니다.

해설 본동사 어휘 문제로, 의미상 "~의 영화가 수상 경력이 있는 출
연진들을 특징으로 하다"의 (D)가 정답이다.

어휘 director 감독 award-winning 상을 받은 destroy 파괴
하다 expect 기대하다, 예상하다

129 부사 자리

온라인 판매는 다음 주 휴일에 급격히 증가할 것이므로, 웹 사
이트가 확실하게 작동하는 것이 매우 중요합니다.

해설 It is important 뒤에 오는 that절 안에 동사는 원형이어야 한
다. 따라서 be functioning이 되었고 function(작동하다)은
자동사이므로 빈칸은 부사 자리이다. 따라서 답은 (B)이다.

어휘 online sales 온라인 판매 sharply 급격히 holiday 휴일
function 작동하다 reliably 확실하게

130 전치사 어휘

Puma Automotive의 섬세함은 차량 전체 라인에 걸쳐 일관
됩니다.

해설 빈칸 뒤에 오는 명사구(its entire line of vehicles)를 이끄는
전치사 어휘 문제로, 의미상 "전체에 걸쳐"의 뜻을 가지고 있는
(B)가 정답이다.

어휘 attention to details 섬세함 consistent 지속적인 entire
전체의 among ~사이에서 across ~에 걸쳐

PART • 6

[131-134] 기사

주택 판매 오름세

전국 부동산 협회(National Real Estate Association)는 연말까지 주
택 판매가 전국 125만 개에 달할 것으로 예상하고 있다. 이는 전년도
수치보다 19% 증가한 것이고 4년 전의 합계를 뛰어넘는 새로운 최
고 기록이다. 협회는 주택 대출 금리의 지속적인 하락을 포함하여 판
매의 꾸준한 상승에 여러 요인이 기인한다고 말했다. 주거 부문이 활
성화되었음에도 불구하고 상업용 부동산 시장은 지난 4년간 거의 성
장하지 못했다. 업계 전문가들은 이런 상반되는 이유에 관해 확신하
지 못하고 있다.

어휘 on the rise 오름세에 expect 예상하다, 기대하다
nationwide 전국적인 reach 도달하다 mean 의미하다
previous 과거의, 이전의 figure 수치 exceed 초과하다
attribute A to B A를 B의 탓으로 돌리다 steady 꾸준한
a number of 수많은 factor 요소 continued 지속적인
interest rate 금리 loan 대출 residential 거주의
sector 부문 commercial 상업용의 real estate 부동산
contrast 대조

131 형용사 어휘

해설 빈칸을 포함한 문장 후반에 전년도 수치와 비교하여 19%가
증가한 것이라는 문맥이 어울리므로 정답은 (C) previous(과
거의)이다.

132 전치사 자리

해설 빈칸 앞에 a number of factors를 부연 설명하는 분사형 전
치사인 (D)가 '~을 포함하여'라는 의미로 정답이다.

133 명사 어휘

해설 앞 문장에서 역접의 의미로 "despite the increasing
activity(활성화에도 불구하고)라는 표현이 나오므로 "has
shown very little growth(거의 성장을 보이지 못했다)"가
의미상 자연스럽다. 따라서 (A)가 정답이다.

134 문맥에 맞는 문장 고르기

(A) 내일 또 다른 주택 하나가 시중에 나올 것이다.
(B) 업계 전문가들은 이런 상반되는 이유에 관해 확신하지 못하고 있다.
(C) 시장에는 상업용 부동산보다 주거용 부동산이 더 많다.
(D) 협회는 주택 융자 금리가 계속 하락할 것으로 예상하고 있다.

해설 바로 앞 문장에서 주택 판매 시장의 오름세와 상업용 부동산 시장의 저조함을 말했으므로 대조적인 상황을 언급하는 (B)가 정답이다.

[135-138] 정보

Zenith 2000 노트북 컴퓨터는 새로운 직장에서 여러분을 위한 가장 중요한 도구가 될 것입니다. 그러므로 항상 원활하게 작동되도록 컴퓨터를 관리하는 것이 중요합니다. 다음은 컴퓨터를 최상의 상태로 유지할 수 있는 저희 제품 관리팀의 유용한 조언입니다. 먼저, 특히 컴퓨터를 청소할 때 Zenith가 승인한 용품만 사용하십시오. 둘째, 충전기를 연결할 때 주의하십시오. 설명서에는 실수로 충격을 주거나 배터리가 소모되지 않도록 지침이 포함되어 있습니다. 셋째, 적절한 안티 바이러스 소프트웨어를 설치하십시오. 적절한 보호는 컴퓨터의 정보를 안전하게 유지 관리하는 데 중요합니다. 마지막으로, 컴퓨터를 수리해야 하는 경우, 인증된 전문 기술자를 선택하는 것이 좋습니다. 이 간단한 단계만 수행하면 컴퓨터의 수명을 연장할 수 있습니다.

어휘 laptop computer 노트북 tool 도구 critical 중요한 take care of 돌보다, 관리하다 run 작동하다 smoothly 원활하게 product care 제품 관리 in great shape 좋은 상태의 approve 승인하다 especially 특히 plug 꼽다 charger 충전기 manual 설명서 contain 포함하다 instruction 설명 accidentally 우연히 drain 소모시키다 install 설치하다 proper 적절한 adequate 적절한 professional 전문적인 technician 기술자 follow 따르다 extend 연장시키다 life 생명, 수명

135 부사 어휘

해설 부사 어휘 문제로, 앞 문장에서 "새로운 직장에서 Zenith 2000 노트북이 가장 중요한 도구가 될 것이다."라고 말하고 빈칸 뒤에 오는 내용은 "원활한 작동을 위해서는 이 컴퓨터를 잘 관리해야 한다."라고 했기 때문에 이를 자연스럽게 연결하는 것은 (D)이다.

136 명사 어휘

해설 빈칸 앞의 형용사 "Zenith-approved(Zenith가 승인한)"의 수식을 받을 수 있는 (B)가 정답이다.

137 문맥에 맞는 문장 고르기

(A) 적절한 보호는 컴퓨터의 정보를 안전하게 관리하는 데 중요합니다.
(B) 컴퓨터에는 사용할 여분의 충전기가 함께 제공됩니다.
(C) 문제가 있을 경우 설명서에 포함된 번호로 문의하십시오.

(D) 정기적으로 청소하면 컴퓨터 내부에 먼지가 쌓이지 않습니다.

해설 바로 앞 문장에서 "make sure to install proper anti-virus software(적절한 안티 바이러스 소프트웨어를 설치하세요.)"라고 나오기 때문에 의미상 (A)가 어울린다.

138 형용사 자리

해설 관사와 명사 사이에 있는 형용사 자리이다. 수식을 받는 professional technician(전문 기술자) 명사 앞에서는 과거분사 certified(증명된, 공인의)가 적합하므로 정답은 (C)이다.

[139-142] 회람

수신: 극장 관계자
발신: 엠. 실버, 연극 감독
날짜: 5월 12일
제목: 새로운 정책

지금 진행 중인 여름 콘서트 시리즈의 좌석 정책을 즉각 변경할 예정임을 알려드립니다. 아시다시피, 많은 관람객이 콘서트 당일에 좌석을 요청합니다. 특히 통로 좌석에서 여분의 다리를 뻗을 수 있는 공간을 원하는 사람들은 더욱 그렇습니다. 이 순간부터 티켓 구매 시에만 좌석 요청을 수락합니다.
콘서트 당일, 여분의 공간을 필요로 하는 방문객은 선착순으로 뒷줄에 앉을 수 있습니다. 거기는 대개 비어 있으니까요. 무대에서 더 멀지만 여분의 다리를 뻗을 수 있는 공간이 있습니다. 이 새로운 정책은 콘서트 전에 사람들을 더 빨리 자리에 앉히고, 공연 중의 불만을 피하는 데 도움이 될 겁니다.

어휘 policy 정책 be underway 진행 중이다 effective 시행되는 immediately 즉시 request 요청 particularly 특히 leg room 다리를 뻗을 수 있는 공간 aisle 복도 accept 수용하다 extra 여분의 space 공간 row 줄 on a first-come first-served basis 선착순으로 empty 텅 빈 complaint 불평, 불만 farther 더 먼

139 명사 어휘

해설 빈칸 뒤에 있는 'policy(정책)'과 함께 어울리는 복합명사 어휘 문제로, 다음 문장에서 'seating requests(좌석 요청)'을 언급하기 때문에 (C)가 정답이다.

140 부사 어휘

해설 부사 어휘 문제로, 의미상 "only at the time of ticket purchase(티켓 구매시에만 가능하다)"는 문맥이 어울리므로 정답은 (A)이다.

141 관계대명사

해설 빈칸 앞에 있는 사람 명사(visitors)를 수식하고, 뒤에 동사 can sit을 고려했을 때 주격 관계대명사와 본동사가 있는 (B)가 정답이다.

142 문맥에 맞는 문장 고르기

(A) 많은 방문자들이 무대에 더 가까워지는 것을 선호합니다.
(B) 우리는 작년보다 방문자가 더 많을 것으로 예상합니다.
(C) 새로운 정책은 다음 달부터 시행됩니다.
(D) 무대에서 더 멀지만 여분의 다리를 뻗을 수 있는 공간이 있습니다.

해설 앞 문제에 대한 부연 설명으로, 선착순으로 뒷줄에 앉는 것이 변경된 정책이고 이에 대한 구체적인 내용을 언급하는 (D)가 문맥상 자연스럽다.

[143-146] 보도 자료

Minton Laboratories는 Massachusetts 주 Waltham에 본사를 둔 민간 연구 기관으로서 식품의약국(FDA)로부터 보조금을 받았다. 이 보조금은 FDA에 제출된 신청서에 부응하여 수여되었다. 기금은 Minton에서 이미 실행되고 있는 폐암 치료를 위한 신약 연구를 발전시키기 위해 사용될 예정이다. <u>Minton은 이미 실험 단계에 진입할 예정인 약을 생산했다.</u> 그러므로 이 보조금은 새로운 기후 제어 시스템과 새로운 시험 장비와 같은 실험실의 실험 시설을 업그레이드하는 데도 사용된다. 이러한 개선 조치 후에 잔액이 남아 있으면 실험실의 다른 부분을 업그레이드하는 데 사용된다. 실험실 책임자인 재니스 하트먼 박사는 FDA의 마크 햄프턴과 협의하여 작업을 감독할 것이다.

어휘 based ~에 본사를 둔 grant 보조금 award 수여하다 in response to ~에 응하여 application 신청서, 지원서 submit 제출하다 fund 자금 further 추후의 conduct 실행하다 drug 약 treatment 치료(법) lung cancer 폐암 therefore 그러므로 laboratory 실험실 facility 시설(물) climate 기후 equipment 장비 remain 남다 portion 부분 in consultation with ~와 협의하여 produce 생산하다 phase 단계

143 문맥에 맞는 문장 고르기

(A) Minton Laboratories는 최근 Boston에서 Waltham으로 이전했다.
(B) Minton은 이미 실험 단계에 진입할 예정인 약을 생산했다.
(C) 햄프턴 씨는 보존 조치를 개발한 경험이 있다.
(D) 효율성을 높이기 위한 에너지 절약형 건축 양식이 인기를 얻고 있다.

해설 빈칸 뒤에서 보조금이 실험 단계에서도 사용될 것이라고 말하므로 실험 단계의 전 단계로 추측할 수 있는 신약 생산에 대한 내용이 문맥상 어울린다. 따라서 정답은 (B)이다.

144 연결어

해설 빈칸 뒤에 예시가 되는 두 가지(a new climate control system and new testing equipment)가 나오므로 정답은 예시를 들 때 쓰이는 (D)이다.

145 명사 어휘

해설 빈칸 바로 앞에 있는 these는 앞 문장에서 언급한 a new climate control system and new testing equipment로, (C) improvements(개선 사항)가 정답이다.

146 동사의 시제

해설 앞 부분에서 보조금 사용 계획을 언급하고 있으므로 맥락상 미래 시제 (A)가 적절하다.

PART • 7

[147-148] 쿠폰

Silver Diner
특별 기념일 쿠폰

다음 방문 시 웨이터 또는 웨이트리스에게 이 쿠폰을 제시하시고 식사 주문과 함께 무료 디저트를 받으십시오! 이 쿠폰은 월요일부터 금요일까지 아무 때나 사용 가능합니다(주말에는 유효하지 않음).

귀하의 의견은 우리에게 중요합니다!

www.silverdiner.com을 방문하여 메뉴 및 향후 행사 목록을 보십시오. 고객 설문 조사를 작성하고 제출하시면 식당의 50달러 상품권 당첨 대상에 들어갈 수 있습니다!

어휘 anniversary 기념일 present 제시하다 visit 방문하다; 방문 complimentary 무료의 order 주문하다; 주문 meal 식사 valid 유효한 opinion 의견 listing 목록 upcoming 다음의 complete 작성하다 submit 제출하다 customer survey 고객 설문조사 drawing 추첨 gift certificate 상품권

147 세부 사항

이 쿠폰을 사용하면 어떤 무료 상품을 얻을 수 있는가?
(A) 식사
(B) 샌드위치
(C) 식기류
(D) 디저트

해설 첫 문장 "Present this coupon to your waiter or waitress during your next visit and receive a complimentary dessert with your order of any meal!"에서 쿠폰을 제시하면 무료 디저트를 받을 수 있다고 나오므로 정답은 (D)이다.

148 세부 사항

고객은 어떻게 상품을 탈 기회를 얻을 수 있는가?
(A) 식당을 10회 방문해서
(B) 이번 주말에 쿠폰을 사용해서
(C) 설문 조사에 응해서
(D) 식당에서 50달러를 써서

해설 마지막 문장을 보면 "Complete and submit our customer survey to be entered into a drawing for a $50 gift certificate to the diner!"라며 고객 설문 조사에 응하면 추첨을 통해 상품권을 받을 수 있다고 나오므로 정답은 (C)이다.

[149-150] 이메일

수신: 샘 와인하트
발신: 질 심슨
날짜: 2월 23일
제목: 휴스턴 사무소

와인하트 씨,

지난 11월 휴스턴 사무소로의 이전을 신청하셨었네요. 그 당시에는 휴스턴에 공석이 없었기 때문에 귀하의 요청을 승인할 수 없었어요. 그러나 방금 휴스턴 사무장과 대화한 결과, 마케팅 부서에 공석이 있다고 들었어요. 그들은 누군가를 내부적으로 데려오는 것을 선호했고, 저는 즉시 당신을 떠올렸어요. 여전히 관심이 있다면 이번 주 수요일까지 알려주시기 바랍니다. 그렇지 않은 경우 회사 웹 사이트에 채용 정보를 게시해야 합니다. 당신의 대답을 기다릴게요.

질 심슨

어휘 apply for 신청하다 transfer 이동하다, 이전하다 approve 승인하다 request 요청하다; 요청 opening 공석 marketing department 마케팅 부서 preference 선호 internally 내부적으로 immediately 즉시 job opening 공석

149 주제/목적

심슨 씨는 왜 와인하트 씨에게 이메일을 보냈는가?
(A) 일을 해달라고 요청하기 위해
(B) 신입 사원을 소개하기 위해
(C) 가능한 공석 자리를 알리기 위해
(D) 그의 이전 요청을 거부하기 위해

해설 지문 초반 "However, I just spoke to the Houston office manager this morning, and they now have an opening in their marketing department."에서 지금 마케팅 부서에 공석이 있음을 알리고 있다. 따라서 정답은 (C)이다. however와 같이 반전을 의미하는 접속부사 뒤에 정답 단서가 잘 나온다는 걸 알아두자.

150 세부 사항

심슨 씨는 무엇을 하려고 기다릴 것인가?
(A) 공고 올리기
(B) 와인하트 씨에게 전화하기
(C) 와인하트 씨를 사무장으로 고용하기
(D) 휴스턴 사무소로 이전하기

해설 마지막 부분 "If not, I will need to post a job opening on our company Web site. I will wait to hear from you."에서 공석에 관심이 없으면 회사 웹 사이트에 올리려고 하니 대답을 달라고 한다. 따라서 정답은 (A)이다.

[151-152] 온라인 채팅

데이비드 정 [10:20 A.M.]
고든 씨, 안녕하세요. 어제 아침에 보내 드린 편지 초안을 확인 중입니다. 당신으로부터 연락을 받지 못해서 그것을 검토하고 있는지 확인하고 싶었습니다.

제인 고든 [10:23 A.M.]
네, 직원 중 한 명이 지금 검토 중입니다. 그가 오늘 이른 오후까지 교정 사본을 준비할 것입니다.

데이비드 정 [10:25 A.M.]
좋아요! 저는 늦어도 내일 아침에 서신을 보내야 하고, 제 상사도 검토해야 합니다.

제인 고든 [10:27 A.M.]
제가 받자마자 교정된 원고를 보내 드리겠습니다. 제안된 교정본에 관한 질문이 있으시면 언제든지 전화주세요.

데이비드 정 [10:31 A.M.]
네, 그러겠습니다. 도와주셔서 고맙습니다.

어휘 draft 초안 make sure 확실하게 하다 review 검토하다 proofread 교정을 보다 at the latest 늦어도 revise 교정하다 as soon as ~하자마자 regarding ~에 관해

151 추론/암시

고든 씨는 어느 사무소에서 일할 것 같은가?
(A) 편집부
(B) 영업부
(C) 마케팅부
(D) 인사부

해설 정 씨가 고든 씨에게 초안 확인을 부탁하자, 그가 부서 직원이 검토 중이라고 했으므로 정답은 (A)이다.

152 의도 파악

오전 10시 31분에, 정 씨가 "그러겠습니다"라고 쓴 의도는 무엇인가?
(A) 그는 고든 씨가 또 다른 글을 검토하길 바란다.
(B) 그는 질문이 있다면 고든 씨에게 연락할 것이다.
(C) 그는 고든 씨의 도움에 고마워한다.
(D) 그는 초고에 관한 질문을 묻기 위해 직원에게 연락할 것이다.

해설 바로 앞 문장에서 "If you have a question regarding any of our suggested revisions, please feel free to give me a call."라며 제안된 교정본에 관한 질문이 있다면 전화 달라는 말에 '그러겠다'라고 한 것이므로 정답은 (B)이다.

[153-154] 광고

북미 변호사 협회(NALC)

최근 몇 년 동안, NALC는 전국의 여러 일류 법률 사무소에서 수천 명의 참석자를 끌어모았습니다. 올해까지 수를 살펴보면, 우리는 새로운 기록에 도전하고 있습니다. 기조 연설자이자 Davis Kronin & Seinfeld의 업무 사원 브라이언 잉그램과 기타 저명한 변호사들과의 많은 흥미로운 프레젠테이션, 포럼 토론 및 법률 워크숍에 참여하십시오. 올해 컨퍼런스의 주제는 진화하는 법률 시스템과 새로운 고객 기대에 적응하는 방법입니다.

법률업계의 동료들에 관한 한, NALC에 참석한 후에 이점을 누릴 수 있을 것입니다. 놓치지 마세요! 4월 28일까지 www.nalc.com에서 사전 등록하고 일반 등록 수수료를 15 % 절약하세요.

어휘 draw 끌다   attendee 참석자   leading 선두의, 일류의   law firm 법률 사무소   so far 지금까지   keynote speaker 기조 연설자   prominent 저명한   legal 법적의   evolve 진화하다   adapt 적응하다   client 고객   expectation 기대   peer 동료   industry 산업   miss 놓치다   preregister 사전 등록하다   registration fee 등록비

153 Not/True 확인

NALC에 대해서 뭐라고 언급하는가?
(A) 유일한 전국 법률 회의다.
(B) 일주일간 열릴 것이다.
(C) 최근 몇 년 동안 참석률이 저조하다.
(D) 변호사들만 참석한다.

해설 북미 변호사들이 참석하는 회의라고 제목에서 언급하고 있으므로 정답은 (D)이다.

154 Not/True 확인

행사에 관련된 어떤 정보가 광고에 제공되지 않는가?
(A) 기조 연설자의 이름
(B) 컨퍼런스의 날짜
(C) 웹 사이트의 주소
(D) 회의 주제

해설 (A) 기조 연설자 이름은 (Brian Ingram), (C) 웹사이트 주소는 (www.nalc.com)와 (D) 회의 주제(the evolving legal system and how to adapt to new client expectations)가 나와 있지만 컨퍼런스의 날짜는 제공되지 않았기 때문에 정답은 (B)이다.

[155-157] 이메일

수신: 사무엘 프레스턴 <smpreston@covington.com>
발신: 레지나 킴 <rekim@freemanlng.com>
날짜: 9월 11일
제목: 환영합니다
첨부: 전근에 도움되는 정보

프레스턴 씨,
Freeman LNG Austin 사무실에 오신 것을 환영합니다. 새 직책은 프로젝트 계획 담당자이며, 프로젝트 관리자에게 직접 보고하게 될 것입니다. 이미 아시다시피, 우리는 최근에 국가 최대 규모의 LNG 프로젝트에 대한 정부의 승인을 얻었으며, 우리는 토대를 마련해 흥분하고 있습니다.

오리엔테이션은 10월 2일 월요일 오전 10시로 잡혔으며, 인사부의 존 그린이 이끌 것입니다. 세션에서 더 큰 프로젝트 그룹에 대한 정보는 물론 혜택 및 기타 고용 세부 사항에 대한 정보를 받게 됩니다. 신분증을 아직 발급 받지 않았으므로 보안 데스크에서 서명하셔야 합니다. 따라서 오리엔테이션 시간에 늦지 않도록 오전 9시 30분까지 오십시오.

첨부된 안내서는 New York 사무실에서 이전하는 데 도움이 되는 몇 가지 정보입니다. 가이드에 포함된 내용은 아직 거주지 마련을 하지 않은 경우에 대비한 몇 가지 제안사항입니다. 도착하기 전에 질문이 있으시면 주저하지 말고 저에게 연락 주십시오.

레지나 킴
인사과 부장
Freeman LNG, Austin 사무소

어휘 report 보고하다   directly 바로, 직접   recently 최근에   government 정부   approval 승인   groundwork 기초   토대 공사   lead 이끌다   human resources 인사(과)   benefit 혜택   details 세부사항   employment 고용   issue 발행하다   identification 신분증   sign in 서명하다   attach 첨부하다   include 포함시키다   housing   arrangement 주택 마련   hesitate 주저하다

155 주제/목적

왜 킴 씨는 이메일을 보냈는가?
(A) 정부 승인을 요청하기 위해
(B) 새로운 직장에 지원하기 위해
(C) 새로운 일에 대한 세부 사항을 제공하기 위해
(D) 신분증을 발급하기 위해

해설 도입부에 "I would like to welcome ~ LNG"라며 환영 인사와 함께 새로 온 직원에게 직책 설명과 오리엔테이션 설명 및 이사에 도움이 되는 정보를 제공하고 있으므로 정답은 (C)이다.

156 Not/True 확인

Freeman LNG에 대해 명시된 것은 무엇인가?
(A) 사무실이 한 군데 이상 있다.
(B) 보스톤에 사무소가 있다.
(C) 더 많은 직원을 고용할 것이다.
(D) 정부 승인을 기다리고 있는 중이다.

해설 첫 문장에서 Austin 사무실에 온 걸 환영한다고 했고, 마지막 문단 첫 문장에서 New York 사무소로부터 이전한다고 언급되어 있으므로 정답은 (A)이다.

157 세부 사항

프레스턴 씨는 무엇을 하도록 권유 받는가?
(A) 오리엔테이션에 일찍 도착하기
(B) 오리엔테이션 전에 그린 씨와 대화하기
(C) 추천서 목록 제공하기
(D) 미리 오리엔테이션 자료 읽기

해설 두 번째 문단에서 오리엔테이션 시간이 10시라고 언급되었고 마지막 부분에 "Therefore, please plan to arrive by 9:30 A.M. so that you are on time for your orientation session." 9시 30분까지 도착해 달라고 했으므로 정답은 (A)이다.

[158-160] 정보

국립 치과 협회
18회 연례 심포지엄, 7월 13-15일
Jefferson 컨벤션 센터 — Las Vegas, Nevada

국립 치과 협회의 18회 연례 심포지엄에 참석하기 위해 등록해 주셔서 감사합니다. 심포지엄 중 점심식사는 컨퍼런스 센터의 메인 로비에 있는 등록 카운터에서 식사권을 구입할 수 있습니다. 3일간의 식사권을 18달러에 구입하거나 개별 식사권을 7달러에 구입할 수 있습니다. 구매 시 심포지엄 등록 번호를 알려 주십시오. 식사권이 없을 경우 표준 가격으로 9달러가 청구됩니다. 식사권은 컨벤션 센터 내에서만 사용 가능합니다.
구내식당은 심포지엄 동안 점심 시간 오전 11시 30분부터 오후 2시 30분까지 개장합니다. 채식 식사 옵션이 필요한 참가자의 경우, 컨벤션 센터 2층에 위치한 Natural Diner가 건강식 채식 식사 옵션을 제공합니다. 다과는 로비의 Rainforest 카페에서 구입할 수 있지만 카페에서는 점심식사를 제공하지 않습니다. 컨벤션 센터의 지도가 심포지엄 자료에 포함되어 있어 길을 찾는 데 어려움이 없습니다.
컨벤션 센터에서 떨어진 곳에서 점심식사를 하는 것을 선호한다면, 운전해서 15분 이내에 갈 수 있는 다양한 레스토랑이 있습니다.
자세한 내용은 등록 카운터에 문의하십시오.

어휘 **register** 등록하다 **attend** 참석하다 **annual** 연례의 **purchase** 구매하다 **meal** 식사 **locate** 위치하다 **option** 선택 **individual** 개인의, 각각의 **make sure** 확실하게 하다 **in the absence of** ~이 없을 때 **valid** 유효한 **location** 위치 **participant** 참석자 **in need of** ~을 필요로 하는 **vegetarian** 채식주의자 **serve** 제공하다 **map** 지도 **include** 포함시키다 **material** 자료 **prefer** 선호하다 **a number of** 많은 **details** 세부 사항

158 Not/True 확인

국립 치과 협회에 대해 사실인 것은 무엇인가?
(A) 항상 심포지엄을 라스베이거스에서 연다.
(B) 18년 전에 처음으로 모임을 가졌다.
(C) 심포지엄에서는 어떠한 음식도 제공하지 않는다.

(D) 등록은 전세계 참가자들에게 열려 있다.

해설 제목에 "18th Annual Syposium"이라고 명시되어 있으므로 정답은 (B)이다.

159 세부 사항

심포지엄 참석자들이 점심식사를 할 수 없는 곳은 어디인가?
(A) Rainforest 카페에서
(B) 구내식당에서
(C) Natural Diner 식당에서
(D) 컨벤션 센터 외부에서

해설 두 번째 문단을 보면 "Refreshments can be purchased at Rainforest Café in the lobby, but the café does not serve lunch."라며 카페에서 다과는 구매 가능하지만 식사는 제공되지 않는다고 언급하므로 정답은 (A)이다.

160 Not/True 확인

심포지엄 외부에서 먹을 수 있는 장소에 대해서 사실인 것은 무엇인가?
(A) 오후 3시까지 점심이 제공된다.
(B) 점심 값이 9달러 이상이다.
(C) 심포지엄 식사권을 받지 않는다.
(D) 컨벤션 센터에서 도보 거리에 있다.

해설 첫 번째 문단 마지막 부분 "Please note that the meal passes are valid for use only at locations within the convention center."에서 식사권은 컨벤션 센터 내에서만 가능하다고 했기 때문에 정답은 (C)이다.

[161-163] 이메일

수신 Joy Toys 모든 직원들
발신 레스터 맨
날짜 9월 10일
제목 보안 접근

보는 식원 여러분께,

우리는 건물에 출입하기 위한 새로운 보안 시스템을 설치했습니다. 다음 주 월요일부터 새로운 시스템이 가동될 것입니다. 변경 사항은 임직원에게 영향을 미치지 않습니다. 그러나 건물 방문자를 확인하는 절차는 다를 것입니다.

이전과 마찬가지로 모든 방문객은 로비 보안 데스크에서 등록해야 합니다. 이전에 사용된 종이로 된 명부는 디지털화된 시스템으로 대체되어 방문자의 사진을 찍고 방문자가 본사 건물에 머무는 동안 항상 보여야 하는 임시 출입증을 발급합니다.

새로운 시스템은 각각의 제조 공장뿐만 아니라 당사의 본사에도 설치되었습니다. 현장 견학으로 우리 공장을 방문하는 학생 단체는 새로운 디지딜 시스템의 대싱이 되지 않습니다. 새 시스템에 대한 질문이 있으면 현재 보안 설명서의 49.3b 부분에서 추가 정보를 찾을 수 있습니다.

레스터 맨
Joy Toys 보안 책임자

어휘 security 보안 in operation 운영 중인 affect 영향을 끼치다 regular employee 정직원 process 절차 previously 과거에 replace 대체하다 digitalize 디지털화하다 issue 발행하다 temporary 임시의 visible 보일 만한 within ~내에 corporate 기업의 headquarters 본사 manufacturing 제조 plant 공장 factory 공장 be subject to ~의 대상이다 additional 추가적인 current 현재의

161 주제/목적

이메일의 목적은 무엇인가?
(A) 주차 불만에 대응하기
(B) 새로운 절차 설명하기
(C) 합병에 관한 문제 해결하기
(D) 새로운 고용 정책 논의하기

해설 글의 목적은 대부분 첫 부분에 나온다. "We have installed a new security system for access to our building."에서 새로운 보안 시스템을 언급하며 설명하고 있으므로 정답은 (B)이다.

162 추론/암시

Joy Toys에 대해 암시된 것은 무엇인가?
(A) 새로운 보안 시스템을 설치할 필요가 있다.
(B) 주말에는 방문자들에게 개방되지 않는다.
(C) 제조 공장이 하나뿐이다.
(D) 더 이상 등록부를 사용하지 않는다.

해설 두 번째 문단을 보면 "The paper sign-in book that was previously used, though, will be replaced by a digitized system that ~"에서 더 이상 종이로 된 등록부를 사용하지 않는다고 언급하고 있기 때문에 정답은 (D)이다.

163 세부 사항

시설 내에 있는 동안 임시 출입증을 소지해야 하는 사람은 누구인가?
(A) 공장 견학을 하는 학생 단체
(B) 보안 직원들
(C) 회사 방문객들
(D) 정규 직원들

해설 두 번째 문단 "a temporary pass card that must be visible at all times during the visitor's stay"에서 회사에 방문하는 방문객들은 임시 출입증을 소지해야 한다고 나오므로 정답은 (C)이다.

[164-167] 기사

맛있는 수박?

10월 21일 - 매년 수박에 대한 소비자 수요가 계속 증가하고 있다. 핀란드, 브라질, 가나, 러시아 등 세계 여러 나라들이 수박을 수출하고 있다. 수박 농민들은 식물 육종의 과학적 진보를 이용하여 최대 수확기를 11개월까지 늘릴 수 있으며 수박은 더 크고 단단해져서 지역 슈퍼마켓까지의 배송이 더 수월해졌다.

그러나, 더 많은 수박을 수확하기 위한 고군분투 끝에 한 가지를 잃었다. 아무도 맛을 고려하지 않는 것 같다. 러시아의 과학자 알렉시스 포르그브는 오늘날 우리가 볼 수 있는 더 크고 더 예쁜 수박은 수년 전에 판매된 수박과 견줄 수 없다고 말한다. "더 큰 예쁜 껍데기를 만들기 위해 수박의 달콤함이 크게 희생되었습니다."라고 그는 말한다.

수박을 수확하는 방식의 변화는 천천히 그리고 점차적으로 나타났다. 포르그브 박사는 과학적 발전의 연속이 수박의 맛을 천천히 감소시켰다고 설명한다. 맛의 감소가 그렇게 장기간 동안 발생했기 때문에 소비자가 차이를 구별할 수 없을 것이다. 소비자들은 결국 수박이 주는 단맛을 잊어버렸을 수도 있다.

포르그브 박사는 현재 우리가 즐기게 된 크기와 모양의 발전을 유지하면서 맛을 다시 수박에 삽입하는 프로젝트를 진행하고 있다. "묶음 당 수박 몇 개를 적게 사용하면 더 좋은 맛을 내는 데 드는 비용이 적게 듭니다."라고 그는 말한다. 포르그브 박사는 매우 인기있는 과학적 번식 방법과는 다르게 자연적 번식 방법의 사용을 지지한다. 그는 자신의 초기 노력이 큰 가능성을 보여준 것이라고 말한다.

어휘 consumer 소비자 demand 수요 continue 계속되다 increase 증가하다 export 수출하다 take advantage of 이용하다 advances 진보, 발전 plant-breeding 식물 육종 harvest 수확 last 지속되다 up to ~까지 capable of ~가능한 survive 살아남다 local 지역의 amidst ~속에 produce 생산하다 consider 고려하다 taste 맛 stack up against 견줄만하다 largely 주로 sacrifice 희생시키다 shell 껍질 explain 설명하다 successive 연속인 reduce 감소시키다 flavor 맛 difference 차이점 take place 발생하다 period 기간 eventually 결국 sweetness 달콤함 currently 현재 insert 삽입하다 maintain 유지하다 outward appearance 외관 batch 배치, 묶음 method 방법 as opposed to ~와는 반대로 promise 가능성

164 주제/목적

기사에서 수박의 어떤 특징에 초점을 두고 있는가?
(A) 수박의 크기
(B) 수박의 단단함
(C) 수박의 모양
(D) 수박의 맛

해설 제목에서 수박의 맛과 달콤함이 사라졌음을 언급하고 있으므로 정답은 (D)이다.

165 세부 사항

수박 농작이 어떻게 바뀌었는가?

(A) 수박은 거의 일년 내내 수확된다.
(B) 수박은 실내에서만 자란다.
(C) 수박은 남미에서만 수출된다.
(D) 수박은 기계로만 수확된다.

해설 첫 번째 문단 "Taking advantage of scientific advances in plant-breeding, watermelon farmers now enjoy a longer harvest season that lasts up to 11 months, ~."에서 보면 수확기가 11개월까지 늘어났음을 알 수 있으므로 답은 (A)이다.

166 Not/True 확인

포르고브 박사에 대해 명시된 내용은 무엇인가?
(A) 그는 현재 가나에서 살고 있다.
(B) 그는 식물 육종을 실험하고 있다.
(C) 그는 수박 농작의 과학적 발전을 담당했다.
(D) 그는 수박에 알레르기가 있다.

해설 마지막 문단을 보면 "Dr. Porgov is currently working on a project to reinsert the flavor back into watermelons, while maintaining the advances in the size and outward appearance we have come to enjoy." 현재 수박의 맛을 예전처럼 살리기 위한 프로젝트를 연구 중인 것으로 나오고 있으므로 정답은 (B)이다.

167 문장 삽입

[1], [2], [3] 및 [4]로 표시된 위치 중 다음 문장이 가장 적합한 곳은 어디인가?
"수박을 수확하는 방식의 변화는 천천히 그리고 점차적으로 나타났다."
(A) [1]
(B) [2]
(C) [3]
(D) [4]

해설 3번의 바로 다음 문장에서 "Dr. Porgov explains that each successive round of scientific advances slowly reduced the watermelon flavor." 수박의 맛이 천천히 감소했다고 말하고 있으므로 해당 문장이 들어갈 위치로는 (C)가 적합하다.

[168-171] 온라인 채팅

그레이스 맨시니: 레이첼, 로버트, 저는 지금 Thacher Corporation으로 가서 새로운 제조 공장의 설계에 대해 논의하려고 하는데 공장 모형을 사무실에 두고 왔다는 것을 알았어요. 둘 중 한 명이 저 좀 도와주시겠어요? [2.22 P.M.]

레이첼 그랜트: 네트워크에 모델을 업로드했어요? 컴퓨터를 사용해서 고객에게 모델을 보여줄 수 있나요? [2:25 P.M.]

그레이스 맨시니: 스크린 샷은 효과 없을 거예요. 그리고 컴퓨터 화면에서는 모든 각도에서 디자인의 세부 사항을 이해하는 것은 어려워요. [2:28 P.M.]

레이첼 그랜트: 그러면 사무실로 돌아와서 모델을 가져가야 해요. [2:28 P.M.]

로버트 젠슨: 제가 도울 수 있을 것 같네요. 저는 지금 Conrad 사무실에 있어요. 다행히 여기에 당신이 만든 복제 모델이 있거든요. [2:29 P.M.]

그레이스 맨시니: 좋아요! 근처 어디에서 만날 수 있을까요? 지금 Conrad 사무실에서 약 20분 거리에 있는 메인 거리에 주차했어요. [2:30 P.M.]

로버트 젠슨: 문제 없어요. 근처에 Conrad 마트 보여요? [2:31 P.M.]

레이첼 그랜트: 로버트, 고객 사무실에서 그레이스를 만나는 게 어때요? [2:32 P.M.]

로버트 젠슨: 저는 사실 오늘 오후에 고객 회의를 위해 사무실로 돌아갈 예정이었어요. Thacher Corporation으로 갈 시간이 없어요. [2:33 P.M.]

그레이스 맨시니: 괜찮아요. Conrad 마트가 보입니다. 5분 내로 그곳에 갈 수 있어요. 서두를 수 있어요? [2:34 P.M.]

로버트 젠슨: 곧 가겠습니다. [2:35 P.M.]

어휘 on the way ~하는 중에 discuss 논의하다 manufacturing 제조 plant 공장 notice 알아 차리다 upload 업로드하다 client 고객 appreciate 고맙게 여기다, 인식하다 details 세부 사항 then 그 다음에, 그러면 grab 붙잡다 duplicate 똑같은, 사본의 nearby 근처 actually 사실상 head 가다, 향하다

168 추론/암시

맨시니 씨는 누구일 것 같은가?
(A) Thacher Corporation의 부장
(B) Conrad 마트의 출납원
(C) 젠슨 씨의 고객
(D) 디자인 회사의 직원

해설 첫 번째 대화 문장에서 맨시니 씨가 "I am on my way now to Thacher Corporation to discuss the designs for their new manufacturing plant and just noticed that I left the plant model in my office." 고객과 제조 공장 디자인을 의논하기 위해 가는 중이라고 했기 때문에 (D)가 답이다.

169 의도 파악

오후 2시 28분에, 맨시니 씨가 "스크린 샷은 효과 없을 거예요"라고 쓴 의미는 무엇인가?
(A) 그녀는 고객에게 실제 모델을 보여 주고 싶어 한다.
(B) 그녀는 사무실 네트워크에 접근하는 방법을 모른다.
(C) 그녀는 오늘 오후 사무실에 오지 않을 것이다.
(D) 그녀는 공장 모델을 사무실 네트워크에 업로드하지 못했다.

해설 인용 표현 바로 앞 문장에서 "Could you show the client the model using a computer?" 컴퓨터를 사용해서 고객에게 보여줄 수 있는지에 대한 응답으로, 컴퓨터로 보여줄 수 없고 실제 모델을 보여줘야 한다는 의미로 답은 (A)이다.

170 세부 사항

맨시니 씨는 어디에 있는가?
(A) Thacher Corporation에
(B) 그녀의 차 안에
(C) Conrad 사무실에
(D) 컴퓨터 앞에

해설 2시 30분에 "Right now, I'm parked on Main Street, about 20 minutes from the Conrad office." 지금 Main 거리에 주차했다고 했으므로 답은 (B)이다.

171 세부 사항

젠슨 씨는 무엇을 하겠다고 제안하는가?
(A) Thacher Corporation에 가기
(B) 맨시니 씨에게 새로운 모델 만들어 주기
(C) 맨시니 씨에게 물건 가져다주기
(D) 회의 일정 다시 잡기

해설 2시 29분에 "Good thing you made a duplicate model to keep here." 젠슨 씨가 복사본이 여기에 있다고 언급했고 맨시니 씨에게 복사본을 가져다주겠다고 말했으므로 정답은 (C)이다.

[172-175] 기사

Dragon Textiles의 새로운 공장 개장

베이징 (3월 17일) — 베이징에 본사를 두고 있는 세계 최대 의류 제조업체 중 하나인 Dragon Textiles는 6월 8일 베트남 Danang에 최신 제조 시설의 개장을 발표했다. 새로운 시설은 Phoenix라는 이름으로 운영될 예정이며, 지역 관리팀이 전적으로 관리할 것이다.

새로운 공장은 Dragon Textiles의 급속한 성장을 상징하며, 아시아 전역에 날개를 펼치고 있다. Dragon Textiles의 CEO인 사이먼 웡은 "베트남의 제조 시설은 우리가 목표로 하는 시장에 보다 쉽게 접근할 수 있게 해줄 것입니다. 이 새로운 위치로 인해, 우리는 이 지역의 경쟁 업체와 비교해서 우리의 입지를 더욱 강화하게 될 것입니다."라고 말했다. 웡 씨는 Danang 공장의 취임식에 회사의 핵심 임원들과 함께 참석할 것이다.

Dragon Textiles는 거의 10년 전에 베이징에서 시작했다. Dragon이 급속도로 확장되면서 중국의 유명 의류 브랜드와 힘을 합쳤다. 그러나 중국의 전체 매출액은 지난해에 정점을 찍고 안정세를 유지하고 있다. 회사는 현지의 의류 생산이 비용을 절감하고 수익을 높일 것이라고 확신하고 있다.

Dragon Textiles은 중국의 Cheng Du에 두 개의 제조 공장을 가지고 있다. 웡 씨는 그의 회사가 인도네시아 정부와 다른 공장의 건설을 협상하고 있다고 언급했다. 그는 새 공장이 내년 말까지 가동될 것이라고 확신했다.

어휘 garment 옷 manufacturer 제조업체 headquartered in ~에 본사를 둔 announce 발표하다 opening 개장, 개업 facility 시설 operate 운영하다 entirely 전체적으로 local 지역의 management 운영 symbolize 상징화하다 rapid 급격한 growth 성장 spread 퍼지다 wing 날개 throughout 전체에 걸쳐 state 언급하다 allow 허용하다 access to ~로의 접근 target 목표, 대상 location 위치, 지점 strengthen 강화시키다 position 위치 competitor 경쟁자 in the region 지역에서 attend 참석하다 inauguration ceremony 취임식 along with ~와 함께 key 주요한 executive 임원 rapidly 급격히 expand 확장하다 overall 전반적인 plateau (안정 상태를) 유지하다 reach 다다르다 peak 최고조 save 절약하다 cost 비용 boost 북돋우다, 신장시키다 be in the process 진행중이다 negotiate 협상하다 construction 건설 government 정부 express 표현하다 confidence 확신 up and running 제대로 작동 중인

172 Not/True 확인

Dragon Textiles에 대해 명시된 것은?
(A) 유럽에 본사를 두고 있다.
(B) 이미 베트남에 공장 하나를 가지고 있다.
(C) 동남 아시아로 확장하기를 원한다.
(D) 3년 동안만 사업을 했다.

해설 두 번째 문단 "The new plant symbolizes the rapid growth of Dragon Textiles, as it continues to spread its wings throughout Asia."에서 아시아 전역에 날개를 펼치고 있다고 언급하므로 정답은 (C)이다.

173 Not/True 확인

웡 씨에 대해 명시된 것은 무엇인가?
(A) 그는 직접 Danang 공장을 운영할 것이다.
(B) 그는 회사를 유럽으로 확장할 계획이다.
(C) 그는 베트남에서 대부분의 시간을 보낸다.
(D) 6월에 Danang에 갈 계획이다.

해설 첫 번째 문단에서 6월 8일에 공장이 개장할 것이라고 언급되어 있고, 두 번째 문단 마지막 "Mr. Wong will attend the inauguration ceremony of the Danang plant, along with key company executives."에서 취임식에 참석할 것이라고 했기 때문에 답은 (D)이다.

174 세부 사항

Dragon Textiles은 다음 생산 시설을 어디에 건설할 것인가?
(A) 베트남에
(B) 인도네시아에
(C) 중국에
(D) 태국에

해설 미래 계획은 보통 마지막 부분에 나온다. 마지막 문단 "Mr. Wong noted his company is in the process of negotiating the construction of another plant with the

Indonesian government."에서 인도네시아 정부와 공장 건설을 협상 중이라고 언급하므로 정답은 (B)이다.

175 문장 삽입

[1], [2], [3] 및 [4]로 표시된 위치 중 다음 문장이 들어가기에 가장 적합한 곳은?
"이 새로운 위치로 인해, 우리는 이 지역의 경쟁 업체와 비교해서 우리의 입지를 더욱 강화하게 될 것입니다."
(A) [1]
(B) [2]
(C) [3]
(D) [4]

해설 앞에서 베트남의 제조 시설을 언급했으므로 이로 인해 기대되는 긍정적인 효과를 덧붙여 언급하는 [1]이 자연스럽다.

[176-180] 이메일 & 탑승권

수신: 마크 브라벨 <mvrabel@konoco.com>
발신: 조던 페이지 <jpage@zoomrailways.com>
날짜: 11월 12일
제목: 귀하의 기차표 예매

브라벨 씨에게,

휴일 때문에 11월은 가장 바쁜 달 중 하나입니다. 내일 보스턴에서 마이애미까지 가는 ZR 32 열차의 승객 수는 엄청날 것입니다. 특별 여행 상품권으로 다른 시간대에 출발하는 열차로 교환할 승객을 찾고 있습니다. 상품권은 6개월 동안 유효하며, 최대 500달러까지 Zoom Railways 기차 티켓으로 사용할 수 있습니다.

실례를 무릅쓰고 귀하가 마이애미로 이동할 수 있는 대체 날짜와 시간을 검색했습니다. 아래에서 언급된 첫 번째 옵션은 원래 출발일과 동일한 날에 출발하지만 워싱턴 DC에서 잠깐 경유합니다.

ZR 22	보스턴	11월 21일 오후 3시 40분	워싱턴 DC	11월 21일 오후 6시 55분
ZR 23	워싱턴 DC	11월 21일 오후 7시 45분	마이애미	11월 21일 오후 11시

또 다른 옵션은 마이애미로 바로 가지만, 하루 뒤에 마이애미로 떠납니다.

ZR 33	보스턴	11월 22일 오후 2시 5분	마이애미	11월 22일 오후 8시 15분

열차를 바꿀 의향이 있으면 예약번호 1-855-338-4891로 전화 주십시오. 원래 예약을 유지하려면 출발하기 전에 웹 사이트(www.zoomrailways.com/reservations)에 로그인하여 여행 정보를 등록하십시오.

항상 그랬듯이, Zoom Railways로 여행해 주셔서 대단히 감사드립니다.

조던 페이지
고객 서비스 담당
Zoom Railways

탑승권			
기차	날짜	탑승 시간	출발 시간
ZR 33	11월 22일	오후 1:45	오후 2:05
출발	도착	승강장	열차/좌석
보스턴	마이애미	3B	CAR 7/SEAT 16A

다른 열차 7의 승객들과 함께 차량에 순서대로 탑승하십시오.
반입 수하물에는 공간이 제한되어 있습니다. 승객은 휴대용 가방 하나를 열차에 가져올 수 있습니다. 다른 가방들을 모두 맡겨야 합니다.

어휘 holiday 휴일   expect 기대하다, 예상하다   seek 찾다   volunteer 지원자   passenger 승객   be willing to 기꺼이 ~하다   switch 바꾸다   depart 출발하다   in exchange for ~을 받는 대가로   voucher 바우처   valid 유효한   redeem (상품권 등을) 현금(상품)으로 바꾸다   up to ~까지   take the liberty of ~ing 실례를 무릅 쓰고 하다   potential 잠재적인   alternative 대체 가능한   layover 도중 하차   directly 바로, 직접   reservation 예약   hotline 직통 전화   prior to ~전에   register 등록하다   board 탑승하다   in order of ~의 순서로   space 공간   limit 제한하다   baggage 수하물, 짐   carry-on 들고 들어갈 수 있는

176 주제/목적

이메일의 목적은 무엇인가?
(A) 승객의 열차 변경을 권장하기 위해
(B) 예약 정보를 확인하기 위해
(C) 예약된 티켓의 지불을 요청하기 위해
(D) 승객에게 새 보안 정책을 알리기 위해

해설 글의 목적은 대부분 첫 부분에 나온다. 첫 번째 문장 "we are seeking volunteers among our ticketed passengers who might be willing to switch to a train departing at a different time in exchange for a special travel voucher."에서 티켓을 변경해 줄 지원자를 찾고 있으므로 정답은 (A)이다.

177 Not/True 확인

상품권에 대해 명시되어 있는 것은 무엇인가?
(A) 아무 열차 티켓으로 사용될 수 있다.
(B) 유효 기간이 있다.
(C) 상품권을 제시하는 사람은 아무나 사용할 수 있다.
(D) 가격은 브라벨 씨가 구입한 티켓과 같다.

해설 이메일 첫 번째 문단 마지막 문장 "The voucher will be valid for six months and may be redeemed for any train ticket with Zoom Railways valued up to $500."에서 6개월 동안 유효하다고 언급하므로 정답은 (B)이다.

178 추론/암시 (연계)

브라벨 씨는 이메일을 받은 후 무엇을 했을 가능성이 가장 높은가?
(A) 열차에 바로 탑승하기
(B) 웹 사이트에 로그인하기
(C) 이메일에 답장 보내기
(D) 예약 핫라인으로 전화하기

해설 첫 번째 지문 이메일에서 "If you are willing to switch trains, please call our reservation hotline at 1-855-338-4891." 열차 시간을 바꿀 의향이 있다면 연락을 달라고 했고, 두 번째 지문 탑승권을 보면 열차 번호가 ZR 33으로 출발 날짜가 바뀐 것을 알 수 있으므로 정답은 (D)이다.

179 Not/True 확인

탑승권은 브라벨 씨의 기차에 대해 무엇을 명시하는가?
(A) 워싱턴 DC에서 출발할 것이다.
(B) 오전에 출발할 것이다.
(C) 승객은 예정된 순서대로 탑승할 것이다.
(D) 승객은 수하물을 들고 탑승할 수 없다.

해설 탑승권을 보면 "Board in order of cars with other Car 7 passengers."라고 언급되어 있으므로 순서대로 탑승해야 한다는 것을 알 수 있다. 따라서 정답은 (C)이다.

180 세부 사항 (연계)

브라벨 씨는 최종 도착지에 몇 시에 도착할 예정인가?
(A) 오후 6시 55분.
(B) 오후 8시 15분
(C) 오후 11시
(D) 오후 2시 5분

해설 탑승권 기차 번호가 ZR 33이고, 첫 번째 이메일에 ZR 33 시간표를 보면 11월 22일 오후 8시 15분에 도착함을 알 수 있다. 따라서 답은 (B)이다.

[181-185] 광고 & 양식

디지털 시대의 마케팅에 관한 비즈니스 세미나

더 넓은 범위의 새로운 고객을 확보할 수 있는 방법을 모색하고 있습니까? 새로운 온라인 소셜 네트워킹 사이트에 익숙해지기 원하십니까? 그렇다면 www.empoweredbusiness.edu를 방문하여 모든 종류의 디지털 미디어를 사용하여 고객에게 마케팅하는 방법을 논의하는 온라인 세미나에 등록할 수 있습니다. 각자 자신의 사업을 운영하는 전문가 패널에 온라인으로 접근할 수 있으며, 그들이 최신 트렌드에 대해 이야기하고 온라인 프로필을 작성하는 방법에 대해 설명할 겁니다. 라이브 세미나는 3월 14일 월요일 오후 1시 30분에서 3시 30분까지 진행됩니다. (동부 표준시)

세미나는 세 가지 프레젠테이션으로 구성됩니다.
• 마크 제이콥스의 "온라인 프로필 작성에 대한 첫걸음"
• 산제이 굽타의 "신세대의 마음을 움직일 가장 인기 있는 온라인 도구"
• 제니퍼 로드리게스의 "신세대를 향한 마케팅: 최신 동향"

온라인으로 등록할 수 없다면 rcassidy@empoweredbusiness.edu로 3월 11일 금요일까지 로저 캐시디에게 이메일을 보내십시오.

라이브 세미나에 참석할 수 없지만 관심이 있는 경우, 온라인 세미나 라이브러리를 방문하십시오. 모든 세미나는 방송 후 48시간 이내에 시청할 수 있습니다.

---

www.empoweredbusiness.edu/seminar3912/evaluation-form

렌 나카야마 씨, 디지털 시대의 마케팅 세미나에 참석해 주셔서 감사합니다. 다음 설문조사를 작성하기 위해 시간을 할애해 주시면 대단히 감사하겠습니다. 이 정보는 우리가 서비스를 지속적으로 개선하는 데 도움이 될 것입니다.

1점(매우 불만족)에서 5점(매우 만족)까지, 다음을 평가해 주세요.

전반적인 세미나 주제	5
각 프레젠테이션의 질	4
유용한 정보의 양	4

세미나에서 가장 좋았던 점은 무엇입니까?

굽타 씨의 프레젠테이션은 제 업무에 특히 유용했습니다. 저는 최신 소셜 네트워킹 사이트에 빠지지 않도록 참아 왔지만, 굽타 씨는 가장 관련성이 높은 정보를 간결하게 요약하고 이를 가장 잘 활용할 수 있도록 해주었습니다.

앞으로 있을 이벤트에 대해서 개선되었으면 하는 점이 있습니까?

세미나에 참가할 수 있는 대체 시간이 있다면 정말 좋겠어요. 제가 로그인했을 때 주어진 시간은 제 사무실이 있는 도쿄는 새벽 2시 30분이어서 실제로 불편했습니다.

어휘 become familiar with ~에 익숙해지다   market 광고하다   manner 방법   expert 전문가   run 운영하다   the latest 가장 최근의   trend 추세, 경향   take place 발생하다   consist of ~로 구성되다   be unable to ~할 수 없다   register 등록하다   broadcast 방송하다   greatly 매우   appreciate 고맙게 여기다   complete 작성하다   improve 향상시키다   scale 등급   dissatisfied 불만족스러워 하는   rate 등급을 매기다   overall 전반적인   particularly 특별히   resist 거부하다   get caught up 사로잡히다   succinctly 간단하게   summarize 요약하다   relevant 관련된   alternate 대체 가능한   available ~가능한   participate 참석하다   actually 사실상   inconvenient 불편한   located 위치한

181 Not/True 확인

세미나에 대해 명시된 것은 무엇인가?
(A) 2일 동안 생방송으로 방송될 것이다.
(B) 온라인으로 방송될 것이다.
(C) 운영 기법에만 초점을 둘 것이다.
(D) 북미 거주자만 이용 가능하다.

해설 첫 번째 지문 마지막 부분 "If you are not able to attend the live seminar but are still interested, you can visit our online seminar library. All seminars are available for viewing within 48 hours of broadcast."에서 온라인 세미나 라이브러리가 있고 방송으로 볼 수 있다고 언급되어 있으므로 정답은 (B)이다.

182 세부 사항

광고에 따르면, 독자들은 왜 캐시디 씨에게 연락해야 하는가?
(A) 등록을 취소하기 위해
(B) 세미나에 접속하기 위해
(C) 설문 조사에 참여하기 위해
(D) 발표자들에 대한 정보를 얻기 위해

해설 첫 번째 지문 "If you are unable to register online, please e-mail Roger Cassidy ~"에서 온라인 등록이 안 될 경우, 이메일로 연락하라고 나와 있으므로 정답은 (B)이다.

183 Not/True 확인

발표자들에 대해 사실은 무엇인가?
(A) 자신의 사업을 운영한 경험이 있다.
(B) 모두 같은 회사에서 일한다.
(C) 예전에 다양한 주제에 대해 수많은 세미나에서 발표했다.
(D) 모두 미국에 살고 있다.

해설 첫 번째 지문에서 "You will have online access to our panel of experts, each of whom runs his or her own business, who will talk about the latest trends and how to go about building your online profile."라며 각각 자신의 사업을 운영하는 전문가 패널들이라고 소개가 나오므로 정답은 (A)이다.

184 추론/암시 (연계)

나카야마 씨에 대해 암시된 것은 무엇인가?
(A) 그는 세미나에 참석할 수 없었다.
(B) 그는 다음 세미나 행사에서 발표하고 싶어 한다.
(C) 그는 굽타 씨와 전에 함께 일했다.
(D) 그는 온라인 도구에 대해 듣는 것을 즐겼다.

해설 두 번째 지문 나카야마 씨가 쓴 설문조사 중 두 번째 박스에서 "Mr. Gupta's presentation was particularly useful for my line of work." 굽타 씨의 발표가 유용했다고 칭찬했다. 첫 번째 지문에서 굽타 씨의 강의는 "The Most Popular Online Tools to Reach the New Generation"이기 때문에 그가 online tools에 대해 들었음을 알 수 있다. 따라서 정답은 (D)이다.

185 세무 사항

나카야마 씨는 세미나의 어떤 측면이 변경되길 제안하는가?
(A) 프레젠테이션의 수
(B) 세미나 주제
(C) 일정
(D) 위치

해설 두 번째 지문 마지막 문단에서 "I would really like it if there were alternate times available for participating in the seminar."라며 다른 시간대가 있었으면 좋겠다고 했으므로 정답은 (C)이다.

[186-190] 임대 계약서 & 양식 & 이메일

SEVEN LOCKS MANAGEMENT 사무소 임대 계약

37 Seven Locks Road, Unit 12
Bethesda, Maryland 20810

임대 약관
귀하는 3월 1일부터 2월 28일까지 12개월 동안 매월 1일까지 1만 4천 달러의 월세를 내며 사무실을 임대하는 것에 동의합니다. 연체료로는 1,000 달러의 벌금이 부과되며 이는 보증금에서 공제될 수 있습니다. 계약 기간이 끝나기 전에 임대 계약을 취소하면 1,000달러의 벌금이 부과되고 보증금에서 공제됩니다. 집세에는 전기, 수도 및 난방을 포함한 모든 공공요금이 포함됩니다. 인터넷 연결 설치와 관련 비용은 귀하의 책임입니다. 또한 귀하의 사무실 바로 앞에 5개의 주차 공간이 임대료에 포함되어 있습니다. 추가 주차 공간이 필요하면 매월 200달러로 임대할 수 있습니다. 또 다른 옵션은 우리 건물에 인접한 주차장에 주차하는 것입니다.

보증금
귀하는 2월 14일에 1개월분의 집세와 동일한 보증금을 지불했습니다. 보증금은 계약 기간 만료 15일 이내에 반환됩니다. 관리팀은 임대 기간 전후에 사무실 공간을 점검합니다. 임대 기간이 시작되기 전에 우리가 발견하는 청소 또는 유지 보수 문제는 문서화되어 사본이 귀하에게 제공됩니다. 임대 기간 이후에 발견되는 문제는 귀하의 보증금에서 차감됩니다.

SEVEN LOCKS MANAGEMENT 점검 양식

일시: 2월 19일
주소: 37 Seven Locks Road, Unit 12

검사에 대한 의견:
모든 설비와 장비는 정상적으로 작동합니다. 입구 근처와 식품 저장실 옆의 카펫에 약간의 변색이 있습니다. 또한, 식품 저장실 벽면의 페인트 중 일부가 떨어져 나갔습니다. Seven Locks Management는 2월 28일까지 이 문제를 해결하도록 준비할 것입니다.

마이클 멘데즈   존 킴
관리자   사무실 세입자

수신: mmendez@sevenlocks.com
발신: jkim32@kmail.net
날짜: 1월 21일
제목: 보증금
첨부: sevenlocks/inspection.form.pdf

멘데즈 씨,
몇 주 전에 12호에 대한 임대 계약을 종료했고, 저는 Seven Locks Management로부터 보증금을 받았습니다. 저는 1,000달러의 공제를 예상했지만, 2,000달러를 추가로 공제했다는 사실에 놀랐습니다. 첨부된 편지에 페인트 작업에 대한 2,000달러의 공제가 있었음을 언급했는데, 필자가 사무실로 이사하기 전에 카펫 청소는 하겠다고 했지만 식품 저장실은 다시 칠하지 않는다고 했습니다. 페인트 칠을 한 적이 없으므로, 2,000달러를 환불해 주기 바랍니다.

존 킴

어휘 **agree to** ~에 동의하다　**rent** 임대료　**late payment** 연체료　**be subject to** ~의 대상이다　**penalty** 벌금　**deduct** 공제하다　**security deposit** 보증금　**lease** 임대　**include** 포함시키다　**utility** 공과금　**set up** 설치하다　**associate** 관련시키다　**fee** 요금　**parking space** 주차 공간　**directly** 바로, 직접　**additional** 추가적인　**adjacent to** ~와 가까운　**pay** 지불하다　**equal to** ~와 동등한　**agreement term** 계약 기간　**inspect** 검사하다, 조사하다　**period** 기간　**document** 문서화하다　**issue** 문제　**spot** 발견하다　**comment** 의견　**upon** ~에 관한　**facility** 시설　**equipment** 장비　**discoloration** 변색　**pantry** 식품 저장실　**chip off** 부서지다, 떨어져 나가다　**arrange** 정리하다, 마련하다　**terminate** 종결시키다　**accompanying** 첨부한　**note** 언급하다　**attached** 첨부된　**recall** 회상하다　**prior to** ~전에

186 Not/True 확인
임대 계약에 대해 명시된 것은 무엇인가?
(A) 사무실은 가구가 완전히 비치되어 있다.
(B) 임대 계약에는 주차 공간이 포함되어 있지 않다.
(C) 계약 기간은 10개월이다.
(D) 세입자는 인터넷 서비스를 별도로 지불해야 한다.

해설 첫 번째 지문인 임대 계약서에 "You are responsible for setting up any Internet connections and associated fees."라고 언급되어 있으므로 정답은 (D)이다.

187 Not/True 확인
Seven Locks Office Building에 대해 사실인 것은 무엇인가?
(A) 주차장 옆에 있다.
(B) 정확히 12개 유닛이 있다.
(C) 지난달에 막 보수가 끝났다.
(D) 내년에 새로운 곳으로 이전할 것이다.

해설 첫 번째 지문 임대 계약서에 "Another option is to park in the parking garage adjacent to our building." 건물 근처에 있는 주차장에 주차할 수 있다고 말하고 있으므로 답은 (A)이다.

188 동의어 찾기
임대 계약서에서, 첫 번째 단락, 두 번째 줄의 "subject to"와 의미상 가장 가까운 것은?
(A) ~에게 배우다
(B) ~을 책임지다
(C) ~에 의해 검사 받다
(D) ~에 관해 알다

해설 subject to의 뜻은 '~의 대상이다'라는 뜻으로 이와 의미상 가장 가까운 것은 '~을 책임지다'라는 뜻의 (B)이다.

189 세부 사항 (연계)
왜 킴 씨는 1,000달러의 벌금이 부과될 것으로 예상했는가?
(A) 추가로 주차 공간을 빌렸다.
(B) 임대료를 늦게 냈다.
(C) 임대 기간 동안 사무실을 손상시켰다.
(D) 임대 기간이 만료되기 전에 이사했다.

해설 임대 계약서에 "If you cancel the lease before the end of the term, you will be subject to a penalty of $1,000, also to be deducted from your security deposit."라고 기간 전에 임대를 취소할 경우 1,000달러의 벌금이 있다고 언급되어 있다. 그리고 이메일에서 "I terminated my rental agreement ~ a couple of weeks ago"에서 계약 종료 시점이 이메일 발신일로 역추적했을 때 계약기간 전임을 알 수 있다.

190 세부 사항 (연계)
점검 양식 내용 중 Seven Locks Management는 무엇을 지키지 않았는가?
(A) 카펫이 올바르게 청소되지 않았다.
(B) 식품 저장실이 칠해지지 않았다.
(C) 관리자가 건물을 조사하지 않았다.
(D) 식품 저장실이 다른 색으로 칠해졌다.

해설 점검 양식에서 식품 저장실의 떨어져 나간 페인트 부분을 칠해 주겠다고 했지만 마지막 지문인 이메일에서 알 수 있듯이, 다시 칠해 준 적이 없으므로 청구된 금액을 줄 수 없다고 주장하고 있다. 따라서 답은 (B)이다.

[191-195] 웹 페이지 & 양식 & 게시글

세계 조류 관찰자 포럼 규정

1. 우리의 포럼은 글의 길이를 제한하지 않지만 조류와 조류의 서식지에만 초점을 맞출 것을 요청합니다. 조류 및 조류 관련 장비 판매에 관해 논의하는 게시물을 적극적으로 찾아 삭제할 것입니다.

2. 모든 게시물은 "조류 유형 (또는 간단한 설명) - 서식지" 형식을 따르는 제목과 쌍을 이루어야 합니다. 우리 회원들은 전세계에서 올리기 때문에 구체적이고 간략해야 한다는 것을 기억하십시오.

좋은 제목 예시: "붉은 꼬리 로빈 - 핀란드 헬싱키"
나쁜 제목 예시: "와우! - 이 새를 봐!"

3. 서면 설명은 때때로 특정 새를 정확하게 확인하기에 충분하지 않을 수 있으므로 모든 게시물에 적어도 사진 한 장을 포함시키는 것이 좋습니다.

4. 활동적인 포럼 회원이 최근에 증가했습니다. 24시간 이내에 게시물을 최대 2개까지만 제한하여 최대한 효율적으로 웹 사이트를 운영할 수 있도록 하십시오. 우리 새 전문가들은 며칠 이내에 귀하의 모든 질문에 대해 답변하도록 열심히 노력하고 있습니다.

세계 조류 관찰자 포럼
회원 등록 양식

이름: *개빈 제닝스*   E-mail: *gjennings@sandmail.com*

조류 관련 분야에서 공식 교육을 받았습니까? *조류학 박사 학위*
가장 최근에 어디에서 일했습니까? *뉴욕 주립 대학교*

회원으로 등록 시 정식 교육이나 현재 고용 상태는 불필요합니다. 우리는 게시물에 대한 답변을 게시할 때 전문가로 간주될 수 있는 회원을 구별하기 위해 이 정보를 사용합니다.

World Bird Watchers Forum에서 정기적으로 이메일을 받고 싶습니다. 예 (✓) 아니오 ( )

개인 정보 정책: 세계 조류 관찰자 포럼(World Bird Watchers Forum)은 안전한 웹 사이트입니다. 회원 정보는 제3자와 공유되거나 판매되지 않습니다.

신규 포럼 게시물 회원 이름: 개빈 제닝스
제목: 이 새의 이름이 뭔지 알려주세요.   날짜: 6월 7일

저는 열한한 조류 관찰자입니다. 올해 초에 은퇴한 후, 저는 브라질로 여행을 갔습니다. 그곳에서 가장 아름다운 점무늬 새를 보았습니다. 검은 반점과 하얀 가슴이 있는 진한 빨간색 새였습니다. 나는 그것이 spatuletail일지도 모른다고 생각했습니다. 그러나 제 이전 학생들 중 한 명이 spatuletail는 빨간 꼬리를 가지고 있다고 지적했습니다. 제가 보았던 새는 분명히 검은 꼬리를 가지고 있었습니다. 누가 이 새 이름을 알려줄 수 있습니까?

첨부된 사진을 보십시오.

_____

Spotted_Bird_05.30

어휘 limit 제한하다 length 길이 posting 게시물 discussion 토론 be focused on ~에 초점을 맞추다 habitat 서식지 aggressively 적극적으로 seek out 찾다 delete 삭제하다 be paired with ~와 병행하다 subject line 제목 follow 따르다 description 설명 location 위치, 지역 specific 구체적인, 명확한 brief 간략한 insufficient 불충분한 accurately 정확하게 identify 확인하다, 알아보다 encourage 격려하다 at least 적어도 increase 증가 active 적극적인 period 기간 operate 운영하다 efficiency 효율성 expert 전문가 respond to 응답하다 inquiry 질문 formal 공식적인 field 분야 register 등록하다 distinguish 구별하다 be considered 고려되다 privacy policy 개인 보호 정책 secure 안전한 avid 열렬한 retire 은퇴하다 spot 점 chest 가슴 former 과거의, 이전의 tail 꼬리 distinct 뚜렷한 attach 첨부하다

191 Not/True 확인
웹 페이지는 포럼에 대해 무엇을 명시하는가?
(A) 해외 제출물을 허용한다.
(B) 생장과 관련된 토론을 특징으로 한다.
(C) 회원들은 등록비를 내야 한다.
(D) 게시물은 한 문단 이상이면 안 된다.

해설 첫 번째 지문 2번에서 "Our members post from all over the world, so please remember to be specific and brief."라고 전 세계 모든 멤버들로부터 게시물을 받는 것을 알 수 있으므로 답은 (A)이다.

192 세부 사항
세계 조류 관찰자 포럼은 회원들에게 무엇을 약속하는가?
(A) 질문 당일에 응답한다.
(B) 조류 관련 일자리를 제공한다.
(C) 등록비를 절대 올리지 않을 것이다.
(D) 개인 정보를 보호한다.

해설 두 번째 지문에서 "Privacy Policy: World Bird Watchers Forum is a secure Web site; member information will not be shared with or sold to third parties." 개인 정보 정책을 통해 (D)가 답임을 알 수 있다.

193 주제/목적
제닝스 씨는 왜 게시물을 올렸는가?
(A) 다른 회원에게 전문가로서 조언하기 위해
(B) 다른 회원 게시물에 응답하기 위해
(C) 추측에 대한 확인 설명을 찾기 위해
(D) 새 모이 주기 설명을 요청하기 위해

해설 세 번째 지문 게시물의 내용을 보면 확실하지 않은 새의 이름을 일고 싶어 한다는 것을 알 수 있으므로 정답은 (C)이다.

194 세부 사항 (연계)
제닝스 씨는 포럼 규칙을 어떻게 지키지 않았는가?
(A) 판매 목적으로 새에 관한 글을 올렸다.

(B) 게시물에 사진을 첨부했다.
(C) 그의 게시물은 길이 요건을 충족시키지 못했다.
(D) 그의 글 제목이 너무 일반적이다.

해설 첫 번째 지문 웹 페이지에서 "All postings should be paired with a subject line that follows the format "bird type (or short description) - location" Our members post from all over the world, so please remember to be specific and brief." 제목 규정을 언급했으나, 세 번째 지문 게시물에 쓰인 제목을 보면 "Please someone help me name this bird"으로 썼기 때문에 정답은 (D)이다.

195 추론/암시 (연계)

제닝스 씨에 대한 사실일 것 같은 것은 무엇인가?
(A) 대학에서 수업을 한 적이 있다.
(B) 브라질로 이사 갈 예정이다.
(C) 현재 교사로 일하는 중이다.
(D) 오랫동안 포럼 회원이었다.

해설 두 번째 지문인 양식에서 박사 학위를 가지고 있음을 알 수 있고, 세 번째 지문 이메일 "I thought it might be a spatuletail, but one of my former students pointed out that spatuletails have red tails, ~"에서 학생 중 한 명이 지적했다는 내용이 나오므로 정답은 (A)이다.

[196-200] 구인 광고 & 정보 & 이메일

직책: *파트타임 언어 강사* 지역: *Northern Virginia(북버지니아)*

워싱턴 DC에서 남서쪽으로 약 25분 거리에 위치한 Morton Industries는 직원들을 대상으로 강의를 진행할 자격을 갖춘 언어 강사를 찾고 있습니다.
관심 있는 언어는 중국어(표준 중국어), 일본어 및 한국어입니다. 관심 있는 강사는 매주 평일 오전 9시 30분 전에 수업을 할 수 있어야 합니다.
수업의 형식과 구조는 강사에게 달려 있습니다. 경력에 상응하는 시간당 요금을 지불할 것입니다.
신청하시려면 humanresources@mortonind.com로 "언어 강사"라는 제목의 이메일을 보내주십시오.
귀하의 전자 메일에는 이력서와 최소한 2부의 추천서가 포함되어야 합니다.

Morton Industries
Falls Church Headquarters

9월 언어 수업 일정

저희 어학센터는 월요일부터 금요일, 오전 7시부터 오후 9시까지 운영됩니다. 현재 제공하고 있는 다음 수업에 등록하실 수 있습니다. 여유 자리가 있으면 미리 등록하지 않고 방문하셔서 참석하실 수도 있습니다. 별도로 명시하지 않는 한 모든 수업은 매일 진행됩니다. 수업명은 교실 외부에 게시됩니다.

시간	수업	강사
오전 7시 ~ 오전 8시	기초 일본어	아츠키 마코
오전 8시 ~ 오전 9시 (수요일, 금요일만 가능)	중급 프랑스어	마고 허브스트
오전 11:30 ~ 오후 12:30	중급 스페인어	후안 도밍게스
오후 6:30 ~ 오후 7:30 (월요일, 목요일만 가능)	기초 러시아어	블라디미르 드라고

모든 직원은 Morton Industries 신분증을 사용하여 언어센터에 출입할 수 있습니다. 다른 Morton 지점에서 근무하는 직원도 센터에 출입할 수 있지만 먼저 안내 데스크에서 서명해야 합니다.

수신: Jame Smith, 어학 센터 부장	
발신: 라울 산체스, 운영팀 부장	
일시: 목요일, 9월 27일	
제목: 신규 언어 수업	

이번 달부터 시작하는 새로운 수업 일정에 대한 보고서를 받았습니다. 많은 직원들이 센터를 잘 활용하고 있다는 소식에 매우 기쁩니다. 저는 매우 잘 배우고 있는 직원들로부터 여러 긍정적인 피드백을 받았습니다. 그러나 몇몇 관리자들로부터 몇 가지 의견을 들었습니다. 사실, 한 가지 일반적인 문제를 제기한 매니저와 지금 막 전화를 끊었습니다. 아시다시피, 점심 시간은 한 시간이지만, 점심시간으로 예정된 수업은 한 시간 내내 진행됩니다. 이 수업에 참석하는 직원들은 언어센터로 오고 가는 데 시간을 더 들여야 하며, 점심을 그들 사무실 책상에서 먹어야 합니다. 또한 회의 시간을 계획하는 어려움에 대해 불만이 있었습니다. 가장 간단한 해결책은 점심 시간 수업을 40분으로 줄이는 것입니다. 그게 가능할까요?

다시 말하지만, 언어 프로그램을 계속 유지해 주셔서 감사 드립니다.

라울 산체스
운영팀 부장
Morton Industries, Falls Church Headquarters

어휘 job title 직책 instructor 강사 located 위치한 seek 찾다 qualified 자격을 갖춘 employee 직원 available 가능한 weekday 주중 format 형식 structure 구조 completely 완전히 be up to ~에 달려있다 pay 지불하다 hourly rates 시간당 급여 commensurate with ~에 상응하는 apply 신청하다, 지원하다 subject line 제목 include 포함시키다 résumé 이력서 reference 이력서, 참조 schedule 일정 sign up 등록하다 following 다음의 currently 현재 space 공간 drop in 들르다 attend 참석하다 register 등록하다 in advance 미리 unless indicated otherwise 달리 명시하지 않는 한 post 공지하다 access 접근하다 report 보고서 be pleased 기쁘다 make good use of 잘 활용하다 positive 긍정적인 feedback 의견 greatly 매우 raise 일으키다 common 일반적인 issue 문제점 lunch break 점심 시간 complaint 불평, 불만 shorten 줄이다 appreciate 고맙게 여기다

196 세부 사항

구인 광고에 따르면, 강사는 무엇을 결정할 것인가?

(A) 수업 형식
(B) 시간 당 급여
(C) 수업에 등록 가능한 학생 수
(D) 수업 일수

해설 첫 번째 지문 구인 광고에서 "The format and structure of the class is completely up to the instructor."라며 수업 형식과 구조는 전적으로 강사의 몫이라고 언급하고 있으므로 답은 (A)이다.

197 추론/암시 (연계)

누가 가장 신규 언어 강사일 것 같은가?

(A) 마코
(B) 허브스트
(C) 도밍게스
(D) 드라고

해설 첫 번째 지문 구인 광고에서 "중국어, 일본어, 한국어 강사"를 찾고 있다고 하고, 두 번째 박스 수업 일정에서 오전 7시에서 오전 8시까지 강의할 일본어 강사인 (A)가 정답이다.

198 Not/True 확인

일정에 나타난 것은 무엇인가?

(A) 직원들은 하나 이상의 수업을 들을 수 있다.
(B) 언어센터에 언어 수업 교실이 하나뿐이다.
(C) 회사의 다른 지점에서 온 직원들도 언어센터를 사용할 수 있다.
(D) 모든 수업을 미리 등록해야 한다.

해설 두번째 지문 마지막 부분을 보면 "Employees visiting from other Morton locations may also access the center, but they will need to first sign in at reception." 다른 지점의 직원들도 센터를 출입할 수 있음을 알 수 있다. 따라서 정답은 (C)이다.

199 세부 사항

이메일에 따르면, 산체스 씨는 누구와 통화했는가?

(A) 언어 강사
(B) 인사부장
(C) 새로운 지원자
(D) 회사 매니저

해설 세 번째 지문 이메일에서 "However, I've also heard from a few of our managers — in fact, I just got off the phone with one now — who have raised one common issue." 매니저 중 한 사람과 통화했다고 언급하고 있으므로 답은 (D)이다.

200 추론/암시 (연계)

무슨 수업의 시간이 줄어들 것 같은가?
(A) 기초 일본어
(B) 중급 프랑스어
(C) 중급 스페인어
(D) 기초 러시아어

해설 마지막 지문 이메일에서 "The simplest solution may be to just shorten the lunchtime class to 40 minutes."라고 제안했고, 두 번째 지문 안에 있는 일정을 확인하면 점심시간 11:30~12:30에 진행하고 있는 수업의 시간이 줄어들 것이므로 (C)가 정답이다.

TEST 3

p.104

LISTENING TEST

01	(D)	02	(C)	03	(C)	04	(A)	05	(D)
06	(B)	07	(B)	08	(C)	09	(A)	10	(C)
11	(A)	12	(C)	13	(B)	14	(C)	15	(B)
16	(A)	17	(B)	18	(A)	19	(B)	20	(C)
21	(B)	22	(C)	23	(B)	24	(C)	25	(A)
26	(A)	27	(C)	28	(A)	29	(C)	30	(A)
31	(A)	32	(D)	33	(B)	34	(C)	35	(B)
36	(C)	37	(C)	38	(A)	39	(D)	40	(D)
41	(C)	42	(D)	43	(B)	44	(C)	45	(A)
46	(C)	47	(D)	48	(C)	49	(B)	50	(C)
51	(C)	52	(D)	53	(A)	54	(C)	55	(B)
56	(B)	57	(A)	58	(D)	59	(A)	60	(C)
61	(C)	62	(C)	63	(A)	64	(C)	65	(D)
66	(C)	67	(C)	68	(A)	69	(B)	70	(A)
71	(A)	72	(A)	73	(C)	74	(C)	75	(D)
76	(C)	77	(D)	78	(B)	79	(A)	80	(A)
81	(B)	82	(C)	83	(A)	84	(C)	85	(D)
86	(C)	87	(D)	88	(B)	89	(B)	90	(C)
91	(C)	92	(A)	93	(C)	94	(B)	95	(A)
96	(D)	97	(D)	98	(A)	99	(B)	100	(C)

READING TEST

101	(A)	102	(D)	103	(B)	104	(C)	105	(D)
106	(C)	107	(D)	108	(A)	109	(A)	110	(C)
111	(D)	112	(A)	113	(B)	114	(C)	115	(A)
116	(C)	117	(D)	118	(B)	119	(A)	120	(C)
121	(C)	122	(B)	123	(D)	124	(C)	125	(B)
126	(C)	127	(A)	128	(A)	129	(C)	130	(D)
131	(A)	132	(B)	133	(C)	134	(D)	135	(D)
136	(C)	137	(C)	138	(C)	139	(B)	140	(B)
141	(D)	142	(A)	143	(C)	144	(B)	145	(D)
146	(A)	147	(C)	148	(B)	149	(C)	150	(A)
151	(D)	152	(C)	153	(C)	154	(C)	155	(D)
156	(B)	157	(C)	158	(C)	159	(A)	160	(B)
161	(C)	162	(C)	163	(B)	164	(C)	165	(C)
166	(B)	167	(B)	168	(D)	169	(A)	170	(A)
171	(B)	172	(C)	173	(A)	174	(C)	175	(C)
176	(C)	177	(D)	178	(D)	179	(B)	180	(A)
181	(C)	182	(A)	183	(D)	184	(C)	185	(A)
186	(C)	187	(A)	188	(D)	189	(B)	190	(B)
191	(A)	192	(A)	193	(A)	194	(C)	195	(C)
196	(C)	197	(D)	198	(D)	199	(D)	200	(B)

PART · 1

1 인물(1인) 사진

(A) She is repairing the guitar.
(B) She is watering the grass.
(C) She is sitting on the staircase.
(D) She is playing an instrument.

(A) 여자가 기타를 수리하고 있다.
(B) 여자가 잔디에 물을 주고 있다.
(C) 여자가 계단에 앉아 있다.
(D) 여자가 악기를 연주하고 있다.

해설 여자가 잔디에 앉아서 기타를 연주하고 있는 모습을 '악기를 연주하고 있다(playing an instrument)'고 표현한 (D)가 정답이다. (A)는 기타는 들고 있으나 수리하고 있지 않으므로 오답이며, (B)는 잔디에 물을 주고 있지 않으므로 오답이다. (C)는 여자가 계단이 아닌 벤치에 앉아 있어서 오답이다.

어휘 water 물을 주다 staircase 계단 instrument 도구, 악기

2 인물(2인 이상) 사진

(A) They are running down the slope in a row.
(B) They are getting out of the building.
(C) They are walking down the stairs.
(D) They are leaning against the railings.

(A) 그들은 비탈길을 한 줄로 뛰어 내려가고 있다.
(B) 그들은 건물 밖으로 나오고 있다.
(C) 그들은 계단을 걸어 내려가고 있다.
(D) 그들은 난간에 기대고 있다.

해설 사람들이 계단을 내려가는 사진이므로 (C)가 정답이다. (A)는 장소가 비탈길이 아닐뿐더러 사람들이 뛰어내려가고 있지 않아서 오답이며, (B)는 건물에서 걸어 나오는 모습이 아니므로 오답이다. (D)는 난간이 사진에 등장하지만 사람들이 기대고 있는 모습이 아니므로 오답이다.

어휘 slope 경사지, 비탈 lean against ~에 기대다 railing 난간

3 인물(2인 이상) 사진

(A) They are unpacking the boxes.
(B) One of the men is turning on the equipment.
(C) They are holding a box with two hands.
(D) They are putting on their uniforms.

(A) 그들은 박스들을 풀고 있다.
(B) 남자들 중 한 명이 장비를 켜고 있다.
(C) 그들은 양손으로 박스를 들고 있다.
(D) 그들은 유니폼을 착용하는 중이다.

해설 두 남자가 박스를 양손으로 들고 있는 사진이므로 (C)가 정답이다. (A)와 (B)는 각각 박스를 푸는 행동과 장비를 켜는 행동을 하지 않아서 오답이며, (D)는 유니폼을 착용하는 '동작'(put on)이 아니므로 오답이다.

어휘 unpack 꺼내다, (짐을) 풀다   turn on ~을 켜다   put on ~을 입다, 착용하다

4 혼합 사진

(A) A woman is making a presentation.
(B) A woman is standing by the speaker.
(C) Some people are pointing at the board.
(D) All of the seats are occupied.

(A) 여자가 발표를 하고 있다.
(B) 여자가 발표자 옆에 서 있다.
(C) 몇몇 사람들이 칠판을 가리키고 있다.
(D) 모든 자리가 찼다.

해설 사진 중앙의 한 여자가 발표하는 사진이므로 (A)가 정답이다. (B)는 서 있는 사람이 발표자 외에는 보이지 않으므로 오답, (C)는 칠판을 가리키는 사람들이 없어서 오답, (D)는 사진 속 자리가 하나 비어 있으므로 오답이다.

어휘 presentation 연설, 발표   point at ~을 가리키다, 지적하다   occupied 사용 중인

5 사물/풍경 사진

(A) Several products are being removed from the store.
(B) Glass bottles are lined up on a table.
(C) Some customers are paying for their purchases.
(D) Products have been stocked on shelves.

(A) 제품들이 가게에서 꺼내지고 있다.
(B) 유리병이 테이블 위에 줄지어 있다.
(C) 고객들이 물건 값을 지불하고 있다.
(D) 제품들이 선반 위에 채워져 있다.

해설 선반에 제품들이 진열되어 있으므로 (D)가 정답이다. stock는 동작동사 뿐만 아니라 상태동사도 된다는 점을 기억해야 한다. 제품을 가게에서 꺼내고 있는 사람과 물건 값을 지불하는 사람이 없으므로 (A)와 (C)는 오답이며, (B)는 사진에 유리병이 등장하지 않으므로 정답이 될 수 없다.

어휘 line up 줄을 세우다   stock 채우다   shelf (pl. shelves) 선반

6 혼합 사진

(A) The rear door of a car is being closed.
(B) Some boxes are loaded into a vehicle.
(C) He is grasping the handle of a cart.
(D) He is looking through a box of tools.

(A) 차 뒷문이 닫히고 있다.
(B) 차에 상자들이 실려 있다.
(C) 그는 카트 손잡이를 잡고 있다.
(D) 그는 공구가 든 상자를 살펴보고 있다.

해설 차 안에 상자들이 실려 있는 사진으로 (B)가 정답이다. 'be being p.p.(현재진행 수동태)'는 사람이 현재 하고 있는 행동을 나타낼 때 쓰이는데, (A)는 남자가 문을 닫고 있지 않아서 오답, (C)는 카트 손잡이를 잡고 있지 않아서 오답, (D)는 사진 속에 공구 상자가 보이지 않으므로 오답이다.

어휘 rear 뒤쪽의   load (짐을) 싣다   look through 살펴보다

7 Where 의문문

Where is Prime Department Store?
(A) About three miles.
(B) It's in front of the post office.
(C) Thirty-seven dollars.

Prime 백화점이 어디에 있나요?
(A) 대략 3마일이요.
(B) 우체국 앞에 있어요.
(C) 37달러입니다.

해설 장소를 묻는 Where 의문문으로, 백화점이 어디에 있는지 묻는 질문에 우체국 앞에 있다고 위치를 정확하게 설명하는 (B)가 정답이다. (A)는 위치가 아닌 거리를 나타내는 표현이며, (C)는 가격을 나타내는 표현으로, How much 질문에 대한 대답이다.

8 선택 의문문

Did you speak to David or his manager?
(A) No, she doesn't.
(B) He will arrive at seven.
(C) Neither of them.

데이비드와 그의 매니저 중 누구한테 얘기했어요?
(A) 아니요, 그녀는 그렇지 않아요.
(B) 그는 7시에 도착할 겁니다.
(C) 둘 다 아니에요.

해설 이야기를 한 사람이 둘 중 누구인지 묻는 질문에, 누구에게도 이야기하지 않았다고 대답하는 (C)가 정답이다. (A)는 주어 및 시제가 맞지 않아서 오답이며, (B)는 시제가 잘못되었고 질문과 관계없는 내용이므로 오답이다.

9 How 의문문

How often do you go to English Bay?
(A) Every Saturday.
(B) I went there with my colleague.
(C) That sounds good.

당신은 English Bay에 얼마나 자주 가나요?
(A) 토요일마다요.
(B) 저는 그곳에 동료와 함께 갔어요.
(C) 좋은 의견입니다.

해설 특정 장소를 방문하는 빈도를 묻는 How often 의문문으로, 매주 토요일, 즉 주 1회 방문한다고 답한 (A)가 정답이다. (B)는 Who 의문문에 적절한 응답이며, (C)는 의견에 대한 반응으로 적합한 응답이다.

어휘 colleague 동료

10 When 의문문

When will the warranty on TV expire?
(A) It's more expensive than mine.
(B) I want to purchase a new television.
(C) Two years from now.

TV 보증 기간이 언제 만료됩니까?
(A) 그것은 제 것보다 더 비싸요.
(B) 저는 새 텔레비전을 구매하고 싶어요.
(C) 지금부터 2년 후에요.

해설 보증 기간 만료 시점을 묻는 When 의문문으로, 2년 후라고 정확한 미래 시점을 언급한 (C)가 정답이다. (A)는 가격에 대한 내용이므로 오답이며, (B)는 TV와 같은 단어인 television을 사용한 오답이다.

어휘 warranty 품질 보증(서) expire 만료되다, 만기가 되다
purchase 구매하다; 구매, 구매품

11 요청 의문문

Can I see the new mobile phone on the shelf?
(A) Sure, I'll get it for you.
(B) I bought the telephone a year ago.
(C) Yes, he can do it now.

선반 위의 새 휴대폰 좀 볼 수 있을까요?
(A) 물론이죠, 제가 가져다드릴게요.
(B) 저는 그 전화기를 1년 전에 구입했어요.
(C) 네, 그는 지금 할 수 있어요.

해설 휴대폰을 보는 것이 가능한지 묻는 질문에, 그것을 가져다주겠다고 말하는 (A)가 정답이다. (B)는 질문의 mobile phone과 비슷한 telephone을 사용한 오답이며, (C)는 질문에 Yes로 대답할 수는 있지만, 뒤의 내용이 질문과 무관하므로 오답이다.

12 제안/권유문

Let me introduce the new employee to you this afternoon.
(A) Yes, I will employ her.
(B) You should attend the orientation for new employees.
(C) Thanks, but I've already met her.

오늘 오후에 당신에게 신입 사원을 소개해 드릴게요.
(A) 네, 저는 그녀를 고용할 겁니다.
(B) 당신은 신입 사원 오리엔테이션에 참석해야 해요.
(C) 고맙지만, 저는 이미 그녀를 만났어요.

해설 신입 사원을 소개해 주겠다는 말에, 이미 만났으니 소개하지 않아도 된다고 간접적으로 말한 (C)가 정답이다. (A)는 질문에 나온 employee와 유사한 단어 employ를 사용한 오답이며, (B)는 employee를 반복 사용했으나 질문과 관계없는 오답이다.

13 Why 의문문

Why is the restaurant closing early next Thursday?
(A) The chef is famous for his daring recipes.
(B) It's a national holiday.
(C)They are always open until 2 P.M.

그 식당은 왜 다음 주 목요일에 일찍 문을 닫나요?
(A) 그 주방장은 대담한 조리법으로 유명해요.
(B) 그날은 국경일이에요.
(C) 그들은 항상 오후 2시까지 영업합니다.

해설 특정일에 식당이 일찍 닫는 이유를 묻는 Why 의문문으로, 국경일이기 때문에 문을 일찍 닫는다고 알려주는 (B)가 정답이다. (A)는 주방장에 관한 질문이 아니기 때문에 오답이며, (C)는 일반적인 영업 시간을 말하는 보기이므로 질문과 관계가 없다.

어휘 chef 주방장 national holiday 국경일, 공휴일

어휘 appointment 예약, 약속 appoint 임명하다

14 What 의문문

What do you think of the new sedan?
(A) The vehicle is made in Germany.
(B) The driver will arrive here by seven.
(C) It looks more luxurious than mine.

신형 세단에 대해 어떻게 생각해요?
(A) 그 차량은 독일에서 만들어졌어요.
(B) 운전자는 여기에 7시까지 도착할 겁니다.
(C) 제 차보다 더 고급스러워 보입니다.

해설 신형 세단에 대한 의견을 묻는 'What do you think of ~?' 형태의 질문에, 자신의 차보다 더 고급스러워 보인다며 견해를 밝힌 (C)가 정답이다. (A)는 의견이 아닌 객관적인 사실을 말하고 있으므로 오답이며, (B)는 질문의 sedan에서 연상할 수 있는 driver를 이용했지만 질문과 상관없는 내용이므로 오답이다.

어휘 sedan 세단형 자동차 vehicle 차량 luxurious 고급스러운, 사치스러운

15 일반 의문문

Are you going to Gary's birthday party on Saturday?
(A) She will visit my office this weekend.
(B) Who else is coming?
(C) It was held at Ocean Hotel.

당신은 토요일에 게리의 생일 파티에 갈 건가요?
(A) 그녀는 이번 주말에 제 사무실을 방문할 겁니다.
(B) 또 누가 오나요?
(C) Ocean Hotel에서 열렸습니다.

해설 생일 파티에 갈 예정인지 묻는 질문에, 참석 여부를 답하기 전에 또 누가 오는지 묻는 (B)가 정답이다. (A)는 Saturday에서 연상할 수 있는 weekend를 이용한 오답이며, (C)는 Where 의문문에 어울리는 대답일 뿐더러 시제도 맞지 않으므로 오답이다.

16 평서문

I have an appointment with Dr. Johnson.
(A) Could you wait a moment, please?
(B) He was appointed the director.
(C) I have met him before.

저는 존슨 박사님과 약속이 있어요.
(A) 잠시만 기다려 주시겠어요?
(B) 그는 관리자로 임명되었어요.
(C) 저는 전에 그를 만난 적이 있어요.

해설 특정 인물과 약속이 있다는 말에, 잠시 기다리라고 하는 (A)가 정답이다. (B)는 질문의 appointment가 파생된 기본형 appoint를 이용한 오답이며, (C)는 질문의 내용과 관계없는 오답이다.

17 요청 의문문

May I close the door because of the wind?
(A) You should try the key on the desk.
(B) Sure, go ahead.
(C) It is close to my office.

바람이 많이 부는데 문 좀 닫아도 될까요?
(A) 책상 위의 열쇠를 사용하세요.
(B) 물론이죠, 그렇게 해요.
(C) 그곳은 제 사무실과 가까워요.

해설 문을 닫아도 되는지 허락을 구하는 질문에, 이를 흔쾌히 승낙하는 (B)가 정답이다. (A)는 door에서 연상되는 어휘 key를 사용한 오답이며, (C)는 질문의 close를 반복한 오답이다.

어휘 try 시도하다, 사용해보다

18 평서문

My flight leaves for London at four o'clock.
(A) I think you should go right now.
(B) I saw Thomas at Vancouver Airport.
(C) I will leave the passport on your desk.

제 항공편이 4시에 런던으로 출발합니다.
(A) 지금 당장 가셔야겠네요.
(B) 저는 밴쿠버 공항에서 토마스를 봤습니다.
(C) 제가 당신 책상에 여권을 둘게요.

해설 자신의 항공편이 출발할 시각을 말하는 평서문에, 늦지 않도록 서두르라고 간접적으로 말한 (A)가 정답이다. (B)는 질문의 flight에서 연상되는 어휘 airport를 이용한 오답이며, (C)는 flight에서 연상되는 leave와 passport를 이용한 오답이다.

어휘 leave for ~로 떠나다 right now 지금 즉시 leave 떠나다, 남겨두다

19 부정 의문문

Isn't the interview taking place tomorrow?
(A) You should send me your résumé.
(B) Let me check that.
(C) I prefer the Paris office.

면접이 내일 있지 않나요?
(A) 저한테 이력서를 보내주셔야 합니다.
(B) 제가 확인해 볼게요.
(C) 저는 파리 지사를 선호해요.

해설 내일 면접이 진행되는지 묻는 부정 의문문에, 확인해 보겠다, 즉 '잘 모르겠다'고 답하는 (B)가 가장 적절히다. (A)는 질문의 interview에서 연상될 수 있는 résumé를 이용한 오답이며, (C)는 선호하는 장소를 말하고 있으므로 Where 또는 Which 의문문에 적절한 대답이다.

어휘 take place 일어나다, 발생하다 résumé 이력서

20 선택 의문문

Did you see all of the items or just a few of them?
(A) I have to pay twenty dollars.
(B) He'll send me the sample soon.
(C) Just the ones in the showroom.

당신은 그 물건들을 다 보셨나요, 아니면 몇 개만 보셨나요?
(A) 저는 20달러를 지불해야 합니다.
(B) 그가 저에게 견본을 곧 보내 줄 거예요.
(C) 전시장 안에 있는 것들만요.

해설 물건들을 전부 다 보았는지, 아니면 일부만 보았는지 묻는 질문으로, 특정 장소에 있는 물건들만 봤다고 대답하는 (C)가 정답이다. (A)는 금액이나 비용을 묻는 질문이 아니므로 오답이며, (B)는 질문에 He가 언급되지 않았으므로 오답이다.

어휘 item 물품, 품목 sample 샘플, 견본 showroom 전시장

21 Which 의문문

Which printer should we order?
(A) Please print the report now.
(B) How about getting a more affordable one?
(C) In three hours.

우리는 어떤 프린터를 주문해야 할까요?
(A) 보고서를 지금 출력해 주세요.
(B) 가격이 더 알맞은 걸 주문하는 게 어때요?
(C) 3시간 후에요.

해설 어떤 프린터를 주문해야 할지 묻고 있으므로, 가격이 적당한 것을 주문하자고 제안하는 (B)가 정답이다. (A)는 질문에 나온 printer와 유사한 print를 사용한 오답이며, (C)는 When 의문문에 어울리는 응답이므로 오답이다.

어휘 affordable (가격이) 알맞은

22 How 의문문

How can we increase the sales?
(A) I'm from the sales department.
(B) Sales are still in the red.
(C) We need to invest in online marketing.

우리가 어떻게 매출을 증가시킬 수 있을까요?
(A) 저는 영업부에서 왔습니다.
(B) 매출이 여전히 적자네요.
(C) 온라인 마케팅에 투자해야 합니다.

해설 매출을 증가시킬 방법을 묻는 How 의문문으로, 온라인 마케팅에 투자할 것을 제안하는 (C)가 정답이다. (A)와 (B)는 질문에서 사용된 어휘 sales를 반복한 오답이다.

어휘 increase 증가하다, 인상시키다 in the red 적자 상태인 invest 투자하다

23 When 의문문

When will the article be published?
(A) For a few hours.
(B) After it's approved.
(C) In the last issue.

그 기사는 언제 출판되나요?
(A) 몇 시간 동안이요.
(B) 승인 받은 후에요.
(C) 지난 호에요.

해설 기사가 출판되는 시점을 묻는 When 의문문으로, 승인된 후에 출판된다고 알려주는 (B)가 정답이다. (A)는 시점이 아닌 기간을 나타내는 표현이어서 오답이며, (C)는 과거의 시점을 말하고 있으므로 미래시제인 질문에 적절하지 않다.

어휘 publish 발행하다, 출판하다 approve 승인하다 issue (잡지, 신문의) 호, 화제

24 부정 의문문

Isn't my weekly news magazine renewing by itself?
(A) I'm thinking of getting a subscription.
(B) Yes, but you have outstanding bills.
(C) I was surprised at the news.

제 시사 주간지는 저절로 갱신되지 않나요?
(A) 저는 구독할까 생각 중입니다.
(B) 네, 그런데 미납된 금액이 있어요.
(C) 저는 그 소식에 놀랐어요.

해설 주간지가 저절로 갱신되는 것이 아닌지 묻는 부정 의문문으로, 미납금이 있다며 이를 납부해야 갱신된다고 돌려 말하는 (B)가 정답이다. (A)는 질문의 news magazine에서 연상되는 어휘 subscription을 사용한 오답이며, (C)는 질문의 news를 반복 사용한 오답이다.

어휘 renew 갱신하다 outstanding 미납의, 두드러진, 뛰어난

25 Why 의문문

Why is there a projector in the meeting room?
(A) The sales representative made a presentation.
(B) Mr. Evans is in charge of the project.
(C) I met the CEO of Ace Company at a conference.

왜 회의실에 프로젝터가 있나요?
(A) 영업 담당자가 프레젠테이션을 했어요.
(B) 에반스 씨가 그 프로젝트를 담당하고 있어요.
(C) 저는 컨퍼런스에서 Ace 사의 대표이사를 만났어요.

해설 회의실에 프로젝터가 있는 이유를 묻는 Why 의문문으로, 영업 담당자가 프레젠테이션을 했기 때문이라고 말하는 (A)가 정답이다. (B)는 질문의 projector와 유사한 어휘 project를 이용한 오답이며, (C)는 질문의 meeting에서 연상되는 어휘 conference를 이용한 오답이다.

어휘 projector 영사기, 프로젝터 representative 담당자, 대표자; 대표하는 in charge of ~을 책임지는, 담당하는

26 Who 의문문

Who knows how to open the cover?

(A) I think Mr. Robinson does.

(B) It can cover your employees to drive.

(C) You should close the door when you go out.

누가 그 덮개를 여는 법을 알고 있나요?

(A) 로빈슨 씨가 알고 있을 거예요.

(B) 그것은 당신의 직원들이 운전하는 것을 보장합니다.

(C) 나갈 때 문을 닫아야 합니다.

해설 덮개를 여는 법을 아는 사람이 누구인지 묻는 Who 의문문으로, 로빈슨 씨가 알 거라고 알려주는 (A)가 정답이다. (B)는 질문에 나온 어휘 cover(덮개)를 다른 의미(보장하다)로 사용한 오답이며, (C)는 질문의 open에서 연상되는 어휘 close를 이용한 오답이다.

어휘 cover 덮개, 표지, 보장하다

27 선택 의문문

Do you want to have lunch at the Korean restaurant or the Japanese one?

(A) I'll make a reservation.

(B) That sounds good to me.

(C) How about the Italian one?

점심을 한식집에서 드시고 싶으세요? 아니면 일식집에서 드시고 싶으세요?

(A) 제가 예약할게요.

(B) 좋은 생각입니다.

(C) 이탈리아 음식점은 어때요?

해설 점심을 먹으러 한식집을 갈지 일식집을 갈지 묻는 질문에, 이탈리아 식당이라는 새로운 선택안을 제안하는 (C)가 정답이다. (A)는 질문의 restaurant에서 연상되는 어휘 reservation을 이용한 오답이며, (B)는 제안하는 말에 적절한 대답이므로 오답이다.

어휘 reservation 예약

28 평서문

We need to hire another Web designer.

(A) Where should we advertise the job opening?

(B) He is an experienced designer.

(C) I will put the picture on the Web site.

웹 디자이너를 한 명 더 고용해야겠어요.

(A) 어디에 구인 광고를 하는 게 좋을까요?

(B) 그는 숙련된 디자이너입니다.

(C) 제가 웹 사이트에 사진을 올릴게요.

해설 웹 디자이너를 새로 고용해야겠다는 평서문에 대한 응답으로, 구인 광고를 어디에 올릴지를 묻는 (A)가 가장 적절하다. (B)는 질문에 주어(He)에 해당하는 사람이 언급되지 않아 오답이며, (C)는 질문에 나온 Web designer의 유사어 Web site를 이용한 오답이다.

어휘 advertise 광고하다, 홍보하다   experienced 능숙한, 숙련된

29 부가 의문문

Donald sent out the meeting schedule, didn't he?

(A) Usually by e-mail.

(B) He is scheduled to meet with a customer.

(C) He hasn't done it yet.

도날드 씨가 회의 일정을 보냈죠, 그렇죠?

(A) 주로 이메일로요.

(B) 그는 고객과 만날 예정입니다.

(C) 아직 보내지 않았어요.

해설 도날드 씨가 회의 일정을 보냈는지 묻는 부가 의문문에, 아직 보내지 않았다고 말하는 (C)가 정답이다. (A)는 수단과 방법을 묻는 How 의문문에 적절한 대답이며, (B)는 질문에 나온 schedule의 유사 발음인 scheduled를 이용한 오답이다.

어휘 schedule 일정, 일정표   be scheduled to V ~하기로 되어 있다

30 요청 의문문

Can you review my documentation soon?

(A) I can finish it by three o'clock.

(B) The view is really good.

(C) He reviewed the article.

제 서류를 곧 검토해 주실 수 있나요?

(A) 3시까지 끝낼 수 있어요.

(B) 전망이 아주 좋아요.

(C) 그가 기사를 검토했습니다.

해설 자신의 서류를 곧 검토해 줄 수 있는지 묻는 질문에, 3시까지 검토를 마칠 수 있다고 응답하는 (A)가 정답이다. (B)는 질문의 review와 유사한 view를 이용한 오답이며, (C)는 질문의 review를 반복했으나 주어가 맞지 않은 오답이다.

어휘 review 검토하다   documentation 서류, 증빙서류   finish 마무리하다

31 일반 의문문

Are you going to accept the management position?

(A) Actually, I start on March 1st.

(B) Ms. Kim is working as a personnel manager.

(C) I retired from the company.

당신은 그 관리직을 수락할 건가요?

(A) 실은 3월 1일에 근무를 시작합니다.

(B) 킴 씨는 인사 부장으로 근무하고 있습니다.

(C) 저는 그 회사에서 퇴직했습니다.

해설 직책 제안을 수락할 것인지 묻는 질문으로, 근무 시작일을 알려주면서 제안을 수락했음을 간접적으로 말하는 (A)가 정답이다. (B)는 질문의 management와 유사한 어휘 manager를 이용한 오답이며, (C)는 과거의 일을 언급하고 있으므로 오답이다.

어휘 management position 관리직

PART 3

[32-34]

M I'm meeting an acquaintance here for lunch. The problem is that we only have half an hour, so we need something that can be prepared as quickly as possible. Could you recommend anything?

W Um… How about the pasta with vegetables? It only takes a few minutes to prepare. Therefore, you can have enough time to have a meal. In addition, we're running a special event on the pasta now. If you order two servings of the pasta, you'll get two glasses of cider at no additional cost.

M That sounds good. My acquaintance asked me to order for her, as she will be here a few minutes later. So, please prepare the pasta for two people.

M 저는 점심식사를 하기 위해 여기서 지인과 만날 예정입니다. 문제는 우리에게 30분 밖에 시간이 없어서 최대한 빨리 준비될 수 있는 음식을 먹어야 한단 거예요. 추천 좀 해주시겠어요?

W 음… 야채가 들어간 파스타는 어때요? 준비하는 데 몇 분 밖에 안 걸려서 손님이 식사하실 시간이 충분할 거예요. 뿐만 아니라, 우리는 지금 파스타 메뉴에 특별 이벤트를 진행하고 있어요. 파스타 2인분을 주문하시면, 추가 비용 없이 사과 주스 두 잔을 받으실 수 있어요.

M 좋아요. 제 지인이 몇 분 후면 여기 도착할 건데 저에게 주문을 해 달라고 요청했어요. 그러니 파스타 2인분을 준비해 주세요.

어휘 acquaintance 지인   serving (음식의) 1인분
at no additional cost 추가 요금 없이   grocery 식료품
inexpensive 저렴한   free of charge 무료로

32   대화 장소

화자들은 어디에 있는가?
(A) 호텔에
(B) 식료품점에
(C) 구내 식당에
(D) 음식점에

해설 대화가 일어나는 장소를 묻는 문제는 주로 지문의 초반에 단서가 나온다. 첫 대사에서 '지인과 이곳에서 식사를 할 것이며 음식이 빨리 준비되어야 한다(I'm meeting an acquaintance here for lunch. The problem is that we only have half an hour, so we need something that can be prepared as quickly as possible.)'고 언급하는 것으로 보아 대화 장소가 음식점이라는 것을 알 수 있다. 따라서 정답은 (D)이다.

33   세부 사항

여자는 왜 파스타를 추천하는가?
(A) 가격이 저렴하다.
(B) 만드는 데 시간이 오래 걸리지 않는다.

(C) 새로 추가된 메뉴이다.
(D) 건강에 매우 좋다.

해설 남자가 빨리 준비될 수 있는 메뉴를 추천해 달라고 요청했고, 이어지는 여자의 대사에서 '준비하는 데 몇 분 밖에 안 걸린다 (It only takes a few minutes to prepare.)'며 파스타를 추천하는 것으로 보아 정답이 (B)임을 알 수 있다.

34   세부 사항

남자가 무료로 얻게 될 것은 무엇인가?
(A) 더 많은 야채
(B) 빵
(C) 음료
(D) 쿠폰

해설 여자의 대사에서 '파스타 2인분 주문 시 추가 비용 없이 사과 주스가 제공된다(If you order two servings of the pasta, you'll get two glasses of cider at no additional cost.)'고 언급되었으므로 정답은 (C)이다. 지문의 "at no additional cost"는 질문의 "free of charge"로, 지문의 "cider"는 보기의 "Drinks"로 바뀐 것에 주목하자.

[35-37]

W This is Sally Edwards calling. I was in your shop to buy a new monitor last Monday. The monitor that I want to buy was out of stock at that time. So, I ordered one, and I was told to call back today to check whether it's available.

M Hello, Ms. Edwards. We'll have it ready for you later today. You can come in anytime after three o'clock to pick it up.

W Okay, great. I'm going to stop by your shop before six. Could you tell me whether I can get a discount? I saw a pamphlet that indicates a special discount event.

M The event doesn't apply to that monitor since it's the newest one. However, we'll give you a 20% discount coupon for your next purchase.

W 저는 샐리 에드워즈라고 합니다. 저는 지난 월요일에 새 모니터를 구입하려고 당신의 매장을 방문했는데요. 그때는 제가 사고 싶은 모니터가 품절되었어요. 그래서 저는 하나를 주문했고, 그것을 가져갈 수 있는지 확인하기 위해 오늘 다시 전화하라고 요청받았습니다.

M 안녕하세요, 에드워즈 씨. 모니터는 오늘 늦게 준비될 겁니다. 3시 이후에 아무 때나 가지러 오시면 됩니다.

W 네, 좋아요. 6시 전에 매장에 들르도록 할게요. 혹시 제가 할인을 받을 수 있는지 알려주시겠어요? 특별 할인 행사가 나와 있는 팸플릿을 봤거든요.

M 그 모니터는 최신 상품이기 때문에 행사에서 적용되지 않아요. 하지만, 저희가 다음 번에 구매할 때 사용할 수 있는 20% 할인 쿠폰을 드릴게요.

어휘 out of stock 품절이 된 available 이용 가능한, 여유가 있는
pick up ~을 가지러 가다, ~를 데리러 가다 pamphlet
(= booklet) 팸플릿, 안내책자 apply to ~에 적용되다
manufacturer 제조업자 voucher 상품권, 할인권, 쿠폰

35 주제/목적

여자가 전화하는 이유는 무엇인가?

(A) 장비를 주문하기 위해

(B) 주문품을 확인하기 위해

(C) 제품을 보내기 위해

(D) 문제를 보고하기 위해

해설 여자의 첫 대사에서 '사고 싶은 모니터가 없어서 주문했고, 물건의 재고가 있는지 확인하기 위해 오늘 다시 전화하라고 요청 받았다(The monitor that I want to buy was out of stock at that time. So, I ordered one, and I was told to call back today to check whether it's available.)'고 하므로 주문품을 확인하기 위해 전화한 것임을 알 수 있다. 따라서 정답은 (B)이다.

36 다음에 할 일

여자는 무엇을 할 것이라고 말하는가?

(A) 매장에 다시 전화한다

(B) 제조업체에 연락한다

(C) 매장에 간다

(D) 쿠폰을 가져온다

해설 여자의 두 번째 대사에서 '6시 전에 매장에 들를 것이다(I'm going to stop by your shop before six.)'라고 말하고 있으므로 정답은 (C)이다.

37 제안

남자는 무엇을 하겠다고 제안하는가?

(A) 여자에게 나중에 전화한다

(B) 제품을 배송한다

(C) 할인권을 제공한다

(D) 할인을 해준다

해설 남자의 마지막 대사에서 '20% 할인 쿠폰을 제공할 것 (we'll give you a 20% discount coupon tor your next purchase.)'임을 알 수 있다. discount coupon이 보기에서는 voucher로 바꿔 표현되었으므로 (C)가 정답이다.

[38-40]

> M Hi, my name is Jason Davies. I'm here in Toronto to attend the economic seminar. I have a reservation at this hotel for two nights.
>
> W Good afternoon, Mr. Davies. Hmm… Unfortunately, it seems that an error occurred in the online reservation system. So, I can't find any information about your reservation. I'm very sorry. All the rooms are occupied.
>
> M How could this happen? I received this booking confirmation message when I booked my room a month ago. And I paid the full amount for the accommodation.
>
> W I really apologize for this inconvenience. I'll give you a refund immediately. And if you want, I can call the Kingdom Hotel near here and ask whether there is any room available.

M 안녕하세요, 저는 제이슨 데이비스라고 합니다. 경제 세미나에 참석하기 위해 여기 토론토에 왔습니다. 저는 이 호텔에 2박 3일을 예약했어요.

W 안녕하세요, 데이비스 씨. 음… 안타깝게도, 온라인 예약 시스템에 오류가 발생했던 것 같아요. 그래서 당신의 예약에 관한 어떠한 정보도 찾을 수가 없네요. 정말 죄송합니다. 모든 방이 다 찼습니다.

M 어떻게 이런 일이 있었죠? 저는 한 달 전에 방을 예약했을 때 이 예약 확인 메시지도 받았어요. 그리고 숙박비도 전액 지불했습니다.

W 불편을 드려 진심으로 사과 드립니다. 즉시 환불해 드릴게요. 그리고 원하신다면, 이 근처에 있는 Kingdom 호텔에 전화해서 남은 방이 있는지 물어볼게요.

어휘 reservation 예약 unfortunately 불행히도, 안타깝게도
occupied 사용 중인 accommodation 숙박, 숙소
immediately 즉시 inspect 점검하다, 검사하다 deposit
예금하다, 보증금을 내다 duplicate 중복의 properly 적절하게 lodging 임시 숙소

38 세부 사항

남자는 왜 토론토에 있는가?

(A) 세미나에 참석하기 위해

(B) 박물관에 방문하기 위해

(C) 호텔을 예약하기 위해

(D) 시스템을 점검하기 위해

해설 남자가 토론토에 있는 이유를 묻는 질문으로, 남자의 말에 주목해야 한다. 남자의 첫 대사에서 '세미나 참석을 위해 토론토에 왔다(I'm here in Toronto to attend the economic seminar.)'는 내용이 나오므로 정답은 (A)이다.

39 문제점

여자의 말에 따르면, 무엇이 문제를 일으켰는가?

(A) 숙박비가 입금되지 않았다.

(B) 중복 예약이 되었다.

(C) 방 번호가 잘못되었다.

(D) 컴퓨터 시스템이 제대로 작동하지 않았다.

해설 여자가 첫 대사에서 '온라인 예약 시스템에 오류가 있었던 것 같다(it seems that an error occurred in the online reservation system.)'고 했으므로 컴퓨터 시스템에 문제가 있었다는 것을 알 수 있다. 따라서 정답은 (D)이다.

TEST 3 정답과 해설

40 제안

여자는 무엇을 하겠다고 제안하는가?
(A) 쿠폰을 제공한다
(B) 방을 업그레이드해준다
(C) 대기 명단에 이름을 올려준다
(D) 숙소 정보를 찾아준다

해설 요청이나 제안을 묻는 질문은 주로 지문의 후반에 답이 나온다. 여자의 마지막 대사에서 '인근 호텔에 남은 방이 있는지 알아봐 줄 수 있다(I can call the Kingdom Hotel near here and ask whether there is any room available.)'고 했으므로 정답은 (D)이다.

[41-43]

> W Hi, Colin. I would like to remind you that we're going to close the store early on Friday to conduct some maintenance work. We will probably have to work until late on that day.
> M I see. I've already put up signs in every doorway to notify the customers of the scheduled work. Is there anything else I should do?
> W No, you don't have anything more to do. Thank you. Well, I'll e-mail you details now on what we have to do on Friday. If you have any questions after checking your e-mail, please contact me.
>
> ---
>
> W 안녕하세요, 콜린 씨. 일부 보수 작업을 하기 위해 금요일에 매장을 일찍 닫는다는 걸 상기시켜 드리고 싶어요. 우리는 아마 그날 늦게까지 작업해야 할 겁니다.
> M 알겠습니다. 저는 고객들에게 예정된 작업을 알리기 위해 이미 모든 출입구에 안내 표지판을 세워 뒀어요. 제가 해야 할 다른 일이 더 있나요?
> W 아뇨, 당신이 더 해야 할 건 없어요. 고마워요. 그럼, 우리가 금요일에 해야 하는 것에 대한 세부 내용을 지금 이메일로 보낼게요. 이메일을 확인한 후에 질문이 있으면 제게 연락하세요.

어휘 remind 상기시키다 maintenance 점검, 관리, 유지 put up 게시하다, 세우다 details 세부 사항 conference 학회, 컨퍼런스 contact 연락하다, 접촉하다 arrange 마련하다, 정리하다, 배열하다

41 대화 장소

화자들이 있는 곳은 어디일 것 같은가?
(A) 회의실에
(B) 도서관에
(C) 매장에
(D) 건설 현장에

해설 대화가 일어나는 장소에 대한 단서는 주로 지문의 초반에 나온다. 여자의 첫 대사를 보면, '금요일에 매장을 일찍 닫을 것(we're going to close the store early on Friday)'이라고 말하는 것으로 보아 대화 장소가 두 사람이 근무하는 매장이라고 추측할 수 있다. 따라서 정답은 (C)이다.

42 세부 사항

남자는 무엇을 했다고 말하는가?
(A) 모든 문을 닫았다
(B) 일부 직원들에게 연락했다
(C) 고객들에게 특별 판매에 대해 알려주었다
(D) 표지판을 설치했다

해설 남자의 대사 중 고객들에게 예정된 작업을 알리기 위해 '모든 출입구에 표지판을 세웠다(I've already put up signs in every doorway to ~)'고 말하고 있으므로 정답은 (D)이다.

43 다음에 할 일

여자가 다음에 할 일은 무엇인가?
(A) 일부 상품들을 교환한다
(B) 세부 정보를 보낸다
(C) 자신의 이메일 주소를 알려준다
(D) 파일을 정리한다

해설 다음에 할 일을 묻는 문제는 주로 지문의 후반부에 단서가 나온다. 여자의 마지막 대사를 보면 '세부 내용을 이메일로 보내겠다(I'll e-mail you details now on what we have to do on Friday.)'는 내용이 있으므로, 정답은 (B)이다.

[44-46]

> W Where should we have the department's end-of-year party? I think the new Japanese restaurant on Robson Street might be a good place for us.
> M Yes, I have already been there, and the food was so great, but the prices are a little expensive. Also, I think they don't have enough space to accommodate our large group.
> W I see. Then, where do you think will be better?
> M In my opinion, the Korean restaurant across from our company would be better. They provided us with excellent service last August. What do you think?
>
> ---
>
> W 우리 부서 연말 파티는 어디서 해야 할까요? 제 생각에는 Robson 가에 새로 생긴 일본 음식점이 우리에게 좋은 장소일 것 같아요.
> M 네, 저는 이미 그곳에 가 봤는데, 음식은 아주 좋았지만 가격이 약간 비쌌어요. 제 생각에는 그곳은 우리의 많은 인원을 수용할 충분한 공간도 없을 것 같아요.
> W 그렇군요. 그럼, 어디가 더 좋을 것 같아요?
> M 제 생각에는, 우리 회사 맞은편에 있는 한국 음식점이 더 좋을 것 같네요. 그들은 지난 8월에 우리에게 훌륭한 서비스를 제공했죠. 어떻게 생각해요?

어휘 banquet 연회, 만찬 accommodate 공간을 제공하다, 수용하다 provide 제공하다 awards ceremony 시상식 orientation 예비 교육 reasonable (가격이) 합리적인 quality 질, 고급, 양질 a variety of 여러 가지의

44 세부 사항

화자들이 계획하고 있는 것은 무엇인가?

(A) 시상식

(B) 연례 파티

(C) 오리엔테이션

(D) 워크숍

해설 여자의 첫 대사에서 '연말 파티를 어디서 해야 할지(Where should we have the department's end-of-year banquet?)'를 묻고 있으므로 정답은 (B)이다.

45 세부 사항

남자는 일본 음식점에 대해 뭐라고 말하는가?

(A) 맛있는 음식을 제공한다.

(B) 회사에서 다소 멀다.

(C) 합리적인 가격에 음식을 제공한다.

(D) 최근에 개업했다.

해설 남자의 첫 대사에서 일본 음식점에 이미 가 본 적이 있고, '음식이 훌륭했다(the food was so great)'고 했으므로 정답은 (A)이다. 최근에 문을 열었다는 말은 여자가 한 말임에 주의해야 한다.

46 문제점

일본 음식점의 문제점은 무엇인가?

(A) 음식의 질

(B) 회사로부터의 거리

(C) 공간의 규모

(D) 요리의 종류

해설 남자의 첫 대사에서 '우리의 많은 인원을 수용하기엔 공간이 충분하지 않다(I think they don't have enough space to accommodate our large group.)'고 언급되었다. 따라서 (C)가 정답이다.

[47-49]

M Excuse me. I need to take bus number 46, and I've been waiting for it for almost an hour. Why isn't the bus coming?

W I think the bus is probably running late due to the International Fireworks Show at Marion Bay this weekend. The festival always causes a lot of delays in the city.

M Oh, that's why I'm waiting for the bus now. The subway station is so far away that I went to the bus stop instead. However, in this case, it might be better to walk to the subway station and take the subway.

W I think so. If you don't want to get there on foot, you can take a taxi and transfer to the subway.

M 실례합니다. 저는 46번 버스를 타야 하는데, 거의 한 시간째 기다리고 있어요. 버스가 왜 이렇게 안 오나요?

W 제 생각에는 이번 주말에 Marion Bay에서 열리는 국제 불꽃 쇼 때문에 버스가 늦는 것 같아요. 그 축제는 항상 시내에 엄청난 지연을 야기해요.

M 아, 그래서 제가 지금 버스를 기다리는 거군요. 지하철역은 너무 멀리 있어서 대신 버스 정류장으로 왔어요. 하지만, 이 경우엔 지하철역까지 걸어가서 지하철을 타는게 나을지도 모르겠네요.

W 제 생각도 그래요. 만약 거기까지 걸어가고 싶지 않으시면, 택시를 타고 가서 지하철로 갈아타면 돼요.

어휘 cause ~을 야기하다 transfer 옮기다, (교통수단을) 갈아타다 traffic accident 교통 사고 ongoing 진행중인 strike 파업 destination 목적지

47 대화 장소

화자들은 어디에 있는 것 같은가?

(A) 지하철역에

(B) 택시 정류장에

(C) 음식점에

(D) 버스 정류장에

해설 대화가 일어나고 있는 장소는 대화의 초반에 단서가 나온다. 남자가 첫 대사에서 '거의 한 시간째 46번 버스를 기다리고 있다(I need to take bus number 46, and I've been waiting for it for almost an hour.)'는 것으로 보아, 대화 장소가 버스 정류장임을 알 수 있다. 따라서 정답은 (D)이다.

48 문제점

여자의 말에 따르면, 무엇이 지연을 야기했는가?

(A) 교통 사고

(B) 계속되는 파업

(C) 지역 행사

(D) 도로 공사

해설 여자의 첫 대사에서 '국제 불꽃 쇼 때문에 버스가 늦는 것 같다(I think the bus is probably running late due to the International Fireworks Show)'고 말하고 있으므로 행사 때문에 버스가 지연된다는 것을 알 수 있다. 따라서 정답은 (C)이다.

49 제안

여자는 남자에게 무엇을 제안하는가?

(A) 더 기다리는 것

(B) 택시를 타는 것

(C) 목적지로 걸어가는 것

(D) 버스 회사에 전화하는 것

해설 제안이나 요청하는 내용은 주로 대화의 후반부에 나온다. 여자의 마지막 대사를 보면, '택시를 타고 가서 지하철로 갈아타는 것(you can take a taxi and transfer to the subway.)'을 남자에게 권유하고 있으므로 정답은 (B)이다.

W Good morning, I'm Shura Brown from Dream Advertising Corporation. I have an appointment at 10 A.M. with the company manager to confirm the final details for your company's product launch.

M Well, I think you've got something wrong. Your meeting is scheduled for 11 A.M. Why don't you check the schedule again?

W Really? Just a moment please. Um… Oh, I was wrong. Sorry, but couldn't the manager meet with me at ten o'clock?

M I'm afraid that he's out of the office now. He'll be back at about 10:30 A.M. at the earliest. Now, it's 9:50 A.M. Would you like to wait here or come back later?

W 안녕하세요, 저는 Dream Advertising 사에서 온 슈라 브라운입니다. 귀사의 제품 출시에 대한 최종 세부 사항을 확정 짓기 위해 회사 매니저와 오전 10시에 만나기로 약속했어요.

M 음, 제 생각엔 뭔가 잘못 알고 계신 것 같은데요. 당신의 약속은 오전 11시로 예정되어 있습니다. 일정을 다시 확인해 보시겠어요?

W 그래요? 잠시만요. 음… 아, 제가 잘못 알고 있었군요. 죄송하지만 매니저와 10시에 만날 수 없을까요?

M 유감이지만 그는 지금 사무실에 안 계십니다. 그는 빨라도 10시 30분은 되어야 돌아오실 겁니다. 지금은 오전 9시 50분이네요. 여기서 기다리실래요? 아니면 나중에 다시 오시겠어요?

어휘 appointment 약속, 임명 confirm 확인하다, 확정하다 be scheduled for ~로 예정되어 있다 at the earliest 빨라도 agency 대리점, 대행사 insurance 보험, 보험업 complaint 불평, 불만 sales representative 영업 담당자 finalize 마무리 짓다

50 화자의 근무지

여자가 어디에서 일하는 것 같은가?
(A) 여행사에서
(B) 케이터링 회사에서
(C) 광고 대행사에서
(D) 보험 회사에서

해설 일반적으로 화자의 신분, 직업은 대화의 초반부에서 알 수 있다. 여자의 첫 대사에서 'Dream Advertising 사에서 왔다(I'm Shura Brown from Dream Advertising Corporation.)'고 말하는 것으로 보아, 여자가 광고 회사 직원임을 알 수 있다. 따라서 정답은 (C)이다.

51 세부 사항

여자가 회사를 방문한 이유는 무엇인가?
(A) 항의를 하기 위해
(B) 영업사원을 만나기 위해
(C) 일에 대한 세부 사항을 마무리 짓기 위해
(D) 일부 제품을 가져가기 위해

해설 여자의 첫 대사에 '귀사의 제품 출시에 대한 최종 세부 사항을 확정 짓기 위해 매니저와 만나기로 했다(I have an appointment at 10 A.M. with the company manager to confirm the final details for your company's product launch.)'고 했으므로 정답은 (C)이다.

52 세부 사항

남자의 말에 따르면, 여자는 언제 매니저와 만나기로 되어 있는가?
(A) 오전 9시 50분
(B) 오전 10시
(C) 오전 10시 30분
(D) 오전 11시

해설 남자의 첫 대사에 '여자의 회의가 오전 11시로 잡혀 있다(Your meeting is scheduled for 11 A.M.)'고 언급되었으므로 정답은 (D)이다. (A) 오전 9시 50분은 현재 대화하고 있는 시각이고, (B) 오전 10시는 여자가 착각한 회의 시간, 그리고 (C) 오전 10시 30분은 매니저가 최대한 일찍 도착할 수 있는 시각이다.

[53-55]

M Hi. I came here to buy some pens and folders yesterday. When I got home, I realized I didn't have my mobile phone. I think I may have dropped it somewhere in this store.

W Well, we cleaned and checked the store this morning. Are you sure you lost it here? No one has found anything.

M Absolutely. I also talked on the phone at this store. I've looked everywhere for my cell phone, but it's nowhere to be seen.

W In that case, I'll let all other employees know about your cell phone.

M I really appreciate your help. Now, I have something urgent to attend to. I'll come by again before eight o'clock.

W I see. I hope that someone will find your lost item by then.

M 안녕하세요. 저는 어제 펜과 서류철을 사러 이곳에 왔는데요. 집에 돌아갔을 때, 제 휴대폰이 없다는 걸 알았어요. 제 생각에는 이 매장 어딘가에 그것을 떨어뜨린 것 같아요.

W 음, 저희는 오늘 아침에 매장을 청소하고 점검했습니다. 여기서 잃어버린 게 확실한가요? 아무도 발견한 것이 없어요.

M 확실합니다. 이 매장에서 전화 통화도 했어요. 휴대폰을 찾으려고 모든 곳을 찾아봤지만, 어디에도 보이지 않습니다.

W 그렇다면, 제가 다른 모든 직원들에게 당신의 휴대폰에 대해 알리겠습니다.

M 도와주셔서 정말 감사합니다. 지금 제가 급하게 처리해야 할 일이 있어요. 8시 전에 다시 들르겠습니다.

W 알겠습니다. 그때쯤에는 누군가 당신의 분실물을 찾길 바랍니다.

어휘 realize 깨닫다, 알아채다 absolutely 전적으로, 틀림없이
urgent 긴급한 come by ~에 들르다 stationery 문구류
appliance 가전제품 damaged 손상된 inform A of B
A에게 B에 대해 알려주다

53 대화 장소

대화가 일어나는 곳은 어디인가?

(A) 문구점에서
(B) 휴대폰 매장에서
(C) 가전제품 수리점에서
(D) 비품 창고에서

해설 대화 장소는 주로 대화의 초반부에 단서가 나온다. 남자의 첫
대사에서 '어제 이 곳에 펜과 서류철을 사러 왔다(I came
here to buy some pens and folders yesterday.)'고 하
는 것을 보면, 대화하고 있는 장소가 문구점인 것을 알 수 있다.
따라서 정답은 (A)이다.

54 의도 파악

여자는 왜 "음, 저희는 오늘 아침에 매장을 청소하고 점검했습
니다"라고 하는가?
(A) 손상된 상품을 발견했다.
(B) 남자가 사려는 펜을 찾기 위해 노력했다.
(C) 모든 제품들을 제자리에 두었다.
(D) 매장 내에서 어떤 분실물도 보지 못했다.

해설 화자의 의도를 묻는 문제는 해당 문장의 앞뒤 문맥을 잘 파악
해야 한다. 주어진 문장의 바로 뒤에 여자가 '여기서 잃어버린
게 확실한가요? 아무도 발견한 것이 없어요(Are you sure
you lost it here? No one has found anything.)'라고 하
는 것을 보아, 정답이 (D)임을 알 수 있다.

55 제안

여자는 무엇을 하겠다고 하는가?
(A) 남자에게 오늘 늦게 전화한다
(B) 직원들에게 분실물에 대해 알린다
(C) 제품을 새것으로 교환한다
(D) 재고를 조사한다

해설 여자의 두 번째 대사에서 '다른 모든 직원들에게 당신의 휴대
폰에 대해 알리겠습니다(I'll let all other employees know
about your cell phone.)'라고 했으므로 정답은 (B)이다. 지
문의 cell phone이 item(물품)으로 표현되었다.

[56-58]

W Eric, there aren't any free parking spaces. Do you
happen to know when the construction will be
finished in the parking lot?
M I expect it to take about three weeks. So, I ride with
my other colleagues. By sharing rides, the parking
situation has become completely different. As the
number of cars is reduced, it's much easier to park.
How about finding someone to share a ride with?

W That sounds good. Do you know anyone else who
wants to carpool?
M Maybe Thomas does. He doesn't live very close to
you, but I don't think that's a big problem.
W Okay. I'll go see Thomas right away.

W 에릭, 무료 주차 공간이 하나도 없네요. 혹시 주차장 공사가 언제
끝나는지 아세요?
M 대략 3주 정도 걸릴 거라고 예상해요. 그래서 저는 다른 동료들과
차를 함께 타고 다닙니다. 차를 같이 타니까 주차 상황이 완전히 달
라졌어요. 자동차 수가 줄어드니, 주차하기 훨씬 더 수월해졌어요.
당신도 차를 함께 탈 사람을 찾는 게 어때요?
W 좋은 생각이에요. 카풀을 원하는 사람을 알고 있나요?
M 아마 토마스가 원할 겁니다. 그는 당신과 그렇게 가까이 살진 않지
만, 큰 문제는 없을 거라고 생각해요.
W 알겠습니다. 지금 당장 토마스를 만나러 가야겠어요.

어휘 parking space 주차 공간 happen to + V 혹시 ~하다,
우연히 ~하다 uncomfortable 불편한 transportation
운송, 수송

56 문제점

여자가 언급한 문제는 무엇인가?
(A) 주차 요금이 너무 비싸다.
(B) 차를 주차하기 어렵다.
(C) 많은 직원들이 회사 차량을 필요로 한다.
(D) 공사가 지연 중이다.

해설 여자의 첫 대사에서 '무료 주차 공간이 하나도 없다(there
aren't any free parking spaces.)'고 하고, 주차장 공사에
대해서도 언급하는 것으로 보아, 주차할 공간이 없어 어려움
을 겪고 있음을 알 수 있다. 따라서 정답은 (B)이다. 공사가 언
제 끝나는지 여자가 초반에 묻고 있지만 공사 지연으로 인한
문제는 아니므로 (D)는 오답이다.

57 의도 파악

남자는 왜 "차를 같이 타니까 주차 상황이 완전히 달라졌어
요"라고 하는가?
(A) 주차 공간을 찾는 것이 쉬워졌다.
(B) 차량 부족으로 그는 불편해졌다.
(C) 교통비가 줄어들었다.
(D) 많은 차량이 필요하다.

해설 화자의 의도를 묻는 문제는 주어진 문장의 앞뒤 문맥을 잘 파
악해야 한다. 해당 문장 앞에는 동료들과 차를 함께 타고 다닌
다고 했고, 뒤 문장에는 '자동차 수가 줄어드니 주차하기가 훨
씬 더 쉬워졌다(As the number of cars is reduced, it's
much easier to park.)'고 하는 것으로 보아, 자동차 수가 줄
어 주차 공간을 찾기가 쉬워졌음을 알 수 있다. 따라서 정답은
(A)이다.

58 세부 사항

토마스에 대해서 알 수 있는 것은?
(A) 큰 차를 가지고 있다.
(B) 운전을 잘한다.
(C) 공사 일정을 알고 있다.
(D) 여자와 가까운 곳에 살지 않는다.

해설 토마스가 언급된 부분을 집중해서 들어야 한다. 남자가 카풀을 원하는 사람으로 토마스를 언급하고, 뒤이어 "그는 당신과 가까이 살지 않지만(He doesn't live very close to you)" 이라고 하는 것을 보아 정답이 (D)임을 알 수 있다.

[59-61] 3인 대화

> W Could you please let me know the progress in entering our golf membership information into the computer?
> M1 It's coming along. I've almost finished creating the computer files for most of the members in our system, and Lucas is in the middle of updating our reservation system.
> M2 Yes. I'm setting it up so that all their information can be processed electronically when our members make a reservation.
> W That's great. Could you finish the work by the end of this month?
> M1 I think it's a little difficult.
> M2 To complete the whole thing by then, we need more people.
> W OK, I'll ask the personnel department if we can hire more employees in our department.
>
> W 우리 골프 회원 정보를 컴퓨터에 입력하는 것에 대한 진행 상황을 알려 줄래요?
> M1 잘 진행되고 있습니다. 저는 우리 시스템에 있는 대부분의 회원들에 대한 컴퓨터 파일을 거의 다 만들었고, 루카스는 예약 시스템을 업데이트하는 중입니다.
> M2 네. 우리 회원들이 예약하면, 그들의 모든 정보가 전자상으로 처리될 수 있도록 설정하고 있습니다.
> W 아주 좋아요. 이번 달 말까지 그 일을 끝낼 수 있겠어요?
> M1 제 생각엔 그건 좀 어려울 것 같아요.
> M2 그때까지 모든 일을 끝내려면, 더 많은 인력이 필요합니다.
> W 알겠어요, 제가 우리 부서에 직원을 더 고용할 수 있는지 인사부에 물어볼게요.

어휘 progress 진행, 진척   enter A into B A를 B에 입력하다   in the middle of ~하는 중인   personnel department 인사부   hire 고용하다   inspect 점검하다, 검사하다   contact 연락하다, 접촉하다   convene 수집하다

59 화자의 근무지

화자들은 어디에서 일하는 것 같은가?
(A) 골프장에서
(B) 병원에서

(C) 컴퓨터 매장에서
(D) 소프트웨어 회사에서

해설 화자들의 직업이나 신분은 대화의 초반에 단서가 나온다. 여자의 첫 대사에서 '우리의 골프 회원 정보를 컴퓨터에 입력하는 것(entering our golf membership information into the computer)'의 진행 상황에 대해 묻는 것을 보아 세 사람이 (A) 골프장에서 근무하고 있음을 알 수 있다.

60 세부 사항

남자들이 하고 있는 일은 무엇인가?
(A) 예약하기
(B) 서류 정리하기
(C) 데이터베이스에 정보 입력하기
(D) 컴퓨터 시스템 점검하기

해설 첫 번째 남자는 '시스템에 있는 회원들에 대한 컴퓨터 파일을 만들고(creating the computer files for most of the members in our system)' 두 번째 남자는 '예약 시, 회원들의 모든 정보가 전자상으로 처리될 수 있도록 설정하고 있다(setting it up so that all their information can be processed electronically when our members make a reservation.)'는 것을 미루어 볼 때, 두 사람이 데이터베이스에 들어가는 회원 정보와 관련된 작업을 하고 있음을 알 수 있다. 따라서 정답은 (C)이다.

61 다음에 할 일

여자가 다음에 할 일은 무엇인가?
(A) 더 많은 직원을 고용한다
(B) 컴퓨터를 수리한다
(C) 다른 부서에 연락한다
(D) 회의를 소집한다

해설 다음에 할 일을 묻는 문제는 대화의 후반부를 집중해서 들어야 한다. 두 번째 남자의 마지막 대사에서 더 많은 인력이 필요하다고 하자 여자가 '인사부에 직원 고용을 할 수 있는지 물어보겠다(I'll ask the personnel department if we can hire more employees in our department.)'고 했으므로 정답은 (C)이다.

[62-64]

> M Hi, I have some great news. The board of directors finally approved our proposal!
> W That's great! I've been waiting a long time for the results to come out. Then, where do you think is the best place to open our new store?
> M That's what I'm most concerned about now. It's really not easy to come to a conclusion.
> W You don't have to worry about that. I have already done a market survey to see which areas have the highest demand for our clothes. If there are no major changes, perhaps we should open our first store in York.

M Good. Then I'll find out what it costs to open a store in the area.

M 안녕하세요, 좋은 소식이 있어요. 이사회가 마침내 우리 제안을 승인했어요!

W 잘됐네요! 그 결과가 나오길 오랫동안 기다렸어요. 그럼, 우리 새로운 매장을 개점하기 가장 좋은 장소가 어디라고 생각해요?

M 그게 지금 제가 가장 걱정하는 부분이에요. 결론을 내기 정말 쉽지 않네요.

W 걱정할 필요 없어요. 제가 이미 우리 의류에 대한 수요가 가장 높은 지역이 어디인지 알아보기 위한 시장조사를 마쳤어요. 큰 변동이 없으면, 아마 York에 우리의 첫 매장을 개점하는 게 좋을 거예요.

M 좋아요. 그럼 저는 그 지역에서 매장을 여는 데 비용이 얼마나 드는지 알아볼게요.

어휘 approve 승인하다 be concerned about ~에 관심을 가지다, 걱정하다 come to a conclusion 종결되다, 결론에 도달하다 market survey 시장조사 demand 수요 real estate 부동산 expand 확장하다 release 공개하다, 출시하다 recruit 모집(채용)하다 figure out 알아내다, 계산하다

62 화자의 직업

화자들은 어떤 산업에서 일하는가?
(A) 금융 서비스업
(B) 마케팅업
(C) 의류업
(D) 부동산업

해설 일반적으로 화자의 직업은 대화의 초반에 언급되지만, 이 문제에서는 여자의 두 번째 대사에 단서가 나온다. '우리 의류에 대한 가장 높은 수요(the highest demand for our clothes)'라는 표현을 통해 두 화자가 의류업계에 종사한다는 것을 알 수 있으므로 정답은 (C)이다.

63 세부 사항

화자들은 무엇을 할 예정인가?
(A) 사업을 확장한다
(B) 신제품을 출시한다
(C) 제품을 광고한다
(D) 새로운 회원들을 모집한다

해설 여자의 첫 대사에서 '새 매장을 개점하기 좋은 장소가 어디일지(where do you think is the best place to open our new store?)' 물어보는 것으로 보아 그들이 사업을 확장하려 한다는 걸 알 수 있다. 따라서 정답은 (A)이다.

64 다음에 할 일

남자가 다음에 할 일은 무엇인가?
(A) 회의를 준비한다
(B) 고객과 만난다
(C) 비용을 계산한다
(D) 장소를 추천한다

해설 다음에 할 일은 주로 대화 후반부에 단서가 나온다. 남자의 마지막 대사를 보면, '비용이 얼마나 드는지 알아보겠다(I'll find out what it costs to open a store in the area.)'고 했으므로 정답은 (C)이다.

[65-67] 대화 & 건물 안내도

W Hello, I'm here because I have a doctor's appointment at 11 A.M. I just parked in the parking lot. What's the hourly rate here?

M Actually, customers visiting any office in this building can park here for free. When you leave later, please show the receipt from the office you visited.

W Okay. Then, this is my first visit to the Denver Clinic in this building, but the clinic's name isn't on the building directory. Could you tell me where to go?

M The clinic just moved in last Saturday, and we haven't had enough time to change the directory from Royal Bank to Denver Clinic.

W 안녕하세요, 오전 11시에 병원 진료 예약이 있어서 왔습니다. 방금 주차장에 주차했어요. 이곳의 주차 요금은 시간당 얼마인가요?

M 사실, 이 건물 사무실에 방문하는 고객들은 이곳에 무료로 주차할 수 있어요. 나중에 나갈 때, 방문하신 사무실의 영수증을 보여 주면 됩니다.

W 알겠습니다. 그런데, 이 건물의 Denver 병원은 처음 오는데, 병원 이름이 건물 안내도에 없어요. 어디로 가야 하는지 알려주실 수 있나요?

M 그 병원은 지난 토요일에 막 입점했고, 우리는 안내도를 Royal 은행에서 Denver 병원으로 변경할 충분한 시간이 없었어요.

사무실	위치
Star 미용실	1105호
Yoon 병원	1125호
Royal 은행	1205호
Blue 법률사무소	1512호

어휘 parking lot 주차장 hourly 매 시간의 for free 무료로 receipt 영수증 directory 명부, 목록 deliver 배달하다, 전달하다 consult 상담하다 duration 기간 discounted 할인된

65 목적

여자가 방문한 목적은 무엇인가?
(A) 변호사를 만나기 위해
(B) 은행 계좌를 개설하기 위해
(C) 물건을 전달하기 위해
(D) 의사의 신료를 받기 위해

해설 여자의 첫 번째 대사에서 '병원 진료 예약이 있다(I have a doctor's appointment)'는 부분을 통해 여자가 의사의 진료를 받으러 왔음을 알 수 있다. 따라서 정답은 (D)이다.

66 세부 사항

남자는 주차에 대해 뭐라고 말하는가?
(A) 주차 시간이 제한되어 있다.
(B) 고객들은 할인된 요금을 지불한다.
(C) 방문객들은 무료로 주차할 수 있다.
(D) 주말에는 주차할 수 없다.

`해설` 남자의 첫 번째 대사에서 '영수증을 보여주면 방문 고객들은 무료로 주차할 수 있다(customers visiting any office in this building can park here for free.)'고 했으므로, 정답은 (C)이다.

67 시각 자료 연계

시각 자료를 보시오. 여자는 건물에서 어디로 갈 것 같은가?
(A) 1105호
(B) 1125호
(C) 1205호
(D) 1512호

`해설` 남자의 마지막 대사에 따르면, 여자가 찾는 병원(Denver Clinic)은 지난 토요일에 막 들어온(just moved in last Saturday) 병원이어서 아직 건물 안내도의 이름이 Royal 은행에서 Denver 병원으로 변경되지 않았다. 따라서 여자는 병원에 가기 위해 Royal 은행이 있었던 곳인 1205호로 가야 하므로 정답은 (C)이다. 병원 진료 예약을 했다는 말만 듣고 (B)를 고르지 않도록 주의한다.

[68-70] 대화 & 평면도

M Lisa, I know you're very busy preparing for the orientation for new employees, but do you have time to approve the room assignment for our renovation?

W No problem. Could you explain how you are planning to assign offices?

M Rooms 1 and 2 have been assigned to our marketing staff. And you've come to use the office next to the staff lounge. In that office, you'll have enough space for meetings.

W Oh, I think it's good for me. If so, the room at the corner is yours, isn't it?

M Yes, I thought it would be nice, as it's close to both the marketing team and you.

W Good! I think everyone will like the plan due to the bigger lounge.

M 리사, 신입 사원 오리엔테이션을 준비하느라 바쁜 거 알고 있습니다만, 개조 작업을 위한 방 배정을 승인해 줄 시간이 있나요?

W 문제 없어요. 사무실을 어떻게 배정할 계획인지 설명해줄 수 있나요?

M 1, 2호실은 우리 마케팅 직원들에게 배정됐어요. 그리고 당신은 직원 휴게실 옆에 있는 사무실을 사용하게 되었습니다. 그 사무실에서 당신은 충분한 회의 공간을 갖게 될 겁니다.

W 아, 저에게 잘된 일인 것 같군요. 그렇다면, 모통이에 있는 방은 당신 사무실이군요, 아닌가요?

M 네, 그곳이 마케팅 팀과 당신 둘 다에 가깝기 때문에 좋을 거라고 생각했어요.

W 좋네요! 더 큰 휴게실이 생겨서 모두 그 계획을 좋아할 거예요.

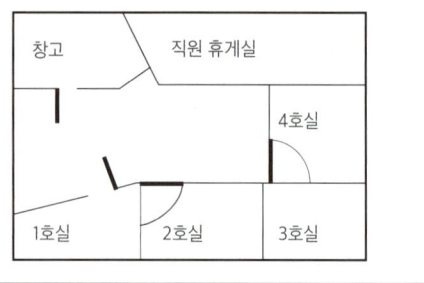

`어휘` be busy -ing ~하느라 바쁘다 assignment 배정 renovation 보수, 수리 assign 할당하다, 배정하다 next to ~옆에 lounge 휴게실, 라운지 both A and B A와 B 둘 다 organize 조직하다, 준비하다

68 세부 사항

여자는 왜 바쁜가?
(A) 그녀는 행사를 준비하고 있다.
(B) 그녀는 개조 작업을 계획하고 있다.
(C) 그녀는 마케팅 회의를 준비하고 있다.
(D) 그녀는 사무실을 청소하고 있다.

`해설` 남자의 첫 대사에서 '신입 사원 오리엔테이션 준비하느라 바쁜 것을 알고 있다(I know you're very busy preparing for the orientation for new employees)'는 부분을 통해 여자가 행사를 준비하느라 바쁘다는 것을 알 수 있다. 따라서 정답은 (A)이다.

69 시각 자료 연계

시각 자료를 보시오. 어떤 방이 여자에게 배정되었는가?
(A) 1호실
(B) 2호실
(C) 3호실
(D) 4호실

`해설` 남자의 두 번째 대사에서 '당신은 직원 휴게실 옆에 있는 사무실을 이용하게 되었다(you've come to use the office next to the staff lounge.)'고 했으므로 (D)가 정답이다.

70 세부 사항

여자의 말에 따르면, 왜 직원들이 그 계획을 좋아할 것인가?
(A) 휴게실이 이전보다 더 크다.
(B) 그들은 넓은 작업 공간을 가질 것이다.
(C) 그들의 사무실이 여자의 사무실과 가깝다.
(D) 그들은 자신들의 사무실에서 회의할 수 있다.

`해설` 여자의 마지막 대사에서 '더 큰 휴게실이 생겨서 모든 직원들이 그 계획을 좋아할 것이다(I think everyone will like the plan due to the bigger lounge.)'라는 부분을 통해 정답이 (A)임을 알 수 있다.

PART 4

[71-73] 회의 발췌

Today, we've had a great gathering to learn some really useful information. Let's give a big hand to Richard for giving us great tips on designing our homepage. Before we end the meeting, I have a few things to tell you. First, it's time to pay the yearly membership fee again. Please send your renewal payment to my account by May 10. Also, remember that we usually meet on the 5th of every month, but the next meeting will be at the Wilton Hotel banquet hall on June 1st. So, please don't forget to update your schedules.

오늘 우리는 정말 유용한 몇 가지 정보를 알게 되는 좋은 모임을 가졌습니다. 우리의 홈페이지를 디자인하는 것에 대한 훌륭한 팁들을 제공해 준 리처드에게 큰 박수를 보냅시다. 모임을 마무리하기 전에, 여러분에게 몇 가지 드릴 말씀이 있어요. 첫 번째, 연회비를 다시 납부할 때가 되었어요. 여러분의 연장 회비를 5월 10일까지 제 계좌로 보내주세요. 또한, 우리 보통 매월 5일에 모이지만, 다음 모임은 6월 1일 Wilton 호텔 연회장에서 있을 예정입니다. 그러니 여러분의 일정을 업데이트하는 것을 잊지 마세요.

어휘 gathering 모임, 수집 give a big hand to ~에게 큰 박수를 보내다 membership fee 회비 renewal 갱신, 연장 update 갱신하다, 최신 정보를 알려주다 patron 고객, 후원자 clerk 직원, 점원

71 청자의 직업

청자들은 누구일 것 같은가?
(A) 모임 회원들
(B) 호텔 손님들
(C) 가게 직원들
(D) 의상 디자이너들

해설 화자나 청자의 신분에 대한 단서는 대부분 지문의 초반에 언급되지만, 해당 지문에서는 중반부에서 힌트가 나온다. 지문의 네 번째 문장에서 '연회비를 다시 납부할 때가 되었다(it's time to pay the yearly membership tee again.)'는 내용이 나오는데, 이를 통해 청자들이 어떤 모임에 소속된 회원들임을 알 수 있다. 따라서 정답은 (A)이다.

72 요청 사항

화자는 청자들에게 무엇을 제출하라고 요청하는가?
(A) 지불금
(B) 계좌 번호
(C) 갱신된 정보
(D) 회원 카드

해설 앞서 화자가 연회비를 납부해야 한다고 언급한 후, '자신의 계좌로 회비를 보내달라(Please send your renewal payment to my account)'고 요청하고 있으므로, 정답이 (A) 지불금임을 알 수 있다.

73 세부 사항

다음 모임은 언제 열릴 것인가?
(A) 5월 5일
(B) 5월 10일
(C) 6월 1일
(D) 6월 10일

해설 지문에서 날짜를 여러 번 언급하기 때문에 질문에서 묻는 내용을 정확히 파악해야 한다. 후반부에 '다음 모임은 6월 1일에 Wilton 호텔 연회장에서 열릴 것(the next meeting will be at the Wilton Hotel banquet hall on June 1st.)'이라고 얘기하고 있으므로, 정답은 (C)이다.

[74-76] 전화 메시지

Hello, this is Jennifer Moore from the management team here at the Stars Electronics production plant. I'm calling to let you know about an inevitable change we need to make to our production schedule. Our supplier just informed me that the shipping of the display panels that was supposed to arrive tomorrow is going to be delayed. They said they'll be able to send us the panels this Thursday. As this postpones our schedule a bit, I'd like to ask you to see if there are any employees who can work on the weekend. Then we will be able to produce the order on time. Thank you.

안녕하세요, 저는 Stars Electronics 생산공장의 관리팀에서 근무하는 제니퍼 무어입니다. 우리의 생산 일정에 불가피한 변동이 필요하다는 점을 알려드리기 위해 전화했어요. 우리 공급업체가 내일 도착하기로 되어 있던 디스플레이 패널의 배송이 지연될 거라고 방금 알려줬습니다. 그들은 이번 주 목요일에 패널을 보내줄 수 있을 거라고 말했어요. 이로 인해 우리의 일정도 조금 늦춰져서, 주말에 근무할 수 있는 직원들이 있는지 알아봐 주길 요청하고 싶습니다. 그러면 우리가 주문품을 제때 생산할 수 있을 겁니다. 감사합니다.

어휘 inevitable 불가피한 panel 판, 금속판 delay(= postpone) 연기하다, 미루다 on time 시간을 어기지 않고, 정각에 facility 설비, 시설 missing 빠뜨린, 분실된 deliver 배달하다, 배달

74 화자의 근무지

화자는 어디에서 근무하는가?
(A) 백화점에서
(B) 배송업체에서
(C) 전자제품 공장에서
(D) 발전소에서

해설 화자의 수속이나 직업은 일반적으로 지문의 초반에 단서가 나온다. 첫 문장에서 화자가 '전자제품 생산공장 소속(from the management team here at the Stars Electronics production plant.)'이라고 언급했으므로, 정답은 (C)이다.

75 문제점

문제가 무엇인가?
(A) 생산 설비가 작동하지 않는다.
(B) 주문품들이 분실되었다.
(C) 잘못된 제품들이 배송되었다.
(D) 배송이 지연될 것이다.

해설 중반부에 '내일 도착하기로 했던 패널의 배송이 지연될 것(the shipping of the display panels that was supposed to arrive tomorrow is going to be delayed.)'이라는 내용이 나오고 그로 인해 일정 변동이 불가피하다는 내용이 이어지므로, 정답은 (D)이다.

76 요청 사항

화자는 청자에게 무엇을 하라고 요청하는가?
(A) 평소보다 제품을 일찍 배송하는 것
(B) 제품이 배송되기를 기다리는 것
(C) 주말에 일할 직원을 찾는 것
(D) 이번 주에 야간 근무하는 것

해설 요청이나 부탁하는 내용은 주로 지문의 후반부에 나온다. 후반부에서 부탁하는 표현(I'd like to ask you ~)이 나온 후 '주말에 일할 수 있는 직원을 찾아봐 달라(I'd like to ask you to see if there are any employees who can work on the weekend.)'고 요청하고 있으므로, 정답은 (C)이다.

[77-79] 방송

Welcome to Innovative Business Strategies on KSJ Radio. On today's show, we've invited special guest Grace Wilson, a professor of business administration at Kings University. She recently made headlines for writing a paper on "Forward-oriented Management". Having enough leisure time is the most important condition for employees to exercise their creativity and enthusiasm, she argued. Today, she will talk about how to use leisure time efficiently. If there is something you would like to ask her while she is with us, please post it on the Web site.

KSJ 라디오의 '혁신적 사업 전략'에 오신 것을 환영합니다. 오늘 방송에서 저희는 Kings 대학교 경영학 교수인 그레이스 윌슨 씨를 특별 손님으로 초대했습니다. 그녀는 최근에 "미래 지향적 경영"에 관한 논문을 써서 화제가 되었죠. 충분한 여가시간을 갖는 것은 직원들이 그들의 창의력과 열정을 발휘하는 데 있어 가장 중요한 조건이라고 그녀는 주장했습니다. 오늘 그녀는 여가시간을 어떻게 효율적으로 활용하는지 이야기할 것입니다. 그녀가 우리와 함께하는 동안 질문이 있으시면, 홈페이지에 게시해 주기 바랍니다.

어휘 innovative 혁신적인 administration 관리 recently 최근에 make headlines 화제가 되다, 대대적으로 보도되다 leisure 여가 condition 상태, 조건, 환경 creativity 창의력 enthusiasm 열정 argue 주장하다 efficiently 효율적으로 hold 쥐다, 개최하다 reward 보상하다 performance 성과 contact 연락하다

77 특정 인물의 신분

그레이스 윌슨은 누구인가?
(A) 라디오 진행자
(B) 기자
(C) 경영인
(D) 교수

해설 지문 초반에 해당 이름이 나오고 '경영학 교수(a professor of business administration)'라고 소개되었으므로 정답은 (D)이다.

78 세부 사항

윌슨 씨에 따르면, 직원들의 창의력을 발휘하게 하는 가장 좋은 방법은 무엇인가?
(A) 워크숍 자주 개최하기
(B) 충분한 자유시간 제공하기
(C) 좋은 실적을 보상하기
(D) 온라인으로 근무하게 하기

해설 중반부에 '여가시간을 충분히 갖는 것이 창의력을 발휘하기에 가장 중요한 조건(Having enough leisure time is the most important condition for employees to exercise their creativity)'이라고 윌슨 씨가 주장했다고 했으므로 정답은 (B)이다.

79 세부 사항

윌슨 씨에게 질문이 있는 청자들은 무엇을 해야 하는가?
(A) 그녀에게 온라인으로 물어본다
(B) 편지를 보낸다
(C) 그녀의 사무실을 방문한다
(D) 방송 후 그녀에게 연락한다

해설 지문의 마지막 문장에서 '윌슨 씨에게 묻고 싶은 것이 있다면 홈페이지에 올려 달라(If there is something you would like to ask her while she is with us, please post it on the Web site.)'는 내용이 나온다. 따라서 on the Web site를 online으로 표현한 (A)가 정답이다.

[80-82] 안내

Good afternoon, and welcome to the Seoul National Art Museum. I'll be your tour guide in the museum today. After a while, you'll see some great exhibits. There are artworks by the sculptor Ace Watson. The most outstanding feature of Mr. Watson's sculptures is that the patterns are very delicate. Many critics expressed surprise at the patterns on the sculptures. The tour will last for about one hour. Before we begin, I recommend leaving your belongings in the lockers beside the front desk. And please remember that you can't take pictures in the museum.

안녕하세요, 서울국립미술관에 오신 것을 환영합니다. 저는 오늘 미술관에서 여러분의 관광 안내원이 될 것입니다. 잠시 후, 여러분은 굉장한 전시품들을 보게 될 것입니다. 조각가 에이스 왓슨의 예술작품들이 전시되어 있습니다. 왓슨 씨의 조각상의 가장 두드러진 특징은 무늬가 매우 섬세하다는 것입니다. 많은 비평가들이 조각상의 무늬에 놀라움을 표했습니다. 견학은 약 1시간 동안 진행될 예정입니다. 시작하기 전에, 여러분의 소지품들은 안내데스크 옆에 있는 개인 보관함에 넣어 두시길 바랍니다. 그리고, 미술관에서 사진 촬영은 할 수 없다는 것을 기억해 주세요.

어휘 exhibit 전시품; 전시하다 artwork 미술작품 sculptor 조각가 outstanding 뛰어난, 두드러진 feature 특징, 특색 sculpture 조각 pattern 패턴, 무늬 delicate 섬세한, 정교한 belongings 소지품 locker 보관함 detailed 구체적인, 상세한, 섬세한 simple 간단한, 단순한 be made of ~으로 만들어지다 identification card 신분증 storage 저장, 저장고, 보관함 brochure 소책자, 안내문

80 화자의 직업

화자는 누구인가?
(A) 관광 안내원
(B) 비평가
(C) 접수 담당자
(D) 예술가

해설 화자의 신분은 주로 지문의 초반에 나온다. 두 번째 문장에서 '저는 오늘 여러분의 관광 안내원이 될 겁니다(I'll be your tour guide in the museum today.)'라는 내용이 있으므로 정답은 (A)이다.

81 세부 사항

화자는 왓슨 씨의 조각상에 대해 뭐라고 말하는가?
(A) 단순하다.
(B) 디자인이 섬세하다.
(C) 매우 유명하다.
(D) 특별한 재료로 만들어졌다.

해설 지문 초반의 '무늬가 매우 섬세하다(The most outstanding feature of Mr. Watson's sculptures is that the patterns are very delicate.)'는 내용을 통해 정답을 쉽게 알 수 있다. delicate를 detailed로, patterns를 designs로 바꿔 표현한 (B)가 정답이다.

82 제안

화자는 청자들에게 무엇을 하라고 제안하는가?
(A) 신분증 제시하기
(B) 안내데스크에서 사진 찍기
(C) 개인 물품을 보관함에 보관하기
(D) 입구에서 안내 책자 가져가기

해설 제안이나 요구사항은 주로 지문의 후반에 답이 나온다. '소지품을 보관함에 넣어 두시길 바랍니다(I recommend leaving your belongings in the lockers beside the front desk.)'라고 하는 것을 보아, 정답은 belongings를 personal items라고 표현한 (C)임을 알 수 있다.

[83-85] 회의 발췌

I'd like to talk to you about our energy-saving campaign. What we should do here at Dream Construction is to be a leader in saving electricity, so we're asking that all employees try to use as little electricity as they can. For example, please be sure to turn off lights and computers when leaving the office. Of course, everyone has managed to do well so far. But I'd like you to be more attentive in the future. Beginning this month, we will introduce a compensation plan for teams that are good at saving energy. Tickets to the Alicia Ruiz concert will be given to the team members who have used the least electricity.

저는 여러분에게 에너지 절약 캠페인에 대해 이야기하고자 합니다. 이곳 Dream Construction 사에서 우리가 해야 할 일은 전기 절약에 앞장서는 것입니다. 그래서 우리는 모든 직원들이 가능한 한 전기를 적게 사용하도록 노력할 것을 요청합니다. 예를 들어, 퇴근할 때 전등과 컴퓨터를 반드시 꺼 주세요. 물론, 모두가 지금까지 그럭저럭 잘해왔습니다. 하지만 앞으로 더 신경 써 주시기 바랍니다. 이번 달부터, 에너지 절약을 잘한 팀을 위한 보상 제도를 도입할 것입니다. 전기를 가장 적게 사용한 팀원들에게는 알리시아 루이즈의 콘서트 티켓이 주어질 것입니다.

어휘 saving 절약 electricity 전기 be sure to 반드시 ~하다 manage to 그럭저럭 ~하다 so far 여태껏, 지금까지 attentive 주의를 기울이는, 신경 쓰는 beginning ~시점 부로 compensation 보상 resource 자원, 재료 share 공유하다 expense 비용 recycle 재활용하다 waste 낭비하다; 폐기물

83 주제

화자는 주로 무엇에 대해 말하고 있는가?
(A) 전기 사용 줄이기
(B) 근무 시간 단축하기
(C) 새로운 에너지 사원 만들기
(D) 사무실 비품 공유하기

해설 초반부에 '에너지 절약 캠페인에 대해 이야기하고자 한다(I'd like to talk to you about our energy-saving campaign)'는 내용이 나오고 그 뒤에도 전기를 절약하자고 요청하는 것으로 보아, 전기 사용을 줄이는 것에 대해 말하고 있음을 알 수 있다. 따라서 정답은 (A)이다.

84 세부 사항

직원들에 대해 알 수 있는 것은?
(A) 비용을 신경 쓰지 않는다.
(B) 비품을 새활용하려고 한다.
(C) 전기를 절약하려고 노력한다.
(D) 많은 에너지를 낭비하곤 했다.

해설 중반부에 '모두가 지금까지 그럭저럭 잘해 왔다(everyone has managed to do well so far.)'고 언급하는 것으로 보아

직원들이 지금까지 전기를 절약하려고 노력했다는 것을 알 수 있다. 따라서 정답은 (C)이다.

85 다음에 할 일

이번 달에 회사는 무엇을 하려고 하는가?
(A) 개회식을 준비한다
(B) 광고 캠페인을 만든다
(C) 시상식을 연다
(D) 보상 제도를 도입한다

해설 마지막 부분에서 '이번 달부터, 에너지 절약을 잘한 팀을 위한 보상 제도를 도입할 것이다(Beginning this month, we will introduce a compensation plan for teams that are good at saving energy.)'라는 내용이 나오므로 정답이 (D) 임을 알 수 있다.

[86-88] 전화 메시지

Hello, Sheryl. This is Daniel from British Electronics. I'm calling about the order for computers that we received from your company last Wednesday. I printed and reviewed your order form, and I would like to check on something with you. You ordered 15 computers which add up to $2,400, but we've received only $1,650. The amount you sent is the equivalent of 15 monitors, not computers. So, we can't send you the products now. I think there might have been some confusion on your end. Would you call or e-mail me to talk about that? Thanks.

....

안녕하세요, 셰릴 씨. 저는 British Electronics 사의 다니엘입니다. 지난 수요일에 당신의 회사에서 받은 컴퓨터 주문에 관하여 전화 드립니다. 저는 당신의 주문서를 출력해서 검토해 보았는데, 당신과 확인하고 싶은 사항이 있습니다. 당신은 총 2,400달러에 달하는 15대의 컴퓨터를 주문했으나, 저희는 1,650달러만 받았습니다. 당신이 보낸 금액은 컴퓨터가 아니라 모니터 15대에 대한 금액과 같습니다. 그래서 저희는 지금 그 제품들을 보내드릴 수 없습니다. 귀사 쪽에서 약간 혼돈이 있었던 것 같습니다. 그 사안에 대해 이야기하기 위해 저에게 전화나 이메일을 주시겠습니까? 감사합니다.

어휘 order form 주문서 amount 양, 총액 equivalent 동등한; 등가물 submit an order 주문하다, 주문서를 제출하다 payment 지불 pay for ~을 지불하다

86 세부 사항

화자는 무슨 주문을 받았는가?
(A) 모니터
(B) 복사기
(C) 컴퓨터
(D) 프린터

해설 지문 초반에 '지난 수요일에 우리가 받은 컴퓨터 주문에 관하여 전화 드린다(I'm calling about the order for computers that we received from your company

last Wednesday.)'는 내용이 나오고, 이어지는 내용에서도 '당신은 15대의 컴퓨터를 주문했다(You ordered 15 computers)'고 언급하고 있으므로, 정답은 (C)이다.

87 의도 파악

화자가 "당신과 확인하고 싶은 사항이 있습니다"라고 말한 의도는 무엇인가?
(A) 제품이 품절되었다.
(B) 그가 잘못된 물품을 보냈다.
(C) 청자가 주문서를 제출하지 않았다.
(D) 지불에 문제가 있다.

해설 해당 문장 뒤에 '당신은 2,400달러에 달하는 15대의 컴퓨터를 주문했는데, 1,650달러만 받았다(You ordered 15 computers which add up to $2,400, but we've received only $1,650.)'는 내용이 나온다. 이는 물품 비용 계산이 잘못되었다는 의미이므로, 정답은 (D)이다.

88 요청 사항

화자는 청자에게 무엇을 하라고 요청하는가?
(A) 주문서를 다시 보내는 것
(B) 그 사안에 대해 논의하기 위해 그에게 연락하는 것
(C) 물품 비용을 당장 지불하는 것
(D) 수리를 위해 공장에 전화하는 것

해설 마지막 문장에서 '그 사안에 대해 이야기하기 위해 전화나 이메일로 연락해 달라(Would you call or e-mail me to talk about that?)'고 청자에게 요청하고 있으므로 정답은 (B)이다.

[89-91] 전화 메시지

Hi, this is Anna from Houston Clinic. I'm calling to remind you that it has been a year since you had a medical checkup. It is time to get a medical checkup again. Customers are able to make appointments online. If you go to www.houstonclinic.com, you can make an appointment easily. Maybe one minute is enough. The Web site is very well designed for your convenience, but if you are not used to using it, you can always call us at 555-1117. Thank you!

....

안녕하세요, 저는 Houston 병원의 안나입니다. 당신이 건강검진을 받은 지 1년이 되었다는 것을 알려 드리기 위해 전화 드립니다. 건강검진을 다시 받으실 시기입니다. 고객들은 온라인으로 예약할 수 있습니다. www.houstonclinic.com에 접속하시면 쉽게 예약할 수 있습니다. 아마 1분이면 충분할 것입니다. 웹 사이트는 여러분의 편의를 위해 매우 잘 설계되어 있지만, 만약 사용하는 데 익숙하지 않으시면, 언제든 555-1117로 전화 주시면 됩니다. 감사합니다!

어휘 remind 상기시키다 medical checkup 건강검진 convenience 편의 be used to ~ing ~하는 것에 익숙하다 look over ~을 훑어보다, 살펴보다 place an order 주문하다 treatment 치료, 대우, 대접 be close to ~에 가깝다

89 화자의 근무지

화자는 어디에서 일하는가?
(A) 의료기기 회사에서
(B) 병원에서
(C) 약국에서
(D) 문화 회관에서

해설 화자의 직업은 주로 지문의 초반에 나온다. 첫 번째 문장에서 화자가 'Houston 병원의 Anna입니다(this is Anna from Houston Clinic.)'라고 소개하고 있으므로, 정답은 (B)이다.

90 세부 사항

화자는 왜 청자에게 웹 사이트를 방문하라고 요청하는가?
(A) 사진을 살펴보기 위해
(B) 정보를 얻기 위해
(C) 예약하기 위해
(D) 주문하기 위해

해설 질문의 키워드인 '웹 사이트' 주소가 들리는 문장을 잘 들으면 답을 찾을 수 있다. 지문 중반에 '웹 사이트에 방문하면 쉽게 예약할 수 있다(If you go to www.houstonclinic.com, you can make an appointment easily.)'고 말하고 있으므로, 정답은 (C)이다.

91 의도 파악

화자가 "아마 1분이면 충분할 것입니다"라고 말한 의도는 무엇인가?
(A) 치료는 오래 걸리지 않는다.
(B) 청자는 충분한 시간이 없다.
(C) 온라인 시스템은 이용하기 쉽다.
(D) 사무실이 청자와 매우 가까운 곳에 있다.

해설 앞서 웹 사이트로 예약하는 것이 쉽다고 했고, 뒤에서도 '웹 사이트는 고객들의 편의를 위해 매우 잘 설계되어 있다(The Web site is very well designed for your convenience)'고 하는 것으로 보아, 해당 문장이 그들의 온라인 시스템은 이용하기 쉽다는 것을 강조하고 있음을 알 수 있다. 따라서 정답은 (C)이다.

[92-94] 안내 & 시간표

Attention, all passengers leaving on the 4 P.M. flight to San Francisco. The storm is so severe that the flight will be canceled. But the storm is moving quickly, so you are expected to be able to leave before seven o'clock. However, if there are not enough seats on the flight, some passengers may have to take a ten o'clock flight. Hotel accommodations will be provided for passengers who don't mind leaving tomorrow. Thanks for your patience, and we apologize for any inconvenience.

오후 4시에 샌프란시스코행 비행기로 떠나는 승객 여러분 주목하세요. 폭풍이 너무 심한 관계로 항공편이 결항될 예정입니다. 하지만 폭풍이 빠르게 이동 중이어서, 7시 전에는 출발할 수 있을 것으로 예상됩니다. 그러나, 비행기에 좌석이 충분하지 않을 경우, 일부 승객들은 10시 비행기를 타야 할 수도 있습니다. 내일 출발해도 되는 승객께는 호텔 숙박이 제공될 것입니다. 양해해 주셔서 감사 드리며, 불편을 끼쳐드려 죄송합니다.

출발	도착
10:00	14:20
12:00	16:20
13:30	17:50
16:00	20:20
18:50	23:10
22:00	02:20

어휘 storm 폭풍 severe 극심한, 혹독한 be expected to ~할 것으로 예상되다 accommodation 숙박시설 apologize for ~에 대해 사과하다 shortage 부족 failure 고장, 실패 interruption 중단, 방해 lodging 숙소 shuttle bus 셔틀버스

92 문제점

무엇이 결항을 야기했는가?
(A) 악천후
(B) 연료 부족
(C) 장비 고장
(D) 통신 중단

해설 지문의 초반에서 '폭풍이 너무 심해서 비행기가 결항될 것(The storm is so severe that the flight will be canceled.)'이라는 내용을 봤을 때 악천후로 인해 결항될 것임을 알 수 있다. 따라서 정답은 (A)이다.

93 시각 자료 연계

시각 자료를 보시오. 청자들은 이르면 몇 시에 떠날 수 있는가?
(A) 10시
(B) 16시
(C) 18시 50분
(D) 22시

해설 지문의 중반에서 '7시 전에는 출발할 수 있을 것으로 예상된다(you are expected to be able to leave before seven o'clock.)'고 했는데, 원래의 출발 시간인 4시 이후에 출발하는 항공편 중 7시 이전에 출발하는 것은 18시 50분 항공편이므로, 정답은 (C)이다.

94 세부 사항

다음 날 출발하는 승객들에게는 무엇이 제공되는가?
(A) 특별 쿠폰
(B) 숙박 시설

(C) 무료 셔틀버스 서비스
(D) 좌석 업그레이드

해설 지문 후반에, '내일 출발해도 되는 승객들께는 호텔 숙박이 제공될 예정(Hotel accommodations will be provided for passengers who don't mind leaving tomorrow.)'이라고 언급되었으므로, 정답은 이를 동의 표현으로 바꾼 (B)이다.

[95-97] 전화 메시지 & 주문서

Hi, Henry. It's Tina from the Maintenance department, and I'm calling about the purchase orders for office supplies. As you can see from the forms, the public relations department says they're running out of black-and-white toner for the printer. And the quality control department says one computer monitor is out of order and two desk lamps are needed. Personnel needs paper for the fax machine. I'm not sure if there are additional items to order. So, before you order them, be sure to show the completed order forms to the departments in advance. You can't place an order without my approval. And since the staff may be missing something, please check all departments again. Thanks.

안녕하세요, Henry. 저는 관리부 티나이고, 사무용품 구매 주문서 때문에 전화 드립니다. 주문서에서 볼 수 있듯이, 홍보부가 프린터에 사용할 흑백 토너를 다 써 간다고 해요. 그리고 품질관리부는 컴퓨터 모니터 하나가 고장 났고, 탁상용 램프 두 개가 필요하다고 합니다. 인사부는 팩스기에 사용할 용지가 필요하고요. 주문할 추가 물품들이 있을지 모르겠어요. 그래서 당신이 주문하기 전에, 작성된 주문서를 부서들에 미리 보여줘야 합니다. 제 승인이 없다면 주문할 수 없어요. 그리고 직원들이 뭔가 빠뜨렸을 수도 있으니까, 모든 부서에 다시 확인해 보세요. 감사합니다.

품목	수량	비용
탁상용 램프		
종이		
토너	2개	40달러
모니터		

어휘 purchase order 구입 주문서 run out of ~을 소진시키다, 다 써버리다 out of order 고장 난 order form 주문 양식 place an order 주문하다 approval 승인 fill out ~을 작성하다

95 시각 자료 연계
시각 자료를 보시오. 어느 부서가 주문서를 작성했는가?
(A) 홍보부
(B) 품질관리부
(C) 인사부
(D) 관리부

해설 주문서를 보면 토너 2개를 주문한다고 작성되어 있는데, 지문 초반에 'the public relations department says they're running out of black-and-white toner for the printer' 홍보부에서 토너를 다 써 간다고 했으므로 홍보부가 주문서를 작성했다는 것을 알 수 있다. 따라서 정답은 (A)이다.

96 요청 사항
청자는 주문하기 전에 무엇을 하도록 요청 받는가?
(A) 회의 참석하기
(B) 가격 확인하기
(C) 팩스로 주문서 보내기
(D) 확인 받기

해설 질문의 'before ordering'이 키워드로, 내용 중간에 'before you order them, be sure to show the completed order forms to the departments in advance' 작성된 주문서를 각 부서에 보여주라고 하고, 그 뒤에 화자의 승인이 없으면 주문할 수 없다고 했으므로 청자는 주문하기 전에 확인을 받아야 함을 알 수 있다. 따라서 정답은 (D)이다.

97 세부 사항
화자는 무슨 일이 일어날 수 있다고 생각하는가?
(A) 예산이 부족할 수도 있다.
(B) 승인이 거절될 수도 있다.
(C) 주문서가 분실될 수도 있다.
(D) 주문 목록이 불완전할 수도 있다.

해설 화자가 예상하거나 추측하는 내용을 묻는 문제이다. 지문 후반부 'since the staff may be missing something, please check all departments again.'에서 직원들이 주문서에 뭔가를 빠뜨릴 수도 있다고 했으므로 정답은 (D)이다.

[98-100] 회의 발췌 & 판매 현황표

During today's monthly sales meeting, the product we are going to focus on is our most popular laptop. The Legender had been selling well at the beginning of the year. However, when our main competitor released a new model, the sales of the Legender decreased sharply. To get through this difficulty, we decided to extend the warranty period from one year to two years. Customers can exchange the laptop for a new one if they encounter any mechanical defect within this period. In the month the policy was implemented, the sales of the laptop doubled from the previous month. And so far, sales have continued to rise.

오늘 월례 영업 회의에서 우리가 집중적으로 다룰 제품은 우리의 가장 인기 있는 노트북 컴퓨터입니다. Legender는 연초에는 잘 팔렸습니다. 그러나 우리 주요 경쟁사가 새로운 모델을 출시했을 때, Legender의 판매는 급격히 하락했어요. 이 어려움을 극복하기 위해, 우리는 보증 기간을 1년에서 2년으로 연장하기로 결정했습니다. 만약 고객들

이 이 기간 내에 기계적인 결함을 발견하면, 노트북 컴퓨터를 새 제품으로 교환할 수 있습니다. 그 정책이 시행된 달에, 그 노트북의 매출은 전 달에 비해 두 배로 증가했습니다. 그리고 지금까지 판매량은 계속 증가하고 있습니다.

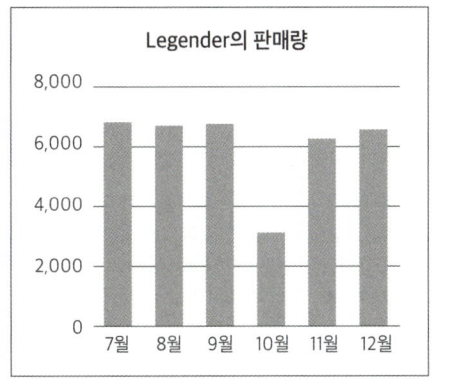

Legender의 판매량

어휘 focus on ~에 초점을 맞추다, 집중하다   at the beginning of the year 연초에   competitor 경쟁자, 경쟁업체   release 출시하다   sharply 급격히   get through ~을 통과하다, 헤쳐 나가다   warranty period 보증 기간   exchange A for B A를 B로 교환하다   encounter 직면하다   defect 결함   implement 시행하다   double 두 배가 되다   previous 이전의   manufacturer 생산업자, 생산업체   launch 출시하다

98 담화 장소
담화는 어디에서 일어나는 것 같은가?
(A) 컴퓨터 제조업체에서
(B) 과학 박물관에서
(C) 광고 대행 업체에서
(D) 자동차 회사에서

해설 담화가 일어나는 장소는 지문의 초반에 단서가 나온다. 첫 번째 문장에서, 회의에서 집중적으로 다룰 제품이 '우리의 가장 인기있는 노트북 컴퓨터(our most popular laptop)'라고 하는 것으로 보아, 담화는 컴퓨터 제조업체에서 일어나고 있다고 유추할 수 있다. 따라서 정답은 (A)이다.

99 세부 사항
화자에 따르면, 왜 매출이 떨어졌는가?
(A) 보증 기간이 충분히 길지 않았다.
(B) 다른 회사가 신제품을 출시했다.
(C) 제품 가격이 인상되었다.
(D) 고객들에 의해 많은 결함이 발견되었다.

해설 지문의 중반에 '주요 경쟁사가 새로운 모델을 발표했을 때, 매출이 급격히 떨어졌다(when our main competitor released a new model, the sales of the Legender decreased sharply.)'는 부분에서 정답이 (B)임을 알 수 있다.

100 시각 자료 연계
시각 자료를 보시오. 업체는 언제 새 정책을 도입했는가?
(A) 7월에
(B) 10월에
(C) 11월에
(D) 12월에

해설 지문의 후반부에 '그 정책이 시행된 달에, 노트북 컴퓨터 판매가 전 달에 비해 두 배로 증가했다(In the month the policy was implemented, the sales of the laptop doubled from the previous month.)'는 내용이 있다. 그래프를 보면 10월(October)에 비해 11월(November)의 판매량이 두 배가 되었으므로 11월에 정책이 도입되었다는 것을 알 수 있다. 따라서 정답은 (C)이다.

PART · 5

101 to부정사 자리
유감스럽게도, 저희는 배송료 인상 때문에 연간 구독료를 올릴 수밖에 없습니다.

해설 to부정사는 [to + 동사원형] 형태로 쓰이므로, 빈칸은 동사원형인 (A)가 정답이다.

어휘 unfortunately 유감스럽게도, 공교롭게도   have no choice but to V ~할 수밖에 없다   annual 연간의   subscription 구독료   delivery 배송

102 형용사 어휘
스미스 씨는 그렇게 친숙한 분위기에서 일하는 것이 정말 행운이라고 확신합니다.

해설 4개의 형용사 보기 중 알맞은 것을 선택하는 문제이다. '(A) 취약한, (B) 결정적인, (C) 상당한, (D) 친숙한' 중에서 '친숙한 환경'이란 의미를 만드는 (D)가 문맥상 가장 적절하다.

어휘 confident 확신하는   really 진심으로   environment 환경

103 명사 자리
연구 부서는 경영진에게 그 제품이 철저히 검사되어야 한다는 것을 상기시켰습니다.

해설 빈칸은 주어 자리이므로 명사가 필요하다. 따라서 '연구 부서'라는 의미를 만드는 (B)가 정답이다. 동명사 (D)는 뒤에 목적어가 필요하므로 답이 될 수 없다.

어휘 management 운영진, 운영   comprehensively 완전히, 철저히   inspect 조사하다   divide 나누다   division 부서, 과

104 전치사 어휘
수용 인원 제한으로 인해, 저희는 추후 공지가 있을 때까지 어떠한 추가 등록도 받을 수 없습니다.

해설 (A) 반전의 전치사(~에도 불구하고), (B) 기간/공간/도구의 전치사(~동안/~에 걸쳐/~을 통해), (C) 시점 전치사(~까지), (D) 장소 전치사(~주위에) 중에서, 빈칸 뒤와 '추후 공지가 있을 때까지'라는 의미를 만드는 시점 전치사 (C)가 정답이다.

어휘 limited 제한된 capacity 수용력 registration 등록 further 향후의

105 대명사
변동이 심한 시장에 대한 대응 전략으로써, 대부분의 회사들은 현재 스스로 구조조정하고 있습니다.

해설 빈칸 앞 restructure은 능동태이므로 빈칸에는 (B), (D)가 목적어로 올 수 있는데, 주어인 '대부분의 회사들'이 그들 자신에 대한 구조조정을 실시한다는 뜻이므로, 주어와 목적어가 동일할 때 사용하는 재귀대명사 (D)가 정답이다.

어휘 strategy 전략 respond to ~에 대응하다, 응답하다 fluctuating 요동치는, 변동의 restructure 구조조정하다

106 부사 어휘
제이미 씨는 퇴임 발표 직후, 25년간 회사에 기여한 것에 대한 영예를 안았습니다.

해설 '(A) ~보다, (B) 충분히, (C) 곧, 바로, (D) 매우'의 부사 중에서, 시간 전치사 after를 앞에서 강조할 수 있는 (C)가 의미상 적절하다.

어휘 honor 명예[영예]를 주다 contribution 기여(도) retirement 퇴임, 퇴사

107 부사 자리
브래들리 우즈 사는 가끔 평판이 좋은 다른 회사들과 최신 정보를 공유합니다.

해설 주어(Bradley Woods Co.)와 동사(shares) 사이에 위치할 수 있는 것은 부사이므로 (D)가 정답이다.

어휘 share 공유하다 up-to-date 최신의 reputable 평판이 좋은

108 형용사 어휘
시험 결과를 받은 후, 에드워즈 씨는 베스의 충고가 그의 해외 취업 준비에 매우 도움이 되었다고 생각했습니다.

해설 '(A) 도움이 되는, (B) 긴, (C) 즉각적인, (D) 홍보의'의 형용사 보기들 중, 베스가 해준 충고가 취업 준비에 '도움이 되었다'는 의미를 만드는 (A)가 문맥상 가장 적절하다.

어휘 find 생각하다, 알게 되다 overseas 해외의

109 동사의 형태
지난주에 발표된 조사는 Huxley 사가 여전히 동아시아에서 높은 브랜드 인지도를 유지하고 있음을 입증했습니다.

해설 빈칸은 명사절 접속사 that절의 동사 자리로, 뒤에 나오는 명사구(its high brand awareness)를 목적어로 취하는 능동태가 나와야 한다. 따라서 (A)가 정답이다.

어휘 survey 조사 release 발표하다, 출시하다 verify 입증하다 awareness 인식, 인지도 maintain 유지하다

110 연결어
Clarion Trading 사는 작은 모임을 여러 번 갖기보다 전 직원들을 위한 연간 행사를 매년 12월에 개최하기로 결정했습니다.

해설 부사절 접속사 (A)와 (D) 뒤에는 완전한 문장이 나와야 하므로 오답, (B)는 '꼭 ~처럼, ~같이'라는 의미의 원급 비교 구문이므로 오답이다. '~보다'의 의미로 접속사 기능을 하는 동시에 구 또는 단어를 연결하는 (C)가 정답이다.

어휘 gathering 모임 hold 개최하다 annual 매년의, 연례의

111 부사 자리
우아하게 옷을 입고 앞줄에 앉아 있는 캐서린 씨가 "올해의 기자" 상을 받을 것입니다.

해설 주격 관계대명사 who 뒤의 동사 dress는 '옷을 입다'라는 의미의 1형식 자동사로, 빈칸에는 동사를 수식할 수 있는 부사가 나와야 한다. 따라서 (D)가 가장 적절하다.

어휘 dress 옷을 입다 sit 앉다 name 이름을 지어주다, 명명하다

112 관계대명사
주차권을 발급받고자 하는 주민들은 건물 관리 사무실에 연락해야 합니다.

해설 문장에 동사 'should contact'가 있으므로 빈칸에는 관계대명사가 나와야 한다. 선행사가 있기 때문에 (D)는 올 수 없고, 관계절에 주어가 없으므로 빈칸에는 주격 관계대명사인 (A)가 나와야 한다.

어휘 contact 연락하다, 접촉하다 administration office 관리 사무실

113 명사 어휘
우리의 주요 관심사는 이번 연례 컨퍼런스를 위해 어떤 장소가 최적이고 우리가 얼마나 많은 예산을 가지고 있는지입니다.

해설 '(A) 원천, 자료, (B) 관심사, 걱정, 문제, (C) 동반자 관계, (D) 중역, 간부'의 명사 어휘들 중에서, '관심사, 문제'라는 의미로 is 뒤의 내용과 동격을 이룰 수 있는 (B)가 문맥상 가장 적절하다.

어휘 chief 주된, 최대의 budget 예산

114 형용사 자리
장 루소의 새로 개봉된 영화는 이전 영화들보다 더 환상적이고 인상적이었지만, 사실 비용은 더 적게 들었습니다.

해설 빈칸은 비교급 more ~ than 사이에 and를 기준으로 fantastic과 대등하게 연결되는 형용사 자리이므로, (B)와 (C)가 올 수 있다. (B) impressed는 감정을 나타내는 수동형 분사로 주로 주체가 사람일 때 사용되므로 오답이며, '인상적인, 훌륭한'의 의미를 지닌 형용사 (C)가 정답이다.

어휘 newly 새로 release 개봉하다 previous 이전의 cost 비용이 들다 less 덜하게, 더 적게

115 동사 어휘

그 일자리는 지원자들에게 관련 분야에서 최소 2년의 경력이 있을 것을 요구합니다.

해설 '(A) 요구하다, (B) 감시하다, (C) 놀라게 하다, (D) 평가하다'의 타동사 어휘들 중에서, 문맥상 지원자가 갖추어야 할 자격 요건을 '요구한다'는 의미의 (A)가 정답이다.

어휘 at least 적어도 work experience 경력 relevant 관련된 field 분야

116 상관 접속사

뉴스에 따르면, Biz Con 사와 Max Stock 사 둘 다 그들의 인수합병에 동의하지 않았습니다.

해설 상관 접속사 neither A nor B 구조로, 빈칸 뒤의 nor과 함께 쓰이는 부사 (C)가 정답이다.

어휘 according to ~에 따르면 accept 수용하다 agreement 합의, 동의 mergers and acquisitions 인수합병(M&A)

117 부사 어휘

추가 장치 없이, XC-200 노트북 컴퓨터는 사용자들이 그들의 텔레비전에 원격으로 연결할 수 있도록 합니다.

해설 '(A) 면밀히, 긴밀히, (B) 결국, (C) 신중하게, (D) 원격으로, 떨어져서'의 부사 어휘 중에서, 노트북 컴퓨터가 텔레비전에 '원격으로' 연결된다는 내용이 자연스러우므로 (D)가 답이다.

어휘 device 장치 enable 가능하게 하다 connect 연결하다, 접속하다

118 동사 어휘

모든 컴퓨터 부속품들이 20퍼센트 할인 중인 반면, 컴퓨터 할인율은 모델 유형에 따라 상이합니다.

해설 빈칸 뒤에 목적어가 없으므로 1형식 자동사가 필요하다. '(A) 수리하다, (B) 서로 다르다, (C) 수행하다, (D) 준수하다'의 동사 어휘들 중 자동사는 (B)와 (D)로, 모델별로 할인율이 '다르다'는 의미를 만드는 (B)가 정답이다.

어휘 accessory 부속품, 액세서리 rate 비율 depending on ~에 따라

119 형용사 자리

현재 시장의 다양한 경제 변수들을 고려하면, 메디나 박사의 발표가 얼마나 신뢰할 만했는지는 아직 명확하지 않습니다.

해설 빈칸은 be동사의 보어 자리이므로 형용사인 (A)가 정답이다.

어휘 clear 명확한 reliable 신뢰할 만한 economic 경제의 variable 변수

120 동사의 형태

글로리아 헤더의 신간 도서는 우리가 일상에서 쉽게 마주할 수 있는 흥미로운 사례들로 잘 구성되고 설명되어 있습니다.

해설 be동사 is 뒤에서 and를 기준으로 수동형 분사 organized 와 연결되는 형태이므로 (C)가 정답이다.

어휘 organize 구성하다 illustrate 설명하다, 분명히 보여주다 interesting 흥미로운 case 사례 face 마주하다

121 명사 어휘

모든 대학원생들이 교육부의 특별 세미나, 포럼 그리고 환영회에 참석하도록 초대 받았습니다.

해설 빈칸 앞 and를 기준으로 '행사'와 관련된 어휘들이 나열되고 있으므로, '(A) 형식상의 절차, (B) 노출, (C) 환영회, (D) 도움'의 명사 어휘들 중에서 (C)가 문맥상 가장 자연스럽다.

어휘 graduate student 대학원생, 졸업생 invite 초대하다, 요청하다

122 동사 어휘

사회 문제들을 줄이는 가장 좋은 방법은 대중이 현재의 법과 규칙을 준수하도록 교육하는 것입니다.

해설 '(A) 통역하다, 해석하다, (B) 교육하다, (C) 보살피다, (D) 참석하다'의 동사 어휘들 중에서, 법과 규칙을 준수하도록 대중을 '교육시킨다'는 의미의 (B)가 정답이다.

어휘 social 사회의 comply with 준수하다 law 법 rule 규칙

123 to부정사 자리

자료를 보호하기 위해 관리자는 회사 내 부서들 간에 정보를 책임감 있게 공유하는 방법에 대해 설명해야 합니다.

해설 문장에 동사 'should explain'이 있으므로 빈칸엔 뒤에 목적어를 취할 수 있는 준동사가 나와야 한다. 보기 중에 '자료를 보호하기 위해'라는 의미를 만드는 목적을 나타내는 to부정사가 위치할 수 있으므로 (D)가 정답이다. 동명사 (C)는 의미상 맞지 않다.

어휘 responsibly 책임감 있게

124 부사절 접속사

그 계약에 대한 이용 약관이 변경될 것이므로, 우리의 모든 고객들은 컴퓨터로 동의서에 전자 서명해야 합니다.

해설 빈칸 뒤에 [주어 + 동사] 형태의 완벽한 절이 있으므로 부사절 접속사 (A)와 (B)가 올 수 있는데, 부사절에 미래시제 will이 있으므로 시간 부사절 접속사 (B)는 불가능하다. 따라서 (A)가 정답이다.

어휘 terms and conditions 이용 약관 sign 서명하다
agreement 동의서 electronically 컴퓨터로, 전자적으로

125 명사 어휘

미국 외 국적을 가진 해외 지원자들이 이곳에서 일하기 위해서는 유효한 비자가 있어야 합니다.

해설 주어 자리에 들어갈 명사를 고르는 문제로, (B) '지원자'와 (C) '지원서' 중에서 비자를 소지해야 하는 주체는 사람이므로 (B)가 정답이다.

어휘 national 국민 valid 유효한 visa 비자 in order to V ~하기 위해서

126 전치사 어휘

구매를 결정하기 전에, 여러분은 다양한 웹 사이트를 통해 가격을 비교해 볼 필요가 있습니다.

해설 '(A) ~에 관하여, (B) ~의, ~중, (C) ~전에, (D) ~안으로'의 전치사들 중에서, '구매를 결정하기 전'이라는 문맥이 자연스러우므로 (C)가 정답이다.

어휘 make a purchase 구매하다 compare 비교하다
through ~을 통해 a variety of 많은, 다양한

127 명사 어휘

연방법에 따르면, 미국에서 판매되는 모든 물품들은 내용물에 대한 생산 일자와 원산지가 표기되어 있어야 합니다.

해설 '(A) 근원, 기원, (B) 사본, (C) 자산, 매물, (D) 종교'의 명사 어휘들 중에서, 'place of origin(원산지)'라는 형태로 사용되는 (A)가 정답이다.

어휘 federal law 연방법 label 라벨(표)를 붙이다 content 내용물

128 동사의 시제

헤더 씨는 이번 3월 우리 본사로 전근 올 때쯤이면 Fairfax 지점에서 10년째 일한 것이 됩니다.

해설 시간 부사절 접속사 by the time 뒤의 시제가 현재면 미래를 나타내므로 주절은 미래 완료 시제가 나와야 한다. 따라서 (A)가 정답이다.

어휘 by the time ~할 때쯤 transfer 전근 가다
headquarters 본사

129 형용사 자리

710-1920으로 인사과에 전화하셔서 당신이 회의 일정에 동의하는지 알려주세요.

해설 빈칸은 be동사 is 뒤의 보어 자리로, '동의하는, 받아들일 수 있는'을 의미하는 형용사 (C)가 정답이다.

어휘 personnel division 인사과

130 전치사 어휘

World Football Championship의 결승전이 이번 주 토요일 밤 JCB 채널을 통해 모든 주에 걸쳐 방송될 것입니다.

해설 '(A) ~(둘) 사이에, (B) ~와 함께, (C) ~안으로, (D) ~을 가로질러'의 전치사들 중에서, 결승전이 모든 주에 '걸쳐' 방송된다는 의미이므로 (D)가 정답이다.

어휘 final 결승전 broadcast 방송하다 state 주

PART • 6

[131-134] 광고

> Florida는 현재 여러분에게 아쿠아리움, 놀이공원 그리고 좋은 식당과 같은 다양한 명소들을 제공하고 있습니다. Special Florida Pass로, 여러분은 주 전역에 있는 모든 종류의 인기 장소들을 합리적인 가격에 즐길 수 있습니다. 여러분이 더 많은 명소를 이용하면, 더 많은 할인을 받을 수 있습니다. 이 할인은 해외 관광객들만 이용하실 수 있습니다. 이용권은 여러분의 나라를 떠나시기 전에 저희 웹 사이트 www.specialflorida.com을 통해서만 구매할 수 있습니다. 여러분이 첫 번째 명소를 방문하면, 구매하신 이용권은 자동으로 활성화될 것입니다. 그것들은 30일 동안 Florida 주의 어느 장소에서나 유효할 것입니다. 그것들을 구매할 때, 여러분은 주 내 아울렛 매장에서 사용할 수 있는 프리미엄 쿠폰북도 받으실 수 있습니다.

어휘 attraction 관광명소 amusement park 놀이공원
reasonable 합리적인 purchase 구매하다 pass 패스, 통행권 activate 활성화시키다 automatically 자동으로

131 동사의 시제

해설 빈칸은 if절의 동사 자리이므로 (A)와 (B)가 올 수 있는데, 주절의 시제가 현재(can get)이므로 현재시제인 (A)가 정답이다.

132 문맥에 맞는 문장 고르기

(A) 많은 여행사들이 여러분에게 가이드 관광을 제공합니다.
(B) 이 할인은 해외 관광객들만 이용하실 수 있습니다.
(C) 특히, Sea World는 외국인 방문객들에게 가장 잘 알려져 있습니다.
(D) 게다가, 여러분은 저희 사무실에 그것을 직접 제출해야 합니다.

해설 빈칸 앞 문장에 할인(discouns)에 관한 내용이 있으므로 이를 지칭하는 This offer가 있는 (B)가 정답이다.

133 형용사 어휘

해설 '(A) 훌륭한, 멋진, (B) 결정적인, (C) 유효한, (D) 열린'의 형용사 어휘들 중에서, 30일 동안 Florida 주에서 입장권이 '유효하다'는 의미를 만드는 (C)가 정답이다.

134 부사 어휘

해설 앞서 언급한 통행권에 대해 계속 설명하고 있으므로 (D)가 정답이다. (A)는 very는 '매우'라는 의미로 형용사/부사를 수식하므로 오답, (B) as well은 '또한'이라는 의미로 문장 맨 끝에 위치해야 하므로 오답, (C) yet은 '아직'이라는 의미로 부정어와 함께 not ~ yet 또는 to부정사와 함께 have yet to V 형태로 사용되므로 오답. (D) also는 '또한'이라는 의미로 주어와 가까운 곳에 나오는데, 빈칸이 주어(you)근처에 있으므로 위치상 적절하다.

[135-138] 이메일

수신: 올라 코너 <u.connor@uccommunication.org>
발신: 제인 리 <j.lee@innobizproduction.net>
날짜: 10월 8일
제목: 9월 30일 워크숍

코너 씨에게,

저는 9월 30일 저희 Nashville 본사에서 존 스왈레 씨가 진행했던 워크숍에 대해 감사드리고자 글을 씁니다. 그의 강연 전에 일부 직원들은 워크숍의 효과에 우려를 나타냈습니다. 이 직원들은 하루 종일 워크숍에 참석했고, 심지어 다음 교육이 열릴지 여부를 묻기도 했습니다. 그래서, 그 후 저희는 향후 워크숍의 수요를 확인하기 위해 참석자들에게 평가서를 작성하도록 요구했습니다. 대부분의 참석자들이 의사소통 능력을 향상시키는 데 좋은 기회였다고 진술하며 그 안건에 긍정적으로 답하였습니다. 다른 참석자들은 더 많은 실전 연습이 필요했다고 말했습니다. 추후 워크숍에 대하여 자세히 논의하기 위해 저희에게 연락 주세요.

행운을 빌며,

제인 리
Innobiz Production 사

어휘 extend 주다, 베풀다, 연장하다 concern 걱정, 염려 effectiveness 효과 lecture 강연 participate in ~에 참석하다 session 교육 evaluation 평가 positively 긍정적으로 respond to ~에 응답하다, 대응하다 improve 개선하다 in detail 자세히

135 명사 자리

해설 빈칸은 소유격 our 뒤의 명사 자리이므로 (D)가 정답이다.

136 동사의 형태, 시제, 수

해설 빈칸 뒤에 목적어(concern)가 있으므로 능동형인 (A), (B), (D) 중 골라야 한다. 해당 문장은 그의 강연(his lecture)이 있

기 전 우려를 나타냈다는 내용으로, 앞 문장에서 강연이 9월 30일, 즉 과거에 진행된 것(John Swale conducted ~ on September 30)을 알 수 있으므로 과거보다 이전 시점을 나타내는 과거완료 (D)가 정답이다.

137 부사 어휘

해설 '(A) 상당히, (B) 보통, (C) 그 뒤에, (D) 자주'의 부사 어휘들 중에서, (A)는 의미상 오답이며, 빈도부사 (B)와 (D)는 동사 근처에서 수식해야 하므로 위치상 답이 될 수 없다. 강연 '이후' 참가자들에게 평가서를 작성하도록 했다는 의미의 (C)가 정답이다.

138 문맥에 맞는 문장 고르기

(A) 워크숍은 다음 달에 준비될 예정이었습니다.
(B) 저희는 당신에게 400달러의 상여금을 수표로 제공할 것입니다.
(C) 다른 참석자들은 더 많은 실전 연습이 필요했다고 말했습니다.
(D) 사장님은 머지않아 당신의 강연을 듣고자 합니다.

해설 바로 앞 문장에서 대부분 참가자들의 의견에 대해 말하고 있으므로 빈칸에 그 외의 다른 사람들을 언급하는 것이 자연스럽다. 따라서 강연에 대한 다른 사람들의 생각을 언급한 (C)가 정답이다.

[139-142] 이메일

수신: 대니 리베라 <d.rivera@boardworld.com>
발신: 브래드 트리아나 <b.triana@uptondesign.com>
날짜: 3월 20일
제목: 정기 주문

우리는 Upton Design 사의 정기 주문에 대해 몇 가지를 변경하고자 합니다. 일부 직원들만 발표에 무광 흑칠판을 사용하고 있어서, 결과적으로 칠판에 쓰는 CH-200 분필의 사용이 줄고 있습니다. 그러므로 다음 딜부터 그 제품의 주문 개수를 딘 10개로 줄여 주시기 바랍니다. 대신에, JX-120 다목적 마커 20개를 추가해 주세요.
우리는 올해 말까지 CH-200 분필 사용을 점차 줄여나갈 것입니다. 그러나, 우리는 그날 전까지 귀사에 계속 공지를 보낼 것입니다. 우리의 월별 주문에 대한 수정된 청구서를 저에게 보내주시겠습니까? 우리 회계 부서에서 그것을 요구할 것입니다.

그럼 이만,

브래드 트리아나
Upton Design 사

어휘 matte 무광의 chalkboard 칠판 presentation 발표 chalk 분필 board 판 instead 대신에 multipurpose 다목적의 marker 마커(펜) gradually 점점 decrease 줄이다 continuous 지속적인 revised 수정된

139 형용사 어휘

해설 '(A) 기한이 지난, (B) 지속적인, 정기의, (C) 과도한, (D) 불필요한'의 형용사 어휘 중에서, 제목의 Regular order(정기 주문)을 통해 '정기적인' 주문에 대한 내용임을 알 수 있으므로 (B)가 정답이다.

140 접속 부사

해설 '(A) 예를 들어, (B) 그러므로, (C) 그럼에도 불구하고, (D) 마찬가지로'의 접속부사들 중에서, 앞 문장에서 CH-200 분필 사용이 감소한다고 했고 뒤 문장에는 분필 주문 개수를 줄여 달라고 했으므로 빈칸에는 원인-결과를 나타내는 (B)가 적절하다.

141 동사의 형태, 시제, 수

해설 4형식 동사 give의 목적어 2개(your company, continuous notices)가 빈칸 뒤에 있으므로 능동형인 (A), (C), (D) 중 선택해야 한다. 해당 문장은 올해 말까지 분필 사용을 줄여 나가고 이에 대해 계속해서 공지를 하겠다는 의미이므로 미래 시제인 (D)가 정답이다.

142 문맥에 맞는 문장 고르기

(A) 우리 회계 부서에서 그것을 요구할 것입니다.
(B) 우리는 그 칠판을 위한 새로운 사업을 시작할 것입니다.
(C) 직원들은 귀사의 제품들에 만족합니다.
(D) 당신은 저희에게 송장 제출을 요구해도 됩니다.

해설 빈칸 앞 문장에서 월별 주문에 대한 수정된 청구서를 요청한다고 했으므로, 청구서를 it으로 받으면서 청구서와 연관된 회계 부서가 언급되는 (A)가 정답이다.

[143-146] 편지

4월 20일

척 콘래드
Haman Utility 사
Albany, New York

콘래드 씨에게,

저희는 Willy Development 사가 Civic Center의 개량 공사에 대한 Haman Utility 사의 입찰 제안을 수락했음을 발표하게 되어 기쁩니다. 공사를 할 귀사의 노동자들은 6월 10일부터 현장에 접근할 수 있을 것입니다. 건물 공사에 관한 정책에 따르면, Haman Utility 사는 필수적인 허가를 받을 책임이 있을 것입니다. 이 편지에 동봉된 문서에서 프로젝트의 배치도를 찾을 수 있습니다. 게다가, 저희의 다른 제휴사 목록도 있으며, 귀사는 전반적인 공사 작업에 그들이 적합하다는 것을 확인하실 수 있습니다. 질문이 있으시거나 추가 정보가 필요하시면 언제든지 저희에게 연락주세요. 귀하에게 가능한 한 빨리 정보를 제공해 드리겠습니다.

진심으로,

존 스벤슨, 부장
Willy Development 사

동봉

어휘 proposal 제안(서) bid 입찰 improvement 개선, 개량 공사 access 접근 policy 정책 take responsibility for ~에 책임을 지다 obtain 확보하다, 얻다 required 필수의 permit 허가(증) layout 배치(도), 개요 enclosed 동봉된 associate 제휴하다 suitability 적합성 overall 전반적인

143 동사의 형태, 시제, 수

해설 빈칸 뒤에 목적어가 있으므로 수동태인 (D)는 오답이다. 편지 내용을 알리는 시점은 현재이고, 입찰 제안이 수락된 것은 과거에 이미 일어났던 사실이므로 현재완료인 (C)가 정답이다.

144 명사 어휘

해설 '(A) 품목, (B) 현장, (C) 날짜, (D) 사람'의 명사 어휘들 중에서, 노동자들이 공사 '현장'에 접근할 수 있다는 내용이 어울리므로 (B)가 정답이다.

145 접속부사

해설 '(A) 그러나, (B) 대신에, (C) 결과적으로, (D) 게다가'의 접속부사 중, 앞 문장에서 동봉된 문서에 배치도가 있다고 했고, 뒤 문장에서는 제휴사 목록도 있다고 추가 정보를 나열하고 있으므로 추가의 접속부사 (D)가 답.

146 문맥에 맞는 문장 고르기

(A) 귀하에게 가능한 한 빨리 정보를 제공해 드리겠습니다.
(B) 귀하는 아래의 주소로 우리 웹 사이트에 접속할 수 있습니다.
(C) 귀하에게 본사를 직접 방문하시기를 요청합니다.
(D) 귀하는 귀사의 결정에 관하여 저희에게 알려주셔야 합니다.

해설 빈칸 앞 문장에서 문의가 있거나 추가 정보가 필요하면 연락해 달라고 했으므로, 빈칸은 가능한 한 빨리 정보를 제공하겠다고 한 (A)가 가장 적절하다.

PART • 7

[147-148] 이메일

수신: 윌리엄 로버트 <w_robert@questmail.com>
발신: 캐서린 브론테 <k_bronte@routledge.net>
날짜: 5월 30일
제목: 표지 디자인

윌리엄 씨에게,

조만간 당신이 Routledge 마케팅 부서에서 이메일을 받게 됨을 알려드리고자 합니다. 당신은 마케팅 과정의 세부 사항을 찾을 수 있고, 작가들을 위한 온라인 설문조사로 연결되는 웹 사이트 주소를 보실 수 있습니다. 비록 마케팅 부장과 디자이너가 당신의 책 표지에 관해 논의할지라도, 그것에 대한 당신만의 의견을 가질 필요가 있습니다. 표지 디자인을 보다 눈에 띄고 독특하게 만들 제안이 있나요? 좋은 아이디어가 있으시면 저에게 알려주세요.

진심으로,

캐서린 브론테
편집장
Routledge 출판사

어휘 notify 알리다, 공지하다 in the near future 조만간, 가까운 장래에 link 연결하다 author 작가 opinion 의견, 견해

147 추론/암시
로버트 씨는 누구일 것 같은가?
(A) 디자이너
(B) 분석가
(C) 작가
(D) 마케팅 담당자

해설 세 번째 문장의 "Although a marketing director and a designer will discuss your book cover"를 봤을 때 수신자인 로버트 씨는 책을 쓴 작가라고 추론할 수 있다. 따라서 (C)가 정답이다.

148 세부 사항
이메일에 따르면, 무엇이 곧 도착하는가?
(A) 도서 샘플 페이지
(B) 마케팅 정보
(C) 설문조사 결과
(D) 서점 목록

해설 첫 번째 문장에서 마케팅 부서로부터 이메일이 올 것이라고 했고, 두 번째 문장 "You can find the details about the marketing process"를 통해 이메일에는 마케팅 과정 세부 사항에 관한 내용이 있다는 것을 알 수 있으므로 (B)가 정답이다.

[149-150] 공지

Bayview 호텔을 선택해 주셔서 감사합니다!

고객들의 지속적인 지지에 대한 보답으로, 저희는 무료 셔틀 버스 서비스를 도심지까지 연장하기로 했습니다. 셔틀 버스는 박물관, 쇼핑 센터, 그리고 모래 해변과 같은 도시의 다양하고 흘륭한 명소에 들를 것입니다. 비록 이 목적지 대부분이 우리 호텔에서 걸어갈 수 있는 거리에 있지만, 셔틀 버스를 이용하면 여러분은 그곳에 더 빨리 도착할 수 있습니다. 이 변화는 신규 고객과 단골 고객 모두에게 좋습니다. 이 셔틀 버스는 계절 행사나 축제가 있을 추가적인 장소에도 들를 것입니다.

셔틀 버스 서비스 일정은 저희 호텔 로비와 웹 사이트에 게시되어 있습니다. 저희 공항 서비스와 마찬가지로, Gold 회원은 셔틀 버스를 사전 예약하실 수 있습니다.

어휘 constant 지속적인 complimentary 무료의 shuttle 셔틀(버스) downtown 도심 district 지역 destination 목적지 within walking distance 걸어갈 수 있는 거리에 seasonal 계절의 post 게시하다 in advance 미리, 사전에

149 세부 사항
무엇이 제공되는가?
(A) 숙박 시설에 대한 할인 요금
(B) 무료 교통 서비스
(C) 명소의 가이드 관광
(D) 회원권 업그레이드 프로그램

해설 첫 번째 문장 중 "we have decided to extend our complimentary shuttle service to the downtown district" 부분에서 도심지로 가는 무료 셔틀 서비스를 연장한다고 하는 것으로 보아 (B)가 정답이다.

150 추론/암시
Bayview 호텔에 대해 암시된 것은 무엇인가?
(A) 도시 중심부 근처에 있다.
(B) 출장 온 손님들에게 인기가 있다.
(C) 역사적 관점에서 매우 가치 있다.
(D) 객실 요금이 그 지역에서 가장 비싸다.

해설 세 번째 문장 "Although most of these destinations are just within walking distance from our hotel"을 보면, 도시의 명소들이 호텔에서 걸어갈 수 있는 거리에 있다고 했으므로 호텔이 도시 중심부와 가깝다는 것을 알 수 있다. 따라서 (A)가 정답이다.

[151-152] 문자 메시지

줄리 메이 [오전 11시 30분]
글렌 씨, 제 기차가 한 시간 정도 지연돼서, 회의에 늦을 지도 모르겠어요. 제가 오후 2시까지 그곳에 도착하지 못하면 저를 대신해서 회의를 준비하고 시작해 주실 수 있나요?

글렌 최 [오전 11시 32분]
물론이죠. 기차역에는 언제 도착하세요?

줄리 메이 [오전 11시 33분]
1시 30분까지는 Penn 역에 도착할 수 없을 것 같아요. 그러면 저는 사무실까지 Red Line 버스를 타고 가야 해요.

글렌 최 [오전 11시 35분]
그럴 필요 없어요. 제가 역으로 태우러 갈게요. 우리가 오후 2시 전에 사무실에 도착할 수 있을 거라 확신해요.

줄리 메이 [오전 11시 37분]
그거 좋네요! 하지만 저는 회의를 위해 컴퓨터 장비들을 준비해야 해요.

어휘 delay 지연시키다 prepare for ~을 준비하다 instead of ~대신 pick up 태우다 set up 설치하다

151 주제/목적

메이 씨는 무엇을 걱정하는가?
(A) 컴퓨터 소프트웨어를 업데이트하는 것
(B) 교통 혼잡을 피하는 것
(C) 회의를 위해 출력물을 준비하는 것
(D) 사무실에 정시에 도착하는 것

해설 첫 메시지에서 "I might be late for the meeting. Could you prepare for it and start instead of me if I don't arrive there by 2 P.M.?"라고 하는 것을 보아, 제시간에 회의 장소에 도착할 수 없을까봐 걱정한다는 것을 알 수 있다. 따라서 (D)가 정답이다.

152 의도 파악

오전 11시 35분에, 최 씨가 "그럴 필요 없어요"라고 쓴 것은 무엇을 의미하는가?
(A) 그들은 Penn 역에서 만날 필요가 없다.
(B) 그들은 컴퓨터를 설치할 필요가 없다.
(C) 메이 씨는 버스를 탈 필요가 없다.
(D) 메이 씨는 회의에 합류할 필요가 없다.

해설 의도 파악 문제는 앞뒤 문장의 문맥을 통해 답을 찾아야 한다. 앞 문장에서 사무실로 가는 버스를 타야 한다고 했고, 뒤 문장에서는 역으로 태우러 간다고 했으므로, 그럴 필요가 없다는 것은 문맥상 버스를 탈 필요가 없다는 의미이다. 따라서 (C)가 정답이다.

[153-155] 기사

Baltimore 비즈니스 위크

BALTIMORE (7월 10일) — Tahoma Max 사는 Baltimore 시에 많은 일자리가 생길 것이라고 월요일에 발표했습니다. 회사 대변인인 시몬 프레이저는 새로운 식당이 8월 20일 Fleming 가 301 번지에 개업할 예정이라고 말했습니다. Baltimore 시 지점장은 개업하기 전에 현재 약 40명의 직원들을 구인 중입니다. 서빙 직원과 요리사부터 매니저와 주방장까지 다양한 일자리가 있습니다. 이 자리들을 채우기 위해, Tahoma Max 사는 7월 20일에 열릴 일일 취업 박람회를 준비하고 있습니다. 참가자들의 지원서를 확인한 다음, 가장 알맞은 후보자들의 면접을 즉석에서 볼 것입니다.

Tahoma Max 사의 새로운 지점은 농작물을 직접 재배하여 요리에 사용하는 Baltimore의 유일한 식당이 될 것입니다. 그들은 현지 농산물을 사용함으로써 지역 메뉴를 후원합니다. "우리는 지역 기반의 업무 환경 발전에 기여하게 되어 진심으로 기쁩니다"라고 Tahoma Max 사의 공동 설립자이자 대표이사인 지안 파누치가 말했습니다. "우리는 열정적이고 전문적인 많은 후보자들이 이 직책들에 지원하기를 희망

합니다. 자격요건에 부합되면, 우리는 장래의 직원들에게 경쟁력 있는 임금과 복지 혜택을 제공합니다." 관심은 있으나 박람회에 참석할 수 없는 후보자들은 www.tahomamax.com/Baltimore에서 온라인으로 대신 지원할 수 있습니다.

어휘 job opening 일자리, 공석 a range of 다양한 job fair 취업 박람회 ideal 이상적인, 가장 알맞은 farm product 농작물 stand behind 후원하다 regional 지역적인 produce 농산물 devote 헌신하다 passionate 열정적인 professional 전문적인 apply for ~에 지원하다 fulfill 충족시키다 requirement 자격요건 prospective 장래의, 앞으로의 competitive 경쟁력 있는 salary 임금 benefits package 복지혜택

153 주제/목적

기사문은 주로 무엇에 관한 것인가?
(A) 지역화된 제품들의 광고
(B) 회사의 사회적 기여
(C) 도시 경제의 성장
(D) 새로운 식당의 취업 기회

해설 첫 문장의 "it will have many job openings in the city of Baltimore"에서 일자리가 있음을 알 수 있고, 두 번째 문장 "The company's spokesman, Simon Fraser, said a new restaurant is scheduled to open ~"에서 새로운 식당의 개업을 말하고 있으므로 식당 취업과 관련된 (D)가 정답이다.

154 추론/암시

7월 20일의 행사에 관하여 암시되는 것은?
(A) 모든 지원자들은 면접에 참여해야 한다.
(B) 도시의 식료품점 소유주만을 위한 것이다.
(C) 참가자들은 회사가 제공할 다양한 음식들을 먹어볼 수 있다.
(D) 지원할 수 있는 직책들이 많을 것이다.

해설 세 번째 문장 "The branch manager of the Baltimore City location is currently looking for about 40 employees before it opens. There is a range of positions from servers and cooks to managers and chefs"를 통해 Baltimore 시 지점에 다양한 일자리가 있음을 알 수 있고, 다섯 번째 문장 "In order to fill these positions, Tahoma Max is organizing a one-day job fair on July 20."에서 이 일자리를 채우기 위해 취업 박람회를 준비한다고 했으므로 (D)가 정답이다.

155 세부 사항

Tahoma Max 사가 특별한 이유는 무엇인가?
(A) 지역 자선단체들에 기부했다.
(B) 사업을 해외로 확장했다.
(C) 최저가에 요리를 제공한다.
(D) 채소와 작물을 직접 재배할 것이다.

해설 두 번째 문단 첫 문장 "The new branch of Tahoma Max will be the only restaurant in Baltimore that grows its own farm products and uses them for its dishes"에서 직접 농작물을 기르고 요리에 이용하는 유일한 식당이 될 것이라 했으므로 (D)가 정답이다.

[156-157] 이메일

수신: douglaird@findsplash.com
발신: customerservice@rossapparel.com
날짜: 3월 12일
제목: 주문 확인 (번호 10984821)

레어드 씨에게,

저희 의류를 구매해 주셔서 감사합니다! 이 이메일은 www.rossap-parel.com에서 귀하의 주문 확인에 관한 것입니다. 의류 회사들 중에, 저희는 전국적으로 잘 알려져 있고, 특히 귀하가 주문하신 요리 복장을 전문으로 합니다.

저희는 현재 귀하의 주문을 처리하는 중입니다. 일반적으로 주문은 영업일 기준 3일 이내에 처리되고 저희 배송 부서로 보내집니다. 그 이후, 저희 직원들은 귀하의 물품을 배송할 준비가 될 것입니다. 물류 창고에서 제품이 발송되면, 귀하는 배송 추적 번호에 대한 업데이트 정보를 포함한 또 다른 이메일을 받을 것입니다.

저희와 거래해 주셔서 감사합니다.

그럼 이만,

주문 및 배송
Ross Apparel

어휘 confirmation 확정, 확인 recognized 인정된, 알려진 nationally 전국적으로 specialize in ~에 특화되다, ~을 진문으로 하다 attire 의복 process 치리히다 generally 일반적으로 tracking number (배송) 추적 번호

156 추론/암시

레어드 씨는 어떤 종류의 사업을 하는 것 같은가?
(A) 의류 회사
(B) 식당
(C) 지역 농장
(D) 배송업체

해설 세 번째 문장의 "we have been well recognized nationally, and we particularly specialized in the attire for cooking that you ordered." 부분에서 레어드 씨가 주문한 것이 요리할 때 입는 옷임을 알 수 있으므로, 보기에서 식당이 가장 유력하다. 따라서 (B)가 성답이나.

157 세부 사항

이메일에 따르면, 레어드 씨는 언제 Ross Apparel로부터 또 다른 이메일을 받을 것인가?

(A) 그가 물품에 대해 지불할 때
(B) 그가 주문을 확인할 때
(C) 그의 주문품이 물류 창고를 떠날 때
(D) 새로운 상품이 입고되었을 때

해설 마지막 문장 "Once your product is shipped from our warehouse, you will receive another e-mail, which will include updated information about your tracking number."을 보면, 물류 창고에서 물건이 발송되면 또 다른 이메일을 받게 될 것이라고 했으므로 (C)가 정답이다.

[158-160] 편지

Bonnie Alyssa
2491 Courtland 대로
Daytona, FL 32118

9월 20일

앨리사 씨에게,

Allo Broadband Net 사와의 서비스 계약 갱신에 감사드립니다. 저희 웹 호스팅 서비스에 대한 분기별 송장을 동봉했습니다. 귀하의 명세서에는 정기 점검 서비스에 대한 15달러의 추가 비용이 보일 것입니다. 저희는 6월에 이미 당신에게 이상에 관해 이메일로 공지했습니다. 다시 말씀드리면, Allo Broadband Net 사는 8월에 귀하의 웹 사이트가 모든 종류의 최신 기기들과 소프트웨어와 호환되도록 하기 위해 업그레이드했습니다. 그리고 이제 웹 사이트를 이용하고 동일한 컨텐츠를 보는 데에 아무런 문제가 없습니다.

저희는 이러한 개선이 귀하의 웹 사이트와 사업에 얼마나 효과적인지에 관한 귀하의 의견을 알고 싶습니다. 귀하의 ABN 계정으로 로그인하고 페이지 하단의 빨간색 배너를 클릭하셔서 저희 온라인 설문지를 작성해 주세요. 이에 대한 감사의 표시로, 향후 요금의 15퍼센트를 할인 받으실 수 있습니다.

귀하의 성원에 감사드립니다!

클라크 데이비슨
Allo Broadband Net

동봉

어휘 renew 갱신하다 contract 계약 quarterly 분기의 invoice 청구서, 송장 Web hosting 웹 호스팅(웹사이트에 저장 공간을 제공하는 것) maintenance 유시 remInder 알림 compatible 호환이 되는 effective 효과적인 questionnaire 설문지 log into 로그인하다 click 클릭하다 banner 배너, 현수막 bottom 하단, 아래 expression 표현 gratitude 감사

158 세부 사항

왜 추가 요금이 부과되었는가?
(A) 앨리사 씨가 그녀의 현재 계정에 웹 사이트를 추가했다.
(B) 앨리사 씨가 그녀의 서비스 요금제를 업그레이드하도록 회사에 요구했다.
(C) Allo Broadband Net 사가 웹 서비스를 개선했다.
(D) Allo Broadband Net 사가 새로운 기술 전문가들을 고용했다.

해설 첫 문단 세 번째 문장 "You will find the additional cost of $15 on your billing statement for our regular maintenance service."를 보면 회사가 정기 점검을 하면서 비용이 추가적으로 발생했다고 했고, 다음에 나오는 "Allo Broadband Net upgraded your Web site"에서 웹 사이트를 업그레이드했다고 했으므로 (C)가 정답이다.

159 세부 사항
데이비슨 씨는 앨리사 씨에게 무엇을 하도록 요구하는가?
(A) 온라인 설문조사 양식을 작성하도록
(B) 그녀의 고객들에게 공지를 보내도록
(C) 그녀의 월간 계약을 갱신하도록
(D) 그녀의 개인 정보를 갱신하도록

해설 두 번째 문단 두 번째 줄의 "Please fill out our online questionnaire"에서 온라인 설문지 작성을 요구하고 있으므로 (A)가 정답이다.

160 문장 삽입
표시된 [1], [2], [3], [4]의 위치들 중에서 다음의 문장이 들어갈 가장 알맞은 곳은?
"저희는 6월에 이미 당신에게 인상에 관해 이메일로 공지했습니다."
(A) [1]
(B) [2]
(C) [3]
(D) [4]

해설 제시된 문장의 this increase를 통해 인상에 관한 내용이 앞서 언급된 것을 알 수 있는데, [2]번 앞 문장에서 "15달러의 추가 비용(the additional cost of $15)"에 대해 이야기했으므로 이에 대한 공지가 이미 있었다는 해당 문장이 (B)에 위치하는 것이 자연스럽다.

[161-163] 이메일

발신: Xpress Sofsys Tech 고객 서비스
수신: BLI 소프트웨어 이용자들
날짜: 7월 15일
제목: 5.2 버전

이번 달 말에, Xpress Sofsys Tech 사는 재고 관리를 위한 온라인 소프트웨어 BLI 5.2 버전을 출시할 것입니다. 7월 31일 자정부터 BLI는 우리 IT 팀이 새로운 버전을 출시하는 동안 일시적으로 서비스가 중단될 것입니다. 여러분은 아무것도 할 필요 없이 그저 완료되기를 기다리면 됩니다. 이 기간 동안, 우리 클라우드 서버는 여러분의 현재 데이터를 자동으로 저장할 것이고, 모든 사용자들은 작업이 완료된 후인 8월 1일 오전 7시에 이 업데이트에 관하여 알림을 받을 것입니다. 이 알림을 받은 이후, 모든 사용자들은 아무 조치 없이 평소처럼 BLI 소프트웨어를 사용할 수 있습니다.

이용자들이 쉽게 기능을 찾게 하는 직관적인 사용자 인터페이스와 그들의 작업 시간을 줄이는 빠른 데이터 처리 엔진을 포함한 새롭고 혁신적인 특징들이 있습니다. 게다가, 기존 사용자들은 새 버전 출시를

기념하는 홍보 이벤트로 100 기가바이트의 웹 클라우드 데이터 저장 공간을 추가로 받을 수 있습니다. 우리는 여러분이 별다른 어려움 없이 이 새로운 기능들을 충분히 즐기실 것이라 확신합니다.

진심으로,

고객 서비스
Xpress Sofsys Tech

어휘 release 출시하다   inventory 재고, 재고 목록   starting ~부터   out of service 서비스가 중단된, 운행이 중단된   roll out 출시하다   save 저장하다   subsequent to ~ 다음에   as usual 늘 그렇듯이, 평소처럼   feature 특징   intuitive 직관적인   function 기능   existing 현존하는, 기존의   storage 창고, 저장소   promotional 홍보의   celebrate 축하하다, 기념하다   release 출시

161 주제/목적
이메일의 목적은 무엇인가?
(A) 국가적인 행사를 홍보하기 위해
(B) 회사 정책을 업데이트하기 위해
(C) 고객들에게 변경사항을 알리기 위해
(D) 구독자들에게 지불을 상기시키기 위해

해설 두 번째 문장 "Starting at midnight on July 31, BLI will be out of service temporarily while our IT team rolls out the new version."에서 새로운 소프트웨어 출시로 인해 서비스 사용이 일시적으로 불가하다고 했고, 네 번째 문장 "During this period, our cloud server will automatically save your current data,"에서 현재 데이터가 자동으로 저장된다고 했다. 두 번째 문단은 새로운 버전의 달라진 점들을 설명하므로, 이메일은 전반적으로 서비스의 변경사항을 알리고 있다고 볼 수 있다. 따라서 (C)가 정답이다.

162 동의어 찾기
첫 번째 문단 세 번째 줄의 "rolls out"이라는 어구와 의미상 가장 가까운 것은
(A) 순환하다
(B) 제거하다
(C) 도입하다
(D) 확장하다

해설 해당 어구는 새로운 버전을 '출시하다'라는 의미이므로 문맥상 가장 가까운 것은 (C)이다.

163 세부 사항
8월 1일에 무슨 일이 일어날 것인가?
(A) 직원이 새로운 버전을 시연할 것이다.
(B) 사용자들은 소프트웨어를 이전처럼 사용할 수 있을 것이다.
(C) Xpress Sofsys Tech 사가 직원을 추가로 고용할 것이다.
(D) 컴퓨터 프로그램 업데이트가 시작될 것이다.

해설 네 번째 문장 "all users will be notified of this update at 7 A.M. on August 1 after the work is finished."에서 소프트웨어 출시 준비가 끝난 후 8월 1일 7시에 업데이트에 관해 알림을 받을 것이라 했고, 다음 문장 "Subsequent to this notification, all users can use our BLI software as usual without any action."에서 알림을 받은 이후 BLI 소프트웨어를 평소대로 사용할 수 있다고 하므로 정답은 (B)이다.

[164-167] 회람

메모

수신: 고객 서비스 직원들
날짜: 10월 20일
제목: 다음 주 월요일 회의

지난주에 우리는 모여서 우리 고객 서비스 품질에 대해 논의했습니다. 우리가 확보한 데이터에 따르면, 대부분의 고객들이 우리 고객 서비스 직원들과의 의사소통에 긍정적인 반응을 보였습니다. 우리 직원들은 포장 서비스, 배송비, 택배 현황 추적에 관한 다양한 문의 응대에 정말 전문적이고 신속했습니다.

우리가 해결해야 할 한 가지는 낮은 지인 추천도입니다. 설문조사에 근거하면, 단지 소수의 고객들만이 우리 서비스의 장점을 타인에게 말했습니다. 대부분의 사람들은 우리의 배송 서비스만 이용하는 단골 고객들이거나 우리를 미디어 기반의 광고를 통해서만 인식합니다. 우리가 추천을 통한 신규 고객 유치에 실패했다는 것이 명확합니다.

그러므로, 다음 주 월요일 회의는 이 문제에 중점을 둘 것입니다. 저는 이 상황을 개선할 몇 가지 방법을 고안할 것입니다. 여러분도 추천도를 높일 수 있는 창의적이고 혁신적인 접근법들을 생각해내면 감사하겠습니다. 제 이메일로 여러분의 제안을 제출하시면 저는 논의를 위해 발표 슬라이드에 그것들을 포함할 것입니다. 여러분 모두에게 연락이 있기를 고대합니다.

로날드 잭슨
고객 시비스 부장

어휘 gather 모으다, 모이다   secure 확보하다   prompt 신속한   various 다양한   packaging 포장   parcel 소포   tracking 추적   settle 해결하다   acquaintance 지인   advantage 장점   advertising 광고   obvious 명확한   attract 끌어들이다   referral 추천, 소개   focus on ~에 집중하다   method 방법   appreciate 감사하다   come up with ~를 제시하다, 생각해내다   creative 창의적인   innovative 혁신적인   approach 접근(법)   look forward to ~하기를 기대하다

164 추론/암시

잭슨 씨가 일하는 곳은 어디일 것 같은가?
(A) 통신 회사
(B) 보험 회사
(C) 물류 회사
(D) 광고 회사

해설 세 번째 문장의 "~ regarding the packaging service, shipping fees, and parcel status tracking"에서 문의가 주로 물류와 관련됨을 알 수 있으므로 (C)가 정답이다.

165 세부 사항

무슨 문제가 언급되었는가?
(A) 고객 서비스 부서에 인력이 부족하다.
(B) 광고 비용이 점차 증가하고 있다.
(C) 다른 사람들에게 회사를 추천하는 고객들이 거의 없다.
(D) 일부 주문이 자주 지연되는 경향이 있다.

해설 두 번째 문단 첫 문장 "One thing that we need to settle is the low level of recommendation to their acquaintances"를 보면 그들이 해결해야 할 한 가지 문제가 지인 추천도가 낮은 것이라고 했으므로 정답은 (C)이다.

166 세부 사항

잭슨 씨는 어떤 정보를 검토했는가?
(A) 재무 대차 대조표
(B) 설문조사 결과
(C) 온라인 광고
(D) 경쟁사 분석

해설 두 번째 문단의 "Based on our survey,"로 미루어 보아, 설문조사 결과를 검토했음을 알 수 있다. 따라서 (B)가 답이다.

167 세부 사항

직원들은 무엇을 하도록 요구되는가?
(A) 첨부된 양식 작성하기
(B) 잭슨 씨에게 문제에 대한 아이디어 보내기
(C) 더 많은 고객 서비스부 직원 채용하기
(D) 회의 날짜 확정하기

해설 세 번째 문단, 네 번째 문장의 "Please submit your suggestions to my e-mail," 부분을 보면 직원들에게 문제 해결을 위한 제안을 보내달라고 요구하고 있으므로 (B)가 정답이다.

[168-171] 온라인 채팅

한나 박 [오전 11시 20분]
여러분은 우리 건물 일부에서 에어컨이 작동되지 않는다는 것을 알 겁니다.

밥 테일러 [오전 11시 21분]
들었어요. 한동안, 점점 덥고 습해졌어요.

한나 박 [오전 11시 22분]
기스 배관에 문제기 좀 있는데, 부품 긍급 문제로 수리가 지연되고 있어요. 지난번에 고장났을 때는 고치는 데 4일 정도 걸렸죠. 아마도 내일 오후 늦게 기술자가 도착할 것입니다. 그때까지 기존에 있는 선풍기를 사용하도록 하세요.

밥 테일러 [오전 11시 25분]
저희 컴퓨터 장비가 과열될까 봐 걱정돼요. 작업물을 임시로 저장할 수 있는 장비가 있나요? 데이터를 잃을까 봐 걱정되네요.

한나 박 [오전 11시 28분]
이 건물에는 없어요. 왓슨 씨의 승인이 있으면, Fleming의 물류 창고에서 여분의 저장 장비를 얻을 수 있을 거예요. 제 생각에는 그곳에 장치가 4~5개 있어요. 빨라도 내일 오후에 가져올 수 있어요.

에이미 왓슨 [오전 11시 30분]
한나, 지금 당장 데이터 보호를 위해 임시 저장 서버 장치를 즉시 구매하도록 허락할게요. 구매 준비가 되는 대로 필요한 장치의 개수와 견적 비용을 저에게 알려줘요.

한나 박 [오전 11시 31분]
지금 당장 시작하겠습니다.

에이미 왓슨 [오전 11시 32분]
오후 3시까지 그것들을 배송해 줄 지역 전자제품 매장을 찾지 못하면, 직접 수령해 오도록 누군가를 바로 보내세요.

어휘 aware 아는, 인식하는 air conditioning 에어컨 part 일부, 부품 for some time 한동안 increasingly 점점 humid 습한 piping 배관 fix 고치다 probably 아마도 fan 선풍기 overheat 과열되다 temporarily 임시로 storage 저장 warehouse (물류) 창고 urgently 긴급히 protect 보호하다 right away 즉각, 곧바로 estimated 견적의, 추측의 appliance 전자제품

168 주제/목적
무엇이 문제인가?
(A) 물류 창고가 사무실에서 너무 멀다.
(B) 구매 허가가 거절되었다.
(C) 배송비가 예상보다 더 비싸다.
(D) 냉방 장치가 작동되지 않는다.

해설 주제는 주로 도입부에 언급된다. 오전 11시 20분 메시지 "the air conditioning is not working"에서 에어컨이 작동되지 않는다고 했으므로, 이를 냉방 장치(cooling system)로 바꿔 표현한 (D)가 정답이다.

169 의도 파악
오전 11시 28분에, 박 씨가 "이 건물에는 없어요"라고 쓴 것은 무엇을 의미하는가?
(A) 근처에 여분의 저장 장치가 없다.
(B) 개선 작업으로 데이터가 더 안전해질 것이다.
(C) 회사 서버는 어느 곳에서나 안정적이다.
(D) 사무용품을 옮기기 위해 소형 트럭이 필요하다.

해설 앞서 11시 25분에 테일러 씨가 임시 저장 장비가 있는지 물어봤고, 박 씨가 "Not in this building"이라고 답한 것은 장비(저장 장치)가 건물에 없다는 의미이므로 정답은 (A)이다.

170 추론/암시
Fleming에 있는 장비에 대해 암시되는 것은?
(A) 사무실에 도착하는 데 너무 오래 걸릴 것이다.
(B) 다른 가게의 추가 부품이 필요하다.
(C) 저장소가 사무실 근처에 위치해 있다.
(D) 설치를 위해 전문가가 필요하다.

해설 11시 28분에 박 씨가 회사 물류 창고에서 장비를 가져올 수 있는 시간이 빨라도 내일 오후라고 하자, 마지막 메시지에서 오후 3시까지 배송이 되지 않으면 직접 수령해 오라고 하는 것으로 보아, 장비가 도착하는 데 시간이 오래 걸리는 상황임을 유추할 수 있다. 따라서 (A)가 가장 적절하다.

171 세부 사항
다음에 어떤 일이 일어날 것 같은가?
(A) 선풍기가 각 사무실에 배치될 것이다.
(B) 박 씨가 주문할 준비가 될 것이다.
(C) 기술자가 새로운 서버를 설치할 것이다.
(D) 테일러 씨가 불필요한 데이터를 삭제할 것이다.

해설 11시 30분 왓슨 씨의 메시지 "Please let me know the number of needed units and estimated costs as soon as you're ready for the purchase."에서 주문할 준비가 되면 알려달라고 하자, 박 씨가 11시 31분 메시지 "I'll get started right now."에서 곧 시작하겠다고 했으므로 (B)가 정답이다.

[172-175] 기사

가상 현실 속으로: 성공의 열쇠

COLUMBUS (5월 2일) — 제인 멜리사는 25년 전 New York 시에 있는 대학교에 입학했을 때 패션 디자인을 전공했던 학생이었습니다. 그러나, 여름방학 동안 작은 의류 매장에서 일했을 때, 그녀는 사업을 시작하길 원했습니다. 새로운 목표를 이루기 위해 그녀는 경영학과로 전과했고, 학위 취득 후, 그녀의 고향 Columbus에서 "Melissa's Open Arms"라는 이름으로 그녀만의 작은 매장을 열었습니다.

20년 후, 멜리사 씨의 매장은 매년 수백만 달러를 벌어들이며 미국 동부에서 가장 빠르게 성장하는 회사로 꾸준히 확장되고 있습니다. 그녀의 인터뷰에 따르면, 이러한 성공은 부분적으로는 7년전에 고용했던 제시카 도리스의 가상 온라인 매장에 관한 제안 덕분이었습니다. 그녀의 아이디어들을 수용함으로써, 멜리사 씨는 디지털 정체성과 부합하도록 본점 이름을 "V-Melissa"로 변경했습니다.

멜리사 씨는 뛰어난 의사소통 능력과 고객들과 직접 상호작용하는 능력을 가지고 있고, 심지어 그들과 감정을 공유하는 것을 매우 좋아합니다. 그녀는 여전히 자신이 할 수 있는 최선의 일은 고객들이 그녀의 오프라인 매장에서 쇼핑할 때 그들의 실질적 요구를 충족시키는 것이라고 믿습니다. 그러나, 그녀는 전자 통신이 발전한 오늘날 온라인 쇼핑이 중요하다는 것을 알고 있습니다. V-Melissa는 웹상에서만 연매출이 2억 달러로 증가할 것으로 예상됩니다. 이 매출의 3분의 1이 영국, 프랑스, 일본, 한국과 같은 미국 외 국가들로부터 비롯될 것입니다.

이러한 확장에 따라, V-Melissa는 가상 온라인 매장을 업데이트 및 관리하며, 미국 내외로 새 지점들을 확장할 준비를 하기 위해 지속적으로 많은 신입 및 경력 직원들을 고용했습니다.

"우리는 시기 적절하게 새로운 지점들을 개점하는 것의 타당성과 수익성을 고려해야 합니다."라고 멜리사 씨는 말했습니다. "우리는 전세계에 우리의 양질의 제품과 서비스를 홍보하는 것이 중요합니다."

마지막으로, 멜리사 씨가 말하길, 비록 그녀가 미래를 정확히 예측할 수는 없지만, 그저 그녀의 믿음직한 직원들과 한걸음씩 나아갈 뿐이라고 했습니다.

어휘 virtual reality 가상 현실 major in ~을 전공으로 하다 get down to ~에 착수하다 achieve 달성하다 degree 학위 steadily 꾸준히 earn 벌다, 얻다 partly 부분적으로 flagship store 본점, 주력 상점 interact with ~와 상호작용하다 in person 직접 aware 알고 있는 in accordance with ~와 일치하여, ~에 따라 experienced 능숙한, 경력이 있는 prepare for ~을 준비하다 state 주 validity 타당성 profitability 수익성 in a timely fashion 시기적절하게 quality 고급의, 양질의

172 주제/목적

기사문의 목적은 무엇인가?
(A) 온라인 판매의 중요성을 강조하기 위해
(B) 새로운 의류 제품들을 광고하기 위해
(C) 회사가 어떻게 성장했는지 설명하기 위해
(D) 최신 패션 트렌드를 논의하기 위해

해설 전반적으로 멜리사 씨의 사업 시작 동기와 회사의 성장에 대해 이야기하고 있다. 특히 두 번째 문단에서 회사의 지속적인 성장과 그 이유에 관해 설명하고 있으므로 (C)가 정답으로 가장 적절하다.

173 Not/True 확인

V-Melissa에 대해 알 수 있는 것은?
(A) 다른 이름으로 운영되었다.
(B) New York 시에 첫 매장을 열었다.
(C) 웹 디자이너들만 고용해 왔다.
(D) 최근에 도리스 씨를 부사장으로 임명했다.

해설 첫 문단 마지막 문장 "she started her own small store in her hometown of Columbus under the name "Melissa's Open Arms"와 두번째 문단 마지막 문장 "Ms. Melissa renamed her flagship store "V-Melissa" to match its digital identity."로 미루어 보아, V-Melissa는 처음에 Melissa's Open Arms라는 이름으로 운영되었고 그 후 V-Melissa로 바뀌었음을 알 수 있다. 따라서 (A)가 정답이다.

174 동의어 찾기

다섯 번째 문단 두 번째 줄의 "fashion"과 의미상 가장 가까운 것은?
(A) 방법
(B) 종류
(C) 기능
(D) 용모

해설 in a timely fashion(시기적절하게)에서 fashion은 '방법'을 의미하므로 보기 중에서 이와 유사한 단어는 (A)이다.

175 문장 삽입

표시된 [1], [2], [3], [4]의 위치들 중에서 다음의 문장이 들어갈 가장 알맞은 곳은?

"그녀는 여전히 자신이 할 수 있는 최선의 일은 고객들이 그녀의 오프라인 매장에서 쇼핑할 때 그들의 실질적 요구를 충족시키는 것이라고 믿습니다."

(A) [1]
(B) [2]
(C) [3]
(D) [4]

해설 제시된 문장이 오프라인 매장에서 고객들의 실질적인 요구를 들어준다는 내용이므로, 이 문장 앞에는 고객들과 직접 만나 이야기를 한다는 내용이 등장하는 것이 문맥상 가장 자연스럽다. 따라서 (C)가 정답이다.

[176-180] 온라인 양식 & 이메일

[http://www.miraclesoftware.com/support_request]

Miracle Software 지원 요청서

이름: 케이티 윤
회사: Wiki 사
이메일: k.yoon@wikicorp.com
제목: 화상 회의 문제

당신이 겪고 있는 문제를 설명해 주세요.
지난 3월 이래로, 우리는 귀사의 웹 기반 화상 회의 소프트웨어를 사용했고, 전반적으로 만족하고 있습니다. 그러나, 우리는 이따금씩 연결이 끊기고, 화면과 음성 일치에 문제가 있습니다. 최근 회의 중에 화면이 갑자기 잡음을 내며 깜빡거렸습니다. 재시작했더니, "서비스 센터에 연락하세요"라는 메시지가 떴습니다. 전 세계의 고객들 중 몇 명이 지난 주간 회의에서 이러한 불편에 불만을 제기해서 우리는 회의 일정을 변경할 수밖에 없었습니다. 이 문제들을 개선하기 위한 즉각적인 조치는 없습니까? 만약 없다면, 우리는 서비스 계약을 곧 종료하고자 합니다. 우리의 프로젝트를 순조롭게 진행할 수 있도록 다시는 이런 일이 발생하지 않을 것이라는 보장을 받고 싶습니다. 저희에게 가능한 한 빨리 해결책을 알려주세요.

수신: 케이티 윤 <k.yoon@wikicorp.com>
발신: Miracle Software 지원 <support@miraclesoftware.com>
날짜: 5월 2일
제목: 서비스 지원 201904128 - 화상 회의 문제

윤 씨에게,

저희에게 귀하의 문제에 대한 정보를 알려주셔서 감사합니다. 귀하가 그 당시에 겪은 문제는 데이터베이스 서버들 간의 충돌로 인해 초래된 것입니다. 이 문제는 저희 IT 지원팀에서 예상하거나, 발견하지 못해서 저희가 고객들에게 사전에 경고할 방법이 없었습니다. 우리 웹 서버상에서 이러한 문제는 매우 드문 일임을 확인합니다.

귀하의 피드백을 고려하여, 저희는 화면의 안내 메시지들을 "서비스 센터에 연락하세요"에서 "서비스 코드 100번"으로 변경하기로 결정했습니다. 이 새로운 메시지는 우리 고객들이 문제를 정확히 알고 웹 상의 유지관리 설명서에서 해결책을 찾을 수 있게 합니다. 그렇게 함으로써, 저희 고객들은 이런 종류의 문제를 쉽게 해결할 수 있습니다. 사실상, 저희 화상 회의 소프트웨어는 모든 면에서 거의 완벽합니다. 이러한 갑작스러운 변수를 고려하여, 저희는 인터넷을 통해 가능한 한 빨리 소프트웨어를 업데이트하겠습니다. 업그레이드가 되는 동안, 소프트웨어는 단 몇 분 동안 접속이 일시적으로 불가능할 것입니다.

이러한 불편을 드려 진심으로 사과드리며, 귀하의 의견에 정말 감사드립니다. 감사의 표시로, 이번 달 청구서에서 100달러를 차감해 드리겠습니다.

안부를 전하며,

스티븐 내쉬
소프트웨어 지원부서
Miracle Software

어휘 be satisfied with ~에 만족하다 overall 전반적으로 intermittently 간헐적으로, 이따금씩 disconnected 끊기는 match 맞추다, 일치시키다 suddenly 갑자기 flicker 깜빡거리다 inconvenience 불편 have no choice but to V ~할 수 밖에 없다 reschedule (일정을) 재조정하다 immediate 즉각적인 action 조치 terminate 종료하다 guarantee 보증, 보장 proceed with ~을 진행하다 smoothly 순조롭게, 부드럽게 solution 해결책 difficulty 어려움, 문제 conflict 충돌 warn 경고하다 in advance 사전에 confident 확신하는 rare 드문 alert 경고 maintenance 유지, 보수 in light of ~를 고려하여 variable 변수 temporarily 임시로 inaccessible 접속 불가능한 sincerely 진심으로 apologize 사과하다 truly 정말로, 진심으로 as a token of one's appreciation 감사의 표시로 deduct 공제하다, 차감하다

176 세부 사항

윤 씨가 온라인 양식에서 요청한 것은 무엇인가?
(A) 새로운 회의 장치
(B) 고객 서비스 전화
(C) 빠른 해결책
(D) 회원권 업그레이드

해설 온라인 양식의 후반부에서, "Don't you have any immediate action for improving these issues?"를 보면 문제에 대한 즉각적인 조치를 요구하고 있으므로 (C)가 정답이다.

177 Not/True 확인

Wiki 사에 관하여 명시된 것은?
(A) Miracle Software와 협업했다.
(B) 소프트웨어 저작권을 소유했다.
(C) 3월 중순부터 운영되고 있다.
(D) 정기적으로 화상 회의 프로그램을 사용한다.

해설 윤 씨는 화상 회의 소프트웨어를 사용하는 회사의 일원으로, 첫 번째 지문의 다섯 번째 문장 "Several of our clients from all over the world complained about this inconvenience in the last weekly conference, so we had no choice but to reschedule it."에서 지난 주간 회의 때 전 세계 고객들이 이것을 사용하는 데 문제가 생겼다는 것으로 보아 고객들과 정기적으로 화상 회의를 한다는 것을 알 수 있으므로 정답은 (D)이다.

178 주제/목적 (연계)

윤 씨가 Miracle Software 사의 프로그램과 관련하여 직면한 문제는 무엇인가?
(A) 그녀의 컴퓨터와 호환되지 않는다.
(B) 그녀의 구체적인 요구사항에 적합하지 않는다.
(C) 다른 경쟁사들보다 더 비싸다.
(D) 서버가 신뢰할 수 없고 불안정하다.

해설 첫 번째 지문의 세 번째 문장 "the screen suddenly flickered with some noise."와 두 번째 지문의 두 번째 문장 "The problem you experienced at that time was caused by some conflicts among database servers."를 보면 서버 문제로 인해 오류가 있었음을 알 수 있다. 따라서 서버가 신뢰할 수 없고 불안정하다는 (D)가 정답이다.

179 세부 사항

내쉬 씨는 Miracle Software가 무엇을 바꿀 것이라고 말하는가?
(A) 이용 약관
(B) 혼란을 주는 메시지
(C) 유지관리 일정
(D) 웹캠과 스피커폰

해설 이메일의 두 번째 문단 첫 문장에서 "we have decided to change our on-screen alert messages from "Call the Service Center" to "Service Code No.100."라고 했으므로 안내 메시지를 변경할 것임을 알 수 있다. 따라서 (B)가 정답이다.

180 추론/암시 (연계)

Miracle Software에 관하여 암시된 것은?
(A) Wiki 사와 계속 거래할 것이다.
(B) 최근에 새로운 기술 전문가를 고용했다.
(C) 고객들의 재무 계획을 관리한다.
(D) 지난달에 서버를 업그레이드했다.

해설 첫 번째 지문에서 윤 씨가 Don't you have any immediate action for improving these issues? If not, we would like to terminate our service contract soon.라며 조치를 취해 주지 않으면 계약을 곧 종료하겠다고 했고, 두 번째 지문에서 내쉬 씨가 해결책을 제시하고 있으므로 윤 씨가 소속된 Wiki 사는 Miracle Software와 계속 거래할 것임을 유추할 수 있다. 따라서 정답은 (A)이다.

[181-185] 이메일 & 지시 사항

발신: Dana Kay, Blue Light 여행사
수신: 앤 니키타
제목: 패션 상품 박람회 출장 계획
날짜: 5월 15일
첨부: LA_New York_일정표.pdf

니키타 씨에게,

요청하신 대로, 저는 귀하의 New York행 왕복 티켓을 예매했습니다. 귀하의 예약 번호는 LM3870401SW입니다. 귀하는 6월 2일 L.A. 국내 공항을 출발하여 6월 5일 New York 공항에서 돌아올 것입니다. 이 일정은 6월에 있을 귀하의 패션 상품 박람회 업무 일정과 겹치지 않을 것입니다. 이 이메일의 첨부파일에서 일정표를 보실 수 있습니다.

소형 가구를 같이 보낼 수 있는지에 대한 귀하의 문의에 대한 회신으로, 의류 거치대는 수하물로 부칠 수 있습니다. South-West 항공사 담당자는 특대 사이즈의 수하물은 각각 100달러의 추가 비용이 발생한다고 저에게 알려주었습니다. 요금을 사전에 납부하시면, 체크인 하실 때 빠른 체크인 기기에 이러한 특대 사이즈의 수하물들을 신속하게 맡길 수 있습니다. 위에 언급된 귀하의 물건들은 무게와 크기 면에서 항공사의 수하물 정책 제한을 초과하지 않습니다. 부치고자 하는 물건이 더 있으시면, 저에게 그것들의 무게와 크기를 이메일로 보내주세요. 그러면, 제가 귀하를 위해 사전에 지불해드릴 수 있습니다.

그럼 이만,

다나 케이
Blue Light 여행사

South-West 항공사

빠른 수하물 체크인 서비스를 위한 지시사항

공항에 도착하자마자, 이 간단한 절차를 따라주세요.

1. 공항의 체크인 기기에서 귀하의 탑승권을 출력하세요.

2. 빠른 체크인 기기에서, 귀하의 물품들을 저울 위에 올려 두세요. 귀하의 사진이 있는 유효한 신분증(여권 또는 운전면허증)과 탑승권을 직원 한 명에게 제시하세요. 그들은 당신이 부치길 원하는 가방이나 다른 물건들의 개수를 물을 것입니다.

3. 우리 직원이 귀하의 수하물에 수하물 표를 붙이고 관련 서류를 줄 것입니다. 그러고 나서, 공항 보안 검색대로 가세요.

주의: 빠른 수하물 수속 서비스는 현재 Chicago, Atlanta, L.A. 공항에서만 이용 가능합니다.

어휘 itinerary 일정(표) make a reservation 예약하다 round-trip 왕복의 domestic 국내의 task 업무 attached 첨부된 in response to ~에 대응하여 inquiry 문의 rack 선반 luggage 짐, 수하물 the person in charge 담당자 oversized 특대의, 너무 큰 express 빠른, 신속한 kiosk 키오스크, 간이 안내소, 가판 beforehand 사전에, 미리 drop off 내려놓다 mention 언급하다 exceed 초과하다 arrival 도착 simple 간단한 procedure 절차 boarding pass 탑승권 scale 저울 valid 유효한 relevant 관련된 security checkpoint 보안 검색대

181 추론/암시

이메일에 따르면, 니키타 씨는 왜 New York 시에 갈 것 같은가?
(A) 패션쇼에 참석하기 위해
(B) 수입 원단 가격을 협상하기 위해
(C) 자신의 회사 제품들을 홍보하기 위해
(D) 고객들과 회의하기 위해

해설 이메일의 제목과 첫 번째 문단 "This schedule does not conflict with your tasks for the June Fashion Merchandise Fair. You can find the itinerary in the attached file of this e-mail"을 보았을 때 니키타 씨가 패션 상품 박람회 일정으로 출장간다는 것을 알 수 있고, 두 번째 문단 clothes racks can be checked as luggage 부분에서 수하물에 의류 거치대가 포함된 것으로 보아 박람회에 제품을 홍보하러 간다는 것을 알 수 있으므로 (C)가 정답이다.

182 Not/True 확인

니키타 씨의 특대 수하물에 관한 설명 중 옳은 것은?
(A) 박람회를 위한 가구로 구성되어 있다.
(B) 무게 제한을 초과했다.
(C) 그녀의 고객들이 구매했다.
(D) 기차로 보내질 것이다.

해설 첫 번째 지문 두 번째 문단 "In response to your inquiry about whether your small furniture can be sent together, clothes racks can be checked as luggage"를 보면, 수하물로 부치는 물건이 의류 거치대 같은 가구라고 했으므로 (A)가 정답이다.

183 세부 사항

케이 씨는 니키타 씨를 위해 무엇을 하겠다고 제안하는가?
(A) 출장 예산을 편성한다
(B) 호텔을 예약한다
(C) 일정을 변경한다
(D) 비용을 처리한다

해설 첫 번째 지문의 마지막 문장 "If so, I can make the payment for you in advance."를 보면, 비용을 사전에 처리해 줄 수 있다고 했으므로 (D)가 정답이다.

184 Not/True 확인

탑승권에 관하여 명시된 것은?
(A) 케이 씨의 이메일에 첨부되어 있다.
(B) 체크인 구역에서 제시되어야 한다.
(C) 집에서 출력되어야 한다.
(D) 보안 검색대에서 요구되지 않는다.

해설 두 번째 지문이 체크인과 관련된 지시사항으로, 두 번째 항목 "Show your valid photo ID (passport or driver's license) and boarding pass to one of our staff."를 보면 직원에게 탑승권을 제시하라고 하였으므로 (B)가 정답이다.

185 추론/암시 (연계)

니키타 씨의 돌아오는 항공편에 대하여 암시되는 것은?
(A) 니키타 씨는 빠른 수하물 수속 서비스를 사용할 수 없다.
(B) 니키타 씨는 밤에 L.A.로 돌아올 것이다.
(C) 니키타 씨는 일정을 변경할 것이다.
(D) 니키타 씨는 추가 수하물이 있을 것이다.

해설 첫 번째 지문 세 번째 문장 "You will depart from the L.A. domestic airport on June 2, and return from the New York airport on June 5."를 보면 니키타 씨의 항공편은 L.A.와 뉴욕 왕복 일정인데, 두 번째 글의 주의사항 "NOTE: The express drop-off service is currently available only in Chicago, Atlanta, and L.A."를 보면 돌아오는 항공편의 출발지인 뉴욕 공항에서는 빠른 수하물 수속 서비스를 이용할 수 없으므로 (A)가 정답이다.

[186-190] 웹페이지 & 이메일 & 기사

http://pennylife.org/donations

Penny Life 매장들은 대중에게 가구, 가전제품, 사무용품 등과 같은 새 물건이나 중고 물건들을 기부하도록 요청합니다. 이것들은 다른 사람들이 사용할 수 있도록 깨끗해야 합니다. 손상되거나 얼룩진 물건은 허용되지 않는다는 점을 유의하세요. 이러한 물건들의 판매를 통해 얻은 수익은 지역사회 개발 프로젝트에 자금을 지원하기 위해 사용되는데, 이는 주택 개조, 교육 프로그램 개설 및 주변 환경 개선을 포함합니다.

기부 절차:
1. 우리 웹 사이트의 메인 페이지 검색창에 당신의 주소를 입력하여 가장 가까운 Penny Life 매장을 찾으세요.

2. 각 매장의 운영 시간과 위치를 웹 사이트에서 확인하세요.

3. 쓸모없고 불필요한 물건들을 직접 가져오시거나, 여러분의 집 또는 회사로부터 큰 물건을 가져갈 일정을 잡기 위해 웹에 있는 번호로 우리 관리자들 중 한 명에게 연락하세요.

발신 : d.ditzel@ditzellodge.com
수신 : k.tyler@pennylife.org
날짜 : 4월 20일
제목 : 기부

타일러 씨에게,

저는 Morgantown에 있는 Ditzel Suite Lodge의 소유주입니다. 저는 다음 달 숙박업을 그만둘 예정입니다.

저는 제 건물에 있는 침대, 책상, 의자, 테이블 등의 많은 좋은 가구들을 기부하고자 합니다. 제 친구 중 한 명이 당신의 기관에 이 재고품들을 기부하라고 조언했습니다. 저는 위치 검색 시스템을 이용해서 Penny Life의 가장 가까운 지점이 Pittsburgh점임을 알았고, 지금 그 지점 관리자의 연락처 정보를 알고 있습니다. 제 위치는 그 지점에서 25마일 정도 떨어진 곳에 있습니다. 이 문제에 관해 가능한 한 빨리 저에게 연락해 주세요.

그럼 이만,

데이비드 디첼
Ditzel Suite Lodge

Ditzel Suite Lodge 폐업

MORGANTOWN (5월 2일) — 데이비드 디첼 씨는 최근에 Penny Life의 트럭들에 의해 Ditzel Suite Lodge에서 많은 숙박시설 가구들이 옮겨지는 것을 보았습니다. 그는 지역 랜드마크인 그 호텔을 50년간 주인으로서 운영했습니다. "저는 오대호 중 하나인 Eire호와 맞닿아 있는 Erie County로 이사하게 되어 정말 행복합니다."라고 Ditzel 씨는 말했습니다. "그리고 저는 제 여생을 봉사와 휴식으로 보낼 계획입니다. 그러나 호텔이 제 삶의 큰 부분이었기 때문에 Morgantown을 떠나는 것은 힘드네요."

Ditzel Suite Lodge 매물은 이미 Max Virginia 개발사에 의해 매입되었습니다. 그 회사는 향후 몇 년 동안 그 건물을 완전히 재건축하고 새로운 쇼핑 단지를 건설할 것으로 보입니다.

어휘 the public 대중 donate 기부하다 pre-owned 중고의 appliance 전자제품 supplies 사무용품 damaged 손상된 stained 얼룩진 profit 수익 fund 자금을 조달하다 surrounding 주변의 redundant 쓸모없는, 남는 unneeded 불필요한 pick up 수령하다, 가지고 오다 accommodation 숙박업소 retire 은퇴하다 inventory 재고 arrange 준비하다, 마련하다 operate 운영하다 landmark 랜드마크, 주요지형지물 border (경계를) 접하다 rest 나머지 property 부동산, 매물 entirely 완전히

186 세부 사항

웹 페이지에 따르면, Penny Life는 받은 물품으로 무엇을 하는가?
(A) 지역 자선단체에 기부하기
(B) 재활용을 위해 세척하기
(C) 대중에게 판매하기
(D) 전시를 위해 수리하기

해설 첫 번째 지문인 웹 페이지의 네 번째 문장 "Profits from the sales of these goods are used to fund local community development projects," 부분에서 판매로 얻

은 수익은 지역사회 개발 프로젝트에 자금을 지원하기 위해 사용된다고 했으므로, 기부 받은 물품을 판매한다는 것을 알 수 있다. 따라서 (C)가 정답이다.

187 세부 사항 (연계)

디첼 씨는 어떻게 Penny Life의 연락 정보를 찾았는가?
(A) 웹 사이트를 방문함으로써
(B) 그의 지인에게 들음으로써
(C) 운영 체제 업데이트를 다운로드함으로써
(D) 본사에 연락함으로써

(해설) 첫 번째 지문의 절차 부분 중 세 번째 항목의 "call one of our managers at the number on the Web"을 보면 웹 사이트에 관리자의 전화번호가 있음을 알 수 있고, 두 번째 지문의 다섯 번째 문장 "I figured out that the nearest branch of Penny Life is the Pittsburgh office when I used the location search system, and I now know the branch manager's contact information there."에서 디첼 씨가 웹 페이지에서 지점 관리자 연락처 정보를 알았다는 것을 알 수 있으므로 (A)가 정답이다.

188 Not/True 확인

이메일에서 디첼 씨에 대해서 명시된 것은?
(A) 새 가구를 판매하고자 한다.
(B) 다른 지점으로 전근 갈 예정이다.
(C) 다른 일자리를 구하고 있다.
(D) 사업을 그만두기로 결정했다.

(해설) 이메일의 두 번째 문장 "I am planning to close my accommodation business next month."를 보면 숙박업을 그만둘 것이라고 했으므로 (D)가 정답이다.

189 추론/암시 (연계)

Pittsburgh의 Penny Life 지점에 관하여 암시된 것은?
(A) 고객들에게 훌륭한 이사 서비스를 제공한다.
(B) 미국에서 가장 큰 지점이다.
(C) 수거 서비스를 위해 디첼 씨의 업체를 방문할 것이다.
(D) 개조 작업을 위해 일시적으로 문을 닫을 것이다.

(해설) 웹 페이지의 기부 질차에서 첫 번째 항목 "Find the nearest Penny Life store"에서 가까운 지점을 찾으라 했고, 세 번째 항목 "~ in order to schedule a pickup time for large items from your home or company."에서 근처 지점들에서 큰 물품들을 수령해 간다고 했다. 두 번째 이메일의 다섯 번째 문장 "I figured out that the nearest branch of Penny Life is the Pittsburgh office"를 보면 가장 가까운 지점이 Pittsburgh라고 하면서 수령해 가길 요청하고 있으므로 (C)가 정답이다.

190 세부 사항

기사문에 따르면, 디첼 씨는 다음에 어디에서 거주할 계획인가?
(A) Pittsburgh에서
(B) Erie에서
(C) Morgantown에서
(D) Virginia에서

(해설) 기사문의 세 번째 문장 "I am really happy to move into Erie County, which borders Lake Erie,"에서 디첼 씨는 Erie로 이사하게 되어 행복하다고 했으므로 (B)가 정답이다.

[191-195] 이메일 & 주문서 & 이메일

수신: 토미 랜서 <t.lancer@blackdots.com>
발신: 그레이스 킴 <g_kim@proassetfinanacial.net>
날짜: 6월 15일
제목: 사무용품 주문
첨부: Orderform.doc

랜서 씨에게,

저는 첨부 양식에 나온 우리가 다음 달에 사용하려는 물품들의 변경에 대해 글을 씁니다. 우리는 Black Dots Supplies에서 정기적으로 주문했고, 매월 1일에 자동으로 물품을 수령하고 있습니다. 하지만 이번에는 우리가 수령하던 잉크 토너를 양식에 명시된 다른 브랜드로 교체하려 한다는 걸 알아주시기 바랍니다. 게다가, 우리는 최근에 신입 회계사들을 추가로 고용했기 때문에 이번에만 LP 350 품목을 평소보다 더 추가하고 싶습니다. 그래서, 우리는 그들을 위한 사무 공간을 준비할 필요가 있습니다. 당신은 기록 내역에서 저희 법인카드 정보를 찾아서 결제에 사용하시면 됩니다.

우리는 귀사의 제품들, 특히 우리 회사 로고가 있는 재생 용지로 만들어진 문구류 품질에 항상 만족하고 있습니다.

행복을 빌며,

그레이스 킴
종무과 관리자
Proasset 금융회사

주문 대상: Proasset 금융회사 　　주문일: 6월 15일
연락처: 그레이스 킴

품목 설명	품목 번호	수량	단가	품목별 총합
레터헤드지	LP 350	10연	40달러	400달러
화이트보드 마커	WM 500	5개 x 8묶음	5.99달러	47.92달러
Maxdova 잉크 토너 카트리지	MI 750	10개	50달러	500달러
Dusittani 지석 화이트보드	DM 900	5개	89.99달러	449.95달러
Black Dots Supplies			세금:	60.13달러
			총합:	1,458달러

수신: 그레이스 킴 <g_kim@proassetfinanacial.net>
발신: 토미 랜서 <t.lancer@blackdots.com>
날짜: 6월 16일
제목: 회신: 사무용품 주문

킴 씨에게,

저희는 귀하의 주문서에 요청된 대로 몇 가지 변경사항을 포함한 귀하의 주문을 처리하게 되어 기쁩니다. 그러나, 귀하가 주문하신 Dusittani 사의 화이트보드가 현재 품절되어 유감입니다. 그것 대신에, 다른 고객들로부터 가장 높은 선호도를 보인 Gannon 사의 화이트보드들을 사용해 보시길 권장하고 싶습니다. 이것은 사무용품 시장에서 최상위 제품입니다. 원래 가격은 개당 95달러 99센트이지만, 저는 기꺼이 귀하에게 Dusittani 자석 화이트보드와 같은 가격으로 다섯 개를 공급해 드릴 것입니다. 이 권유에 동의하시면, 이 이메일로 저에게 알려주세요.

진심으로,

토미 랜서
Black Dots Supplies

어휘 place an order 주문하다 on a regular basis 정기적으로 automatically 자동으로 replace 교체하다 indicate 명시하다 accountant 회계사 especially 특히 ream 연(종이를 세는 단위) process 처리하다 regretful 유감인 out of stock 품절된 instead of ~대신에 preference 선호(도) top-ranked 최상위의 be willing to V 기꺼이 ~하다

191 주제/목적

첫 번째 이메일의 목적은 무엇인가?
(A) 정기 주문을 변경하기 위해
(B) 제품에 불만을 제기하기 위해
(C) 제조업자에게 연락하기 위해
(D) 예정된 배송일을 확인하기 위해

해설 첫 번째 이메일의 첫 문장 "I am writing about some changes of items we want to use for the next month on the attached form." 부분을 통해 주문에 대한 변경사항을 알리기 위해 쓴 글임을 알 수 있다. 따라서 (A)가 정답이다.

192 Not/True 확인

첫 번째 이메일에서, Proasset 금융회사에 대하여 명시된 것은?
(A) 현재 확장 중이다.
(B) 사무실 이전을 준비하고 있다.
(C) 최근에 새로운 판매 사원을 고용했다.
(D) 일부 사무 기기를 업그레이드했다.

해설 첫 번째 문단의 후반부 "because new accountants have been recently employed. So, we need to prepare some office spaces for them."을 보면 신입 회계사들이 추가로 고용되었고, 이들을 위한 추가 공간이 필요하다는 것으로 보아 사세가 확장되고 있다는 (A)가 정답이다.

193 세부 사항 (연계)

킴 씨가 특히 만족한 제품은 무엇인가?
(A) 레터헤드 용지
(B) 화이트보드 마커
(C) Maxdova 잉크 토너 카트리지
(D) Dusittani 자석 화이트보드

해설 첫 번째 이메일의 마지막 문장 "We have been always satisfied with the quality of your items, especially the recycled paper-based stationery with our company's logo."를 보면, 회사의 로고가 박힌 종이 제품에 특히 만족한다고 했는데, 주문서에서 이에 해당하는 것은 레터헤드 용지이므로 (A)가 정답이다.

194 세부 사항 (연계)

정기적으로 주문되는 제품들 중 교체품의 품목 번호는 무엇인가?
(A) LP 350
(B) WM 500
(C) MI 750
(D) DM 900

해설 첫 번째 지문의 세 번째 문장에서 "we would like to replace the ink toner we have received with a different brand, as indicated on the form." 부분을 보면 잉크 토너를 다른 브랜드로 교체한다고 했으므로, 주문서에서 잉크 토너 카트리지의 품목 번호인 (C) MI 750이 정답이다.

195 세부 사항 (연계)

회사는 Gannon 브랜드의 화이트보드에 각각 얼마를 지불할 것인가?
(A) 47.92달러
(B) 60.13달러
(C) 89.99달러
(D) 95.99달러

해설 세 번째 지문의 다섯 번째 문장 "The original price is $95.99 each, but I am willing to supply you with five at the same price as the Dusittani magnetic whiteboard."에서 해당 제품의 원래 가격은 95.99달러이지만, Dusittani 자석 화이트보드와 동일한 가격으로 제공할 것이라 했으므로 주문서에서 이에 해당하는 금액인 (C) 89.99달러가 정답이다.

[196-200] 일정표 & 이메일 & 이메일

Benjamin 기업

컨퍼런스 룸 일정표
7월 매주 금요일

아래는 우리 컨퍼런스 룸에 예약된 회의 및 새로운 회의의 이용 가능한 시간에 대한 일정표입니다. 7월 매주 금요일에는 예약된 회의와 컨퍼런스만 회의실 이용이 가능합니다. 경영진이 회의실을 긴급히 요

청할 경우를 대비한 것이니 여러분의 양해 부탁드립니다. 이러한 상황이 발생하면, k_rodgers@benjaminco.com으로 케니 로저스 씨에게 연락하여 우리 구내의 다른 건물에서 회의실을 이용할 수 있는지 문의해 주세요.

시간대	201호 (수용인원: 30명)	202호 (수용인원: 60명)
오전 1 오전 9:30~10:30	이용 가능	영업팀
오전 2 오전 10:50~11:50	인사과	홍보 기획
오후 1 오후 2:20~3:20	고객 서비스	IT 지원 센터
오후 2 오후 3:40~4:40	이용 가능	마케팅 그룹

수신: 부서 관리자들
발신: 케니 로저스
날짜: 6월 29일
제목: 컨퍼런스 룸 일정

회사의 다가오는 총회를 위한 경영진의 사전 세미나가 있을 것이기 때문에, 7월 10일 금요일 하루 동안 Franklin 건물의 두 개의 컨퍼런스 룸 모두 사용할 수 없게 되었습니다. 이는 10시에 시작할 것이고, 우리가 시간표에 정해 놓은 시간도 초과할 예정입니다. 이 날짜에 회의실을 사용하고자 하는 분은 이 이메일을 통해 이번 주 금요일까지 저에게 알려 주셔야 합니다. 회의실은 선착순으로 예약될 것입니다.

감사합니다,

케니 로저스
비서실장

수신: 전 직원
발신: 케니 로저스
날짜: 7월 3일
제목: 금요일 일정 변경

7월 10일 중요한 임원진 회의로 인해 일정표에 다음의 변경사항이 있다는 것을 확인하세요.

아래는 해당 날짜에 예약된 회의실입니다.
- 701호와 702호에서 오전 1 시간대에 회의가 진행될 예정입니다.
- 오후 1 시간대에, 마케팅 그룹이 502호에서 모일 예정입니다.

여러분은 제한된 수용 인원과 컨퍼런스 장비를 다시 확인해야 하고, 변경해야 하거나 장비가 필요하면 저에게 이메일을 보내 주세요. 위에 명시되지 않은 회의는 회사 정책과 공지에 따라 모두 취소됩니다. 이 사안에 대한 모든 문의는 여러분의 직속 관리자들에게 직접 보고되어야 합니다. 회의 또는 컨퍼런스 내용은 회의를 놓친 사람들을 위해 우리 인트라넷 게시판에 게시될 것입니다.

케니 로저스
비서실장

어휘 timetable 시간표, 계획표　chart 표　reserved 예약된　case 경우, 사례　happen 발생하다　availability 이용 가능성　premise 구내, 부지　slot 위치, 장소, 칸　capacity 용량, 수용력　the entire day 하루 종일　preliminary 사전의　management 운영진　general meeting 총회　on a first-come, first-served basis 선착순으로　gather 모으다　immediate 직속의

196 Not/True 확인

일정표에 따르면, Benjamin 기업에 관한 설명 중 옳은 것은?
(A) 직원들은 한 달에 한 번 만난다.
(B) 확장할 계획이 있다.
(C) 여러 건물을 소유하고 있다.
(D) 연간 회의실 일정을 게시한다.

해설 일정표의 마지막 문장 "If this happens, please contact Kenny Rodgers at k_rodgers@benjaminco.com to inquire about the availability of rooms in other buildings on our premises." 부분을 보면, other buildings라고 했으므로 건물이 여러 채 있음을 알 수 있다. 따라서 (C)가 정답이다.

197 세부 사항

부서 관리자들은 왜 첫 번째 이메일에 답장을 보내야 하는가?
(A) 경영진과 만나기 위해
(B) 일자리를 문의하기 위해
(C) 추가 직원 고용을 요구하기 위해
(D) 회의실을 확보하기 위해

해설 일정표 중반에 경영진 회의로 인해 회의실 사용에 제약이 있다고 했고, 마지막 문장 "If this happens, please contact Kenny Rodgers at k_rodgers@benjaminco.com to inquire about the availability of rooms ~" 부분에서 그러한 일이 발생하면 회의실을 이용할 수 있는지 문의하기 위해 이메일을 보내라고 했으므로 (D)가 정답이다.

198 추론/암시 (연계)

경영진 세미나는 언제 끝날 것 같은가?
(A) 오전 11시 50분에
(B) 오후 3시 20분에
(C) 오후 4시 40분에
(D) 오후 5시 40분에

해설 두 번째 지문의 두 번째 문장 "These are scheduled to begin at ten o'clock and are expected to exceed the time we appointed on the timetable."을 보면 끝나는 시간은 시간표에 정해져 있는 시간을 초과할 것이라고 언급한다. 첫 번째 지문의 표를 보면 마지막 일정의 끝나는 시간이 오후 4시 40분이므로, 보기 중 이를 초과하는 시간인 (D) 오후 5시 40분이 정답이다.

199 세부 사항 (연계)

어떤 그룹이 7월 10일에 회의를 하지 않는가?

(A) 영업팀
(B) 마케팅 그룹
(C) 경영진
(D) 인사과

해설 두 번째 지문에서 7월 10일에 경영진 회의가 있다고 했으므로 (C)는 제외해야 하고, 세 번째 지문을 보면 오전 1시간대에 회의가 있다고 했고, 오전 1은 시간표상에서 영업팀이었으므로 (A)도 제외해야 한다. 오후 1시간대에 마케팅 그룹이 들어간다고 했으므로 (B)도 제외한다. 표에 있던 인사과의 회의 변경은 언급되지 않았으므로 (D)가 정답이다.

200 Not/True 확인

회의에 참석하지 않는 직원들에 관하여 알 수 있는 것은?

(A) 불참 사유서를 관리자에게 제출해야 한다.
(B) 웹 사이트에서 회의 정보를 찾을 수 있다.
(C) 다음 회의에 참석할 수 있다.
(D) 로저스 씨의 회의록을 요청해야 한다.

해설 세 번째 지문의 마지막 문장 "Meeting or conference contents will be posted on our intranet bulletin board for those who miss a meeting."에서 회의에 참석하지 못한 사람들을 위해 사내 인트라넷 게시판에 회의 내용이 게시된다고 했으므로 (B)가 정답이다.

Memo

TEST 4

p.148

LISTENING TEST

01 (A)	02 (B)	03 (D)	04 (B)	05 (D)
06 (D)	07 (C)	08 (B)	09 (C)	10 (A)
11 (C)	12 (A)	13 (B)	14 (C)	15 (B)
16 (A)	17 (C)	18 (A)	19 (C)	20 (B)
21 (A)	22 (B)	23 (A)	24 (B)	25 (C)
26 (C)	27 (A)	28 (B)	29 (B)	30 (B)
31 (A)	32 (B)	33 (D)	34 (A)	35 (C)
36 (B)	37 (D)	38 (B)	39 (D)	40 (C)
41 (D)	42 (A)	43 (D)	44 (D)	45 (C)
46 (B)	47 (D)	48 (B)	49 (A)	50 (C)
51 (C)	52 (B)	53 (D)	54 (B)	55 (A)
56 (D)	57 (A)	58 (C)	59 (B)	60 (A)
61 (B)	62 (C)	63 (A)	64 (C)	65 (B)
66 (D)	67 (C)	68 (D)	69 (B)	70 (A)
71 (D)	72 (C)	73 (A)	74 (D)	75 (C)
76 (B)	77 (C)	78 (B)	79 (A)	80 (B)
81 (D)	82 (A)	83 (B)	84 (A)	85 (C)
86 (D)	87 (C)	88 (D)	89 (C)	90 (A)
91 (D)	92 (C)	93 (D)	94 (A)	95 (D)
96 (D)	97 (B)	98 (B)	99 (D)	100 (A)

READING TEST

101 (B)	102 (A)	103 (D)	104 (C)	105 (A)
106 (B)	107 (C)	108 (B)	109 (A)	110 (A)
111 (A)	112 (C)	113 (B)	114 (B)	115 (D)
116 (D)	117 (B)	118 (C)	119 (A)	120 (C)
121 (B)	122 (B)	123 (D)	124 (A)	125 (A)
126 (B)	127 (B)	128 (D)	129 (A)	130 (A)
131 (B)	132 (A)	133 (B)	134 (C)	135 (D)
136 (B)	137 (A)	138 (D)	139 (B)	140 (C)
141 (B)	142 (A)	143 (A)	144 (B)	145 (A)
146 (C)	147 (A)	148 (A)	149 (B)	150 (D)
151 (B)	152 (C)	153 (B)	154 (A)	155 (C)
156 (C)	157 (B)	158 (B)	159 (D)	160 (B)
161 (D)	162 (B)	163 (A)	164 (D)	165 (A)
166 (D)	167 (A)	168 (C)	169 (D)	170 (A)
171 (A)	172 (D)	173 (B)	174 (D)	175 (A)
176 (C)	177 (D)	178 (A)	179 (C)	180 (A)
181 (B)	182 (D)	183 (A)	184 (A)	185 (B)
186 (B)	187 (C)	188 (C)	189 (A)	190 (C)
191 (A)	192 (C)	193 (C)	194 (C)	195 (D)
196 (D)	197 (D)	198 (A)	199 (A)	200 (A)

PART • 1

1 인물(2인 이상) 사진

(A) They are looking at the same page.
(B) They are facing each other.
(C) One of the men is pointing at the papers.
(D) They are staring into the distance.

(A) 그들은 같은 페이지를 보고 있는 중이다.
(B) 그들은 서로 바라보고 있는 중이다.
(C) 남자들 중 한 명이 서류를 가리키고 있다.
(D) 그들은 먼 곳을 바라보고 있는 중이다.

> **해설** (B)는 서로 마주 보고 있지 않으므로 오답, 사람들이 같은 페이지를 보고 있으므로 (A)가 정답이다. (C)는 여자가 서류를 가리키고 있으므로 오답이고, (D)는 동사 stare(응시하다)가 나오지만 바로 앞에 있는 서류를 보고 있으므로 오답이다.

> **어휘** look at 쳐다보다   same 같은   face 직면하다   stare into ~을 응시하다

2 사물/풍경 사진

(A) The trees are being planted by the street.
(B) The chairs are facing the tables.
(C) The chairs are being stacked up.
(D) The customers are currently being served.

(A) 길 옆에 나무들을 심고 있는 중이다.
(B) 의자들이 테이블을 바라보고 있다.
(C) 의자들이 쌓이고 있다.
(D) 손님들이 서빙을 받는 중이다.

> **해설** (A)는 나무를 심는 동작을 하는 사람이 없기 때문에 오답이고, (C)는 의자는 보이지만 사람이 의자를 쌓고 있는 중이 아니며, (D)는 서빙을 받는 중인 손님이나 서빙하는 종업원이 보이지 않으므로 오답이다. 실외에 있는 의자들이 전부 다 테이블을 향해 놓여 있기 때문에 정답은 (B)이다.

> **어휘** plant 심다   street 거리   stack up 쌓다   serve (음식을) 제공하다

TEST 4
정답과 해설

3 인물(2인 이상) 사진

(A) They are putting on a jogging suit.
(B) They are walking away from each other.
(C) They are looking out at the field.
(D) They are running in the same direction.

(A) 그들은 조깅복을 입고 있는 중이다.
(B) 그들은 서로 반대 방향으로 걸어가는 중이다.
(C) 그들은 들판을 내다 보고 있는 중이다.
(D) 그들은 같은 방향으로 달리고 있는 중이다.

해설 (A)는 'put on(옷을 입다)'는 행동을 나타내는 동사로 시험에 자주 등장하지만 이미 옷을 입고 있기 때문에 'wear(입고 있다)'가 어울리므로 오답이다. (B)는 반대 방향으로 걸어가는 사진이 아니므로 오답이다. (C)는 '내다 보고 있다'라는 행동 묘사가 잘못되었다. 같은 방향으로 뛰고 있다는 (D)가 정답이다.

어휘 put on 입다   each other 서로   field 들판   direction 방향

4 혼합 사진

(A) The car is being displayed in a showroom.
(B) The man is checking under the hood of the car.
(C) The man is on their way to work.
(D) The wheels are being replaced by the man.

(A) 자동차가 쇼룸에 전시되고 있다.
(B) 남자가 자동차 덮개 아래에서 점검 중이다.
(C) 남자가 직장으로 가고 있다.
(D) 바퀴가 남자에 의해 교체되고 있다.

해설 (A)는 동사와 장소 모두 맞지 않고 (C)는 '직장으로 가다'라는 동작이 틀리다. (D)는 사진에 교체 중인 바퀴가 보이지 않아서 틀렸다. 자동차 덮개 아래에서 점검 중이라고 한 (B)가 정답이다.

어휘 display 전시하다   on one's way ~하는 중인   wheel 바퀴
replace 교체하다

5 인물(2인 이상) 사진

(A) They are looking at the chart.
(B) They are taking notes on the paper.
(C) They are standing in a line.
(D) They are taking part in a meeting.

(A) 그들은 차트를 보고 있다.
(B) 그들은 종이에 필기하고 있다.
(C) 그들은 줄을 서 있다.
(D) 그들은 회의에 참석 중이다.

해설 (A)는 차트를 보고 있는 동작 묘사 오류, (B)는 사람들이 필기하는 동작이 아니고 (C)는 한 줄로 서 있는 사진이 아니므로 오답이다. 회의에 참석하고 있는 상황이므로 정답은 (D)다.

어휘 take notes 메모하다   stand in a line 줄을 서다   take
part in ~에 참석하다

6 사물/풍경 사진

(A) Workers are operating cranes.
(B) A truck is being loaded with items.
(C) Boats are moving away from the dock.
(D) The containers are stacked beside a truck.

(A) 일꾼들이 기중기를 작동시키고 있다.
(B) 트럭에 짐을 싣고 있다.
(C) 배들이 부두에서 멀어지고 있다.
(D) 컨테이너들이 트럭 옆에 쌓여 있다.

해설 (A)는 기중기를 작동시키고 있는 인부들이 보이지 않아서 오답, (B)는 물건들이 트럭에 실리고 있지 않아 오답이다. (C)는 사진에 배나 부두는 보이지 않으므로 오답이다. 컨테이너들이 트럭 옆에 쌓여 있으므로 정답은 (D)다.

어휘 crane 기중기   load 싣다   item 물건   dock 부두

PART • 2

7 일반 의문문

Does this elevator go to the top floor?
(A) I live on the top floor.
(B) The elevator is here.
(C) Yes, it does.

이 엘리베이터가 맨 위층까지 가나요?
(A) 저는 맨 위층에 살아요.
(B) 엘리베이터가 여기 있어요.
(C) 네, 맞아요.

해설 do동사 의문문은 특정 사실을 확인하는 의문문이므로 yes 또는 no로 응답이 가능하기 때문에 (C)가 정답이다.

어휘 elevator 엘리베이터   floor 층

8 Where 의문문

Where did she buy those flowers?
(A) Just this morning.
(B) At the store across the street.
(C) It's her birthday today.

그녀는 저 꽃을 어디에서 샀나요?
(A) 바로 오늘 아침이요.
(B) 길 건너에 있는 가게에서요.
(C) 오늘이 그녀의 생일이에요.

해설 Where 의문문은 장소에 관련된 의문문이므로 장소를 언급한 (B)가 정답이다.

어휘 across 건너에 있는

9 How 의문문

How was the technology convention last month?
(A) Yes, I work with technology.
(B) I attended the convention.
(C) It was very crowded.

지난달에 열린 기술 컨벤션은 어땠습니까?
(A) 네, 저는 기술 관련된 일을 합니다.
(B) 저는 컨벤션에 참석했습니다.
(C) 사람들로 꽉 찼어요.

해설 의견이나 상태를 묻는 How 의문문으로, 컨벤션이 어땠냐는 질문에, 사람들로 꽉 찼다고 한 (C)가 정답이다.

어휘 technology 기술 convention 컨벤션 last 지난 attend 참석하다 be crowded 붐비다, 꽉 차다

10 Who 의문문

Who's handling the Steinberg project?
(A) Ms. Jennings is.
(B) I handed it to her this morning.
(C) Mr. Stelnberg called yesterday.

누가 Steinberg 프로젝트를 담당하나요?
(A) 제닝스 씨요.
(B) 제가 오늘 아침에 그녀에게 건네주었어요.
(C) 스테인버그 씨가 어제 전화했어요.

해설 Who 의문문으로, 프로젝트 담당자가 누군지 묻는 질문에, 이름을 말하는 (A)가 정답이다. (B)의 hand는 질문에 있는 handle과 유사 발음으로 혼동을 주고 있다. (C)는 고유명사 중복 오답이다.

어휘 handle 다루다, 해결하다, 취급하다 hand 건네주다

11 When 의무문

When is the final meeting report due?
(A) The meeting is on the second floor.
(B) Yes, the report is due.
(C) In one week.

최종 회의 보고서 제출 기한이 언제입니까?
(A) 회의는 2층에서 열립니다.
(B) 네, 보고서 제출 마감입니다.
(C) 일주일 후입니다.

해설 제출기한을 묻는 When 의문문으로, 구체적인 기간을 나타내는 (C)가 정답이다. (A)는 장소에 관련된 답이고, (B)는 질문에 나온 report가 반복된 오답 함정이다.

어휘 final 최종의 due 예정된, ~하기로 되어 있는

12 Which 의문문

Which restaurant did you reserve for the party?
(A) The Greek restaurant on Grover Lane.
(B) The reservation is for twelve people.
(C) I was there last night.

파티를 위해 어떤 레스토랑을 예약했나요?
(A) Grover Lane에 있는 그리스 레스토랑이요.
(B) 12명 예약입니다.
(C) 저는 어젯밤 그곳에 있었어요.

해설 어떤 레스토랑을 예약했는지 묻고 있다. 구체적인 식당 종류를 제시한 (A)가 정답이다.

어휘 reserve 예약하다

13 제안/권유 의문문

Would you like any help preparing the agenda for the meeting?
(A) No, I didn't attend the meeting.
(B) I have already completed it.
(C) It is generally available.

회의 의제 준비에 도움이 필요한가요?
(A) 아니요, 저는 회의에 참석하지 않았습니다.
(B) 이미 다 끝냈어요.
(C) 일반적으로 이용 가능합니다

해설 도움이 필요한지 묻는 질문에, 이미 끝내서 괜찮다는 (B)가 정답이다. (A)는 meeting을 반복한 오답 함정, (C)는 질문과 관련 없는 내용이다.

어휘 prepare 준비하나 agenda 의제 complete 완수하다, 작성하다 generally 주로, 보통

14 How 의문문

How long is the flight to Boston?
(A) I am leaving tomorrow morning.
(B) It has been delayed.
(C) About two hours.

비행기로 Boston까시 얼마나 걸리나요?
(A) 내일 오전에 출발합니다.
(B) 지연되었습니다.
(C) 대략 2시간이요.

해설 How long으로 시작하는 기간을 묻는 의문문이므로, 구체적인 시간을 말하는 (C)가 정답이다.

어휘 flight 비행, 항공편   delay 지연시키다

15 Why 의문문

Why is the Houston office closed today?
(A) Starting Tuesday.
(B) Due to area flooding.
(C) It is close to the Dallas office.

Houston 사무실은 왜 오늘 닫았나요?
(A) 화요일부터요.
(B) 지역 홍수 때문이에요.
(C) Dallas 사무실과 가까워요.

해설 사무실이 문을 닫은 이유를 묻는 Why 의문문에, 홍수 때문이라고 답하는 (B)가 정답이다. (C)는 질문의 office를 반복한 오답이다.

어휘 flooding 홍수

16 조동사 의문문

Have all the samples been sent to the client?
(A) Glen from the warehouse will know.
(B) Two boxes.
(C) No, it is only a sample.

모든 샘플이 고객에게 전달되었나요?
(A) 재고 담당인 글렌이 알 거예요.
(B) 2박스요.
(C) 아니요, 그냥 샘플이에요.

해설 Have 의문문은 경험이나 완료 여부를 묻는 질문으로, 제3자가 알 거라고 하는 "몰라요" 유형의 (A)가 정답이다. (C)는 질문에 나온 sample을 반복한 오답이다.

어휘 warehouse 창고

17 What 의문문

What is the company vacation policy?
(A) Just five days.
(B) I am leaving tomorrow.
(C) It's on the Web site.

회사 휴가 정책이 뭔가요?
(A) 단 5일이요.
(B) 저는 내일 떠나요.
(C) 웹 사이트에 있어요.

해설 정책을 묻는 What 의문문으로, 웹사이트에 정보가 있다, 즉 본인은 모른다는 (C)가 정답이다.

어휘 policy 정책

18 제안/권유 의문문

Why don't we make a few extra copies of the brochure?
(A) Sure, I'll do that right away.
(B) No, I am not.
(C) Yes, the copy machine is broken.

책자를 몇 권 더 만드는 게 어때요?
(A) 물론이죠, 바로 할게요.
(B) 아니요, 전 아니에요.
(C) 네, 복사기가 고장 났어요.

해설 Why don't we~ ?(~하는 게 어때요?)는 제안을 나타내는 질문이므로 그렇게 하겠다며 제안을 받아들이는 (A)가 정답이다.

어휘 brochure 책자   copy machine 복사기   be broken 고장이 나다

19 부정 의문문

Aren't we supposed to e-mail the report to Mr. Johnson?
(A) No, it leaves tomorrow night.
(B) She is at a meeting.
(C) I was told to send copies to his assistant.

존슨 씨한테 보고서를 이메일로 보내야 하지 않나요?
(A) 아니요, 내일 밤에 떠나요.
(B) 그녀는 회의 중이에요.
(C) 그의 조수에게 복사본을 보내라고 들었어요.

해설 존슨 씨에게 보고서 발송 여부를 확인하는 부정 의문문으로, 그의 조수에게 보내라고 들었다며 추가 정보를 제공하는 (C)가 정답이다.

어휘 be supposed to ~하기로 되어 있다   assistant 조수

20 평서문

I heard that Allison moved to the Billing Department in May.
(A) Yes, I can call him now.
(B) Yes, she's now on my team.
(C) No, the bill is due next month.

앨리슨이 5월에 경리 부서로 옮겼다고 들었어요.
(A) 네, 지금 그에게 전화할 수 있어요.
(B) 네, 그녀는 이제 제 팀이에요.
(C) 아니요, 청구서는 다음 달까지예요.

해설 부서 이동 소식을 언급하는 평서문에 대한 답으로, 지금은 자기 팀이라고 추가 내용을 전달하는 (B)가 적합하다. (C)는 질문의 Billing과 유사 발음인 bill로 혼동을 주고 있다.

어휘 move 움직이다, 옮기다   billing department 경리 부서

21 선택 의문문

Is he planning on giving the presentation in person or online?
(A) He will be there in person.
(B) We have an excellent online program.
(C) Sometime early next week.

그는 직접 발표할 계획인가요? 아니면 온라인으로 하나요?
(A) 그는 직접 갈 겁니다.
(B) 우리는 훌륭한 온라인 프로그램을 가지고 있어요.
(C) 다음 주 초쯤에요.

해설 선택 의문문으로, 정답은 '둘 중에 하나를 선택, 둘 다 선택, 또는 둘 다 부정하는 선택지'가 등장한다. 정답은 둘 중 하나를 택한 (A)이다.

어휘 give a presentation 발표하다 in person 직접 online 온라인 상으로 excellent 뛰어난, 훌륭한 sometimes 언젠가

22 요청 의문문

Would you prepare a summary of the discussion yesterday?
(A) We discussed for almost two hours.
(B) I can get that to you later today.
(C) I am on vacation starting tomorrow.

어제 있었던 토론 요약본을 준비해 줄 수 있나요?
(A) 거의 2시간 동안 토론했습니다.
(B) 오늘 이따가 드릴게요.
(C) 내일부터 저는 휴가입니다.

해설 요약본을 준비해 달라는 요청에, 이따가 주겠다는 (B)가 정답이다. (A)는 질문에 나온 discuss를 반복한 오답이다.

어휘 summary 요약 discussion 토론 vacation 휴가

23 When 의문문

When do you want to discuss staffing for the new project?
(A) I'm free anytime this morning.
(B) Yes, I am a new manager.
(C) Some of the staff have gone home for the day.

언제 새 프로젝트에 대한 인력 파견을 논의할까요?
(A) 전 오늘 오전 아무 때나 괜찮습니다.
(B) 네, 제가 신임 매니저입니다.
(C) 직원들 중 일부는 퇴근했습니다.

해설 원하는 논의 시기를 묻는 질문에, 구체적인 시기를 언급하는 (A)가 정답이다. (B)는 질문의 new를 반복, (C)는 질문의 staffing과 유사 발음인 staff로 혼동을 주고 있다.

어휘 discuss 의논하다 anytime 아무 때나

24 일반 의문문

Are any tables available for lunch?
(A) Yes, I have a reservation.
(B) We're fully booked today.
(C) I've already eaten.

점심 때 이용 가능한 테이블이 있습니까?
(A) 네, 제가 예약했습니다.
(B) 오늘은 전부 예약이 찼습니다.
(C) 전 이미 먹었습니다.

해설 예약 가능 여부를 묻는 일반 의문문으로, 오늘은 예약이 다 찼다는 (B)가 정답이다. (A), (C)는 질문의 lunch의 연상어인 reservation, eaten으로 혼동을 노린 오답이다.

어휘 reservation 예약 fully 완전히 book 예약하다

25 부가 의문문

You've been to Tokyo before, haven't you?
(A) I enjoy shopping.
(B) I am not Japanese.
(C) I was there four years ago.

전에 도쿄에 가본 적 있죠, 그렇죠?
(A) 저는 쇼핑을 좋아합니다.
(B) 저는 일본인이 아닙니다.
(C) 4년 전에 갔어요.

해설 사실을 확인하거나 상대방의 동의를 구하는 부가 의문문으로, 도쿄에 가봤냐는 질문에, 4년 전에 갔다고 하는 (C)가 정답이다. (B)는 Tokyo의 연상어인 Japanase로 혼동을 주고 있다.

어휘 have been to ~에 가 본 적 있다

26 Who 의문문

Who can I speak with to return this audio system?
(A) I already own an audio system.
(B) Do you have a reservation?
(C) I'll bring the manager over.

이 오디오 시스템을 반납하려면 누구와 이야기해야 하나요?
(A) 이미 오디오 시스템을 가지고 있습니다.
(B) 예약하셨나요?
(C) 제가 매니저를 데려오겠습니다.

해설 반납을 위해 누구와 이야기해야 하는지 묻는 질문에, 매니저를 데려오겠다는 (C)가 응답으로 적절하다.

어휘 return 반납하다 reservation 예약 bring over 데려오다

27 부정 의문문

Shouldn't we recruit more staff members?
(A) We have five on the team already.
(B) In about two hours.
(C) Yes, mine is less expensive.

더 많은 직원을 뽑아야 하지 않을까요?

(A) 이미 5명이 팀에 있어요.

(B) 대략 2시간 후에요.

(C) 네, 제 것은 덜 비싸요.

해설 추가 고용에 대한 의견을 묻는 부정 의문문으로, 이미 인력이 충분하다는 문맥의 (A)가 정답이다.

어휘 recruit 채용하다   staff member 직원   expensive 비싼

28   How 의문문

How often does Ms. Clark want to schedule these meetings?

(A) I cannot attend tomorrow's meeting.

(B) What did she do last year?

(C) We are right on time.

클라크 씨는 얼마나 자주 회의 일정을 잡길 원하나요?

(A) 내일 회의에는 참석할 수 없습니다.

(B) 그녀가 작년에는 어떻게 했나요?

(C) 우리는 딱 정시에 왔어요.

해설 회의 주기를 묻는 How often ~? 의문문으로, 구체적인 답을 하는 대신 작년에는 어땠는지 되묻는 (B)가 정답이다. (A)는 질문의 meeting을 반복한 오답 함정이다.

어휘 schedule 일정을 잡다

29   부가 의문문

We don't have to work this weekend, do we?

(A) I just arrived ten minutes ago.

(B) No, the deadline was extended.

(C) Yes, I heard that too.

이번 주말에 일할 필요 없죠, 그렇죠?

(A) 저는 10분 전에 막 도착했어요.

(B) 아니요(일할 필요 없어요), 마감일이 연장됐어요.

(C) 네, 저도 그 얘기를 들었어요.

해설 부가 의문문으로, 사실을 확인하며 상대방의 동의를 구하고 있다. 응답이 긍정이면 yes로, 부정이면 no로 말한다. 주말 근무 여부를 묻는 말에, 마감일이 연장됐다, 즉 주말 근무를 하지 않아도 된다는 (B)가 정답이다.

어휘 deadline 마감일   extend 연장시키다

30   선택 의문문

Should I order a new chair or just have this one repaired?

(A) I am heading over there now.

(B) I know a good furniture repair shop.

(C) No, we don't have enough chairs.

새 의자를 주문할까요? 아니면 이 의자를 수리해야 할까요?

(A) 저는 지금 그곳으로 가고 있습니다.

(B) 제가 좋은 가구 수리점을 알고 있어요.

(C) 아니요, 의자가 충분하지 않아요.

해설 선택 의문문은 둘 중에 하나를 고르거나, 전체 긍정 또는 부정하는 선택지가 답이 될 수 있다. 수리하는 게 좋겠다고 우회적으로 언급하는 (B)가 정답이다.

어휘 head ~를 향해 가다   furniture 가구   repair shop 수리점

31   평서문

It's probably too late to make changes to the contract.

(A) I think we still can.

(B) Yes, I bought one last week.

(C) I don't have any change.

계약서를 변경하기에는 너무 늦은 것 같아요.

(A) 아직 할 수 있을 것 같은데요.

(B) 네, 지난주에 하나 샀어요.

(C) 잔돈이 없어요.

해설 계약서를 변경하기에 너무 늦었다는 말에, 아직 변경 가능할 거라고 하는 (A)가 정답이다. (C)는 질문에 나온 change가 반복된 오답으로 여기서는 '잔돈'이라는 전혀 다른 뜻으로 쓰였다.

어휘 probably 아마도   make changes 변경하다   contract 계약(서)

PART • 3

[32-34]

M Hello. My name is Robert Crane. I made an appointment with Dr. Kim for 9 A.M.

W Good morning, Mr. Crane. Dr. Kim is on her way in, but you will need to wait just a few minutes. I see that this is your first visit to our clinic.

M That's right. I downloaded the registration form from your Web site. Here is the completed form.

W Perfect! This will save us a lot of time. I would appreciate it if you would tell me how you were referred to us. We ask this of all our new patients.

M 안녕하세요. 제 이름은 로버트 크레인입니다. 저는 김 박사님과 오전 9시에 약속이 있습니다.

W 안녕하세요, 크레인 씨. 김 박사님이 들어 오시는 중이지만, 몇 분 정도 기다리셔야 합니다. 저희 병원을 처음 방문하시는 거네요.

M 맞습니다. 웹 사이트에서 등록 양식을 다운로드했어요. 작성한 양식을 가져왔어요.

W 완벽합니다! 이렇게 하면 많은 시간을 절약할 수 있어요. 저희 병원을 어떻게 알게 되었는지 말씀해 주시면 고맙겠습니다. 처음 오시는 모든 분들께 하는 질문이에요.

어휘 make an appointment 약속하다   on one's way ~가 가는 중   visit 방문; 방문하다   clinic 병원   download 다운로드하다   registration 등록   complete 작성하다   form 양식   perfect 완벽한   save 절약하다, 구하다   appreciate 고맙게 여기다

32 대화 장소

화자들은 어디에 있는 것 같은가?
(A) 컨벤션 센터에
(B) 병원에
(C) 레스토랑에
(D) 극장에

해설 여자의 첫 대사 중, "I see that this is your first visit to our clinic." 부분을 보면 병원에 방문한 것을 알 수 있으므로 정답은 (B)이다.

33 세부 사항

남자는 무엇을 가지고 왔는가?
(A) 예약증
(B) 작업 지시서
(C) 영수증
(D) 양식

해설 남자의 두 번째 대사 중, "Here is the completed form."에서 양식을 가져왔음을 알 수 있기 때문에 정답은 (D)이다.

34 세부 사항

여자는 남자에게 무엇을 묻는가?
(A) 어떻게 병원을 알았는지
(B) 무슨 용무로 한 예약인지
(C) 김 박사에 대해서 언제 처음 들었는지
(D) 그의 예약 시간이 언제인지

해설 여자의 마지막 대사 중 "I would appreciate it if you would tell me how you were referred to us."에서 병원에 대해 어떻게 알게 되었는지 물었기 때문에 정답은 (A)이다.

[35-37]

M Hello, I will be attending the marketing seminar that you're hosting in Cleveland in May. I'm calling because I wanted to know if there are any tourist activities in the area that you might recommend.

W Of course. As a matter of fact, there is a new exhibit at the modern art museum in downtown Cleveland. All seminar attendees will be receiving a free admission pass for the museum.

M That sounds great. I will actually be arriving in town a few days before the seminar. Would it be possible to receive the pass earlier so I can go before the date of the seminar?

W I'm sorry to say that the passes are valid only during the days of the seminar. Unfortunately, we are not able to change that. Sorry for the inconvenience.

M 안녕하세요, 저는 5월에 Cleveland에서 당신이 주최하는 마케팅 세미나에 참석할 것입니다. 그 지역에서 추천해 주실 만한 관광 활동이 있는지 알고자 전화했어요.

W 물론이죠. 사실, Cleveland 도심의 현대 미술관에서 새로운 전시회가 있습니다. 모든 세미나 참석자는 박물관 무료 입장권을 받게 됩니다.

M 좋네요. 저는 사실 세미나 시작 며칠 전에 도시에 도착할 거예요. 세미나 전에 갈 수 있도록 세미나 이전에 출입증을 받을 수 있을까요?

W 유감스럽게도 출입증은 세미나 당일에만 유효합니다. 안타깝게도, 변경해 드릴 수 없어요. 불편을 드려 죄송합니다.

어휘 host 열다, 개최하다　activity 활동　area 지역　recommend 추천하다　as a matter of fact 사실　exhibit 전시(회)　modern art museum 현대 미술관　attendee 참석자　admission 입장료　pass 출입증, 통행증　sound ~하게 들리다　actually 사실상　possible 가능한　valid 유효한　unfortunately 불행히도, 안타깝게도　inconvenience 불편

35 주제/목적

남자는 왜 전화하는가?
(A) 비행기를 예약하기 위해
(B) 세미나에 관심을 표현하기 위해
(C) 지역 활동에 대해 묻기 위해
(D) 오류에 대해 불평하기 위해

해설 대화의 목적은 보통 첫 부분에 나온다. 남자가 "I'm calling because I wanted to know if there are any tourist activities in the area that you might recommend."라고 말하는 부분에서 관광객이 할 수 있는 활동이 있는지 묻고 있기 때문에 정답은 (C)이다.

36 세부 사항

여자는 무엇이 배포될 거라고 하는가?
(A) 책자
(B) 입장권
(C) 무료 식사
(D) 상

해설 여자가 한 말 중 "All seminar attendees will be receiving a free admission pass for the museum."에서 모든 참석자에게 입장권이 배포될 것이라고 했으므로 정답은 (B)이다.

37 세부 사항

여자는 왜 사과하는가?
(A) 세미나가 취소되었다.
(B) 등록이 끝났다.
(C) 비행편이 지연되었다.
(D) 몇몇 날짜는 변경할 수 없다.

해설 마지막 부분 "Unfortunately, we are not able to change that."에서 날짜는 변경될 수 없다고 말하기 때문에 정답은 (D)이다.

[38-40]

M Jane, I just got out of a meeting with our show's producers, and they told me they've booked an exotic animal trainer Gordon Rabinsky to appear on our morning show next month. He will be promoting his TV show on rare animals.

W That's great! He's a hard man to line up. I hope he will be bringing with him some interesting animals on our show.

M Of course! We've been asked to work with our staff to build the set in accordance with Gordon's specifications. He will be sending them over sometime next week.

W No problem. I will watch for his e-mail.

M 제인, 방금 공연 프로듀서들과 회의를 마치고 나왔어요. 그들은 다음 달 오전 쇼에 희귀 동물 트레이너 고든 라빈스키와 예약을 잡아줬어요. 그가 희귀 동물에 대한 TV 프로그램을 홍보할 예정입니다.

W 좋군요! 그는 방송에 세우는 것이 힘든 사람이에요. 그가 우리 쇼에 흥미로운 동물들을 데려오면 좋겠네요.

M 물론이에요! 우리는 직원들과 고든의 특정 사항에 따라 세트를 제작하도록 요청 받았어요. 그는 다음 쯤 그걸 보내줄 거예요.

W 문제 없어요. 이메일을 기다릴게요.

어휘 get out of ~에서 나오다 producer 프로듀서 exotic 이국적인 rare 드문, 희귀한 specification 특정 사항 in accordance with ~에 따라 send over 보내다

38 화자의 근무지

화자들은 어디에서 일하는가?
(A) 동물원에서
(B) 방송국에서
(C) 국립 공원에서
(D) 출판사에서

해설 남자의 첫 번째 대화 "I just got out of a meeting with our show's producers, ~ our morning show next month." 에서 제작자, 쇼, TV프로그램 등이 나오므로 정답은 (B)이다.

39 세부 사항

여자는 고든 라빈스키가 무엇을 하길 바라는가?
(A) 쇼를 연장한다
(B) 세트를 짓기 위해 직원들을 보낸다
(C) 다음 여행에 그녀를 데리고 간다
(D) 흥미로운 동물을 소개한다

해설 여자가 한 말 중에서 "I hope he will be bringing with him some interesting animals on our show" 흥미로운 동물을 데리고 오길 희망한다고 하므로 정답은 (D)이다.

40 다음에 할 일

그녀는 다음 주에 무엇을 할 거라고 말하는가?
(A) 책을 읽는다
(B) 고든 라빈스키의 사무실을 방문한다
(C) 이메일을 기다린다
(D) 고든 라빈스키와 점심을 먹는다

해설 미래에 대한 계획은 보통 마지막에 나온다. "I will watch for his e-mail."라고 말하므로 정답은 (C)이다.

[41-43]

W Hi, David. Have you seen the report on product sales last quarter? Demand for our new line of toys has dropped off significantly.

M I just saw it yesterday. Do you have any suggestions for how we can bring sales back up?

W We need to expand our marketing efforts. Perhaps we can look into partnering with a company that sells children's cereals or other foods and including discount coupons as prizes in cereal boxes.

M You know, that's a pretty good idea. The management meeting is next Wednesday. You should consider bringing up your idea at that meeting.

W 안녕하세요, 데이비드. 지난 분기 제품 판매 보고서를 보셨어요? 우리의 새 장난감 제품 라인에 수요가 크게 떨어졌습니다.

M 어제 봤어요. 우리가 판매를 되살리는 방법에 대한 제안이 있나요?

W 우리는 마케팅을 확장해야 합니다. 어린이 시리얼 또는 음식을 판매하는 회사와 파트너를 맺어서 시리얼 박스 안에 상품으로 할인 쿠폰을 넣는 방법이 있어요.

M 꽤 좋은 생각이네요. 운영진 회의는 다음 주 수요일이에요. 그 회의에서 아이디어를 제기할 것을 고려해 주세요.

어휘 product 제품 sales 판매 last 지난 quarter 분기 demand 수요 drop off 떨어지다 significantly 상당히 suggestion 의견 expand 확장시키다 perhaps 아마도 look into 조사하다 partner with ~와 파트너십을 갖다 include 포함시키다 prize 상 management 운영진 consider 고려하다 bring up 꺼내다

41 주제/목적

화자들은 어떤 문제를 논의하고 있는가?
(A) 주요 직원들이 일을 그만두었다.
(B) 공장에서 사고가 있었다.
(C) 어린이들이 더 이상 그들의 시리얼을 즐겨 먹지 않는다.
(D) 제품 판매량이 감소했다.

해설 대화의 목적은 보통 첫 부분에 나온다. "Demand for our new line of toys has dropped off significantly."에서 제품 수요가 줄었음을 알 수 있으므로 정답은 (D)이다.

42 제안

여자는 무엇을 제안하는가?

(A) 마케팅 확장하기
(B) 새로운 장난감 제품 만들기
(C) 신입 사원 채용하기
(D) 새로운 시리얼 제품 출시하기

해설 여자가 한 말 중에서 "We need to expand our marketing efforts."을 통해 마케팅을 확대해야 한다고 제안하고 있음을 알 수 있다. 따라서 정답은 (A)이다.

43 세부 사항

다음 주 수요일에 무슨 일이 일어나는가?
(A) 시리얼 회사와 회의
(B) 공장 안전 점검
(C) 제품 시연
(D) 운영진 회의

해설 문제의 키워드는 '수요일'로, 키워드가 언급된 부분 "The management meeting is next Wednesday."에서 운영진 회의가 다음 주 수요일로 예정되어 있음을 알 수 있다. 따라서 정답은 (D)이다.

[44-46]

> W George, I know you've taken the day off on Friday, but it looks like we will need some extra help that day. A large engagement party had their caterer cancel at the last minute, and they've asked whether we could cater.
> M I have a plumber scheduled to come to my house around lunchtime to fix my sink. I have been having problems with my pipes for weeks.
> W The engagement party is at lunchtime on Friday, so that won't work.
> M Sorry about that. Have you tried Santif? He just told me the other day that he could use more hours.
> ⋯⋯⋯⋯⋯⋯⋯⋯⋯⋯⋯⋯⋯⋯⋯⋯⋯⋯⋯⋯⋯⋯⋯⋯⋯
> W 조지, 금요일에 쉬는 날인 건 알지만, 그날 도움이 좀 필요할 것 같아요. 큰 약혼 파티의 출장 연회 서비스가 막판에 취소되었고 그들은 우리가 음식을 제공할 수 있는지 물었어요.
> M 싱크대를 고치기 위해 점심 시간 때쯤 집으로 배관공이 올 예정이에요. 몇 주 동안 파이프에 문제가 있었거든요.
> W 그러면 안 되겠네요. 약혼 파티가 금요일 점심 시간에 있거든요.
> M 미안해요. 산티프와 이야기해 봤어요? 그가 지난번에 더 많은 시간을 할애할 수 있다고 말했어요.

어휘 day off 휴일 extra 추가의 engagement 약혼 caterer 출장 연회 서비스 at the last minute 막판에 whether ~인지 아닌지 plumber 배관공 schedule 일정을 잡다 fix 고치다 sink 싱크대 the other day 지난번에

44 화자의 직업

화자들은 어느 업계에서 일하는가?
(A) 배관
(B) 부동산
(C) 교육
(D) 음식 서비스

해설 여자의 첫 대화 "they've asked whther we could cater"에서 출장 연회 서비스 요청을 받았다고 말하고 있으므로 정답은 (D)이다.

45 의도 파악

남자가 "몇 주 동안 파이프에 문제가 있었어요."라고 말하는 의도는 무엇인가?
(A) 그는 금요일에 일하고 싶지 않다.
(B) 그는 직업에 만족하지 않는다.
(C) 그의 집은 보수가 필요하다.
(D) 그는 약혼할 예정이다.

해설 주어진 문장의 바로 앞 문장 "I have a plumber scheduled to come to my house around lunchtime to fix my sink."과의 문맥을 통해 집에 보수가 필요하다는 것을 알 수 있다. 따라서 정답은 (C)이다.

46 세부 사항

남자는 산티프에 대해서 뭐라고 말하는가?
(A) 그는 최근에 일을 시작했다.
(B) 그는 더 많이 일하고 싶어 한다.
(C) 그는 이 일에 능숙하다.
(D) 그는 다른 부서로 옮겼다.

해설 산티프의 이름이 언급된 마지막 부분에 "He just told me the other day that he could use more hours."에서 그가 더 일하고 싶어 한다는 걸 알 수 있으므로 정답은 (B)이다.

[47-49] 3인 대화

> M That concludes our tour of the building. If you follow me, we will now head over to the Human Resources Department to get your new hire paperwork organized. Do you have any questions before we head over there?
> W1 How do we sign up to use the gym facilities?
> M Sign-up is not necessary. All employees can access the gym until 11 P.M. every weekday and until 9 P.M. on weekends. You just need to swipe your company ID card to enter. Anything else?
> W2 Will we have a chance to go back to the Sales Department once we've completed our paperwork? I would like the chance to meet our new team members.
> M Of course. I know the team is just as excited to meet you.
> ⋯⋯⋯⋯⋯⋯⋯⋯⋯⋯⋯⋯⋯⋯⋯⋯⋯⋯⋯⋯⋯⋯⋯⋯⋯

M 건물 견학이 끝났어요. 저를 따라오시면 인사과로 가서 정리된 신입 사원 채용 서류를 받을 거예요. 거기 가기 전에 질문이 있나요?
W1 헬스장 시설을 이용하려면 어떻게 가입해야 하나요?
M 가입은 필요하지 않아요. 모든 직원은 매주 평일은 오후 11시까지 그리고 주말은 오후 9시까지 헬스장에 갈 수 있어요. 들어가기 위해 인식기에 사원증만 대면 돼요. 또 질문 있나요?
W2 서류 작업이 끝나면 영업부로 돌아갈 건가요? 새로운 팀원들을 만날 기회를 갖고 싶어요.
M 물론이죠. 제가 알기로는 영업부에서도 당신들을 만나기를 기대하고 있는 걸요.

어휘 conclude 마치다, 끝내다   tour 견학   follow 따라가다   head over ~을 향해 가다   human resource department 인사과   hire 고용하다   paperwork 서류   organize 준비하다   sign up 서명하다   gym facility 헬스장 시설   necessary 필요한   access 접근하다   weekday 평일   weekend 주말   swipe (카드를 인식기에) 대다   complete 완수하다, 작성하다

47 화자의 직업
남자가 말하고 있는 대상은 누구인 것 같은가?
(A) 여행 가이드
(B) 안전 요원
(C) 운동 선수 트레이너
(D) 신입 사원

해설 남자의 첫 번째 대화문 "we will now head over to the Human Resource Department to get your new hire paperwork organized"에서 남자가 인사과에 신입 사원 채용 서류를 받으러 간다고 했기 때문에 (D)가 정답이다.

48 세부 사항
남자는 운동 시설에 대해서 뭐라고 말하는가?
(A) 평일에만 연다.
(B) 사원증으로 이용할 수 있다.
(C) 보수 중이다.
(D) 임원들만 이용 가능하다.

해설 남자의 두 번째 대사 중 "You just need to swipe your company ID card to enter"에서 사원증만 대면 된다고 언급하므로 정답은 (B)이다.

49 다음에 할 일
여자들은 다음에 무엇을 할 것 같은가?
(A) 서류를 작성한다
(B) 팀원들을 안내한다
(C) 헬스장을 방문한다
(D) 퇴근해서 집으로 간다

해설 마지막에 여자가 한 말 "Will we have a chance to go back to the Sales Department once we've completed our paperwork?"에서 서류 작성 후 영업부로 갈 수 있냐고 질문하고 있다. 따라서 대화 후에 서류를 작성할 것으로 추측할 수 있으므로 정답은 (A)이다.

[50-52]

M Hello, I'm Michael. Thanks for coming to my house on such short notice. Let me show you to the kitchen. It really needs a lot of work.
W Thank you for calling us. We specialize in kitchen renovations and always welcome a lot of work! I see what you mean… We will have to start by getting rid of a lot of what is in here. Then, we can install new cabinets and appliances.
M That sounds right. You should know that I'm hosting a party here in about two weeks, and the kitchen will need to be ready by then. Do you think that's possible?
W That should be doable if I can get started first thing tomorrow. Would you be able to make a quick decision if I send you my estimate later this afternoon?
M Yes. If it's reasonable, I can let you know immediately.

M 안녕하세요, 저는 마이클입니다. 갑작스런 요청에도 집에 오겠다고 해 주셔서 고맙습니다. 부엌을 보여 드릴게요. 정말 많은 작업이 필요합니다.
W 전화해 주셔서 감사합니다. 저희는 부엌 개조를 전문으로 항상 많은 작업을 환영합니다! 무슨 말씀인지 알 것 같네요… 여기에 있는 것을 많이 없앤 다음, 새 서랍장과 가전제품을 설치해야겠네요.
M 맞아요. 제가 여기에서 약 2주 후에 파티를 열어야 해서 부엌이 그때까지 준비되어야 하는데요. 그게 가능할까요?
W 내일 당장 작업을 시작할 수 있다면 그렇게 할 수 있어요. 제가 오늘 오후에 견적을 보내신 신속하게 결정하실 수 있나요?
M 네, 가격이 합리적이라면 즉시 알려 드릴게요.

어휘 short notice 촉박한 통보   specialize in ~을 전문으로 하다   renovation 보수   get rid of 제거하다   install 설치하다   appliance 가전제품   sound ~하게 들리다   host 개최하다   doable 할 수 있는   make a decision 결정하다   estimate 견적(서)   reasonable 합리적인   immediately 바로, 즉시

50 주제/목적
화자들은 무엇을 논의하고 있는가?
(A) 새 집 짓기
(B) 은퇴 기념 파티 열기
(C) 부엌 보수하기
(D) 새 가구 재배치하기

해설 대화문 첫 문장 "Let me show you to the kitchen. It really needs a lot of work"에서 부엌에 고칠 것들이 많다고 언급되어 있으므로 정답은 (C)이다.

51 세부 사항

약 2주 후에 무슨 일이 일어날 것인가?
(A) 집을 팔려고 내놓을 것이다.
(B) 남자는 견적을 받을 것이다.
(C) 파티가 열릴 것이다.
(D) 남자는 휴가를 떠날 것이다.

해설 문제의 키워드 '약 2주 후'가 들어가 있는 "You should know that I'm hosting a party here in about two weeks, ~." 부분에서 파티가 있음을 알 수 있기 때문에 정답은 (C)이다.

52 다음에 할 일

여자는 오늘 오후에 무엇을 보낼 거라고 말하는가?
(A) 디자인 계약서
(B) 견적서
(C) 캐비닛 사진들
(D) 실내 디자이너

해설 미래에 할 일은 마지막 부분에 주로 나온다. "Would you be able to make a quick decision if I send you my estimate later this afternoon?" 견적서를 보내면 빨리 결정해 줄 수 있냐고 물어봤으므로 정답은 (B)이다.

[53-55]

W Mark, you're working on the new mobile application for our real estate listings, right? Is that coming along alright?

M Yes, I have the entire mobile section of the technology department supporting me. We're still working through some of the final kinks, but we should have it up and running soon.

W That's great. When do you think the app will be ready?

M <u>I would suggest you check with someone in the technology department</u>. They've said it should be ready any day now, but…

W Okay, I'll check with them. Our scheduled launch is less than a month away, and I'm just worried because we still need to do consumer testing, which may take a while.

W 마크, 부동산 목록을 위한 새 모바일 애플리케이션을 제작 중이시죠. 잘 진행되고 있나요?

M 네, 기술부의 전체 모바일 섹션에서 저를 지원합니다. 우리는 여전히 몇 가지 최종 결함을 해결하기 위해 노력하고 있지만 곧 작동될 것입니다.

W 좋아요. 앱이 언제 준비될 거라고 생각하나요?

M 기술 부서의 직원에게 확인해 보세요. 그들은 거의 다 되었다고 말했지만…

W 알겠어요. 제가 그들에게 확인해 볼게요. 예정된 출시는 한 달도 남지 않았고, 꽤 시간이 걸리는 소비자 테스트를 해야 하기 때문에 걱정이네요.

어휘 work on (일을) 수행하다 application 애플리케이션 come along 되어 가다 real estate 부동산 listing 목록 entire 전체의 technology department 기술부 support 지지하다, 후원하다 kink 꼬임 up and running 제대로 작동하는 scheduled 예정된 and day now 곧 launch 출시 consumer 소비자 take a while (시간이) 걸리다

53 세부 사항

남자는 무슨 일을 진행 중인가?
(A) 예산 보고서
(B) 새로운 교육용 소프트웨어
(C) 채용 지침
(D) 모바일 애플리케이션

해설 초반 대화문 "you're working on the new mobile application ~, Is that coming along alright?"에서 여자가 모바일 앱이 잘 진행되고 있는지 물었고 남자가 그렇다고 답했기 때문에 정답은 (D)이다.

54 의도 파악

남자가 "기술 부서의 직원에게 확인해 보세요"라고 말한 의도는 무엇인가?
(A) 현재 그는 기술부서로 가는 중이다.
(B) 그는 답을 모른다.
(C) 그는 고객과 통화 중이다.
(D) 그는 다른 팀으로 옮기고 싶어 한다.

해설 주어진 문장 앞에서 "When do you think the app will be ready?"라고 질문했고 이에 대해 다른 사람에게 물어보라고 하는 것은 본인은 정확한 답을 모른다는 의미임을 유추할 수 있다. 따라서 (B)가 정답이다.

55 문제점

여자가 걱정하는 것은 무엇인가?
(A) 빠듯한 기한
(B) 예산 초과
(C) 고객 불만
(D) 부족한 사원

해설 마지막 대화문 중 "Our scheduled launch is less than a month away, and I'm just worried ~"에서 여자가 출시 일정이 한 달도 안 남았고 소비자 테스트가 남아서 걱정된다고 말하므로 정답은 (A)이다.

TEST 4 정답과 해설

[56-58]

W Greg, how was the culinary exposition that you attended last week? Was there anything that we could adapt here at the bistro?

M Actually, yes. One of the booths at the exposition had an intriguing demonstration on different kinds of marinades for meats using only organic ingredients. There are a number of them that we can use to introduce new flavorful meat dishes in our menu.

W That's great! We have received quite a bit of customer feedback wanting new flavors in our menu items.

M Precisely. After the lunch rush today, perhaps I can create a few of the marinades I learned so you can taste them. We can then choose ones which will fit in with our menu.

W 그렉, 지난주 참석한 요리 설명회는 어땠나요? 거기서 우리 레스토랑에 적용할 만한 게 있었나요?

M 사실, 그렇습니다. 박람회 부스 중 하나는 유기농 재료만을 쓴 다양한 육류용 양념으로 흥미로운 시연을 했습니다. 우리 메뉴에 새로운 고기 요리를 선보이는 데 사용할 많은 양념이 있어요.

W 좋습니다! 메뉴 항목에 새로운 양념들을 원한다는 고객 의견을 많이 받았어요.

M 그러니까요. 오늘 바쁜 점심 시간이 지나면 배운 양념을 몇 가지 만들어 당신이 맛볼 수 있게 할게요. 그런 다음 메뉴에 무엇이 적합할지 선택할 수 있을 거예요.

어휘 culinary 요리의 exposition 설명회, 전시회, 박람회 adapt 각색하다, 적합시키다 bistro 작은 식당 booth 부스 intriguing 흥미로운 demonstration 시연 marinade 양념장 meat 고기 organic 유기농의 ingredient 재료 introduce 소개하다 flavor 양념 dish 요리 receive 받다 quite a bit of 꽤 많은 customer feedback 고객 의견 precisely 정확히 perhaps 아마도 create 만들다 taste 맛보다 fit 맞다

56 세부 사항

남자는 최근에 어떤 행사에 참가했는가?
(A) 가족 결혼식
(B) 레스토랑 개업식
(C) 졸업식
(D) 박람회

해설 여자가 첫 대화문에서 남자에게 "the culinary exposition" 요리 설명회에 다녀온 건 어땠는지 묻기 때문에 정답은 (D)이다.

57 세부 사항

여자에 따르면, 고객들은 무엇을 요청하는가?
(A) 더 다양한 양념
(B) 더 많은 유기농 재료
(C) 더 많은 와인 목록
(D) 더 나은 서비스

해설 키워드 customer가 있는 대화문 "We have received quite a bit of customer feedback wanting new flavors in our menu items."에서 메뉴 항목에 새로운 양념을 원한다는 고객 후기가 있었다고 했으므로 정답은 (A)이다.

58 다음에 할 일

남자는 점심 이후에 무엇을 할 거라고 말하는가?
(A) 예약하기
(B) 부엌 치우기
(C) 소스 만들기
(D) 고객들에게 연락하기

해설 미래의 할 일은 마지막 부분에 나온다. 남자의 마지막 대사 중 "After the lunch rush today, perhaps I can create a few of the marinades I learned"에서 시연 때 배운 양념 몇 가지를 만들어 보겠다고 했으므로 정답은 (C)이다.

[59-61]

M Hi, I'm Sam calling from customer service at Portable Technologies. I'm responding to an e-mail you sent us asking for information about our new line of automatic sprinkler systems.

W Yes, thank you for calling. I have a very large yard, and I have been looking for help with keeping the moisture level of my lawn even and balanced.

M Our newest product, Morton 2300 has automatic sensors that regularly measure the moisture levels of your lawn throughout the day, administering an appropriate amount of water whenever necessary to maintain good moisture balance.

W That sounds like the system for me. The price seems a bit high, though.

M Not to worry. We can offer you a payment plan on the Morton 2300 that is just $50 per month.

W That sounds reasonable. Let me discuss that first with my family and get back to you. Please let me know where I can reach you.

M 안녕하세요, 저는 샘이고 Portable Technologies의 고객 서비스팀에서 전화 드립니다. 새로운 자동 스프링클러 시스템 라인에 대한 정보를 요청하는 귀하의 이메일에 대한 답변을 드립니다.

W 네, 전화해 줘서 고마워요. 저는 커다란 마당을 가지고 있고, 잔디밭의 수분 함량을 균일하게 맞추는 데 도움이 될 만한 걸 찾고 있어요.

M 우리 회사의 신제품인 Morton 2300은 하루 종일 잔디의 수분 함량을 정기적으로 측정하여, 필요한 경우 적절한 수분 균형을 유지하기 위해 필요한 양의 물을 분사하는 자동 센서가 있습니다.

W 제가 원하는 시스템인 것 같네요. 그런데 가격이 약간 높긴 하네요.

M 걱정 마세요. 매월 딱 50달러의 지불 방식으로 Morton 2300을 제공해 드릴 수 있습니다.

W 그건 합리적인 것 같네요. 먼저 가족과 이야기하고 다시 연락 드리겠습니다. 어디로 연락하면 되는지 알려 주세요.

어휘 customer service 고객 서비스 respond to 대답하다

information 정보 automatic 자동적인 sprinkler
스프링클러 yard 정원 keep 유지하다 moisture 수분
balanced 균형을 갖춘 product 상품 regularly 정기적으로
measure 측정하다 throughout 내내 administer 집행
하다, 처리하다 appropriate 적당한 necessary 필요한
maintain 유지하다 good 적절한 payment 지불
per ~마다 reasonable 합리적인 discuss 논의하다
reach 연락하다

59 **화자의 직업**

남자는 누구인가?
(A) 정원사
(B) 고객 서비스 직원
(C) 재정 상담가
(D) 기술자

해설 첫 대화문 "I'm Sam calling from customer service ~"에
서 남자가 고객 서비스 팀에서 연락한다고 소개하므로 정답은
(B)이다.

60 **세부 사항**

남자는 Morton 2300에 대해 뭐라고 말하는가?
(A) 수분 수준을 측정한다.
(B) 해로운 곤충을 잡는다.
(C) 밤에만 자동으로 작동한다.
(D) 잔디밭에 누군가 들어가면 알람이 울린다.

해설 남자가 제품을 설명하는 부분 중 "~ automatic sensors
that regularly measure the moisture levels of your
lawn throughout the day, ~."에서 수분 함량을 정기적으
로 측정한다고 했으므로 정답은 (A)이다.

61 **세부 사항**

왜 여자는 나중에 다시 연락한다고 말하는가?
(A) 그녀는 나가는 중이다.
(B) 그녀는 가족과 의논할 필요가 있다.
(C) 그녀는 Morton 2300이 그녀가 찾던 것이라고 생각하지
않는다.
(D) 그녀는 은행에 확인해 볼 필요가 있다.

해설 미래에 할 일은 마지막 부분에 나온다. "Let me discuss
that first with my family and get back to you."에서 여자
가 가족과 먼저 이야기해 보겠다고 했으므로 정답은 (B)이다.

[62-64] 대화 & 보고서

M I've been going over our cosmetic company's most
recent quarterly report. Take a look at this.
W It seems that our expenses have gone up again this
quarter. That is now four quarters in a row. Where
can we make some spending reductions?
M Some of our lip gloss products come with overly
intricate packaging. While visually pleasing, we
could probably save costs by making it simpler.

W OK, I will find out how much we may be able to save
there.

M 우리 화장품 회사의 최근 분기 보고서를 검토했습니다. 이것 좀
보세요.
W 이번 분기에 우리 비용이 다시 올라간 것 같네요. 4분기 연속이네
요. 지출 삭감은 어디에서 할 수 있나요?
M 립글로스 제품 중 일부는 지나치게 복잡한 포장과 함께 제공됩
니다. 시각적으로는 예쁘지만 더 단순한 포장으로 바꾸면 절약할
수 있어요.
W 좋아요, 제가 얼마나 절감할 수 있는지 알아볼게요.

공장 유지	15,000달러
사무실 렌탈	9,000달러
포장	20,000달러
자재	35,000달러

어휘 go over 검토하다 cosmetic 화장품 quarterly 분기별의
report 보고서 take a look 살펴 보다 expense 비용
in a row 연속해서 spending 지출 reduction 감소
overly 몹시 intricate 정교한 packaging 포장 visually
시각적으로 pleasing 기쁜, 기분 좋게 하는 probably
아마도 save 절약하다 find out 찾아내다 maintenance
유지 material 재료

62 **세부 사항**

회사는 어떤 제품을 만드는가?
(A) 신발
(B) 장난감
(C) 화장품
(D) 의류

해설 첫 대화문에서 'cosmetic company(화장품 회사)'라고 언급
하므로 정답은 (C)이다.

63 **세부 사항**

여자는 보고서에 대해 무엇을 지적하는가?
(A) 비용이 증가했다.
(B) 보고서가 불완전하다.
(C) 몇몇 비용이 누락됐다.
(D) 재료 비용이 감소했다.

해설 여자의 첫 번째 대화문 "It seems that our expenses
have gone up again this quarter"에서 비용이 증가했음
을 알 수 있다. 따라서 정답은 (A)이다.

64 **시각 자료 연계**

시각 자료를 보시오. 남자는 어떤 금액이 변할 거라고 말하
는가?

(A) 15,000달러
(B) 9,000달러
(C) 20,000달러
(D) 35,000달러

해설 남자가 "Some of our lip gloss products come with overly intricate packaging, ~ we could probably save costs by making it simpler."라며 포장 비용이 너무 많이 들어가니 더 심플하게 바꾸면 비용이 줄 것 같다고 언급했다. 따라서 도표에 나와 있는 포장 비용인 (C) $20,000가 정답이다.

[65-67] 대화 & 도표

W You're a lifesaver, Paul. I didn't know how I was going to get to work while my car is being repaired. Thank you for agreeing to pick me up.

M I live only a few blocks away, so it's really no big deal. I just remembered, though, that the annual Springfield Marathon is taking place today. Some of the roads going into the office will be closed to traffic.

W Oh, that's right. Well... I just looked up road closings on my mobile phone. Here are the four roads that we can take to the office. It looks like we're only going to be able to take one of them this morning.

M You're right. This is the road we can take because it's 7:30 A.M.

....

W 당신은 구세주예요, 폴. 저는 제 차가 수리되는 동안 어떻게 출근해야 할지 몰랐어요. 저를 데리러 와 줘서 고마워요.

M 몇 블록 밖에 안 떨어진 곳에 살아서 정말 별일 아니에요. 그런데 연례 스프링필드 마라톤 행사가 오늘 열린다는 게 생각났어요. 사무실로 들어가는 도로 중 일부는 통행이 차단될 거예요.

W 맞다, 그랬죠! 음… 휴대 전화로 지금 막 도로 폐쇄를 찾아 봤어요. 이게 우리가 사무실로 갈 수 있는 네 가지 길이죠. 오늘 아침엔 그 중 한 길로만 갈 수 있을 것 같아요.

M 그렇군요. 지금이 오전 7시 반이니까 이 길로 가야겠어요.

Main Street	오전 6시에서 오후 3시까지 폐쇄
Gordon Boulevard	오전 7시에서 오후 1시까지 폐쇄
Seven Locks Road	오전 7시 30분에서 오후 5시까지 폐쇄
Bethany Street	오전 9시 30분에서 오후 3시까지 폐쇄

어휘 lifesaver 생명의 은인 be repaired 수리되다 pick up 태우다 It's no big deal 큰일이 아니다 take place 발생하다, 일어나다 look up 찾아 보다

65 세부 사항
남자는 여자를 왜 태워 주는가?
(A) 그녀는 사무실에 가는 방법을 모른다.
(B) 그녀의 차가 수리 중이다.
(C) 그녀는 짐이 많다.
(D) 그녀는 회의에 늦었다.

해설 여자의 첫 번째 대화문 중 "I didn't know how I was going to get to work while my car is being repaired."에서 차가 수리 중이라고 말하므로 정답은 (B)이다.

66 세부 사항
남자에 따르면, 오늘 어떤 행사가 있는가?
(A) 봄 축제
(B) 회사 야유회
(C) 음악 축제
(D) 달리기 경기

해설 남자의 첫 번째 대사 중에서 "the annual Springfield Marathon(연례 스프링필드 마라톤)"라는 행사 이름이 언급되므로 정답은 (D)이다.

67 시각 자료 연계
시각 자료를 보시오. 화자들은 어떤 길로 갈 것인가?
(A) Main Street
(B) Gordon Boulevard
(C) Seven Locks Road
(D) Bethany Street

해설 남자의 마지막 대사 중, "This is the road we can take because it's 7:30 A.M."에서 지금이 오전 7시 30분이니 이 길로 가야 한다고 했다. 시각 자료에서 해당 시간에 폐쇄되지 않는 도로는 (D)이다.

[68-70] 대화 & 일정표

W I'm glad we were able to get everyone together on short notice.

M It sure was. We've operated this restaurant for ten years, and all of a sudden we are opening four new restaurants. If we are going to pull this off, we need everyone to be on the same page at all times.

W You know, I saw your e-mail about the opening dates for the new restaurants. It all looks great, but one thing needs to be changed. The opening in Somersville will be delayed a couple of weeks.

M Oh no. What happened?

W Haven't you read about the recent snowstorm in that area? The site got completely snowed in, so construction has been delayed.

....

W 긴급한 통보에도 우리가 한자리에 모이게 되어 기쁘게 생각합니다.

M 그렇습니다. 우리는 이 식당을 10년 동안 운영했고 갑자기 네 곳의 식당을 새로 개업하게 되었어요. 이 일을 해내려면 모든 사람들이 항상 합심해야 합니다.

W 새 레스토랑 개업 날짜에 대한 이메일을 봤어요. 모든 것이 훌륭해 보이지만, 한 가지를 바꿔야 합니다. Somersville의 개업식은 2주 정도 지연될 거예요.

M 저런. 무슨 일이에요?

W 최근 그 지역의 눈보라에 대해 읽지 않았나요? 그 일대가 완전히 눈에 파묻혀서 공사가 지연되었어요.

위치	개업일
Cranston	1월 28일
Somersville	2월 18일
Silver City	4월 4일
Maytown	5월 22일

어휘 short notice 촉박한 통보 operate 운영하다 sudden 갑작스러운 opening 개업 pull something off 해내다 on the same page 합심한 at all times 항상 delay 지연시키다 a couple of 둘 정도의, 몇 개의 happen 일어나다 snowstorm 눈보라 site 현장 completely 완전히 be snowed in 눈에 갇히다 construction 공사

68 주제/목적

화자들은 무엇을 하고 있는가?
(A) 회의 일정 변경하기
(B) 직원 회의에 참석하기
(C) 가이드가 있는 관광하기
(D) 약속 잡기

해설 대화 첫부분 "I'm glad we were able to get everyone together on short notice."에서 화자들이 긴급한 통보에 한 자리에 모였음을 알 수 있고, 전반적으로 레스토랑 일정에 대해 논의하고 있으므로 정답은 (B)이다.

69 시각 자료 연계

시각 자료를 보시오. 어떤 날짜가 변경되어야 하는가?
(A) 1월 28일
(B) 2월 18일
(C) 4월 4일
(D) 5월 22일

해설 대화 후반부 "The opening in Somersville will be delayed a couple of weeks."에서 Somersville 지역의 레스토랑 개업일이 지연되었다고 하므로 정답은 (B)이다.

70 문제점

무엇이 공사 지연의 원인이 되었는가?
(A) 날씨가 안 좋았다.
(B) 도시 승인을 받지 못했다.
(C) 공사 현장 직원들이 아팠다.
(D) 예산이 초과되었다.

해설 질문의 키워드 "delay(지연)"가 언급된 문장 "The site got completely snowed in, so construction has been delayed."에서 눈 때문에 지연되었음을 알 수 있다. 따라서 정답은 (A)이다.

PART • 4

[71-73] 전화 메시지

Good morning, Jennifer. This is Brian Cassidy calling from Software Development. I know you wanted to stop by later this afternoon to discuss the status of the upgrades to our online catalog. Unfortunately, I've just been asked to set everything aside this afternoon and lead the orientation for our recent new hires. I know you mentioned that you need the information today, so I would suggest that you reach out to Mike Breen in my department. He knows as much about the upgrades as I do, so he should be able to get you the information you need.

좋은 아침입니다, 제니퍼. 저는 소프트웨어 개발팀에서 일하는 브라이언 캐시디입니다. 오늘 오후에 온라인 카탈로그 업그레이드 상태를 논의하기 위해 저를 만나고 싶어 하신다고 들었습니다. 불행히도, 제가 오늘 오후에는 모든 것을 미루고 저희 회사의 신입 사원 오리엔테이션을 이끌도록 요청 받았습니다. 귀하께서 오늘 정보가 필요하다고 하신 걸로 알고 있으므로 제 부서의 마이크 브린에게 연락할 것을 제안합니다. 그도 저만큼 업그레이드에 대해 많이 알고 있기 때문에 필요한 정보를 얻으실 수 있을 겁니다.

어휘 stop by 들르다 discuss 논의하다 status 상태 unfortunately 불행히도 set aside ~을 한쪽으로 미루다 hire 신입 사원 lead 이끌다 mention 언급하다 information 정보 reach 연락하다 department 부서

71 주제/목적

화자는 왜 전화하는가?
(A) 회의를 요청하기 위해
(B) 면접을 보기 위해
(C) 프로그램의 기술 세부 사항을 논외하기 위해
(D) 면담을 거절하기 위해

해설 카탈로그 업그레이드를 논의하기 위해 만나길 원하는 고객에게, 다른 일이 있어 불가능하므로 부서의 다른 사람에게 연락할 것을 권유하는 메시지이다. 따라서 정답은 (D)이다.

72 다음에 할 일

화자는 오늘 오후에 무엇을 하는가?
(A) 병원에 간다
(B) 온라인 카탈로그를 작업한다
(C) 신입 사원들과 만난다
(D) 출장차 해외로 간다

해설 키워드 "this afternoon"이 들어가 있는 "Unfortunately, I've just been asked to set everything aside this afternoon and lead the orientation for our recent new hires."에서 신입 사원들과 만날 것을 알 수 있으므로 정답은 (C)이다.

73 제안

화자는 청자가 무엇을 하도록 제안하는가?

(A) 다른 회사 동료에게 연락하기
(B) 발표에 참석하기
(C) 내일 그와 함께 점심 식사하기
(D) 전화 기다리기

해설 미래에 할 일은 마지막 부분에 나온다. 화자 대신 마이크 브린에게 연락할 것을 권유하므로 정답은 (A)이다.

[74-76] 회의 발췌

Let's move on to talk about our recent project, Panda Ping pre-made dumplings. As you know, following numerous compliments and requests from customers, we began packaging and selling our most popular dumplings at each of our restaurant locations. The immediate response was extremely positive, and during the year, we ended up selling almost as many pre-packaged dumplings as we did in our restaurants. We're now hoping to leverage the success we've had and expand into a larger market. We have begun discussions with Quality Foods Supermarkets about carrying our dumplings in their frozen foods sections. We first need to convince their marketing manager that customers will buy our dumplings in a supermarket. To do that, starting Monday, we will be conducting customer surveys at a few of their supermarket locations.

우리의 최근 프로젝트인 Panda Ping의 조리 식품인 만두에 대해 이야기하겠습니다. 알다시피, 고객의 많은 칭찬과 요청에 따라, 우리는 가장 인기 있는 만두를 각 레스토랑 지점에서 포장해서 판매하기 시작했습니다. 즉각적인 반응은 매우 긍정적이었고, 일 년 동안 우리는 식당에서 파는 것처럼 포장된 만두를 많이 팔았습니다. 지금 우리가 이룬 성공을 극대화하고 더 큰 시장으로 확장하기 바랍니다. 우리는 냉동 식품 코너에 우리의 만두를 진열하는 것에 대해 Quality Foods 슈퍼마켓과 논의하기 시작했습니다. 우리는 먼저 소비자들이 슈퍼마켓에서 우리 만두를 살 것이라고 마케팅 매니저를 확신시켜야 합니다. 그러기 위해, 월요일부터 우리는 몇 개의 슈퍼마켓 지점에서 고객 설문 조사를 실시할 것입니다.

어휘 pre-made 사전 제작된 dumpling 만두 numerous 수 많은 compliment 칭찬 request 요청 customer 소비자 package 포장하다 location 지점, 위치 immediate 즉각적인 response 응답 extremely 매우 positive 긍정적인 end up 결국 ~로 끝나다 leverage 강화하다, 추진하다 expand into ~로 확장하다 discussion 토론 convince 확신시키다 conduct 실시하다 customer survey 고객 설문 조사

74 화자의 근무지

화자는 어떤 회사에서 일하는가?

(A) 슈퍼마켓 체인점
(B) 마케팅 에이전시
(C) 요리 학교
(D) 레스토랑 체인점

해설 도입부 "~ we began packaging and selling our most popular dumplings at each of our restaurant locations."에서 화자가 레스토랑에서 일하고 있음을 알 수 있으므로 정답은 (D)이다. (A)는 제품 진열을 논의한 업체에 해당된다.

75 세부 사항

화자는 어떤 사업 계획을 논의하고 있는가?

(A) 배달 사업 시작하기
(B) 경쟁업체와 합병하기
(C) 유통 확장하기
(D) 새로운 마케팅 매니저 고용하기

해설 담화 중반부의 "We're now hoping to leverage the success we've had and expand into a larger market."에서 사업을 더 큰 시장으로 확장하고자 하므로 정답은 (C)이다.

76 다음에 할 일

청자들은 월요일에 무엇을 할 것인가?

(A) 사업 계획을 변경한다
(B) 고객 설문조사를 실시한다
(C) 새로운 가게를 연다
(D) 예산 제안서를 수정한다

해설 미래의 할 일은 마지막 부분에 나온다. "To do that, starting Monday, we will be conducting customer surveys at a few of their supermarket locations." 고객 설문 조사를 실시할 것이라고 했으므로 정답은 (B)이다.

[77-79] 안내

I'd like to start by welcoming each of you to today's session. My name is Rachel Kim, and I've spent over 17 years as a speech therapist, both coaching individual speakers and writing books. While I have experience working with a variety of different issues relating to speech, my joy is helping people, just like you, overcome their fear of public speaking. After today's session, each of you will receive a complimentary copy of my new book, which discusses in depth many of the themes we will be covering here today. Now, the first thing we will do is have each of you complete the questionnaire you see in front of you. This will help you identify and verbalize what you believe to be your strengths and weaknesses when it comes to speaking in public.

저는 오늘 여러분을 환영하는 것으로 시작하고 싶습니다. 저는 레이첼 킴입니다. 저는 17년 동안 언어 치료사로 일하면서 개인 연설 코치와 책 쓰는 일을 동시에 했습니다. 연설과 관련된 여러 가지 다른 문제를 경험하면서, 저의 기쁨은 여러분들과 같이 대중 연설에 대한 두려움을 극복하고자 하는 분들에게 도움을 주는 것입니다. 오늘 과정이 끝난 후, 여러분은 오늘 우리가 여기서 다루게 될 많은 주제에 대해 깊이 다룬 저의 새로운 책을 무료로 받게 될 것입니다. 이제 우리가 할 첫 번째 일은 각자 앞에 놓인 설문지를 작성하는 것입니다. 이것은 대중 연설에 있어 강점과 약점이라고 믿는 것을 식별하고 말로 표현하는 데 도움이 될 것입니다.

어휘 spend (시간을) 보내다 therapist 치료사 coach 코치하다 individual 개인의 a variety of 다양한 relating to ~에 관하여 overcome 극복하다 fear 공포 public speaking 대중 연설 complimentary 무료의 copy 사본 in depth 깊이 있게 theme 주제 cover 다루다 complete 작성하다 questionnaire 설문지 identify 입증시키다 verbalize 말로 표현하다 strength 강점 weakness 약점

77 주제/목적
워크숍은 주로 무엇을 다루는가?
(A) 소프트웨어 프로그램 만들기
(B) 취업 면접 능력 강화하기
(C) 대중 연설 배우기
(D) 쓰기 능력 향상하기

해설 언어 치료사라고 본인을 소개하면서 오늘의 주제를 말하고 있다. "~ my joy is helping people, just like you, overcome their fear of public speaking." 대중 연설에 대한 두려움을 극복하도록 사람들을 돕는 것이 기쁘다고 했으므로 정답은 (C)이다.

78 세부 사항
화자가 청자들에게 무엇을 줄 것인가?
(A) 서명
(B) 책
(C) 안내책자
(D) 일자리

해설 담화 중반부에 "After today's session, each of you will receive a complimentary copy of my new book, ⋯"에서 무료로 책을 준다고 했으므로 정답은 (B)이다.

79 다음에 할 일
청자들은 다음에 무엇을 할 것인가?
(A) 몇 가지 질문에 답하기
(B) 그룹 별로 모이기
(C) 책 읽기
(D) 각자 소개하기

해설 미래의 할 일은 마지막 부분에 나온다. "Now, the first thing we will do is have each of you complete the questionnaire you see in front of you."에서 고객 설문 조사지를 작성해 달라고 말하고 있다. 따라서 정답은 (A)이다.

[80-82] 회의 발췌

Let's go ahead and get started with the meeting. We will be introducing a new security policy for the building. As you know, we have had some incidents recently, and the responsibility is ours as the security guards for the building to make safety our number one priority. Right now, all office tenants can access the elevator banks by swiping their company ID cards through the card reader. Starting on Monday, ID cards will also need to be swiped inside the elevator to access the tenant's floor. Tenants will no longer be allowed access to other floors of the building. To implement this new policy, we will need to issue new ID cards to all tenants, with barcodes embedded in them for the elevators. Here is a sample of the new ID card. Let's move over to the elevators so I can show you how this works.

회의를 시작하겠습니다. 우리는 건물에 새로운 보안 정책을 도입할 예정입니다. 알다시피 최근 몇 건의 사고가 있었으며, 안전 요원으로서 건물 안전이 최우선 사항이 되도록 저희가 책임지겠습니다. 현재 모든 사무실 세입자는 회사 사원증을 카드 리더기에 대면 엘리베이터를 탈 수 있습니다. 월요일부터는 세입자 층에 가기 위해 엘리베이터 안에서도 사원증을 대야 합니다. 세입자는 더 이상 건물의 다른 층에 출입할 수 없게 됩니다. 이 새로운 정책을 시행하기 위해 모든 세입자에게 엘리베이터용 바코드가 내장된 사원증을 발급해야 합니다. 새로운 사원증의 샘플이 여기 있습니다. 여러분에게 어떻게 작동하는지 보여드릴 테니 엘리베이터로 이동합시다.

어휘 go ahead 시작하다 introduce 소개하다 security policy 보안 정책 incident 사고 recently 최근에 responsibility 책임 priority 우선 순위 tenant 세입자 access 접근하다 swipe 대다 starting on ~부터 시작해서 allow 허용하다 implement 실행하다 issue 발행하다 embedded 내장된 work 작동하다

80 청자의 근무지
청자들은 어디에서 일하는가?
(A) 학교에서
(B) 사무실 건물에서
(C) 레스토랑에서
(D) 부동산 중개업소에서

해설 담화 초반에 "~ the responsibility is ours as the security guards for the building to make safety our number one priority."에서 건물 안전 요원이 청자들의 직업임을 알 수 있고, 사무실 세입자들을 위한 보안 정책을 설명하고 있으므로 정답은 (B)이다.

81 세부 사항
화자에 따르면, 무엇이 변경되는가?
(A) 사건 보고를 위한 절차
(B) 보안 직원들의 수
(C) 로비의 보수 작업 일정
(D) 건물 접근 제한

해설 담화 초반 "We will be introducing a new security policy ~"에서 새로운 보안 정책을 도입할 예정이라고 언급하

며, 월요일부터 엘리베이터 안에서도 신분증을 대야 원하는 층으로 이동할 수 있다고 말하고 있다. 따라서 정답은 (D)이다.

82 다음에 할 일

청자들은 이후에 무엇을 할 것인가?

(A) 시연 보기
(B) 안내 데스크에서 등록하기
(C) 일하러 돌아가기
(D) 점심 먹으러 이동하기

해설 미래에 관련된 내용은 마지막 부분에 주로 나온다. 마지막 문장 "Let's move over to the elevators so I can show you how this works."에서 어떻게 작동하는지 엘리베이터로 가서 보여주겠다고 제안하므로 정답은 (A)이다.

[83-85] 전화 메시지

> Karen, it's Dennis. I'm on my way to the office now, but there's been a terrible accident up ahead on the freeway. Traffic is really backed up, and it looks like I might be stuck here for a while. I can't remember whether I sent you the latest version of the agenda, but I'll e-mail it to you now so that you can start the meeting on time. Nancy is going to have to take the meeting minutes today. I'll give her a call after I e-mail you the agenda. She's done it before, so I don't think there will be a problem. See you when I get in.
>
> ----
>
> 카렌, 저 데니스예요. 지금 사무실에 가고 있는데 고속 도로에서 끔찍한 사고가 발생했어요. 차가 꽉 막혀 있고 제 생각에 한동안 이렇게 정체 속에 있어야 할 것 같아요. 제가 최근 회의 안건을 보내 주었는지 기억나지 않지만 지금 이메일을 보내면 제시간에 회의를 시작할 수 있어요. 낸시가 오늘 회의에서 회의록을 적어야 할 거예요. 제가 당신한테 이메일을 보내고 나서 그녀에게 전화를 걸게요. 그녀가 전에 해본 적이 있기 때문에 문제없을 거예요. 도착하면 봅시다.

어휘 on one's way 가는 도중인 terrible 끔찍한 accident 사고 freeway 고속 도로 traffic 교통 be backed up 꽉 막히다 look like ~해 보이다 stuck 갇힌 for a while 한동안 remember 기억하다 whether ~인지 아닌지 the latest 최신의 agenda 안건 on time 정시에 meeting minute 회의록 give a call 전화를 걸다

83 의도 파악

화자가 "차가 꽉 막혔어요"라고 말할 때 의도하는 것은 무엇인가?

(A) 그는 반대편으로 운전 중이다.
(B) 그가 사무실에 늦게 도착할 것이다.
(C) 그는 지금 기차를 타고 있다.
(D) 그는 오늘 사무실에 가지 않을 것이다.

해설 주어진 문장 바로 앞 "I'm on my way to the office now, but there's been a terrible accident ~"에서 사무실로 가고 있는데 교통 사고가 발생해 차가 꽉 막혀 있다고 말하므로 화자가 늦게 도착한다는 걸 알 수 있다. 따라서 정답은 (B)이다.

84 세부 사항

화자는 청자에게 무엇을 이메일로 보낼 것인가?

(A) 안건
(B) 회의록
(C) 계약서
(D) 영수증

해설 키워드 "e-mail(이메일을 보내다)"이 있는 부분 "I can't remember whether I sent you the latest version of the agenda, but I'll e-mail it to you now so that you can start the meeting on time."에서 안건을 보내 줄 것임을 알 수 있으므로 정답은 (A)이다.

85 요청 사항

화자는 낸시에게 무엇을 하도록 요청할 것인가?

(A) 점심 주문하기
(B) 회의 안건 준비하기
(C) 노트 작성하기
(D) 고객에게 전화하기

해설 "Nancy is going to have to take the meeting minutes today."을 통해 회의록을 작성할 것을 알 수 있으므로 정답은 (C)이다.

[86-88] 회의 발췌

> I see we're missing a couple of people, but I want to get started before it gets too late. We're here today to continue discussing plans for the upcoming technology expo. We sent out requests for industry sponsors almost three months ago, and I am told we have received only 17 positive responses so far. While this number is a bit lower than this time last year, I would like to remind all of you that we landed Horizon Tech as a sponsor this year, which is a huge win. In the interim, I would like to put together a small team to be in charge of organizing the attendees list and sending out periodic e-mail reminders. If you would like to volunteer for this group, please talk to me after the meeting.
>
> ----
>
> 몇몇 분들이 아직 안 온 걸 알지만, 너무 늦기 전에 시작하겠습니다. 우리는 오늘 다가오는 기술 박람회에 대한 계획을 계속 논의하기 위해 이곳에 왔습니다. 우리는 거의 3개월 전에 업계 후원자들에게 요청을 보냈는데, 지금까지 단 17개의 긍정적인 응답만 받았다고 들었습니다. 이 숫자는 작년 이맘때에 비해 약간 적지만, 올해 Horizon Tech가 후원하게 되었고 이 일이 매우 큰 업적이라는 걸 여러분 모두에게 다시 알려 드리고자 합니다. 그동안에 참석자 목록을 구성하고 주기적으로 이메일 알림을 보내도록 소규모 팀을 구성하고자 합니다. 이 팀에 자원하는 사람은 회의가 끝나면 저에게 말해 주세요.

어휘 a couple of 몇몇의 continue 지속하다 discuss 논의하다 plan 계획 upcoming 다가오는 expo 박람회 request 요청 industry 산업, 업계 sponsor 후원자 positive 긍정적인 response 반응, 응답 so far 지금까지 huge 거대한 win 승리 in the interim 그러는 동안에 land 상륙하다, 획득하다, ~을 잡다 be in charge of 책임지다, 담당하다

organize 준비하다   attendee 참석자   list 목록   send
out 발송하다   periodic 주기적인   reminder 알림
volunteer 지원자

86   청자의 직업

청자들은 누구일 것 같은가?
(A) 시 공무원들
(B) 은행 대출 담당 직원들
(C) 신문 기자들
(D) 컨퍼런스 기획자들

해설 청자들의 직업은 보통 첫 부분에 나온다. "We're here
today to continue discussing plans for the upcoming
technology expo."에서 다가오는 기술 박람회 준비를 위한
회의를 하고 있음을 알 수 있다. 따라서 정답은 (D)이다.

87   의도 파악

남자가 "올해 Horizon Tech가 후원하게 되었고 이 일은 매우
큰 업적입니다"라고 말한 의도는 무엇인가?
(A) 그들은 대회에서 우승했다.
(B) 청자들은 스스로 자랑스럽게 여겨야 한다.
(C) 청자들은 걱정할 필요가 없다.
(D) 청자들은 Horizon Tech에 연락해야 한다.

해설 바로 앞 문장 "I am told we have received 17 positive
response so far. While this number is a bit lower than
this time ~"에서 17군데의 업체들만이 긍정적인 답변을 보
냈다고 말하고, 작년에 비해 낮은 숫자라고 말한 후, Horizon
Tech가 후원하게 되어 매우 큰 업적이라고 했으므로 이는 걱
정할 필요가 없다고 청자들을 안심시키기 위해 하는 말임을 알
수 있다. 따라서 정답은 (C)이다.

88   세부 사항

왜 청자들은 회의 후에 화자에게 말을 걸어야 하는가?
(A) 박람회를 후원하는 데 동의하기 위해
(B) 다음 회의 날짜를 듣기 위해
(C) 내회에 참가하기 위해
(D) 작업 팀에 들어가기 위해

해설 마지막 부분 "If you would like to volunteer for this
group, please talk to me after the meeting."에서 자원
하는 사람들은 회의 후에 말해 달라고 하기 때문에 정답은 (D)
이다.

[89-91] 광고

Have you been searching for a cost-efficient vehicle
that is also a friend of the environment? Cyon Motors
introduces the newest line of solar-powered cars that
can save you quite a bit on fuel costs. The Solarla
GS, with its sleek design, is powered entirely through
solar panels on the roof of the vehicle. Imagine how
much you can save on gas! On days without sunlight,
the vehicle's internal battery automatically kicks in so

that you are never left without power. Visit our Web site
today to learn more and sign up for a test drive.

친환경적이면서 비용 효율적인 차량을 찾고 계십니까? Cyon Motors
는 당신에게 연료비를 상당히 절약할 수 있는 태양열 자동차의 최신
라인을 소개합니다. 날렵한 디자인의 Solaria GS는 자동차 루프 위에
있는 태양열 패널을 통해서 전체 전력을 공급 받습니다. 얼마나 연료
를 절약할 수 있는지 상상해 보십시오! 햇빛이 없는 날에는 차량의 내
부 배터리가 자동으로 작동하여 절대로 전원이 나가지 않습니다. 더 많
은 정보를 얻고 시운전에 등록하려면 오늘 웹사이트를 방문하십시오.

어휘 search for ~를 찾다   cost-efficient 비용 효율적인
environment 환경   introduce 소개하다   solar-powered
태양열의   save 절약하다   fuel 연료   sleek 매끈한, 날렵한
roof 지붕   imagine 상상하다   sunlight 햇빛   internal
내부의   automatically 자동적으로   kick in 작동하다, 효과가
나다   charge 충전하다

89   주제/목적

무엇이 광고되고 있는가?
(A) 식기 세척기
(B) 휴대폰
(C) 자동차
(D) 컴퓨터

해설 담화 도입부에서 "Have you been searching for a cost-
effective vehicle ~?"라며 광고 대상을 언급하고 있다. 따라
서 정답은 (C)이다.

90   세부 사항

화자는 제품의 무엇을 강조하는가?
(A) 비용 효율성
(B) 가격
(C) 편리성
(D) 색상 배합

해설 도입부의 "cost-efficient vehicle(비용 효율적인 차량)",
"Cyon Motors introduces the newest line of solar-
powered cars that can save you quite a bit on fuel
costs."에서 연료 비용을 꽤 줄일 수 있는 태양열 자동차라고
소개하므로 정답은 (A)이다.

91   세부 사항

청자들은 왜 웹 사이트를 방문해야 하는가?
(A) 고객 서비스 직원과 대화하기 위해
(B) 가까운 지점을 찾기 위해
(C) 무료 쿠폰을 받기 위해
(D) 시운전을 신청하기 위해

해설 담화 후반부의 "Visit our Web site today to learn more
and sign up for a test drive."에서 사이트에 들어가서 시운
전에 등록하라는 내용을 확인할 수 있다. 따라서 정답은 (D)이
다.

[92-94] 방송

Good afternoon, everyone! Welcome to No Place Like Home, Channel 5's show about arts and culture around town. Our first story is about the local art museum and its ongoing project to create an online digital catalog of all their artwork. Museum curator Noelle Baptiste points to the many benefits that will stem from this project, including the ability for everyone to appreciate local artwork from the comfort of their own homes. Ms. Baptiste is not yet certain about when the digitization project will be finished, <u>considering the sheer number of art pieces at the museum</u>.

모두들, 안녕하세요! 도시 주변의 예술과 문화에 관한 Channel 5의 쇼인 "No Place Like Home"에 오신 것을 환영합니다. 우리의 첫 번째 이야기는 지역 미술관과 진행 중인 모든 예술품의 온라인 디지털 카탈로그를 만드는 프로젝트입니다. 박물관 큐레이터인 노엘 밥티스트는 모든 사람들이 자신의 집에서 편안하게 지역 미술 작품을 감상할 수 있는 점을 포함해서 이 프로젝트에서 비롯되는 많은 혜택을 시사합니다. 밥티스트 씨는 미술관의 수많은 예술 작품 수를 고려하여 언제 디지털화 프로젝트가 완료될지 확신하지 못하고 있습니다.

어휘 art museum 미술관 ongoing 진행 중의 create 만들다 catalog 카탈로그 artwork 미술 작품 point to 나타내다, 시사하다 benefit 혜택 stem from ~로부터 비롯되다 include 포함시키다 appreciate 고맙게 여기다 comfort 편안함 interesting 흥미로운 catch 사로잡다 in person 직접 certain 확신하다 the sheer number of 수많은

92 주제/목적

화자는 무슨 기관에 대해 말하는가?
(A) 시청
(B) 대학교
(C) 미술관
(D) 야구 경기장

해설 초반부의 "Our first story is about the local art museum and its ongoing project to create an online digital catalog of all their artwork."에서 미술관의 진행 중인 프로젝트를 말하고 있으므로 정답은 (C)이다.

93 세부 사항

화자에 따르면, 프로젝트는 대중에게 무슨 혜택을 제공하는가?
(A) 예술가들을 직접 만날 기회
(B) 더 많은 일자리 기회
(C) 입장료 할인
(D) 미술 작품에 더 쉬운 접근

해설 중반부의 "Museum curator Noelle Baptiste points to the many benefits that will stem from this project, including the ability for everyone to appreciate local artwork from the comfort of their own homes."에서 편하게 미술 작품을 감상할 수 있다고 했으므로 정답은 (D)이다.

94 의도 파악

여자가 "미술관의 수많은 예술작품 수를 고려하여"라고 말한 의도는 무엇인가?
(A) 많은 시간이 소요될지도 모른다.
(B) 프로젝트가 아직 시작되지 않았다.
(C) 온라인 접속에 비용이 든다.
(D) 더 많은 공간이 필요하다.

해설 인용 표현 바로 앞 문장 "Ms. Baptiste is not yet certain about when the digitization project will be finished, ~."에서 디지털화하는 프로젝트가 언제 완료될지 모르겠다고 하고, 그 이유로 수많은 예술 작품의 수 때문이라고 하므로 정답은 (A)이다.

[95-97] 회의 발췌 & 제품 정보

Let's get this meeting started. First on the agenda is customer feedback we have received on our new mobile phone. We've been offering customers various options to personalize their phones and make them more suitable for their daily lives, including size, color, amount of memory, and shape. Surprisingly, customers have really liked that we offer phones in different shapes and would like to see more options, so we will be releasing three more shapes in August. Now, for some bad news: a number of customers have reported issues with the phone's battery. We declared that battery life is good for six hours of continuous use, but it seems a number of batteries are dying in less than one hour. We will need to get to the bottom of this immediately.

이제 회의를 시작합시다. 첫 번째 안건은 우리의 새로운 휴대 전화에 대한 고객 의견입니다. 우리는 고객에게 휴대 전화를 개인의 필요에 맞추기 위해 크기, 색상, 메모리 용량 및 모양 등을 포함해서 일상 생활에 더 적합하도록 다양한 옵션을 제공하고 있습니다. 놀랍게도 고객들은 실제로 다양한 모양의 휴대폰을 제공받는 걸 좋아했고, 더 많은 옵션을 보고 싶어 하므로 8월에 세 가지 모양을 추가로 출시할 예정입니다. 이제 몇 가지 나쁜 소식을 말하자면, 많은 고객이 휴대 전화의 배터리 문제에 대해 말했습니다. 우리는 배터리 수명이 6시간 지속 사용이 가능하다고 했지만 수많은 배터리의 수명이 1시간 이내인 것으로 보입니다. 우리는 즉시 이 문제부터 해결해야 합니다.

고객 맞춤형 휴대폰	
크기	3가지 옵션 - 소, 중, 대
색상	6가지 옵션 - 하양, 검정, 은색, 금색, 분홍, 초록
메모리 용량	4가지 옵션 - 64GB, 128GB, 256GB, 512GB
모양	2가지 옵션 - 직사각형, 원형

어휘 agenda 안건 customer 소비자 feedback 의견 receive 받다 option 선택 personalize 개인화하다 suitable 적합한 daily lives 일상 생활 include 포함시키다 surprisingly 놀랍게도 release 출시하다 a number of 많은 report 보고하다 battery 배터리

declare 선언하다 life 수명 continuous 지속적인 get to the bottom of ~의 원인을 알아내다 immediately 즉시, 바로

95 주제/목적

화자는 주로 무엇을 논의하고 있는가?
(A) 공사 프로젝트
(B) 다가오는 세미나
(C) 연간 매출액
(D) 소비자 의견

해설 담화 초반에 "First on the agenda is customer feedback we have received on our new mobile phone."에서 소비자 의견이 첫 번째 회의 안건이라고 말하므로 정답은 (D)이다.

96 시각 자료 연계

도표를 보시오. 8월에 어떤 옵션의 양이 증가할 것인가?
(A) 3옵션
(B) 6옵션
(C) 4옵션
(D) 2옵션

해설 키워드는 'August'로, "customers have really liked that we offer phones in different shapes and would like to see more options, so we will be releasing three more shapes in August."에서 shape이 더 많은 모양으로 출시될 것이라고 했다. 시각 자료에서 이에 해당하는 것은 (D)이다.

97 문제점

화자가 우려하는 것은 무엇인가?
(A) 물건이 잘 안 팔린다.
(B) 배터리에 문제가 있다.
(C) 고객들이 컬러 옵션을 좋아하지 않는다.
(D) 제품 배송 시간이 너무 오래 걸린다.

해설 후반부의 "Now, for some bad news: a number of customers have reported issues with the phone's battery."에서 배터리 수명에 대한 문제가 많이 보고되었다고 하므로 정답은 (B)이다.

[98-100] 전화 메시지 & 지도

Hi, this is Martin from Riverside Realtors. I'm calling to let you know I think I've found the perfect property for your new restaurant. It just came on the market and is located downtown directly across the street from Fancy Dry Cleaning. With a movie theater right next door and an increasing number of people spending time downtown following recent renovations, you are sure to get a lot of customers. I just got off the phone with the owner, and he said he's already getting a lot of inquiries about the property. The listed price is a bit higher than the budget you gave me, but I thought I would run it by you anyway because I think the extra cost might be worth it. Please let me know your thoughts.

안녕하세요, 리버 사이드 부동산 중개소의 마틴입니다. 귀하의 새로운 식당을 위한 완벽한 장소를 찾았다는 걸 알려 드리고자 연락합니다. 이제 막 부동산 시장에 나왔으며, Fancy 세탁소에서 길 건너편에 바로 위치해 있습니다. 바로 옆에 있는 영화관이 최근 개조 공사를 마친 후 시내에서 시간을 보내는 사람들이 늘어나면서 많은 고객을 확보하게 될 거라고 생각합니다. 방금 주인과 전화 통화를 마쳤고 그는 이미 많은 문의를 받고 있다고 말했습니다. 게시된 가격은 당신이 저에게 제시한 예산보다 조금 더 높습니다만, 저는 그 이상의 비용이 그만한 가치가 있다고 생각하기 때문에 어쨌든 당신과 상의해 보는 것입니다. 당신의 생각을 저에게 말씀해 주세요.

어휘 property 부동산, 자산 on the market 시중에 나와 있는 locate 위치하다 directly 바로, 직접 across 건너편에 movie theater 극장 increase 증가하다 spend (시간을) 보내다 renovation 보수 customer 고객 get off the phone 전화를 끊다 inquiry 문의 사항 listed 올려진 budget 예산 run by 설명하다 anyway 어쨌든 extra cost 추가 비용 worth 가치가 있는 thought 생각, 의견

98 화자의 직업

화자는 누구일 것 같은가?
(A) 교수
(B) 부동산 중개인
(C) 가게 주인
(D) 음식 평론가

해설 보통 화자의 직업은 첫 부분에 나온다. "Hi, this is Martin from Riverside Realtors."에서 자신이 중개소 직원이라고 소개하기 때문에 정답은 (B)이다.

99 시각 자료 연계

시각 자료를 보시오. 화자가 말하는 곳은 어디인가?
(A) Fancy 세탁소
(B) Jim의 슈퍼마켓
(C) Lucky Strike 볼링장
(D) Sam의 편의점

해설 담화 초반부의 "~ located in downtown directly across the street from Fancy Dry Cleaning. With a movie theater right next door"에서 위치가 세탁소 건너편이고 극장 바로 옆이라고 설명했으므로 정답은 (D)이다.

100 세부 사항

화자는 어떤 계획을 변경하길 제안하는가?

(A) 예산
(B) 위치
(C) 부동산 규모
(D) 공사 일정

해설 마지막 부분 "The listed price is a bit higher than the budget you gave me, but I thought I would run it by you anyway because I think the extra cost might be worth it."에서 예산보다 비싸지만 가치가 있으니 생각해 보라고 제안하고 있으므로 정답은 (A)이다.

PART • 5

101 명사 자리

뉴욕의 두 회사가 서로 합병할 의도가 없다는 것은 사실입니다.

해설 타동사 have의 목적어로서 수량 형용사 any의 수식을 받는 명사가 필요하므로, (A) 동사, (B) 명사, (C) 동명사/분사, (D) 동사/분사 중 (B)가 정답이다.

어휘 intention 의도   merge with ~와 합병하다

102 분사

다음 호를 위한 내용을 편집하면서, 에드먼즈 씨는 그것의 삽화들에서 많은 오류를 발견했습니다.

해설 빈칸부터 콤마(,)까지는 수식어로, 빈칸 뒤 명사(the contents)가 분사의 목적어 역할을 하므로 (A)가 정답이다.

어휘 content 내용   issue (정기 간행물의) 권, 호   illustration 삽화

103 대명사

이번 회의에서, 곧 있을 홍보 행사에 관한 그의 견해는 제 견해와 그렇게 다르지 않습니다.

해설 비교 대상이 '그의 견해'이기 때문에 빈칸에는 '나의 견해(my opinion)'가 와야 한다. '나의 것'이라는 의미의 소유대명사 (D) mine이 나와야 한다.

어휘 promotional event 홍보 행사   be different from ~와 다르다

104 전치사

그 건물은 수리로 인해 6개월 동안 임시로 폐쇄될 예정입니다.

해설 빈칸 뒤에 기간이 숫자로 표현(six months)되어 있으므로 (C) for가 가장 적절하다. during 또한 기간을 나타내는 전치사이지만 뒤에 숫자가 아니라 특정 기간이 와야 한다.

어휘 be scheduled to ~할 예정이다   temporarily 임시로 renovation 수리

105 명사 어휘

우리 웹 사이트는 회원들에게 좋은 정보를 제공하기 위해 전 연령대를 위한 매우 다양한 신간 도서와 중고 서적들을 보여 줍니다.

해설 보기는 (A) 선택, (B) 거래/양, (C) 결론, (D) 시행이라는 뜻의 명사들로, <a ---- of + 복수명사>의 구조로 사용되어 '많은/다양한'을 의미하는 (A) selection이 정답이 된다. a (great) deal of의 경우 셀 수 없는 명사와 함께 쓰이므로 (B)는 답이 될 수 없다.

어휘 show 보여 주다   used 중고의

106 부사 자리

4세대 트렌드에 관한 마크의 기사문은 대부분의 분석가들에게 긍정적으로 평가 받았습니다.

해설 빈칸은 be동사(been)와 수동형 분사(reviewed) 사이의 부사 자리이므로 (B)가 정답이다.

어휘 positively 긍정적으로   analyst 분석가

107 부사 어휘

일 년에 한 번, Tahoma 사는 다음 시즌을 위해 본사에서 총회를 개최합니다.

해설 [------ + a + 시간 명사]의 구조로, a year과 함께 쓰여 빈도를 나타내는 (C) Once가 정답이다.

어휘 general meeting 총회   headquarters 본사

108 동사의 형태, 시제, 수

Max Resolution 사는 고객이 구매한 불량품들을 가능한 한 빨리 회수하겠다고 발표했습니다.

해설 문장에 동사가 없으므로 빈칸에는 동사가 와야 하며, 단수 주어와 수 일치해야 한다. (C)와 (D)는 동사가 아니며, (A)는 단수 동사(announces)가 아니므로 오답이다. 따라서 과거형 (B) announced가 정답이다.

어휘 recall 회수하다   faulty 결함이 있는, 잘못된

109 형용사 자리

5월에 출시된 그들의 신제품은 그들이 판매했던 이전 제품들보다 훨씬 더 비쌉니다.

해설 [(much) more ------- than] 구조의 빈칸에는 형용사 (A)와 부사 (B)가 모두 가능한데, (much) more과 than 이하를 생략하면 빈칸에 나올 품사를 알 수 있다. 위의 문장에서 이들을 생략하면 [~ are ------] 구조가 되므로 be동사 뒤에서 보어 역할을 할 수 있는 형용사 (A)가 정답이다.

어휘 expensive 비싼   previous 이전의

110 대명사

대부분의 직원들은 인사과로부터 새로 개정된 규정들을 통보 받습니다.

해설 of 뒤에 복수 명사가 있고, 복수 동사 are이 쓰인 것으로 보아 주어를 단수로 만드는 (B) Each는 오답이다. (C) Little은 셀 수 없는 명사 앞에 위치하므로 오답이고, (D)는 부사이므로 답이 될 수 없다. 따라서 (A) Most가 가장 적절하다.

어휘 notify 알리다, 통보하다   revised 개정된

111 전치사 어휘

코너 씨는 공상 과학 소설 분야에서 창의적인 작가로 널리 알려져 있습니다.

해설 빈칸 뒤 명사(a creative writer)가 주어의 신분/직책을 나타내므로 (A) as가 정답이다.

어휘 widely 널리   be known as ~로 알려져 있다   creative 창의적인

112 명사 어휘

지방 정부는 많은 교통량에 대처하기 위해 새로운 도로가 건설되어야 한다는 합의에 마침내 이르렀습니다.

해설 보기가 모두 명사인 명사 어휘 문제로, (A) 단서, (B) 보상, (C) 합의, (D) 모순 중에서 새로운 도로 건설에 대한 '합의'에 이르렀다는 의미의 (C)가 가장 적절하다.

어휘 government 정부   reach 도달하다

113 형용사 어휘

특허청이 정해진 기간 동안 개발자에게 그들의 발명에 대한 독점권을 주는 것은 타당합니다.

해설 보기가 모두 형용사인 형용사 어휘 문제이다. (A) 포괄적인, (B) 독점적인, (C) 명백한, (D) 의존하는 중에서, 개발자들에게 '독점적인' 권리를 줘야 한다는 (B)가 의미상 가장 적절하다.

어휘 reasonable 합리적인, 타당한   patent 특허권   inventor 개발자, 발명가   right 권리

114 부사절 접속사

우리는 새로운 센터를 건설하길 간절히 원했음에도 불구하고, 부동산을 개발할 기회를 놓쳤습니다.

해설 (A) 비유(마치~인 것처럼), (B) 반전(비록 ~일지라도), (C) 조건(오직 ~한 경우에), (D) 시간(마침 ~할 때)의 부사절 접속사 중, '원했지만 기회를 놓쳤다'는 문맥을 만드는 반전의 접속사 (B) even though가 정답이다.

어휘 property 부동산   eager 열렬한, 간절히 바라는

115 형용사 어휘

UPS 매장에서 사서함을 만들면, 누군가가 당신이 우편물을 받아서 그것을 안전하게 보관하도록 돕고, 당신을 대신하여 소포에 대해 서명을 합니다.

해설 (A) 주의하는, (B) 취약한, (C) 까다로운, (D) 안전한의 형용사 어휘들 중에서, 개인의 우편물을 '안전한' 상태로 보관한다는 문맥을 만드는 (D)가 가장 적절하다.

어휘 keep ~한 상태로 두다   package 소포   instead of ~ 대신에

116 부사 어휘

블랙 프라이데이 주간 동안, 대부분의 아울렛 매장들은 고객들에게 최대 80퍼센트까지 할인된 가격에 제품들을 제공할 것입니다.

해설 빈칸 뒤 80%를 수식할 수 있는 숫자 강조 부사 (D) up to(~까지)가 정답이다.

어휘 offer 제공하다   product 제품

117 동사 어휘

그들의 새로운 고객 서비스 규정은 현재의 서비스를 개선함으로써 직원들이 고객의 요구에 효율적으로 대응할 수 있게 합니다.

해설 (A) 마주치다, (B) 가능하게 하다, (C) 불러일으키다, (D) 설명하다의 보기 중 구조에 알맞은 동사를 고르는 문제이다. 사람 목적어(staff) 뒤에 to부정사가 나왔으므로 enable A to V (A가 ~할 수 있게 하다)의 구조로 사용될 수 있는 (B)가 정답이다.

어휘 regulation 규정   effectively 효율적으로   improve 개선하다

118 명사 어휘

지금까지, Holly Motors는 미국에서 판매 부족으로 인해 공장 폐쇄를 발표한 유일한 제조업체입니다.

해설 (A) 고장, (B) 금지, (C) 폐쇄, (D) 건설을 의미하는 명사 어휘들 중에서, 빈칸에는 plant와 함께 쓰일 수 있는 복합 명사가 나와야 하므로 '폐쇄'를 뜻하는 (C) shutdowns가 의미상 가장 적합하다.

어휘 so far 지금까지   manufacturer 제조업자   shortage 부족

119 전치사 자리

마케팅의 성공에도 불구하고, 우리의 매출액은 눈에 띄게 증가하지 않았습니다.

해설 (A) 전치사, (B) 접속사, (C) 부사, (D) 부사 중에서, 빈칸에는 뒤의 명사(the success)를 연결하는 전치사가 필요하므로 (A)가 정답이다.

어휘 sales figures 매출액   remarkably 눈에 띄게

120 부사 어휘

그 연구 기업은 인터넷과 신문 광고 수입 간의 격차가 내년에 급격하게 증가할 것이라고 예측합니다.

해설 (A) 열정적으로, (B) 설세하게, (C) 급격히, (D) 관대하게의 부사 어휘들 중에서, 빈칸 앞 동사(increase)를 수식하여 '급격하게 증가하다'라는 의미를 만드는 (C) drastically가 가장 적절하다.

어휘 predict 예측하다   gap 차이, 격차

121 동사의 형태

대학원 과정을 밟고 있는 모든 학생들은 다가오는 이번 학술 포럼에 예외 없이 참석하도록 요구됩니다.

해설 보기의 require는 5형식 '시키다' 류의 동사로, [require + 목적어 + to부정사] 구조로 사용되는데, 빈칸 뒤에는 목적어 없이 바로 to부정사가 나왔으므로 수동형인 (B)가 정답이다.

어휘 graduate course 대학원 과정   scholar 학술, 학자
exception 예외

122 동사의 시제

저희 직원 중 한 명과 회의 일정을 잡으시려면, 먼저 저희 고객 서비스 센터에 연락주세요.

해설 if는 조건의 접속사이므로, 주절에 미래(will) 시제가 나오려면 if절에는 현재 시제가 나와야 하므로 (B)가 정답이다.

어휘 schedule 일정을 잡다

123 명사 어휘

관리자들은 휴대폰 공장의 생산력을 증가시키는 방법에 관한 조언을 요청했습니다.

해설 (A) 흥미/이자, (B) 제안, (C) 중요성, (D) 조언의 명사 어휘들 중에서, 증가시키는 방법에 대한 '조언'을 구한다는 의미를 만드는 (D)가 문맥상 가장 적절하다.

어휘 ask for ~을 요구하다   capacity 규모, 용량, 능력   plant 공장

124 부사절 접속사

그 기사를 신중히 검토했을 때, 존 씨는 그 내용에서 몇 가지 심각한 오류들을 발견했습니다.

해설 빈칸 뒤는 [주어+동사]의 구조가 아닌 현재 분사가 있으므로, 이를 연결해 주는 시간/조건 부사절 접속사가 필요하다. 문맥상 '~할 때'라는 의미의 When이 오는 것이 가장 적절하므로 정답은 (A)이다.

어휘 severe 심각한   content 내용

125 to부정사 자리

우리는 할인을 포함한 다양한 홍보 행사를 개최하는 것과 같이 더 많은 고객들을 끌어들일 계획을 가지고 있어야 합니다.

해설 빈칸 앞의 plan은 앞으로 ~할 것이라는 미래의 의미가 내포된 명사이므로 to부정사가 뒤에서 수식해야 한다. 따라서 정답은 (A)이다.

어휘 attract 끌어들이다, 유치하다   various 다양한
promotional 홍보의

126 관계대명사

1990년에 설립된 Best Neighbors는 아프리카의 가난한 사람들을 도와주는 임무를 가진 단체입니다.

해설 빈칸 뒤는 완전한 구조이므로 불완전한 절을 이끄는 (A) which, (C) who는 오답이다. 빈칸 앞에 선행사가 있기 때문

에 (D) that 또한 관계대명사로서 불완전한 절을 이끌어야 하므로 적절하지 못하다. 따라서 앞뒤에 명사가 나올 수 있고, 완전한 절을 이끄는 소유격 관계대명사 (B) whose가 정답이다.

어휘 organization 조직, 단체   mission 임무

127 동사의 형태

지구 온난화 문제에 관한 케빈의 논문은 우리 학술지에서 논문을 출간하기 위한 기준 양식으로 참고됩니다.

해설 refer to(~을 참고하다)에서 전치사 to 뒤에 명사(전치사의 목적어)가 없으므로 수동태인 (B)가 정답이다.

어휘 standard 표준의   journal 신문, 학술지

128 부사 어휘

많은 자원의 낭비 없이, 효율적으로 건축된 건물들은 원자재와 에너지의 양을 줄이는 친환경적 사무실을 가지고 있습니다.

해설 (A) 부드럽게, (B) 편리하게, (C) 원격으로, (D) 효율적으로를 뜻하는 부사 어휘들 중에서, 건물이 원자재와 에너지의 양을 줄이는 친환경적인 사무실을 갖고 있다는 것은 효율적으로 건축되었다는 것을 의미하므로 (D)가 가장 적절하다.

어휘 resource 자원   eco-friendly 친환경적인   raw material 원자재

129 동사 어휘

우리는 우리의 모든 고객이 새로 도입된 서비스에 계속 만족하도록 최선을 다해야 합니다.

해설 (A) ~한 상태로 두다, (B) 요구하다, (C) 알리다, 통지하다, (D) 방해하다의 타동사들 중에서, [------ + 목적어 + 분사 (satisfied)]의 5형식 구조에 알맞은 동사가 필요하므로 목적 보어로 형용사/분사를 취하는 (A) keep이 정답이다.

어휘 do one's best 최선을 다하다   satisfied 만족한   newly 새롭게

130 명사 어휘

우리는 원자재를 더 낮은 가격에 대량으로 구매하는 명확한 사업 네트워크를 가지고 있어서, 고객들에게 좋은 품질이지만 더 저렴한 제품들을 제공할 수 있습니다.

해설 (A) 규모/양, (B) 양, (C) 통행료, (D) 요금의 명사 어휘들 중에, 좋은 품질에 싼 제품을 제공하기 위해서는 원자재를 대량으로 구매해야 하므로 in bulk(대량으로)로 사용되는 (A)가 가장 적절하다.

어휘 concrete 명확한   raw material 원자재

PART 6

[131-134] 공지

망 중립성에 대한 입장 선택

미연방 통신 위원회(FCC)는 지지자들이 소비자, 서비스 제공자, 그리고 투자자들의 이익을 보호할 수 있다고 말하는 논란이 많은 인터넷에 대한 새로운 법안을 화요일에 승인했다.

통신 위원회의 회원들은 인터넷 서비스 제공업체들이 주파수폭 혹은 소비자의 인터넷 접근을 선택적으로 제한하는 것을 주로 막는 일련의 법안을 승인하기 위해 마침내 투표했다.

위원회 의장인 제임스 쿠퍼는 강력하지만 유연성 있는 인터넷의 미래 체계를 만들어내기 위하여 그가 '망 중립성'이라고도 부르는 지침을 내놓았다.

조항에 의거하여, Veracast 또는 AC&T와 같은 네트워크는 고주파수나 경쟁사의 사이트로부터 인터넷 통신을 느리게 하거나 막아서는 안 된다. 위원회 일부 회원들이 그러한 행위의 법적 승인과 규제적 필요성에 의문을 제기하면서 이러한 움직임에 반대했음에도 불구하고, 이 법안은 인터넷 서비스 제공업자(ISP)들이 더 높은 가격에 훨씬 빠른 속도와 큰 용량을 제공하면서 다양한 계층적 서비스를 제공할 수 있게 할 것이다. 하지만, *Common Times Journal*은 이 법안이 "유료 고속도로"와 같은 서비스를 좌절시킬 것이라고 보고했다.

어휘 bar 막다, 금지하다 selectively 선택적으로 restrict 제한하다 bandwidth (주파수)대 tiered (배)열의, 층층의 question 의문을 제기하다 authority 승인 discourage 좌절시키다, 낙담시키다

131 부사 어휘

해설 조동사와 동사 사이에 올 수 있는 부사를 묻는 문제로, 문맥상 '법안이 주로 막는다'는 의미가 자연스러우므로 '주로'를 의미하는 (B) largely가 적합하다.

132 형용사 어휘

해설 빈칸 앞의 but은 역접의 접속사로, strong(강건한/곧은)에 상응하는 의미인 (A) flexible(유연한/유연성 있는)이 적절하다.

133 비교급 강조 부사

해설 빈칸 뒤에 비교급 greater가 있기 때문에 비교급을 수식하는 부사인 (B) far가 적절하다. 비교급을 수식하는 부사로는 far, a lot, still, even, much가 있다는 것을 알아두자.

134 문맥에 맞는 문장 고르기

(A) 게다가, 그들의 인터넷 서비스는 품질과 가격 면에서 다른 경쟁사에 비해 매우 뛰어나다.

(B) 예를 들어, 많은 회사들의 인터넷 서비스는 그늘이 최신 보안 소프트웨어로 업데이트될 것이다.

(C) 하지만, <Common Times Journal>은 이 법안이 "유료 고속도로"와 같은 서비스를 좌절시킬 것이라고 보고했다.

(D) 더욱이, 웹 기반의 보호 시스템 또한 그들의 모든 잠재 고객들에게 주어진다.

해설 빈칸 앞 문장에서 법안으로 인해 빠른 속도와 큰 용량이 제공될 것이라는 장점을 설명했지만, 이와 관련된 법적 승인과 규제적 필요성에 대한 문제가 있음을 암시하고 있다. 각 보기의 접속부사를 고려했을 때, 도리어 그 법안이 이를 좌절시킬 수도 있음을 나타내는 (C)가 문맥상 가장 적절하다.

[135-138] 이메일

수신: 제시카 개리슨
발신: 존 파누치
날짜: 5월 18일
제목: 유의해 주세요

제시카에게,

최근의 집 내부 검사 동안, 당신의 카펫에 얼룩이 있다는 것이 발견되었습니다. 아파트를 좋은 상태로 유지하기 위한 노력으로, 각 아파트 세입자들은 얼룩이 땅바닥의 흙으로 인해 야기되는 영구적인 손상을 피하기 위해 주기적으로 카펫을 세탁하도록 강력히 권고됩니다. 만약 카펫에 과도한 얼룩이 있고 적당한 시간 내에 이러한 얼룩을 제거하기 위한 시도가 없다면, 카펫의 수명이 단축되고 아파트의 상태는 나빠질 것입니다. 임대 기간 동안 예방 조치가 취해진다면 심각한 손상 및 카펫 교체를 피할 수 있습니다. 만약 Copper Beach 아파트에서 당신의 카펫을 세탁하기 위해 일정을 잡고 그 비용을 지불하길 원한다면 언제든지 사무실로 연락 바랍니다.

진심으로,

존 파누치
Copper Beach Apartment

어휘 inspection 검사 shampoo (세제로) 청소하다 periodically 주기적으로 excessive 과도한 shorten 단축시키다, 줄이다 downgrade 격하시키다, 저하시키다

135 문맥에 맞는 문장 고르기

(A) 우리는 Copper Beach 아파트에 거주하기 시작한 모든 분들을 환영합니다.

(B) 우리의 청소 서비스는 펜실베이니아 주에서 완성도로 널리 알려져 있습니다.

(C) 다음달, 우리는 우리의 거주 지역을 효율적으로 유지하는 방법에 관한 세미나를 개최할 것입니다.

(D) 최근의 집 내부 검사 동안, 당신의 카펫에 얼룩이 있다는 것이 발견되었습니다.

해설 빈칸 뒤 문장의 내용에서, 아파트를 좋은 상태로 유지하기 위해 카펫을 주기적으로 세척하기를 권장한다고 하고 있다. 이는 현재 카펫의 상태가 좋지 않기 때문에 그 관리 방법을 설명하고 있는 것이므로 빈칸에는 문맥상 (D)가 적절하다.

136 형용사 어휘

해설 (A) 긴, (B) 영구적인, (C) 결석한, (D) 계절적인의 형용사 어휘들 중에서, 빈칸 뒤 내용인 얼룩이나 흙에 의해 야기되는 손상과 문맥상 가장 잘 어울리는 것을 골라야 한다. 따라서 '영구적인'이라는 의미의 (B)가 가장 적절하다.

137 형용사 자리

해설 빈칸 뒤에 명사 measures(조치)가 있으므로 앞에는 이를 수식할 수 있는 형용사가 나와야 한다. 따라서 (A)가 답이다. (D)를 현재분사 수식어로 볼 수도 있지만 의미상 적절하지 않다.

138 과거분사

해설 have는 사역 동사로 『have + 목적어(사물) + 동사원형/p.p.(-ed)』의 형태로 사용된다. 여기서는 카펫이 '세탁이 되는' 것이기 때문에 과거분사 형태의 (D)가 정답이다.

[139-142] 광고

> **Ameriprise Financial이 당신에게 적합한가요?**
>
> 사람들은 다양한 이유로 재정 계획 및 조언을 구합니다. 일부 사람들은 퇴직 계획 혹은 구체적인 미래 재정 목표에 대해 도움을 구하고 있습니다; 다른 사람들은 어떻게 계획할지 혹은 어떻게 적응할지 확신하지 못하는 삶의 변화 또는 시장 변화를 경험합니다. 모든 사람들은 그들의 일생 동안 현명한 재무 결정을 확실히 하고 싶어 합니다.
>
> 금융 조언과 장기 계획을 소중히 여기세요!
> 만약 당신이 장기 재정 목표 달성에 전념하고 몇 가지 지침을 활용할 수 있다면, 우리가 도와 드릴 수 있습니다. 당신이 받으실 금융 조언의 수준은 귀하의 요구와 선호 사항에 달려 있습니다. 다른 사람의 의견이나 더 많은 정보를 사용하면서 재정을 직접 관리할 수 있습니까? 대부분의 재정 문제를 전문가에게 맡기길 원하십니까? 귀하의 개인 재정 방식이 무엇이든 간에, 우리는 귀하가 평생 동안 건실한 금융 결정을 하도록 도와드릴 수 있습니다.

어휘 retirement 퇴직, 은퇴 throughout ~동안, 내내 adapt to ~에 적응하다 informative 유익한 value 소중히 여기다 long-term 장기간의 depend on ~에 달려있다, 좌우되다 preference 선호(도) turn ~ over to... …에게 ~을 넘기다

139 대명사

해설 [Some ~. Others ~.] 구조이다. some은 일부 사람들을 의미하고, others는 (일부 사람들을 제외한 남은) 다른 사람들을 의미하므로 (B)가 정답이다.

140 동명사 자리

해설 『be committed to -ing (~에 전념하다, 헌신하다)』 구문으로, 빈칸 앞의 to는 전치사이다. 따라서 빈칸에는 명사 또는 동명사가 와야 하므로 (C) working이 정답이다.

141 문맥에 맞는 문장 고르기

(A) 우리의 웹 사이트를 통해서, 여러분은 많은 주식 정보를 다운로드 할 수 있습니다.
(B) 귀하께서 받으실 금융 조언의 수준은 귀하의 요구와 선호 사항에 달려 있습니다.
(C) 최근 재정 위기는 무리한 투자로 인해 초래되었습니다.
(D) 우리 전문가들과 함께, 여러분은 수익성 높은 사업에 투자할 수 있습니다.

해설 빈칸 앞 문장에서 '지침이 필요하면 우리가 도와줄 수 있다'고 하고, 빈칸 뒤에서 일부 도움을 받기 원하는지 대부분을 맡기고 싶은지 구체적인 요구와 선호사항의 예시가 나온다. 따라서 요구와 선호사항에 따라 조언의 수준이 결정된다고 하는 (B)가 가장 적절하다.

142 형용사 어휘

해설 (A) 건실한, 굳건한, (B) 생기 넘치는, (C) 사소한, (D) 부유한의 형용사 어휘들 중에서, decision(결정)을 수식하는 형용사로 '건실한/굳건한'이라는 뜻의 (A) sound가 적절하다.

[143-146] 편지

> 2월 20일
> 부모님, 보호자 그리고 학생 여러분께,
>
> 인디아나 지역의 학군은 곤충, 쥐, 그리고 잡초 관리를 위해 통합해충관리(IPM) 접근법을 사용합니다. 우리의 목표는 해충 관리를 위해 통합해충관리 접근법을 이용함으로써 모든 학생들을 살충제 노출로부터 보호하는 것입니다. 우리의 통합해충관리 접근법은 먹이와 물의 공급원을 없애고 그들의 은신처와 번식지를 제거함으로써 학교 건물과 토양을 이러한 해충들에게 적합하지 않은 서식지로 만드는 데 중점을 두고 있습니다.
> 우리는 청소와 유지 보수를 통해 이를 해 왔습니다. 우리는 존재하는 해충들을 탐지하기 위해서 정기적으로 학교 건물과 토양을 모니터하고 있습니다. 해충 발견은 "해충 문제"를 평가하고 그 문제를 처리하기 위해 적절한 해충 관리 기술을 결정하는 통합해충관리 매니저에게 보고됩니다.
> 기술들은 증진된 위생 관리, 보관 절차 수정, 입구 밀폐, 해충의 물리적 제거 등을 포함합니다. 학군은 매년 새로운 신고소를 마련할 것입니다. 질문이 있으시면, 통합해충관리 매니저 존 파팔에게 (724) 463-7591로 연락 주시기 바랍니다.
>
> 진심으로,
>
> 캐슬린 R. 켈리
> 학교 관리자

어휘 integrated 통합적인 rodent 설치류, 쥐 pesticide 살충제 exposure 노출 pest 해충 habitat 서식지 accomplish 성취하다 routinely 일상적으로, 정기적으로 evaluate 평가하다 sanitation 위생 시설 (관리) seal 봉합하다 physically 물리적으로 notification 통보, 알림 registry 등록소

143 동사 어휘

해설 (A) 제거하는, (B) 포함하는, (C) 평가하는, (D) 더하는의 동명사 어휘 중에서 '서식지를 제거함으로써'의 의미가 가장 자연스러우므로 (A)가 정답이다.

144 동사 어휘

해설 (A) 제어하다, (B) 감시하다, (C) 찾다, (D) 등록하다의 동사 어휘들 중에서, 해충을 탐지하기 위해 학교 건물과 토양을 '감시한다'는 의미의 (B)가 가장 적절하다.

145 동사 어휘

해설 빈칸 뒤 목적어가 한 개가 있으므로 3형식 타동사가 필요하다. (B)와 (C)는 각각 4형식 타동사, 1형식 자동사이므로 오답이다. (A) 처리하다, (D) 말하다 중에서, 문맥상 '문제(the problem)를 처리하기 위해' 해충 관리 기술을 결정한다는 것이 자연스러우므로 정답은 (A)이다.

146 문맥에 맞는 문장 고르기

(A) 다음 주, 우리는 위생 검사관에 대한 구인광고를 게시할 것입니다.
(B) 정부는 주립 학교들의 운동장 확장을 위한 기금을 지원했습니다.
(C) 학군은 매년 새로운 신고소를 마련할 것입니다.
(D) 우리는 여러분에게 위생 만족도에 관한 설문조사 양식을 작성하도록 요구했습니다.

해설 빈칸 앞 문장에서 해충 문제 해결을 위한 방법이 나와 있으므로, 이와 관련된 신고소 설치 내용이 (C)에 나오는 것이 가장 적절하다.

PART • 7

[147-148] 쿠폰

> **Doria's 카페**
> **여러분의 성원에 감사 드립니다.**
>
> 다음에 이곳에 방문할 때 계산대에서 이 쿠폰을 보여 주세요. 그렇게 하시면, 여러분은 버거, 샐러드, 또는 케이크 주문 시, 무료 음료를 받으실 수 있습니다. 월요일부터 금요일까지, 주중에 언제든지 쿠폰을 사용하세요.
> (* 주말에는 유효하지 않음)
>
> **저희는 여러분의 피드백을 기다립니다!**
>
> 더 많은 홍보 행사에 관해 알고 싶다면, 저희 웹 사이트 www.doriascafe.net에서 확인하실 수 있습니다. 온라인 설문조사 양식을 작성하면 자동으로 50달러 상당의 Doria's 카페 상품권 추첨에 응모됩니다. 여러분의 많은 참여 부탁 드립니다.

어휘 counter 계산대 beverage 음료 weekday 평일 fill out 작성하다 automatically 자동으로 draw 추첨

147 세부 사항

쿠폰 소지자에게는 어떤 종류의 무료 품목이 주어질 수 있는가?
(A) 음료
(B) 버거
(C) 샐러드
(D) 케이크

해설 두 번째 문장 "If you do so, you can get a free beverage with your other orders such as a burger, salad, or cake."에서 무료 음료(free beverage)가 주어지는 것을 알 수 있으므로 (A)가 정답이다.

148 세부 사항

고객들은 어떻게 상품권을 얻을 수 있는가?
(A) 설문지를 작성함으로써
(B) 이 쿠폰을 제시함으로써
(C) 행사에 참여함으로써
(D) 다른 고객들을 소개함으로써

해설 두 번째 문단 두 번째 줄 "Please fill out the online survey form, and you will be automatically entered for our drawing for a $50 Doria's Café Card."에서 온라인으로 설문지를 작성하면 상품권 추첨에 자동 응모된다고 했으므로 (A)가 정답이다.

[149-150] 문자 메시지

> 헬렌 클라이머 [오전 10:20]
> 레논 씨, 사무실에 계시나요? 지금 면접자들이 기다리고 있어요.
>
> 제레미 레논 [오전 10:21]
> 미안해요! Penn 고속도로가 공사 중이어서, 교통 체증이 약간 있어요. 저는 20분 정도 늦을 것 같아요. 괜찮으시다면, 저 없이 면접을 진행해 주시겠어요?
>
> 헬렌 클라이머 [오전 10:23]
> 물론이죠! 카렌 도슨 씨부터 먼저 면접할게요.
>
> 제레미 레논 [오전 10:25]
> 고마워요. 그녀는 온라인 광고에 경력이 있는 사람이에요.
>
> 헬렌 클라이머 [오전 10:26]
> 알겠어요. 우리 회사의 빠른 성장으로 인해 추가 마케팅 직원을 채용해야 한다니 믿기지 않네요.
>
> 제레미 레논 [오전 10:29]
> 맞아요! 곧 봅시다!

어휘 interviewee 면접자 highway 고속도로 under construction 공사 중인 congestion 혼잡 rapid 급격한, 빠른

149 세부 사항

레논 씨는 클라이머 씨가 무엇을 하기를 원하는가?
(A) 몇 가지 주문하기
(B) 입사 지원자와 이야기하기
(C) 웹상에 채용 공고 게시하기
(D) 다른 직원의 참여 부탁하기

해설 10시 21분 문자 메시지의 "can you take care of the interview without me?"에서 지원자와 면접을 먼저 시작할 것을 요구하므로 (B)가 정답이다.

150 의도 파악

오전 10시 29분에 레논 씨가 "맞아요"라고 쓴 의미는 무엇인가?
(A) 그는 10분 뒤에 도착할 것을 확신한다.
(B) 그는 회사에 공격적인 마케팅이 필요하다고 생각했다.
(C) 그는 도슨 씨를 이전에 만난 적이 있다.
(D) 그도 회사의 성장이 놀랍다.

해설 해당 문자 메시지 전에 온 10시 26분 메시지를 보면, 회사의 빠른 성장으로 추가 직원을 뽑는 게 믿기지 않는다, 즉 놀랍다는 반응을 보이고 있고, 이에 레논 씨가 맞다고 동의하고 있으므로 그 또한 회사 성장에 놀라워한다는 것을 알 수 있다. 따라서 정답은 (D)이다.

[151-152] 정보

Pacific Union 연구소의 지시 사항들
구매 요청서에 관하여

- 가능하다면, 구매할 물품들을 제품 코드 번호를 포함하여 설명하세요.
- 특정 브랜드가 필요하면, 양식의 "지정 상품"에 체크하고, 아래의 네모 칸에 그 이유를 작성하세요.
- 판매 업체의 이름과 웹 사이트 주소 또는 전화번호와 같은 연락처 정보를 기재하세요.
- 양식 하단에 서명하고 총무실에 제출하세요. 서명이 없으면, 주문이 처리될 수 없습니다.
- 당신의 팀의 각 분기별 예산 보고서를 신중하게 검토하세요.

* 구매 비용은 주문이 되자마자 당신의 팀 예산에서 공제될 것입니다.

어휘 require 요구하다 designated 지정된 vendor 판매 회사 general affairs office 총무실 process 처리하다 subtract 빼다, 공제하다

151 세부 사항

지시 사항에 따르면, 모든 구매 요청서에 반드시 제시되어야 하는 것은 어떤 정보인가?
(A) 판매자 연락처
(B) 구매자의 서명
(C) 구매 이유
(D) 제품 일련 번호

해설 네 번째 항목 "Sign the form at the bottom"에서 구매자의 서명을 요청하고 있고, "Without a signature, the order cannot be processed."에서 서명이 필수적임을 강조하고 있으므로 (B)가 정답이다.

152 추론/암시

총무부에 관해 암시되고 있는 것은?
(A) 약간의 가격 협상이 필요하다고 생각한다.
(B) 믿을 만한 판매 업체의 목록을 제시한다.
(C) 각 팀의 예산에서 비용을 공제할 수 있다.
(D) 직원들에게 보안 출입증을 발행한다.

해설 네 번째 항목의 "submit it to the general affairs office."에서 구매 요청서가 총무부에 제출된다는 것을 알 수 있고, 마지막 문장에서 "The expense of the purchase will be subtracted from your team budget as soon as the order has been placed." 구매 비용이 팀 예산에서 공제된다고 했으므로 (C)가 정답이다.

[153-155] 공지

공지

애리조나 Tucson 역사 박물관의 방문객 여러분 주목하세요.

6월 1일부터 8월 20일까지 'Arizona의 항공 역사'라 불리는 특별 전시회를 준비하고 있는 관계로, 헤리티지 전시실은 일시적으로 폐쇄됩니다. 저희는 이 혁신적이고 눈부신 전시회를 여러분이 경험하시길 바라는데, 이는 공군 장비와 사진, 비행기, 그리고 미국 국방부의 후원을 받은 기술적인 자원들을 특별히 포함합니다. 특히, 여러분은 이전의 공군 장교였던 맥클러스터 씨와 당시 그의 전우들이었던 데인 씨와 콘도르 씨가 함께 진행하는 국방 체계의 역사적 가치에 관한 강연을 포함하여 세계 2차 대전 동안 사용된 다양한 군용장비들을 보실 수 있습니다. 게다가, 미국의 미사일 방어 체계를 감독하는 책임지며 이 분야의 권위로 널리 존경 받는 라이스 씨에 의해 신기술들이 소개될 것입니다. 이 행사에 관해 보다 세부적인 정보가 필요하시면, 우리 웹 사이트 www.tucsonmuseum.org로 접속하거나, 박물관 입구에 있는 특별 안내 책자를 가져가세요.

어휘 temporarily 임시로 organize 준비하다, 조직하다 exhibit 전시(회) brilliant 눈부신 feature ~을 특별히 포함하다 Air Force 공군 Department of Defense 국방부 especially 특히 hardware 장비 lecture 강연 value 가치 national defense 국방 fellow soldier 전우 supervise 감독하다 regard 존경하다, 간주하다 authority 권위, 권위자 access 접근하다, 접속하다

153 추론/암시

박물관에 관하여 암시되는 것은?
(A) 보안 시스템으로 인정받고 있다.
(B) 다음 전시회를 홍보하고 있다.
(C) 수리 계획으로 폐쇄될 것이다.
(D) 항상 군대의 역사적 특징들을 보여준다.

해설 첫 문장의 "because we are organizing a special exhibit called "Arizona Aviation History" there from June 1 to August 20."와 두 번째 문장의 "We would like you to experience this innovative and brilliant exhibit."을 볼 때, 다음 특별 전시회 참여를 독려하며 이를 홍보하고 있음을 알 수 있다. 따라서 정답은 (B)이다.

154 세부 사항

맥클러스터 씨는 누구인가?
(A) 퇴역 군인
(B) 기자
(C) 예술 비평가
(D) 박물관 관장

해설 지문 중간의 "Mr. McCluster, a former Air Force General, with his fellow soldiers, Mr. Dane and Mr. Condor, at that time."에서 맥클러스터 씨가 이전에 공군 장교였음을 알 수 있으므로 퇴역 군인을 의미하는 (A) veteran 이 정답이다.

155 세부 사항

공지문에 따르면, 대중에게 존경 받는 사람은 누구인가?
(A) 콘도르 씨
(B) 맥클러스터 씨
(C) 라이스 씨
(D) 데인 씨

해설 후반부의 "Ms. Rice, who is responsible for supervising the state's missile defense system and is widely regarded due to her authority in this field." 부분을 보면, 라이스 씨가 국방 분야에서의 권위로 존경을 받는다고 언급하고 있으므로 (C)가 정답이다.

[156-157] 양식

Pennsylvania Appalachian 연구소
보안 통행권 요청서

1. 요청 이유
   [ ] 통행권 신규 발급   [V] 통행권 분실   [ ] 통행권 변경

2. 직원 정보
   이름: <u>아놀드 린더만</u>
   부서: <u>지질학</u>
   직위: <u>수석 연구원</u>
   소재지: <u>Stapleton Hall</u>
   고용 형태: [V] 정규직   [ ] 임시직

3. 보안 통행권을 분실한 경우, 그것이 어떻게 발생했는지 설명하세요 (날짜와 시간 요함)
   <u>저는 5월 10일 금요일 오후 4시쯤 Acher 강당에서 총회에 참석했을 때 제 보안 통행권을 분실했습니다. 사무실에서 나와 저녁 7시쯤 주차장에 도착했을 때 저는 통행권을 분실했다는 것을 알았습니다. 강당으로 돌아갔지만, 문이 잠겨 있었습니다. 아침에 출근하여 다시 강당에 들러서 통행권을 샅샅이 찾아봤음에도 불구하고 그것을</u>

<u>찾을 수 없습니다. 그래서 저는 그것을 주차장으로 가는 길이나 강당 근처에서 잃어버린 것으로 추정합니다.</u>

4. 보안 통행권 소지자 확인
   제공된 정보는 전적으로 사실이며 정확하다는 것을 인정하는 바입니다. 제 과실일 경우 통행권 재발급에 대한 위약금 100달러를 지불해야 한다는 것을 이해합니다.

   * 일주일 내로 분실된 통행권이 발견될 경우 해당 금액이 환불될 것입니다.

   통행권 소지자 서명: <u>*아놀드 린더만*</u>   날짜: <u>5월 11일</u>

5. 공무에만 사용
   승인: 캐서린 존스
   신규 통행권 발행일: <u>5월 11일</u>

어휘 lab 실험실   security pass 보안 통행권   geology 지질학   participate in ~에 참석하다   general conference 총회   auditorium 강당   realize 인식하다   missing 없어진, 잃어버린   stop by 들르다   thoroughly 철저히, 샅샅이   assume 추정하다, 가정하다   acknowledge 인정하다   penalty 벌금, 위약금   reissue 재발행하다   in the event that ~할 경우에

156 추론/암시

린더만 씨에 대해 암시된 것은?
(A) 그는 퇴근 후에 동료와 만났다.
(B) 그는 누군가에게 강당을 열어 달라고 요청했다.
(C) 그는 저녁에 Stapleton Hall을 떠났다.
(D) 그는 최근에 실험실에서의 일을 시작했다.

해설 직원 정보를 통해 린더만 씨가 Stapleton Hall에서 근무하는 연구원임을 알 수 있고, 세 번째 항목의 "When I left my office and arrived at the parking lot around 7 P.M.,"에서 그가 저녁 7시에 Stapleton Hall을 떠났다는 것을 알 수 있다. 따라서 (C)가 정답이다.

157 Not/True 확인

5월 11일에 일어나지 않은 일은 무엇인가?
(A) 통행권을 위해 돈이 지불되었다.
(B) 잃어버린 통행권이 발견되었다.
(C) 서류가 제출되었다.
(D) 새로운 통행권의 효력이 발생했다

해설 "Pass holder signature: Arnold Linderman / Date: May 11"에서 통행권 소지자의 서명이 5월 11일에 되어 있으므로 해당 날짜에 (C) 문서가 제출되었음을 알 수 있고, "I understand that I must pay a penalty of $100 for reissuing the replacement pass in case of it being my fault."를 통해 (A) 신청자의 과실로 돈이 지불되었음을 알 수 있다. 또한, 5번 항목에서 신규 통행권의 발행일이 5월 11일이라고 되어 있으므로 (D) 신규 통행권이 그날에 즉시 효력을 발휘한다는 것을 알 수 있다. 따라서 정답은 (B)이다.

[158-160] 이메일

수신: j_foster@zmobile.co.uk
발신: t_svenson@wef.org.uk
제목: 등록 및 접수
날짜: 8월 20일

포스터 씨에게,

이 이메일은 올해 영국에서의 세계경제포럼(WEF)에 대한 당신의 지불과 양식을 포함한 등록 상태를 확인했음을 확정하기 위한 것입니다. 우리는 당신의 정기적인 참여를 진심으로 환영합니다.

저는 당신에게서 알고자 하는 사항이 하나 더 있습니다. 저희가 당신의 양식을 확인했을 때, 당신이 포럼 저녁식사의 식단 선택에 관한 세부 사항을 포함하지 않은 것을 발견했습니다. 저는 레스토랑의 관리 책임자에게 해당 정보를 제공해야 합니다. 그렇게 함으로써, 조리팀이 행사 참가자들의 식사 준비를 시작할 수 있습니다. 육류나 해산물 선택 외에도, 호텔 레스토랑은 채식주의자를 위한 선택권 또한 제공합니다. 이러한 선택권에 대한 추가 정보는 우리 웹 사이트 www.wef.org/uk2018에 게시되어 있습니다. 가능한 한 빨리 이 이메일에 답장을 주셔서 저에게 당신의 식단 선택을 알려주시겠어요?

당신의 등록 지불액에 이 저녁식사 금액이 포함되어 있음을 알아 두시기 바랍니다. 추가 비용은 부과되지 않을 것입니다.

행운을 빌며,

톰 스벤슨
세계경제포럼-영국

어휘 confirm 확정하다 registration 등록 status 상태
sincerely 진심으로 attendance 참석, 출석
specification 세부사항 dietary 식단의 meal 식사
option 선택(권) vegetarian 채식주의자 post 게시하다

158 추론/암시

스벤슨 씨는 누구일 것 같은가?
(A) 식당 관리자
(B) 컨퍼런스 관계자
(C) 호텔 요리사
(D) 웹 마스터

해설 스벤슨 씨가 이메일의 발신자이고, 두 번째 문단의 둘째 줄 "I should provide that information to the restaurant chief manager."를 보면 스벤슨 씨가 행사 참가자들의 식단 정보를 레스토랑 관리자에게 알리는 일을 담당하고 있음을 알 수 있다. 따라서 (B) 컨퍼런스 관계자임을 유추할 수 있다.

159 세부 사항

포스터 씨는 무엇을 하도록 요구 받는가?
(A) 양식을 작성한다
(B) 예약을 확인한다
(C) 좌석을 선택한다
(D) 음식 선택을 명시한다

해설 후반부의 "Could you reply to this e-mail as soon as possible and let me know about your meal choice?" 에서 식단 선택을 알려달라고 하고 있으므로 (D)가 정답이다.

160 문장 삽입

표시된 [1], [2], [3], [4]의 위치들 중 다음 문장이 가장 잘 어울리는 곳은?
"저는 당신에게서 알고자 하는 사항이 하나 더 있습니다."
(A) [1]
(B) [2]
(C) [3]
(D) [4]

해설 발신자가 알고자 하는 것이 있다고 했으므로 그 다음에는 그 사항에 대해 언급하는 문장이 나올 것이다. [2]번 뒤의 "you did not include specifications about your dietary choice for the forum dinner."에서 식단 선택에 대한 항목을 포함하지 않았다며 이에 대한 정보를 요구하고 있으므로 정답은 (B)이다.

[161-163] 기사

Strousberg (4월 5일) — Master Electronics 사는 지난주에 Superb Technology 사를 성공적으로 인수했다고 발표했습니다. Master Electronics 사가 Strousberg에 위치한 Superb 공장의 재건축을 곧 시작한다는 것은 그 지역 주민들에게 매우 중요합니다.

Superb 지역 공장은 지역 사회에 많은 일자리를 제공하면서 대량 생산을 처리하기 위해 운영되었습니다. 그러나 일 년 전 그들의 예산 관련 문제들이 발생했고, 지역 공장은 작업을 축소하기 시작했습니다. Master 사의 대변인 킴 이사벨은 어제 그 시설의 수리 프로젝트가 몇 달 내로 완료될 것이며, 그때 새로운 고용 절차가 시작될 것이라고 말했습니다.

"우리의 임무는 10월까지 그 시설의 운영과 직원 채용을 완전히 정상화하는 것입니다."라고 이사벨은 말했습니다. "아마도 그 시설은 12월까지 전면 가동될 것입니다."라고 그녀는 덧붙였습니다.

게다가, 그곳에서는 Superb 사의 가장 인기 있는 물품들을 그들의 원래 브랜드로 제조할 것이며, Master 사의 새로 개발된 개인 컴퓨터용 SSD를 생산할 것입니다.

Master Electronics 사는 지난 몇 년간의 노력으로 3년 전 미국의 전자산업 분야에서 선도 기업이 되었습니다. 본사는 현재 Pittsburgh 시에 위치해 있습니다.

어휘 successfully 성공적으로 purchase 구입하다
renovation 재건축, 수리 plant 공장 operate 운영하다, 가동하다 massive 대량의 community 공동체, 지역 사회
deputy 대변인, 대리인 normalize 정상화하다 at full capacity 전면으로, 완전히 leading 선두의 preceding 이전의

161 주제/목적

기사문의 목적은 무엇인가?
(A) 새로운 사업 개시를 발표하기 위해
(B) 전자 산업의 시장 동향을 설명하기 위해
(C) 공장이 폐쇄된 이유를 설명하기 위해
(D) 인수 합병에 대한 정보를 제공하기 위해

해설 첫 문장 "Master Electronics Co. announced that it successfully purchased Superb Technology last week."에서 인수했다(purchased)는 키워드를 통해 기사가 회사의 인수(합병)에 대해 설명하고 있음을 알 수 있다. 따라서 (D)가 정답이다.

162 세부 사항

이사벨 씨에 따르면, 10월에 무슨 일이 일어날 것인가?
(A) 공장이 완전히 무너질 것이다.
(B) 회사가 더 많은 직원을 고용할 것이다.
(C) 새로운 품목이 출시될 것이다.
(D) 협상이 완료될 것이다.

해설 세 번째 문단의 첫 문장 "Our mission is to normalize the facility's operation and staffing completely by October," said Isabel."에서 10월까지 시설 운영과 직원 채용을 정상화하는 것이 임무라고 언급하고 있으므로 (B)가 정답이다.

163 Not/True 확인

Master Electronics 사에 관해 명시된 것은?
(A) 컴퓨터 관련 저장 장치를 생산할 것이다.
(B) Pittsburgh로 이전할 것이다.
(C) Strousberg에 더 많은 지점이 있다.
(D) 더 큰 회사에 의해 인수되었다.

해설 네 번째 문단의 "In addition, it will manufacture Superb's most popular items under its original brand and produce Master's newly developed Solid State Drive(SSD) for personal computers there."에서 Master 사에서 컴퓨터 저장 드라이브(SSD)를 생산하는 것을 알 수 있으므로 (A)가 가장 적절하다.

[164-167] 웹 페이지

◀ ▶ https://www.appletonartcenter.net

Appleton 예술 센터

Florida Appleton 예술 센터의 봄

Appleton 예술 센터를 찾아 주신 모든 분들을 환영합니다. 저희의 연장된 봄 시즌 운영 시간을 확인하시고, 다양한 강연을 경험하고 이전에 어디에서도 듣지 못했던 특별한 것들을 배우세요.

예술 센터 운영 시간

화요일부터 토요일까지, 오전 9시 ~ 오후 6시
일요일, 오후 12시 ~ 오후 7시 30분
월요일 휴무

봄 전시회

· 브루노 제임스: 19세기 미국의 풍경화
· 루이스 티파니: 영화, 화폭, 그리고 종이에 대한 감명
· 휴 맥킨: 예술 기계

센터 강연

3월 28일 오후 7시
North Carolina에 위치한 Slippery Rock 박물관의 큐레이터 베스 한센 씨가 이번 봄 내내 사진들이 전시되는 유명한 사진작가 브루노 제임스의 전기와 경력에 대해 이야기하려고 방문할 것입니다.

4월 10일 오후 3시
Appleton의 큐레이터인 릴리 사보바 씨는 그녀의 경험과 기법에 대한 가벼운 논의를 통해 우리 주의 유명한 예술가인 루이스 티파니 씨와 함께할 것입니다. 그 다음에 사보바 씨는 센터 사무실을 돌면서 우리 센터를 소개할 것입니다.

5월 17일 오후 3시
Northern Florida 대학 부교수인 켄 하이랜드 씨는 Appleton 예술 센터의 다양한 예술 기계에 관련된 추가적인 정보에 대해 이야기할 것이고, 이것은 우리 메인 갤러리에서 예술 기법 발전의 역사를 보여줄 것입니다.

어휘 extended 연장된 operation hours 운영 시간 experience 경험하다 talk 강연, 회담 landscape 조경 impression 감명, 인상 canvas 화폭 biography 전기 display 전시 join 합류하다, 함께 하다 give a tour 구경을 시켜 주다 associate professor 부교수

164 Not/True 확인

Appleton 예술 센터에 대해서 명시된 것은?
(A) 주 정부에 의해 운영된다.
(B) 지역 예술가들의 작품만 전시한다.
(C) 많은 유명 화가들을 두고 있다.
(D) 일요일에는 더 늦게까지 문을 연다.

해설 예술 센터 운영 시간(Art Center Hours)을 보면 "Tuesday through Saturday, 9:00 A.M. - 6:00 P.M. / Sunday, 12:00 P.M. - 7:30 P.M."일요일에는 평소보다 더 늦게까지 문을 연다는 것을 알 수 있으므로 (D)가 정답이다.

165 Not/True 확인

Appleton 센터의 전시회 주제로 언급되지 않은 것은?
(A) 연극을 위한 무대 디자인
(B) 19세기 미국의 그림
(C) 영화와 그림에 대한 느낌
(D) 예술을 위한 장비와 기법

해설 Spring Exhibitions 부분을 보면 Bruno James: 19th Century - American Landscapes(19세기 미국의 풍경화) / Louis Tiffany: Impressions on Film, Canvas, and Paper(영화, 화폭, 그리고 종이에 대한 감명) / Hugh McKean: The Art Machine(예술 기계)가 나와 있으므로 언급되지 않은 (A)가 정답이다.

166 세부 사항

티파니 씨는 누구인가?
(A) 관광 가이드
(B) 센터 큐레이터
(C) 대학 강사
(D) 지역 예술가

해설 4월 10일 강연 부분의 "Appleton's curator, Lily Savova, will join Louis Tiffany, famous artist in our state,"에서 티파니 씨가 주의 유명한 예술가라고 언급되어 있으므로 (D) 가 정답이다.

167 세부 사항

5월에 있는 논의는 주로 무엇에 관한 것인가?
(A) 예술 기법의 역사
(B) 예술가들의 창의성
(C) 지역 예술가들의 삶
(D) 미국의 풍경 변화

해설 5월 17일 강연 부분의 "Ken Hyland, associate professor of Northern Florida College, will talk about additional information regarding the Appleton Art Center's variety of art machines,"에서 예술 기계가 해당 강연 의 주된 소재임을 알 수 있고, "can show history of art technique development"에서 이것이 예술 기법 발전의 역 사를 보여준다고 언급하고 있으므로 (A)가 정답이다.

[168-171] 이메일

수신 반다르 살레; 마시아타 밤바; 치아키 첸; 산드라 바지즈
발신 인다 카레라
날짜 3월 20일
제목 할당 업무
첨부 position_list.doc; compensation_benefits_info.doc; contact_info.doc

여러분 모두에게,

6월 10일 목요일에 뉴델리에서 지점을 개점하는 우리의 자회사 Giant Logistics 사와 관련된 이 프로젝트에 자원해 주신 여러분의 지원에 진심으로 감사드립니다. 지금부터, 우리는 그 날짜 전까지 해야 할 일들이 많습니다. 제가 지난 회의에서 설명 드렸듯이, 새로운 지점에 50 개의 새로운 일자리들이 채워져야 합니다. 여러분은 다음 업무들을 담당하는데, 이는 공지된 마감 기간까지 반드시 완료되어야 합니다.

반다르 살레: 4월 20일까지 각 직책에 대한 자격 요건과 업무 목록 에 관한 최종안을 작성하세요. (첨부된 직책 목록 확인)
마시아타 밤바: 제공될 임금과 복지 혜택에 관한 데이터 표를 만드세 요. (첨부파일 활용)
치아키 첸: 주내의 모든 취업알선 회사에 공석에 관해 공지하세요. (첨부된 연락처 활용)
반다르 살레: 우리 회사 웹 사이트에 공지문과 발표문을 게시하세요. (정보부의 하지즈 씨에게 이메일로 원고 전달)
산드라 바지즈: 사무실 개업과 구인 자리를 알리기 위한 광고물과 그 매체를 제안하세요. (4월 15일까지 사무엘 존스 씨에 게 제안서 제출)

우리는 4월 10일에 이 업무들에 관한 여러분의 진행 상태를 검토하고 논의하기 위해 모일 것입니다. 질문 있으시거나, 문제가 생기면 주저 말고 저에게 연락주세요.

인다 카레라
인사 담당자

어휘 appreciate 고마워하다 volunteer 자원하다 related 관련된 subsidiary 자회사 in charge of ~을 담당하는 task 업무 make out 작성하다 final draft 최종안 qualification 자격 요건 responsibility 책임, 업무 wage 임금, 급여 benefits package 복지 혜택 agency 중개소, 대리점 come up with ~을 생각해내다, 제안하다 vacancy 빈자리, 공석 assignment 임무, 업무

168 세부 사항

직무 설명에 대한 마감은 언제인가?
(A) 4월 10일
(B) 4월 15일
(C) 4월 20일
(D) 6월 10일

해설 반다르 살레의 업무에서 "Make out a final draft about the list of qualifications and responsibilities for each position by April 20." 자격 요건 및 업무 목록에 관한 최종 안, 즉 직무 설명의 마감일이 4월 20일이라고 언급되었으므 로, 정답은 (C)이다.

169 Not/True 확인

첨부 파일을 사용할 필요가 없는 사람은 누구인가?
(A) 반다르 살레
(B) 마시아타 밤바
(C) 치아키 첸
(D) 산드라 바지즈

해설 Bandar Saleh는 "See attached the list of positions", Massiata Bamba는 "Using attached file", 치아키 첸은 "Using attached contact information"을 통해 첨부 파 일을 사용하라고 언급되었지만, 산드라 바지즈는 "Submit your proposals to Samuel Jones by June 11" 제출 지 령만 있으므로 (D)가 정답이다.

170 세부 사항

카레라 씨는 수신자들에게 다음 회의 전까지 무엇을 하도록 요구하였는가?
(A) 그녀에게 언제든지 문제에 관해 묻기
(B) 본사에 직접 방문하기
(C) 서로 긴밀하게 협력하기
(D) 자원봉사 업무 신청하기

해설 마지막 문장 "If you have any questions, or whenever you face some problems, do not hesitate to contact me."에서 질문이나 문제가 있으면 주저하지 말고 연락하라고 말하고 있으므로 (A)가 정답이다.

171 문장 삽입

표시된 [1], [2], [3], [4]의 위치들 중에서 다음 문장이 가장 잘 어울리는 곳은?

"지금부터, 우리는 그 날짜 전까지 해야 할 일들이 많습니다."

(A) [1]
(B) [2]
(C) [3]
(D) [4]

해설 주어진 문장에서 that date가 있는 것으로 보아 특정 날짜가 이전에 언급되어야 하며, '할 일이 많다'고 한 후, 그 뒤에 업무가 나열된다는 것이 자연스럽다. 업무에 관한 내용을 처음 언급한 것은 "지난 회의(last meeting)에서 50개의 새로운 일자리를 채워야 한다"고 이야기하는 부분이므로 그 앞 문장에 해당하는 (A) [1]이 정답이다.

[172-175] 온라인 채팅

> **앨런 슈니처 [오전 11:15]**
> 여러분 좋은 아침입니다. 금요일에 있을 우리의 다음 팀 미팅에 관해서 생각해 봤으면 합니다. 현재로서는 판매 실적이 좋지 않습니다. 우리는 새로운 방향을 고려해야 해요.
>
> **로이드 알리사 [오전 11:16]**
> 저희가 무엇을 준비하면 되죠?
>
> **앨런 슈니처 [오전 11:17]**
> 기능성 화장품에 대한 수요가 급격히 줄어서, 제 생각에는 현재 시장 경향을 조사해야 할 것 같아요.
>
> **닉 덴튼 [오전 11:18]**
> 그렇다면, 우리는 먼저 고객들을 연령, 성별, 작업 환경 등과 같은 몇 개의 범주로 나눠야겠군요.
>
> **달튼 레베카 [오전 11:20]**
> 저는 이것이 우리가 신제품들을 개발하고 출시하는 데 매우 중요하다고 생각해요. 그런데, 우리는 먼저 소비자가 현재 제품들을 외면한 이유부터 알아야 해요.
>
> **로이드 알리사 [오전 11:21]**
> 전적으로 동의해요. 신제품 개발을 위해선 시장 조사 전에 원인 분석을 마쳐야 해요.
>
> **앨런 슈니처 [오전 11:22]**
> 모두 좋은 생각이에요. 회의에서, 저는 여러분의 생각을 듣고 싶어요. 제가 여러분의 이메일 주소로 보낸 현재 데이터와 잠재적인 정보를 활용해서 각자 발표 준비를 시작하세요. 또한, 저는 수요 감소에 대한 분석 데이터 정보가 필요합니다.
>
> **달튼 레베카 [오전 11:23]**
> 네. 제가 그것을 처리할게요.
>
> **앨런 슈니처 [오전 11:24]**
> 질문 있으면 알려줘요. 회의 지침에 대한 다른 첨부파일을 이메일로 보낼게요.

어휘 sales figure 판매 수치 prepare for ~을 준비하다 functional 기능의, 기능적인 cosmetics 화장품 sharply 급격히 divide 나누다 category 범주 gender 성별 release 출시하다 turn one's back on ~에 등을 돌리다 take advantage of ~을 활용하다, 이용하다 potential 잠재적인

172 의도 파악

오전 11시 15분에 슈니처 씨가 "우리는 새로운 방향을 고려해야 해요"라고 쓴 의도는 무엇인가?

(A) 그 회사는 사무실을 다른 장소로 이전할 필요가 있다.
(B) 그 회사는 본사에서 총회를 개최할 예정이다.
(C) 그 회사는 그들의 현재 사업을 다른 분야로 변경하는 데 집중해야 한다.
(D) 그 회사는 매출을 증진시킬 전략을 세워야 한다.

해설 11시 15분 메시지에서 "Sales figures are not good for now. We should consider moving in a new direction." 판매 실적이 좋지 않아 새로운 방향을 고려해야 한다고 말한 뒤, 원인 분석, 판매 증대를 위한 방안들과 절차를 논의하는 것으로 보아 (D)가 정답임을 알 수 있다.

173 추론/암시

그들은 어떤 업종에서 일하고 있는가?

(A) 데이터 분석 사무소
(B) 화장품 회사
(C) 연구소
(D) 이사업체

해설 11시 17분 메시지를 보면 "Because the demand for functional cosmetics is sharply decreasing, we need to research the current market trend, I think." 기능성 화장품 수요 급감으로 인해 시장 경향을 조사해야 한다는 것은 그들이 화장품 회사에서 일하고 있음을 유추할 수 있으므로 정답은 (B)이다.

174 세부 사항

레베카 씨가 다음에 할 일은 무엇인가?

(A) 그녀는 출력물을 나눠줄 것이다.
(B) 그녀는 데이터를 분석할 것이다.
(C) 그녀는 대표이사에게 이메일을 보낼 것이다.
(D) 그녀는 제안서를 준비할 것이다.

해설 11시 22분 메시지 "In addition, I will need the information about the analysis data for the reduced demand."에서 데이터 분석의 필요가 언급되자, 다음 레베카 씨의 메시지 "OK. I will handle that."에서 본인이 처리하겠다고 했으므로 정답은 (B)이다.

175 세부 사항

슈니처 씨는 팀원들에게 무엇을 줄 것인가?

(A) 다음 회의를 위한 지시 사항
(B) 최근 구매와 주문 목록

(C) 제품 개선을 위한 세부 계획
(D) 신입 사원 고용을 위한 제안

> **해설** 마지막 메시지 "Let me know if you have any questions. I'll send another attached file for our meeting guidelines by e-mail."를 보면, 슈니처 씨가 회의 지침 (meeting guidelines)을 보내겠다고 했으므로 이와 관련된 (A)가 정답이다.

[176-180] 이메일 & 이메일

> 수신: 데이비드 로빈슨 <d.robinson@zetamai.com>
> 발신: AUTOINSU <autoservice@autoinsu.com>
> 날짜: 2024년 4월 26일
> 제목: 확인
>
> 이 이메일은 다음의 확인 번호를 참조합니다: 1GHAK-3QPZ-3K4LC
> **AUTOINSU 손해 보험사**
>
> 로빈슨 씨에게,
>
> AUTOINSU의 온라인 서비스를 이용해 주셔서 감사드립니다. 저희는 귀하께서 요청하신 정책 변경사항들을 처리했습니다. 귀하의 보험료에는 변경이 없을 것입니다. 업데이트된 정책 정보는 24시간 이내에 온라인에서 확인하실 수 있습니다. 귀하는 www.autoInsu.com/mypolicy에서 AUTOINSU 보험 가입자 서비스센터에 로그인해서 변경사항들을 보실 수 있습니다.
> 귀하가 저희 Paperless Policy(종이를 쓰지 않는 정책) 서비스에 등록하시면, 온라인에서 업데이트된 정책 문서를 이용할 수 있을 때 이메일로 받게 될 것입니다.
> 도움이 필요하시면, 이 이메일에 답장 보내 주세요. 저희는 일주일 내내 하루 24시간 이용 가능합니다.
> 저희의 적절한 대응을 위해, 이 메시지에 답변하실 때 제목 영역에 있는 귀하의 확인 번호나 회신 주소를 변경하지 마세요.
> 귀하에게 훌륭한 서비스를 제공하는 것이 저희의 목표입니다. 귀하의 거래와 충성에 감사 드리며, 앞으로 오랫동안 귀하의 요구에 맞는 서비스를 제공하기를 기대합니다.
>
> 진심으로,
>
> 존 월러
>
> ――――――――――――
> AUTOINSU고객 서비스
> 1-800-813-3340
> ――――――――――――
>
> [주의사항]
> 귀하의 개인 정보를 보호하기 위해, 운전면허증 번호, 사회보장번호, 출생일, 또는 주소 세부사항과 같은 개인정보는 이메일 안에 포함하지 마세요. 이러한 정보를 저희에게 제공해야 한다면, 저희 웹 사이트에 로그인해서 My Resource Center 탭 밑에 있는 Contact Us 를 클릭하세요. 원하시면, 차량 보험 정책을 위해 1-800-861-8380 으로, 원동기(오토바이) 정책을 위해 1-800-442-9253으로 전화하셔도 됩니다.

> 수신: AUTOINSU <autoservice@autoinsu.com>
> 발신: 데이비드 로빈슨 <d.robinson@zetamai.com>
> 날짜: 2024년 4월 26일
> 제목: 회신: 확인
>
> 관계자분들께,
>
> 귀하가 저에게 보내주신 제 온라인 정보에 무언가를 요청하기 위해 이 글을 씁니다. 대부분의 정책과 내용들이 제대로 업데이트되었지만, 주소 정보가 잘못되었습니다. 이전에 거기 직원과의 라이브채팅 서비스를 통해 요청했듯이, 저는 최근에 이전 주소지 근처의 다른 곳으로 이사했습니다. 당신이 제 새 주소, 1038 Courtland Road, Indiana, PA로 변경해 주길 바랍니다. 저는 제 신분증 재발급을 위해 거주 증명서로 확인서를 제출해야 하므로, 저에게 변경사항을 가능한 한 빨리 알려 주세요.
>
> 그럼 이만,
>
> 데이비드 로빈슨

> **어휘** casualty insurance 손해 보험 process 처리하다
> premium 보험료 policyholder 보험계약자 enroll in
> ~에 등록하다 privacy 사생활 previous 이전의
> certificate 증명서 reissue 재발행하다 identification
> 신분(증)

176 주제/목적

첫 번째 이메일의 목적은 무엇인가?
(A) 서비스 홍보 코드를 제공하기 위해
(B) 회사의 새로운 서비스를 광고하기 위해
(C) 고객 정책 업데이트를 확인하기 위해
(D) 온라인 서비스 접속 방법을 설명하기 위해

> **해설** 제목과 도입부의 "We processed the policy changes you requested."를 통해 이 이메일은 고객의 정책 업데이트를 확인하기 위한 것임을 알 수 있으므로 (C)가 정답이다.

177 Not/True 확인

AUTOINSU의 온라인 서비스에 관하여 언급되지 않은 것은?
(A) 고객들은 직원들의 도움을 받을 수 있다.
(B) 고객들의 상태를 온라인으로 확인할 수 있다.
(C) 고객들은 그들의 정보를 변경할 수 있다.
(D) 고객들은 할인을 받을 수 있다.

> **해설** (A)는 "If you need assistance, please reply to this e-mail.", (B)는 "your updated policy information will be available online", (C)는 "We processed the policy changes you requested."을 통해 확인할 수 있지만, 할인 정책은 언급되지 않았으므로 (D)가 정답이다.

178 주제/목적

왜 로빈슨 씨는 두 번째 이메일을 보냈는가?
(A) 그의 주소 변경을 요청하려고
(B) 홍보 코드를 받으려고
(C) 그의 새로운 신분증을 신청하려고
(D) 온라인 채팅 프로그램을 설치하려고

해설 다섯 번째 줄의 "I would like you to change to my new address"을 통해 주소 변경을 요청하고자 함을 알 수 있으므로 (A)가 정답이다.

179 Not/True 확인

로빈슨 씨에 대해 명시된 것은?
(A) 그는 그의 서비스 업그레이드를 원한다.
(B) 그는 다른 사무실로 이전했다.
(C) 그는 온라인으로 직원과 전에 이야기했다.
(D) 그는 그의 확인 번호를 잊어버렸다.

해설 두 번째 이메일의 세 번째 문장 "As I requested before through the live-chat service with your staff, ~"을 통해, 라이브 채팅 서비스로 직원과 이전에 이야기를 나누었음을 알 수 있다. 따라서 (C)가 정답이다.

180 세부 사항 (연계)

두 번째 이메일에서, 어떤 정보가 문제가 될 수 있는가?
(A) 집 주소
(B) 확인 번호
(C) 이메일 주소
(D) 정책 정보

해설 첫 번째 이메일 "주의(NOTE)" 부분에 "In order to protect your privacy, please do not include personal information such as your driver's license number, social security number, date of birth, or address details in your e-mail." 개인 정보 보호의 일환으로 개인 정보 관련 내용을 포함시키지 말라고 했는데 두 번째 이메일에서 주소 변경을 요청하면서, "I would like you to change to my new address,1038 Courtland Road, Indiana, PA." 라고 언급했으므로 문제의 소지가 있을 수 있다. 따라서 정답은 (A)이다.

[181-185] 광고 & 이메일

The Grand Cascade Hotel & Conference Center

예약하세요!
The Grand Cascade Hotel & Conference Center의 넓고 다양한 회의실들이 이용 가능합니다.
4가지 유형의 특실 중에서 선택하세요.

회의실	좌석	특징 및 장비	비용
Tahoma Room	임원용 회전 의자 20개	대형 회의 테이블	200 파운드
Edu Room	컴퓨터 작업 공간 15개	무료 인터넷 접속, 시연을 위한 일반 소프트웨어 설치	230 파운드
Tech Room	컴퓨터 작업 공간 30개	칠판, 프로젝터, 무료 인터넷 접속, 시연을 위한 일반 소프트웨어 설치	250 파운드
Innobiz Room	100~150명을 위한 강당 좌석	연단, 마이크, 프로젝터, 스크린, 컴퓨터	300 파운드

The Grand Cascade Hotel & Conference Center의 각 회의실은 화이트보드와 마커 펜, 종이, 그리고 펜이 구비되어 있습니다.

** 가격은 (오전/오후) 최대 5시간 사용 가격이고 최소 일주일 전에 회의실을 예약하고 비용을 지불해야 합니다.
** 세션당 50파운드로, 우리의 IT 지원 직원들이 컴퓨터가 구비된 세 개의 회의실 중 한 곳에 있을 것입니다. 회의 대표자는 사전에 소프트웨어와 장비 사용에 관한 세부 지시사항을 받을 수 있습니다. 우리 전문가 중 한 명으로부터 기술적인 도움을 받고자 하시면, 그들은 회의 동안 함께 할 것입니다. 전문가들은 컴퓨터 관련 산업에서 10년 이상의 경력을 가지고 있습니다.
이 서비스를 예약하시려면 871-222-0047로 전화주세요.

수신: maxdavis@manchesteruniv.co.uk
발신: lindawood@grandcascade.co.uk
날짜: 9월 10일
제목: 회의실

데이비스 씨에게,

저는 230파운드에 예약된 당신의 예약 번호 1284를 확인하기 위해 이 이메일을 작성합니다. 당신이 이 예약을 하셨을 때, 저는 9월 18일에 Edu Room에서 카펫 청소 서비스가 예정되어 있다는 것을 알지 못했습니다. 제가 기억하기로는, 당신은 이 날짜에만 회의가 가능합니다. 그래서, 저는 당신에게 요금 변경 없이 Tech Room을 대신 제공하고자 합니다. 게다가, 우리 전문가의 도움이 필요하시면, 한 분을 원래 가격의 절반인 25파운드에 제공할 수 있습니다. 우리 전문가인 코스타 씨는 당신의 그룹을 도와주게 되어 기쁠 것입니다.

추가 절차를 논의하시려면 저에게 871-222-1017로 편하게 연락주세요.

진심으로,

린다 우드
호텔 지배인

어휘 type 유형 workstation 작업대, 작업상 demonstration 시연 podium 지휘대, 연단 be equipped with ~이 구비되다 expert 전문가 aware 알고 있는 procedure 절차

181 Not/True 확인

광고에서, 회의실에 관하여 명시된 것은?
(A) 일주일 전에 점검되어야 한다.
(B) 필기 도구가 구비될 것이다.
(C) 건물 수리로 전부 폐쇄될 것이다.
(D) 웹 사이트를 통해 예약할 수 있다.

해설 광고의 표 하단 "Each room at the Grand Cascade Hotel & Conference Center is equipped with whiteboards, marker pens, paper and pens."에서 펜과 종이가 구비되었다고 했으므로, (B)가 정답이다.

182 세부 사항

80명 참석 강연에 가장 적합한 회의실은 무엇인가?
(A) Tahoma Room
(B) Edu Room
(C) Tech Room
(D) Innobiz Room

해설 Tahoma Room은 20개의 의자, Edu Room은 15개의 작업대, Tech Room은 30개의 작업대가 있으므로 80명을 수용할 수 없다. Innobiz Room은 100명에서 150명까지 수용할 수 있으므로 가장 적합한 회의실은 (D)이다.

183 주제/목적

이메일의 목적은 무엇인가?
(A) 예약에 대한 대안을 제안하기 위해
(B) 수신자에게 전액 지불을 알리기 위해
(C) 전문가가 필요한지 문의하기 위해
(D) 참가자 수를 묻기 위해

해설 예약일에 해당 회의실에서 카펫 청소가 예정되어 이용이 불가능한 상황으로, "So, I would like to offer you the Tech Room instead without any change in fee."에서 추가 비용 없이 더 큰 방으로 대체하는 것을 제안하고 있으므로 (A)가 정답이다.

184 세부 사항

이메일에 따르면, Tech Room을 이용하기 위해 데이비스 씨에게 얼마가 부과될 것인가?
(A) 200파운드
(B) 230파운드
(C) 250파운드
(D) 300파운드

해설 데이비스 씨는 원래 Edu Room을 예약했지만, 사용이 불가하여 추가 요금 없이 Tech Room을 대신 제공한다고 했으므로 Edu Room 가격인 (B) 230 파운드가 정답이다.

185 추론/암시 (연계)

코스타 씨에 대해 암시된 것은?
(A) 그는 행사를 위한 모든 종류의 업무를 돕고 있다.
(B) 그는 컴퓨터를 다루는 것에 매우 능숙하다.
(C) 그는 주제를 논의하기 위해 데이비스 씨에게 연락하길 원한다.
(D) 그는 회의 동안에는 도움을 줄 수 없다.

해설 광고의 마지막 부분 "The experts have more than 10 years of experience in the computer-related industry."에서 그들의 전문가들은 모두 컴퓨터 관련 산업에서 경력이 10년 이상이라고 했고, 이메일에서 그 전문가 중 한 사람으로 코스타 씨가 언급되어 있으므로 (B)가 정답이다.

[186-190] 이메일 & 전단지 & 문자 메시지

발신: 로빈 밀러
수신: 예비 졸업생들
날짜: 5월 25일
제목: 연설

학생 여러분께,

저는 아쓰시 씨가 이번 여름에 우리의 연설 시리즈에 참여하기로 결정한 것을 알리게 되어 정말 기쁩니다. 여러분의 인턴십 프로그램의 일환으로, 여러분은 6월 10일부터 30일까지 있을 그의 교내 연설 일정을 확인해야 하고, 여러분의 과정 증명서를 받기 위해 모든 필수 문서 작업을 완료하고 승인 받아야 합니다. 여러분은 또한 최종 발표를 위해 회의실을 예약해야 할 것입니다. 저는 여러분에게 Leonard Hall을 예약할 것을 권장하는데, 이는 가장 많은 인원을 수용할 수 있고, 시청각 장비들이 잘 구비되어 있기 때문입니다. 하지만 그 건물의 다른 회의실들도 괜찮을 것입니다.

게다가, 아쓰시 씨가 그의 잠정적인 연설 일정을 제공하자마자, 여러분은 전단지를 만들어서 교내 곳곳의 모든 건물에 게시하는 것을 포함한 활동들에 참여하게 될 것입니다. 저는 여러분 다섯 명이서 아무 문제 없이 임무들을 완수할 수 있을 것이라 믿습니다.

감사합니다.

밀러 박사
인문과학대학 학장

인문과학대학
연설 시리즈 발표

일다 아쓰시
부사장, 일본 기업 Osaka Progressive Asset

M&A 기술과 팁 개발
6월 15일 오후 3시
Charlton Room

M&A라는 용어는 합병과 인수의 약어입니다. 합병이란 두 사업체의 결합인 반면, 인수는 한 사업체의 소유권을 다른 사업체가 구매하는 것입니다. 새로운 정보 기술의 도래와 함께, 노동력 기반의 산업들은 경쟁력이 낮아졌고, 중소기업들은 회사 운영에 어려움을 겪고 있습니다. 이 문제에 대한 가능한 해결책 중 하나가 인수합병(M&A) 전략입니다. 그러나, 이것 또한 체계적인 합의 없이 진행된다면 역효과가 일어날 수도 있습니다. 그래서 아쓰시 씨는 이 분야에서 자신만의 노하우와 일본에서 그의 실제 사례들과 함께 오랜 시간에 걸쳐 증명된 승리 전략들을 전수해 줄 것이고, 그 다음에 어떻게 이러한 기술들을 우리 경제 상황에 적용할 수 있는지에 관해 논의할 것입니다.

수신: 이사야 콜린
발신: 도널드 험프리
수신일: 6월 2일 오후 5시

콜린 씨, 저는 컴퓨터실에서 당신이 보내준 전단지를 출력하고 있는데, 오류를 발견했습니다. 아쓰시 씨의 프로필 정보가 전단지에서 삭제되었어요! 이것을 수정해서 저에게 즉시 다시 보내줄 수 있나요? 컴퓨터실이 20분 후에 문을 닫아서, 밀러 박사님이 강조했던 전단지를 오늘 저녁에 게시하지 못할 수도 있어요.

어휘 participate in ~에 참석하다 **paperwork** 문서 작업 **certificate** 인증서, 증명서 **accommodate** 수용하다 **tentative** 잠정적인 **take part in** 참여하다 **activity** 활동 **post** 게시하다 **dean** 학장 **vice president** 부사장 **abbreviation** 약어, 축약형 **merger** 합병 **acquisition** 인수 **ownership** 소유권 **advent** 등장, 도래 **workforce** 노동력 **competitive** 경쟁력 있는 **have difficulty -ing** ~하는 데 어려움을 겪다 **matter** 문제 **strategy** 전략 **side effect** 역효과, 부작용 **time-tested** 세월에 걸쳐 증명된 **winning** 승리한 **case** 사례

186 추론/암시

Charlton Room에 대해서 암시된 것은?
(A) 인문과학 건물 외부에 위치해 있다.
(B) Leonard Hall보다 작다.
(C) 이번 연설 시리즈를 위한 유일한 회의실이다.
(D) 여름 동안 개조될 것이다.

해설 첫번째 이메일의 "I advise you to book Leonard Hall because it can accommodate the most people"을 통해 Leonard Hall이 가장 많은 사람들을 수용하는 가장 큰 회의실임을 알 수 있으므로 같은 건물의 Charlton Room은 이보다 작다는 것을 유추할 수 있다. 따라서 (B)가 정답이다.

187 동의어 찾기

이메일에서, 두 번째 문단 세 번째 줄의 "issues"와 의미상 가장 가까운 것은?
(A) 주제
(B) 책
(C) 갈등
(D) 간행물

해설 "I believe that you will be able to finish the tasks among the five of you without any issues."에서 다섯 명이 아무 문제 없이 임무를 완수할 수 있을 것이라고 믿는다 했고, 이는 문맥상 의견의 충돌이나 갈등을 의미하므로 (C)가 가장 적절하다.

188 세부 사항

아쓰시 씨의 발표는 무엇에 관한 것인가?
(A) 인턴십 프로그램의 중요성
(B) 추천서에 관한 조언
(C) 기업 인수 조언
(D) 경영학 석사 과정 설명

해설 전단지에서 연설 제목이 "Developing M&A Techniques and Tips"라고 나와 있으므로 M&A(인수합병)에 대해 발표한다는 것을 알 수 있다. 따라서 정답은 (C)이다.

189 세부 사항

험프리 씨는 어떤 문제를 언급하는가?
(A) 전단지에서 누락된 정보
(B) 철자가 잘못된 이름과 그 위치
(C) 마감 기한 맞추기 실패
(D) 회의실 예약 오류

해설 문자 메시지의 두 번째 문장을 보면, "Mr. Atsushi's profile information was deleted from the flyer!"라고 되어 있으므로 전단지에서 정보가 누락되었음을 알 수 있다. 따라서 (A)가 정답이다.

190 추론/암시 (연계)

콜린 씨는 누구인 것 같은가?
(A) 연설 시리즈의 발표자
(B) 아쓰시 씨의 조교
(C) 인문과학대학 학생
(D) 교내 컴퓨터실 직원

해설 문자 메시지의 첫 번째 문장 "Ms. Colen, I'm in the computer lab, printing the flyer you sent to me,"와 두 번째 문장 "Mr. Atsushi's profile information was deleted from the flyer!"에서 콜린 씨가 아쓰시 씨와 관련된 전단지를 보내주었음을 알 수 있다. 아쓰시 씨와 관련된 전단지를 만들고 배포하는 것은 첫 번째 이메일에서 언급된 인문과학대학 졸업 예정자들이 해야 할 활동이므로, 콜린 씨는 (C) 인문과학대학의 학생임을 알 수 있다.

[191–195] 이메일 & 가격표 & 이메일

수신: r.steve@tubecare.net
발신: j.mckenzie@styleathome.com
날짜: 4월 10일
제목: 회신: Style at Home의 광고
첨부: 가격 목록_styleathome.doc

스티브 씨에게,

Style at Home에 대한 당신의 관심에 감사 드립니다. 저희 잡지는 한 달에 두 번 시드니의 수많은 가정으로 보내지기 때문에 저희 잡지에서 광고를 진행하는 것은 귀하의 제품들과 서비스를 홍보하는 최고의 방법이라고 강하게 믿습니다. 이 이메일에 첨부된 가격표 파일을 참고하시면, 저희의 합리적이고 표준적인 광고 비용을 보실 수 있습니다. 게다가, 저희는 모든 광고주분들에게 다음을 알려드리고자 합니다.:

• Style at Home은 흑백으로 출판됩니다. 가독성을 보장하기 위해, 사진과 삽화들은 단순해야 합니다.
• 저희는 당신이 보내주신 어떠한 이미지도 변경하지 않을 것입니다. 그러므로, 당신은 마감 전까지 저희에게 정확한 이미지들을 보내주셔야 합니다.
• 광고가 나가기 전에 요금 전액을 지불하셔야 합니다.

문의가 있으시면 주저 말고 연락주세요. 저희는 당신의 좋은 품질의 제품들과 서비스를 저희 잡지에 싣기를 매우 고대합니다.

신심으로,

존 맥켄지
광고 담당 이사

Style at Home
광고비 목록

크기	1권	6권 (3개월)	12권 (6개월)
1/4 페이지	500달러	2,600달러	5,400달러
1/2 페이지	1,000달러	5,500달러	10,500달러
전체 페이지	2,000달러	11,000달러	21,000달러

** 참고: 이 가격은 세금이 포함된 가격입니다. (변경 시, 사전에 알려드립니다)
당신의 추가 요청에 따라, 추가 비용이 발생할 수 있습니다.

수신: j.mckenzie@styleathome.com
발신: r.steve@tubecare.net
날짜: 4월 15일
제목: 회사: 회신: Style at Home의 광고
첨부: tubecare_image.png

맥켄지 씨에게,

당신의 상세한 설명에 감사 드립니다. 저는 앞으로의 여섯 호 동안 당신의 회사와 광고를 진행하고자 합니다. 우선, 저는 우리 광고를 1/2 페이지 사이즈로 올리길 원하며, 향후 사이즈를 늘릴지 아니면 광고 기간을 연장할지 고려할 것입니다. 그리고 결제는 어떻게 해야 하는지 알려 주세요.

행운을 빕니다.

랜달 스티브
Tubecare 사, 홍보부

어휘 strongly 강하게 proceed with ~을 진행하다 promote 홍보하다 standard 표준의 advertiser 광고주 greyscale 흑백의 readability 가독성 illustration 삽화 hence 그러므로 correct 수정하다 in full 전액으로 feature 특별히 포함하다, 특징으로 삼다 issue (정기 간행물의) 호 enlarge 확장하다, 확대하다 extend 연장하다 term 기간

191 주제/목적

첫 번째 이메일의 목적은 무엇인가?
(A) 잠재 고객에게 세부 사항을 제공하기 위해
(B) 시민들에게 그들의 잡지를 광고하기 위해
(C) 장식 세트의 비용을 설명하기 위해
(D) 출판물에 더 많은 구독자를 끌어 모으기 위해

해설 첫 번째 이메일의 "Thank you for your interest in *Style at Home*."에서 관심에 감사하다는 표현으로 보아 수신자가 예비 고객임을 알 수 있고, 잡지에 광고를 진행하는 과정과 지시사항 등을 알려주는 내용이 이어지므로 (A)가 정답이다.

192 세부 사항

맥켄지 씨는 고객에게 무엇을 하도록 요구하는가?
(A) 팀에게 많은 정보 보내기
(B) 사진 크기와 텍스트 길이 조정하기
(C) 광고 제출 전 이미지 검토하기
(D) 광고 오류 수정하기

해설 첫 번째 이메일에 나열된 항목 중 "We will not change any images you send. Hence, you should send the correct images to us before the deadline."을 보면 이미지 변경이 불가하니 반드시 정확한 이미지를 보내라고 요구하고 있다. 즉, 제출하기 전에 미리 검토하여 정확한 이미지를 보내라는 말이므로 (C)가 적절하다.

193 추론/암시

두 번째 이메일에서 스티브 씨에 대해 암시된 것은?
(A) 그는 새로운 사업을 시작할 예정이다.
(B) 그는 최근 시드니 지역으로 이사했다.
(C) 그는 나중에 광고의 크기와 기간을 변경할 수도 있다.
(D) 그는 잡지의 정규 회원으로 가입할 것이다.

해설 두 번째 이메일 중반부에서 "we will consider whether to enlarge the size or extend the term of this advertising in the future." 향후 광고의 크기 변경과 기간 연장을 고려하겠다고 언급하고 있으므로 (C)가 정답이다.

194 세부 사항 (연계)

스티브 씨는 얼마를 부과 받을 것 같은가?
(A) 1,000 달러
(B) 2,600 달러
(C) 5,500 달러
(D) 10,500 달러

해설 두 번째 이메일에서 "I would like to go forward with the advertisement with your company for the next six issues." 앞으로의 여섯 호 동안 광고하길 희망한다고 했고, 그 다음 문장에서 "I want to post our advertisement with a half page size" 절반(1/2)사이즈를 원한다고 했으므로 가격표에서 이에 해당하는 가격은 (C)$5,500이다.

195 동의어 찾기

두 번째 이메일에서, 첫 번째 문단 세 번째 줄의 "term"과 의미상 가장 가까운 것은?
(A) 합의
(B) 표현
(C) 조건
(D) 기간

해설 term 앞에 쓰인 extend(연장하다)를 참고해 볼 때, term이 '기간'을 연장한다는 의미로 사용되었음을 알 수 있다. 따라서 (D)가 정답이다.

[196-200] 편지 & 송장 & 이메일

Gourmet Catering

3317 Hamilton Boulevard, Allentown
PA 18104
610-770-8888

모니카 씨에게,

우리 출장 뷔페 서비스를 주문해 주셔서 감사드립니다. 우리는 우리의 음식과 음료로 모든 고객을 만족시키기 위해 최선의 노력을 기울입니다. 여러분에게 건강에 좋은 유기농 음식을 제공하기 위해, 우리는 항상 모든 식재료들을 원산지에서 공수합니다.

이 편지에 동봉된 송장을 주의 깊게 검토해 보시고, 주문에 문제가 있다면, 저희에게 610-770-888 또는 cs3317@gourmetcatering. com으로 연락하세요. 당신의 주문 번호가 참조용으로 포함되어야 한다는 것을 알아두세요.

* 접시, 컵, 냅킨, 그리고 식기 도구는 모든 주문에 포함됩니다.

존 밀턴
예약 부서

송장

고객 성명: Lehigh Valley 부동산의 앤 모니카
주소: 1146 S Cedar Crest Drive 302, Allentown, PA
배송일: 11월 10일 오후 1시 30분
주문 번호: NOV391501

품목	크기	수량	가격	총합
그리스식 샐러드와 소고기 구이	라지	1	50달러	50달러
칠리 소스를 곁들인 신선한 상추 랩 샌드위치	더즌	4	15달러	60달러
커피와 차	1인당	20	3달러	60달러

배송 및 준비 : 12.00달러
총액 : 182.00달러
지불액 : -182.00달러
잔액 : 0달러

11월 6일 이후로 주문 변경을 원하시면, 우리의 주문 정책 하에 늦은 변경에 대한 30달러를 지불해야 한다는 것을 주의하세요.

수신: cs3317@gourmetcatering.com
발신: a_monica@lehighvalleyrt.net
날짜: 11월 7일
제목: 주문 번호 NOV391501

저는 11월 10일 Cedar Crest Drive 302로 배송되는 제 주문번호 NOV391501에 관하여 글을 씁니다. 우리 직원에게 메뉴를 보여 주었는데, 유감스럽게도 직원 한 명이 채식주의자라는 것을 알게 되었습니다. 야채 볶음 요리로 교체할 수 있을까요? 저는 같은 가격의 음식을 보았고, 그래서 기존 음식을 그 음식으로 대체하기를 원합니다. 업데이트된 송장을 보내 주시면 감사하겠습니다.

진심으로,

앤 모니카

---

196 주제/목적

편지는 왜 발송되었는가?
(A) 정책 개정을 알리려고
(B) 늦은 변경으로 인한 요금을 요구하려고
(C) 현재 영수증을 업데이트하려고
(D) 최근 주문을 확인하려고

해설 첫 번째 편지에 송장이 동봉되어 있고, 주문에 대한 확정 사안과 주의사항들을 기술하는 내용이 담겨 있으므로 수신자가 최근에 한 주문을 확인하고자 한다는 것을 알 수 있다. 따라서 (D)가 정답이다.

197 세부 사항

Gourmet Catering 사는 질문이 있을 때 고객에게 무엇을 하라고 요구하는가?
(A) 영업 시간에만 사업체에 연락한다
(B) 그녀의 영수증 사본을 포함한다
(C) 그들의 매장에 직접 방문한다
(D) 그녀의 주문 번호를 언급한다

해설 첫 번째 지문인 편지 후반부 "Please be aware that you should include your order number for reference."를 보면 문의할 때 참고를 위해 주문번호를 꼭 포함하라고 요청하고 있으므로 (D)가 정답이다.

198 추론/암시 (연계)

모니카 씨에 대해 암시된 것은?
(A) 그녀는 직원들을 위한 점심 식사를 준비하고 있다.
(B) 그녀는 불필요한 비용을 줄이려 하고 있다.
(C) 그녀는 Gourmet Catering 사의 서비스를 자주 이용한다.
(D) 그녀는 새로운 지점을 개점할 예정이다.

해설 이메일의 "I have shown the menu to our staff, and unfortunately I just found out that one employee is a vegetarian."을 보면 직원들을 위해 메뉴를 주문했음을 알 수 있고, 송장에서 배송 시간이 오후 1시 30분임을 감안해 볼 때, 모니카 씨는 점심 식사를 주문했다는 것을 알 수 있으므로 (A)가 정답이다.

199 추론/암시 (연계)

모니카 씨는 Gourmet Catering 사에 무엇을 보내야 할 것 같은가?
(A) 추가 요금
(B) 서명된 주문서
(C) 업데이트된 메뉴
(D) 그녀의 직원 목록

해설 송장의 마지막 문장을 보면 "if you want to change your order after November 6, you should pay $30 for the late change under our order policy."에서 11월 6일 이후 주문 변경 시 추가 지불이 발생한다고 했다. 모니카 씨의 변경 요청 이메일은 11월 7일에 발신된 것이므로(Date: November 7) 추가 금액을 지불해야 함을 유추할 수 있다. 따라서 (A)가 정답이다.

200 세부 사항

모니카 씨가 더 이상 원하지 않는 요리는 무엇인가?
(A) 소고기 구이
(B) 신선한 랩 샌드위치
(C) 커피
(D) 야채 볶음 요리

해설 직원 중 한 명이 채식주의자여서 메뉴 변경을 요청했으므로 고기가 들어간 음식인 (A) Grilled Beef가 정답이다.

Memo

TEST 5

p.192

LISTENING TEST

01	(A)	02	(D)	03	(B)	04	(B)	05	(C)
06	(C)	07	(A)	08	(B)	09	(C)	10	(C)
11	(B)	12	(A)	13	(C)	14	(A)	15	(B)
16	(C)	17	(B)	18	(B)	19	(C)	20	(B)
21	(A)	22	(A)	23	(C)	24	(B)	25	(A)
26	(B)	27	(C)	28	(B)	29	(C)	30	(A)
31	(C)	32	(B)	33	(A)	34	(B)	35	(D)
36	(B)	37	(A)	38	(B)	39	(B)	40	(C)
41	(A)	42	(B)	43	(C)	44	(B)	45	(B)
46	(C)	47	(C)	48	(A)	49	(B)	50	(D)
51	(B)	52	(C)	53	(B)	54	(D)	55	(A)
56	(C)	57	(A)	58	(D)	59	(A)	60	(B)
61	(B)	62	(C)	63	(D)	64	(B)	65	(A)
66	(D)	67	(C)	68	(A)	69	(B)	70	(D)
71	(C)	72	(B)	73	(D)	74	(C)	75	(C)
76	(C)	77	(B)	78	(D)	79	(D)	80	(B)
81	(C)	82	(D)	83	(B)	84	(D)	85	(A)
86	(D)	87	(C)	88	(D)	89	(A)	90	(C)
91	(C)	92	(B)	93	(C)	94	(A)	95	(A)
96	(C)	97	(B)	98	(B)	99	(D)	100	(C)

READING TEST

101	(B)	102	(C)	103	(D)	104	(B)	105	(C)
106	(A)	107	(C)	108	(A)	109	(D)	110	(B)
111	(C)	112	(B)	113	(B)	114	(D)	115	(D)
116	(A)	117	(A)	118	(A)	119	(D)	120	(D)
121	(B)	122	(B)	123	(A)	124	(A)	125	(B)
126	(A)	127	(B)	128	(A)	129	(B)	130	(B)
131	(C)	132	(A)	133	(C)	134	(B)	135	(B)
136	(A)	137	(C)	138	(D)	139	(B)	140	(C)
141	(B)	142	(A)	143	(C)	144	(A)	145	(D)
146	(A)	147	(B)	148	(A)	149	(B)	150	(B)
151	(D)	152	(C)	153	(B)	154	(D)	155	(C)
156	(B)	157	(C)	158	(C)	159	(B)	160	(A)
161	(A)	162	(D)	163	(A)	164	(B)	165	(D)
166	(A)	167	(C)	168	(A)	169	(B)	170	(B)
171	(C)	172	(B)	173	(C)	174	(B)	175	(C)
176	(A)	177	(C)	178	(D)	179	(B)	180	(C)
181	(C)	182	(D)	183	(D)	184	(B)	185	(B)
186	(D)	187	(C)	188	(B)	189	(D)	190	(D)
191	(C)	192	(D)	193	(C)	194	(B)	195	(C)
196	(D)	197	(B)	198	(D)	199	(B)	200	(D)

PART • 1

1 인물(1인) 사진

(A) The man is holding some clothes.
(B) The man is hanging up a shirt.
(C) The man is removing an item from a shelf.
(D) The man is putting on a jacket.

(A) 남자가 옷을 들고 있다.
(B) 남자가 셔츠를 걸고 있다.
(C) 남자가 선반에서 물건을 꺼내고 있다.
(D) 남자가 재킷을 입고 있다.

> **해설** 남자가 옷을 들고 있는 모습을 묘사한 (A)가 정답이다. (B)는 사진 속에 셔츠는 있지만 걸고 있지 않으므로 오답, (C)는 선반에서 물건을 꺼내는 동작이 없으므로 오답, (D)는 남자가 재킷를 입는 동작이 아니므로 오답이다. 이미 입은 '상태'를 묘사할 때에는 동사 "wear"로 표현한다는 것을 기억해 두자.

> **어휘** hang up ~을 걸다   remove 꺼내다   put on ~을 입다(동작)

2 사물/풍경 사진

(A) A mechanic is working on a car in a garage.
(B) Some tires are being examined.
(C) A car door is being opened.
(D) A car has been lifted for repairs.

(A) 정비공이 차고에서 차를 수리하고 있다.
(B) 타이어가 점검 중이다.
(C) 자동차 문이 열리고 있다.
(D) 자동차가 수리를 위해 올려져 있다.

> **해설** 자동차가 올려져 있는 상태를 현재완료 수동태 "has been lifted"로 표현한 (D)가 정답이다. 사물 사진에는 수동태(be p.p.)와 현재완료 수동태(has/have been p.p.)가 자주 사용된다는 것을 기억해 두자. (A)는 차를 수리 중인 인물이 없으므로 오답, (B)는 타이어를 점검하는 인물이 없으므로 오답, (C)는 자동차 문이 열려 있지 않고 여는 행동도 없으므로 오답이다.

> **어휘** mechanic 정비공   garage 차고   vehicle 자동차   open 열다; 열린   lift 올리다   repair 수리; 수리하다

3 인물(1인) 사진

(A) The woman is typing on a keyboard.
(B) The woman is sitting behind a desk.
(C) The woman is wiping off the monitor screen.
(D) The woman is reaching for a coffee mug.

(A) 여자가 키보드를 치고 있다.
(B) 여자가 책상 뒤에 앉아 있다.
(C) 여자가 모니터 화면을 닦고 있다.
(D) 여자가 커피 잔에 손을 뻗고 있다.

해설 책상에 앉아서 작업하는 여자에 대해, 여자의 행동을 묘사하지 않고 '책상 뒤에 앉아 있다'고 위치를 설명한 (B)가 정답이다. (A)는 키보드는 있지만 타자를 치고 있지 않으므로 오답, (C)는 모니터가 있지만 화면을 닦고 있지 않고, (D)는 커피 잔이 있지만 손을 뻗는 행동도 없으므로 오답이다.

어휘 **type** 타자 치다   **behind** 뒤에   **wipe off** ~을 닦아내다
reach for ~에 손을 뻗다

4 혼합 사진

(A) They are exiting a building.
(B) They are standing in a line outside.
(C) Maintenance work is being done on a staircase.
(D) The door to a building has been left open.

(A) 그들은 건물을 나가고 있다.
(B) 그들은 야외에서 한 줄로 서 있다.
(C) 계단에서 보수 공사가 진행되고 있다.
(D) 건물의 문이 열려 있다.

해설 사람들이 모여 있는 모습을 서다(stand)라는 동사로 표현한 (B)가 정답이다. (A)는 건물에서 나오고 있는 사람이 없으므로 오답, (C)는 계단이 있지만 공사가 진행되는 모습을 볼 수 없고, (D)는 건물의 문이 닫혀 있으므로 오답이다.

어휘 **exit** 나가다   **stand in a line** 일렬로 서다   **maintenance work** 보수 공사

5 혼합 사진

(A) The woman is painting the wall.
(B) The woman is turning on a light.
(C) Some pictures are hanging on the wall.
(D) Floors are being cleaned for an exhibit.

(A) 여자가 벽에 페인트칠하고 있다.
(B) 여자가 불을 켜고 있다.
(C) 그림들이 벽에 걸려 있다.
(D) 전시회를 위해 바닥이 청소되고 있다.

해설 혼합 사진 문제로, 벽에 그림들이 걸려 있는 배경을 묘사한 (C)가 정답이다. (A)는 벽(wall)에 그림(painting)이 있지만, painting이 페인트칠한다는 의미로 쓰였으므로 오답, (B)는 불을 켜고 있는 사람이 없고, (D)는 바닥을 청소하는 동작이 없으므로 오답이다.

어휘 **paint** 페인트칠하다   **turn on** 켜다   **hang** ~에 달려 있다
floor 바닥   **clean** 청소하다; 깨끗한   **exhibit** 전시품, 전시회

6 사물/풍경 사진

(A) Some display racks are being emptied.
(B) A banner is suspended from the ceiling.
(C) Products have been stocked on shelves.
(D) There are cushions scattered on the floor.

(A) 진열 선반이 비워지고 있다.
(B) 현수막이 천장에 매달려 있다.
(C) 선반에 물건들로 채워져 있다.
(D) 바닥에 쿠션들이 흩어져 있다.

해설 진열 선반에 제품들이 놓여 있는 모습을 묘사한 (C)가 정답이다. (A)는 진열 선반을 비우는 동작을 하는 인물이 없으므로 오답, (B)는 현수막이 보이지 않고, 천장에 매달려 있는 것은 조명이므로 오답, (D)는 바닥에 쿠션이 없으므로 오답이다.

어휘 **empty** 비우다   **banner** 현수막   **suspend** 매달다   **stock** 채우다   **scatter** 흩뿌리다

PART • **2**

7 Who 의문문

Who will be interviewing the candidates?
(A) I'll ask David to do it.
(B) It has a nice view.
(C) Today at eleven o'clock.

누가 지원자들을 인터뷰할 건가요?
(A) 데이비드에게 요청할 겁니다.
(B) 그곳은 전망이 좋습니다.
(C) 오늘 11시요.

해설 Who 의문문으로, 누가 인터뷰를 진행할 것인지 묻고 있다. 따라서 '데이비드에게' 요청할 거라고 알려주는 (A)가 정답이다. (B)는 질문의 interviewing과 비슷한 발음의 view를 사용한 오답이고, (C)는 의문사 when에 대한 대답이므로 오답이다.

어휘 interview 인터뷰하다 candidate 후보자, 지원자 ask 부탁하다, 요청하다 view 전망; 보다

8 What 의문문

What time does the next bus to Boston leave?
(A) About three dollars.
(B) In half an hour.
(C) At the next stop.

Boston으로 가는 다음 버스가 몇 시에 출발하나요?
(A) 약 3달러요.
(B) 30분 후에요.
(C) 다음 정류장에서요.

해설 시간을 묻는 "What + time" 의문문으로, 30분 후에 출발한다고 버스의 출발 시간을 말한 (B)가 정답이다. (A)는 How much 의문문의 대답으로 적합하고, (C)는 bus에서 연상되는 단어 stop(정류장)을 이용했지만 의문사 Where의 대답으로 적합하므로 오답이다.

어휘 leave 떠나다, 출발하다 half 반, 절반 next 다음의 stop 정류장

9 How 의문문

How long have you worked at the company?
(A) Ten dollars per kilo.
(B) At five o'clock.
(C) Nearly ten years.

당신은 그 회사에서 얼마나 오랫동안 일했나요?
(A) 킬로당 10달러입니다.
(B) 5시에요.
(C) 거의 10년이요.

해설 How long 의문문으로, 현재완료 시제를 사용하여 얼마나 오랫동안 회사에서 근무했는지 묻고 있다. 따라서 구체적인 근무 기간을 언급한 (C)가 정답이다. (A)는 가격을 묻는 How much 의문문에, (B)는 시점을 묻는 When 의문문에 대한 대답으로 적합하다.

어휘 per ~당, 마다 nearly 거의

10 Where 의문문

Where did you get the printer paper?
(A) The newspaper is delivered at seven every morning.

(B) We should buy a new laser printer.
(C) From the supply closet.

어디에서 프린터 용지를 가져왔나요?
(A) 신문은 매일 아침 7시에 배달됩니다.
(B) 우리는 새 레이저 프린터를 구입해야 해요.
(C) 비품 창고에서요.

해설 어디에서 프린터 용지를 가져왔는지 묻는 Where 의문문에, '비품 창고에서 가져왔다'고 장소를 언급한 (C)가 정답이다. (A)는 질문의 paper와 발음이 유사한 newspaper를 이용한 오답이며, (B)는 질문에 사용된 printer를 반복한 오답이다.

어휘 get 구하다, 얻다 printer paper 프린터 용지 newspaper 신문 deliver 배달하다 supply closet 비품 창고

11 선택 의문문

Is it better to travel to Jasper by train or by bus?
(A) No, it is not too late.
(B) The bus is more convenient.
(C) I think they do a good job.

Jasper까지 기차로 가는 게 낫나요, 아니면 버스로 가는 게 낫나요?
(A) 아니요, 너무 늦지 않았어요.
(B) 버스가 더 편리해요.
(C) 저는 그들이 잘한다고 생각해요.

해설 선택 의문문으로, 기차와 버스 중 어느 교통편이 나은지 묻는 질문에 '버스가 더 편리하다'고 둘 중 하나를 골라 응답한 (B)가 정답이다. (A)는 Yes/No 의문문의 응답으로 적절하며, (C)는 주어가 복수인 일반동사 의문문의 응답으로 적절하다.

어휘 better 더 나은 travel 여행하다 convenient 편리한

12 When 의문문

When can I get the research results?
(A) After the monthly meeting.
(B) I looked for it everywhere.
(C) In the conference room.

제가 언제 연구 결과를 받아볼 수 있나요?
(A) 월례 회의 후에요.
(B) 모든 곳을 다 찾아 보았습니다.
(C) 회의실에서요.

해설 의문사 When으로 시작하는 의문문으로, 연구 결과를 언제 받을 수 있는지 묻고 있다. 이에 '회의 후'라고 특정 시점을 언급한 (A)가 정답이다. (B)는 research에서 연상되는 look for (찾다)를 이용한 오답이며, (C)는 장소를 묻는 Where 의문문의 대답으로 적합하다.

어휘 get 받다 research 연구 result 결과 monthly 매일의 look for ~을 찾다 conference 회담, 회의

13 명령문

Please watch your step as you board the boat.
(A) At the next board meeting.
(B) About thirty minutes.
(C) Sure, I'll be careful.

배에 탑승 시 계단을 조심하세요.
(A) 다음 이사회에서요.
(B) 약 30분이요.
(C) 물론이죠, 조심할게요.

해설 주의 사항을 알려주는 명령문에, "그렇게 하겠다"고 하는 (C)가 정답이다. (A)는 질문의 board를 반복했지만 내용상 관계가 없으며, (B)는 의문사 How long의 대답으로 적합하다.

어휘 watch 지켜보다, 조심하다 step 계단 board 탑승하다; 이사회 careful 조심하는

14 Why 의문문

Why do you go to work so early?
(A) To avoid the heavy traffic.
(B) No later than 9 A.M.
(C) I'll go with you on Friday.

왜 이렇게 일찍 출근하나요?
(A) 교통 체증을 피하려고요.
(B) 늦어도 오전 9시까지요.
(C) 금요일에 당신과 함께 갈게요.

해설 일찍 출근하는 이유를 묻는 Why 의문문에, '교통 체증을 피하기 위해서'라고 응답하는 (A)가 정답이다. to부정사는 목적이나 이유를 말할 때 자주 쓰인다는 것을 알아 두자. (B)는 시간을 묻는 의문문에 적합하고, (C)는 질문의 go를 반복한 오답이다.

어휘 go to work 출근하다 avoid 피하다 heavy traffic 교통 체증 no later than 늦어도 ~까지

15 일반 의문문

Do you think you can finish the report by Friday?
(A) Close it when you leave.
(B) Yes, if I work quickly.
(C) The office opens early on Friday.

보고서를 금요일까지 끝낼 수 있을 것 같나요?
(A) 나갈 때 그것을 닫으세요.
(B) 네, 제가 빨리 한다면요.
(C) 사무실은 금요일에 일찍 문을 엽니다.

해설 금요일까지 보고서를 끝낼 수 있는지 묻는 일반 의문문으로, "Yes + 세부 내용"을 언급한 (B)가 정답이다. (A)는 내용상 관계가 없고, (C)는 질문의 Friday를 반복함으로써 혼동을 주는 오답이다.

어휘 finish 끝내다 leave 출발하다, 떠나다

16 요청 의문문

Can you please tell me where I can buy a subway ticket?
(A) That's at 11 P.M.
(B) By bus, I guess.
(C) Over at those machines.

지하철 표를 어디에서 구입할 수 있는지 알려줄 수 있나요?
(A) 그건 오후 11시예요.
(B) 제 생각에는 버스로요.
(C) 저기 있는 기계에서요.

해설 "Could you tell me ~?"의 형태로, 의문사 Where 뒤의 내용에 집중해야 한다. 표를 살 수 있는 장소를 묻고 있으므로, 정답은 '저쪽에 있는 기계에서'라고 장소를 설명한 (C)이다. (A)는 시점을 묻는 의문사 When의 대답으로 적합하며, (B)는 질문의 subway에서 연상될 수 있는 bus를 이용한 오답이다.

어휘 subway ticket 지하철 표 guess 추측하다, 짐작하다 machine 기계

17 요청 의문문

Would you mind working an extra shift at the restaurant?
(A) Thanks, but we've already ordered.
(B) Which day will you need me?
(C) The customers at table five need a menu.

식당에서 추가 근무해줄 수 있나요?
(A) 고마워요, 하지만 저희는 벌써 주문했어요.
(B) 무슨 요일에 제가 필요한가요?
(C) 5번 테이블에 있는 손님들은 메뉴판이 필요해요.

해설 'Would you mind ~ing?'는 '~해도 괜찮습니까?'라는 의미로, 승낙이면 부정(No)으로, 거절이면 긍정(Yes)으로 대답해야 한다. 여기서는 추가 근무를 부탁하는 질문에 Yes/No로 답하지 않고 어떤 요일에 추가 근무를 해야 하는지 되묻는 (B)가 정답이다.

어휘 mind 꺼리다, 싫어하다 extra 추가의 shift 교대 근무 order 주문하다 day 요일 menu 메뉴(판)

18 Why 의문문

Why isn't my money transfer on my account statement?
(A) Yes, I think that's true.
(B) I'll find out and call you back.
(C) There is no trouble in my account.

제 계좌 명세서에 왜 송금 내역이 나와 있지 않죠?
(A) 네, 전 그것이 사실이라고 생각해요.
(B) 제가 알아보고 다시 연락 드리겠습니다.
(C) 제 계좌에는 아무 문제가 없습니다.

해설 송금 내역이 명세서에 나오지 않는 이유를 묻는 Why 의문문으로, 이에 "몰라요" 유형인 "알아보고 다시 전화 주겠다"고 응답한 (B)가 정답이다. "몰라요"의 다양한 형태는 매 시험에 출

제되니 반드시 기억해 두도록 하자. (A)는 Yes/No 응답으로 의문사 의문문에는 부적절하며, (C)는 질문의 account를 반복한 오답이다.

어휘 money transfer 송금 account statement 계좌 명세서 find out 알아내다 call someone back ~에게 다시 전화하다 trouble 문제

19 평서문

I'd like to cancel our meeting this week.
(A) No, I've never met her before.
(B) For a reasonable price.
(C) Would you like to reschedule it for next week?

이번 주 회의를 취소하고 싶습니다.
(A) 아니요, 저는 이전에 그녀를 만난 적이 없습니다.
(B) 합리적인 가격으로요.
(C) 다음 주로 일정을 변경하고 싶으신가요?

해설 금주의 회의를 취소하길 원한다는 평서문에, 다음 주로 일정을 조정하고 싶은지 묻는 (C)가 정답이다. 평서문은 Yes/No로 대답이 가능하며, 조건이나 반문의 형태로도 답할 수 있음을 알아 두자. (A)는 질문과 무관한 her가 등장해서 오답이며, (B)는 이유나 목적을 묻는 질문에 대한 응답으로 적절하다.

어휘 cancel 취소하다 reschedule 일정을 바꾸다

20 Which 의문문

Which newspaper should we publish our advertisement in?
(A) About three hundred words.
(B) Let's try the *Daily Times*.
(C) I've already subscribed to it.

어떤 신문에 우리 광고를 실어야 할까요?
(A) 약 300자요.
(B) <Daily Times>에 해 보죠.
(C) 저는 이미 그것을 구독했어요.

해설 "Which + 명사"의 형태로, 여러 신문 중에서 어떤 신문을 선택해야 하는지 묻는 문제이다. 정답은 신문사의 이름을 언급하며 선택을 제안하는 (B)이다. Which 의문문은 특징 이름을 언급하거나 "The one ~"의 형태로 선택 사항 중 하나를 말하는 것이 일반적이다. (A)는 글의 길이를 묻는 질문의 응답으로 적절하며, (C)는 질문의 newspaper에서 연상할 수 있는 subscribe를 이용한 오답이다.

어휘 newspaper 신문 publish 출판하다 advertisement 광고 subscribe to ~를 구독하다

21 부정 의문문

Aren't the supervisors usually in the office on Mondays?
(A) Yes, from nine to five.
(B) All the offices on the fifth floor.
(C) It starts at ten o'clock on Monday.

관리자들은 월요일에 보통 사무실에 있지 않나요?
(A) 네, 9시부터 5시까지요.
(B) 5층에 있는 모든 사무실이요.
(C) 그것은 월요일 10시에 시작합니다.

해설 부정 의문문은 상대방의 동의를 구하거나 사실을 확인하기 위해 사용된다. 질문에서는 관리자들이 월요일에 주로 사무실에 있지 않은지 묻고 있고, 정답은 그렇다고 알려주며 그들의 근무 시간을 설명한 (A)이다. (B)는 질문의 office를, (C)는 질문의 Monday를 반복한 오답이다.

어휘 supervisor 관리자, 상사 usually 대개, 보통 office 사무실

22 평서문

We should leave soon in case there's heavy traffic.
(A) I'll be ready in a few minutes.
(B) From the radio update.
(C) I'm afraid I left it at home.

교통이 막힐 경우를 대비해서 우리는 곧 출발해야 해요.
(A) 저는 몇 분 후면 준비돼요.
(B) 라디오 뉴스에서요.
(C) 제가 그것을 집에 두고 온 것 같아요.

해설 곧 출발해야 한다는 평서문에, "Yes"를 생략하고 "곧 준비된다"고 말한 (A)가 정답이다. (B)는 질문의 traffic에서 연상되는 radio update를 사용한 오답이며, (C)는 질문에 나온 leave의 과거형을 사용했지만, "(물건을) 두다/놓다"라는 전혀 다른 의미로 사용한 오답이다.

어휘 leave 떠나다, 놓다 in case ~의 경우에 a few 몇몇의 update 업데이트

23 제안/권유 의문문

Would you like me to make an extra copy of the file?
(A) File them in the cabinet.
(B) No, we don't have any extra money.
(C) Yes, do you have time?

제가 그 파일의 추가 사본을 만들까요?
(A) 그것들을 캐비닛에 보관하세요.
(B) 아니요, 우리는 여윳돈이 없어요.
(C) 네, 시간 되시나요?

해설 'Would you like me ~?'로 시작하는 제안/권유 의문문으로, 추가 사본을 만들길 원하는지 묻는 질문에 "Yes + 세부 내용"의 형태로 그렇게 해줄 시간이 있는지 반문한 (C)가 정답이다. (A)와 (B)는 각각 질문의 file과 extra를 반복한 오답이다.

어휘 extra 추가의, 여분의 copy 사본; 복사하다 file 파일; 보관하다 cabinet 장

24 What 의문문

What was Mr. Moreno's final offer?
(A) Yes, at last.
(B) Twenty thousand dollars.
(C) Sorry, we only accept cash.

모레노 씨가 최종적으로 얼마를 제안했나요?
(A) 네, 마침내요.
(B) 2만 달러요.
(C) 죄송합니다, 저희는 현금만 받습니다.

해설 What으로 시작하는 의문문은 뒤에 연결되는 명사에 따라 의미가 다양하다. offer는 "제안"이라는 의미 외에도 입찰 등에서 "제안하는 가격"이라는 의미로 사용될 수 있다. 질문은 모레노 씨가 최종적으로 제안한 가격을 묻고 있으므로, 이에 2만 달러라고 말한 (B)가 정답이다. (A)는 질문의 final에서 연상되는 last를 사용된 오답이며, (C)는 돈과 관련된 표현을 사용했지만 내용과는 무관하다.

어휘 final 최종의   offer 제안, 제의한 액수   at last 드디어, 마침내   accept 받다   cash 현금

25 부가 의문문

The copier's still broken, isn't it?
(A) I'll get it fixed this afternoon.
(B) He hasn't spoken yet.
(C) I want it to be printed in colors.

복사기가 여전히 고장이죠, 그렇죠?
(A) 제가 오늘 오후에 수리할 거예요.
(B) 그는 아직 말하지 않았습니다.
(C) 그것을 컬러로 인쇄하고 싶습니다.

해설 복사기가 여전히 고장인지 묻는 부가 의문문이다. 부가 의문문이나 부정 의문문은 추궁이나 확인을 하는 의미로 등장하는 경우가 많다. 정답은 '(아직 고장이지만) 내가 오늘 오후에 수리할 것이다'라는 의미의 (A)이다. (B)는 질문과 무관한 He가 나와 오답이며, (C)는 copier에서 연상되는 어휘 print를 이용한 오답이다.

어휘 copier 복사기   broken 고장 난   fix 고치다

26 일반 의문문

Is that your phone ringing?
(A) Yes, I like singing.
(B) Not mine. Mine is in silent mode.
(C) She will call today.

당신의 전화기가 울리는 건가요?
(A) 네, 저는 노래 부르는 것을 좋아해요.
(B) 제 것이 아니에요. 제 것은 무음으로 되어 있어요.
(C) 그녀가 오늘 전화할 겁니다.

해설 상대방의 휴대폰이 울리고 있는지 묻는 질문에, "No"를 생략하고 자신의 전화기가 아니라고 설명하는 (B)가 정답이다. (A)는 질문의 ringing과 발음이 유사한 singing으로 오답을 유

도하고 있고, (C)는 질문의 phone에서 연상되는 어휘 call을 이용한 오답이다.

어휘 silent 무음의, 조용한   mode 방법, 모드

27 평서문

I'm going to do some errands during lunch.
(A) I've already checked the report for errors.
(B) That's what I have for lunch.
(C) Where are you going?

저는 점심 시간에 용무를 처리할 거예요.
(A) 제가 이미 보고서에 오류가 있는지 확인했어요.
(B) 그것은 제가 점심 때 먹는 거예요.
(C) 어디로 가실 건가요?

해설 점심 시간에 용무를 처리할 거라는 평서문에, 용무를 보러 어디로 갈 건지 묻는 (C)가 정답이다. (A)는 질문의 errand(심부름, 용무)와 발음이 유사한 error를 이용한 오답, (B)는 질문의 lunch를 반복한 오답이다.

어휘 errand 심부름, 용무   during ~동안에   check 확인하다   report 보고서   error 실수, 오류

28 선택 의문문

Should I put this package on Mr. Rosella's desk or somewhere else?
(A) No, I couldn't find them anywhere.
(B) You can leave it at the reception desk.
(C) Thanks, but I'm not finished packing.

이 소포를 로셀라 씨의 책상에 놓을까요, 아니면 다른 곳에 둘까요?
(A) 아니요, 저는 그것들을 어디에서도 찾을 수 없었어요.
(B) 접수처에 두시면 됩니다.
(C) 감사하지만, 저는 포장을 끝내지 못했습니다.

해설 선택 의문문으로, 소포를 특정 인물의 책상에 둘 지, 아니면 다른 곳에 둘 지 묻고 있다. 정답은 새로운 선택지인 '접수처에 두면 된다'는 (B)이다. (A)는 질문의 somewhere과 유사한 anywhere를 이용한 오답이고, (C)는 질문의 package와 유사한 packing을 이용한 오답이다.

어휘 package 소포, 꾸러미   leave 남기다, 두다   reception desk 접수 데스크   packing 포장

29 부정 의문문

Wouldn't it be nice to take the clients out for dinner?
(A) Usually at six o'clock.
(B) The office is on the ninth floor.
(C) I couldn't agree with you more.

고객들을 데리고 나가서 저녁식사를 대접하는 게 좋지 않을까요?
(A) 보통 6시에요.

(B) 사무실은 9층에 있습니다.

(C) 당신 말에 전적으로 동의합니다.

해설 'Wouldn't it be nice to ~?' 형태의 부정 의문문으로, 고객들을 데리고 나가는 게 좋을지 묻고 있다. 정답은 "전적으로 동의한다"는 의미의 관용적 표현인 (C)이다. (A)는 dinner에서 연상할 수 있는 시간 표현 six o'clock을 이용한 오답이며, (B)는 Where 의문문에 적절한 응답이다.

어휘 take somebody out ~를 데리고 나가다 client 고객 usually 보통, 대개 agree with ~에 동의하다

30 Who 의문문

Who will manage the accounting division after Steve leaves?

(A) I thought he decided to stay.

(B) The calculation has no errors.

(C) In the commercial district.

스티브가 떠난 후에 누가 회계 부서를 관리할 건가요?

(A) 저는 그가 계속 있기로 결정한 걸로 아는데요.

(B) 그 계산에는 오류가 없습니다.

(C) 상업 지구에서요.

해설 Who 의문문의 전형적인 대답은 사람의 이름이나 직급을 언급하는 것이 일반적이지만, 그렇지 않은 경우 보기 중 가장 적절한 것을 골라야 한다. 스티브가 나가면 누가 관리하냐는 질문에, 나가지 않고 계속 있을 거라고 말하는 (A)가 정답이다. (B)는 accounting에서 연상되는 calculation을 사용했지만 내용과 무관하며, (C)는 division과 발음이 유사한 district를 이용한 오답이다.

어휘 manage 관리하다 accounting 회계 division 부서 leave 떠나다 stay 머무르다, 계속 있다 calculation 계산 error 실수, 오류 commercial 상업의 district 구역, 구

31 평서문

The engineering department has a larger budget this quarter.

(A) It was designed by a famous engineer.

(B) Isn't Mandy at the technology conference now?

(C) Now they can hire more staff.

기술부는 이번 분기에 예산이 더 늘었어요.

(A) 그것은 유명한 기술자가 설계했어요.

(B) 맨디는 지금 기술 컨퍼런스에 있지 않나요?

(C) 이제 그들은 더 많은 직원들을 고용할 수 있겠네요.

해설 부서의 늘어난 예산에 대해 말하는 평서문에, "늘어난 예산으로 직원을 고용할 수 있다"고 세부 내용을 말한 (C)가 정답이다. (A)는 질문이 engineering과 유사한 engineer를 사용한 오답이며, (B)는 engineering에서 연상되는 단어 technology를 사용했지만 내용상 관계가 없다.

어휘 department 부서 budget 예산 quarter 분기 design 디자인하다, 설계하다 famous 유명한 hire 고용하다

PART ● **3**

[32-34]

> W Hi, I'd like to know where the new Wendy Fox CD is. I think it was just released this week.
>
> M Yes, we have plenty of those in stock in the newly released section on the far wall.
>
> W Thank you. I also need a CD of the audio book, *The Road to Happiness* by Dr. John Abrams.
>
> M Hmm… The computer system is showing that we're out of stock at this location, but there are two copies at our southside store. I can call over there and have them put one on hold for you until tomorrow. It's only about a twenty-minute drive from here.
>
> ---
>
> W 안녕하세요, 새로 나온 Wendy Fox의 CD가 어디 있는지 알고 싶습니다. 그건 이번 주에 막 발매된 것 같아요.
>
> M 네, 저쪽 벽에 있는 신규 발매 섹션에 그것의 재고가 많이 있어요.
>
> W 감사합니다. 저는 존 아브람스 박사의 오디오북 CD인 <행복으로 가는 길>도 필요해요.
>
> M 음… 컴퓨터 시스템상에서는 이 지점에 재고가 없다고 나오는데요, 하지만 남쪽에 있는 매장에 2장이 있네요. 제가 그곳에 전화해서 당신을 위해 한 장을 내일까지 보관해 달라고 할 수 있어요. 그곳은 여기서 차로 대략 20분이면 갈 수 있어요.

어휘 release 출시하다, 발매하다 plenty of 많은 in stock 재고가 있는 section 구획, 칸 far 저쪽의, 멀리 show 보여주다 out of stock 재고가 떨어진 location 위치 put ~ on hold ~을 예약하다 likely ~할 것 같은 offer 제공하다, 제안하다 ship 배송하다 reserve 예약하다 copy 권, 부 discount 할인

32 대화 장소

화자들은 어디에 있는 것 같은가?

(A) 사무실에

(B) 도서관에

(C) 상점에

(D) 콘서트 홀에

해설 장소를 묻는 질문은 주로 본문 초반에서 힌트를 찾을 수 있다. 여자의 첫 대사 'Hi, I'd like to know where the new Wendy Fox CD is. I think it was just released this week.'에서 대화가 일어나는 장소가 CD 판매점, 즉 상점임을 알 수 있다. 따라서 정답은 (C)이다.

33 세부 사항

여자는 무엇을 찾고 있는가?

(A) CD

(B) 책

(C) 콘서트 티켓

(D) 컴퓨터

TEST 5 정답과 해설

여자의 대사 중 'Hi, I'd like to know where the new Wendy Fox CD is.'와 'I also need a CD of the audio book' 부분을 통해 여자가 새로 발매된 CD와 오디오북 CD를 찾고 있음을 알 수 있으므로 정답은 (A)이다.

34 제안

남자는 여자를 위해 무엇을 하겠다고 제안하는가?
(A) 그녀의 집으로 물건을 배송한다
(B) 다른 매장에 물건을 예약한다
(C) 제조업체에 전화한다
(D) 그녀에게 할인을 제공한다

남자의 두 번째 대사 'I can call over there and have them put one on hold for you until tomorrow.'에서 다른 매장에 CD가 남아 있으니 그곳에 전화해서 보관해 달라고 하겠다고 했으므로 정답은 (B)이다.

[35-37]

W Hello, Mr. Kingsley. I'm calling from the National Science Foundation. I'd like to thank you for your generous donation. We're putting short introductions of our donors on our Web site, and we'd like to set up a phone interview to learn more about you.

M That's fine, I guess. I'm available this Saturday at four o'clock. Will that work for you?

W Yes, Mr. Kingsley. And could you please send me a recent photo of yourself? We'll put it alongside your story on our donor page.

M I'd be happy to. Then we'll talk more on Saturday.

W 안녕하세요, 킹슬리 씨. 국립 과학 재단에서 전화 드립니다. 당신의 후한 기부에 감사드리고 싶습니다. 저희가 웹 사이트에 기부자들에 대한 짧은 소개를 올리려고 하는데, 당신에 대해 더 알기 위해 전화 인터뷰 약속을 잡고 싶습니다.

M 괜찮을 것 같아요. 저는 이번 주 토요일 4시에 가능합니다. 그 시간에 괜찮을까요?

W 네, 킹슬리 씨. 그리고 당신의 최근 사진을 하나 보내 줄 수 있나요? 저희 기부자 페이지에서 당신의 이야기 옆에 넣으려고요.

M 물론이죠. 그럼 토요일에 더 얘기하도록 하죠.

foundation 재단 generous 후한, 관대한 introduction 소개 donor 기부자, 기증자 learn about ~에 대해 배우다 available 가능한, 시간이 있다 work 효과가 있다 recent 최근의 alongside ~옆에, 나란히 agree 동의하다 work overtime 야근하다, 시간 외 근무하다 fundraiser 모금 행사 donation 기부, 헌금 arrange 잡다, 계획하다 finalize 마무리 짓다, 완결하다 contact number 연락처 reference 참조, 추천

35 세부 사항

여자는 왜 남자에게 고마워하는가?
(A) 그는 잔업하는 데 동의했다.
(B) 그는 그녀를 위해 웹 사이트를 디자인했다.
(C) 그는 모금 행사를 준비했다.
(D) 그는 기부를 했다.

여자의 첫 대사 "I'm calling from the National Science Foundation. I'd like to thank you for your generous donation."에서 남자가 기부한 것에 대해 감사하고 있음을 알 수 있다. 따라서 정답은 (D)이다.

36 주제/목적

여자는 왜 전화하는가?
(A) 주제에 대해 논의하기 위해
(B) 인터뷰를 잡기 위해
(C) 일자리를 제안하기 위해
(D) 예산을 마무리 짓기 위해

목적을 묻는 문제로, 본문 초반에서 힌트를 찾을 수 있다. 여자의 초반 대사 "we'd like to set up a phone interview to learn more about you." 부분에서 인터뷰 약속을 잡기 위해 전화했음을 알 수 있다. 따라서 정답은 (B)이다.

37 요청 사항

여자는 남자에게 무엇을 제공하라고 요구하는가?
(A) 사진
(B) 연락처
(C) 추천서
(D) 행사 일정표

여자의 마지막 대사 "could you please send me a recent photo of yourself?" 부분에서 남자에게 최근 사진을 보내달라고 요청하고 있으므로 (A)가 정답이다.

[38-40]

M Hello, Sunrise Enterprises. How can I help you?

W Hi, I'm Tina Simmons, the business manager of YG Electronics. May I speak to Jimmy Hender in the sales department? There's a problem with the shipment of the latest headsets I ordered from you.

M Oh, I'm afraid Mr. Hender and the other representatives are having a meeting at the moment. But I can give you his mobile number in case you want to talk to him personally in the afternoon.

W Okay, I'd appreciate that. I need to get in touch with him as soon as possible.

M 안녕하세요, Sunrise Enterprises입니다. 무엇을 도와드릴까요?

W 안녕하세요, 저는 YG 전자의 사업 매니저인 티나 시몬스입니다. 영업부의 지미 헨더 씨와 이야기할 수 있을까요? 당신의 회사에서 주문한 최신 헤드폰 배송에 문제가 있어요.

M 아, 안타깝게도 헨더 씨와 다른 직원들은 지금 회의 중입니다. 하지만 당신이 오후에 그분과 개인적으로 통화하고 싶으시다면 휴대폰 번호를 드릴 수 있어요.
W 네, 그렇게 해주시면 감사하겠습니다. 가능한 한 빨리 그와 연락해야 하거든요.

enterprise 기업, 회사 shipment 배송 latest 최신의 headset 헤드폰 at the moment 현재 personally 개인적으로 appreciate 고마워하다, 감사하다 get in touch with ~와 연락하다 order 주문하다 extra 추가의, 여유의 supplies 용품, 물품 inquire 묻다 contact number 연락 번호 defective 결함 있는, 불량의 client 고객 sales representative 영업 사원 personnel 인사부 leave 남기다

38 주제/목적

여자는 왜 전화하고 있는가?
(A) 추가 물품을 주문하기 위해
(B) 주문품에 대해 문의하기 위해
(C) 연락처를 알아내기 위해
(D) 불량품을 환불받기 위해

해설 여자의 첫 대사 "May I speak to Jimmy Hender in the sales department? There's a problem with the shipment of the latest headsets I ordered from you." 부분에서 여자의 주문에 문제가 있고, 이에 대해 문의하기 위해 전화했음을 알 수 있다. 따라서 정답은 (B)이다.

39 세부 사항

여자는 누구와 말하고 싶어 하는가?
(A) 고객
(B) 영업 사원
(C) 비서
(D) 인사 부장

해설 여자가 "May I speak to Jimmy Hender in the sales department?"라고 말하는 부분에서 영입부 직원인 헨더 씨와 말하고 싶어함을 알 수 있다. 또한 대화 중반 남자의 대사 "I'm afraid Mr. Hender and the other representatives are having a meeting at the moment."에서 헨디 씨와 다른 직원들은 회의 중이다'라고 했으므로 여자가 통화하고 싶은 사람은 '영업 사원'임을 알 수 있다. 따라서 정답은 (B)이다.

40 다음에 할 일

여자는 무엇을 할 것 같은가?
(A) 메시지를 남긴다
(B) 가게를 방문한다
(C) 다른 번호로 전화한다
(D) 남자에게 전화번호를 준다

해설 여자가 이후에 할 일에 대해서 묻고 있다. 남자가 "But I can give you his mobile number in case you want to talk to him personally in the afternoon." 그의 핸드폰 번호를 줄 수 있다고 말하자 여자가 "Okay, I'd appreciate that. I

need to get in touch with him as soon as possible." 그에게 가능한 한 빨리 연락해야 한다고 했으므로 다른 번호로 전화를 걸 것임을 알 수 있다. 따라서 정답은 (C)이다.

[41-43] 3인 대화

M1 I really need to buy a new suitcase. My old one is broken, and I have to get a new one for my trip next week. Natasha, Ben, do you have any suggestions?
W I recently bought a bag from a brand called Travel Pro, and I'm really happy with it. It is much lighter than other bags and easy to carry.
M2 Oh, I agree with this suggestion. You know, I recently got an e-mail about a special offer. If you buy the large suitcase from Travel Pro, you can get a carrying case for a laptop for free.
W That is a great deal for business travelers like us.
M1 Yes, that sounds perfect for me. Will you forward me the e-mail with that offer, Ben?
M2 Absolutely, Mr. Kim.

M1 저는 여행 가방을 새로 사야 해요. 예전 것이 망가져서 다음 주 여행을 위해 새것을 사야 하거든요. 나타샤 씨, 벤 씨, 추천해줄 게 있으신가요?
W 제가 최근에 Travel Pro라는 브랜드의 가방을 샀는데요, 정말 만족하고 있어요. 다른 가방들보다 훨씬 가볍고, 들고 다니기 편해요.
M2 오, 저도 그 제안에 동의해요. 있잖아요, 제가 최근에 특별 할인에 대한 이메일을 받았어요. Travel Pro에서 대형 여행 가방을 사면, 노트북 케이스를 무료로 받을 수 있어요.
W 우리처럼 출장을 다니는 사람들에게 정말 좋은 제안이네요.
M1 그러게요, 저한테 딱 좋을 것 같네요. 벤 씨, 그 할인에 관한 이메일을 저에게 전달해 줄 수 있어요?
M2 물론이죠, 킴 씨.

suitcase 여행용 가방 broken 고장 난 suggestion 제안 recently 최근에 carry 휴대하다, 가지고 다니다 special offer 특가 판매, 특별 할인 for free 무료로 deal 거래 perfect 완벽한, 아주 좋은 absolutely 물론 luggage 가방, 짐 itinerary 일정 reservation 예약 lightweight 가벼운 import 수입하다 different 다른, 다양한 purchase 구매 forward 전달하다, 보내다 lend 빌려주다 item 물건

41 주제/목적

무엇이 논의되고 있는가?
(A) 여행 가방
(B) 여행 일정
(C) 저녁 식사 예약
(D) 노트북 컴퓨터

해설 남자 1의 첫 대사 "I really need to buy a new suitcase." 에서 여행 가방을 사야 한다고 했고, 그 뒤에도 여행 가방을 사는 것에 대해 말하고 있으므로 정답은 suitcase를 luggage로 바꾼 (A)이다.

TEST 5 정답과 해설

42 세부 사항

여자는 왜 그 상품을 좋아하는가?
(A) 그것은 작다.
(B) 그것은 가볍다.
(C) 그것은 다른 나라에서 수입된다.
(D) 그것은 다양한 색으로 나온다.

해설 여자가 "I'm really happy with it. It is much lighter than other bags and easy to carry."라고 하는 부분에서 가방이 가볍고 들고 다니기 편해서 좋아한다는 것을 알 수 있다. 따라서 정답은 (B)이다.

43 요청 사항

벤은 무엇을 하라고 요청 받았는가?
(A) 구매하기
(B) 매장에 들르기
(C) 메시지 전달하기
(D) 물건 빌려주기

해설 지문 마지막 부분 "Will you forward me the e-mail with that offer, Ben?"에서 이메일을 전달해 달라는 킴 씨의 부탁에 벤은 "Absolutely, Mr. Kim."이라고 승낙하고 있다. 따라서 정답은 (C)이다.

[44-46]

M Hi, Laura. It's James. I'm glad I called you before you left your house. Could you give me a ride to the office this morning?
W Actually, <u>I'm already at the office.</u> I came here a little bit early today to prepare for our meeting. Do you think you can make it in time for that?
M I'm not sure. I can't get my car to start.
W I'm sorry to hear that. I would like to pick you up, but our clients from Acadia Pharmaceuticals will be here soon. Why don't you try to contact David? He usually comes in later, and I think he lives in your area.
M Okay, I'll do that. I hope I can be there before the meeting starts.

M 안녕하세요, 로라. 저는 제임스입니다. 당신이 집에서 출발하기 전에 제가 전화해서 다행이에요. 오늘 아침에 저를 사무실까지 태워다 줄 수 있을까요?
W 실은, 저는 이미 사무실에 있어요. 회의 준비 때문에 오늘은 좀 일찍 왔어요. 당신은 회의 시간에 맞춰서 올 수 있을 것 같아요?
M 잘 모르겠어요. 제 차에 시동이 걸리지 않아요.
W 유감이네요. 제가 데리러 가고 싶지만, Acadia 제약회사의 고객들이 곧 올 거예요. 데이비드에게 연락해 보는 건 어때요? 그는 보통 늦게 출근하는데, 당신 동네에 살 거예요.
M 알았어요, 그렇게 할게요. 회의 시작 전에 도착할 수 있으면 좋겠네요.

어휘 give ~ a ride ~를 태워 주다 a little bit 약간 prepare for ~를 준비하다 make it 도착하다 in time 제시간에

pharmaceuticals 제약 회사 area 지역 extra 추가의, 여유분의 copy (책, 신문 등의) 부, 권 revision 개정, 수정 agenda 안건, 일정 contact information 연락처 imply 암시하다 accident 사고 client 고객 confused 혼란스러운, 당황하는 postpone 연기하다 set up 세팅하다, 잡다 conference call 전화 회의 contact 연락하다 colleague 동료 location 위치

44 요청 사항

남자는 무엇을 요청하는가?
(A) 보고서 추가 사본
(B) 사무실까지 태워다 주기
(C) 안건 수정
(D) 고객 연락처

해설 남자의 첫 대사 "Could you give me a ride to the office this morning?"에서 여자에게 사무실까지 태워다 달라고 요청하는 것으로 보아 정답이 (B)임을 알 수 있다.

45 의도 파악

여자가 "저는 이미 사무실에 있어요"라고 말하는 의미는 무엇인가?
(A) 그녀는 차 사고에 대해 걱정한다.
(B) 그녀는 남자를 도울 수 없다.
(C) 그녀는 남자를 위해 다른 고객들에게 전화할 것이다.
(D) 그녀는 회의 시간에 대해 혼동하고 있다.

해설 차를 태워 달라는 남자의 부탁에 "난 이미 출근했다"고 하는 것은 태워다 줄 수 없다, 즉 남자를 도와줄 수 없다는 의미이다. 따라서 (B)가 가장 적합하다.

46 제안

여자는 남자에게 무엇을 하라고 제안하는가?
(A) 회의를 연기한다
(B) 전화 회의를 잡는다
(C) 다른 동료에게 연락한다
(D) 다른 장소에서 일한다

해설 차에 시동이 걸리지 않는다는 남자의 말에 여자가 "Why don't you try to contact David? He usually comes in later, and I think he lives in your area."라고 말하며 다른 동료인 데이비드에게 연락할 것을 권하고 있으므로 정답은 (C)이다.

[47-49]

M Who's next?
W Actually, Dr. Palmer, I wanted to let you know that your last patient of the day, Mr. Wong, just canceled. I was able to fit him in for next week.
M Good. I'm glad you were able to set up another appointment for him so soon. So, why don't we close up the office a bit early today? We've been very busy recently.

W Thanks. Oh, there's one thing I have to tell you —
the new cleaning service is starting tonight. They'll
be coming in after hours twice a week, Wednesdays
and Fridays, to clean the building.

M 다음 환자 분?
W 파머 박사님, 실은 오늘 마지막 환자인 웡 씨가 좀 전에 취소했다는
걸 알려드리고 싶었어요. 그 일정을 다음 주로 맞출 수 있었어요.
M 잘됐네요. 그 환자와 다른 약속을 그렇게 빨리 잡을 수 있었다니 다
행이네요. 그러면, 오늘은 병원을 좀 일찍 닫을까요? 우리는 최근
에 굉장히 바빴잖아요.
W 감사합니다. 아, 말씀 드릴 게 한 가지 있어요. 새로운 청소 서비스
가 오늘 밤에 시작돼요. 그들은 일주일에 두 번, 수요일과 금요일에
영업 시간이 끝나면 건물을 청소하러 올 거예요.

어휘 last 마지막의 patient 환자 fit 억지로 넣다, 맞추다
recently 최근에 after hours 영업시간 후에, 폐점 후에
twice a week 일주일에 두 번 restock 다시 채우다,
보충하다 supplies 용품, 물품 mail 우편으로 보내다
invoice 송장 medical 의학의 additional 추가의
suggest 암시하다 install 설치하다 facility 시설, 건물
contract 계약서 sign 서명하다 renovation 개조, 개축

47 세부 사항
여자는 무엇을 했다고 말하는가?
(A) 물품을 보충했다
(B) 송장을 우편으로 보냈다
(C) 약속을 변경했다
(D) 새로운 의사들을 면접했다

해설 여자의 대사 "your last patient of the day, Mr. Wong,
just canceled. I was able to fit him in for next week."
에서 마지막 환자가 약속을 취소해서 일정을 다음 주로 변경했
다고 했으므로 정답은 (C)이다.

48 세부 사항
남자는 무엇을 하기를 원하는가?
(A) 사무실 일찍 닫기
(B) 의학 회의 참석하기
(C) 추가 서비스 제공하기
(D) 사무실 직접 청소하기

해설 남자가 "why don't we close up the office a bit early
today?"라고 권유하는 것을 통해 병원(doctor's office)을 빨
리 닫기를 원한다는 것을 알 수 있다. 따라서 정답은 (A)이다.

49 세부 사항
여자는 오늘 밤에 무슨 일이 있을 것이라 말하는가?
(A) 새 일정 관리 소프트웨어가 설치될 것이다.
(B) 시설이 청소될 것이다.
(C) 계약서에 서명될 것이다.
(D) 건물 개조가 시작될 것이다.

해설 여자의 마지막 대사 "there's one thing I have to tell you
— the new cleaning service is starting tonight."에서
오늘 밤에 청소 서비스가 시작될 것이라는 내용을 확인할 수
있으므로, 보기에서 병원을 시설(facility)로 바꾼 (B)가 정답
이다.

[50-52]

W Hi, Robert. I hope you're enjoying your first day
working here. Have you been able to fill out all of
your new hire forms online?
M Actually, I filled out the forms I'm supposed to
complete, but something's wrong with the system.
It is not saving correctly. The information isn't there
when I reopen the file.
W Well, your computer probably has an outdated
version of file reader software. I'll ask Mr. Garcia,
our tech specialist, to install the correct version.
M Thank you. Ms. Cantor.
W Also, a few of us are going out together for dinner
after work. Would you like to join us? It's a great way
to get to know more people from other teams.

W 안녕하세요, 로버트. 당신이 이곳에서의 근무 첫날을 즐기고 있으
면 좋겠네요. 온라인으로 신입 사원 양식을 다 작성했나요?
M 실은, 제가 작성해야 하는 양식을 채워 넣었는데, 시스템이 뭔가
잘못된 것 같아요. 저장이 제대로 안 돼요. 파일을 다시 열면 정보
가 거기에 없어요.
W 글쎄요, 아마 당신의 컴퓨터에는 구 버전의 파일 리더 소프트웨어
가 설치되어 있는 것 같네요. 제가 기술 전문가인 가르시아 씨에게
적절한 버전을 설치해 달라고 부탁할게요.
M 감사합니다. 칸토어 씨.
W 또한, 저희는 퇴근 후에 같이 저녁식사를 하러 갈 거예요. 당신
도 함께 갈래요? 다른 팀의 더 많은 사람들을 알게 되는 좋은 방
법이에요.

어휘 fill out(= complete) 작성하다 new hire 신입사원
form 양식 outdated 오래된, 구식의 version 버전, 양식
specialist 전문가 mention 언급하다 be ready 준비되다
signature 서명 access 들어가다, 이용하다 save 저장
하다 correctly 올바르게 follow-up 추후, 후속 install
설치하다 arrange 잡다, 계획하다 tour 견학 contact
연락하다 personnel 인사의 submit 제출하다 recent
최근의 gathering 모임, 행사

50 문제점
남자는 어떤 문제점을 언급하는가?
(A) 서류가 아직 준비되지 않았다.
(B) 양식에 서명이 빠져 있다.
(C) 일부 구역에 들어갈 수 없다.
(D) 파일이 제대로 저장되지 않는다.

양식을 작성했는지 묻는 여자의 질문에 남자가 "Actually, I filled out the forms I'm supposed to complete, but something's wrong with the system. It is not saving correctly."라며 작성을 완료했지만 저장이 제대로 되지 않는다고 하는 것으로 보아 (D)가 정답임을 알 수 있다.

51 요청 사항

여자는 가르시아 씨에게 무엇을 하라고 할 것인가?
(A) 추후 면접 일정을 잡으라고
(B) 소프트웨어를 설치하라고
(C) 회사 견학을 준비하라고
(D) 인사 부장에게 연락하라고

여자의 두 번째 대사 "I'll ask Mr. Garcia, our tech specialist, to install the correct version."에서 가르시아 씨에게 적절한 버전의 소프트웨어 설치를 부탁하겠다고 했으므로 (B)가 정답이다.

52 제안

여자는 남자에게 무엇을 하라고 제안하는가?
(A) 최근 사진을 제출하라고
(B) 컴퓨터를 재시작하라고
(C) 특별 모임에 참석하라고
(D) 저녁식사를 예약하라고

여자의 마지막 문장 "a few of us are going out together for dinner after work. Would you like to join us?"에서 직원들의 저녁식사에 남자를 초대하고 있으므로, 저녁식사를 gathering이라고 표현한 (C)가 정답이다.

[53-55]

W This is the Museum of Contemporary Art. How can I help you?
M Hello, this is Samid calling from BioTech Inc. We want to find out if the museum has any programs specifically for businesses.
W Yes, we have the After-Hours programs. The museum stays open late on Wednesdays, and visitors go on a guided tour of one of the galleries. Then, there's a reception with a networking event.
M That is exactly what we are looking for. My company just moved here, and my colleagues want to get to know the area. Do we need to buy tickets?
W No, the admission is free, but you need to register so we know how many people are coming.
M Okay, I'll talk to my coworkers and get back to you as soon as possible. Thanks.

W 현대 미술 박물관입니다. 무엇을 도와드릴까요?
M 안녕하세요, 저는 BioTech 사의 사미드입니다. 저희는 박물관에 특히 기업을 위한 프로그램이 있는지 알고 싶습니다.
W 네, 저희는 '일과 후' 프로그램이 있어요. 박물관은 매주 수요일에 늦게까지 문을 여는데, 방문객들은 갤러리 중 한 곳을 가이드와 함께 견학합니다. 그 다음에, 인맥을 쌓을 수 있는 행사가 포함된 환영회가 있어요.
M 저희가 찾는 게 바로 그런 거예요. 저희 회사는 이곳으로 막 이전했고, 제 동료들은 이 지역에 대해 알고 싶어 해요. 저희가 티켓을 사야 하나요?
W 아니요, 입장료는 무료지만, 몇 명이 참석하는지 저희가 알 수 있도록 등록해 주셔야 합니다.
M 알겠습니다, 제 동료들과 이야기하고 되도록 빨리 연락 드리도록 하죠. 감사합니다.

museum 박물관, 미술관 contemporary 현대의 specially 특별히, 특히 after-hours 근무시간 후의 guided tour 가이드와 함께하는 견학 reception 환영회, 파티 networking 인맥 쌓기 colleague 동료 admission 입장 as soon as possible 가능한 한, 빨리 pharmacy 약국 travel agency 여행사 artwork 미술작품, 예술작품 entrepreneurship 기업가 정신, 창업 정신 solicit 요청하다 fund 자금 local 지역의 promote 장려하다, 촉진하다 sign up(= register) 등록하다 material 자료, 재료 association 협회 business card 명함

53 화자의 근무지

여자는 어디에서 일하는가?
(A) 약국에서
(B) 박물관에서
(C) 여행사에서
(D) 영화관에서

여자가 일하는 곳을 묻는 질문으로, 본문의 앞쪽에서 힌트를 주는 것이 일반적이다. 여자의 첫 대사 "This is the Museum of Contemporary Art. How can I help you?"에서 여자가 일하는 곳이 (B) 박물관임을 알 수 있다.

54 세부 사항

프로그램의 목적은 무엇인가?
(A) 예술품을 팔기 위해
(B) 기업가 능력을 가르치기 위해
(C) 지역 예술가들을 위한 자금을 요청하기 위해
(D) 인맥 형성을 고취하기 위해

여자가 프로그램을 설명하는 "visitors go on a guided tour of one of the galleries. Then, there's a reception with a networking event." 부분에서 인맥을 형성하는 것이 목적 중 하나라는 것을 알 수 있다. 따라서 정답은 (D)이다.

55 세부 사항

여자의 말에 따르면, 남자는 무엇을 해야 하는가?
(A) 행사에 등록하기
(B) 홍보 자료 가져가기
(C) 협회에 가입하기
(D) 명함 가져오기

해설 여자의 마지막 문장 "you need to register so we know how many people are coming."에서 행사에 참여하려면 등록해야 한다고 말하고 있으므로 (A)가 정답이다.

[56-58]

M Yuri, let me give you an overview of the work your remodeling team will be doing on this house. Follow me to the living room.

W Wow, look at this carpet. It must be thirty years old or even older. It would look so out of place with the new design of the house.

M And the wallpaper is not much better. It doesn't match the modern look of the redesign at all. That's why you'll be peeling off the wallpaper today and cleaning up the walls for the new materials.

W Hmm... This is a really big room. Are we still planning to paint the garden fences today?

M No, that job has been pushed back to tomorrow. Once I check the size of the living room, you will start working on the walls in here.

- -

M 유리, 당신의 리모델링 팀이 이 집에서 할 작업에 대해 전반적으로 알려 드릴게요. 거실로 따라오세요.

W 와, 이 카펫을 보세요. 30년 이상은 됐겠는데요. 이 집의 새로운 디자인과 너무 안 어울릴 것 같아요.

M 벽지도 그다지 좋지 않아요. 새 디자인의 현대적인 스타일과 전혀 어울리지 않아요. 그래서 오늘 당신들은 벽지를 다 벗겨내고 새 벽지를 위해 벽을 청소할 거예요.

W 음... 이 방은 정말 크네요. 여전히 오늘 정원 울타리에 페인트칠도 할 계획인가요?

M 아니요, 그 작업은 내일로 미뤄졌어요. 제가 거실 크기를 확인하면, 당신들은 여기서 벽에 대한 작업을 시작할 거예요.

어휘 overview 개요, 개관 follow 따라가다 out of place 맞지 않는 wallpaper 벽지 match 어울리다 redesign 다시 디자인하다; 재설계 peel off 벗기다 fence 울타리 push back(=delay) 연기하다, 미루다 check 확인하다 construction 공사 vehicle 차량 renovation 개조, 개축 expense 비용 outdated 구식의, 시간이 지난 store 보관하다, 저장하다 basement 지하층 deliver 배달하다 remove 없애다 reschedule 일정을 변경하다 task 작업, 일 take 시간이 걸리다 complete 완성하다

56 주제/목적

화자들은 무엇에 대해 이야기하고 있는가?
(A) 광고 캠페인
(B) 공사 차량
(C) 개조 작업
(D) 이사 비용

해설 첫 문장 "let me give you an overview of the work your remodeling team will be doing on this house."에서 대화 주제가 리모델링팀의 작업, 즉 리모델링인 것을 알 수 있다. 따라서 정답은 이를 renovation으로 바꿔 표현한 (C)이다.

57 세부 사항

여자는 카펫에 대해서 뭐라고 말하는가?
(A) 낡아 보인다.
(B) 너무 비싸다.
(C) 지하실에 보관되어 있다.
(D) 내일 배송될 것이다.

해설 여자가 카펫에 대해 말하는 부분 "Wow, look at this carpet. It must be thirty years old or even older."에서 카펫이 오래되었을 거라고 말하고 있다. 따라서 정답은 (A)이다.

58 의도 파악

여자가 "이 방은 정말 크네요"라고 말하는 의미는 무엇인가?
(A) 가구들이 옮겨져야 한다.
(B) 더 많은 사람들이 초대되어야 한다.
(C) 발표 일정이 변경되어야 한다.
(D) 작업을 완료하는 데 시간이 더 걸릴 것이다.

해설 화자의 의도는 주어진 문장의 앞뒤 문맥을 파악하는 것이 중요하다. 벽지를 뜯어내라는 지시를 듣고 "방이 크다"고 말하는 것은 결국 작업량이 많다는 것을 우회적으로 말하는 것이다. 따라서 정답은 작업을 완료하기까지 시간이 더 걸릴 것이라는 (D)가 가장 적절하다.

[59-61]

W Thank you for coming in today, Mr. Garrison.

M Wow, your office is huge. I thought you were running a one-person company.

W We actually have almost 30 financial advisors on our staff. Okay, why don't we get started? I'm very pleased to have this opportunity to explain our services to you. Hopefully, by the end of this meeting, you'll be ready to hire me as your financial advisor.

M Well, I'd like to know more about your services for small businesses. My restaurant is very successful, but it's still a small operation. What experience do you have working with small businesses like mine?

W Mr. Garrison, I personally advise over thirty clients who own small businesses. You have nothing to worry about.

- -

W 오늘 와 주셔서 감사합니다, 개리슨 씨.

M 와, 사무실이 정말 크네요. 저는 당신이 1인 기업을 운영하는 줄 알았어요.

W 실은 거의 30명의 재정 고문들이 직원으로 있어요. 자, 그럼 시작할까요? 당신에게 저희 서비스를 설명할 기회를 갖게 되어 정말 기쁩니다. 바라건대, 이 회의가 끝날 때면 저를 귀사의 재정 고문관으로 고용할 준비가 되실 겁니다.

M 음, 저는 당신 회사의 소기업 대상 서비스에 대해 더 알고 싶네요. 저희 식당은 굉장히 성공적이지만, 아직은 소규모 업체예요. 저희와 같은 소기업과 일한 경험이 있으신가요?

W 개리슨 씨, 저는 소기업을 소유한 30명이 넘는 고객들에게 직접 자문해 드립니다. 걱정하실 것 없어요.

어휘 huge 거대한 actually 실은 financial advisor 재정 고문관 opportunity 기회 operation 사업체, 기업 experience 경력, 경험 personally 개인적으로 own 소유하다 be surprised 놀라다 office space 사무실 공간, 사무실 expensive 비싼 relocate 이전하다 business 사업체, 회사 hire 고용하다 apply for 지원하다 position 자리, 직책 regularly 정기적으로 acquire 인수하다 location 위치, 지점

59 세부 사항

남자는 왜 놀라는가?
(A) 사무실 공간이 크다.
(B) 서비스가 비싸다.
(C) 회사가 이전했다.
(D) 방에 사람이 많다.

해설 남자의 첫 대사 "Wow, your office is huge."에서 여자의 사무실이 커서 놀란 것을 알 수 있다. 따라서 정답은 (A)이다.

60 세부 사항

남자는 왜 여자와 만나는가?
(A) 그는 사업체 매각에 관심이 있다.
(B) 그는 재정 고문관을 고용하길 원한다.
(C) 그는 새로운 사무실 공간을 찾아야 한다.
(D) 그는 여자의 회사에 지원할 것이다.

해설 여자의 대사 "by the end of this meeting, you'll be ready to hire me as your financial advisor."에서 남자가 재정 고문관을 고용하기 위해 여자와 만난다는 것을 알 수 있다. 따라서 정답은 (B)이다.

61 세부 사항

여자는 자신의 고객들에 대해 뭐라고 말하는가?
(A) 그들과 정기적으로 만난다.
(B) 그들 중 많은 사람들이 소기업을 가지고 있다.
(C) 그들 중 많은 사람들이 단골 손님을 확보했다.
(D) 그들 중 일부는 새 지점을 개점해야 한다.

해설 여자의 대사 "I personally advise over thirty clients who own small businesses."에서 자신의 고객들 중 30명 이상이 소규모 업체를 소유하고 있다고 말하는 것을 통해 (B)가 정답임을 알 수 있다.

[62-64] 대화 & 가격표

> W Devon & Jones clothing company. How may I help you?
> M Hi, I'm looking at your online clothing catalog right now, and I'd like to order a sweater. My sister is currently working in Asia, and I'm wondering if you can ship it there.
> W Let's see... Yes, we can. It's in our International Zone 2.

> M Great. I'd like to order a blue sweater, model number 3952 in the medium size, please.
> W Hold on for a second. Yes, everything is all set now. I've added the international shipping charge to your total.
> M Okay. Let me give you the address to ship the sweater to.

W Devon &Jones 의류 회사입니다. 무엇을 도와드릴까요?
M 안녕하세요, 제가 지금 당신 회사의 온라인 의류 카탈로그를 보고 있는데요, 스웨터를 하나 주문하고 싶어요. 제 여동생이 지금 아시아에서 일하고 있는데 그곳으로 배송이 가능한지 궁금해요.
W 어디 봅시다... 네, 할 수 있어요. 그곳은 저희 국제 지역 2에 있거든요.
M 잘됐네요. 저는 모델 번호 3952의 파란색 스웨터를 미디엄 사이즈로 주문하고 싶어요.
W 잠시만 기다려 주세요. 네, 이제 모두 준비되었습니다. 당신의 총액에 해외 배송비를 추가했습니다.
M 알겠어요. 스웨터를 배송할 주소를 알려드릴게요.

배송비		
국내 지역	미국	3달러
유럽 지역	유럽	5달러
국제 지역 1	아프리카	7달러
국제 지역 2	아시아	10달러

어휘 clothing 의류 order 주문하다 currently 현재 wonder 궁금해하다 zone 구역, 지역 second 초, 잠깐 set 세팅하다, 준비하다 add 추가하다 charge 비용, 요금 total 합계, 총액 address 주소 shipping rate 배송비 postal 우편의 customer service 고객 서비스 representative 직원 banker 은행가 choose 선택하다 review 논평, 평가

62 화자의 직업

여자는 누구인 것 같은가?
(A) 우체국 직원
(B) 의류 디자이너
(C) 고객 서비스 직원
(D) 국제 은행가

해설 여자가 누구인지 물어보는 질문으로, 지문 초반에서 힌트를 얻을 수 있다. 여자의 첫 대사 "Devon & Jones clothing company. How may I help you?"에서 여자가 의류회사에서 전화를 받는 업무를 맡고 있음을 알 수 있다. 따라서 (C) 고객 서비스 직원이 가장 적절하다. (B)는 여자가 의류 회사에서 근무하지만 디자이너인지는 알 수 없다.

63 시각 자료 연계

시각 자료를 보시오. 남자는 배송비로 얼마를 지불할 것인가?
(A) 3달러
(B) 5달러
(C) 7달러
(D) 10달러

여자의 말에 따르면 남자가 스웨터를 보낼 아시아는 국제 지역 2에 해당한다. 표에서 해당 구역의 배송비는 10달러라고 나와 있으므로 정답은 (D)이다.

64 **다음에 할 일**
남자는 다음에 무엇을 할 것 같은가?
(A) 디자인을 선택한다
(B) 정보를 제공한다
(C) 카탈로그를 주문한다
(D) 고객 후기를 작성한다

다음에 할 일을 묻는 문제는 주로 지문의 후반부에 단서가 나올 가능성이 크다. 남자의 마지막 대사 "Let me give you the address to ship the sweater to."에서 여자에게 주소를 알려줄 것임을 알 수 있다. 따라서 정답은 정보를 제공한다는 (B)이다.

[65-67] 대화 & 가격표

> M Rose Paradise Hotel, Raymond speaking. How may I help you?
> W Hi, I saw your ad in the paper today, and I'd like to make a reservation for three people next Saturday.
> M Of course. As you can see in the ad, we have several tea packages available for you. Which one did you have in mind?
> W I'd like to reserve the 50-dollar tea package for my mother. She just retired from her job, so I want to do something special for her.
> M Certainly. The 50-dollar package is an excellent choice. Customers absolutely love it.
> ⋯⋯⋯⋯⋯⋯⋯⋯⋯⋯⋯⋯⋯⋯⋯⋯⋯⋯
> M Rose Paradise 호텔의 레이먼드입니다. 무엇을 도와드릴까요?
> W 안녕하세요, 제가 오늘 신문에서 당신의 광고를 봤는데요, 다음 주 토요일에 세 사람을 예약하고 싶어요.
> M 알겠습니다. 광고에서 보실 수 있듯이, 이용할 수 있는 티 패키지가 여럿 있습니다. 어떤 것을 생각하고 계신가요?
> W 저희 어머니를 위해서 50달러짜리 티 패키지를 예약하고 싶어요. 얼마 전에 은퇴하셨는데, 그녀를 위해 뭔가 특별한 것을 해 드리고 싶어서요.
> M 물론이죠. 50달러짜리 패키지는 아주 좋은 선택입니다. 손님들이 정말 좋아해요.

>
> ### Rose Paradise 호텔
> ### 티타임을 즐겨보세요!!
>
> 티, 샌드위치 - 매일 굽는 빵
>
> | | |
> |---|---|
> | 클래식 티 | 18달러 |
> | 프리미엄 티 | 25달러 |
> | 패밀리 티 | 30달러 |
> | 로열 티 | 50달러 |

make a reservation(= reserve) 예약하다 package 패키지, 세트 available 이용할 수 있는, 준비되어 있는 have in mind ~을 염두에 두다 retire 은퇴하다 special 특별한 excellent 뛰어난, 탁월한 choice 선택 absolutely 전적으로, 틀림없이 baked goods 빵, 제과 learn about ~에 대해 배우다 colleague 동료 travel agency 여행사 celebrate 축하하다 retirement 은퇴 promotion 승진

65 **세부 사항**
여자는 어떻게 티타임 패키지를 알았는가?
(A) 신문에서
(B) 동료에게서
(C) 웹 사이트에서
(D) 여행사에서

여자의 첫 문장 "Hi, I saw your ad in the paper today"에서 신문에서 패키지 정보를 봤다는 것을 알 수 있으므로 정답은 (A)이다.

66 **시각 자료 연계**
시각 자료를 보시오. 어떤 티타임 패키지가 선택되었는가?
(A) 클래식 티
(B) 프리미엄 티
(C) 패밀리 티
(D) 로열 티

여자가 "I'd like to reserve the 50-dollar tea package" 라고 말했으므로 표에서 50달러에 해당하는 로열 티를 선택했음을 알 수 있다. 따라서 (D)가 정답이다.

67 **세부 사항**
여자는 왜 티 패키지를 예약하는가?
(A) 그녀의 동료들과 회의를 하기 위해
(B) 그녀의 어머니의 은퇴를 기념하기 위해
(C) 동료의 승진을 축하하기 위해
(D) 고객을 대접하기 위해

여자의 대사 "I'd like to reserve the 50-dollar tea package for my mother. She just retired from her job, so I want to do something special for her."를 통해 어머니의 은퇴를 축하하기 위해 티 패키지를 예약한다는 것을 추측할 수 있다. 따라서 정답은 (B)이다.

[68-70] 대화 & 표지판

> M Hi, Jenny. I wanted to let you know that the managers appreciate the fact that you and your team stayed late last night and finished the rush order. You all did a great job.
> W No problem. We knew the work was for an important customer.
> M Thanks again. By the way, I see you have some bread there with you.
> W Yeah, I slept in this morning and didn't have time to eat breakfast.

M Well, I'm afraid you'll have to take it to the break room. The rule says that there can't be any food on the factory floor.
W Oh, all right. Sorry, I'll be right back.

M 안녕하세요, 제니. 당신과 당신 팀이 어젯밤 늦게까지 남아 급한 주문을 마무리한 것에 대해 관리자들이 고마워한다는 걸 알려주고 싶었어요. 모두들 정말 잘했어요.
W 괜찮아요. 우리는 그 일이 중요한 고객을 위한 것임을 알고 있었어요.
M 다시 한번 고마워요. 그런데, 빵을 가지고 왔네요.
W 네, 오늘 아침에 늦잠을 자서 아침 먹을 시간이 없었어요.
M 음, 미안하지만 당신은 그것을 휴게실로 가져가야 할 거예요. 규정에 의하면 작업 현장에는 음식이 있으면 안 돼요.
W 아, 알겠어요. 죄송합니다. 금방 돌아올게요.

작업 현장 안전 규정
1. 안전모 착용
2. 안전 장갑 및 신발 착용
3. 휴대폰 사용 금지
4. 식사 금지

어휘 appreciate 감사하다 rush order 긴급 주문 customer 고객 break room 휴게실 safety rules 안전 규정 wear 입다, 쓰다 hardhat 안전모 footwear 신발(류) mobile phone 휴대폰 work overtime 야근하다, 추가 근무하다 extra 추가의, 여유분의 supply 용품, 물품 bring 가지고 오다

68 세부 사항
남자는 여자에게 무엇에 대해서 감사하는가?
(A) 야근을 한 것
(B) 추가 물품을 주문한 것
(C) 서류를 업데이트한 것
(D) 신입사원들을 도와준 것

해설 남자의 첫 대사 "I wanted to let you know that the managers appreciate the fact that you and your team stayed late last night and finished the rush order."에서 늦게까지 남아서 주문을 마무리한 것에 대해 여자에게 고마워한다는 걸 알 수 있다. 따라서 이를 동의 표현으로 바꾼 (A)가 정답이다.

69 세부 사항
오늘 아침에 여자에게 무슨 일이 있었는가?
(A) 서류 가져오는 것을 잊어버렸다.
(B) 늦게 일어났다.
(C) 고객과 만났다.
(D) 점심을 집에 두고 왔다.

해설 대화의 중반에 남자가 여자가 가지고 있는 빵에 대해 묻자 여자가 "I slept in this morning and didn't have time to eat breakfast."라며 오늘 아침에 늦잠을 자서 아침을 못 먹었다고 했으므로 (B)가 정답이다.

70 시각 자료 연계
시각 자료를 보시오. 화자들은 어떤 안전 규정에 대해 이야기하고 있는가?
(A) 1번 규정
(B) 2번 규정
(C) 3번 규정
(D) 4번 규정

해설 빵을 들고 있는 여자에게 남자가 "The rule says that there can't be any food on the factory floor."라며 작업 현장에 음식물이 있으면 안 된다고 했고, 이에 해당하는 내용은 4번 규정이므로 정답은 (D)이다.

PART • 4

[71-73] 전화 메시지

Hello, Ms. Yang. This is Leslie from Spick & Span Cleaning Service. I'm calling about the cleaning appointment at your house tomorrow. We'll be there at nine, and we'll start by vacuuming the floors and cleaning the kitchen and bathrooms as usual. You mentioned that you also would like us to shampoo your carpets this time. We are planning to do that, but just make sure that you move all items and small furniture off of the carpets so that we can clean as best as possible. Also, keep in mind that the carpets will be damp for approximately twelve hours. If you need to reschedule for any reason, please call our office at 555-4810 and leave a message. Otherwise, we'll be there tomorrow morning at nine o'clock. Thank you.

안녕하세요, 양 씨. 저는 Spick & Span 청소 서비스 사의 레슬리입니다. 내일 당신의 집 청소 예약 때문에 전화 드립니다. 저희는 내일 9시에 방문할 것이고, 평소와 마찬가지로 진공청소기로 바닥을 밀고 주방과 욕실을 청소하는 것부터 시작할 것입니다. 당신은 이번에 카펫을 세탁하고 싶다고 하셨습니다. 저희는 그렇게 할 계획이고, 저희가 가능한 한 깨끗이 청소할 수 있도록 반드시 모든 물건과 작은 가구들을 카펫에서 치워주세요. 또한 카펫이 약 12시간 동안 축축할 것임을 명심해 주세요. 어떤 이유로든 일정을 변경해야 한다면, 555-4810으로 저희 사무실에 전화해서 메시지를 남겨 주세요. 그렇지 않으면, 저희는 내일 오전 9시에 그곳을 방문하겠습니다. 감사합니다.

어휘 vacuum (진공청소기로) 청소하다 as usual 평소와 마찬가지로 mention 언급하다 shampoo 청소하다 move 옮기다 item 물건, 품목 keep in mind 명심하다 damp 젖은, 축축한 approximately 거의 reschedule 일정을 변경하다 otherwise 그렇지 않으면 purpose 목적 promote 홍보하다 confirm 확인하다 work plan 작업 계획 flooring 마루, 바닥재 delivery 배달 repair 수리; 수리하다 president 사장 leave 남기다

71 주제/목적

메시지의 목적은 무엇인가?
(A) 새로운 사업을 홍보하기 위해
(B) 가재도구를 판매하기 위해
(C) 작업 계획을 확인하기 위해
(D) 약속을 취소하기 위해

해설 전화 메시지의 목적을 묻는 질문으로, 메시지 초반 'I'm calling about the cleaning appointment at your house tomorrow.'에서 청소 예약을 확인하기 위해 전화했다는 것을 알 수 있다. 따라서 정답은 (C)이다.

72 화자의 직업

화자는 어떤 업종에서 근무하고 있는가?
(A) 바닥재 납품업체
(B) 청소업체
(C) 택배업체
(D) 주택 수리업체

해설 화자가 어떤 업종에서 근무하는지 묻는 질문으로, 'This is Leslie from Spick & Span Cleaning Service. I'm calling about the cleaning appointment at your house tomorrow.'에서 청소 용역 업체에서 근무하는 사람이라는 것을 알 수 있다. 따라서 정답은 (B)이다.

73 세부 사항

청자는 약속을 변경하려면 무엇을 해야 하는가?
(A) 가게를 방문한다
(B) 웹 사이트에 접속한다
(C) 업체 사장에게 전화한다
(D) 전화 메시지를 남긴다

해설 화자의 당부 내용은 지문 후반부에 나오는 것이 일반적이다. 메시지 후반의 "If you need to reschedule for any reason, please call our office at 555-4810 and leave a message."에서 전화해서 메시지를 남겨야 약속을 변경할 수 있다는 것을 알 수 있다. 따라서 정답은 (D)이다.

[74-76] 방송

And now, the Altra Mountain Radio Calendar of Events. This weekend, Mountain Elementary School will be hosting their annual charity sale of books, and they're asking for help from the community. If you have any used books or even new ones that you're willing to donate to the event, please drop them off at the elementary school's main office by Wednesday afternoon. The other event on the calendar is the first annual Altra Mountain Five Kilometer Marathon, which is scheduled for Saturday. Stay tuned for more details on the race. On that note, let's go to the weather.

이어서, Altra Mountain 라디오의 행사 일정입니다. 이번 주말에, Mountain 초등학교가 연례 도서 자선 바자회를 여는데, 그들은 지역 주민들에게 도움을 요청하고 있습니다. 행사에 기부하고 싶은 중고 책이나 새 책이 있다면, 수요일 오후까지 초등학교 본관에 맡겨 주세요. 일정표에 있는 다른 행사는 토요일에 예정된 제 1회 연례 Altra Mountain 5km 마라톤입니다. 경주에 대한 더 자세한 정보를 위해 채널을 고정해 주세요. 그런 의미에서, 날씨를 확인해 보죠.

어휘 calendar 달력, 일정표 host 주최하다 annual 연례의 charity 자선 community 주민, 지역 공동체 drop off 맡기다 stay tuned 채널 고정하다 broadcast 방송 local 지역의 author 작가 condition 상황 upcoming 다가오는 event 행사 opportunity 기회 complete 완성하다 application 지원, 지원서 donation 기부, 헌금 organization 조직, 단체

74 주제/목적

방송은 주로 무엇에 대한 것인가?
(A) 지역 작가
(B) 교통 상황
(C) 다가오는 행사
(D) 취업 기회

해설 화자는 "the Altra Mountain Radio Calendar of Events."라며 코너를 소개하고, 이후 도서 바자회 및 마라톤 행사에 대해 설명하고 있으므로 (C)가 정답이다.

75 세부 사항

청자들은 수요일 오후까지 무엇을 하라고 요구 받는가?
(A) 경기에 참가하라고
(B) 신청서를 작성하라고
(C) 기부하라고
(D) 단체에 가입하라고

해설 질문의 키워드는 Wednesday afternoon으로, 화자는 도서 바자회에 내해 말하면서 "please drop them off at the elementary school's main office by Wednesday afternoon." 수요일 오후까지 기부할 책을 본관에 맡겨달라, 즉 책을 기부하라고 했으므로 정답은 (C)이다.

76 다음에 할 일

청자는 다음에 무엇을 들을 것인가?
(A) 교통 정보
(B) 광고
(C) 일기 예보
(D) 인터뷰

해설 지문 마지막 문장 "let's go to the weather."에서 날씨를 확인해 보자고 하므로, 이후 일기 예보가 이어질 것을 알 수 있다. 따라서 정답은 (C)이다.

Asher, it's Mary. I received some user feedback on the new accounting management software my team's been working on. The program has a few problems. They're all related to how the numbers are calculated. Helen suggested I call you because you've worked on these kinds of problems before. She said you'd know how to solve these issues. They all need to be corrected by the end of the month, and a lot of people on my team are on vacation. Give me a call back when you have time. Thanks.

어서 씨, 메리입니다. 저희 팀이 작업하고 있는 새로운 회계 관리 소프트웨어에 대한 사용자 피드백을 받았는데요. 프로그램에 몇 가지 문제가 있어요. 그것들은 모두 숫자가 계산되는 방식과 관련되어 있네요. 헬렌은 당신이 이런 종류의 문제를 이전에 다루어 본 적이 있기 때문에 당신에게 전화하라고 제안했어요. 당신이 이 문제를 해결할 방법을 알 거라고 하더군요. 이번 달 말까지 모든 것이 수정되어야 하는데, 저희 팀의 많은 사람들이 휴가를 갔어요. 시간 날 때 전화 주세요. 감사합니다.

어휘 feedback 피드백, 의견　accounting 회계　a few 몇몇의　be related 관련되다　calculate 계산하다　suggest 제안하다　solve 해결하다　issue 이슈, 문제　correct 수정하다　vacation 휴가　budget 예산　workshop 워크숍, 훈련　recommend 추천하다　conduct 실시하다, 수행하다　training 훈련　session 시간, 수업　connection 관계, 연줄　industry 업계, 분야　experience 경력, 경험　similar 유사한　propose 제안하다　decline 거절하다　accept 받아들이다　revision 수정

77 세부 사항

화자의 팀은 무엇을 작업하고 있는가?
(A) 회계 예산
(B) 컴퓨터 프로그램
(C) 여행 일정
(D) 경영진 워크숍

해설 화자는 첫 문장 "I received some user feedback on the new accounting management software my team's been working on."에서 자신의 팀이 회계 관리 소프트웨어를 작업하고 있다고 말하고 있다. 따라서 정답은 이를 컴퓨터 프로그램이라고 표현한 (B)이다.

78 세부 사항

화자에 의하면, 청자는 왜 추천되었는가?
(A) 그는 교육을 실시할 수 있다.
(B) 그는 신제품에 할인을 제공할 수 있다.
(C) 그는 그 업계에 사업상 인맥이 있다.
(D) 그는 비슷한 문제를 경험했다.

해설 지문 중반 "Helen suggested I call you because you've worked on these kinds of problems before. She said you'd know how to solve these issues."에서 헬렌이 남자와 비슷한 문제를 겪었으니 해결책을 알 것이라며 그를 추천했다는 것을 알 수 있다. 따라서 정답은 (D)이다.

79 의도 파악

화자는 왜 "저희 팀의 많은 사람들이 휴가를 갔어요"라고 말하는가?
(A) 일정 변경을 제안하기 위해
(B) 제안을 거절하기 위해
(C) 요청된 수정 사항을 받아들이기 위해
(D) 왜 도움이 필요한지 설명하기 위해

해설 의도 문제는 해당 문장의 앞뒤 문맥을 파악해야 한다. 화자는 자신이 겪고 있는 문제 때문에 청자에게 연락했고, 주어진 문장에서 많은 팀원들이 휴가를 갔다고 한 것은 청자의 도움이 필요한 상황임을 설명하기 위해서다. 따라서 정답은 (D)이다.

The next topic we will discuss is the electric wiring work in the building that will be done next week. You have probably noticed electricians have been walking around since Monday. They performed an extensive inspection of the whole building and found some problems that could be potentially hazardous to our safety. The problem areas are mostly in the basement, including the company cafeteria and main conference hall. We have decided to do some repair work and rewire the entire basement. That means we have to turn the electricity off on Thursday for a total of five hours. Lunch will be served as usual in the cafeteria, but employees are not allowed to stay there after three o'clock and should leave earlier on that day. Everything should be back to normal on Friday. If you have any questions, you can contact Mr. Tim Butler, the maintenance supervisor.

우리가 논의할 다음 주제는 다음 주에 완료될 건물 내 전기 배선 작업에 관한 것입니다. 아마 여러분도 월요일부터 전기 기사들이 돌아다니는 걸 아셨을 겁니다. 그들은 건물 전체에 대한 대규모 검사를 실시했고, 잠재적으로 우리의 안전에 위협이 될 수 있는 몇 가지 문제들을 발견했습니다. 문제가 되는 장소는 대부분 지하에 있는데, 구내식당과 본 회의실을 포함합니다. 우리는 수리 작업을 하고, 지하 전체 전선을 갈기로 결정했습니다. 이는 목요일에 총 다섯 시간 동안 전기를 꺼야 한다는 것을 의미합니다. 점심 식사는 평소처럼 구내식당에서 제공될 것이지만, 그날에는 3시 이후로 직원들이 그곳에 있을 수 없고 더 일찍 나가야 합니다. 금요일에는 모든 것이 정상으로 돌아올 것입니다. 질문 있으시면, 시설관리 부장 팀 버틀러 씨에게 연락하시면 됩니다.

어휘 topic 주제　discuss 토론하다, 논의하다　electric 전기의　notice 알아채다, 알아보다　electrician 전기 기사　perform

실시하다 extensive 광범위한, 대규모의 inspection 검사 potentially 잠재적으로 hazardous 위험한 safety 안전 area 지역 mostly 대부분 basement 지하 cafeteria 구내식당 rewire 전선을 갈다 entire 전체의 turn off 끄다 a total of 총, 전부 as usual 평소와 같이 be allowed to ~이 허용되다 normal 평소의, 보통의 contact 연락하다 supervisor 관리자 equipment 장비, 기계 encourage 독려하다, 권고하다 save 절약하다, 지축하다

80 주제/목적

담화의 목적은 무엇인가?
(A) 새로운 장비를 설명하기 위해
(B) 정비 작업을 알리기 위해
(C) 구내 식당 개조를 위한 기금을 마련하기 위해
(D) 전기 절약을 권고하기 위해

해설 담화의 목적은 주로 본문의 앞에서 확인할 수 있다. 첫 문장 "The next topic we will discuss is the electric wiring work in the building"에서 건물 정비 작업에 대해 공지하는 내용임을 알 수 있다. 따라서 답은 (B)이다.

81 세부 사항

작업은 언제 완료될 것인가?
(A) 월요일에
(B) 수요일에
(C) 목요일에
(D) 금요일에

해설 발표의 중간 부분 "That means we have to turn the electricity off on Thursday for a total of five hours."에서 목요일에는 정전이 되는 것으로 보아 그날에 작업한다는 것을 알 수 있다. 그리고, "Everything should be back to normal on Friday."에서 금요일에는 모든 것이 정상으로 돌아온다고 했으므로 작업은 목요일 안에 완료된다고 볼 수 있다. 따라서 정답은 (C)이다.

82 요청 사항

청자들은 무엇을 하도록 요청 받는가?
(A) 경비원에게 보고하라고
(B) 금요일에 하루 쉬라고
(C) 문제가 있으면 전기 기사에게 연락하라고
(D) 구내 식당을 평소보다 빨리 떠나라고

해설 발표의 마지막 부분 "but employees are not allowed to stay there after three o'clock and should leave earlier on that day."에서 목요일에는 수리 작업으로 인해 평소보다 구내식당에서 빨리 나가야 한다고 했으므로 정답은 (D)이다.

[83-85] 안내

> Ladies and gentlemen, may I have your attention for a moment, please? There has been a slight change to today's agenda. Due to some unforeseen circumstances, our motivational speaker will be presenting at 4 P.M. instead of one o'clock as originally scheduled. We apologize for the postponement of this popular presentation. There aren't any more changes to the rest of the schedule. A buffet lunch will be available in the second-floor banquet hall at 12:30 P.M. as planned. After lunch, Ted Leopold will be giving the keynote speech entitled "Networking 101: How to Grow Your Client Base." We apologize again for the inconvenience and hope you enjoy the rest of the conference. Thank you.

신사 숙녀 여러분, 잠깐 주목해 주시겠습니까? 오늘 일정에 약간의 변동이 생겼습니다. 예기치 못한 상황으로 인해, 저희 동기 부여 강사가 원래 예정되었던 1시 대신 오후 4시에 발표할 것입니다. 이 인기 강연이 연기된 것에 대해 사과 드립니다. 나머지 일정에는 더 이상 변동 사항이 없습니다. 점심 식사 뷔페는 예정대로 오후 12시 30분에 2층 연회실에서 이용 가능합니다. 점심 식사 후에는 테드 레오폴드 씨가 '인맥 관리 기초: 고객 기반을 확충하는 법'이라는 제목의 기조연설을 할 것입니다. 불편을 드려 다시 한 번 사과 드리며 남은 컨퍼런스를 즐기시길 바랍니다. 감사합니다.

어휘 attention 주의, 집중 for a moment 잠시 동안 slight 약간의 unforeseen 예기치 않은 circumstance 상황 present 발표하다 instead of ~대신에 originally 원래 scheduled 예정된 apologize 사과하다 postponement 연기 rest 나머지 banquet 연회 entitled ~ ~라는 제목의 inconvenience 불편 announcement 발표 location 위치 updated 업데이트된, 개선된 building plan 건물 도면 postpone 연기하다 registration 등록 deadline 마감 시한 departure 출발 motivational 동기를 부여하는 speech 연설 keynote speaker 기조 연설자

83 주제/목적

발표는 무엇에 관한 것인가?
(A) 식당의 위치
(B) 컨퍼런스 일정
(C) 업데이트된 건물 도면
(D) 새로운 회의 장소

해설 초반부의 "There has been a slight change to today's agenda."에서 일정에 약간의 변동이 생겼음을 공지하고 있다. 따라서 정답은 (B)이다. agenda라는 어휘는 '안건' 외에 '일정(schedule, plan)'이라는 의미도 있다는 것을 기억해 두자. 선택지에서는 schedule로 패러프레이징되었다.

84 세부 사항

무엇이 연기되었는가?
(A) 등록 마감일
(B) 출발 시간
(C) 업무상 점심 식사
(D) 동기 부여 연설

해설 "Due to some unforeseen circumstances, our motivational speaker will be presenting at 4 P.M. instead of one o'clock as originally scheduled."에서 예기치 못한 상황으로 동기 부여 강사가 원래 예정된 시각보다 늦게 발표하게 되었다고 했으므로, (D) 동기 부여 연설이 연기되었음을 알 수 있다.

85 다음에 할 일

청자들은 오후에 무엇을 할 것인가?
(A) 발표를 듣는다
(B) 프로그램에 등록한다
(C) 구내식당에 간다
(D) 기조 연설자와 대화한다

해설 지문 마지막의 "After lunch, Ted Leopold will be giving the keynote speech ~" 부분을 통해 청자들이 오후에 기조 연설을 들을 것임을 알 수 있다. 따라서 정답은 (A)이다.

[86-88] 설명/소개

Welcome to this event sponsored by the city's Department of Business Development. Today's seminar is aimed at making local business owners like you aware of the funding available through our department. This money will help you take your businesses to the next level. <u>Did you know that this program received only five applications last year?</u> We hope to change that this year. Local businesses can use the financial grants to expand their operations and increase their profits. Now, let's begin by watching a short video about how a local paper company used this fund to increase its capacity.

시당국 사업개발 부서에서 후원하는 이번 행사에 오신 것을 환영합니다. 오늘의 세미나는 여러분과 같은 지역 사업가들이 저희 부서를 통해 사용 가능한 자금이 있다는 것을 인식시키기 위한 것입니다. 이 자금은 여러분의 사업이 다음 단계로 나아갈 수 있도록 도움을 줄 것입니다. 작년에는 이 프로그램에서 신청서를 다섯 개밖에 못 받았다는 것을 알고 계세요? 저희는 올해 이것이 바뀌길 기대하고 있습니다. 지역 사업체들은 운영을 확장하고 수익을 증가시키기 위해 재정 보조금을 사용할 수 있습니다. 지금부터, 한 지역 제지 회사가 물량을 늘리기 위해 이 자금을 어떻게 활용했는지 짧은 동영상을 보는 것으로 시작하도록 하죠.

어휘 sponsor 후원하다 department 부서 aim 목표로 하다 local 지역의 owner 소유자 aware 알고 있는, 인지하고 있는 funding 자금 financial 재정의 grant 보조금

operation 운영 increase 증가시키다 profit 수익 paper company 제지 회사 capacity 물량, 능력, 용량 government 정부 factory 공장 competitive 경쟁력이 높은 well-known 잘 알려진, 유명한 budget 예산 discuss 토론하다, 이야기하다 strategy 전략 review 검토하다 material 자료, 재료 film 영화

86 청자의 직업

청자들은 누구일 것 같은가?
(A) 소프트웨어 프로그래머
(B) 정부 직원
(C) 공장 직원
(D) 사업주

해설 청자가 누구인지 묻는 질문은 주로 본문 초반에 힌트를 얻을 수 있다. 두 번째 문장 "Today's seminar is aimed at making local business owners like you aware of the funding available through our department."에서 청자들이 행사에 온 지역 사업가들임을 알 수 있다. 따라서 정답은 (D)이다.

87 의도 파악

화자가 "작년에는 이 프로그램에서 신청서를 다섯 개밖에 못 받았다는 것을 알고 계세요?"라고 말하는 의미는 무엇인가?
(A) 그 프로그램은 매우 경쟁력이 있다.
(B) 그 프로그램은 취소되어야 한다.
(C) 그 프로그램은 별로 알려지지 않았다.
(D) 그 프로그램은 예산이 많지 않다.

해설 화자의 의도 문제는 주어진 문장의 앞뒤 문맥을 파악해야 한다. 남자가 지역 사업가를 돕는 재정 보조금에 대해 소개하면서 이 프로그램이 작년에는 신청서를 다섯 개만 받았다고 하는 것은 사람들이 프로그램에 대해 잘 알지 못한다는 것을 의미한다. 따라서 가장 적절한 것은 (C)이다.

88 다음에 할 일

청자들은 다음에 무엇을 할 것인가?
(A) 몇 가지 질문을 한다
(B) 사업 전략을 논의한다
(C) 추가 자료를 검토한다
(D) 영상을 본다

해설 지문 마지막 문장 "Now, let's begin by watching a short video about how a local paper company used this fund to increase its capacity." 부분에서 동영상을 통해 특정 회사의 성공 사례를 볼 것임을 알 수 있다. 따라서 정답은 video의 동의어 film을 사용한 (D)이다.

[89-91] 안내

Welcome to NYK Enterprises. I am Jennifer Kim from the personnel department. Today I will show you around the production plant and help you get used to your new working environment at our company. I know what it's like on your first day of a new job, so feel free to ask any questions or share any concerns you may have. We will first have a look at the publication room, where we print out and package all of our magazines before national distribution. Then, we will move to the editorial room and meet our designers and writers. Lastly, I'll take you to my office in the personnel department to distribute your identification badges. Now, follow me, please.

NYK 기업에 오신 것을 환영합니다. 저는 인사부의 제니퍼 킴입니다. 오늘 저는 여러분께 생산 공장을 보여드리고, 여러분이 회사의 새로운 작업 환경에 적응하도록 도와 드릴 것입니다. 새 직장에서의 첫날이 어떤지 알고 있으니, 어떤 질문이든 편하게 하시고, 걱정거리가 있으면 공유해 주시기 바랍니다. 여러분께서는 우선 저희 잡지가 전국에 배포되기 전에 인쇄되고 포장되는 출판실을 볼 것입니다. 그 다음, 편집실로 이동해서 저희 디자이너들과 작가들을 만날 겁니다. 마지막으로, 여러분의 사원증을 나눠 드리기 위해 인사부에 있는 제 사무실로 여러분을 안내할 겁니다. 이제, 저를 따라오세요.

어휘 enterprise 기업, 사업 personnel department 인사부 show ~ around ~에게 구경시켜 주다 production 생산, 제조 plant 공장 environment 환경 publication 발행, 출판 national 전국적인, 국가의 distribution 유통, 배급 move 움직이다, 이동하다 editorial 편집의 writer 작가 lastly 마지막으로 take 데리고 가다 badge 명찰, 배지 follow 따라가다 public relations 홍보 shipping 배송 journalist 기자, 언론인 subscriber 구독자 apply for ~에 지원하다 position 자리, 직책 sign 서명하다 contract 계약서 identification 신분, 신분증 division 부서

89 화자의 직업

화자는 어떤 부서에서 일하고 있는가?
(A) 인사부
(B) 해외 영업부
(C) 홍보부
(D) 배송부

해설 화자가 도입부에서 'I am Jennifer Kim from the personnel department.'라며 자신이 인사부 소속임을 밝히고 있으므로 정답은 (A)이다.

90 청자의 직업

화자는 누구에게 이야기하고 있는가?
(A) 투자자들
(B) 기자들
(C) 신입 사원들
(D) 잡지 구독자들

해설 화자가 이야기하는 대상을 묻는 질문이다. 화자의 두 번째 대사 "Today I will show you around the production plant and help you get used to your new working environment"에서 회사를 안내하고 새로운 작업 환경에 익숙해지도록 돕겠다고 언급하고, "I know what it's like on your first day of a new job, ~"에서 새 직장의 첫날이라고 하는 것으로 보아 화자가 신입 사원들을 인솔하고 있음을 알 수 있다. 따라서 정답은 (C)이다.

91 세부 사항

청자들은 왜 화자의 사무실을 방문하도록 요구되는가?
(A) 공석에 지원하기 위해
(B) 고용 계약서에 서명하기 위해
(C) 사원증을 받기 위해
(D) 다른 부서의 직원들을 만나기 위해

해설 본문 후반부의 "Lastly, I'll take you to my office in the personnel department to distribute your identification badges."에서 청자들이 사원증을 받기 위해 인사부에 방문할 것임을 알 수 있다. 따라서 정답은 (C)이다.

[92-94] 회의 발췌

I've called this meeting to inform you of an expansion of our shipping service. As you know, we were offering delivery service only to the southern part of the U.S. However, we decided to expand our service into all parts of the country since interest in our products has grown significantly. Now, we finally have the infrastructure in place to meet the needs of customers. And we will be very busy next week when we start to ship our products throughout the country.

우리 배송 서비스 확대를 알려드리기 위해 이번 회의를 소집했습니다. 아시다시피, 우리는 미국 남부 지역에만 배송 서비스를 제공하고 있었습니다. 하지만 우리 제품에 대한 관심이 상당히 증가해서, 우리는 배송 서비스를 전국 각지로 확장하기로 결정했습니다. 이제, 마침내 고객들의 요구를 만족시킬 수 있는 기반 시설이 마련되었습니다. 그리고 전국에 제품 배송을 시작하는 다음 주에는 아주 바빠질 것입니다.

어휘 call a meeting 회의를 소집하다 inform A of B A에게 B에 대해 알리다 expansion 확대, 확장 expand 확대하다, 확장하다 significantly 상당히, 크게 infrastructure 사회[공공] 기반 시설 in place ~을 위한 준비가 되어 있는 throughout 도처에, 내내

92 주제/목적

무엇이 주로 논의되고 있는가?
(A) 배송비 절감
(B) 서비스 확대
(C) 새로운 지점 개점
(D) 신입 직원 채용

해설 지문의 전반적인 내용을 파악해야 하는 문제이다. 첫 번째 문장 "I've called this meeting to inform you of an expansion of our shipping service"에서 배송 서비스의 확대를 알리기 위해 회의를 소집했다고 하고, 지문 중반 "we decided to expand our service into all parts of the country"에서 제품에 대한 관심이 높아짐에 따라 전국으로 서비스를 확장하기로 했다고 하므로 정답은 (B)이다.

93 세부 사항

회사는 왜 변화를 줬는가?
(A) 경쟁이 심해졌다.
(B) 고객 불만이 증가했다.
(C) 제품이 인기를 얻었다.
(D) 기름값이 급증했다.

해설 지문 중반의 "However, we decided to expand our service into all parts of the country since interest in our products has grown significantly."를 보면, 제품에 대한 관심이 높아져서, 즉 제품이 인기를 얻어서 서비스를 전국적으로 확대하기로 했다고 하므로 정답은 (C)이다.

94 다음에 할 일

다음 주에 무슨 일이 일어날 것인가?
(A) 회사가 더 많은 지역을 다룰 것이다.
(B) 회사가 사무실을 수리할 것이다.
(C) 회사가 다음 회의를 소집할 것이다.
(D) 회사가 신제품을 출시할 것이다.

해설 앞으로 일어날 일에 대한 단서는 주로 지문의 후반에 나온다. 문제의 키워드인 "next week"이 나오는 문장 "And we will be very busy next week when we start to ship our products throughout the country."를 보면, 다음 주에 전국적으로 배송을 시작하기 때문에 바쁠 것이라고 하므로 정답은 (A)이다.

[95-97] 전화 메시지 & 조사 보고서

Hi, this is Clare Anderson from the clothing manufacturer Red Monkey Company. You came to do a safety inspection at our factory last week. I am calling because I just reviewed your report, and I have some questions about it. On the left side of the report, everything looks like it was checked out fine. But on the right side, there was no explanation as to why we failed the inspection. We need to know exactly why our machinery couldn't pass the inspection so we can fix the problem as quickly as possible. I'm worried because we have a large order to fill soon. Would it be safe to resume our production? Please call me back at your earliest convenience.

안녕하세요, 저는 의류 제조업체 Red Monkey 사의 클레어 앤더슨입니다. 당신은 지난주에 안전 검사를 하러 저희 공장에 오셨는데요. 방금 전 당신의 보고서를 검토했고 그것에 대해 질문이 있어서 전화 드립니다. 보고서 좌측에는 모든 것이 잘 체크된 것으로 보입니다. 하지만 우측에는, 우리가 왜 검사에 불합격했는지 설명이 없었습니다.

저희 기계가 검사에 통과하지 못한 이유를 정확히 알아야 그 문제를 최대한 빨리 해결할 수 있습니다. 저희는 곧 대량 주문을 처리해야 해서 걱정입니다. 생산을 재개해도 안전할까요? 되도록 빨리 연락 주시기 바랍니다.

안전 검사			
회사명 : Red Monkey 사		**의견 :** 검사 불합격 - 기계류	
체크리스트 : ☑ 장비 ☑ 바닥 ☑ 조명 ☑ 비상구		**검사관 :** 아담 왈츠	

어휘 clothing 의류 safety 안전 inspection 검사 just 방금 전에 review 검토하다 report 보고서 fine 잘, 괜찮게 explanation 설명 as to ~에 관한 fail 실패하다, 불합격하다 exactly 정확하게 pass 통과하다 fix 고치다 as quickly as possible 되도록 빨리 fill 채우다 resume 다시 시작하다 production 생산 at one's earliest convenience 형편 닿는 대로, 되도록 일찍 comment 의견, 코멘트 equipment 장비 inspector 검사관 manufacturing 제조 moving 이사 be concerned about ~에 대해 걱정하다 order 주문; 주문하다 complete 완성시키다 keep track of ~을 기억하다, 추적하다 inventory 재고, 물건 penalty 벌금

95 화자의 근무지

화자는 어디에서 일하는가?
(A) 제조 회사에서
(B) 이사업체에서
(C) 디자인 회사에서
(D) 배송업체에서

해설 화자가 일하는 곳을 묻는 질문으로, 본문 초반에서 힌트를 확인할 수 있다. 지문 첫 문장인 "Hi, this is Clare Anderson from the clothing manufacturer Red Monkey Company."에서 화자가 의류 제조업체에서 일한다고 밝혔으므로 정답은 (A)이다.

96 시각 자료 연계

시각 자료를 보시오. 화자는 보고서의 어떤 부분에 대해 질문하는가?
(A) 회사명
(B) 체크리스트
(C) 의견
(D) 검사관

해설 본문 중간의 "But on the right side, there was no explanation as to why we failed the inspection."에서 표의 우측에 불합격 이유가 나와 있지 않다고 했고, 보고서에서 이에 해당되는 부분은 Comments(의견)이므로, 정답은 (C)이다.

97 문제점

화자는 무엇에 대해 걱정하는가?
(A) 새로운 장비 주문하기
(B) 주문 완료하기
(C) 재고 확인하기
(D) 벌금 내기

해설 본문의 마지막 "I'm worried because we have a large order to fill soon."에서 화자가 곧 대량 주문을 처리해야 하는 것에 대해 걱정하고 있음을 알 수 있다. 따라서 정답은 (B)이다.

[98-100] 안내 & 진열 케이스

Good morning, Shop & Lite Grocery Store customers. To celebrate the grand opening of this store, we're offering discounts on a lot of great items for today. We'll be announcing additional price cuts every hour until we close tonight. Right now, check out our bakery department because its cases are full of delicious baked goods from the store ovens—cakes, pies, cookies, and muffins. And we just reduced the price of cookies by another 20 percent.

좋은 아침입니다, Shop & Lite 식료품점 고객 여러분. 가게 개업을 축하하기 위해, 저희는 오늘 많은 훌륭한 제품에 할인을 제공하고 있습니다. 저희는 오늘 밤 마감할 때까지 매 시간마다 추가 할인을 발표할 것입니다. 바로 지금, 저희 베이커리 코너를 확인해 주세요. 진열장은 오븐에서 구운 맛있는 빵들로 가득 차 있으니까요. - 케익, 파이, 쿠키, 머핀이 있습니다. 그리고 저희는 지금 쿠키 가격을 20퍼센트 더 인하했습니다.

1번 칸	케이크
2번 칸	파이
3번 칸	쿠키
4번 칸	머핀

어휘 grocery store 식료품점 celebrate 축하하다 grand opening 개업 announce 발표하다 additional 추가의 price cut 가격 할인 check out 확인하다 delicious 맛있는 holiday 휴일 release 출시하다 upcoming 다가오는 merger 합병 contain 포함하다

98 세부 사항

가게는 무엇을 축하하고 있는가?
(A) 국경일
(B) 개업
(C) 새로 출시된 제품
(D) 다가오는 합병

해설 지문 초반의 "To celebrate the grand opening of this store, we're offering discounts on a lot of great items for today."에서 가게의 개업을 축하한다는 것을 알 수 있다.

따라서 정답은 (B)이다.

99 세부 사항

행사는 언제 끝나는가?
(A) 다음 달
(B) 다음 주
(C) 이틀 후
(D) 오늘 밤

해설 지문의 중간 "We'll be announcing additional price cuts every hour until we close tonight."에서 할인 행사가 오늘 밤 마감할 때까지 진행된다고 했으므로 (D)가 정답임을 알 수 있다.

100 시각 자료 연계

시각 자료를 보시오. 어떤 칸에 추가 할인 제품이 들어 있는가?
(A) 1번 칸
(B) 2번 칸
(C) 3번 칸
(D) 4번 칸

해설 지문 마지막에 "And we just reduced the price of cookies by another 20 percent."에서 쿠키에 추가 할인을 제공한다고 했고, 도표에서 쿠키가 있는 곳은 3번 칸이므로 정답은 (C)이다.

PART · 5

101 대명사

연례 학술 포럼에 참석하고 싶은 사람들은 본인의 사진이 부착된 신분증을 회의장에 가지고 와야 합니다.

해설 빈칸은 사람을 선행사로 하는 관계대명사 who 앞에 있으므로, '사람들'의 의미를 가지는 (B) Those가 정답이다. 나머지는 사물을 대신하는 대명사이므로 오답이다.

어휘 identification card 신분증

102 형용사 자리

금융당국은 민간 기업들과 협력하면서, 현재의 시장 위기를 시기적절하게 해결해야 합니다.

해설 빈칸은 명사(manner)를 수식하는 자리이므로 형용사가 위치해야 한다. 명사 time 뒤에 '-ly'를 붙이면 형용사가 되므로 (C) timely가 정답이다.

어휘 Financial Services Authority 금융당국 crisis 위기 in a timely manner 시기적절하게

103 최상급

온라인으로 주문하는 것은 우리 제품을 구매하는 방법 중 당신의 물건을 받는 가장 빠른 방법입니다.

해설 빈칸은 명사 way 앞 형용사가 필요한 자리이다. 문장 마지막

[among + 복수명사]는 최상급 표현과 함께 '~ 중에서 가장 ~한'의 뜻으로 쓰인다. 따라서 정답은 (D)이다.

어휘 place an order 주문하다   method 방법

104 동사 어휘

기사에서 오류를 발견하면 그 문제들을 처리하기 위해 편집장에게 연락해 주세요.

해설 (A) 다루다 (B) 처리하다 (C) 수정하다 (D) 개정하다의 동사 어휘 중에서, 빈칸 뒤 전치사 with와 함께 쓰여 1형식 자동사 '~을 처리하다'를 나타내는 (B) deal이 정답이다. (A) handle도 의미는 유사하지만 뒤에 바로 목적어를 취하는 타동사이다.

어휘 article 기사   chief editor 편집장

105 동명사 자리

Ebensburgh 공장의 새로 임명된 감독관은 우리의 업무 효율을 개선하는 데 전념하고 있습니다.

해설 contributed 뒤의 to는 전치사이므로 빈칸에는 명사 혹은 동명사가 위치해야 한다. 빈칸 뒤에 명사가 나왔으므로 이를 목적어로 취하는 동사의 역할을 하는 동시에 명사 역할도 하는 동명사 (C)가 답이다.

어휘 appointed 임명된   work efficiency 업무 효율

106 형용사 어휘

30년 고정 금리 대출의 이율이 약 5% 증가할 것이고, 그것만으로도 40만 달러의 주택에 대한 기존의 담보 대출금에 매달 120달러가 추가될 것입니다.

해설 (A) 원래의 (B) 보편적인 (C) 내부의 (D) 평상시의/우연한의 형용사 중에서, 이율이 오르기 때문에 '기존 대출금'에서 금액이 더 추가된다는 의미로 (A)가 문맥상 가장 적절하다.

어휘 loan 대출   about 거의, 대략   alone ~하나만으로도   mortgage 담보 대출

107 동사 어휘

그 계약은 세입자들이 그들의 아파트 임대 계약을 갱신하길 원하면 집주인에게 작은 파손이나 큰 구조 변경에 대해 통보해야 한다는 것을 규정합니다.

해설 (A) 악화되다 (B) 제어하다 (C) 규정하다 (D) 간과하다의 동사 어휘 중, 계약이 집주인에게 파손이나 구조 변경을 알려야 한다는 것을 '규정한다'는 것이 자연스러우므로 (C)가 정답이다.

어휘 tenant 세입자   landlord 주인   structural 구조상의   renew 갱신하다   lease 임대차 계약

108 동사의 수

생산성을 증가시키는 새로운 방법들을 만들어 내는 것은 우리 회사를 위한 가장 중요한 단계입니다.

해설 동명사 Creating new methods가 주어이고 문장에 동사가 없으므로, 빈칸에는 단수 동사가 나와야 한다. 따라서 (A) is가 정답이다.

어휘 method 방법   productivity 생산성   stage 단계

109 재귀대명사

베이커 씨는 회사 총회에 참석한 그의 동료들의 부재로 인해 모든 관련 문서의 오류를 직접 수정했습니다.

해설 빈칸 앞이 완전한 문장이므로 빈칸에는 부사가 나와야 한다. 부사 자리에 들어갈 수 있는 대명사는 재귀대명사밖에 없으므로 (D)가 정답이다.

어휘 related 관련된   absence 부재   general conference 총회

110 부사의 기능

Skavolo 사의 경영진은 회사의 긴축 재정 정책으로 인해 추가 자금을 편성해야 할지 아직 결정하지 못했습니다.

해설 부정어 not의 위치로 보아, [not ~ yet] 구조를 이루는 (B)가 정답이다.

어휘 organize 편성하다, 조직하다   supplementary fund 추가 자금   fiscal policy 재정 정책

111 동사의 형태

대학원생들은 프로그램 코디네이터로부터 그들의 논문을 학술지에 출간할 수 있다는 통지를 받았습니다.

해설 보기에 제시된 inform(알리다, 통지하다)은 2개의 목적어가 필요한 4형식 타동사로, 빈칸 뒤 목적어가 that절 하나인 것으로 보아 inform이 수동태로 쓰였음을 알 수 있다. 따라서 정답은 (C) were informed이다.

어휘 publish 출판하다   journal 학술지

112 명사절 접속사

우리 관리자들은 부산 지점에 더 많은 직원들을 모집할 계획인지 알고 싶어 합니다.

해설 빈칸 뒤 to부정사(to plan)를 연결할 의문사가 필요하다. while은 '반면에, 동시에', whereas는 '반면에'라는 의미의 부사절 접속사이다. that은 to부정사와 함께 쓸 수 없다. [whether to V] 형태로, '~할지 말지'의 의미인 (B)가 정답이다.

어휘 would like to ~을 하고 싶다   recruit 모집하다

113 명사 어휘

Xenon 306 컬러 레이저 프린터는 우수한 품질로 당신의 출력에 혁신을 일으킬 작고, 유연하며, 전문적인 컬러 인쇄를 제공합니다.

해설 (A) 농산물 (B) 출력 (C) 수확량 (D) 창조(물)의 명사 어휘 중에서, 프린터가 우수한 품질로 '출력'에 혁신을 일으킨다는 것이 자연스러우므로 정답은 (B)이다.

어휘 compact 작은, 소형의   flexible 유연한   revolutionize 혁신을 일으키다   exceptional (이례적일 정도로) 우수한, 특출한

114 형용사 어휘

비행기 예약이 초과되었기 때문에, 예약이 확인된 사람조차도 좌석을 이용하지 못할 가능성이 있습니다.

해설 (A) 발달한 (B) 통지를 받은 (C) 취소된 (D) 확인된의 분사 어휘 중에서, 예약이 '확인된' 사람조차도 좌석 이용이 불가능할 수 있다는 문맥이므로 (D)가 가장 적절하다.

어휘 overbook 초과하여 예약을 받다 even 심지어, ~조차

115 동사의 시제

IT 지원 센터의 기술자가 우리 서버를 수리할 때쯤, 전 직원들은 우리 웹 사이트에 다시 접속할 것입니다.

해설 시간을 나타내는 부사절 접속사 by the time 절의 시제가 현재이므로 주절은 미래(완료)시제가 나와야 한다. 따라서 (D)가 정답이다.

어휘 repair 수리하다 connect 접속하다, 연결하다

116 수량 형용사

모든 직원들은 다음 시즌을 위한 홍보 캠페인에 어떠한 예외 없이 참여해야 합니다.

해설 빈칸 뒤에 단수 명사 employee가 위치해 있으므로, 복수 명사를 수식하는 (B) A few는 오답이다. (C) All은 복수 명사나 불가산 명사를 수식하므로 오답이고, (D) Whole은 the 또는 소유격의 한정사와 함께 쓰이므로 오답이다. (A) Every는 단수 명사를 수식하므로 정답으로 적절하다.

어휘 participate in ~에 참석하다 promotional 홍보의, 판촉의

117 동사의 형식

Alpha Apparel 사의 CEO는 회사가 곧 현재의 복장 규정을 변경할 것이라고 모든 직원들에게 통지했습니다.

해설 빈칸 뒤 사람 명사(all the employees)와 that절이 목적어로 사용된 4형식 구조이므로 3형식 동사 (B), (C), (D)는 오답이고, 4형식 동사인 (A) notified가 정답이다.

어휘 dress code 복장 규정 soon 곧

118 to부정사 자리

불필요한 비용을 줄이기 위해, Tahoma Electronics 사의 모든 직원들은 주문하기 전에 재고량을 확인해야 합니다.

해설 불필요한 비용을 '줄이기 위해' 재고량을 확인해야 한다는 내용이므로 목적을 나타내는 to부정사 (A)가 정답이다.

어휘 redundant 불필요한, 쓸모 없는 supply 비품, 물품

119 형용사 어휘

많은 주요 신용카드 발행사들은 최근 그들이 외환 거래에 청구하는 비용의 액수를 상당히 증가시키셨습니다.

해설 (A) 배려하는 (B) 중요한 (C) 승낙하는 (D) 상당한의 형용사 어휘 중, 빈칸 뒤 명사 increases를 수식하는 형용사로는 문맥상 (D) substantial이 가장 적절하다.

어휘 issuer 발행처 amount 액수 transaction 거래

120 전치사

HT Tech 사는 시연 단계를 완료한 후 작은 다기능 태블릿 PC를 3월 10일에 마침내 판매하기 시작했습니다.

해설 빈칸 뒤 날짜 March 10과 함께 쓰일 수 있는 전치사는 on이므로 정답은 (D)이다.

어휘 multi-functional 다기능의 demonstration 시연

121 전치사

그 분야의 전문가들을 제외하고는 아무도 어떤 도움 없이 이 카메라를 다루는 방법을 이해할 수 없습니다.

해설 (A) ~때문에 (B) ~을 제외하고 (C) ~옆에 (D) ~다음에의 전치사 중, 전문가를 '제외한' 누구도 이해할 수 없다는 문맥이 어울리므로 (B)가 정답이다.

어휘 professional 전문가 handle 다루다

122 불가산 명사

생산 효율성을 높이기 위해, 우리는 새로운 기계를 구매할 계획을 가지고 있습니다.

해설 명사 (A), (B)의 의미가 비슷해 보이지만, (A)는 '기계'라는 뜻의 가산 명사이므로 관사 없이 단독으로 사용할 수 없다. (B)는 '기계(류)'라는 의미의 불가산 명사로 단독 사용이 가능하므로 (B) machinery가 정답이다.

어휘 production 생산 efficiency 효율 purchase 구매하다

123 부사 어휘

<노인과 바다>를 관람하는 모든 관객들은 공연 직전에 그들의 전자기기를 꺼야 합니다.

해설 (A) 즉시, 바로 (B) 한 번, 한때 (C) 또한 (D) 너무의 부사 중에서, 빈칸 뒤 시간 전치사 before를 수식할 수 있는 것은 (A) right이다.

어휘 audience 관객 device 장치, 기기

124 명사 어휘

고객들이 상품권을 받아서 그것들을 상품으로 교환하게 함으로써, 증가된 선물 카드 상환이 소매업자들의 매출을 신장시킬 수 있습니다.

해설 (A) 상환 (B) 보증(서) (C) 가격 (D) 지불의 명사 어휘 중에서, 상품권을 받고 그것을 상품으로 바꾼다는 것은 '상환'을 의미하므로 (A)가 문맥상 가장 적절하다.

어휘 gift certificate 상품권 merchandise 상품 boost 신장시키다

125 무사설 접속사

우리의 혁신적인 광고가 다른 광고업주들에게 호평을 받은 동시에, 대중들로부터 많은 긍정적인 피드백 또한 받았습니다.

해설 (A) 조건 접속사(~라면) (B) 시간 접속사(~동안) (C) 원인 접속사(~때문에) (D) 목적 접속사(~하기 위해서) 중에서, '그들

이 긍정적인 피드백도 받았다'고 했으므로 동시에 일어난 일을 열거할 때 사용하는 (B)가 문맥상 적절하다.

어휘 innovative 혁신적인 positive 긍정적인

126 전치사 어휘

모든 직원들은 유급 휴가를 포함해서 추가 휴가를 받을 자격이 있습니다.

해설 빈칸 뒤의 a paid holiday(유급 휴가)는 추가 휴가의 한 종류이므로, 유급 휴가를 '포함하는' 추가 휴가라는 의미를 만드는 (A) including이 정답이다. (B), (C), (D)는 모두 시점의 전치사이다.

어휘 be eligible for ~할 자격이 있다 paid holiday 유급 휴가

127 부사 어휘

한 시청 직원이 건설 공사가 긴 주말 연휴로 인해 일시적으로 중단되었다고 발표했습니다.

해설 (A) 두드러지게 (B) 일시적으로 (C) 동시에 (D) 상대적으로 부사 어휘 중에서, 긴 주말 연휴 때문에 공사가 '일시적으로' 중단되었다는 의미를 만드는 (B)가 적절하다.

어휘 municipal 시의 officer 관리, 공무원 suspend 중단하다

128 전치사 어휘

물품 분실을 방지하기 위해 수영장에 입장하기 전에 귀하의 귀중품을 접수처에 맡겨주세요.

해설 빈칸 뒤 분사 entering이 있기 때문에 빈칸에는 시간을 나타내는 전치사이자 접속사인 (A)와 (B)가 나올 수 있다. 문맥상 귀중품은 수영장에 입장하기 '전에' 맡기라고 하는 것이 자연스러우므로 정답은 (A)이다.

어휘 leave 맡기다, 남기다 valuables 귀중품

129 부사 어휘

임원들이 지난 달 만장일치로 인수합병에 동의해서 우리는 새로운 상황에 준비해야 합니다.

해설 (A) 만장일치로 (B) 급격히 (C) 의식적으로 (D) 느리게 부사 어휘 중에서, 인수합병에 '만장일치로' 동의했다는 문맥을 만드는 (A)가 정답이다.

어휘 agree on ~에 동의하다 prepare for ~를 준비하다

130 부사 어휘

모든 직원들은 안전 교육을 위해 오후 5시 정각에 강당에 모이도록 지시를 받았습니다.

해설 (A) 마음속으로 (B) 정각에 (C) 매우 (D) 극도로 부사 중, 문맥 상 강당에 5시 '정각에' 모인다는 뜻을 만드는 (B)가 가장 적절하다.

어휘 instruct 지시하다, 교육하다 auditorium 강당

PART • 6

[131-134] 이메일

수신: t_hiddlestone@clemson.edu
발신: g.mckane@generalbooks.com
날짜: 6월 1일
제목: 방문 가능성

히들스턴 씨에게,

2주 전 대학교 컨퍼런스에서 당신의 연설을 듣게 되어 정말 행운이었습니다. 제 동료들과 저는 당신의 발언이 통찰력 있을 뿐만 아니라 영감을 준다고 생각했습니다. 우리는 당신이 우리의 더 많은 직원들에게도 동기를 부여하는 것이 좋은 계획일 것이라고 생각했습니다. 저희 사무실에 방문하여 월례 총회에서 간단하게 연설해 주실 수 있을까요? 학기가 얼마 전에 끝나서 학생들의 성적 채점을 마무리하느라 바쁠 것이라 생각합니다. 따라서 지금 당장은 방문할 시간을 내기가 어려울 것입니다. 여름방학이 시작되고 2~3주 후에 방문 일정을 잡는 것은 어떠십니까? 가능한 날짜를 논의하기 위해 당신과 통화로 짧게 이야기를 나누고 싶습니다. 다음 주에 제가 당신에게 전화해도 되는지 알려주십시오.

진심으로,

조지 맥케인
대표이사, General Books

어휘 remark 발언 inspiring 격려하는, 영감을 주는 insightful 통찰력 있는 general assembly 총회 semester 학기 grading 점수 매기기 summer break 여름방학 brief 짧은

131 동사 어휘

해설 (A) 금지하다 (B) 칭송하다 (C) 여기다, 생각하다 (D) 발생시키다 타동사 어휘 중, 히들스턴 씨의 연설이 영감을 준다고 '생각한다'는 의미를 만드는 5형식 동사 (C) considered가 정답이다.

132 to부정사

해설 의미상 주어 for you 뒤에는 to부정사가 나오므로 빈칸은 동사 원형의 자리이다. 따라서 (A)가 정답이다.

133 접속 부사

해설 (A) 그러나 (B) 예를 들어 (C) 그러므로 (D) 대조적으로 접속 부사 중, 빈칸 앞뒤 문장은 성적 채점으로 바쁘다, '그러므로' 당장 방문하는 것은 힘들다는 원인과 결과의 관계이므로 이를 연결하는 (C)가 정답이다.

134 문맥에 맞는 문장 고르기

(A) 약속을 잡기 위해, 당신은 저희에게 언제든지 연락하실 수 있습니다.
(B) 교내의 모든 학생들이 당신의 성품을 매우 존경합니다.

(C) 당신의 연설을 듣고 우리는 모두 판매를 증가시키도록 독려되었습니다.

(D) 가능한 날짜를 논의하기 위해 당신과 통화로 짧게 이야기를 나누고 싶습니다.

> 해설 빈칸 앞 문장에서 여름 방학이 시작한 후 2~3주 안에 방문 일정을 잡는 것이 어떤지 물어보았고, 다음 문장에서 다음 주에 통화를 할 수 있는지 알려달라고 했으므로 빈칸에는 "통화하자"는 내용의 (D)가 가장 적절하다.

[135-138] 편지

친구들에게,

연례 Pitt Three Rivers Cleanup 프로그램이 올해는 4월 5일에 시작한다는 것을 알려드리게 되어 기쁩니다. 올해 참가를 희망하는 기존 자원봉사자들과 새로운 자원봉사자들은 보호 장비를 사용하도록 요구될 것입니다. 장비를 요청하려면 아래의 자원봉사자 등록 양식을 작성해주십시오.

이틀간의 강 청소 작업이 Yellow Creek에서 계획되어 있으며, 뒤이어 Three Rivers에서 이틀간 진행됩니다. 또한, 다양한 팀들이 물가에서 회수한 쓰레기를 시 매립지로 운반하기 위해 환경부와 함께 작업할 것입니다. 여러분도 이 중요한 계획에 참여하길 바랍니다. 여러분의 도움으로 올해의 청소 작업은 또 하나의 주요 성공 사례가 될 것입니다. 그곳에서 뵙겠습니다!

진심으로,

제임스 리베라, 관리자
Pitt Recycling 프로그램

> 어휘 annual 연례의 cleanup 청소, 정화 volunteer 자원봉사자 protective gear 보호 장비 fill in 작성하다 registration 등록 retrieve 회수하다 waterfront 물가 landfill 매립지 participate in ~에 참가하다 initiative 계획

135 형용사 자리

> 해설 빈칸은 명사 gear 앞 형용사 자리이므로 (B)가 정답이다. protective gear는 '보호 장비'라는 뜻으로 토익에서 자주 출제되니 꼭 알아두어야 한다.

136 접속 부사

> 해설 (A) 게다가 (B) 우선 (C) 대신에 (D) 그럼에도 불구하고 접속 부사 중, 앞 문장에서는 청소 작업이 이틀 동안 지속될 것이라고 했고, 빈칸 뒤에서는 다양한 팀들이 쓰레기를 옮길 것이라고 활동 내용을 열거했으므로 비슷한 내용을 추가할 때 사용하는 (A)가 가장 적절하다.

137 문맥에 맞는 문장 고르기

(A) 쓰레기를 제거함으로써, 당신은 그 일에 대한 보수를 받을 수 있습니다.

(B) 그 곳에 가기 위해 당신은 21번 Oak Drive 도로를 타셔야 합니다.

(C) 여러분도 이 중요한 계획에 참여하길 바랍니다.

(D) 그들은 지난 두 달 동안 이 행사를 홍보했습니다.

> 해설 앞 문장에는 자원 봉사에 대한 활동 내용들이, 뒤 문장에는 여러분의 도움으로 크게 성공할 것이라는 내용이 나왔으므로 빈칸에는 사람들의 참여를 독려하는 (C)가 가장 적절하다.

138 동사의 시제

> 해설 지문의 전반적인 내용이 미래에 일어날 청소 작업에 대한 것이고, 이것이 성공적인 일이 되는 것 역시 미래의 일이므로 빈칸에는 미래시제가 나와야 한다. 따라서 정답은 (D)이다.

[139-142] 이메일

수신: 존 메이어 <jmayer@eurocar.com>
발신: 모니카 베스 <mbeth@eurocar.com>
날짜: 1월 30일
제목: 회신: 우수한 고객 평가

메이어 씨에게,

상임 이사진들은 최근 고객 만족도 설문조사의 긍정적 결과를 보고 만족했습니다. 이는 대체로 귀하의 Euro Car Rentals 사에 대한 우수한 관리 덕분이라고 생각합니다. 감사의 표시로, 저희는 3월 1일부터 당신에게 그 직책에 대한 영구 계약을 제안하게 되어 기쁩니다. 게다가, 저희는 정규직 보험료와 출장 경비를 포함하여 더 높은 보수를 제공할 것입니다. 귀하가 6개월 전 최고 운영 책임자로서 업무를 시작한 이래로 자동차 임대는 3배가 되었으며, 이 중 40%는 단골 손님에 의한 것입니다. 고객 설문조사에서 우리에 대한 평가도 상당히 개선되었습니다. 이 모든 것들은 Euro 사가 매우 유능한 사람의 손에 맡겨져 있다는 것을 나타내며, 우리는 이를 유지하길 원합니다. 축하합니다!

모니카 베스
인사과

> 어휘 executive board 이사회 satisfaction 만족(도) recognize 인정하다 exceptional 우수한 appreciation 감사 permanent 영구적인 compensation 보상 repeat client 단골 손님 indicate 나타내다 capable 유능한 in one's capable hands 유능한 사람(솜씨)에 의해 remain 유지하다

139 과거 분사

> 해설 문맥상 이사진들이 만족했다는 뜻이므로 과거분사형인 satisfied가 사용되어야 한다. 따라서 정답은 (B)이다.

140 부사 어휘

> 해설 (A) 신중하게 (B) 즉시, 바로 (C) 주로, 대체로 (D) 곧 부사 어휘 중에서, '이는 귀하의 Euro Car Rentals에 대한 우수한 관리 덕분이다'라는 문맥을 수식할 수 있는 부사로 '주로'를 뜻하는 (C) largely가 가장 자연스럽다.

141 문맥에 맞는 문장 고르기

(A) 그러나, 이번에는 승진을 위한 자리가 없다는 것을 당신에게 알리게 되어 유감입니다.
(B) 게다가, 저희는 정규직 보험료와 출장 경비를 포함하여 더 높은 보수를 제공할 것입니다.
(C) 우리 단골 고객들의 피드백과 지지보다 더 가치 있는 것은 없습니다.
(D) 설명하자면, 2분기 판매 수치가 산업 관련 경쟁사들 사이에서 최고입니다.

해설 빈칸 앞 문장의 "감사의 표시로 3월부터 영구 계약을 제안하게 되어 기쁩니다"에 대한 추가 혜택을 서술한 (B)가 문맥 상 가장 적절하다.

142 부사절 접속사

해설 (A) ~이래로 (B) ~때문에 (C) 비록 ~일지라도 (D) ~할 때 부사절 접속사 중, [------ + 주어 + 과거동사, 주어 + 현재완료]의 구조에서 사용되는 것은 Since이다. 또한 문맥상 '~이래로'로 해석되는 것이 가장 자연스러우므로 정답은 (A)이다.

[143-146] 웹 페이지

Golden Save Card

Golden Save Card는 모든 슈퍼마켓 포인트 적립 카드 중에서 적용 범위가 가장 포괄적입니다. 카드 소지자들은 식료품부터 차량 정비까지 모든 것에 대한 포인트를 받습니다. 당신은 일주일 중 아무 때나 카드를 사용하여 특별 선정 물품에 대해 두 배 또는 세 배의 포인트를 받을 수 있습니다. 포인트는 쇼핑, 휘발유 구입, 자동차 렌트나 호텔 예약에 사용할 수 있습니다. 게다가, 저희는 당신의 쇼핑 습관과 선호에 맞는 쿠폰을 제공하기 위해 당신의 쇼핑 방식도 확인합니다. 옷이나 스포츠 장비를 구매하는 것을 좋아하십니까? 저희는 당신의 쿠폰을 맞춤화하고 해당 품목 세일 때마다 당신에게 알림을 전송할 것입니다. 이 모든 서비스들을 이용하는 데에는 추가 비용이 전혀 들지 않습니다. 저희 포인트 적립 카드가 가장 인기 있는 것은 당연한 일입니다.

어휘 comprehensive 종합적인, 포괄적인 coverage 적용 범위 loyalty card 고객 카드, 포인트 적립 카드 holder 소지자 credit 신용, 포인트 groceries 식료품 selected 선정된 purchase 구매하다 book 예약하다 preference 선호(도) equipment 장비 customize 맞춤화하다, 주문 제작하다 alert 알림 absolutely 틀림없이, 전혀 charge 요금

143 형용사 자리

해설 빈칸은 명사 앞 형용사 자리로, 형용사에 해당하는 보기는 (B)와 (C)이다. '(B) 이해할 수 있는, (C) 종합적인, 포괄적인' 중에서, 뒤의 명사 coverage(적용 범위)를 문맥에 맞게 수식할 수 있는 형용사는 (C)이다.

144 문맥에 맞는 문장 고르기

(A) 카드 소지자들은 식료품부터 차량 정비까지 모든 것에 대한 포인트를 받습니다.

(B) 그것들을 신청하시려면, 저희 등록 부서에 연락주세요.
(C) 그것의 혜택 덕분에, 우리의 카드 판매가 이번 분기에 급격히 증가했습니다.
(D) 당신의 신용 정보를 보호하기 위해, 당신은 최신 보안 소프트웨어를 설치해야 합니다.

해설 빈칸 앞 문장과 뒤 문장 모두 카드의 장점과 혜택을 설명하고 있으므로 빈칸에는 이러한 혜택과 관련된 내용의 (A)가 가장 적절하다.

145 동사 어휘

해설 (A) 활성화시키다 (B) 배상하다 (C) 공제하다 (D) 제공하다 타동사 어휘 중, 당신의 쇼핑 습관과 선호에 맞는 쿠폰을 '제공한다'는 문맥으로 (D)가 가장 적절하다.

146 명사 자리

해설 4형식 동사 send는 [send + 간접목적어(사람) + 직접목적어(사물)]의 구조로 사용되는데, 빈칸에는 사물 목적어에 해당하는 명사가 들어가야 하므로 (A)가 정답이다.

PART • 7

[147-148] 정보

DAA

INNOCREATE Awards는 자동차 디자인 분야에서 주목할 만한 업적을 인정하기 위해 매년 주어집니다. 그 상은 Detroit 자동차 협회의 후원을 받고, Detroit 시의 지역 회사들에게 독점적으로 수여됩니다. 그 상은 4개의 부문으로 나뉘며 11월에 Detroit 자동차 박람회에서 발표됩니다. 모든 그래픽 디자인 회사들은 고려 대상으로 작품들을 제출하도록 장려됩니다. 시상 부문에 관한 더 많은 정보와 제출 절차에 대한 세부 사항을 원하시면 DAA 웹 사이트를 방문해 주세요.

어휘 annually 매년 acknowledge 인정하다, 감사를 표하다 remarkable 놀라운, 주목할 만한 accomplishment 업적, 달성 automobile 자동차 sponsor 후원하다 award (상을) 수여하다 exclusively 독점적으로 divide 나누다 category 범주, 카테고리 encourage 장려하다 consideration 고려

147 Not/True 확인

INNOCREATE Awards에 대해 언급된 것은?
(A) 엄청난 금액의 상금을 포함한다.
(B) 2년에 한 번씩 수여된다.
(C) 디자인 분야와 관련된 사람들에게 주어진다.
(D) 국제 재단의 후원을 받는다.

해설 첫 번째 줄 "~ are given annually to acknowledge remarkable accomplishments in automobile design." 을 통해 자동차 디자인 분야에서 주어지는 상임을 알 수 있으므로 (C)가 정답이다.

148 세부 사항

독자들은 무엇을 하도록 권유받는가?
(A) 대회에 참가한다
(B) 피드백을 준다
(C) 시상식에 참석한다
(D) 행사를 준비한다

해설 다섯 번째 줄 "All graphic design companies are encouraged to submit their works for consideration."을 보면 독자들에게(회사들에게) 작품을 제출하도록 권유하고 있으므로 (A)가 정답이다.

[149-150] 증명서

South Dakota 주립 대학
예측 분석학 교육 프로그램

수료증

수여자:
애니 에블린

비즈니스, 마케팅 및 연구에 대한 예측 분석학 이수를 증명합니다.

그녀의 교육 과정은 수업 참여자들에 의해 "우수" 등급을 받았습니다.

수여일: 2024년 6월 20일

존 스왈레

존 스왈레, 박사, 교수
SUSD 연구소 프로그램 코디네이터

어휘 predictive 예측하는 analytics 분석학 certificate 인증서
certify 증명하다

149 세부 사항

에블린 씨는 6월 20일에 무엇을 했는가?
(A) 대학원 프로그램에 등록했다.
(B) South Dakota로 출장을 갔다.
(C) 수료증을 받았다.
(D) 수업 중 하나를 가르쳤다.

해설 수료증의 수여 일자에 6월 20일이라고 나와 있으므로, 에블린 씨가 그 날 수료증을 받았음을 알 수 있다. 따라서 정답은 (C)이다.

150 추론/암시

에블린 씨는 누구일 것 같은가?
(A) 대학원 조교
(B) 시장 조사원
(C) 컴퓨터 기술자
(D) 프로그램 관리자

해설 수료증의 프로그램이 비즈니스, 마케팅, 연구에 대한 예측 분석학이므로 이와 가장 가까운 직종은 (B)이다.

[151-152] 문자 메시지

데이브 디첼 [오후 3:20]
아직 Stapleton Room이에요?

스텔라 라니 [오후 3:23]
네. 강연자가 이제 막 연설을 끝냈어요.

데이브 디첼 [오후 3:24]
알았어요. 저는 "언어와 문화"에 관한 하만 씨의 발표에 가고 있어요. 저랑 같이 갈래요? 2층의 Sutton Hall에서 열려요.

스텔라 라니 [오후 3:25]
놓칠 수 없죠. 매우 흥미롭겠어요.

데이브 디첼 [오후 3:27]
물론이죠. 그건 정말 유익하기도 할 거예요.

데이브 디첼 [오후 3:28]
앞줄에 있는 제 자리 근처에 자리 맡아줄까요?

스텔라 라니 [오후 3:30]
그래주면 좋죠! 고마워요.

어휘 miss 놓치다 interesting 흥미로운 informative 유익한
front row 앞줄

151 의도 파악

오후 3시 27분, 디첼 씨가 "물론이죠"라고 쓴 의미는 무엇일 것 같은가?
(A) 모든 포럼 참가자들이 환영회에 참석하길 원한다.
(B) Stapleton Room에서의 연설은 매우 흥미롭다.
(C) 그는 발표에 참여하지 못한 것을 후회한다.
(D) 그는 하만 씨의 발표에 대한 라니 씨의 의견에 전적으로 동의한다.

해설 바로 앞 메시지에서 라니 씨가 하만 씨이 발표에 대해 흥미로워서 놓치기 싫다고 했고, 이후 디첼 씨가 그것은 유익하기도 하다고 한 것으로 보아 앞선 라니 씨의 말에 동의한다는 것을 알 수 있다. 따라서 (D)가 정답이다. (B)는 Stapleton Room이 아닌 Sutton Hall에서 열리는 발표에 대해서 이야기하고 있으므로 오답이다.

152 Not/True 확인

디첼 씨에 대한 설명으로 옳은 것은?
(A) 그는 하만 씨의 조수로 고용되었다.
(B) 그는 발표 참가자들을 안내했다.
(C) 그는 라니 씨보다 먼저 Sutton Hall에 도착할 예정이다.
(D) 그는 Sutton Hall에서의 그의 발표를 준비했다.

해설 3시 28분 메시지 "Should I save you a seat near me in the front row?"에서 디첼 씨가 라니 씨의 자리를 맡아 주겠다고 하는 것을 보아, 그가 그녀보다 먼저 도착한다는 것을 알 수 있다. 따라서 (C)가 정답이다.

**36시간 전화 카드 세일
전 품목 5% 할인!**

여름이 다가오고 있습니다! 학생들은 수업 마지막 주를 보내고 있고, 사람들은 여름 해외여행 계획을 짜고 있습니다. 그래서 Speed Tel은 모든 전화 카드 사용자들을 위해 최고의 요금을 계속해서 제공할 것입니다. 여러분의 착신지에 대한 최신 요금을 알아보려면 오늘 요금을 검색해 보세요.
그리고 Speed Tel로부터 가장 최신 소식과 카드 업데이트를 받기 위해 저희 소셜 네트워크 서비스인 INSTABOOK에 "좋아요"를 누르는 것을 잊지 마세요.

- **5%를 즉시 절약하세요**
  현재 매장 전체가 세일 중입니다. 충전을 포함한 모든 것이 5% 할인됩니다. 쿠폰은 필요하지 않습니다.

- **Speed Tel 이동통신 - 네 번의 터치로 충전**
  저희 모바일 인터페이스로 단 네 번만 클릭하여 당신의 스마트폰에서 전화 카드를 충전하세요.

어휘 phone card 전화 카드 rate 요금, 비율 calling destination 착신지, 통화 목적지 up-to-date 최신의 instantly 즉시, 바로 on sale 세일 중인 mark down 인하하다 recharging 재충전

153 Not/True 확인

Speed Tel에 관하여 명시된 것은?
(A) 고객들은 할인 받기 위해 웹 사이트에 로그인해야 한다.
(B) 다른 자격 조건 없이 고객들에게 할인을 제공한다.
(C) 소셜 네트워크 서비스를 통해, 고객들은 그들의 카드를 충전할 수 있다.
(D) 학생들만 이러한 제안을 이용할 수 있다.

해설 지문 후반부 "Everything is marked down 5%, including recharging. No coupon required."에서 쿠폰 없이도 모든 것이 5% 할인된다고 했으므로, 별도의 자격 없이 할인을 이용할 수 있음을 알 수 있다. 따라서 (B)가 정답이다.

154 Not/True 확인

광고에서 제공되지 않은 정보는 무엇인가?
(A) 할인율
(B) 충전 방식
(C) 사회관계망
(D) 회사의 위치

해설 (A) 할인율은 제목에 5%라고 제시되어 있고, (B) 충전 방식은 두 번째 항목에 스마트폰을 통해 카드 충전이 가능하다고 언급되었다. (C) 사회 관계망은 소셜 네트워크 서비스인 INSTABOOK으로 언급되어 있다. 하지만 회사의 위치는 나와 있지 않으므로 (D)가 정답이다.

수신: 희선 윤 <y_heesun@advancedone.ca>
발신: 루벤 앤더슨 <a.reuben@kinneyunionco.com>
제목: 정보
날짜: 3월 10일
첨부: move_details.doc

윤 씨에게,

Kinney Union 사 기획 매니저로서 새로운 직책에 당신을 환영합니다. 시애틀 지사 건물이 효율성 개선을 위해 재건축되었습니다. 이것이 그 지점을 미국에서 가장 발전된 Kinney 사의 시설 중 하나로 만듭니다.

인사과의 샐리 베스 씨가 3월 30일 월요일 오전 10시에 당신을 직원 오리엔테이션으로 안내할 것입니다. Beth 씨는 우리 회사의 구조, 임금, 복지제도 그리고 다른 세부사항들을 친절히 설명할 것입니다. 당신은 아직 사원증을 받지 않아서 보안과에서 그것을 신청해야 할 것입니다. 3월 30일 오전 9시 30분까지 그곳에 도착하길 부탁드립니다.

저는 당신이 밴쿠버에서 시애틀로 이사하는 것을 도울 수 있는 정보를 첨부했습니다. 당신이 적당한 거주지를 찾지 못했을 경우에 대비하여, 파일 안에 몇 가지 추천사항들이 있습니다. 문의가 있으시면, 언제든지 저에게 전화나 이메일로 연락주세요.

진심으로,

루벤 앤더슨
인사과 부장
Kinney Union 사
샌프란시스코 본사

어휘 planning 기획 renovate 재건축하다, 개조하다 efficiency 효율성 advanced 발전된 lead 이끌다, 안내하다 kindly 친절히 wage 임금 benefit 복지, 혜택 identification card 신분증 register for ~에 등록하다 attach 첨부하다 recommendation 추천(사항) in the event that ~의 경우에 suitable 적당한 residential space 주거 공간

155 주제/목적

앤더슨 씨는 왜 이메일을 보냈는가?
(A) 지원 절차를 설명하기 위해
(B) 개인 정보를 요청하기 위해
(C) 새 직책에 관한 세부사항을 제공하기 위해
(D) 회사의 신규 사업을 설명하기 위해

해설 첫 줄의 "I would like to welcome you to your new position"과 두 번째 문단의 "Ms. Beth will kindly explain our company's structures, wages, benefits, and other details."를 미루어 볼 때 새 직책에 관한 세부사항을 제공하기 위해 이메일을 보냈음을 알 수 있다. 따라서 (C)가 정답이다.

156 Not/True 확인

Kinney Union 사에 관해 명시된 것은?
(A) 밴쿠버로 곧 이전할 것이다.
(B) 한 군데 이상의 지사를 가지고 있다.
(C) 추가 직원을 고용할 계획이 있다.
(D) 다른 산업으로 사업을 확장했다.

> **해설** 두 번째 줄의 "The branch building in Seattle"에서 시애틀에 지사가 있음을 알 수 있고, 다음 문장 "It can make the branch one of the most advanced Kinney facilities in the U.S."를 통해 미국 내에 여러 지사가 있음을 알 수 있다. 따라서 (B)가 가장 적절하다.

157 세부 사항

윤 씨는 무엇을 하도록 요구 받는가?
(A) 인사과에 양식 제출하기
(B) 가능한 한 빨리 베스 씨에게 연락하기
(C) 오리엔테이션에 미리 도착하기
(D) 보안과에 전화하기

> **해설** 직원 오리엔테이션은 10시에 있지만, 두 번째 문단 마지막 문장 "I ask you to arrive there by 9:30 A.M. on March 30."에서 사원증을 신청하기 위해 9시 30분까지 도착해 달라고 했으므로 (C)가 정답이다.

[158-160] 전단지

10월 13일
Valentino's 레스토랑의 재개업식에
당신을 초대합니다.

저희 레스토랑의 재개업을 기념하기 위해, Valentino's는 재개업식 첫날에 모든 손님에게 저녁식사와 함께 마실 수 있는 와인 한 병을 무료로 제공합니다. 가족과 같이 동행해서 저희가 엄선한 와인들을 시음해 보세요. 다음을 포함한 20여개국의 와인 중에서 골라보세요.

- 남아프리카
- 프랑스
- 이탈리아
- 뉴질랜드
- 영국

Valentino's는 Hill 식낭과 Mason's 백화점 맞은편인 라틴구에 위치해 있습니다. 저희는 주 6일, 오전 11시부터 새벽 2시까지 영업합니다.

Valentino's의 소유주인 세르히오 메시 씨는 재개업을 홍보하기 위해 9월 30일 텔레비전에 출연할 것입니다.

와인 무료 제공은 예약 1회당 한 병으로 제한됩니다.

> **어휘** reopening 재개업 celebrate 기념하다, 축하하다 accompany 동반하다, 수반하다 try out 시도하다 a selection of 엄선된 be situated in ~에 위치하다 Latin Quarter (파리의) 라틴구 opposite ~맞은편의 brasserie (별로 비싸지 않은 프랑스풍) 식당 appear 나타나다, 출연하다 promote 홍보하다 grand 웅장한; 대규모의 limited 제한된 per ~당 booking 예약

158 세부 사항

Valentino's에서 판매되는 것은 무엇인가?
(A) 식기류
(B) 유니폼
(C) 식사
(D) 식료품

> **해설** 지문 상단의 "the Reopening of Valentino's Restaurant"에서 Valentino's가 식당임을 알 수 있다. 따라서 정답은 (C)이다.

159 세부 사항

손님들은 10월 13일에 무엇을 할 수 있는가?
(A) 온라인으로 테이블 예약하기
(B) 무료 알코올 음료 받기
(C) 10% 할인 쿠폰 받기
(D) 1회 식사 구매 후 무료 식사 받기

> **해설** October 13th가 키워드로, "the Reopening of Valentino's Restaurant on October 13th"에서 그 날에 재개업한다는 것을 알 수 있고, "To celebrate the reopening of our restaurant, Valentino's is offering every customer a free bottle of wine to accompany any dinner on the first day of reopening"에서 재개업 날에 와인 한 병을 무료로 증정함을 알 수 있다. 따라서 정답은 (B)이다.

160 세부 사항

Valentino's에 대해 언급된 것은 무엇인가?
(A) 다른 나라에서 온 다양한 와인이 있다.
(B) 금융 지구에 위치해 있다.
(C) 소유주를 잡지에서 다룰 것이다.
(D) 일주일 내내 영업할 것이다.

> **해설** "Choose from over 20 countries including ~"에서 20여개국의 와인을 제공하고 있다는 것을 안 수 있으므로 정답은 (A)이다.

[161-163] 편지

AT 헬스케어

Wong Chan 대로
인도네시아

7월 2일
인차우 쑤이 씨
5454 Kwon 가, 인도네시아 IN 435

쑤이 씨에게,

AT 헬스케어에 지원해 주셔서 대단히 감사드립니다. 수석 등록관인 하네스 씨가 당신을 저희 병원의 수간호사 직책에 적합한 후보자로 추천했습니다. 7월 22일 월요일 오후 1시 30분에 면접을 보러 오시기

바랍니다. 이 일정을 확인하시려면 제 개인 비서인 레오네 티아 씨에게 연락 주세요. 그녀의 전화번호는 195-3530234입니다.

당신의 추천서 사본도 보내주실 수 있나요? 유감스럽게도, 당신이 보내주신 추천서 원본이 최근에 새 시설로 이전하는 과정에 분실되었습니다.

마지막으로, 작성을 완료해서 면접에 지참해야 하는 첨부 양식을 확인해 주세요. 당신을 만나길 기대합니다.

진심으로,

선 로챈
채용 담당자

동봉

어휘 Boulevard 대로 application 지원, 지원서 recommend 추천하다 senior registrar 수석 등록관 candidate 후보자 position 직책 PA (Personal Assistant) 개인 비서 confirm 확인하다 appointment 예약 일정 reference 추천서 unfortunately 안타깝게도, 아쉽게도 original 원래의, 원본의 misplace 분실하다 recent 최근의 relocation 이전 lastly 마지막으로 attached 첨부된 complete 완성하다 bring along ~을 지참하다 recruitment 채용 enclosure 동봉

161 주제/목적

로챈 씨가 쑤이 씨에게 편지를 쓰는 이유는 무엇인가?

(A) 면접을 잡기 위해
(B) 직책에 관해 문의를 하기 위해
(C) 비자 서류를 요청하기 위해
(D) 위치 변경을 제안하기 위해

해설 편지의 목적을 묻는 문제로, 단서는 주로 도입부에 제시된다. "We would like to invite you for an interview on Monday, July 22nd at 1:30 P.M."에서 지원자에게 면접 일정을 알리고 있으므로 정답은 (A)이다.

162 세부 사항

쑤이 씨가 연락해야 할 사람은 누구인가?

(A) 수석 등록관
(B) 보건 담당자
(C) 하네스 씨
(D) 티아 씨

해설 수신자가 연락해야 할 사람을 묻는 문제로, "Please contact my PA, Leone Tia to confirm this appointment."에서 면접 일정을 확인하려면 Tia 씨에게 연락해야 함을 알 수 있다. 따라서 정답은 (D)이다.

163 세부 사항

로챈 씨가 언급하는 문제는 무엇인가?

(A) 몇몇 서류가 최근 이전 중에 분실되었다.
(B) 병원의 웹 사이트가 제대로 작동하지 않는다.
(C) 쑤이 씨를 면접할 사람에게 연락이 닿지 않는다.
(D) 지원서가 마감일 후에 수신되었다.

해설 언급한 문제점을 묻는 문제로, "Unfortunately, the original references you submitted have been misplaced in our recent relocation to the new facility"에서 새 시설로 이동하는 중에 서류를 잃어버렸다는 것을 확인할 수 있다. 따라서 (A)가 정답이다.

[164-167] 기사

수퍼푸드!
전 세계의 녹차

4월 10일 — 다양한 건강 관련 서적에서 녹차의 효능들이 널리 다루어지면서, 그것의 수요 또한 수년 동안 증가하고 있습니다. 녹차는 차나무 잎으로 만들어진 차의 한 종류로, 중국, 한국, 일본과 같은 동아시아 국가에서 유래되었습니다. 이것의 생육 환경, 재배 방법, 그리고 생산 공정에 따라 그 식물 종에는 굉장히 다양한 녹차가 있습니다. 다양한 재배 방법의 발전과 함께, 그것은 최근 전 세계의 많은 다른 국가들로 퍼져나갔습니다.

몇몇 논문에 따르면, 매일 녹차를 마시는 것은 몸에 항암 효과와 콜레스테롤을 낮추는 효과를 갖고 있습니다. 게다가, 이것은 몸이 신진대사 활동을 증진시키도록 합니다. 그러나, 너무 많이 마시는 것은 다른 심각한 건강 문제를 초래할 수 있습니다. 그래서, 여러분은 하루에 세 번 이내로 적당히 마셔야 합니다.

마시는 방법 중 하나는 뜨거운 물에 티백을 담그는 것입니다. 다른 하나는 뜨거운 물이 담긴 차 주전자를 사용하여 녹차 잎을 끓이는 것입니다. 물의 온도가 너무 높으면 녹차 잎의 원래 영양소를 파괴할 수도 있습니다. 그러니 60도에서 90도까지의 적정 온도를 유지하여 티백을 뜨거운 물에 5분마다 30초씩, 약 3번을 담가야 합니다.

녹차의 맛은 전적으로 그것을 담그고 끓이는 기술에 달려 있습니다. 그러므로 녹차에 대한 적절한 정보가 대중들에게 전해지는 것이 매우 중요한데, 이는 그것이 우리의 건강을 유지시킬 수도, 해칠 수도 있기 때문입니다. 우리 웹 사이트 www.ourvoicemagazine.com/health에서 그것에 대한 자세한 정보를 찾아볼 수 있습니다.

어휘 effect 효과, 효능 a variety of 많은, 다양한 demand 수요 as well 또한 originate 유래하다, 비롯되다 cultivation 경작, 재배 processing 처리, 공정 various 다양한 spread 확산되다 journal 저널, 논문 anti-cancer 항암의 impact 영향 metabolism 신진대사 moderately 적당히 steep 담그다 brew 끓이다 recognize 인식하다, 알다 temperature 온도 destroy 파괴하다 nutrient 영양소 maintain 유지하다 proper 적절한 entirely 전적으로

164 세부 사항

글쓴이는 녹차에 관한 어떤 측면을 설명했는가?

(A) 녹차의 발견의 역사
(B) 녹차의 생산 과정
(C) 녹차의 식물학적 중요성
(D) 녹차를 마시는 방법

해설 세 번째 문단을 보면 녹차를 마시는 두 가지 방법을 설명하면 서 이것이 건강에도 중요한 영향을 미칠 수 있음을 언급하고 있으므로 (D)가 가장 적절하다.

165 Not/True 확인

녹차의 의학적 효능에 관하여 언급되지 않은 것은?
(A) 콜레스테롤 낮추기
(B) 암의 위험 줄이기
(C) 신진대사 활동 돕기
(D) 식욕 억제하기

해설 두 번째 문단의 "drinking green tea daily has anti-cancer effects and cholesterol-lowering impacts on the body. In addition, it can enable the body to enhance metabolism activities."에서 (A), (B), (C)는 언 급되었지만, (D) 식욕 억제와 관련된 내용은 언급되지 않았다.

166 Not/True 확인

녹차에 대하여 명시된 것은?
(A) 우리의 건강에 악영향을 줄 수 있다.
(B) 그것의 기원은 많은 고서에서 발견되었다.
(C) 그것의 색은 현대 기술로 변할 수 있다.
(D) 일반 대중들은 그것의 맛을 좋아하지 않는다.

해설 두 번째 문단 마지막 문장 "So, you should drink it moderately, no more than three times a day."에 서 녹차를 적당히 마시라고 했고, 마지막 문단 두 번째 문장 "because it can help maintain or damage our health." 에서는 그것이 건강을 유지할 수도, 해칠 수도 있다고 했으므 로 녹차가 건강에 악영향을 미칠 수 있다는 (A)가 정답이다.

167 문장 삽입

다음 표시된 [1], [2], [3], [4] 중에서 다음 문장이 들어갈 가 장 알맞은 위치는?
"그러나, 너무 많이 마시는 것은 다른 심각한 건강 문제를 초 래할 수 있습니다."
(A) [1]
(B) [2]
(C) [3]
(D) [4]

해설 해당 문장은 녹차를 지나치게 많이 마실 경우 생길 수 있는 부 정적인 영향에 대해 말하고 있고, 역접을 나타내는 접속부사 However로 시작하는 것으로 보아 앞서 녹차의 긍정적인 영 향을 언급했을 것이라 추론할 수 있다. [3]의 앞 문장에서 녹 차의 효능들을 열거했고, 그 뒤 문장은 녹차를 적당히 마시라 고 하고 있으므로 해당 문장은 (C) [3]에 위치하는 것이 가장 적절하다.

[168-171] 온라인 채팅

엠마 린 [오전 10:35]
여러분 좋은 아침입니다! Pitt 사업 단지에 관한 소식을 들은 사람이 있나요?

조이스 로슈 [오전 10:36]
제가 지난 화요일에 스미스 씨와 이야기했어요. 그가 말하길 이번 주 수요일까지 결정할 예정이라고 했는데, 우리는 아직 아무것도 들은 게 없네요.

엠마 린 [오전 10:37]
음, 철강과 시멘트를 주문하지 않으면, 우리가 이미 청사진을 만들었음 에도 불구하고 마감 기한을 지키지 못할 거예요.

스콧 윌리엄 [오전 10:38]
제가 어제 이미 주문했어요.

엠마 린 [오전 10:40]
그것은 문제가 될 수도 있겠네요. 계약을 따내지 못하면, 우리가 건 축 자재를 사용할 수 없을지라도 그것들에 대한 비용을 지불해야 해 요. 추가 비용을 내지 않으려면 우리가 언제까지 취소해야 하는지 알 고 싶네요.

스콧 윌리엄 [오전 10:41]
변수를 고려하면 그것을 계산하는 데 시간이 좀 필요해요. 제가 확 인해 볼게요.

엠마 린 [오전 10:42]
로슈 씨, 스미스 씨에게 전화해서 지금 어떻게 진행되고 있는지 물 어볼래요?

스콧 윌리엄 [오전 10:43]
내일까지는 다른 위약금 없이 그것들을 취소할 수 있어요.

조이스 로슈 [오전 10:46]
윌리엄 씨, 저 대신에 그것 좀 해줄래요? 그리고 린 씨, 방금 스미스 씨 의 비서인 제이드 씨로부터 전화를 받았어요. 그녀가 말하길 스미스 씨가 이번에는 Cornwell 개발사와 함께 하기로 결정했대요.

엠마 린 [오전 10:48]
너무나 실망스럽지만, 낙담하지는 맙시다! 다음에는 더 좋은 결과가 있을 거예요.

어휘 complex 단지, 상가 deadline 마감 기한 blueprint 청사진 contract 계약 construction material 건축 자재 figure out 알아내다, 계산하다 penalty 벌금, 위약금 discourage 낙담시키다

168 추론/암시

그들은 어떤 업종에서 일하고 있는 것 같은가?
(A) 건설
(B) 조경
(C) 출장연회 서비스
(D) 유통

TEST 5 정답과 해설

해설 10시 37분 메시지의 blueprint(청사진), 40분 메시지의 construction materials(건축 자재)를 통해, 건설과 관련된 일하는 것으로 유추할 수 있으므로 (A)가 가장 적절하다.

169 의도 파악

오전 10시 41분에, 윌리엄 씨가 "제가 확인해 볼게요"라고 말한 의도는?
(A) 그는 자재 비용을 추산할 것이다.
(B) 그는 배송 일정을 재조정할 것이다.
(C) 그는 반품 마감 기한을 계산할 것이다.
(D) 그는 회원 수를 셀 것이다.

해설 바로 앞 린 씨의 메시지 "By when do we have to cancel them to avoid being charged?"에서 추가 비용 없이 취소할 수 있는 기한을 묻고 있고, 이에 윌리엄 씨가 확인해 보겠다고 말한 후 43분에 "We can cancel them without any penalty by the end of tomorrow."라며 본인이 계산한 기한을 이야기했으므로 (C)가 정답이다.

170 세부 사항

제이드 씨는 어떤 정보를 제공했는가?
(A) 계약을 따내는 방법
(B) 누가 스미스 씨의 매물을 개발할 것인지
(C) 언제 공사가 시작될 것인지
(D) 왜 결정이 연기되었는지

해설 10시 46분 로슈 씨의 메시지 "She said Mr. Smith decided to go with Cornwell Development Co. this time."에서 제이드 씨와 통화 후, 스미스 씨와 공사를 함께할 다른 회사를 언급하고 있으므로 (B)가 정답이다.

171 추론/암시

윌리엄 씨는 다음에 무엇을 할 것 같은가?
(A) 스미스 씨에게 다시 연락한다
(B) 그들의 제안서를 제출한다
(C) 그들의 주문을 취소한다
(D) 그들의 청사진을 보여준다

해설 10시 43분 메시지 "We can cancel them without any penalty by the end of tomorrow."에서 윌리엄 씨가 내일까지 주문을 취소해야 위약금이 발생하지 않는다고 했고, 이에 로슈 씨가 그것을 해달라고 부탁했으므로 윌리엄 씨가 주문을 취소할 것임을 알 수 있다. 따라서 (C)가 정답이다.

[172-175] 기사

New Orleans 방문

폴 케이 작성

뉴올리언스 (6월 10일) —20일부터 24일까지, 많은 작가와 교사, 그리고 교수들이 다가오는 제 10회 현대 작문 컨퍼런스에 참가할 것입니다. 이번 컨퍼런스에는 여러 참가자들이 있을 예정이라, 작문 분야에서 가장 큰 행사들 중 하나가 될 것입니다.

저명한 언어학자이자 작가인 안드레아 카르나레 씨는 New York Tribune에 컨퍼런스를 칭찬하는 칼럼을 게시했습니다. 그 글 덕분에 대중의 관심이 상당히 높아졌습니다. "컨퍼런스에 등록하기 위해 많은 사람들이 우리에게 매일 이메일을 보냈습니다."라고 이 행사를 처음 기획하고 감독한 존 스웨인 씨가 말했습니다. 작년에는, 약 100명의 작가들과 교사들이 이 컨퍼런스에 참석했고, 총 등록 인원이 350명을 넘었습니다. 올해는 이 수치가 둘 다 약 3배가 될 것이라 예상합니다.

올해의 컨퍼런스는 작문 분야의 다양한 장르에 초점을 둘 것입니다. "우리는 다양한 문학 작품들과 제2언어 작문 교육에 관한 접근법을 보여주고자 합니다."라고 프로그램 코디네이터인 제리 타나키토가 말했습니다. 작품을 선보일 작가 지망생들은 전 세계 20개의 다른 나라에서 옵니다. 컨퍼런스가 매우 유익하고 성공적일 것이라고 굳게 믿습니다.

행사에 대한 더 많은 정보를 원하시면, 웹 사이트 www.CWC.org를 방문해 주세요.

어휘 professor 교수 contemporary 동시대의, 현대의 a variety of 다양한, 많은 prominent 저명한, 유명한 linguist 언어학자 post 게시하다 complimentary 칭찬하는 column (신문, 잡지의) 칼럼, 정기 기고란 organize 조직하다 direct 감독하다 for the first time 처음으로 participate in ~에 참석하다 registrant 등록자 various 다양한 genre 장르 literary work 문학 작품 approach 접근법 prospective 장래의

172 세부 사항

누가 컨퍼런스가 더 유명해지도록 도왔는가?
(A) 케이 씨
(B) 카르나레 씨
(C) 스웨인 씨
(D) 타나키토 씨

해설 두 번째 문단 "Andrea Carnale, a prominent linguist and writer, posted the complimentary column about the conference on the New York Tribune. Thanks to that writing, public's interest has considerably increased."에서 카르나레 씨의 칼럼 덕분에 대중의 관심이 증가했다고 했으므로 (B)가 정답이다.

173 Not/True 확인

컨퍼런스에 대해 명시된 것은?
(A) 표는 온라인으로만 구매되어야 한다.
(B) 뉴올리언스는 컨퍼런스를 처음 개최한다.
(C) 올해는 새로운 감독이 있다.
(D) 일주일 동안 지속된다.

해설 두 번째 문단의 세 번째 문장 "John Swain, who is organizing and directing this event for the first time."에서 스웨인 씨가 처음 행사를 기획하고 감독한다고 했으므로, 그가 새로운 감독으로 투입되었음을 알 수 있다. 따라서 (C)가 정답이다.

174 세부 사항

컨퍼런스의 작가들에 관하여 언급된 것은?
(A) 그들은 이미 유명하다.
(B) 그들은 특정 회사로부터 후원을 받았다.
(C) 그들은 인증된 자격증이 있다.
(D) 그들은 다양한 나라에서 온다.

해설 세 번째 문단의 세 번째 문장 "Prospective writers presenting their works are from twenty different countries throughout the world."에서 작가 지망생들이 다양한 나라에서 온다고 했으므로 (D)가 정답이다.

175 문장 삽입

다음 표시된 위치 [1], [2], [3], [4] 중에서 다음 문장이 들어갈 가장 알맞은 위치는?
"올해는 이 수치가 둘 다 약 3배가 될 것이라 예상합니다."
(A) [1]
(B) [2]
(C) [3]
(D) [4]

해설 제시된 문장의 both of these figures를 통해 앞 문장에서 두 가지 수치가 나왔음을 추측할 수 있다. [3]의 앞 문장 "Last year, around 100 writers and teachers participated in the conference, and the total number of registrants was over 350."에서 100명의 작가 및 교사들과 350명 이상의 총 등록 인원 수치가 언급되었으므로 (C)가 정답이다.

[176-180] 광고 & 이메일

채용 기회 - INNOBIZ Services		
	날짜: 10월 5일	참고 번호: 2922513
직책	사무실 정비 기술자	
고용 형태	정규직 (종신직)	
자격 요건	지원자들은 전자기기와 기계에 대한 폭넓은 지식과 최소 2년의 복사기 수리 경력이 있어야 하며, 영업용 트럭을 운전할 수 있는 자격이 있어야 합니다.	
직무 설명	우리는 복사기 및 다른 사무기기 수리를 회사에 제공합니다.	
추가 정보	우리가 다루는 지역이 매우 넓으므로, 지원자들은 우리 서비스 지역의 가장 중심지인 Slippery Rock 근처에 거주하는 것이 필수입니다.	
연락처	헨리 케인 INNOBIZ Services - 인사부 391 Washington Drive, Pittsburgh, PA 15712 h_kane@innobizservices.com	
면접 일정	사전 면접: 10월 15일 ~ 10월 20일	
근무 시작일	10월 30일	

수신: 제인 포스터 <j_foster@innobizservices.com>
발신: 헨리 케인 <h_kane@innobizservices.com>
날짜: 10월 10일
제목: 새로운 기술자

포스터 씨에게,

현재, 기술직에 대한 많은 지원서들이 제출되고 있습니다. 관심을 보인 처음 몇 명의 지원자들이 회사가 숙소를 제공해 주는지 여부를 물었습니다.
아마도 우리 구인 광고에 있는 숙소에 관한 세부 사항이 지원자들에게는 명확하지 않나 봅니다. 사전 인터뷰가 시작되기 전까지 광고의 이 부분을 업데이트 해주시기 바랍니다.

더하여, 저는 우리 네트워크의 데이터베이스로 모든 세부 정보를 자동으로 보내는 온라인 지원 양식을 만드는 것이 가능할지 묻고 싶습니다. 우리의 현재 시스템은 지원자들의 정보를 직접 받고 그것을 고용 데이터베이스에 입력해야 해서, 많은 오류가 생길 수 있습니다.

진심으로,

헨리 케인
인사과 부장
INNOBIZ Services

어휘 employment 취업, 고용 reference 참고 permanent 영구적인, 종신의 extensive 폭넓은 certify 인증하다, 증명하다 commercial 상업의 preliminary 사전의 accommodation 숙소 unclear 불명확한, 분명하지 않은 automatically 자동으로 in person 직접

176 Not/True 확인

직책의 자격 요건으로 나열되지 않은 것은?
(A) 대학 학위
(B) 전자 기술 사전 지식
(C) 장비 수리 경험
(D) 상업용 차량 운전 허가증

해설 Qualifications(자격 요건) 부분을 보면, (B)는 "extensive knowledge of electronic devices", (C)는 "at least two years of experience in photocopier repair", (D)는 "be certified to operate a commercial truck"이라고 언급되어 있지만 학위에 대한 언급은 없으므로 (A)가 정답이다.

177 주제/목적

이메일의 목적 중 하나는 무엇인가?
(A) 요청을 승인하기 위해
(B) 약속을 확인하기 위해
(C) 새로운 시스템을 제안하기 위해
(D) 일자리를 제안하기 위해

해설 이메일의 세 번째 문단 첫 문장의 "I want to ask whether it would be possible to create an online application form that automatically sends all detailed information to a database on our network."에서 특정 기능을 가진 온라인 지원 양식이 개발 가능한지 묻는 것으로 보아 이메일의

목적 중 하나는 새 시스템을 제안하는 것임을 알 수 있다. 따라서 (C)가 정답이다.

178 세부 사항

숙소 정보는 언제까지 업데이트될 것인가?
(A) 10월 5일
(B) 10월 14일
(C) 10월 16일
(D) 10월 20일

해설 이메일의 두 번째 문단 "Please update this part of the advertisement before the preliminary interviews start."에서 숙소에 대한 정보를 사전 면접이 시작되기 전까지 업데이트해 달라고 요청했고, 광고에서 사전 인터뷰는 10월 15일에서 20일까지 진행된다고 나와 있으므로 정답은 (B)이다. 광고 작성 날짜가 10월 5일이고, 업데이트를 요청한 이메일의 작성 날짜는 10일이기 때문에 (A)는 정답이 될 수 없다.

179 추론/암시

케인 씨는 누구일 것 같은가?
(A) 대학생
(B) 부장
(C) 컴퓨터 전문가
(D) 구직자

해설 케인 씨가 보낸 이메일의 마지막 부분 "Director, Personnel Division, INNOBIZ Services"에서 인사과 부장이라고 명시되어 있으므로 정답은 (B)이다.

180 세부 사항 (연계)

케인 씨는 광고의 어느 부분을 언급하는가?
(A) 자격 요건
(B) 고용 형태
(C) 추가 정보
(D) 연락처

해설 케인 씨가 보낸 이메일에서 구인 광고의 숙소와 관련된 내용을 업데이트하라고 요구했고, 광고에서 이와 관련된 내용은 추가 정보에 해당하므로 (C)가 가장 적절하다.

[181-185] 공지 & 이메일

Stony Grand 호텔

회원 혜택

월간 회비: BLUE - 30달러, RED - 50달러, BLACK - 70달러

	BLUE	RED	BLACK
무료 주차	Yes	Yes	Yes
수영장과 스파	Yes	Yes	Yes
호텔 헬스장	Yes	Yes	Yes
무료 셔틀	Yes	Yes	Yes
특별 행사 할인	No	Yes	Yes
손님용 입장권	No	No	Yes

1일 등록비는 80달러로, BLACK 회원권의 서비스들을 이용할 수 있습니다. 이 지불금은 등록을 변경하거나 취소할 경우 환불되지 않습니다. 정기 회원권을 등록하시면, 요금은 등록 후 2개월 이내에 환불 가능합니다.

* 특별 행사에 관한 추가 정보와 일정을 보려면, 저희 웹 사이트 www. stonygrandhotel.com으로 방문하세요.

발신: 멜리사 밀턴 <m.milton@stonygrandhotel.com>
수신: 게리 제이콥 <g.jacob@gammanet.com>
제목: 회신: 손님용 입장권
날짜: 7월 10일
첨부: 영수증

제이콥 씨에게,

Stony Grand 호텔의 회원이 되신 것에 다시 한번 감사드립니다. 당신의 전액 지불금인 360달러에 대한 영수증을 첨부했고, 이는 한달에 30달러씩, 12개월의 회비를 반영한 것입니다.

귀하는 7월 30일에 휴가를 가는 친구들을 위해 손님용 입장권을 발행해 달라고 저희 쪽에 요청했습니다. 유감스럽지만, 귀하의 BLUE 회원권은 요청하신 손님용 무료 입장권을 포함하지 않습니다. 귀하의 패키지에 이와 함께 다른 혜택들을 신청하기 위해서는 회원권을 프리미엄 수준으로 업그레이드 해야 합니다. 귀하의 서비스를 BLACK 요금제로 변경하시려면, 480달러의 차액을 지불하셔야 합니다. 하지만 귀하가 BLACK 요금제로 업그레이드 하고 원하지 않으시면, 친구분들은 똑같은 회원권 자격을 받을 수 없습니다. 이러한 경우, 귀하의 친구분들은 1층에 있는 리셉션 데스크에서 1일 입장권을 구매해야 합니다.

멜리사 밀턴
서비스 수석 부장

어휘 complimentary 무료의   registration 등록   pament 지불, 비용   take advantage of ~을 이용하다   non-refundable 환불되지 않는   enrollment 등록   receipt 영수증   reflect 반영하다, 나타내다   due 회비   difference 차액, 차이   be entitled to ~할 권리가 있다

181 Not/True 확인

Stony Grand Hotel 서비스에 관해 옳은 것은?
(A) 다른 호텔들보다 더 비싸다.
(B) 웹상에서만 적용된다.
(C) 비회원에게도 개방된다.
(D) 지역 사회에 의해 운영된다.

해설 공지문 하단의 "Please note that the one-day registration payment is $80, and you can take advantage of our BLACK membership services."에서 1일 등록비에 관한 부분이 명시되어 있으므로 회원권 없이도 호텔 서비스를 이용할 수 있다는 것을 알 수 있다. 따라서 정답은 (C)이다.

182 동의어 찾기

이메일에서, 첫 번째 문단 두 번째 줄의 "reflects"와 의미상 가장 가까운 것은?
(A) 설명하다
(B) 비추다
(C) 나타내다
(D) 고려하다

해설 해당 부분은 영수증의 360달러가 한달에 30달러씩 총 12개월의 요금을 "반영한다"는 의미이므로, "나타내다"를 뜻하는 (C) represents가 의미상 가장 가깝다.

183 세부 사항 (연계)

제이콥 씨가 Stony Grand Hotel에서 할 수 없는 것은?
(A) 호텔 체육관에서 운동한다
(B) 도심지로 가는 무료 셔틀 버스를 탄다
(C) 호텔 주차장에 그의 차를 주차한다
(D) 할인된 가격으로 행사에 참석한다

해설 이메일을 통해 제이콥 씨가 한 달에 30달러를 내는 BLUE 회원권에 등록했음을 알 수 있고, 공지문을 보면 BLUE 회원권은 특별 행사 할인과 손님용 입장권을 포함하지 않으므로 이에 해당하는 (D)가 정답이다.

184 세부 사항

제이콥 씨가 친구들을 도우려면 어떤 요금제로 업그레이드 해야 하는가?
(A) BLUE
(B) RED
(C) BLACK
(D) 1일 입장권

해설 이메일에서 친구들을 위해 손님용 입장권을 사용하려면 프리미엄 수준인 BLACK 회원권으로 업그레이드 해야 한다고 했으므로 (C)가 정답이다. (D)의 1일 입장권은 BLACK 회원권과 같은 서비스를 이용할 수는 있지만, 제이콥 씨의 BLUE 회원권에서 업그레이드하는 것은 아니므로 답이 될 수 없다.

185 Not/True 확인 (연계)

프리미엄 레벨 회원의 손님에 관하여 알 수 있는 것은?
(A) 그들은 회원 한 명을 동반해야 한다.
(B) 그들은 호텔에서 모든 시설과 서비스를 이용할 수 있다.
(C) 그들은 특정 날짜에만 호텔에 머물 수 있다.
(D) 그들은 프론트에서 입장권을 제시해야 한다.

해설 이메일에서 프리미엄 수준의 회원권은 BLACK 회원권이라고 언급했다. 공지문의 표를 보면 BLACK 회원권의 혜택에 손님용 입장권이 포함되어 있고, 모든 서비스를 이용할 수 있다고 표시되어 있으므로 (B)가 정답임을 알 수 있다.

[186-190] 책자 & 일정표 & 기사

Global Vision 재단
기업가 개발 교육

Global Vision 재단은 온라인 마케팅을 통해 운영 전략을 더 혁신적이고 창의적으로 만들고자 하는 기업가들을 위해 다양한 강연과 세미나들을 준비하고 있습니다. 다가오는 이번 행사는 7월 10일부터 13일까지 Kovalchick 컨벤션 센터에서 열릴 예정입니다.

마케팅 전문가인 얀센 게이지 씨는 회사 제품 홍보를 위한 기본적인 요소들에 관하여 이야기할 것입니다. GVF에서 근무하는 온라인 전문가 캐서린 업튼 씨는 합리적인 예산으로 인터넷 기반 운영에 대한 효율성을 증진시키도록 참가자들을 지도할 것입니다. 행사 마지막 날, 효율성과 잠재 성장의 정도에 맞는 사업 계획을 고안하는 모의 훈련은 저희가 가진 모든 자료들을 기반으로 하여 참가자들을 분석할 것입니다.

프로그램 등록비는 15달러가 부과되는 모의 훈련을 제외하고 모두 무료입니다. www.gvf.org/EDTprograms를 방문하셔서 지금 등록하세요.

GVF 프로그램 일정
기업가 개발 교육

주제	시간	장소
7월 10일 월요일		
초보자를 위한 마케팅 전략	오후 4시	Sutton Hall
온라인 홍보 방법	오후 5시	Sutton Hall
1:1 코칭 프로그램	오후 6시	IT 지원센터
7월 11일 화요일		
온라인 마케팅 예산 절약하기	오후 5시	Sutton Hall
1:1 코칭 프로그램	오후 6시	IT 지원센터
7월 12일 수요일		
웹상에서 브랜드 인지도 개선하기	오후 5시	Sutton Hall
1:1 코칭 프로그램	오후 6시	IT 지원센터
7월 13일 목요일		
모의 훈련	오후 6시	Unity Grand Ballroom

GVF가 권위 있는 프로그램을 주최하다

Johnstown (7월 14일) — Global Vision 재단(GVF) 덕분에, 전도유망한 기업가들이 그들의 현재 온라인 사업 방식을 확립하고 개선하도록 하는 다양한 강연과 세미나, 활동들이 있는 4일간의 행사에 참여했다.

최근에 공간 임대 서비스를 시작한 말콤 해리슨 씨는 세미나에 매우 만족했다. "이런 종류의 프로그램들은 저와 같은 소기업을 운영하는 경영주들이 신사업에 대한 위험을 줄임으로써 온라인 홍보 전략의 중요성을 이해하도록 도왔습니다"라고 그는 말했다.

배송 네트워크 사업을 준비하고 있는 안젤라 베스 씨는 특히 모의 훈련에 감명을 받았는데, 이는 SWOT 분석(강점, 약점, 기회, 위협)을 활용했다. "전문가들에게 받은 평가서는 제가 잠재 고객들에게 어떻게 접근해야 하는지 알려줄 것입니다"라고 그녀는 말했다.

GVF 이사인 라이먼 페이스 씨는 행사의 참여도에 매우 놀랐고, 이런 종류의 행사가 12월에 다시 고려되고 있다고 말했다.

어휘 entrepreneur 기업가, 사업가 organize 조직하다 a variety of 다양한 operation 운영 strategy 전략 innovative 혁신적인 creative 창의적인 upcoming 다가오는 be scheduled to V ~할 예정이다 element 요소, 성분 instruct 지시하다, 가르치다 attendee 참가자 efficiency 효율성 reasonable 합리적인 simulation 모의 practice 연습 devise 고안하다, 계획을 세우다 degree 정도 effectiveness 효율성 potential 잠재적인 analyze 분석하다 material 자료, 재료 charge 부과하다 beginner 초보자 save 절약하다 awareness 인지(도) promising 전도유망한 join 참여하다, 합류하다 activity 활동 establish 설립하다, 확립하다 satisfied 만족한 risk 위험 prepare for ~를 준비하다 especially 특히 impressed 감명받은 utilize 활용하다 strength 강점 weakness 약점 threat 위협 evaluation 평가 approach 접근하다 prospective 장래의

186 주제/목적

책자에 따르면, 행사는 주로 무엇에 관한 것인가?
(A) 온라인 서버 관리의 중요성 발표하기
(B) 다가오는 행사 준비를 위한 추가 직원 채용하기
(C) Global Vision 재단의 브랜드 인지도 개선하기
(D) 기업가들에게 웹 기반 전략의 사용법 알려주기

해설 책자의 첫 문장 "~ for entrepreneurs who need to make their operation strategies more innovative and creative through the online marketing."에서 온라인 마케팅을 통해 운영 전략을 개선하고자 하는 기업가들을 위한 강연과 세미나를 준비했다고 했으므로 답이 (D)임을 알 수 있다.

187 동의어 찾기

책자에서, 두번째 문단, 네 번째 줄의 "devise"와 의미상 가장 가까운 것은?
(A) 철회하다
(B) 소집하다
(C) 고안하다
(D) 제조하다

해설 devise는 "고안하다, 계획하다"의 의미로, 해당 문장은 효율성과 잠재 성장의 정도에 맞는 사업 계획을 "고안/계획한다"는 뜻이다. 따라서 (C)가 문맥상 가장 가깝다.

188 추론/암시

프로그램 일정에 관하여 추론할 수 있는 것은?
(A) 매일 하나의 교육만 열린다.
(B) 참가자들은 여러 번의 기회를 가질 수 있다.
(C) 모의 훈련은 다른 행사 전에 시작될 것이다.
(D) 모든 교육들은 같은 홀에서 열릴 것이다.

해설 두 번째 일정표를 보면 "Coaching Program - 1:1"이 월요일/화요일/수요일 오후 6시에 예정되었고, 이는 참가자들이 코칭을 받을 기회가 다양하다는 것이므로 (B)가 가장 적절하다.

189 추론/암시 (연계)

베스 씨에 관해 암시된 것은?
(A) 그녀는 예산 고문을 만났다.
(B) 그녀는 재단과 협업하고 있다.
(C) 그녀는 평가서를 제출했다.
(D) 그녀는 GVF에 돈을 지불했다.

해설 기사문의 세 번째 문단에서 "Angela Beth, ~ was especially impressed with the simulation practice," 부분을 보면 베스 씨가 모의 훈련에 참여했음을 알 수 있고, 첫 번째 지문인 책자 마지막 문단 "The program registration fees are all free except for the simulation practice which will be charged $15." 부분에서 모의 훈련은 15달러가 부과된다고 했으므로, 베스 씨가 모의 훈련에 참여하기 위해 GVF에 돈을 지불했을 것임을 추측할 수 있다. 따라서 답은 (D)이다.

190 추론/암시

GVF에 대해 암시되는 것은?
(A) 해리슨 씨를 새로운 이사로 임명할 것이다.
(B) 모든 신생 기업에 재정 지원을 제공했다.
(C) 재단을 홍보하는 데 총력을 기울였다.
(D) 올해 말에 비슷한 행사를 개최할 것이다.

해설 기사문 마지막 줄의 "~ told that this kind of event is being considered again for December."에서 올해 말인 12월에 이런 종류의 행사가 다시 고려되고 있다고 했으므로 (D)가 가장 적절하다.

[191-195] 이메일 & 티켓 & 이메일

발신: confirmation@ticketexpress.com
수신: c.hunter@betamail.com
날짜: 2024년 5월 18일
제목: 귀하의 주문
첨부: ticket_may_cleveland.pdf

이 메시지는 www.ticketexpress.com에서 현재 처리 중인 당신의 주문에 대해 자동으로 생성된 이메일 영수증입니다.

TicketExpress에서 주문해 주셔서 감사합니다.

*** 개인 식별 번호 정보 ***
당신은 www.ticketexpress.com/myticket에서 저희의 추적 시스템을 이용하여 언제든지 당신의 주문 상태를 조회할 수 있습니다. 당신의 주문 건에 접속하기 위해, 이 주문에 대한 개인 식별 번호뿐만 아니라, 주문할 때 사용된 이메일 주소도 입력해야 합니다. 이 주문에 대한 당신의 개인 식별 번호는 29981524입니다.

주문 정보
주문 번호: 7592591 - 2024년 5월 18일 오후 3시 7분

티켓: 2장, 각 35달러	70달러
티켓 현장 수령:	15달러
총액:	85달러

추가 구매 정보:
당신의 신용카드에 미국 달러로 청구될 것입니다.
* 총액은 해당 주세, 지방세 또는 다른 판매세를 포함하지 않습니다.

영수증에 관하여 문의가 있으시면, 언제든지 저희에게 연락주시고 제목란에 당신의 개인 식별 번호를 명시해 주세요.

주문 확인 부서

이것은 당신의 티켓입니다.

성명: 콜린 헌터 & 써니 베일

구역	열	좌석	경기
183	V	10/11	Cleveland vs Pittsburgh

Progressive 경기장   2024년 5월 25일 토요일 오후 4시 30분

이번 시즌 Progressive 경기장에서 Reds를 놓치지 마세요!

더 많은 정보를 위해, www.TheReds.com를 방문하세요

중요 시시 사항:
 바코드는 한 번 읽히면, 재입장이 불가합니다.
- 이 티켓의 무단 복제나 판매는 당신의 경기 입장을 금지할 수 있습니다.
- 경기장 내부에는 외부 음식이나 음료 반입이 허용되지 않습니다. (야구장 안의 스낵바에서 음식을 구매하실 수 있습니다.)

** 티켓 소지자는 경기 전후와 경기 도중에 야구 경기에서 있을 수 있는 모든 위험들을 감수합니다.

발신: c.hunter@betamail.com
수신: info@ticketexpress.com
날짜: 2024년 5월 19일
제목: 문의

이메일과 야구 경기 티켓을 보내주셔서 감사합니다. 제 주문 건에 대한 세부사항을 주의 깊게 읽었습니다. 그러나, 저는 "Will-Call"이 무엇인지 이해되지 않습니다. 저는 분명 아무 선택 사항 없이 두 장의 티켓만 주문했고, 제 신용카드로 70달러를 지불했습니다. 그런데 "Will-Call"

의 15달러가 제 주문 영수증에 있습니다. 그것이 무엇이고 왜 추가되었는지 설명해 주시겠습니까?

행운을 빌며,

콜린 헌터

** "Will-Call"이란 인터넷으로 주문한 티켓을 현장에서 수령하는 것으로, 이때 추가 금액이 발생할 수 있다.

어휘 automatically 자동으로 generate 발생시키다 receipt 영수증 PIN(personal identification number) 개인 식별 번호 track 추적하다 status 상태 USD(U.S. Dollar) 미국 달러 row 열, 줄 stadium 경기장 entry 입장 unauthorized 승인되지 않은 duplication 복사, 복제 prohibit 금지하다 admittance 입장 ballpark 야구장 incidental 우연한, 의도치 않은, 부수적인 definitely 확실히

191 Not/True 확인
첫 번째 이메일에서 어떤 정보가 진술되었는가?
(A) 고객의 개인 신분이 공개되었다.
(B) 구매자의 연락처 정보에 문제가 있다.
(C) 티켓이 이메일을 통해 전달되었다.
(D) 구매에는 신용카드만 허용된다.

해설 첫 번째 이메일 상단에서 첨부(Attachments)의 "ticket_may_cleveland.pdf"를 통해 티켓을 이메일로 보냈음을 알 수 있다. 따라서 (C)가 정답이다.

192 추론/암시 (연계)
티켓에 관하여 암시되는 것은?
(A) 쿠폰 번호가 포함되어 있다.
(B) 시즌 동안 언제든지 사용될 수 있다.
(C) 타인에게 양도될 수 있다.
(D) 하나의 표는 누 좌석을 포함한다.

해설 첫 번째 지문의 구매 정보에서 2장을 구매했다고 했고, 티켓의 "Name: Colin Hunter & Sunny Bale" 부분과 "SEAT 10/11" 부분을 보면 한 장의 티켓에 두 명의 좌석이 포함되어 있음을 알 수 있으므로 (D)가 정답이다.

193 세부 사항
사람들은 무엇을 하는 것이 금지되는가?
(A) 경기 중 사진 찍기
(B) 경기 도중에 경기장 나가기
(C) 야구장에 간식 가져오기
(D) 각 좌석에서 맥주 마시기

해설 티켓 하난의 지시 사항들을 보면, "No outside food or drink allowed inside the stadium"에서 음식 및 음료 반입은 허용되지 않는다고 했으므로 (C)가 정답이다.

194 동의어 찾기

티켓 하단에, 네 번째 줄의 "take"와 의미상 가장 가까운 것은?
(A) 가장하다
(B) 유지하다
(C) 믿다
(D) 받아들이다

해설 해당 문맥은 모든 위험을 "감수한다"는 의미이므로, "받아들이다"라는 의미의 (D)가 의미상 가장 가깝다.

195 세부 사항 (연계)

두 번째 이메일에는 어떤 정보가 빠져 있는가?
(A) 좌석 번호
(B) 신용카드 번호
(C) 개인 식별 번호
(D) 전화 번호

해설 첫 번째 이메일의 후반부에서 "If you have any questions about the receipt, please feel free to contact us and state your PIN on the subject line." 문의가 있으면 제목란에 PIN(개인 식별 번호)을 명시하라고 했지만, 두 번째 이메일에 이 정보가 누락되어 있으므로 (C)가 정답이다.

[196-200] 광고 & 편지 & 이메일

마케팅 부장 모집

Whitewall 출판사는 최근 출판업계에서 널리 인정받는 Mastermind Group에 의해 인수되었기 때문에, 경력이 있는 마케팅 부장을 추가로 모집하고 있습니다. 마케팅 부장으로서, 이 직책은 'Mastermind Whitewall 대책 위원회'라고 불리는 신규 팀을 담당할 것입니다. 그 또는 그녀는 인문학 도서 목록에 대한 우리의 다가오는 특별 행사를 준비하고 광고함으로써 새로운 직원들과 출판 홍보 절차를 감독할 것입니다. 합격자는 마케팅과 홍보 분야에서 최소 2년의 경력을 가지고 있어야 합니다. 게다가, 이 직책을 맡은 사람은 창의적이고 분석적으로 사고하고, 팀원들을 체계적으로 이끌도록 요구됩니다. 전반적인 관리를 위해 인문학에 관한 높은 수준의 지식 또한 필요합니다. 마지막으로, 최근의 모바일 기반 시대에 적응하기 위해 소셜 미디어 툴에 대한 전문 지식을 보유하는 것이 매우 선호됩니다.
문의가 있거나 우리의 복지 혜택에 관해 알고 싶으시면, 저희에게 mw_taskforce@mastermind.com으로 연락 주세요.
이 직책에 지원하시려면, www.mastermind/application/mw_taskforce으로 방문하세요.

* 지원서는 3월 10일까지 제출되어야 합니다.

Whitewall 출판사
1038 Washington 가
Newark, New Jersey

3월 4일

관계자분들께,

아만다 캐롤린 씨는 Corner Media 사에서 4년 동안 제 팀원으로 있었습니다. 그녀는 판촉 행사들을 위한 다양한 소셜 미디어 활용에 있어

매우 헌신적이고, 능숙하며, 전문적입니다. 비록 부장으로서의 경력은 아직 없지만, 그녀는 부서의 차장으로서 저와 제 직원들과 긴밀하게 일해 왔습니다. 그녀는 심지어 East Virginia 대학에서 인문학과 디지털 미디어를 복수 전공했습니다. 그녀의 학력과 더불어, 그녀는 판매 증대로 이어진 다양한 창의적 광고 및 홍보를 만들어냈습니다. 특히, 그녀는 두 달 전, Washington 대학에서 글로리아 박사의 연설 시리즈를 감독하고 관리했는데, 이는 전국적인 잡지들에서 호평을 받았습니다. 게다가, 그녀의 동료 및 고객들과의 의사소통 능력은 다른 직원들 사이에서도 단연 돋보입니다.

저는 그녀의 능률이 귀사의 신설 부서를 지원하는 데 도움이 될 것이라 희망합니다.

진심으로,

제임스 블랜차드
이사장
Corner Media 사

발신: 패트릭 업튼 <p_upton@mastermind.com>
수신: 아만다 캐롤린 <a.caroline@cornermedia.net>
날짜: 3월 15일
제목: 마케팅 부장 직책

캐롤린 씨에게,

Mastermind Group 신규 팀의 마케팅 부장 직책에 지원해 주셔서 감사합니다. 당신의 자격들은 매우 흥미롭고, 블랜차드 씨의 추천서는 매우 인상적입니다. 사실 저는 1월 2일에 글로리아 씨의 연설 시리즈에 참석했었습니다. 그것은 매우 흥미로웠고 유익했습니다.

저희는 그 직책에 대해 당신과 면접을 진행하고자 합니다. 저는 당신이 3월 20일 오후 2시에 Virginia 사무실 건물로 방문하도록 잠정적으로 일정을 잡았습니다. 이 이메일에 회신하셔서 그 시간이 당신에게 편한지 알려주세요.

행운을 빕니다,

패트릭 업튼
부장, 인사과
Whitewall 출판사, Mastermind Group

어휘 wanted 구하는 experienced 능숙한, 경험이 있는 acquire 인수하다, 얻다 recognized 인정된, 알려진 be in charge of ~을 담당하다 publication 출판 promotion 홍보 humanities 인문학 field 분야 creatively 창의적으로 analytically 분석적으로 systematically 체계적으로 standard 기준, 수준 expertise 전문기술, 지식 highly 매우 era 시대 dedicated 헌신적인 professional 전문적인 career 경력 closely 긴밀하게 deputy 대리인, 차장 double major 복수 전공 favorably 호의적으로 notable 눈에 띄는, 돋보이는 qualification 자격 reference 추천(서) tentatively 잠정적으로

196 Not/True 확인

Whitewall 출판사에 관하여 명시되어 있는 것은?
(A) 신규 팀을 위한 몇 개의 일자리가 필요하다.
(B) 인문학의 중요성을 홍보했다.
(C) 아시아 지역으로 사업을 확장했다.
(D) Mastermind Group에 의해 인수되었다.

해설 광고 첫 문장의 "because it has recently been acquired by the Mastermind Group"을 통해 해당 출판사가 Mastermind Group에 의해 인수되었음을 알 수 있으므로 (D)가 정답이다.

197 세부 사항 (연계)

캐롤린 씨는 그 직책에 대한 어떤 자격요건을 충족했는가?
(A) 뛰어난 교육 및 학업 성과들
(B) 마케팅을 위한 소셜 미디어 도구 활용 능력
(C) 사업의 인수 합병에 관한 지식
(D) 미디어 관련 부서와의 좋은 관계

해설 광고의 첫 번째 문단 마지막 부분 "having expertise in social media tools is highly preferred in order to fit into the recent mobile-based era."에서 소셜 미디어 도구에 대한 전문 지식을 요구하고 있고, 두 번째 지문인 편지의 "She is very dedicated, experienced, and professional in using a variety of social media for promotional events." 부분을 통해 캐롤린 씨가 소셜 미디어를 능숙하게 활용한다는 것을 알 수 있으므로 (B)가 정답이다.

198 주제/목적

편지의 목적은 무엇인가?
(A) 직책을 제안하기 위해
(B) 저자를 만나기 위해
(C) 행사를 논의하기 위해
(D) 사람을 추천하기 위해

해설 편지의 첫 문장 "Amanda Caroline has been a member of my team at Corner Media for four years."에서 캐롤린 씨를 소개하고 있고, 마지막 문장 "I hope that her efficiency will help to support your newly-organized department."에서 그녀가 부서에 도움이 되길 바란다고 하는 것을 보아 그녀를 추천하는 추천서임을 알 수 있다. 따라서 (D)가 정답이다.

199 추론/암시

업튼 씨가 1월 2일에 참석했을 것 같은 행사는?
(A) Virginia 무역 박람회
(B) Washington 대학 강연
(C) Mastermind 사 대표이사의 연설
(D) 소셜 미니어 컨퍼런스

해설 두 번째 지문인 편지의 "she directed and supervised Dr. Gloria's speech series at Washington College"에서 캐롤린 씨가 Washington 대학에서 글로리아 박사의 강연을 감독했다고 언급했고, 세 번째 지문인 이메일의

"I had actually attended Ms. Gloria's speech series on January 2."에서 업튼 씨가 글로리아 박사의 연설에 참석했다고 하는 것으로 보아 그가 참석한 행사는 Washington 대학 강연임을 알 수 있다. 따라서 (B)가 정답이다.

200 세부 사항

업튼 씨는 캐롤린 씨에게 무엇을 하라고 요구하는가?
(A) 온라인으로 새로운 계정 개설하기
(B) 개인 정보 제공하기
(C) 제안서 제출하기
(D) 약속 확정하기

해설 이메일의 마지막 문장 "Please reply to this e-mail to let me know if that time is convenient for you."에서 잠정적으로 정한 면접 시간이 편한지 알려달라고 했고, 이는 약속 시간을 확정하길 요청하는 것이므로 (D)가 정답이다.

○ 점수 환산표

LISTENING (맞은 개수)	LISTENING (환산 점수)	READING (맞은 개수)	READING (환산 점수)
96-100	475-495	96-100	460-495
91-95	435-495	91-95	425-490
86-90	405-470	86-90	400-465
81-85	370-450	81-85	375-440
76-80	345-420	76-80	340-415
71-75	320-390	71-75	310-390
66-70	290-360	66-70	285-370
61-65	265-335	61-65	255-340
56-60	240-310	56-60	230-310
51-55	215-280	51-55	200-275
46-50	190-225	46-50	170-245
41-45	160-230	41-45	140-215
36-40	130-205	36-40	115-180
31-35	105-175	31-35	95-150
26-30	85-145	26-30	75-120
21-25	60-115	21-25	60-95
16-20	30-90	16-20	45-75
11-15	5-70	11-15	30-55
6-10	5-60	6-10	10-40
1-5	5-50	1-5	5-30
0	5-35	0	5-15

books. english. co. kr

books. english. co. kr

books. english. co. kr

books. english. co. kr